WISC-V Assessment and Interpretation

Scientist–Practitioner Perspectives

WISC-V Assessment and Interpretation

Scientist–Practitioner Perspectives

Lawrence G. Weiss
Pearson Clinical Assessment,
San Antonio, Texas, USA

Donald H. Saklofske
Department of Psychology,
University of Western Ontario,
London, Ontario, Canada

James A. Holdnack
Pearson Clinical Assessment,
Bear, Delaware, USA

Aurelio Prifitera
Pearson Clinical Assessment,
Upper Saddle River, New Jersey, USA

AMSTERDAM • BOSTON • HEIDELBERG • LONDON
NEW YORK • OXFORD • PARIS • SAN DIEGO
SAN FRANCISCO • SINGAPORE • SYDNEY • TOKYO
Academic Press is an imprint of Elsevier

Academic Press is an imprint of Elsevier
125, London Wall, EC2Y 5AS
525 B Street, Suite 1800, San Diego, CA 92101-4495, USA
225 Wyman Street, Waltham, MA 02451, USA
The Boulevard, Langford Lane, Kidlington, Oxford OX5 1GB, UK

Notices
Knowledge and best practice in this field are constantly changing. As new research and experience broaden our understanding, changes in research methods, professional practices, or medical treatment may become necessary.

Practitioners and researchers must always rely on their own experience and knowledge in evaluating and using any information, methods, compounds, or experiments described herein. In using such information or methods they should be mindful of their own safety and the safety of others, including parties for whom they have a professional responsibility.

To the fullest extent of the law, neither the Publisher nor the authors, contributors, or editors, assume any liability for any injury and/or damage to persons or property as a matter of products liability, negligence or otherwise, or from any use or operation of any methods, products, instructions, or ideas contained in the material herein.

ISBN: 978-0-12-404697-9

British Library Cataloguing-in-Publication Data
A catalogue record for this book is available from the British Library

Library of Congress Cataloging-in-Publication Data
A catalog record for this book is available from the Library of Congress

For information on all Academic Press publications
visit our website at http://store.elsevier.com/

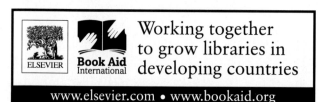

Working together
to grow libraries in
developing countries

www.elsevier.com • www.bookaid.org

Publisher: Nikki Levy
Acquisition Editor: Nikki Levy
Editorial Project Manager: Barbara Makinster
Production Project Manager: Melissa Read
Designer: Greg Harris

Dedication

This book is dedicated to:

Judy Ann, my wife of 30 years – **L.G.W.**

My father Harold and the memory of my beautiful mother Frances Annette – **D.H.S.**

My family Tina, Julia, and Adam, for their support – **J.A.H.**

The memory of my father-in-law Dr. Richard Matré and of my brother-in-law Frank Ivaldi who both inspired me in their own ways to pursue the professional career path I have taken – **A.P.**

We also wish to dedicate this book to the family of David Wechsler. They have given their unwavering support to our work over the years to update, improve, and revise the WISC. David's sons Adam and Len, and Adam's two children Daniel and Neil, have generously engaged in the many updates and revisions to the scales over the years. They have been especially supportive of moving to the digital format through Q-interactive which we could not have done without their support and encouragement. They have helped make the work of carrying on the legacy of David Wechsler's contributions to assessment both a pleasure and honor.

Contents

Part I
Applied Considerations
1. WISC-V: Advances in the Assessment of Intelligence

*Lawrence G. Weiss, Donald H. Saklofske, James A. Holdnack,
and Aurelio Prifitera*

2. Practical Issues in WISC-V Administration and Scoring

Dustin Wahlstrom, Lawrence G. Weiss, and Donald H. Saklofske

3. Practical Considerations in WISC-V Interpretation and Intervention

A. Lynne Beal, James A. Holdnack, Donald H. Saklofske, and Lawrence G. Weiss

Part II
Theoretical Considerations

4. Theoretical and Clinical Foundations of the WISC-V Index Scores

Lawrence G. Weiss, James A. Holdnack, Donald H. Saklofske, and Aurelio Prifitera

5. WISC-V Use in Societal Context

Lawrence G. Weiss, Victoria Locke, Tianshu Pan, Jossette G. Harris, Donald H. Saklofske, and Aurelio Prifitera

6. **The Flynn Effect and Its Clinical Implications**

Jacques Grégoire, Mark Daniel, Antolin M. Llorente, and Lawrence G. Weiss

Part III
Clinical Considerations

7. **Testing Hispanics with WISC-V and WISC-IV Spanish**

Lawrence G. Weiss, Maria R. Munoz, and Aurelio Prifitera

8. **WISC-V and the Evolving Role of Intelligence Testing in the Assessment of Learning Disabilities**

Donald H. Saklofske, Lawrence G. Weiss, Kristina Breaux, and A. Lynne Beal

9. Translating Scientific Progress in Dyslexia into Twenty-first Century Diagnosis and Interventions

Bennett A. Shaywitz, Lawrence G. Weiss, Donald H. Saklofske, and Sally E. Shaywitz

10. Issues Related to the WISC-V Assessment of Cognitive Functioning in Clinical and Special Groups

Jessie L. Miller, Donald H. Saklofske, Lawrence G. Weiss, Lisa Drozdick, Antolin M. Llorente, James A. Holdnack, and Aurelio Prifitera

Part IV
Current and Future Directions

11. Digital Assessment with Q-interactive

Dustin Wahlstrom, Mark Daniel, Lawrence G. Weiss, and Aurelio Prifitera

12. WISC-V and the Personalized Assessment Approach

James A. Holdnack, Aurelio Prifitera, Lawrence G. Weiss, and Donald H. Saklofske

List of Contributors

A. Lynne Beal Private Practice, Toronto, Ontario, Canada

Kristina Breaux Pearson Clinical Assessment, San Antonio, TX, USA

Mark Daniel Pearson Clinical Assessment, Bloomington, MN, USA

Lisa Drozdick Pearson Clinical Assessment, San Antonio, TX, USA

Jacques Grégoire Université Catholique de Louvain, Psychological Sciences Research Institute, Louvain-la-Neuve, Belgium

Jossette G. Harris Department of Psychiatry, University of Colorado School of Medicine, Denver, CO, USA

James A. Holdnack Pearson Clinical Assessment, Bear, DE, USA

Antolin M. Llorente Penn State Hershey College of Medicine, Hershey, PA, USA

Victoria Locke Pearson Clinical Assessment, San Antonio, TX, USA

Jessie L. Miller Pearson Clinical Assessment, Toronto, Ontario, Canada

Maria R. Munoz Pearson Clinical Assessment, San Antonio, TX, USA

Tianshu Pan Pearson Clinical Assessment, San Antonio, TX, USA

Aurelio Prifitera Pearson Clinical Assessment, Upper Saddle River, NJ, USA

Donald H. Saklofske Department of Psychology, University of Western Ontario, London, Ontario, Canada

Bennett A. Shaywitz Yale Center for Dyslexia & Creativity, Yale University School of Medicine, New Haven, CT, USA

Sally E. Shaywitz Yale Center for Dyslexia & Creativity, Yale University School of Medicine, New Haven, CT, USA

Dustin Wahlstrom Pearson Clinical Assessment, San Antonio, TX, USA

Lawrence G. Weiss Pearson Clinical Assessment, San Antonio, TX, USA

About the Authors

The authoring team of Weiss, Saklofske, Holdnack, and Prifitera has a long history of successful collaboration. This is the seventh text book written by two or more members of the team.

Lawrence G. Weiss, Ph.D. is Vice President of Global Research and Development at Pearson Clinical Assessment. He began his career with The Psychological Corporation 25 years ago and now oversees a department of more than 150 professionals in 11 countries across 4 continents for Pearson. Dr. Weiss is responsible for all research and test development activities related to the company's clinical assessment instruments, including the Wechsler scales. In addition, he has authored or coauthored approximately 100 books, book chapters, technical reports, and research articles in peer reviewed professional journals including two special issues devoted to his work.

Donald H. Saklofske, Ph.D. is a professor in the Department of Psychology, University of Western Ontario, Canada. He holds visiting and adjunct professorships at universities in Canada and China and serves on several professional psychology association boards. He has served on WISC and WAIS advisory panels and has published more than 270 books, book chapters and journal articles on topics including intelligence, personality, individual differences, emotional intelligence, resiliency and psychological assessment. Don is editor of the *Journal of Psychoeducational Assessment, Canadian Journal of School Psychology* and Associate Editor of *Personality and Individual Differences*; he also co-edits the Springer book series on Human Exceptionality. He is an elected fellow of the Association for Psychological Science and the Canadian Psychological Association.

James A. Holdnack, Ph.D. is Senior Scientist in the Global Research and Development group at Pearson Clinical Assessment. Dr. Holdnack is a licensed psychologist with a specialty in clinical neuropsychology. He has worked in the test development industry for more than 15 years and has contributed either as development lead, co-lead, or consultant on over 20 clinical products. As Senior Scientist, he provides research consultation and support to the Pearson Clinical Assessment research directors. He has published over 50 books, book chapters, and peer reviewed research articles and speaks regularly at national conferences.

Aurelio Prifitera, Ph.D. is Managing Director at Pearson leading the clinical assessment group. In addition to his psychology training, he holds an MBA degree. Aurelio was trained as a clinical psychologist and worked in clinical settings and private practice, and taught graduate level assessment courses prior to working in the test development field over 25 years ago. He has led several major clinical assessment projects over the years prior to his current role and has helped grow the availability of assessments outside the US in many international markets. He has published numerous peer-reviewed research articles, books and book chapters in the area of assessment. Dr. Prifitera is the founding editor and author of this WISC clinical book series first published in 1998 by Academic Press.

Foreword

The publication of the WISC-V marks a milestone in children's test development. It was published during a year—2014—when other state-of-the-art intelligence tests were also published, namely the CHC-based Woodcock-Johnson IV (Schrank, McGrew, Mather, & Woodcock, 2014) and the Luria-based Cognitive Assessment System—2nd edition (CAS2) (Naglieri, Das, & Goldstein, 2014). The competition for supremacy is steep and the WISC-V has met the challenge. The battery is comprehensive, versatile, child oriented, and clinically rich. It is steeped in a variety of well-researched and well-articulated theories that have roots in cognitive neuroscience, neuropsychological processing, and the CHC model that has expanded from a simple Cattell-Horn fluid-crystallized dichotomy (not unlike Wechsler's original Verbal-Performance distinction) to an array of important cognitive abilities. The developers of the WISC-V have met the challenges of this RTI-dominated and theory-driven decade with much the same goal-directed and ingenious fervor that characterized the great Dr. David Wechsler more than 75 years ago.

Indeed, Dr. Wechsler challenged the Stanford-Binet in the 1930s when no one else had either the courage or the inspiration. The original Stanford-Binet, published in 1916 by Lewis Terman, had many challengers (e.g., Goddard-Binet, Kuhlmann-Binet), all of whom were tied to Alfred Binet's groundbreaking age-based scale normed on Paris students. After Terman triumphed, largely because he had the insight to rearrange the Binet tasks assigned to each age level based on American data, and to actually obtain norms for children and adolescents living in the United States, his Binet test reigned as the measure of IQ.

That reign solidified in 1937 when Terman added a coauthor (Maud Merrill—like Terman, a professor at Stanford), an alternate form (the new Binet boasted Forms L and M), and a sophisticated statistical treatment of the data, thanks in large part to Dr. Quinn McNemar. Noted educator Ellwood P. Cubberly (1937) wrote in the Editor's Introduction to the test manual, "after ten years of painstaking research, two new and equivalent scales, each more extensive than the original both in range and in number of tests, and each providing for greater objectivity in scoring, are at last ready for public use" (pp. vi–vii).

Dr. Wechsler was not intimidated by the thoroughly revised and expanded Binet, touted in its own manual as the IQ test to end all IQ tests. He had vision. He insisted that a Performance Scale was just as necessary as a Verbal Scale to gain a full understanding of a person's mental functioning. Never mind the critics who asked unabashedly, "Why would anyone waste 3 minutes administering a single puzzle to an English-speaking person when a dozen or more Vocabulary words can be administered in the same time frame?" He offered the sophisticated standard score statistic to replace the antiquated and inadequate MA/CA X 100 formula. Terman and Merrill (1937) were well aware of standard scores; they provided a table that converted IQs to standard scores in the test manual, and praised the metric: "From the statistical point of view, every advantage is in favor of the standard score" (p. 27). Yet they continued to derive IQs by formula because "the majority of teachers, school administrators, social workers, physicians, and others who utilize mental test results have not learned to think in statistical terms. To such a person a rating expressed as ' +2 sigma' is just so much Greek" (Terman and Merrill, 1937: 27–28).

Dr. Wechsler, never condescending to test users, knew better. When he published the Wechsler-Bellevue for children and adults (Wechsler, 1939), a scant 2 years after the revised Binet became available, he included state-of-the-art Performance subtests as a featured IQ scale and he never doubted that clinicians were smart enough to "speak Greek." Those two departures from tradition moved the field of intellectual assessment a couple of light years forward.

Dr. Wechsler single-handedly changed the face of intellectual assessment from psychometric to clinical. The Binet tradition, as expounded by Terman and McNemar, was psychometric in orientation. Dr. Wechsler changed that when he published the Wechsler-Bellevue in 1939 and wrote incisively about how to interpret his tests in clinical practice (Wechsler, 1939, 1950, 1958; see also Chapters 8–10 of this book). The field of clinical assessment was born, and, except for some purists who insist that subtest profile interpretation and qualitative analysis of test scores are sacrilegious (for example, McDermott, Fantuzzo, & Glutting, 1990), the practices of clinical assessment have thrived internationally and span the domains of clinical psychology, neuropsychology, and school psychology. Any time a child, adolescent, or adult is tested anywhere in the world, the imprint of Dr. Wechsler reverberates.

Dr. Wechsler's tests continue to dominate the IQ scene. More than 75 years after the original Wechsler-Bellevue was published, Wechsler's scales stand at the very top of the assessment dome for the assessment across the lifespan, from preschool to old age. The WISC-IV has clearly been the most popular IQ measure for children and adolescents, but it has had some company on the assessment scene in schools, clinics, and private practices. Other acronyms have also been tossed about over the past decade when choosing a children's test for this or that type of referral, such as the CAS (Naglieri & Das, 1997) and now the CAS2 (Naglieri et al., 2014); the DAS-II (Elliott, 2007), KABC-II (Kaufman & Kaufman, 2004), RIAS (Reynolds & Kamphaus, 2003), and SB-5 (Roid, 2003); and the WJ-IV (Schrank et al., 2014). However, despite the raising of the bar to unprecedented heights, the WISC-V will undoubtedly continue to carry the international torch of intellectual assessment in the school-age range.

How Dr. Wechsler's legacy lives on! The chapters in this book attest to the WISC-V's superior psychometric and practical features, and demonstrate the test's contextual role within the theoretical, clinical, and research domains of assessment and, more broadly, within society. This volume, authored by the excellent team of Larry Weiss, Don Saklofske, Jim Holdnack, and Aurelio Prifitera, provides a compelling story of the WISC-V and its clinical use and interpretation. They and the varied contributors to this book represent some of the best that the field of intellectual assessment has to offer from the clinical, neuropsychological, and psychometric realms.

In Chapter 1, Weiss et al. offer a compelling introduction to the historical evolution of the WISC. Major innovations in the test model have characterized each revision of the scale. The development of the scale is traced from its origins in the Wechsler-Bellevue Intelligence Scale (Wechsler, 1939) to the present-day WISC-V (Wechsler, 2014), the subject of this book. The authors note that while the scale's evolution has been guided at The Psychological Corporation/Pearson through an emphasis on clinical research in neuropsychology and information processing, theory-based approaches to analysis derive "surprisingly similar models of intelligence based on different lines of research." Furthermore, Weiss et al. provide a history of the new fluid reasoning index, which has "been a systematic research goal since 1997, leading to the development and validation of three fluid reasoning subtests introduced successively in various subsequent editions; Matrix Reasoning, Picture Concepts, and Figure Weights." The chapter concludes with an overview of the test structure, which is at its heart familiar but contains a host of ancillary and complementary measures that enhance the clinical utility of the test for special uses.

In addition to the noticeable changes to the test structure, the WISC-V provides the option of a digital version on Q-interactive, which is a platform that provides the capability to administer tests on iPads and other tablets. Chapter 11 provides an overview of the Q-interactive system and examples of how the subtests are administered within the digital format. Wahlstrom and colleagues review the accumulated evidence of equivalence of the digital and paper versions of both the WISC-IV and the WISC-V, and discuss the implications on the potential to engage the child more readily as well as the potential for future data capture to measure constructs impossible to measure within a paper-and-pencil format.

In Chapter 5, the authors answer the "simple" psychometric question of the size of the ethnic differences for the Full Scale IQ and each primary index score. A regression approach is then used to explain increasingly the variability gaps in Full Scale IQs by race/ethnicity with other factors previously discussed, the distributions of which *also* have been shown to vary across racial/ethnic groups, such as marital status of parents and the number of parents in the home. Dr. Wechsler would have been fascinated by this research because he was always impressed that factor analyses of his scales only accounted for about 60% of the variance.

Dr. Wechsler was convinced that much of the remaining variance could be accounted for by "conative" variables (i.e., noncognitive variables such as motivation and perseverance), and he tried to support his point empirically by including the conative "Level of Aspiration" subtest in the standardization of the WAIS-R. Analyses of this experimental task did not solve the riddle of the unexplained variance, and the task was left on the cutting board. ("Level of Aspiration, which was studied as a possible means of broadening the coverage of the WAIS-R to include a measure of nonintellective ability, had a number of interesting features, but seemed to require further research before it could be added as a regular member of the battery"; Wechsler, 1981: 10). To the publisher, the decision to eliminate the conative task was undoubtedly an objective, simple decision because of weak data. However, to Dr. Wechsler the decision was deeply emotional. In Chapter 5, the authors present analyses that provide evidence that parental attitudes and expectations explain more variance in the Full Scale IQ than do parent education and income combined, and that the influence of parent education and income are reduced by half due to the effect of parental expectations! These results may have provided some satisfaction to Dr. Wechsler, who expressed great disappointment to Alan Kaufman at not being able to prove with data what he knew axiomatically to be true with every aspect of his being—that a person's Full Scale IQ and profile of test scores always reflect a dynamic integration of the person's intellectual and personality variables. He so hoped to be able to demonstrate the integral link between cognitive and conative abilities, and what would have a greater impact on children's motivation and perseverance than their own parents' beliefs about them?

Current best practice for intelligence test interpretation involves interpretation of test results through grounding them in theory (Kamphaus, Winsor, Rowe, & Kim, 2012), as Alan first advocated in *Intelligent Testing with the WISC-R* (Kaufman, 1979). While the WISC-V is not explicitly linked to a single theory, it is far from atheoretical. The myth that the Wechsler scales are atheoretical was perpetuated by several psychologists in the past, including Alan, who has since reconsidered his stance on the lack of a theoretical framework for Wechsler's scales: "Though not specifically developed from CHC [Cattell-Horn-Carroll] theory, Wechsler's modern-day tests were specifically revised in the 1990s and 2000s to incorporate CHC theory and state-of-the-art research on working memory and other executive functions" (Kaufman, 2009: 101). The WISC-V is no different; it was developed with specific theoretical foundations in mind. Its revision reflects the latest knowledge from literature in the areas of structural theories of intelligence, working memory models, information processing theory, and cognitive neuroscience. With respect to interpretation from a theory-grounded perspective, the reader will undoubtedly enjoy Weiss et al.'s Chapter 4, which provides theory-based perspectives on interpretation of each primary and secondary subtest and primary index score from an information-processing theory and cognitive neuroscience perspective. This chapter, additionally, discusses the WISC-V within the context of "an integrative, neurologically and ecologically valid model of cognitive information processing" with fluid and crystallized intelligence (as in the original Cattell-Horn model) holding special status in the "epicenter…and the remaining broad abilities plus executive functions" operating in their service.

The new appealing and theoretically relevant measures of visual–spatial processing (*Gv*-Vz; Visual Puzzles), fluid reasoning (*Gf*-RQ; Figure Weights), *Gwm/Gv*-MV (Picture Span), *Glr*-NA (Naming Speed subtests), and *Glr*-MA (the Symbol Translation subtests) are important innovations that facilitate the application of theory. Wahlstrom and colleagues' Chapter 2 provides sections on administration and scoring of all subtests, including these new measures, and provides a review of the literature that emphasizes the key postulate that results are reliant on administration and scoring that are error free. The subtest sections provide a number of tips for administration and scoring that will be valuable, and the literature demonstrates that students and practitioners alike should heed the "cautionary tale" told in this chapter about the importance of accurate administration and scoring.

Beal et al. (the authors of Chapter 3) manage a delicate balancing act in their discussion of interpretive considerations, concluding that both the Full Scale IQ and the primary index scores are important and clinically useful: the Full Scale IQ for predicting relevant behaviors, and the primary index scores for characterizing the child's unique pattern of strengths and weaknesses. The authors provide a brilliant analogy that may be used to summarize the abilities measured by the primary index scores in this chapter. In this analogy, the ability corresponding to each primary index score is conceptualized as a team member with an occupational specialty: verbal comprehension as a librarian, visual–spatial as an architect, fluid reasoning as a detective, working memory as a general manager, and processing speed as a clerk. The reader will be treated to these descriptions and will undoubtedly find them invaluable when attempting to explain the primary index scores to associated professionals from other fields and to parents. The chapter concludes with an excellent selection of classroom indicators of low scores on each of these five abilities, as well as a host of interventions, accommodations, and instructional strategies for children with low scores on each of these abilities. All of these bits of insight will be extremely useful in generating recommendations for psychological evaluations.

A special issue encountered in intellectual ability testing, the Flynn effect (i.e., a 3-point rise in Full Scale IQ points per decade), is approached in Chapter 6. Grégoire et al. provide a review of the Flynn effect across editions of the WPPSI and WISC, demonstrating that the effect is more complex and varied than originally thought. They provide a well-reasoned explanation for the varied impact of the Flynn effect across domains, particularly the Processing Speed subtests, as well as guidelines for clinical practice that will be of use to clinicians attempting to compare results across the WISC-IV and WISC-V.

Also in Chapter 5, Weiss and colleagues include a brilliant and in-depth treatise on the societal and contextual factors that must be internalized by examiners if racial/ethnic differences for children and adolescents on cognitive measures are to be understood and interpreted. This chapter reviews the extant literature on the roles of mental health status, physical health status, education, income, home environment, cognitive stimulation, and individual differences on intellectual development, and they discuss the implications of these demographic differences in various areas of life. The Chapter 5 authors have replaced the simple psychometric question, "How many IQ points does one ethnic group score higher than another?" with a complex society-driven and research-driven question: "How can we best interpret ethnic differences on the WISC-V in terms of opportunities for cognitive growth and development and with regard to a plethora of key SES and health variables?" These questions, which Weiss and colleagues have answered in similar, ingenious fashion concerning previous editions of Wechsler's scales, should be read and used in tandem with (a) the data on race/ethnicity, and (b) Chapter 7, which provides an account for best practices in testing Hispanics with the WISC-V and offers WISC-V base rates for Hispanic children to supplement information derived from the FSIQ.

Assessment of learning problems is a major purpose of any intelligence test for school-age children, and this book provides two excellent chapters to address assessment of learning problems with the WISC-V. Chapter 9 provides a thorough review of current literature on specific learning disability identification, and a coherent explanation of the learning disability subtyping literature. It additionally provides an explanation of the practical application of a pattern of strengths and weaknesses approach to identification of specific learning disabilities using the WISC-V and the *Kaufman Test of Educational Achievement* (KTEA-3; Kaufman & Kaufman, 2014) or the *Wechsler Individual Achievement Test—Third Edition* (WIAT-III; Pearson, 2009). In Chapter 10, Shaywitz summarizes the historical and current relevance of intellectual ability testing of individuals with dyslexia, and offers best-practice recommendations for involving assessment to ensure accurate diagnosis and intervention.

In Chapter 12, Holdnack and colleagues describe a personalized assessment approach to each individual child through integrating background information during pre-assessment planning to select measures from the WISC-V and other tests to tailor an assessment based on needs in the areas of language functioning, attention and executive functioning, working memory, academic skills, social cognition and pragmatic language skills, memory, processing speed, visual–spatial and fluid reasoning, and sensory and motor functioning. They describe the flexibility of digitally assisted assessment with real-time scoring, where on-the-fly adjustments can be made to the battery at a moment's notice so that only necessary domains are tested and unnecessary measures are not pursued. Holdnack et al. highlight other sophisticated and advanced measurement concepts important to this approach, including interpretation of multivariate data and statistical and clinical expectations about variability.

The chapters of this book, taken together, place the WISC-V firmly within societal, clinical, educational, neuropsychological, computer-based, and psychometric contexts that define today's assessment scene. The WISC-V yields a plethora of composite scores, process scores, error scores, and scaled scores—an array that is so rich and so vast that it will dazzle both the novice examiner and the wizened clinician. There is so much of value in the WISC-V, *and in the diverse, insightful chapters that comprise this book*, that can be put directly to address Dr. Wechsler's original goal when he developed the Wechsler-Bellevue Form II in 1946 (revised to become the WISC in 1949): to help, truly help, solve the child's problems and make a difference in the child's life. This book makes a difference. The WISC-V makes a difference, undoubtedly more so than any revised edition of any Wechsler scale in history. Dr. Wechsler would be awed by his heritage.

Susan Engi Raiford
Pearson Clinical Assessment, San Antonio, Texas, USA

Alan S. Kaufman
Yale Child Study Center, School of Medicine, New Haven, Connecticut, USA

REFERENCES

Cubberly, E. P. (1937). Editor's introduction. In L. M. Terman, & M. A. Merrill, (Eds.), *Measuring intelligence* (pp. v–vii). Boston, MA: Houghton Mifflin.

Elliott, C. (2007). *Differential abilities scale* (2nd ed.). Bloomington, MN: Pearson.

Kamphaus, R. W., Winsor, A. P., Rowe, E. W., & Kim, S. (2012). A history of intelligence test interpretation. In D. P. Flanagan & P. L. Harrison (Eds.), *Contemporary intellectual assessment: Theories, tests, and issues* (pp. 56–70, 3rd ed.). New York, NY: Guilford Press.

Kaufman, A. S. (1979). *Intelligent testing with the WISC–R*. New York, NY: Wiley.

Kaufman, A. S. (2009). *IQ testing 101*. New York, NY: Springer.

Kaufman, A. S., & Kaufman, N. L. (2004). *Kaufman assessment battery for children (KABC-II)* (2nd ed.). Circle Pines, MN: American Guidance Service.

Kaufman, A. S., & Kaufman, N. L. (2014). *Kaufman test of educational achievement (KTEA–3)*. Bloomington, MN: Pearson.

McDermott, P. A., Fantuzzo, J. W., & Glutting, J. J. (1990). Just say no to subtest analysis: A critique on Wechsler theory and practice. *Journal of Psychoeducational Assessment, 8*, 290–302.

Naglieri, J. A., & Das, J. P. (1997). *Cognitive assessment system*. Chicago, IL: Riverside.

Naglieri, J. A., Das, J. P., & Goldstein, S. (2014). *Cognitive assessment system* (2nd ed.). Rolling Meadows, IL: Riverside Publishing.

Pearson, (2009). *Wechsler individual achievement test* (3rd ed.). Bloomington, MN: Pearson.

Reynolds, C. R., & Kamphaus, R. W. (2003). *Reynolds intellectual assessment scales (RIAS)*. Lutz, FL: Psychological Assessment Resources.

Roid, G. (2003). *Stanford-Binet intelligence scales* (5th ed.). Itasca, IL: Riverside.

Schrank, F. A., McGrew, K. S., Mather, N., & Woodcock, R. W. (2014). *Woodcock-Johnson* (4th ed.). Rolling Meadows, IL: Riverside Publishing.

Terman, L. D. (1916). *The measurement of intelligence*. Boston, MA: Houghton Mifflin.

Terman, L. M., & Merrill, M. A. (1937). *Measuring intelligence*. Boston, MA: Houghton Mifflin.

Wechsler, D. (1939). *Measurement of adult intelligence*. Baltimore, MD: Williams & Wilkins.

Wechsler, D. (1950). Cognitive, conative and non-intellective intelligence. *American Psychologist,* *5,* 7–83.

Wechsler, D. (1958). *Measurement and appraisal of adult intelligence* (4th ed.). Baltimore, MD: Williams & Wilkins.

Wechsler, D. (1981). *Wechsler adult intelligence scale—revised (WAIS-R).* San Antonio, TX: The Psychological Corporation.

Wechsler, D. (2014). *Wechsler intelligence scale for children* (5th ed.). Bloomington, MN: Pearson.

Preface

Beginning with the third revision of the Wechsler Intelligence Scale for Children in 1990, we have developed an accompanying book with chapters on important clinical and research topics cast within the scientist-practitioner framework. While the evidence for the psychometric integrity and clinical efficacy of the Wechsler intelligence scales is vast, given the number of published articles that have included the scales, bringing the information together in such a way to address some of the key clinical and practice issues has always been the main driver of this Academic Press series on the Wechsler intelligence tests.

We have attempted always to give a balance between the empirical basis established during the extensive standardization studies and subsequent published research studies with clinical practice and utility. The editors of the series, some of whom worked directly on the revisions to the WISC-V and earlier versions, have also included editors and chapter authors who were not part of the extensive test development process. We believe this balance of in-depth information of the process of test development as well as the perspective of those from clinical, professional training and research settings has resulted in a unique perspective and insights into the testing and assessment process using the Wechsler scales. We have been pleased with the positive response we have received to all of the volumes in this series and thank our readers for their support. We are also most grateful to the numerous authors who have contributed to the chapters over the years, and this book in particular.

Most importantly, we owe so much to David Wechsler for his genius and dedication to the psychological assessment of children, youth, and adults. His original conceptualization of the Wechsler tests was visionary and has allowed the scales to continue to evolve as valuable, leading assessment tools in the field of psychology since the original Wechsler-Bellevue published in 1939. There are only a handful of instruments in the field of psychological and psychoeducational assessment that have lasted that long and we, the editors of this series, are proud to be able to have participated to a small degree in that long legacy of excellence in cognitive assessment.

One reason the Wechsler tests have endured is because of the openness to change from revision to revision and the significant resources and investment that have gone into those revisions. The amount of investment into the Wechsler scales has been second to none in the testing field. The scales have also benefited from the wisdom of David Wechsler himself through the first revisions, to his family's support on the later revisions after his death in 1981. In addition, others who have worked on various aspects of the tests over the years such as Joseph Matarazzo and Alan Kaufman have paved the road for these later test revisions. The tradition has continued and those of us who have also worked inside the organizations responsible for the revisions have been fortunate to have the unwavering support and freedom to do what we thought was best for the assessment of intelligence and cognitive abilities.

The iconic Wechsler scales, even with all their success and changes, are not immune to a multitude of factors that have shaped and will continue to impact both psychological tests and the assessment of intelligence and cognitive processes. We see already on the horizon a significant shift in the future direction of the scales, how they will be used, and the changes that will be different in the next generation of assessments. One of the main drivers of the change is the move from paper towards digital assessment. Although the WISC-V is available in both paper and digital modes, it is fairly clear that the usage patterns are changing rapidly and clinicians are adopting the digital administration. We are just now seeing some of the benefits of a digital modality through the Q-interactive application and we know there are more advantages that will emerge that are not apparent today. In addition to the clear advantages such as portability, ease of use, lower entry costs for tests, faster administration and scoring and ease of accessibility of tests, a digital format will allow for many more benefits in the near future. One of the main benefits is the flexibility that will let the psychologist choose to give a subset of the tests most relevant to addressing the key clinical questions. It is also very easy to give a set of subtests from across various tests on the Q-interactive system that are custom selected for the assessment needs of particular children. This allows for greater personalization of the test battery and for much more flexibility in the approach to assessment. A digital format will also allow the measurement of variables that could not be measured in a paper and pencil format.

Introducing a digital format brings new challenges and measurement issues into the test development process such as validating task equivalence with paper versions but also the need for understanding and incorporation of design and usability into the development so that the testing experience is valid and optimized. Additions and new information on interpretation, meaning of score patterns, norms and new tests can be easily added and accessed through a digital format. This, we believe, will give the clinician and researcher unprecedented access to tools, data, and analysis. This overall more "flexible" approach concept (now enabled with technology) was originally proposed by Edith Kaplan and advocated through her many students including Dean Delis who is carrying that model forward. With access to these data, the empirical basis of score patterns and levels will be more readily available and reach users of the test more quickly.

Another major change over the years has been the growth of international editions of the WISC. One of the most powerful aspects to the Wechsler model of intelligence is that it is fairly robust, consistent, and congruent in terms of the constructs measured and factor structures replicated across different cultures.

The WISC-IV is now available with country norms in at least a dozen countries, and WISC-V standardization data are being collected in six countries as we write. As the world shrinks due to technology and mass communication, the ability to use these tests consistently and compare results across various cultures brings a new dimension in the understanding of intelligence and various clinical conditions. The usage of the Wechsler scales has grown significantly outside the US over the past 25 year to the point where usage now is higher outside than inside the US.

Finally, the ways of interpreting the WISC will see continuing evolution. Much of it due to the impact of digital capabilities mentioned above and the ability to quickly access data from a variety of sources globally. This "big data" capability will have enormous impact and benefit to the research base and clinical understanding and interpretation of these tests. Also, with each revision there has been a steady movement away from simple reliance on summary IQ scores (i.e., Verbal IQ, Performance IQ, and Full Scale IQ) to more sophisticated and nuanced views of the five major domains of cognitive ability now built into WISC-V (i.e., verbal comprehension, visual spatial, fluid reasoning, working memory, and processing speed) and their combination. The neuropsychologist and author Muriel Lezak was a major force advocating this approach in her writings. These newer approaches to interpretation have been greatly influenced by approaches such as the "process" approach advocated by Edith Kaplan, Dean Delis and others and the "Processing Strengths and Weakness" approach advocated by, among others, Hale and Fiorello. Finally longitudinal research by Sally Shaywitz documenting dyslexia as an unexpected difficulty in reading relative to intelligence, as well as research similar to the work done by Virginia Berninger linking patterns of performance to brain imaging and interventions for specific disorders is changing how tests are used and interpreted. These new approaches share a focus of looking at all tests within the context of other tests and not just those in a particular test battery, are driven by hypothesis testing and discover, and are based on solid understanding of the cognitive processes and clinical conditions. We expect this next edition of this book series to follow this dynamic change in interpretative process and benefit from the digital transformation in testing that is just beginning.

We end here by thanking our contributing authors who added a depth of knowledge that has made those chapters much richer in both empirical and practice information. As always, we thank Nikki Levy and Barbara Makinster who have so professionally guided all of our Wechsler books to publication. We also appreciate the professional editing work of Melissa Read seen throughout this book. Finally, our hope is that you, the readers of this book, will find it an important and useful resource both in your use of the WISC-V and the assessment of children's intelligence.

Lawrence G. Weiss
Donald H. Saklofske
James A. Holdnack
Aurelio Prifitera

Part I

Applied Considerations

Chapter 1

WISC-V: Advances in the Assessment of Intelligence

Lawrence G. Weiss[1], Donald H. Saklofske[2], James A. Holdnack[3], and Aurelio Prifitera[4]

[1]*Pearson Clinical Assessment, San Antonio, TX, USA*, [2]*Department of Psychology, University of Western Ontario, London, Ontario, Canada*, [3]*Pearson Clinical Assessment, Bear, DE, USA*, [4]*Pearson Clinical Assessment, Upper Saddle River, NJ, USA*

INTRODUCTION

The Wechsler scales are the most widely used measures of intelligence, and have been translated, adapted, and standardized in dozens of countries around the world. Since first introduced in the Wechlser–Bellevue Intelligence Scale (WBIS), the Wechsler model has evolved substantially, but remains grounded in Dr. Wechsler's foundational definition of intelligence:

> ...*the aggregate or global capacity of the individual to act purposefully, to think rationally, and to deal effectively with his (or her) environment.*
>
> (Wechsler, 1939, p. 3)

A BRIEF HISTORICAL RECAP

The Wechsler series of tests consists of the WISC for school-aged children, the WPPSI for preschool children, and the WAIS for adults. Each of these tests has undergone multiple revisions over several decades. This book is about the fifth edition of the WISC. As we discuss the evolution of the WISC-V, we must necessarily refer to various editions of the WPPSI and WAIS as the evolution of these assessment tools are interrelated theoretically and conceptually as part of the contemporary Wechsler model of intelligence.

Some readers may recall that the original Wechsler model was based on a two part structure comprised of the Verbal Intelligence Quotient (VIQ) and Performance Intelligence Quotient (PIQ), which combined to form the Full Scale Intelligence Quotient (FSIQ). In a series of major theoretical shifts from

L. G. Weiss, D. H. Saklofske, J. A. Holdnack and A. Prifitera (Eds): WISC-V Assessment and Interpretation.
DOI: http://dx.doi.org/10.1016/B978-0-12-404697-9.00001-7

the original Wechsler model described in 1939, the Wechsler tests have evolved with each version. The WISC-V is based on a five part structure, and the resulting five, factor-based index scores have become the primary level of clinical interpretation. The contemporary Wechsler theoretical model measures the following five domains of cognitive ability: verbal conceptualization, visual–spatial organization, fluid reasoning, working memory, and processing speed.

The modern expansion of the Wechsler model began in 1991 when the WISC-III became the first of the Wechsler scales to offer four factor-based index scores as an optional alternative to the traditional VIQ/PIQ structure: verbal comprehension, perceptual organization, freedom from distractibility, and processing speed. The WAIS-III followed suit in 1997 with the same dual model in which those four index scores were offered but considered supplemental to main VIQ, PIQ, and FSIQ scores. At that time, working memory was referred to as "freedom from distractibility"—an older term that reflected the incomplete understanding of the construct at that time.

Following from advances in cognitive psychology, neuropsychology, and clinical psychology, in 2003 the scientific caretakers of the Wechsler Scales at PsychCorp/Pearson broke the proverbial "apron strings" tying the Wechsler tests to the VIQ and PIQ model proposed by David Wechsler in the original WBIS. The VIQ and PIQ were eliminated completely from the WISC-IV, along with changing the name of the freedom from distractibility index to the working memory index to reflect the improved understanding of that construct, and changing the name of the perceptual organization index to the perceptual reasoning index to reflect the increased focus on fluid reasoning among the newly created perceptual subtests. The WISC-IV elevated the four index scores to the primary level of clinical interpretation. The WAIS-IV followed this model in 2008. In 2012, the WPPSI-IV (Wechsler, 2012) introduced the first five factor Wechsler model for children ages 4 to 7 years. To accomplish this, new subtests were created and combined with selected perceptual reasoning and working memory subtests to create a fluid reasoning factor.

FROM THE PAST TO THE PRESENT

The 75-year (1939–2014) history of the Wechsler tests has seen major changes from a focus on general mental ability complemented by verbal and performance IQ scores to either a four (WISC-IV, WAIS-IV) or a five (WPPSI-IV) factor structure. The debate over both the empirical foundations and clinical utility of a four versus five factor structure was the focus of an influential set of papers published in a special issue of the *Journal of Psychoeducational Assessment* (*JPA*) (Tobin, 2013). This five factor model was shown to fit the data slightly better than the four factor model for both WISC-IV and WAIS-IV (Weiss, Keith, Zhu, & Chen, 2013a, 2013b). The fifth factor, of course, was fluid reasoning (FR), which was formed by some subtests previously assigned to the perceptual reasoning and working memory factors.

Another key finding from these papers was that the five factor solution fit the data well in large samples of mixed clinical subjects for both WISC-IV and WAIS-IV, thus supporting the clinical application of the model. As the two target papers in the special issue of *JPA*, these papers were subject to invited critiques by eight prominent researchers, and generally positively reviewed (see Kaufman, 2013 for a summary and discussion of the reviews, and see Weiss, Keith, Zhu, & Chen, 2013c for a rejoinder). Thus, these papers served as the catalyst for a five factor model of WISC-V.

The Wechsler five factor model overlaps substantially with the Cattell–Horn–Carroll (CHC) theory of intelligence that predates it (Carroll, 1993). As a result, recent literature concerning a fifth Wechsler factor has sometimes been cast as a contest between the Wechsler and CHC models of intelligence (Benson, Hulac, & Kranzler, 2010; Ward, Bergman, & Herbert, 2011). However, adding working memory and processing speed factors to the original two factor Wechsler model has been a systematic research goal for the Wechsler test development team, which began in 1990 with the third editions and was fully implemented in the fourth editions (Weiss, Saklofske, Coalson, & Raiford, 2010; Weiss, Saklofske, Prifitera, & Holdnack, 2006). Similarly, adding a fluid reasoning factor to the Wechsler model has also been a systematic research goal since 1997, leading to the development and validation of three fluid reasoning subtests introduced successively in various subsequent editions: Matrix Reasoning, Picture Concepts, and Figure Weights.

While the psychometric fit of the third and fourth editions of the Wechsler series to a four factor model has been well established for decades, the continuous evolution of the contemporary Wechsler scales to a five factor theoretical model has been guided less by CHC-related factor analytic findings and more by ongoing clinical research in neuropsychology and cognitive information processing, as described in Chapter 5. The good news for our science is that independent research labs have derived surprisingly similar models of intelligence based on different lines of research, and this is ultimately confirming the progress the field is making in better understanding the nature of intellectual functioning.

To be fair to Dr. Wechsler's legacy, his model has always included subtests that researchers now understand as measures of working memory, processing speed, and fluid reasoning. These were buried inside the VIQ and PIQ depending on whether the stimuli and response processes were verbal or visual–perceptual, respectively. Still, Dr. Wechsler knew that mental manipulation of numbers was importantly related to intelligence and that is why he included the Arithmetic and Digit Span subtests in the VIQ. Similarly, he knew that quick visual scanning played an important role in cognition and so he included the Coding subtests as part of the PIQ. As we have also seen, with the addition of newer subtests to reflect contemporary models of and research on intelligence, subtests such as Arithmetic have emerged from being initially included in the VIQ to being a key subtest tapping working memory and now finding a place as an optional subtest on the Fluid Reasoning domain.

Present-day researchers have developed well-articulated theories about the underlying neurocognitive processes tapped by these tasks and how they are related to intelligence. Much like the well-known aspirin that continues to be found relevant in the treatment of many more health issues than initially considered, Digit Span is now understood as tapping working memory, especially when digits are recalled in reverse or rearranged in an ordered sequence. Coding is now understood as a measure of cognitive processing speed rather than just simple copying or hand-eye coordination. As more has been learned about these areas, the Wechsler tests have changed over time such that these constructs have been disentangled from VIQ and PIQ, and stand alone. Furthermore, new tasks such as Letter-Number Sequencing and Cancellation were added to elaborate the assessment of working memory and processing speed, respectively. Also, Digit Span was significantly revised in the WAIS-IV and now WISC-V by adding the digit sequencing items to make it a better measure of working memory based on our current understanding of that construct.

Similarly, although the term fluid reasoning was not used in Dr. Wechsler's time, some of the original Wechsler subtests were believed to be related to the ability to solve novel problems (i.e., Similarities, Block Design). It was very much the seminal contributions of Horn and Cattell (1966) that led to describing and distinguishing between fluid (Gf) and crystallized (Gc) intelligence somewhat in comparison to Wechsler's VIQ and PIQ. Although most intelligence tests going back to the early Binet measures seem to have amply covered the more crystallized side, further research on fluid reasoning led to the development of four new Wechsler subtests that measure this construct more directly. Specifically, Matrix Reasoning (which first appeared in WISC-III and was then added to WAIS-III and WISC-IV, and retained in WAIS-IV and WISC-V), Picture Concepts (which first appeared in WISC-IV and was then added to WPPSI-III), and Figure Weights (which appeared for the first time in WAIS-IV, and has now been added to WISC-V).

The key point of this brief 75-year historical backdrop is that the Wechsler scales have changed substantially over the decades, keeping pace with rapid advances in the understanding of intelligence. Yet, without Dr. Wechsler's far-reaching clinical insights, the field of intellectual assessment would not be where it is today. The WISC-V is a very different test than the one that Dr. Wechsler gave us—one that builds upon multiple modern theories of cognitive neuroscience informed by ongoing clinical and neuropsychological research.

STRUCTURE AND CONTENT OF THE WISC-V

Psychologists have come to recognize that while general mental ability measured by the FSIQ is a powerful metric for more global descriptions of a person's cognitive abilities, the greatest clinical usefulness comes from an analysis of the index scores; those "primary" mental abilities that more specifically describe the key or most important components of intellectual and cognitive functioning.

As we often state at workshops, 100 children all with FSIQs of 100 can show many different patterns of strengths and weaknesses among the primary cognitive abilities, leading to considerable variability in school achievement and many other facets of behavior in which intelligence plays a major role.

The WISC-V consists of five primary index scores: Verbal Comprehension Index (VCI), Visual–Spatial Index (VSI), Fluid Reasoning Index (FRI), Working Memory Index (WMI), and Processing Speed Index (PSI). Each of these five index scores is defined and measured by two primary subtests. Most of these five domains include secondary subtests, which are optional and when administered may provide additional information regarding performance in the respective domain. In later chapters we will more fully describe the index scores and their relevance in diagnostic assessment and program-intervention planning. The focus here is to provide an overview of the "parts" or subtests that comprise the "whole" as reflected in both the index scores and the FSIQ. As those familiar with the Wechsler tests will note, many of the subtests included in the WISC-V are psychometrically and clinically improved versions from earlier editions of the WISC and WAIS tests, whereas others were specifically developed to enhance the five factor model that now defines the newest addition to the Wechsler family. Figure 1.1 shows the structure of the WISC-V as defined by basic composition of the FSIQ, the five primary index scores, the five ancillary index scores, and the three complementary index scores.

THE WISC-V PRIMARY INDEXES AND SUBTESTS

Verbal Comprehension Index

The VCI is formed by the two primary verbal comprehension subtests: Similarities and Vocabulary. There are also two secondary verbal comprehension subtests: Information and Comprehension. All four subtests have demonstrated their largest contribution to this index in earlier versions of the WISC.

Similarities

For Similarities, the child is read two words that represent common objects or concepts and describes how they are similar. The subtest is designed to measure verbal concept formation and abstract reasoning. It also involves crystallized intelligence, word knowledge, cognitive flexibility, auditory comprehension, long-term memory, associative and categorical thinking, distinction between nonessential and essential features, and verbal expression (Flanagan & Kaufman, 2009; Groth-Marnat, 2009; Sattler, 2008b; Wechsler, 2014).

Vocabulary

Vocabulary has both picture and verbal items. For picture items, the child names simple objects depicted. For verbal items, the child defines more difficult words that are read aloud by the examiner. Vocabulary is designed to measure word knowledge and verbal concept formation. It also measures crystallized

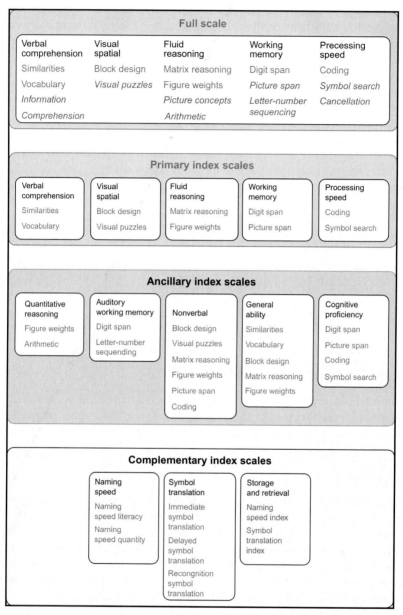

FIGURE 1.1 Structure of the WISC-V as defined by basic composition of the FSIQ, the five primary index scores, the five ancillary index scores, and the three complementary index scores. Subtest descriptions are reused with permission from the WISC-V Manual (Wechsler, 2014).

intelligence, fund of knowledge, learning ability, verbal expression, long-term memory, and degree of vocabulary development. Other abilities that may be used during this task include auditory perception and comprehension, and abstract thinking (Flanagan & Kaufman, 2009; Groth-Marnat, 2009; Sattler, 2008b; Wechsler, 2014).

Information

For Information, the child answers questions about a broad range of general-knowledge topics. The subtest is designed to measure a child's ability to acquire, retain, and retrieve general factual knowledge. It involves crystallized intelligence, long-term memory, and the ability to retain and retrieve knowledge from the environment and/or school. Other skills used include verbal perception, comprehension, and expression (Flanagan & Kaufman, 2009; Groth-Marnat, 2009; Sattler, 2008b; Wechsler, 2014).

Comprehension

For Comprehension, the child answers questions based on his or her understanding of general principles and social situations. Comprehension is designed to measure verbal reasoning and conceptualization, verbal comprehension and expression, the ability to evaluate and use past experience, and the ability to demonstrate practical knowledge and judgment. It also involves crystallized intelligence, knowledge of conventional standards of behavior, social judgment, long-term memory, and common sense (Flanagan & Kaufman, 2009; Groth-Marnat, 2009; Sattler, 2008b; Wechsler, 2014).

Visual–Spatial Index

The VSI is formed by two primary visual–spatial subtests: the long-standing Block Design and newly created Visual Puzzles. There are no secondary visual–spatial subtests.

Block Design

Working within a specified time limit, the child views a model and/or a picture and uses two-color blocks to construct the design. The Block Design subtest is designed to measure the ability to analyze and synthesize abstract visual stimuli. It also involves nonverbal concept formation and reasoning, broad visual intelligence, visual perception and organization, simultaneous processing, visual–motor coordination, learning, and the ability to separate figure-ground in visual stimuli (Carroll, 1993; Flanagan & Kaufman, 2009; Groth-Marnat, 2009; Sattler, 2008b; Wechsler, 2014).

Visual Puzzles

Visual Puzzles is a new WISC-V subtest adapted for children from the WAIS-IV. Working within a specified time limit, the child views a completed puzzle and selects three response options that, when combined, reconstruct the puzzle. The subtest is designed to measure mental, nonmotor, construction ability, which requires visual and spatial reasoning, mental rotation, visual working memory, understanding part–whole relationships, and the ability to analyze and synthesize abstract visual stimuli. Similar measures, such as the WPPSI-IV Object Assembly task and the *Revised Minnesota Paper Form Board Test* (Likert & Quasha, 1995), involve visual perception, broad visual intelligence, fluid intelligence, simultaneous processing, spatial visualization and manipulation, and the ability to anticipate relationships among parts (Carroll, 1993; Groth-Marnat, 2009; Kaufman & Lichtenberger, 2006; Likert & Quasha, 1995; Sattler, 2008b). It is described as measuring visual processing and acuity, spatial relations, integration and synthesis of part–whole relationships, nonverbal reasoning, and trial-and-error learning (Flanagan & Kaufman, 2009; Flanagan, Alfonso, & Ortiz, 2012; Sattler, 2008b, Wechsler, 2014).

The WISC-V Fluid Reasoning Index

The FRI is a major and new addition to the WISC-V. It is formed by two primary fluid reasoning subtests: Matrix Reasoning and Figure Weights. Matrix Reasoning was an established subtest in both the WISC-IV and WAIS-IV, while Figure Weights first appeared in the WAIS-IV. There are also two secondary fluid reasoning subtests: Picture Concepts and Arithmetic, both of which will be known to those familiar with the Wechsler tests.

Matrix Reasoning

For Matrix Reasoning, the child views an incomplete matrix or series and selects the response option that completes the matrix or series. The task requires the child to use visual–spatial information to identify the underlying conceptual rule that links all the stimuli and then apply the underlying concept to select the correct response. The subtest is designed to measure fluid intelligence, broad visual intelligence, classification and spatial ability, knowledge of part–whole relationships, and simultaneous processing (Flanagan & Kaufman, 2009; Groth-Marnat, 2009; Sattler, 2008b; Wechsler, 2014). Additionally, the test requires attention to visual detail and working memory.

Figure Weights

Figure Weights is a new WISC-V subtest adapted for children from the WAIS-IV. Working within a specified time limit, the child views one or two scales balanced by weights and a scale with missing weight(s) and then selects the weight(s) that keep the scale balanced from the response options. This task requires the child to apply the quantitative concept of equality to understand the relationship among objects and apply the concepts of matching, addition, and/or multiplication to identify the correct response. The subtest measures quantitative fluid reasoning and induction (Flanagan et al., 2012; Flanagan & Kaufman, 2009; Sattler & Ryan, 2009; Wechsler, 2014). Quantitative reasoning tasks involve reasoning processes that can be expressed mathematically, emphasizing inductive or deductive logic (Carroll, 1993). Although Figure Weights involves working memory to some extent, it reduces this involvement relative to typical quantitative tasks (e.g., the Arithmetic subtest), by using visual items so that the child can refresh her or his memory as necessary.

Picture Concepts

For Picture Concepts, the child views two or three rows of pictures and selects one picture from each row to form a group with a common characteristic. No image appears more than once within the subtest. This test requires the child to use the semantic representations of nameable objects to identify the underlying conceptual relationship among the objects and to apply that concept to select the correct answer. The subtest is designed to measure fluid and inductive reasoning, visual–perceptual recognition and processing, and conceptual thinking (Flanagan & Kaufman, 2009; Sattler, 2008b; Wechsler, 2014). It may also involve crystallized knowledge (Sattler, 2008b). Additionally, this task requires visual scanning, working memory, and abstract reasoning.

Arithmetic

For this subtest the child mentally solves arithmetic problems that are presented verbally by the examiner as word problems, within a specified time limit. Arithmetic involves mental manipulation, concentration, brief focused attention, short- and long-term memory, numerical reasoning ability, applied computational ability, and mental alertness. It may also involve sequential processing; fluid, quantitative, and logical reasoning; and quantitative knowledge (Groth-Marnat, 2009; Kaufman & Lichtenberger, 2006; Sattler, 2008b; Wechsler, 2014). Additionally, this task requires intact auditory/linguistic processes, including discrimination, comprehension, and to a lesser degree expression.

Working Memory Index

The WMI is formed by two primary working memory subtests: Digit Span and Picture Span. There is one secondary working memory subtest: Letter-Number Sequencing.

Digit Span

This subtest consists of three parts. The child is read a sequence of numbers and recalls the numbers in the same order (Digit Span Forward), reverse order (Digit Span Backward), and ascending order (Digit Span Sequencing). The latter condition was adapted for children from the WAIS-IV, and is intended to increase the working memory demands of the subtest.

The shift from one Digit Span task to another requires cognitive flexibility and mental alertness. All Digit Span tasks require registration of information, brief focused attention, auditory discrimination, and auditory rehearsal. Digit Span Forward assesses auditory rehearsal and temporary storage capacity in working memory. Digit Span Backward involves working memory, transformation of information, mental manipulation, and may involve visuospatial imaging (Groth-Marnat, 2009; Flanagan & Kaufman, 2009; Reynolds, 1997; Sattler, 2008b; Wechsler, 2014).

Digit Span Sequencing, a new task for the WISC-V, is similar to other tasks designed to measure working memory and mental manipulation (MacDonald, Almor, Henderson, Kempler, & Andersen, 2001; Werheid et al., 2002). Digit Span Sequencing is included to increase the cognitive complexity demands of the subtest. Both the backward and sequencing tasks require the resequencing of information; the primary difference between the tasks is how the sequence is determined. In the backward task, the location of the number in the sequence must be maintained in working memory for proper resequencing to occur. In the sequencing task, the quantitative value of the number must be maintained in working memory and compared to numbers before and after its occurrence. In this task, the child does not know where the number will occur in the response until all the numbers are administered.

The total raw score for Digit Span subtest is based on the Digit Span Forward, Digit Span Backward, and Digit Span Sequencing raw scores. This total score enters the WMI and the FSIQ. Digit Span Forward must be administered, as the omission of this task results in lower Digit Span Backward scores for some children (possibly due to the loss of instructional progression). Retaining Digit Span Forward ensures sufficient floor items for children with intellectual disability or low cognitive ability.

The child's performance on Digit Span Forward, Backward, and Sequencing can also be examined separately using the Digit Span process scores. These process scores provide information about relative variability in performance across the three Digit Span tasks.

Picture Span

For Picture Span, a new Wechsler subtest, the child views a stimulus page with one or more pictures of nameable objects for a specified time and then selects the picture(s) (in sequential order, if possible) from options on a response page. Picture Span measures visual working memory and working memory capacity. Similar tasks are thought also to involve attention, visual processing, visual immediate memory, and response inhibition (Flanagan et al., 2012; Flanagan, Alfonso, Ortiz, & Dynda, 2010; Miller, 2010, 2013). The subtest is constructed similarly to existing visual working memory tasks (Hartshorne, 2008; Makovski & Jiang, 2008; Wechsler, 2009), but it is relatively novel in its use of semantically meaningful stimuli. The use of these stimuli may activate verbal working memory as well. The working memory demands of Picture Span stem from the use of proactive interference as well as sequencing requirements. Proactive interference is introduced by occasionally repeating pictures across items, sometimes alternating whether the repeated picture is the target or a distractor.

Letter-Number Sequencing

For Letter-Number Sequencing, the child is read a sequence of numbers and letters and recalls the numbers in ascending order and then the letters in alphabetical order. Like the Digit Span task, the Letter-Number Sequencing task requires some basic cognitive processes such as auditory discrimination, brief focused attention, concentration, registration, and auditory rehearsal. Additionally, the task involves sequential processing, the ability to compare stimuli based on quantity or alphabetic principles, working memory capacity, and mental manipulation. It may also involve information processing, cognitive flexibility, and fluid intelligence (Crowe, 2000; Flanagan & Kaufman, 2009; Groth-Marnat, 2009; Sattler, 2008b; Wechsler, 2014). The latter skills represent executive control and resource allocation functions in working memory. Two qualifying items are given to establish that the child has the prerequisite counting and alphabet skills to perform the task.

Processing Speed Index

The PSI is formed by two well-established primary processing speed subtests: Coding and Symbol Search. There is one secondary processing speed subtest: Cancellation.

Coding

For Coding, the child works within a specified time limit and uses a key to copy symbols that correspond with simple geometric shapes or numbers. In addition to processing speed, the subtest measures short-term visual memory, procedural and incidental learning ability, psychomotor speed, visual perception, visual–motor coordination, visual scanning ability, cognitive flexibility, attention, concentration, and motivation. It may also involve visual sequential processing and fluid intelligence (Flanagan & Kaufman, 2009; Groth-Marnat, 2009; Sattler, 2008b; Wechsler, 2014).

Symbol Search

For Symbol Search, the child scans search groups and indicates if target symbols are present, while working within a specified time limit. In addition to visual–perceptual (e.g., visual identification and matching) and decision-making speed, the subtest involves short-term visual memory, visual–motor coordination, inhibitory control, visual discrimination, psychomotor speed, sustained attention, and concentration. It may also measure perceptual organization, fluid intelligence, and planning and learning ability (Flanagan & Kaufman, 2009; Groth-Marnat, 2009; Sattler, 2008b; Wechsler, 2014).

Cancellation

For Cancellation, the child scans two arrangements of objects (one random, one structured) and marks target objects while working within a specified time limit. The subtest measures rate of test taking, speed of visual–perceptual processing and decision-making, visual scanning ability, and visual–perceptual recognition and discrimination (Flanagan & Kaufman, 2009; Sattler, 2008b; Wechsler, 2014). It may also involve attention, concentration, and visual recall (Sattler, 2008a). Cancellation tasks have been used extensively in neuropsychological settings as measures of visual neglect, response inhibition, and motor perseveration (Lezak, Howieson, & Loring, 2004).

THE WISC-V FULL SCALE INTELLIGENCE QUOTIENT

The FSIQ is one of the most established measures in psychology, reflecting general mental ability as described by numerous experts in the study of intelligence spanning the decades from Spearman, Wechsler, and Vernon to Carroll, Horn, and Cattell. General intelligence has been consistently shown to be associated with many important outcomes in life, and is thus of considerable applied importance in the assessment of children's potential; predicting school achievement, higher educational attainment, job advancement, and career success (Deary, Whiteman, Starr, Whalley & Fox, 2004; Gottfredson & Saklofske, 2009; Squalli & Wilson, 2014; Lubinski, 2004; Sternberg & Grigorenko, 2002). As practicing psychologists often voice, intelligence as assessed by the Wechsler scales contains both the breadth and depth of critical information needed to understand a person's overall cognitive capacity to successfully interact with the world around them.

The FSIQ is composed of seven of the 10 primary subtests described above: two verbal comprehension subtests, one visual–spatial subtest, two fluid reasoning subtests, one working memory subtest, and one processing speed subtest. Extensive empirical analyses revealed that this weighting of the five factors yields the optimal balance of predicting school achievement and key clinical criteria while maintaining high reliability and other psychometric standards.

As shown in Figure 1.1, the FSIQ is composed of the following seven primary subtests: Similarities, Vocabulary, Block Design, Matrix Reasoning, Figure Weights, Digit Span, and Coding. Best practice is to administer all 10 primary subtests in order to obtain the FSIQ and the five primary index scores: VCI, VSI, FRI, WMI, and PSI.

THE WISC-V ANCILLARY INDEXES AND SUBTESTS

In this section we review the five ancillary indexes: the General Ability, Cognitive Proficiency, Nonverbal, Quantitative Reasoning, and Auditory

Working Memory Indexes. The ancillary indexes are optional. They allow the clinician to explore specific cognitive hypotheses related to children's WISC-V scores in the context of their performance in the real world of the classroom, in daily interactions, and in everyday demands. Some but not all of these composites require administration of selected secondary subtests beyond the 10 primary subtests required to obtain the five primary index scores. Figure 1.1 shows the subtest composition of each of the five ancillary index scores.

The General Ability Index

The General ability index (GAI) is a composite score that summarizes performance on all FSIQ subtests except Digit Span and Coding into a single number. The WISC-V GAI differs from FSIQ in that it excludes the contributions of working memory and processing speed. Thus, GAI and FSIQ can lead to different impressions of a child's overall ability when there is variability across the five primary indexes. The GAI is comprised of five of the seven primary subtest scores that enter the FSIQ: Similarities, Vocabulary, Block Design, Matrix Reasoning, and Figure Weights. No secondary subtests are necessary to calculate the GAI.

We originally developed GAI with WISC-III, specifically for use in ability-achievement discrepancy analyses because many learning disabled and ADHD students exhibit cognitive processing deficits in working memory and processing speed concomitant with their learning disabilities (Prifitera, Weiss, & Saklofske, 1998). Lowered performance on WM and PS subtests in turn lowers the FSIQ for many learning disabled students, which decreases the magnitude of the discrepancy between ability and achievement weaknesses, and may result in denial of needed special education services when that model is used for special education eligibility determinations. In those situations, the GAI may be used in the ability-achievement discrepancy analysis in order to better identify eligible students. Other uses for the GAI have since been identified. For similar reasons to those described above, it also may be appropriate to use GAI when evaluating the extent to which general memory functions are commensurate with overall intelligence for children with LD or ADHD. Further, GAI may be an appropriate estimate of overall ability when physical or sensory disorders invalidate performance on the working memory or processing speed tasks, or both.

For these reasons, we previously suggested that some practitioners may prefer the GAI as an alternative way of summarizing overall ability (Saklofske, Prifitera, Weiss, Rolfhus, & Zhu, 2005). However, this suggestion has led to an increasing number of psychological evaluations in which the GAI is described as a better estimate of overall ability than FSIQ whenever the child scores significantly lower on the working memory or processing speed subtests. We subsequently clarified that this is not what we intended, and can be a very problematic practice (Weiss, Beal, Saklofske, Alloway, & Prifitera, 2008). Ultimately, we believe that working memory and processing speed are essential components of intelligence, and excluding them from the estimate of overall intelligence simply because the child scored low on those subtests is poor practice. Such practice will result in unrealistically high estimates of intelligence for those students and possibly create expectations which they cannot live up to without accommodations. To be clear, it is sometimes appropriate to report GAI and compare it to other scores such as achievement and memory. It is not good practice to describe GAI as a better estimate of overall intelligence than FSIQ solely because the child scored poorly on Digit Span or Coding.

The Cognitive Proficiency Index

The Cognitive proficiency index (CPI) summarizes performance on the primary working memory and processing speed subtests of the WISC-V into a single score. The CPI is comprised of four of the 10 primary subtests. No secondary subtests are required to calculate the CPI. Creating a new composite by combining WMI and PSI was first suggested in relation to WISC-III by Dumont and Willis (2001), and subsequently extended to WISC-IV by Weiss et al. (2006) and WAIS-IV by Weiss et al. (2010). In WISC-V, the CPI is included as part of the test's manual (Wechsler, 2014).

The CPI represents a set of functions whose common element is the proficiency with which one processes certain types of cognitive information. As we explain in more detail in Chapter 5, the abilities represented in the CPI are central to the fluid reasoning process. Proficient processing—through quick visual speed and good mental control—facilitates fluid reasoning and the acquisition of new material by reducing the cognitive demands of novel or higher order tasks. More simply, efficient cognitive processing facilitates learning and problem-solving by "freeing up" cognitive resources for more advanced, higher level skills.

The WISC-V CPI excludes the contributions of verbal comprehension, visual–spatial organization, and fluid reasoning. Thus, CPI and GAI can provide different views into a child's cognitive abilities when there is significant variability across the relevant index scores. Both views are sometimes necessary to form a complete picture of an individual's strengths and weaknesses that is not distorted by combining a set of diverse abilities into a single overall FSIQ score. Rather than reporting GAI as the best estimate of overall ability when the profile of subtest scores is diverse, it is sometimes better practice to describe both the GAI and CPI in the psychological evaluation and discuss how deficits in proficient cognitive processing interfere with the expression of the child's general ability.

Nonverbal Index

The Nonverbal index (NVI) is formed by six subtests: Block Design, Visual Puzzles, Matrix Reasoning, Figure Weights, Picture Span, and Coding. All of these are primary subtests, but Visual Puzzles is not a FSIQ subtest. Thus, calculating the NVI requires administration of one secondary subtest.

This index substantially minimizes but does not eliminate verbal comprehension because the subtests still require the child to understand the directions that are spoken verbally and certainly such tasks can be mediated by oral language or private and internal silent speech.

In a sample of English language learners in which the WISC-V FSIQ was 8.3 points lower than matched controls, the WISC-V NVI was only 1.8 points lower (Wechsler, 2014). Thus, the NVI can be useful in a variety of situations in which English language skills are either underdeveloped or impaired.

Quantitative Reasoning Index

The Quantitative reasoning index (QRI) is formed by combining the Arithmetic and Figure Weights subtests. Thus, calculation of QRI requires administration of one secondary subtest (Arithmetic) beyond the 10 primary subtests. The Arithmetic subtest involves mentally solving arithmetic problems presented verbally as word problems. The Figure Weights subtest involves estimation of relative quantities of abstract symbols based on learning and applying their quantitative relationships to each other.

Quantitative reasoning is a type of fluid reasoning. That is, quantitative reasoning is fluid reasoning using quantitative concepts. Further research is needed on the relationship of quantitative reasoning to achievement in higher order mathematics.

Auditory Working Memory Index

The primary WMI is composed of Digit Span and Picture Span, which are auditory and visual working memory tasks, respectively. The WMI allows full construct coverage of working memory across both sensory modalities (visual and auditory). The auditory working memory index (AWMI) removes the contribution of visual working memory by replacing Picture Span with Letter-Number Sequencing. Thus, the AWMI consists of Digit Span and Letter-Number Sequencing, which are both auditory working memory tasks. Calculation of the AWMI requires administration of one secondary subtest (Letter-Number Sequencing). In clinical situations in which the visual modality is impaired, the AWMI allows better evaluation of working memory functions than the WMI.

THE WISC-V COMPLEMENTARY INDEXES AND SUBTESTS

Complementary indexes and subtests are new to WISC-V. They are different from the primary and ancillary indexes because they are not part of any of the broad cognitive abilities measured by the WISC-V. Rather, they are designed to provide examiners with more detailed information relevant to psychoeducational evaluations of children referred for specific learning disorders such as in reading and mathematics.

Naming Speed Index

The Naming Speed Index is comprised of two optional subtests: Naming Speed Literacy and Naming Speed Quantity.

Naming Speed Literacy

In the Naming Speed Literacy subtest the child names elements of various stimuli as quickly as possible. The tasks utilize stimuli and elements that are traditional within rapid naming task paradigms (e.g., colors, objects, letters, and numbers) and that have shown sensitivity to reading and written expression skills and to specific learning disorders in reading and written expression. Similar tasks are closely associated with reading and spelling skill development, with reading achievement, and with a number of variables related to reading and spelling, and have shown sensitivity to specific learning disorder in reading (Crews & D'Amato, 2009; Korkman, Barron-Linnankoski, & Lahti-Nuuttila, 1999; Korkman, Kirk, & Kemp, 2007; Powell, Stainthorp, Stuart, Garwood, & Quinlan, 2007; Willburger, Fussenegger, Moll, Wood, & Landerl, 2008). Some studies suggest they are also related to mathematics skills, specific learning disorder–mathematics, and a number of other clinical conditions (McGrew & Wendling, 2010; Pauly et al., 2011; Willburger et al., 2008; Wise et al., 2008). In order to ensure sensitivity beyond very early grades, the tasks involve naming multiple dimensions simultaneously and alternating stimuli. Such tasks are also sensitive to a wide variety of other neurodevelopmental conditions such as ADHD (Korkman et al., 2007), language disorders in both monolingual and bilingual children (Korkman et al., 2012), and autism spectrum disorder (Korkman et al., 2007). Children at risk for neurodevelopmental issues have been reported to score lower on similar measures (Lind et al., 2011), which are described as measuring storage and retrieval fluency, and naming facility (Flanagan et al., 2012). These subtests specifically measure the automaticity of visual–verbal associations, which should be well developed in school-aged children.

Naming Speed Quantity

In the Naming Speed Quantity subtest the child names the quantity of squares inside a series of boxes as quickly as possible. The subtest is similar to tasks in the experimental literature that show greater sensitivity to mathematics skills and specific learning disorders in mathematics than do the traditional rapid automatized naming tasks that are more closely associated with reading- and writing-related variables (Pauly et al., 2011; van der Sluis, de Jong, & van der Leij, 2004; Willburger et al., 2008). Tasks that involve rapid naming of stimuli are described as measuring naming facility, and storage and retrieval fluency (Flanagan et al., 2012).

Symbol Translation Index

The Symbol Translation Index measures learning associations between unfamiliar symbols and their meanings, and applying them in novel ways. The subtest consists of three conditions: immediate, delayed, and recognition.

Immediate Symbol Translation

In the Immediate Symbol Translation subtests the child learns visual–verbal pairs and then translates symbol strings into phrases or sentences. Tasks similar to Immediate Symbol Translation are described as measuring verbal–visual associative memory or paired associates learning, storage and retrieval fluency and accuracy, and immediate recall (Flanagan et al., 2012). This is a cued memory paradigm, that is, the child recalls information related to a specific visual cue.

Visual–verbal associative memory tasks similar to the Symbol Translation subtests are closely associated with reading decoding skills, word reading accuracy and fluency, text reading, and reading comprehension (Elliott, Hale, Fiorello, Dorvil, & Moldovan, 2010; Evans, Floyd, McGrew, & Leforgee, 2001; Floyd, Keith, Taub, & McGrew, 2007; Hulme, Goetz, Gooch, Adams, & Snowling, 2007; Lervåg, Bråten, & Hulme, 2009; Litt, de Jong, van Bergen, & Nation, 2013). Furthermore, they are sensitive to dyslexia when they require verbal output (Gang & Siegel, 2002; Li, Shu, McBride-Chang, Lui, & Xue, 2009; Litt & Nation, 2014). Visual–verbal associative memory tasks are also related to math calculation skills and math reasoning (Floyd, Evans, & McGrew, 2003; McGrew & Wendling, 2010).

Delayed Symbol Translation

In the Delayed Symbol Translation condition the child translates symbol strings into sentences using visual–verbal pairs previously learned during the Immediate Symbol Translation condition. Tasks similar to Delayed Symbol Translation are described as measuring verbal–visual associative memory or paired associates learning, storage and retrieval fluency and accuracy, and delayed recall (Flanagan et al., 2012). This task is a cued memory paradigm.

Recognition Symbol Translation

In the Recognition Symbol Translation subtest the child views a symbol and selects the correct translation from response options the examiner reads aloud, using visual–verbal pairs recalled from the Immediate Symbol Translation condition. Tasks similar to Recognition Symbol Translation are described as measuring verbal–visual associative memory or paired associates learning, storage and retrieval fluency and accuracy, and delayed recognition (Flanagan et al., 2012). This task constrains the child's responses to words that have been presented in the task and therefore eliminates the possibility of an erroneous word being recalled. This task allows the examiner to identify the strength of the associate learning and not the learning of content (e.g., correct words). The examiner may compare performance on this task to the delayed condition to determine the impact of constraining recall on memory performance.

Storage and Retrieval Index

The Storage and Retrieval Index is formed by combining the scores from the Naming Speed Index and the Symbol Translation Index. This provides an overall measure of the child's ability to store and retrieve learned information quickly and efficiently.

SUMMARY

In this chapter we have shown how the contemporary Wechsler model has evolved and expanded from two to five factors based on a careful research program spanning decades and multiple editions of the various Wechsler tests (WPPSI, WISC, and WAIS). We have described the WISC-V subtests related to each of the five primary and five ancillary cognitive indexes, as well as the three complementary indexes designed to assist psychologists with psychoeducational evaluations of specific learning disabilities. As with all tests, including the WISC-V, they are based on theory and empirical findings from research as well as clinical practice, and are intended to provide the clinician with a standardized measure to aid in the assessment process including diagnosis, planning, and prescription of the child or adolescent. The very nature of the WISC-V should contribute to guiding, informing, and confirming clinical hypotheses in the very complex process of clinical and psychoeducational assessment when the definition of problem areas and solutions are not readily apparent. Yet, the WISC-V, as sophisticated and important as it may be in the psychological assessment of children and adolescents, does not make decisions…psychologists do!

REFERENCES

Benson, N., Hulac, D. M., & Kranzler, J. H. (2010). Independent examination of Wechsler Adult Intelligence Scale—Fourth Edition (WAIS-IV): What does the WAIS-IV measure? *Psychological Assessment, 22*(1), 121–130.

Carroll, J. B. (1993). *Human cognitive abilities: A survey of factor-analytic studies.* New York: Cambridge University Press.

Crews, K. J., & D'Amato, R. C. (2009). Subtyping children's reading disabilities using a comprehensive neuropsychological measure. *International Journal of Neuroscience, 119*, 1615–1639.

Crowe, S. F. (2000). Does the letter number sequencing task measure anything more than digit span? *Assessment, 7*(2), 113–117.

Deary, I. J., Whiteman, M. C., Starr, J. M., Whalley, Lawrence J., & Fox, H. C. (2004). The impact of childhood intelligence on later life: Following up the Scottish mental surveys of 1932 and 1947. *Journal of Personality and Social Psychology, 86*(1), 130–147.

Dumont, R., & Willis, J. (2001). Use of the Tellegen & Briggs formula to determine the Dumont-Willis Indexes (DWI-1 & DWI-2) for the WISC-III. Available at: http://alpha.fdu.edu/psychology/.

Elliott, C. D., Hale, J. B., Fiorello, C. A., Dorvil, C., & Moldovan, J. (2010). Differential Ability Scales–II prediction of reading performance: Global scores are not enough. *Psychology in the Schools, 47*(7), 698–720.

Evans, J. J., Floyd, R. G., McGrew, K. S., & Leforgee, M. H. (2001). The relations between measures of Cattell-Horn-Carroll (CHC) cognitive abilities and reading achievement during childhood and adolescence. *School Psychology Review, 31*(2), 246–262.

Flanagan, D. P., & Kaufman, A. S. (2009). *Essentials of WISC-IV assessment* (2nd ed.). Hoboken, NJ: John Wiley & Sons.

Flanagan, D. P., Alfonso, V. C., Ortiz, S. O., & Dynda, A. M. (2010). Integrating cognitive assessment in school neuropsychological evaluations. In D. C. Miller (Ed.), *Best practices in school neuropsychology: Guidelines for effective practice, assessment, and evidence-based intervention* (pp. 101–140). Hoboken, NJ: John Wiley & Sons.

Flanagan, D. P., Alfonso, V. C., & Ortiz, S. O. (2012). The cross-battery assessment approach: An overview, historical perspective, and current directions. In D. P. Flanagan & P. L. Harrison (Eds.), *Contemporary intellectual assessment: Theories, tests, and issues* (3rd ed.). pp. 459–483. New York, NY: The Guilford Press.

Floyd, R. G., Evans, J. J., & McGrew, K. S. (2003). Relations between measures of Cattell-Horn-Carroll (CHC) cognitive abilities and mathematics achievement across the school-age years. *Psychology in the Schools, 40*(2), 155–171.

Floyd, R. G., Keith, T. Z., Taub, G. E., & McGrew, K. S. (2007). Cattell-Horn-Carroll cognitive abilities and their effects on reading decoding skills: g has indirect effects, more specific abilities have direct effects. *School Psychology Quarterly, 22*(2), 200–233.

Gang, M., & Siegel, L. S. (2002). Sound-symbol learning in children with dyslexia. *Journal of Learning Disabilities, 35*(2), 137–157.

Gottfredson, L. S., & Saklofske, D. H. (2009). Intelligence: Foundations and issues in assessment. *Psychologie canadienne, 50*(3), 183–195.

Groth-Marnat, G. (2009). *Handbook of psychological assessment* (5th ed.). New York, NY: John Wiley & Sons.

Hartshorne, J. K. (2008). Visual working memory capacity and proactive interference. *PLoS ONE, 3*(7), e2716.

Horn, J. L., & Cattell, R. B. (1966). Refinement and test of the theory of fluid and crystallized general intelligences. *Journal of Educational Psychology, 57*, 253–270.

Hulme, C., Goetz, K., Gooch, D., Adams, J., & Snowling, M. J. (2007). Paired-associate learning, phoneme awareness, and learning to read. *Journal of Experimental Child Psychology, 96*, 150–166.

Kaufman, A. S. (2013). Intelligent testing with Wechsler's fourth editions: Perspectives on the Weiss et al. studies and the eight commentaries. *Journal of Psychoeducational Assessment, 31*(2), 224–234.

Kaufman, A. S., & Lichtenberger, E. O. (2006). *Assessing adolescent and adult intelligence* (3rd ed.). Hoboken, NJ: John Wiley & Sons.

Korkman, M., Barron-Linnankoski, S., & Lahti-Nuuttila, P. (1999). Effects of age and duration of reading instruction on the development of phonological awareness, rapid naming, and verbal memory span. *Developmental Neuropsychology, 16*(3), 415–431.

Korkman, M., Kirk, U., & Kemp, S. (2007). *NEPSY–II*. Bloomington, MN: Pearson.

Korkman, M., Stenroos, M., Mickos, A., Westman, M., Ekholm, P., & Byring, R. (2012). Does simultaneous bilingualism aggravate children's specific language problems? *Acta Pædiatrica, 101*, 946–952.

Lervåg, A., Bråten, I., & Hulme, C. (2009). The cognitive and linguistic foundations of early reading development: A Norwegian latent variable longitudinal study. *Developmental Psychology*, *45*(3), 764–781.

Lezak, M.D., Howieson, D.B., & Loring, D.W. (with Hannay, H. J., & Fischer, J. S.) (2004). *Neuropsychological assessment* (4th ed.). New York, NY: Oxford University Press.

Li, H., Shu, H., McBride-Chang, C., Liu, H. Y., & Xue, J. (2009). Paired associate learning in Chinese children with dyslexia. *Journal of Experimental Child Psychology*, *103*, 135–151.

Likert, R., & Quasha, W. H. (1995). *Revised Minnesota paper form board test manual* (2nd ed.). San Antonio, TX: The Psychological Corporation.

Lind, A., Korkman, M., Lehtonen, L., Lapinleimu, H., Parkkola, R., Matomäki, J., et al. (2011). Cognitive and neuropsychological outcomes at 5 years of age in preterm children born in the 2000s. *Developmental Medicine & Child Neurology*, *53*(3), 256–262.

Litt, R. A., de Jong, P. F., van Bergen, E., & Nation, K. (2013). Dissociating crossmodal and verbal demands in paired associate learning (PAL): What drives the PAL–reading relationship? *Journal of Experimental Child Psychology*, *115*, 137–149.

Litt, R. A., & Nation, K. (2014). The nature and specificity of paired associate learning deficits in children with dyslexia. *Journal of Memory and Language*, *71*, 71–88.

Lubinski, D. (Ed.), (2004). Cognitive abilities: 100 years after Spearman's (1904) "General intelligence. objectively determined and measured" (Special section). *Journal of Personality and Social Psychology*, *86*, 96–199.

MacDonald, M. C., Almor, A., Henderson, V. W., Kempler, D., & Andersen, E. S. (2001). Assessing working memory and language comprehension in Alzheimer's disease. *Brain and Language*, *78*, 17–42.

Makovski, T., & Jiang, Y. V. (2008). Proactive interference from items previously stored in visual working memory. *Memory & Cognition*, *36*(1), 43–52.

McGrew, K. S., & Wendling, B. J. (2010). Cattell–Horn–Carroll cognitive-achievement relations: What we have learned from the past 20 years of research. *Psychology in the Schools*, *47*(7), 651–675.

Miller, D. C. (2010). *Best practices in school neuropsychology: Guidelines for effective practice, assessment, and evidence-based intervention.* Hoboken, NJ: John Wiley & Sons.

Miller, D. C. (2013). *Essentials of school neuropsychological assessment* (2nd ed.). Hoboken, NJ: John Wiley & Sons.

Pauly, H., Linkersdörfer, J., Lindberg, S., Woerner, W., Hasselhorn, M., & Lonnemann, J. (2011). Domain-specific rapid automatized naming deficits in children at risk for learning disabilities. *Journal of Neurolinguistics*, *24*, 602–610.

Powell, D., Stainthorp, R., Stuart, M., Garwood, H., & Quinlan, P. (2007). An experimental comparison between rival theories of rapid automatized naming performance and its relationship to reading. *Journal of Experimental Child Psychology*, *98*(1), 46–68.

Prifitera, A., Weiss, L. G., & Saklofske, D. H. (1998). The WISC-III in context. In A. Prifitera & D. H. Saklofske (Eds.), *WISC-III clinical use and interpretation: Scientist–practitioner perspectives* (pp. 1–38). San Diego: Academic Press.

Reynolds, C. R. (1997). Forward and backward memory span should not be combined for clinical analysis. *Archives of Clinical Neuropsychology*, *12*, 29–40.

Saklofske, D. H., Prifitera, A., Weiss, L. G., Rolfhus, E., & Zhu, J. (2005). Clinical interpretation of the WISC-IV FSIQ and GAI. In A. Prifitera, D. H. Saklofske, & L. G. Weiss (Eds.), *WISC-IV clinical use and interpretation: Scientist–practitioner perspectives.* San Diego: Academic Press.

Sattler, J. M. (2008a). *Assessment of children: Cognitive foundations* (5th ed.). San Diego, CA: Author.

Sattler, J. M. (2008b). *Resource guide to accompany assessment of children: Cognitive foundations* (5th ed.). San Diego, CA: Author.

Sattler, J. M., & Ryan, J. J. (2009). *Assessment with the WAIS-IV*. La Mesa, CA: Author.

Sternberg, R. J., & Grigorenko, E. L. (Eds.), (2002). *The general intelligence factor: How general is it?* Mahwah, NJ: Erlbaum.

Squalli, J., & Wilson, K. (2014). Intelligence, creativity, and innovation. *Intelligence, 46*, 250–257.

Tobin, R. M. (2013). The Wechsler intelligence tests: Revisiting theory and practice. *Journal of Psychoeducational Assessment, 31*(2), 91–94.

van der Sluis, S., de Jong, P. F., & van der Leij, A. (2004). Inhibition and shifting in children with learning deficits in arithmetic and reading. *Journal of Experimental Child Psychology, 87*(3), 239–266.

Ward, L. C., Bergman, M. A., & Herbert, K. R. (2011). WAIS-IV subtest covariance structure: Conceptual and statistical considerations. *Psychological Assessment*, Advance online publication.

Wechsler, D. (1939). *The measurement of adult intelligence*. Baltimore, MD: Williams & Wilkins.

Wechsler, D. (2009). *Wechsler memory scale* (4th ed.). Bloomington, MN: Pearson.

Wechsler, D. (2012). *Manual for the Wechsler preschool and primary scales of intelligence* (4th ed.). San Antonio: Pearson.

Wechsler, D. (2014). *Technical manual for the Wechsler intelligence scale for children* (5th ed.). San Antonio: Pearson.

Weiss, L. G., Beal, A. L., Saklofske, D. H., Alloway, T. P., & Prifitera, A. (2008). Interpretation and intervention with WISC-IV in the clinical assessment context. In A. Prifitera, D. H. Saklofske, & L. G. Weiss (Eds.), *WISC-IV clinical assessment and intervention*. San Diego: Academic Press.

Weiss, L. G., Keith, T. Z., Zhu, J., & Chen, H. (2013a). WAIS-IV clinical validation of the four- and five-factor interpretive approaches. *Journal of Psychoeducational Assessment, 31*(2), 114–131.

Weiss, L. G., Keith, T. Z., Zhu, J., & Chen, H. (2013b). WISC-IV clinical validation of the four- and five-factor interpretive approaches. *Journal of Psychoeducational Assessment, 31*(2), 94–113.

Weiss, L. G., Keith, T. Z., Zhu, J., & Chen, H. (2013c). Technical and practical issues in the structure and clinical invariance of the Wechsler scales: A rejoinder to commentaries. *Journal of Psychoeducational Assessment, 31*(2), 235–243.

Weiss, L. G., Saklofske, D. H., Coalson, D., & Raiford, S. E. (2010). *WAIS-IV clinical use and interpretation*. San Diego: Academic Press.

Weiss, L. G., Saklofske, D. H., Prifitera, A., & Holdnack, J. A. (2006). *WISC-IV: Advanced clinical interpretation*. San Diego: Academic Press.

Werheid, K., Hoppe, C., Thöne, A., Müller, U., Müngersdorf, M., & von Cramon, D. Y. (2002). The adaptive digit ordering test: Clinical application, reliability, and validity of a verbal working memory test. *Archives of Clinical Neuropsychology, 17*, 547–565.

Willburger, E., Fussenegger, B., Moll, K., Wood, G., & Landerl, K. (2008). Naming speed in dyslexia and dyscalculia. *Learning and Individual Differences, 18*, 224–236.

Wise, J. C., Pae, H. K., Wolfe, G. B., Seucik, R. A., Morris, R. D., Lovett, M., et al. (2008). Phonological awareness and rapid naming skills of children with reading disabilities and children with reading disabilities who are at risk for mathematical disabilities. *Learning Disabilities Research and Practice, 23*(3), 125–136.

Chapter 2

Practical Issues in WISC-V Administration and Scoring

Dustin Wahlstrom[1], Lawrence G. Weiss[1], and Donald H. Saklofske[2]
[1]*Pearson Clinical Assessment, San Antonio, TX, USA,* [2]*Department of Psychology, University of Western Ontario, London, Ontario, Canada*

INTRODUCTION

The purpose of this chapter is to provide information that will guide both new and experienced practitioners through the nuances of WISC-V administration and scoring. Simplicity and ease of use have always been tenants of the Wechsler tests, but everyone will find parts of the WISC-V unfamiliar given the substantial changes that were made to it relative to its predecessor. Drawing from research literature, feedback from field examiners, and the experience of internal development teams, this chapter summarizes general WISC-V administration and scoring guidelines, describes details of individual subtest administration (noting new subtests), and provides answers to frequently asked questions. Basic subtest administration tips are highlighted in tables throughout the chapter for quick access, and major changes to subtests that were included in the WISC-IV are listed in an appendix at the conclusion. The goal for this chapter is to supplement the *WISC-V Administration and Scoring Manual*, providing practitioners with additional tips and insight based on the experience of those who helped to develop the measure. It is recommended that students and examiners new to the WISC read this chapter in its entirety and give equal attention to all sections. Examiners familiar with the WISC will also benefit from all sections but should pay special attention to the appendix at the end of the chapter, as well as the highlight tables throughout the chapter that summarize the subtest administration rules.

Regardless of experience, careful attention to the seemingly basic information provided in this chapter and the *WISC-V Administration and Scoring Manual* is important. Almost all intelligence test protocols analyzed in studies on examiner accuracy have contained at least one administration or scoring error, regardless of whether they were completed by students or practicing practitioners

L. G. Weiss, D. H. Saklofske, J. A. Holdnack and A. Prifitera (Eds): WISC-V Assessment and Interpretation.
DOI: http://dx.doi.org/10.1016/B978-0-12-404697-9.00002-9

(Belk, LoBello, Ray, & Zachar, 2002; Ryan & Schnakenberg-Ott, 2003; Slate & Chick, 1989). Furthermore, basic experience and practice have been ineffective at significantly reducing these mistakes (Slate & Jones, 1990a, 1990b; but see Platt, Zachar, Ray, Underhill, & LoBello, 2007 for slight improvements). This is a cautionary tale for practitioners, who routinely incorporate test data into high stakes decisions yet are unlikely to have these potential pitfalls in the forefront of consciousness during a typical administration. The first step to interpretable and meaningful WISC-V results is an accurate score, and the data strongly suggest that none of us are exempt from mistakes. The following sections are intended to help readers avoid the most common mistakes and increase the reliability of their WISC-V administrations by highlighting the areas of Wechsler administration and scoring that are the most frequent sources of examiner questions and errors.

GENERAL WISC-V ADMINISTRATION AND SCORING TIPS

WISC-V Administration

The majority of this chapter is organized by subtests and cognitive domains, as most of the administration and scoring rules in the WISC-V vary by those categories. However, there are general aspects of WISC-V administration that do bear mentioning at the outset. First is the proper application of start points, reverse rules, discontinue rules, and stop points, which specify what item to begin on and when to stop testing (with the purpose of limiting the number of items given to reduce frustration or boredom). Students beginning their assessment careers will quickly become familiar with these requirements, as they represent a primary focus of training programs. Similarly, most practitioners feel very familiar with them based on their years of experience, as the basic structure of the rules is consistent across the Wechsler tests. Despite this emphasis, mistakes in this area represent some of the more commonly made errors on the Wechsler intelligence scales (Belk et al., 2002; Loe, Kadlubek, & Marks, 2007). Graduate students often start at the incorrect items, fail to establish basal sets, discontinue subtest administration too early, and forget to give credit to items prior to the start point. A full examination of these rules is outside the scope of this chapter, so it is important that readers know where to find this critical information. First, all WISC-V examiners should consult Chapter 2 of the *WISC-V Administration and Scoring Manual* for a comprehensive and clear explanation of how administration rules should be applied. Pay close attention to this section because it explains how various "edge cases" should be handled (e.g., what happens if the child reaches a discontinue point in the process of reversing?). While these scenarios are relatively rare, they do lead to examiner confusion. Second, in this chapter are tables that summarize the start point, reverse rule, and discontinue rule for each WISC-V subtest. This information can be used during training or as a quick reference when administering the WISC-V (but note that the Record Form has very brief summaries of the rules as well). Overall, mistakes in this area can invalidate subtests, so new examiners are encouraged to utilize them as necessary until they are well versed in the nuances of WISC-V administration rules.

A second issue common across all Wechsler intelligence scales is proper recording of responses and response times. Examiners and graduate students often forget to record completion time for subtests like Arithmetic, verbatim responses for Verbal Comprehension subtests like Vocabulary, and responses for subtests that do not require verbal responses like Matrix Reasoning or Block Design (Loe et al., 2007). Recording this information is best practice for several reasons. First, it provides important qualitative information that seasoned practitioners can use to supplement test scores (e.g., are there certain language deficits that can be identified from the quality of a child's verbal responses?). Second, it offers a solid record of what occurred in the testing session, which can be useful in forensic and training sessions where Record Forms are scrutinized closely. Lastly, it ensures more comprehensive records are available if examiners need to reference them when finalizing scores or writing the report. In general, it is always better to have more information than less, and while we understand the pressure to test quickly in the current professional environment, failing to completely fill out the Record Form is not an effective way to increase efficiency.

Finally, the WISC-V subtests share similar requirements for the recording of behavioral observations. Children display common behaviors when taking the WISC-V—they will often say, "I don't know" or fail to respond at all when items increase in difficulty, request the examiner to repeat questions, self-correct when providing answers, or exhibit other behaviors that necessitate prompting. It is important for examiners to record these behaviors by making notes in the Record Form (e.g., "DK," "NR," "R," etc.). Historically, these observations have been used to provide qualitative insights into a child's problem-solving style or personality that cannot be obtained by traditional test scores alone. For example, it may be important to note that a child gave up easily when the difficulty of items increased, as he may display similar behaviors in the classroom that are interfering with success and could be a focus of intervention. Similarly, a child who frequently asks for repetition might have language or auditory problems that require follow-up. The WISC-V has expanded upon this traditional use of behavioral observations by norming these common behaviors. During standardization, examiners recorded "Don't know" responses, lack of responses, self-corrections, requests for repetitions, and subvocalizations (silent lip movement or perceptible self-talk) for various WISC-V subtests, and the total observations per subtest were converted into base rates. Thus, examiners can now track these observations and use Appendix D of the *WISC-V Technical and Interpretive Manual* to derive scores that add an additional dimension to their interpretation.

WISC-V Scoring

Scoring the WISC involves two primary activities: (1) the item-level action of *scoring* a child's response, a process that may or may not require subjective judgment on the part of the examiner, and (2) *clerical* tasks such as summing item scores, converting subtest raw scores into scaled scores via lookup tables, etc. (Klassen & Kishor, 1996). The requirements for the first type of scoring vary by subtest and are covered elsewhere in this chapter; for that reason, they are not described in detail here. The clerical aspect of scoring does warrant special mention, however, because it is a relatively simple task that can result in significant changes in scores if done incorrectly. Research suggests that clerical mistakes are made less frequently than item-level scoring errors (Hopwood & Richard, 2005) but have a much greater impact on Full Scale Intelligence Quotient (FSIQ) and index scores (Belk et al., 2002). This is hardly a surprise—assigning an additional raw score point to a single Vocabulary item is unlikely to significantly impact the FSIQ once Vocabulary is converted into a subtest scaled score and summed with other subtests to generate composite scores (though it should be noted that the consequences of numerous errors of this type might be more severe). Conversely, looking up the incorrect cell in a table or adding the sum of scaled scores incorrectly could cause scores to vary considerably depending on how egregious the error is. Hopwood and Richard (2005) found that item scoring errors had little impact on FSIQ scores, whereas clerical errors when looking up scaled scores in tables resulted in an average FSIQ change of 5.5 points *per error*.

What should practitioners do to remedy this problem? Recent research revealed that the simple act of double-checking protocols resulted in more than a 50% decrease in errors, tripled the number of error-free protocols, and reduced the number of inaccurate FSIQ scores by two-thirds (Kuentzel, Hetterscheidt, & Barnett, 2011). These findings highlight the potential power of double-checking Wechsler protocols, a simple and widely used data entry technique that takes little to no training to implement. In a professional climate where more and more testing is expected in less and less time, we understand the urge to score quickly and move on to other aspects of testing. The short time taken to verify the accuracy of scoring and recording is more than justified by providing the precision and accuracy expected when clinically important decisions are to be based on data. Given the relative ease of double-checking scores and the potential impacts of mis-scoring, it is suggested that protocol reviews be utilized where appropriate and strongly considered in training clinics staffed by practicum students and interns.

One important data point from the Kuentzel et al. study is that almost a third of all protocols had errors even after the double-checking procedures were employed, a surprising number that highlights the human error inherent in any simple case review process. There are now a number of digital systems available to assist in the administration and scoring of the WISC-V, with one of their benefits being the reduction of clerical scoring errors. Q-global™ is a web-based scoring platform that replaces the traditional scoring assistant software that is available with the Wechsler kits. The use of this software requires examiners to enter subtest total raw scores into the system, so as Kuentzel and colleagues rightfully point out, this system cannot militate against any errors that were made getting to those subtest raw scores. Alternatively, Q-interactive™ allows the examiner to administer the WISC-V using two tablet devices that are connected via Bluetooth: one is used by the child, and the other by the examiner. The examiner's tablet allows her or him to view and control what is seen on the child's tablet. In Q-interactive, all item scores are determined by the examiner, but from there all other scores (and all start points, reverse rules, and discontinue rules) are automated by the system, thus removing many sources of common scoring problems. Chapter 11 contains a more detailed description of the Q-interactive system, so suffice it to say here that accuracy is a key benefit that testing technology promises to provide in the future. Furthermore, unlike double-checking procedures, technology is free of human error and provides increased accuracy without any additional time investment (in fact, typically less). As systems such as Q-global and Q-interactive become more prevalent, we expect that the data on testing errors will reflect a decrease in the number of mistakes made on intelligence test protocols.

Finally, the organization of the WISC-V index scores in relation to the FSIQ bears mentioning in this section. As described in the preceding chapter, the WISC-V differs from its predecessor in that there are 10 subtests required to obtain the five primary index scores (i.e., the primary subtests), and seven of those primary subtests were used to derive the FSIQ normative information (i.e., FSIQ subtests). Examiners should pay careful attention, especially while familiarizing themselves with the WISC-V, to ensure that they have administered the correct number of subtests for the scores they need. Each primary index requires two subtests to calculate, and no proration or substitutions are allowed when deriving these index scores. Omitting one of the 10 primary subtests will thus prevent a primary index score from being calculated. Furthermore, examiners should be sure that the right subtest scores are being used to calculate the FSIQ when hand scoring. Only one substitution or proration is allowed for the FSIQ. These rules are simplified and stricter compared to WISC-IV, so examiners are advised to plan accordingly.

ADMINISTERING THE WISC-V SUBTESTS

Verbal Comprehension Subtests

General Instructions

The Verbal Comprehension domain consists of Similarities, Vocabulary, Information, and Comprehension. Similarities and Vocabulary are the two primary subtests that combine to form the VCI and contribute to the FSIQ. Information and Comprehension are secondary Verbal Comprehension subtests. Their administration rules are summarized in Tables 2.1–2.4. All four share a similar administration workflow whereby the examiner records the child's open-ended verbal responses and compares them to sample responses in the manual to

TABLE 2.1 Highlights—Similarities Administration Tips

Start Points:

- Ages 6–7: Sample, then Item 1
- Ages 8–11: Sample, then Item 5
- Ages 12–16: Sample, then Item 8

Reverse Rule:

- If the child obtains an imperfect score on either of the first two items administered, proceed in reverse order until the child obtains two perfect scores in a row.

Discontinue Rule:

- Discontinue when the child obtains a score of 0 on three consecutive items.

Reminders:

On more difficult items, children sometimes provide answers based on the properties of the words themselves (e.g., "Both words start with *S*"). Items in which this is more likely to happen are marked with an asterisk; pay close attention to these items to ensure you query them appropriately.

TABLE 2.2 Highlights—Vocabulary Administration Tips

Start Points:

- Ages 6–7: Item 1
- Ages 8–11: Item 5
- Ages 12–16: Item 9

Reverse Rule:

- If the child obtains an imperfect score on either of the first two items administered, proceed in reverse order until the child obtains two perfect scores in a row.

Discontinue Rule:

- Discontinue when the child obtains a score of 0 on three consecutive items.

Reminders:

- Vocabulary is a verbal subtest but still requires the Stimulus Book for Items 1–4, which require the child to name pictures.
- Many items are marked with an asterisk. Pay close attention, because they indicate words that were sometimes misheard by children during standardization and require a unique query.

TABLE 2.3 Highlights—Information Administration Tips

Start Points:

- Ages 6–8: Item 1
- Ages 9–16: Item 8

Reverse Rule:

- If the child obtains an imperfect score on either of the first two items administered, proceed in reverse order until the child obtains two perfect scores in a row.

Discontinue Rule:

- Discontinue when the child obtains a score of 0 on three consecutive items.

Reminders:

- A number of Information items have special queries for specific responses that require additional follow-up. While not necessary to memorize all of these queries, you should familiarize yourself with them to ensure a fluent, efficient administration pace.

TABLE 2.4 Highlights—Comprehension Administration Tips

Start Points:

- Ages 6–11: Item 1
- Ages 12–16: Item 3

Reverse Rule:

- If the child obtains an imperfect score on either of the first two items administered, proceed in reverse order until the child obtains two perfect scores in a row.

Discontinue Rule:

- Discontinue when the child obtains a score of 0 on three consecutive items.

Reminders:

- Items 5, 7, and 18 require the child to describe more than one correct concept in order to receive 2 points. For these items, you should query for additional concepts if the child's additional response only covers one.

assign a score. Given the subjective nature of this workflow, as well as the nearly infinite variation of possible responses that a child may provide, it is not surprising that the highest number of administration and scoring errors are found on Verbal Comprehension subtests (Belk et al., 2002; Loe et al., 2007; Patterson, Slate, Jones, & Steger, 1995; Slate, Jones, & Murray, 1991). However, the inter-rater reliabilities are quite high (Wechsler, 2014), so the scoring criteria can be reliably applied even by those inexperienced with their application. One of the most common errors made by practitioners is assigning the incorrect number of points to a response (Loe et al., 2007), with overestimation of scores occurring slightly more often than underestimation of scores. In our experience, familiarity with the sample responses is the only way to prevent these types of mistakes and ensure a fluid, timely administration of Verbal Comprehension subtests. In general, the responses that were provided most frequently in the standardization sample are listed first, with all responses requiring a query (Q) in the top section. The purpose of this organization is to promote efficient scanning, with a priority placed on those responses that require immediate action by the examiner (e.g., queries). We strongly advise all WISC-V examiners to review these sample responses in detail to ensure that they understand the nuances differentiating responses of different point values. It is also critical to note that the sample responses are not an exhaustive list, but rather are intended to provide illustrations of the general scoring rules so examiners can better understand and apply them based on the level of abstraction of the child's responses. There will be cases in which a child's response is not listed in the manual, and in these cases it is important to read the general scoring rules and compare the response to those samples to which it seems to be conceptually similar.

It is safe to say that knowing when and when not to query verbal responses is also one of the hardest parts of giving the WISC. Failing to query responses that should be queried is one of the most commonly made errors on the Wechsler tests (Alfonso, Johnson, Patinella, & Rader, 1998; Loe et al., 2007), and querying responses that should not be queried does not fall far behind (Slate, Jones, Murray, & Coulter, 1993). The following rules summarize when and when not to query responses on WISC-V Verbal Comprehension subtests:

- ALWAYS query responses that obviously correspond to a sample response *with* a (Q) next to it in the manual.
- DO NOT query responses that obviously correspond to a sample response *without* a (Q) next to it in the manual.
- If you are unable to identify a sample response in the manual that corresponds to the child's response, it is acceptable but not required to query for additional information.
- Unless the item instructions indicate a specific query is given for a particular response, do not query a second time if a first query fails to improve a response scored 0 or 1.

The correct application of these rules is critical for obtaining valid scores on Verbal Comprehension subtests. Failing to query responses reduces the number of opportunities the child has to obtain a better score, which could artificially decrease scores; conversely, querying too often results in additional opportunities to obtain better scores and could potentially inflate results. Furthermore, it could become frustrating for the child and damage rapport.

Finally, although less troublesome than querying, the WISC development team has noticed that the concept of spoiled responses sometimes causes confusion with examiners. A spoiled response occurs when the first response to an item receives either 1 or 2 points (e.g., in response to "How are a CAT and HORSE alike?" the child responds "They are living things"), but the follow-up response to that changes the interpretation of what was meant in the initial response (e.g., "They are living things that grow in the ground"). A spoiled response does *not* refer to cases in which a child provides a 1- or 2-point response followed by another response that is simply wrong. While responses like this may cause an examiner to question the child's understanding of the concept, the best response is always scored, no matter how incorrect one of the responses may be.

Similarities

On Similarities, the child is presented with two words that represent common concepts and asked to describe how they are alike (e.g., "In what way are fish and birds alike?"). Items are scored 2, 1, or 0 points.

Vocabulary

Vocabulary consists of both picture naming and word definition items. For picture naming items (Items 1–4), the child names the object presented visually. For word definition items (Items 5–29), the child defines words that are read aloud by the examiner (e.g., "What does *conceive* mean?"). Picture items are scored 1 or 0 points and verbal items scored 2, 1, or 0 points. The Stimulus Book is used to show the child stimuli for the pictures but is not required for the verbal items; remember to remove the book from the child's view when transitioning to the verbal items. Vocabulary contains a few items marked by asterisks in the *WISC-V Administration and Scoring Manual* and Record Form. These asterisks denote words that children in the standardization sample sometimes misheard (e.g., "CORD" instead of "CARD"). In the manual, the asterisks are placed next to the sample response(s) that corresponds to the misheard word as a reminder that you should clearly restate the item, emphasizing the correct word. Although the discontinue rule on Vocabulary is shorter relative to WISC-IV and the subtest contains fewer items, it is still one of the longer subtests to administer. Familiarity with the sample responses and prompts will help ensure an efficient and engaging administration.

Information

Information requires the child to answer questions that address a broad range of general knowledge topics (e.g., "Name the country that launched the first man-made satellite"). Information may be the easiest Verbal Comprehension subtest to administer because the verbatim responses are short relative to the other subtests. In addition, it is the only Verbal Comprehension subtest for which all items are scored 1 or 0 points. Similar to Vocabulary, many of the items on Information are marked with an asterisk. The reasons for this vary; they may call out responses that are too literal (e.g., in response to "What day of the week comes before Sunday?" the child responds "Tomorrow"), responses that are incomplete (e.g., in response to "Name the four presidents on Mount Rushmore" the child responds with the first three). Although varied, these asterisks are intended to help examiners clarify responses that were frequently provided during standardization from children that could answer correctly once queried. It is likely that examiners in the field will come across similar types of responses, and thus familiarity with these specific queries is essential for a smooth and accurate administration.

Comprehension

Comprehension requires the child to answer questions based on his or her understanding of general principles and social situations (e.g., "What are some advantages of keeping money in a bank?"). The WISC-V introduces a number of new items that are focused on school and other concepts specifically relevant for children. Even though Comprehension is not a primary subtest, these items can provide a glimpse into how the child processes his or her environment and thus yield rich clinical information. Similar to Similarities and Vocabulary, Comprehension is scored 2, 1, or 0 points. However, one difference on Comprehension is that three items require the child to provide answers that cover two general concepts specific to those items to receive perfect scores (e.g., for the question above, the child would have to say "In order to earn interest" *and* "To keep it safe"). Answers that cover just one of the general concepts are awarded one point. These multiple general concept items introduce a unique querying requirement. On these items, a special prompt is provided if the child's initial response does not cover both general concepts (say, "Tell me more (things you should do, reasons why) [rephrase item appropriately]"). After that, you are also allowed to query any responses marked with a (Q) in each general concept that the child provides.

Visual–Spatial Subtests

As discussed in the previous chapter, one of the biggest changes in WISC-V is the split of the WISC-IV Perceptual Reasoning Index into the WISC-V Visual–Spatial Index and Fluid Reasoning Index. There are two Visual–Spatial subtests—Block Design and Visual Puzzles—and these combine to form the Visual–Spatial Index. Only Block Design contributes to the FSIQ. The administration rules for these subtests are highlighted in Tables 2.5 and 2.6.

Block Design

Block Design requires the child to view a constructed model or a picture in the Stimulus Book and to use one-color or two-color blocks to recreate the

TABLE 2.5 Highlights—Block Design Administration Tips

Start Points:

- Ages 6–7: Item 1
- Ages 8–16: Item 3

Reverse Rule:

- If the child obtains an imperfect score on either of the first two items administered, proceed in reverse order until the child obtains two perfect scores in a row.

Discontinue Rule:

- Discontinue when the child obtains a score of 0 on two consecutive items.

Reminders:

- Accurate timing is essential. Children who recreate the design correctly are awarded bonus points based on total completion time.
- Make sure the blocks are placed in front of the child correctly. For 2-block items, the blocks should have different sides facing up. For 4-block items, exactly one side should be half-red and half-white. For 9-block items, exactly two sides should be facing up.
- Do not award credit if the child rotates the design more than 30°, half-red and half-white and provide corrective feedback the first time a rotation occurs. Do *not* correct subsequent rotations.

TABLE 2.6 Highlights—Visual Puzzles Administration Tips

Start Points:

- Ages 6–8: Demonstration, Sample, then Item 1
- Ages 9–11: Demonstration, Sample, then Item 5
- Ages 12–16: Demonstration, Sample, then Item 8

Reverse Rule:

- If the child obtains an imperfect score on either of the first two items administered, proceed in reverse order until the child obtains two perfect scores in a row.

Discontinue Rule:

- Discontinue when the child obtains a score of 0 on three consecutive items.

Reminders:

- Visual Puzzles has a strict 30-second time limit. After 20 seconds, you should prompt the child to provide a response. Provide this response *as many times as necessary.*

design within a specified time limit. It is one of the more difficult subtests for new examiners to master because it requires skillful management of various materials—the Manual, Stimulus Book, Blocks, Record Form, and a timer are all used to administer this subtest. Furthermore, the administration and scoring procedures, especially for the first four items, vary widely. Keep in mind that the following variables may change from item to item: (1) the time limit, (2) the number of blocks required to complete the design, (3) the number of trials, and (4) whether you model the correct design or simply show the child the design in the Stimulus Book.

Block Design yields three different types of scores. The standard scoring procedures apply an "all-or-none" method whereby the child receives credit for a correct design and no credit for an incorrect design, with time bonus points awarded for performance on Items 10–13 (up to 3 additional points). The standard Block Design scoring procedure is always used when calculating the VSI and FSIQ.

There are two additional "process" scoring methods that can be employed on Block Design, as well as two base rate scores that quantify the occurrence in the normative sample of common errors made on the subtest. The first process score is a No Time Bonus score in which the time bonuses are not applied to Items 10–13. This score may aid the interpretation of scores for children who have slow, deliberate problem-solving styles that may not lend themselves well to speeded tests. Second is a Partial score, in which each correct block completed within the time limit is awarded credit (as opposed to the all-or-none standard scoring method). This score also reduces the emphasis on speed, providing partial credit to children to complete a majority of the blocks within the time limit. It also reduces the emphasis on attention to detail, as credit is awarded for any part of the design that is constructed correctly. The Rotation Errors score is calculated by summing the number of items in which the child rotated the design more than 30° as part of his or her final response, and the Dimensions Errors score is the sum of items in which the child breaks the standard organization of blocks (e.g., 2×2, 3×3, etc.) *at any time* during the construction of the design. These optional scores provide examiners with useful interpretive information. However, Block Design process scores may not be used to calculate the VSI or FSIQ.

New examiners should pay close attention to other administration nuances and practice them until they are routine. One of the more common errors on Block Design is failure to present the blocks in the correct orientation. The manual provides specific instructions regarding what faces of the blocks should be facing up—for Item 1, the two blocks should have different sides facing up, for the four block items, there should only be one block with the red-and-white side facing up, and for the nine block items, there should be two blocks with the red-and-white sides facing up. For the four and nine block items, the other sides facing up should be a mix of all red and all white. In addition to block presentation, correct handling of rotation errors is an additional subtle administration nuance. If a child makes a rotation error by rotating the design more than 30°, you are supposed to turn it to the correct orientation and say, "See, it goes this way." This prompt should only be provided the *first time* a child makes a rotation error, and the item should still be scored 0 points. For all subsequent rotation errors, the item should be scored 0 and no feedback provided.

Visual Puzzles

Visual Puzzles is a test of visuospatial construction that requires the child to reproduce a geometric image by choosing three of six available responses. Each item is scored 1 or 0 points, and the child must select *all three* correct responses to receive credit. Visual Puzzles requires careful attention to timing. All items have a hard limit of 30 seconds each, but there is an additional prompt that must be given after 20 seconds if the child has not responded. In these situations, say, "Do you have an answer?" but do not stop the timer. If the child does not respond and time expires, move on to the next item by saying, "Let's try another one." Visual Puzzles contains numerous prompts with which examiners should become familiar, many of which are related to the requirement that the child choose three response options per item. If the child selects fewer than three responses you should say, "Choose *three* pieces to make the puzzle." If the child selects more than three responses, say, "What three pieces did you mean?" The response options on Visual Puzzles are numbered, and children sometimes ask if the responses should be provided in numerical order. If this occurs, you should say, "You do not have to choose them in order." Children are also sometimes confused by the orientation of response options, wondering if they are incorrectly positioned because they do not match how they would need to be positioned to be a part of the target image. If a child asks about the orientation of a response option, you should say, "You may have to turn a piece in your mind to make it fit." These prompts can be given as many times as necessary. If the child self-corrects a response within the time limit, score it as correct.

Fluid Reasoning Subtests

The two primary Fluid Reasoning subtests are Matrix Reasoning and Figure Weights. These two subtests combine to form the FRI, and both contribute to the FSIQ. There are also two secondary Fluid Reasoning subtests: Picture Concepts and Arithmetic. Tables 2.7–2.10 highlight the administration rules for the four Fluid Reasoning subtests.

Matrix Reasoning

On Matrix Reasoning, the child looks at an incomplete matrix and selects the missing portion from various response options. Matrix Reasoning is a relatively easy subtest to administer, as the only recording requirement is circling the number corresponding to the child's response, which is scored 1 or 0 points. Matrix Reasoning has a soft 30-second guideline for children who do not appear to benefit from additional problem-solving time. You may prompt children after

TABLE 2.7 Highlights—Matrix Reasoning Administration Tips

Start Points:

- Ages 6–8: Samples A and B, then Item 1
- Ages 9–11: Samples A and B, then Item 5
- Ages 12–16: Samples A and B, then Item 9

Reverse Rule:

- If the child obtains an imperfect score on either of the first two items administered, proceed in reverse order until the child obtains two perfect scores in a row.

Discontinue Rule:

- Discontinue when the child obtains a score of 0 on three consecutive items.

Reminders:

- The 30-second time limit is not strict. If the child exhibits a pattern of providing delayed but correct responses as the item difficulty increases, allow additional time.

TABLE 2.8 Highlights—Figure Weights Administration Tips

Start Points:

- Ages 6–8: Sample A, then Item 1
- Ages 9–16: Sample B, then Item 4

Reverse Rule:

- If the child obtains an imperfect score on either of the first two items administered, proceed in reverse order until the child obtains two perfect scores in a row.

Discontinue Rule:

- Discontinue when the child obtains a score of 0 on three consecutive items.

Reminders:

- Figure Weights has a strict 30-second time limit. After 20 seconds, you should prompt the child to provide a response. Provide this response *as many times as necessary*.
- Items 27–34 have three scales. Prior to Item 27, do not forget to read new instructions that introduce the 3 three-scale items.

approximately 30 seconds by saying, "Do you have an answer?" If the child does not respond, you should say, "Let's try another one" and move on to the next item. Remember, this time limit should *not* be applied rigidly. Unlike some of the other subtests like Visual Puzzles and Figure Weights, where there is a 30-second time limit, the time limit is flexible on Matrix Reasoning. Its purpose is to assist

---

TABLE 2.9 Highlights—Picture Concepts Administration Tips

Start Points:

- Ages 6–8: Sample Items A and B, then Item 1
- Ages 9–11: Sample Items A and B, then Item 4
- Ages 12–16: Sample Items A and B, then Item 7

Reverse Rule:

- If the child obtains an imperfect score on either of the first two items administered, proceed in reverse order until the child obtains two perfect scores in a row.

Discontinue Rule:

- Discontinue when the child obtains a score of 0 on three consecutive items.

Reminders:

- The 30-second time limit is not strict. If the child exhibits a pattern of providing delayed but correct responses as the item difficulty increases, allow additional time.

TABLE 2.10 Highlights—Arithmetic Administration Tips

Start Points:

- Ages 6–7: Item 3
- Ages 8–9: Item 8
- Ages 10–16: Item 11

Reverse Rule:

- If the child obtains an imperfect score on either of the first two items administered, proceed in reverse order until the child obtains two perfect scores in a row.

Discontinue Rule:

- Discontinue when the child obtains a score of 0 on three consecutive items.

Reminders:

- Arithmetic has a strict 30-second time limit. After 20 seconds, you should prompt the child to provide a response. Provide this response *as many times as necessary.*
- You are not allowed to repeat Items 1–19 but can repeat Items 20–34 *one time only.* Stop timing while repeating Items 20–34, but do *not* stop the timer if you tell the child that you cannot repeat the item on Items 1–19.

---

in timely administration and improve rapport for children who do not provide answers or benefit from additional time to solve problems. If the child selects more than one response on Matrix Reasoning, say, "You (said, pointed to) [*insert child's response*], and you (said, pointed to) [*insert child's response*]. Which one did you mean?" This prompt is also used for Figure Weights and Picture Concepts.

Figure Weights

Figure Weights is a measure of quantitative reasoning in which children must balance a scale by identifying the correct response option within a specified time limit. In order to determine the correct response, the child must figure out the relationships between shapes that balanced a previous scale and apply these relationships to the incomplete scale. The number corresponding to the child's response is recorded, and each item is scored 1 or 0 points. Similar to Visual Puzzles, examiners should pay close attention to timing on Figure Weights. Items 1–18 have a strict limit of 20 seconds, and Items 19–34 have a strict limit of 30 seconds. Timing should begin as soon as instructions have been given, or as soon as the item is shown if instructions have been eliminated. Similar to Visual Puzzles, you should prompt the child if he or she has not responded with only 10 seconds remaining. Note that for Items 1–18 this prompt is given after only 10 seconds, so be careful to track the time closely.

Figure Weights is unique in that there is a special introduction prior to Item 27. This item represents the transition to items that have three scales to balance, so an introduction is required to instruct the child to look at all three scales to find the answer. Do not forget to read this instruction. When providing instructions on all items, it is critical that you point to the visual stimuli and response options as appropriate, as it is a critical piece in communicating the problem that has to be solved. As mentioned above, children can self-correct their responses on Figure Weights. For Figure Weights and Visual Puzzles (described above), do not stop the timer while providing this prompt. Some children may attempt to correct a response after a Stimulus Book page has been turned and the timer stopped. These types of corrections are allowable if in your judgment the allotted time has not elapsed.

Picture Concepts

On Picture Concepts, the child is presented with two or three rows of pictures and chooses one picture from each row to form a group with a common characteristic. Recording and scoring requirements are similar to Visual Puzzles and Matrix Reasoning—circle the child's responses and score each item as 1 or 0 points. Picture Concepts requires multiple responses similar to Visual Puzzles, but does not have a time limit—similar to Matrix Reasoning there is a soft 30-second guideline. Again, the limit is only a suggestion for children that do not appear to benefit from additional time and should not be applied rigidly. Some children will not know what every picture on an item is. It is acceptable to name the object for the child but do not describe it, as that description may cue the child to the concept underlying the correct answer.

Arithmetic

In Arithmetic, the child mentally solves a series of orally presented arithmetic problems within a specified time limit (e.g., "Jim buys 5 apples and his mother gives him 2 more. He then eats 1. How many apples does he have left?"). The first five items include images in the Stimulus Book to supplement the verbal instructions. Each item is scored 1 or 0 points. Arithmetic has a strict 30-second time limit. Prompt the child to provide an answer after 20 seconds by saying, "Do you have an answer?" If the child does not respond within the 30-second limit, score the item 0 points and proceed to the next item by saying, "Let's try another one." Because Arithmetic taps working memory resources, examiners need to pay close attention to rules governing whether items can be repeated. Repetitions are *not* allowed for Items 1–19. If the child requests that the item be repeated, you should say, "I can't say it again." Do not stop the timer to provide that feedback. For items 20–34, you are allowed to repeat the item *one time only*. This repetition should only be provided at the request of the child, do not repeat the item solely because the child appears to be struggling with it. While the item is being repeated the timer should be stopped—stop it prior to reading the first words of the item and restart it immediately upon completing the repetition. Do *not* repeat the item a second time. If the child asks for a second repetition, say, "I can't say it again." Do not stop timing to provide this prompt.

Working Memory Subtests

General Instructions

There are two primary Working Memory subtests on the WISC-V: Digit Span and Picture Span. These two subtests combine to form the Working Memory Index (WMI). Only Digit Span contributes to the FSIQ. Letter-Number Sequencing is a secondary Working Memory subtest. Digit Span and Letter-Number Sequencing are primarily auditory working memory tasks, whereas Picture Span is primarily a visual working memory task. Their basic administration rules are summarized in Tables 2.11–2.13.

Digit Span

Digit Span traditionally has been comprised of two parts on the WISC: Digit Span Forward and Digit Span Backward. Digit Span Forward requires the child to repeat numbers in the same order as read aloud by the examiner, and Digit Span Backward requires the child to repeat the numbers in the reverse order of that presented by the examiner. As on the WAIS-IV, WISC-V introduces Digit Span Sequencing, which requires children to sequentially order the numbers presented by the examiner. All three tasks must be given in order to calculate the overall Digit Span scaled score, which is required to calculate the WMI and FSIQ. Every item on Digit Span consists of two trials, each of which is scored 1 or 0 points. Pacing of the item stimuli is critical on Digit Span, as variations in how quickly or slowly they are provided can greatly impact item difficulty. The numbers are read at the rate of one per second, and there are a number of techniques that examiners use to establish an accurate, consistent pace.

TABLE 2.11 Highlights—Digit Span Administration Tips

Start Points:

- Digit Span Forward
  - Ages 6–16: Item 1
- Digit Span Backward
  - Ages 6–16: Sample Item, then item 1
- Digit Span Sequencing
  - Ages 6–7: Qualifying Item, Sample Items A and B, then Item 1
  - Ages 8–16: Sample Items A and B, then Item 1

Reverse Rule:

- None

Discontinue Rule:

- Digit Span Forward
  - Ages 6–16: Discontinue when the child obtains a score of 0 on both trials of an item.
- Digit Span Backward
  - Ages 6–16: Discontinue when the child obtains a score of 0 on both trials of an item.
- Digit Span Sequencing
  - Ages 6–7: Discontinue after an incorrect response to the qualifying item or when the child obtains a score of 0 on both trials of an item.
  - Ages 8–16: Discontinue when the child obtains a score of 0 on both trials of an item.

Reminders:

- Do *not* repeat the sequences. If the child asks for an item to be repeated, say, "I can only say them one time. Just take your best guess."
- Numbers should be read at a rate of one per second. Use tricks such as tapping your foot or using a stopwatch to ensure appropriate pacing.
- All three conditions must be administered to obtain the overall Digit Span scaled score, which is required to calculate the FSIQ.

For example, some use stopwatches and match the total presentation time to the number of stimuli (e.g., 5 numbers should take 5 seconds to say), and others tap their feet to help establish a consistent cadence prior to saying the stimuli out loud. Individuals vary in what works best, but novice examiners are strongly encouraged to practice the pacing using a stopwatch prior to administering them in a clinical setting. Because it is a Working Memory subtest, repetition is not allowed on Digit Span. If the child asks you to repeat the sequence, say, "I can only say them one time, just take your best guess."

TABLE 2.12 Highlights—Picture Span Administration Tips

Start Points:

• Ages 6–16: Samples B and C, then Item 4

Reverse Rule:

• If the child obtains an imperfect score on either of the first two items administered, proceed in reverse order until the child obtains two perfect scores in a row.

Discontinue Rule:

• Discontinue when the child obtains a score of 0 on three consecutive items.

Reminders:

• All children begin on Sample Item B. However, if you have a child that is lower functioning, it is appropriate to start on Sample A, after which you would proceed to Item 1.
• For Sample A through Item 3, the stimulus page should be exposed for 3 seconds. For all other items, expose the stimuli for 5 seconds.

TABLE 2.13 Highlights—Letter-Number Sequencing Administration Tips

Start Points:

• Ages 6–7: Qualifying Items, Demonstration Item A, Sample Item A, then Item 1
• Ages 8–16: Demonstration Item A, Sample Item A, then Item 1

Reverse Rule:

• None

Discontinue Rule:

• Ages 6–7: If the child obtains an incorrect response to either Qualifying Item or after scores of 0 on all three trials of an item.
• Ages 8–16: If the child scores 0 on all three trials of an item.

Reminders:

• Do *not* repeat the sequences. If the child asks for an item to be repeated, say, "I can only say them one time. Just take your best guess."
• Numbers should be read at a rate of one per second. Use tricks such as tapping your foot or using a stopwatch to ensure appropriate pacing.
• For Items 1 and 2, the child must say the number before the letters to receive credit. For all other items, credit is awarded if the numbers or letters are said first, as long as they are in ascending and alphabetical order, respectively.

Picture Span

Picture Span is a measure of visual working memory in which the child is shown a stimulus image(s) for a predefined period, after which the image(s) must be recalled (in the order presented, if possible) from a group of distractors. For items with multiple stimulus images, children are awarded 2 points for selecting the correct images in the correct order, 1 point for the correct images in the incorrect order, and 0 points if they fail to remember all of the images or select an incorrect image. Pay close attention to the start point rules. All children start with Sample Items B and C, then proceed to Item 4. The only reason for administering Items 1–3 is if the child obtains a score of 0 on Items 4 or 5 and has to reverse. Timing is also critical for Picture Span, as there are strict rules about how long the stimulus pages should be shown to the child. For Items 1–3 the stimuli should be shown for 3 seconds, and for Items 4–26 the stimuli should be shown for 5 seconds. These time limits refer to how long the stimuli is exposed to the child—begin timing once the stimuli are in view, and turn the page immediately when the exposure time has been met. Timing consistency is critical, as the length of time the image is exposed impacts how easy or difficult the stimuli are to remember. We recommend that new examiners practice flipping through the stimulus pages to ensure accurate, smooth administration of Picture Span.

Because exposure time is so critical to the administration of this subtest, make sure that the child is attentive and ready prior to showing the stimuli. If the child attempts to turn the page before time expires, stop him or her and say, "Keep looking at this page. I'll turn the page when it's time." Do not stop timing while providing this prompt. Similarly, the stimulus page can only be shown *one* time. If the child asks to see it again, say, "I can only show it one time. Just take your best guess." Children are instructed to memorize the stimulus images in order from left to right. However, some will memorize them in the opposite order, and if this happens you should correct the child by saying, "Remember the pictures in order, starting with this one (point to the first stimulus picture)."

Letter-Number Sequencing

In Letter-Number Sequencing, the examiner reads a sequence of numbers and letters to the child, who recalls the numbers in ascending order and the letters in alphabetical order. The overall administration instructions are very similar to Digit Span. Each item consists of three trials, and the trials are scored 1 or 0 points. The letters and numbers should be read at 1 second per character, and repetition of the item content is *not* allowed. Children are instructed to repeat the numbers first, followed by the letters, but note that this impacts scoring on Items 1 and 2 only (which consist of only one number and one letter, e.g., A–1). For Items 3–10, the child can repeat the letters before the numbers and receive credit, provided the numbers are repeated in ascending order and the letters in alphabetical order. Practitioners often wonder why this rule exists, as opposed to only providing credit for sequences that correctly begin with numbers. The reason is that data analyses indicate no differences in ability for those individuals who repeat the letters first. Hence, the critical variable in Letter-Number Sequencing is being able to sequence within the letters and numbers, not whether letters or numbers are said first.

Processing Speed Subtests

The Processing Speed domain consists of three subtests: Coding, Symbol Search, and Cancellation. Coding and Symbol Search are primary subtests that combine to form the PSI. Only Coding contributes to the FSIQ. Cancellation is a secondary subtest. Their administration rules are summarized in Tables 2.14–2.16.

Coding

Coding requires the child to copy symbols that are paired with shapes or numbers. Using a key, the child draws a symbol in each shape or numbered box within a 120-second time limit. The total raw score for the subtest is calculated from the number of correct symbols completed, and credit should be awarded for a response if it is clear that the child intended to draw the correct symbol. In addition, a Rotation Errors process score is calculated by totaling the numbers of symbols that the child rotates between 90 and 270°, which is converted

---

TABLE 2.14 Highlights—Coding Administration Tips

Start Points:

- Ages 6–7: Form A Demonstration Items, Sample Items, then Test Items
- Ages 8–16: Form B Demonstration Items, Sample Items, then Test Items

Reverse Rule:

- None

Discontinue Rule:

- Discontinue after 120 seconds.

Reminders:

- Left-handed children sometimes partially block the key at the top of the page. If you notice this on the Sample Item, place an additional Response Booklet to the right of the child's. Line the keys up horizontally and let the child complete the Sample Item that way so he or she is comfortable with the arrangement on the test items.
- Pay close attention to ensure that the child does not skip any items or rows. If you notice this occurring, say, "Do them in order. Don't skip any." Point to the first omitted item and say, "Do this one next." Do not stop the timer while providing this instruction.

TABLE 2.15 Highlights—Symbol Search Administration Tips

Start Points:

- Ages 6–7: Form A Demonstration Items, Sample Items, then Test Items
- Ages 8–16: Form B Demonstration Items, Sample Items, then Test Items

Reverse Rule:

- None

Discontinue Rule:

- Discontinue after 120 seconds.

Reminders:

- Each item contains two specific distracters: (1) a rotated version of one of the targets, and (2) an image that is visually similar to one of the targets. Both distracters yield process scores, so be sure to indicate these types of errors as you are scoring the subtest.

TABLE 2.16 Highlights—Cancellation Administration Tips

Start Points:

- Ages 6–16: Demonstration Items, Sample Item, then Item 1

Reverse Rule:

- None

Discontinue Rule:

- Discontinue after 45 seconds for each item.

Reminders:

- Self-corrections are allowed on Cancellation and the other Processing Speed tasks, but watch carefully to ensure that it is not occurring too often and interfering with performance. If so, it is acceptable to discourage the behavior.

into a base rate. Coding has different Forms depending on the age of the child, with 6–7-year-olds taking an easier version of the test than 8–16-year-olds. This was done to ensure developmental appropriateness of the test content and ensure adequate measurement of lower functioning individuals.

New examiners should ensure that they are very comfortable with the initial instructions for Coding. They require the examiner to point to various locations on the Response Booklet and write responses while simultaneously providing instructions, and this requires practice to do elegantly. There are also several prompts to be aware of on Coding. First, children are not provided an eraser, so it is common for them to ask what to do if they make a mistake. If this occurs, say, "That's OK. Just keep working as fast as you can." You should not prevent the child from correcting responses unless it appears to be negatively impacting overall performance. Second, knowing that they are being timed, children will sometimes start test items before the examiner has finished reading all of the instructions. In this case, stop the child and say, "Wait until I say, 'Go' to start." Children are allowed to self-correct on all Processing Speed subtests, but if their tendency to do so repeatedly interferes with performance, feel free to discourage the behavior.

Symbol Search

Symbol Search requires the child to scan a group of symbols and indicate whether the target symbol(s) match(es) any of the symbols in the group within a 120-second time limit. Similar to Coding, there is a simpler Form of the task for 6–7-year-old children in order to ensure developmental appropriateness of the task. Symbol Search is scored by subtracting total incorrect responses from correct responses in order to get the total raw score. In addition, each item on Symbol Search has a distractor image that is visually similar to the correct response (i.e., Set Errors) or identical to the correct response but rotated (i.e., Rotation Errors). Set and Rotation Errors, respectively, are summed across the subtest and converted into separate process scores. Symbol Search contains the same prompts that are described above for Coding, and special attention should be paid to the corrective feedback provided on the sample item. Due to the different types of errors described above, feedback needs to be tailored to the responses that the child provides. Thus, examiners need to watch closely in order to match the child's incorrect response to the appropriate feedback in the manual.

Cancellation

Cancellation requires the child to identify animals among an array of distractor objects. There are two items—Item 1 arranges the objects in a random array, and Item 2 arranges them in a structured array (e.g., rows and columns). Children take each item and have 45 seconds to complete them; they are discontinued after 45 seconds have elapsed or if the child identifies all of the correct responses, whichever comes first. The total raw score for each item is calculated by subtracting the total number of incorrect responses from the total number of correct responses. In addition to an overall scaled score, Cancellation also yields process scores for the random and structured items. Like Symbol Search, Cancellation has unique corrective feedback on the sample item depending on the type of error that the child makes, so pay careful attention to ensure that the feedback matches the error made by the child.

Complementary Subtests

The WISC-V contains five new subtests that are intended to provide information regarding cognitive processes related to learning disability. Due to their specialized use, these subtests do not contribute to the FSIQ, nor are they used to calculate a primary index score. Rather, they are for use in learning disability evaluations in which the examiner wants to obtain information regarding cognitive strengths and weaknesses that may relate to learning problems. As readers will see below, there are several unique administration procedures for each subtest. It is also important to note here that these subtests yield standard scores ($M = 100$, $SD = 15$), which is different than the scaled scores associated with the primary and secondary subtests.

Naming Speed Subtests

The Naming Speed subtests assess the ability to quickly perceive and name visual stimuli, a skill that has long been linked to fluent reading and reading disorders (Bowers & Wolf, 1993; Kail & Hall, 1994; Schatschneider, Carlson, Francis, Foorman, & Fletcher, 2002). There are two Naming Speed subtests: Naming Speed Literacy (NSL) and Naming Speed Quantity (NSQ). NSL contains three items: (1) Color-Object Naming, which requires the child to name simple objects of varying colors (e.g., "green cat"), (2) Size-Color-Object Naming, which adds the dimension of size (e.g., "big green cat"), and (3) Letter-Number Naming, which requires the child to name individual letters or numbers. For NSQ, the child must name the number of boxes inside a larger box (there are two items, one in which the number of boxes varies from 1 to 4 and another in which the number varies from 1 to 5). The number of items administered to the child is determined by age (see Table 2.17). On NSL, children aged 6 are administered Color-Object Naming and Size-Color-Object Naming, children aged 7–8 years take Size-Color-Object Naming and Letter-Number Naming, and children aged 9–16 years take Letter-Number Naming. On NSQ, children aged 6 take Quantity Naming 1–4, and children aged 7–16 are administered Quantity Naming 1–5. Most Wechsler subtests allow you to start at alternative start points for various reasons (e.g., you may start at a lower start point if you suspect a lower functioning child of intellectual disability); however, because the different age groups take unique sets of items, this cannot be done on NSL or NSQ if a normative score is desired. Of course, out of age testing can be conducted after the entire WISC-V is complete for the purposes of limit testing, but raw scores are the only scores that are yielded in that scenario.

Each Naming Speed item consists of two trials in which the child says the stimuli as fast as possible without making errors. There is a 300-second time limit per trial; the examiner records any errors and self-corrections that are made and notes the final completion time. The raw score for an item is derived from the total time it takes to complete both trials, and there are additional process scores that are calculated by summing up the total number of errors

---

TABLE 2.17 Highlights—Naming Speed Literacy Administration Tips

Start Points:

- Naming Speed Literacy
  - Age 6: Demonstration Item A, Sample Item A, then Item 1
  - Ages 7–8: Demonstration Item B, Sample Item B, then Item 2
  - Ages 9–16: Sample Item C, then Item 3
- Naming Speed Quantity
  - Age 6: Sample Item A, then Item 1
  - Ages 7–16: Sample Item B, then Item 2

Reverse Rule:

- None

Discontinue Rule:

- Discontinue after administering both item(s) for each age group.

Reminders:

- You must give all of the age-appropriate items in order to obtain a Naming Speed scaled score. Administering out of age items is allowed for limit testing, but if done in lieu of the age-appropriate task no normative scores will be available.
- All children can use their fingers to track their progress along the rows, but 6–8-year-olds are required to. If the child does not use finger tracking, say, "Use your finger to keep your place."

---

for each item and across each subtest. Examiners are encouraged to pay close attention to the child while he or she completes each item, as there are a number of prompts that address behaviors noticed during piloting. First, note that children aged 6–8 are required to track their progress across the rows with their finger. If a child forgets, remind him or her by saying, "Use your finger to keep your place." Do not stop timing to give this prompt. If the child begins reading before you finish reading the instructions, say, "Wait until I say 'Go' to start." It is sometimes difficult to track where in a row the child is, especially if he or she is making a lot of errors. There are two prompts that help address these issues. First, if the child makes two errors in a row, point to the second error and say, "Keep going from here." Give this same prompt if the child skips a row or appears to complete a row in reverse order. In all cases, do not stop timing. Finally, there are two prompts that encourage the child to continue if they pause at the end of a row or element. If the child pauses at the end of a row, say, "Go on to the next row." If the child pauses in the middle of a row, after 5 seconds say, "Go on to the next one." These prompts help avoid unfairly penalizing children who stop because of confusion or some other reason not related to the constructs being assessed by the task.

TABLE 2.18 Highlights—Symbol Translation Administration Tips

Start Points:

• Ages 6–16: Item 1

Reverse Rule:

• None

Discontinue Rule:

• Immediate Symbol Translation (IST)
  ○ Discontinue after Item 6 if score is less than or equal to 9.
  ○ Discontinue after Item 10 if score is less than or equal to 20.
  ○ Discontinue after Item 14 if score is less than or equal to 30.
• Delayed Symbol Translation (DST)
  ○ Discontinue after Item 6 if discontinued on Item 6 on IST.
  ○ Discontinue after Item 10 if discontinued on Item 10 on IST.
  ○ Discontinue after Item 14 if discontinued on Item 14 on IST.
• Recognition Symbol Translation (RST)
  ○ Discontinue after Item 8 if discontinued on Item 6 on IST.
  ○ Discontinue after Item 16 if discontinued on Item 10 on IST.
  ○ Discontinue after Item 24 if discontinued on Item 14 on IST.

Reminders:

• DST should be given 20–30 minutes after IST. You should not stop the administration of another subtest in order to fit DST within that window, so watch the time carefully after administering DST.
• "And" and "The" are awarded credit on the first six items of IST and DST only. For Items 7–21, a point is *not* awarded for correctly translating these two words.

Symbol Translation Subtests

The Symbol Translation (Table 2.18) subtests assess the ability to store and retrieve newly learned information. The child is shown a series of words and taught that each word is associated with a simple symbol, after which he or she is asked to "read" sentences by naming a series of drawings arranged in a particular order. New word–symbol associations are learned and sentences grow in length throughout the subtest to increase difficulty. There are three Symbol Translation subtests: Immediate (IST), Delayed (DST), and Recognition (RST). For IST, the child is taught the associations and asked to "read" increasingly difficult phrases or sentences. DST, which is administered 20–30 minutes after IST, requires the child to "read" words, phrases, or sentences from memory (i.e., they are not provided the word–symbol associations again and must rely on their memory of the associations from IST). After DST is RST, in which the child is shown an image and must select the word it matches from one of four options. For IST and DST, the child receives 1 point for each correct translation on an item (but note that the words "And" and "The" do not receive credit starting on Item 7). For RST, items are scored 1 or 0 points depending on whether the child provides a correct response.

Due to the novelty of these subtests, examiners should study the administration workflow closely before administering in a clinical setting. Because new word–symbol associations are introduced periodically throughout the subtest, not all items have the same structure. For some, you first teach new associations (e.g., "This one means BEAR, and this one means JUMP. BEAR...JUMP") and then flip the Stimulus Book page to display a sentence that the child must read (e.g., "Start here and tell me what each one means"). Other items do not require teaching, and you go straight to asking the child to read a sentence. The first three items on IST contain two trials. If the child translates all of the associations correctly on Trial 1, you proceed to the next item without administering Trial 2. If the child gets *any* of the translations incorrect, administer Trial 2 and score the trial with the highest number of points. There is no requirement to record incorrect responses verbatim on any of the Symbol Translation subtests. Simply check the boxes corresponding to the correct translations on the Record Form and assign one point per correct translation. There are several prompts to be aware of on IST. If the child takes more than 5 seconds to respond to a picture or says he or she does not know the answer, prompt him or her to continue to the next picture by saying, "Go on to the next one." This helps ensure a steady pace of administration. In addition, Pilot and Tryout data suggested that children sometimes lost their place in the translation string and/or the examiner got so many translations incorrect that the examiner lost track of where in the string they were. There are two prompts to help address these issues. If the child begins to "read" the sentence from right to left, point to the first picture and say, "Start again from here." Similarly, if you are unsure of the child's location in the string, say, "Start again from here."

Symbol Translation requires the examiner to monitor the time between subtests carefully. It is important to administer DST within a 20–30-minute window after IST is complete, as it is based on empirical evidence and ensures that test results are not artificially inflated or deflated. For tasks similar to the Symbol Translation subtests, an adequate period of time between immediate and delayed conditions is required to ensure that long-term memory is being assessed, as briefer intervals may allow for strategies such as rehearsal and thus better reflect short-term memory. Alternatively, the ability to recall information from long-term memory stores is negatively impacted by interference, and so going over the 30-minute limit could depress scores due to the increased interference that occurs as the interval between immediate and delay conditions expands. Plan the subtests in between IST and DST carefully and monitor the time as you go. It is *not* advised that you stop halfway through a subtest to administer DST, so be sure not to start a subtest close to the 20-minute mark that could take longer than 10 minutes to administer. RST should be administered directly following DST.

For IST, all children start on Item 1. It is important to point out that examiners experienced with the Wechsler tests will encounter a new type of discontinue rule for all Symbol Translation subtests. It uses a cumulative score procedure whereby the examiner must stop at various decision points throughout the subtest and determine whether the child's total raw score exceeds a particular threshold. If so, administration continues to the next decision point, where the same analysis is completed again. If not, the subtest is discontinued. The Record Form contains three separate decision points after Items 6, 10, and 14. When you arrive at these items, you should quickly tally up the cumulative score to that point to decide whether to continue. The cumulative score refers to all items starting from Item 1, as opposed to just the items since the last decision point (e.g., for Decision Point B, tally up scores from Items 1–10, rather than just 7–10). It is critical that these decision points are recorded, because they must be used at a later point to determine the stop points on DST and RST. For these, children start on Item 1 and stop at stop points defined by the decision point in which administration was discontinued on IST. For example, if you discontinue administration after Decision Point A, stop at Stop Point A on both DST and RST.

CONCLUDING COMMENTS

There are multiple factors that contribute to an effective psychological or educational assessment—tests must be properly matched to the referral question, solid qualitative observations should be noted, results should be interpreted carefully within empirically supported theoretical models, and interventions should be linked closely to test results. Fundamental to this process are reliable test results, which are directly linked to the extent that an individual examiner is familiar with the administration and scoring procedures of a test. This familiarity does more than simply increase accuracy of scores, however. It decreases testing time, promotes rapport with children, and reduces the cognitive load on the examiner, thus allowing for more insightful observation of the child and better on-the-fly decision-making as the assessment session unfolds. To that end, new and existing examiners are encouraged to study this chapter and the *WISC-V Administration and Scoring Manual*, which should pay dividends for all future assessments involving the WISC-V.

APPENDIX 2A. FREQUENTLY ASKED QUESTIONS

This section contains some of the more frequent administration and scoring questions that the WISC-V development team receives from examiners. It is not an exhaustive list. Students and other practitioners new to the WISC-V should consult the administration and technical manuals for a complete understanding of the issues related to WISC-V assessment. They are also encouraged to consult other textbooks that cover basic assessment principles in detail (Kaufman, 2009; Sattler, 2008).

1. *Why do only some of the sample responses need to be queried?*
   All of the sample responses in the manual were provided by children in the standardization sample. The development team analyzed each response in the 1 and 0 point categories to determine whether children were able to improve their responses when queried. Those items in which a query resulted in improved differentiation among children of varied ability levels or could conceivably improve to a similar response of a higher point value are marked with a (Q).

2. *How did you decide whether certain sample responses are worth 2, 1, or 0 points?*
   In general, 1-point responses are correct but indicate only a basic or concrete understanding of a concept. Two-point responses indicate a deeper or more abstract understanding of the concept. Zero-point responses are either incorrect or indicate a severely limited understanding of a concept. In addition, both qualitative and quantitative analyses contribute to more nuanced decisions about a response's point value. Qualitatively, the development team is careful to ensure that responses are organized in a logical manner that is face valid (e.g., typically, descriptions that include two core characteristics of a word receive higher value than those with one). Statistically, the team is able to analyze whether the credit given to particular responses has positive or negative impacts on the item's psychometric properties and adjusts the organization of the responses accordingly.

3. *How have the substitution and proration rules changed for WISC-V?*
   The rules for substituting and prorating have changed in WISC-V due to the revised test structure. Because the primary index scores (e.g., VCI, FRI, etc.) are comprised of only two subtests, no proration or substitution is allowed when calculating these scores. In fact, the only score for which proration or substitution is allowed is the FSIQ. See Table 2.19 for a list of subtests and their allowable substitutions.

4. *When should I administer secondary subtests?*
   There are several reasons for administering a secondary subtest. First, you may find that a subtest is spoiled for some reason, in which case a secondary subtest could be substituted to obtain an FSIQ score (e.g., an event such as a fire alarm spoils Vocabulary, in which case you could substitute Information). Second, you may decide *a priori* that substitution is necessary because the primary subtest would be an inaccurate reflection of a child's ability. For example, a child with motor problems may not be able to complete Block Design, which may necessitate the substitution of Visual Puzzles into the FSIQ. Finally, there may be specific clinical questions that can be answered by administering a secondary subtest in addition to the primary subtests (e.g., giving Figure Weights and Arithmetic in order to obtain a measure of quantitative reasoning). It is *not* appropriate to substitute secondary subtests based solely on preference or a desire to meet qualification requirements.

TABLE 2.19 Supplemental Subtests That Can Be Substituted into the FSIQ for Each Core Subtest

Core FSIQ	Subtest allowable substitutions
Vocabulary	Information and Comprehension
Similarities	Information and Comprehension
Block Design	Visual Puzzles
Matrix Reasoning	Picture Concepts
Figure Weights	Picture Concepts and Arithmetic
Digit Span	Picture Span and Letter-Number Sequencing
Coding	Symbol Search and Cancellation

5. *Why don't Naming Speed and Symbol Translation contribute to the FSIQ?*
   The purpose of these five subtests is to provide insight into cognitive processes related to learning difficulties. One of the primary uses of the WISC-V is the identification of specific learning disabilities, and these subtests are designed for analyses of strengths and weaknesses related to learning problems. That said, the constructs they measure, while related to intelligence, do not fit within the core theoretical model of the WISC-V, nor do they hold together within any index such as the VCI or FRI. Thus, although they can be combined to create the Naming Speed Index, Symbol Translation Index, and/or Storage and Retrieval Index, they are not used within the FSIQ.
6. *What is the new Nonverbal Index for, and if I want to use it for a student with language problems, should the administration procedures be changed to minimize language demands?*
   The Nonverbal Index (NVI) is an additional index score that minimizes the impact of expressive language demands. It contains subtests from all primary index scores except the VCI. The NVI may represent a more appropriate measure of overall cognitive functioning for children with severe expressive language delays or other clinical conditions with known language deficits (e.g., autism). Similarly, it may be useful for children who are deaf or hard of hearing, as well as children who are English language learners. The directions for the subtests should not change just because the NVI is being calculated. This is because the subtests may also be used to calculate other index scores in addition to NVI and thus must be administered according to standardized procedures. Given that the directions must still be understood, the NVI should not be considered a "language-free" measure.

7. *Why is the FSIQ lower than any of the primary index scores?*
   The phenomenon you are noticing is related to regression to the mean. First, remember that the FSIQ is used to predict the student's true intelligence and does not correlate perfectly with it. Then consider that the primary index scores are composed of fewer subtests than the FSIQ score and do not correlate perfectly with the FSIQ. In this case, if the student's true FSIQ is 57, then his or her primary index scores should be higher than 57 due to the effect of regression toward the mean. At the other end of the continuum, the opposite is true. If a student's FSIQ is 147, there is a greater probability that his or her index scores will be lower than the FSIQ. There are several factors that impact the strength of the effect, including the number of the distance of the subtest scores from the mean and the correlation among those subtests.

8. *Should I administer the Color-Object or Size-Color-Object items of Naming Speed to children with colorblindness?*
   The development team made every effort to ensure that WISC-V items were free of bias against these individuals. During the early stages of development, items were reviewed by color-perception differences experts and individuals with color-perception differences. In addition, acetate overlays were utilized to help test developers to understand the appearance of the stimuli to individuals with various color-perception differences. Items were also copied in black and white to check appearance to those with monochromatic color perception. All items were subjected to an electronic "color-blindness" simulator, to check item appearance with every type of color-perception difference and ensure that the intensity and saturation of colors were not confused or resulted in different responses. The colors on Naming Speed are yellow, blue, and red. Green is not included. They are very pure colors with no mix of other colors; this means that for the most common color blindness (green/red, which is 7–10% of boys), the children will be able to take it without a problem.

9. *I had to administer the WISC-V over the course of two testing sessions, and the child had a birthday in between. What age do I use to calculate her scores?*
   The child's birthdate at the time of the initial session should be used for subtests administered during both sessions, as this was the procedure used in the standardization sample. Examiners should ensure that as little time as possible transpires between the two sessions. Furthermore, if an event that may impact cognitive scores takes place between the sessions, it might be more appropriate to use a different age for the second session. Use your clinical judgment to determine when this procedure is appropriate.

10. *Why is there a strict time limit for Visual Puzzles and Figure Weights but a suggested time limit for Matrix Reasoning and Picture Concepts?*
    Children of higher ability tend to perform Visual Puzzles and Figure Weights items more quickly. However, given enough time, children of

lower ability can eventually respond to items correctly as well. This is not the case with Matrix Reasoning. The 30-second guideline was established because completion time data indicated that the vast majority of children who will respond correctly do so within 30 seconds, but giving additional time to children of low ability did not result in correct scores. A strict time limit is therefore unnecessary.

APPENDIX 2B. HOW IS WISC-V DIFFERENT FROM WISC-IV?

Similarities

- In order to ensure that all children are given similar opportunity for corrective feedback, there are a greater number of teaching items on the WISC-V version of Similarities. Rather than just Items 1 and 2, the start-point items are now teaching items (Items 1, 2, 5, 6, 8, and 9). Remembering to provide this corrective feedback is essential.
- The introduction to the subtest has been shortened. The phrase "I am going to say two words and ask you how they are alike" is no longer included in the instructions. Make sure not to include it despite the fact that it may feel routine based on experience with the WISC-IV.

Vocabulary

- The words are not printed on a page for any age ranges in WISC-V. This was to reduce any construct-irrelevant variance that may be introduced by variations in reading competency.
- Because the words are not printed and to reduce the incidence of misheard words, the administration procedures for administering Vocabulary have changed slightly. First, the word is read, and then there is a request to define the word (e.g., "COW. What is a COW?").
- Words that are more likely to be misheard are marked with an asterisk in the Manual and Record Form. If words on these items are misheard, say, "Listen carefully" and repeat the item emphasizing the misheard word.
- Like Similarities, all start-point items are now teaching items. This includes Items 1, 5, 6, 9, and 10.

Information

- Like other Verbal Comprehension subtests, all start-point items are now teaching items. This includes Items 1, 2, 8, and 9.
- There are numerous specific queries on Information. Each item containing a specific query is marked with an asterisk. Familiarize yourself with these queries to ensure a smooth flow to administration.

Comprehension

- The introduction to the subtest has been shortened. The phrase "Now I am going to ask you some questions, and I would like for you to tell me the answers" is no longer included in the instructions. Make sure not to include it despite the fact that it may feel routine based on experience with the WISC-IV.
- Item 1 was the only teaching item on the WISC-IV. There are now four teaching items on the WISC-V, two for each of the start points (Items 1, 2, 3, and 4).
- As in the WISC-IV, Comprehension still has items in which the child is required to provide responses that cover two general concepts. The rules for prompting these items have changed. Similar to the WISC-IV, if the child provides a response covering a single concept you should prompt for another by saying, "Tell me more (thing you should do, reasons why) [*rephrase item appropriately*]." However, if the child's second response refers to the same general concept, you no longer prompt for an additional response. Score the item and continue to the next appropriate item.

Block Design

- The ceiling item is shaped like an "X," rather than the typical square or diamond design seen in earlier iterations of Block Design.
- All items now require the examiner to show the child an image in the Stimulus Book (in the WISC-IV, Items 1 and 2 used the model only). For Items 1–3, model the picture for the child and place the model to the side of the Stimulus Book that matches the child's dominant hand.
- There is a new prompt for children that attempt to duplicate the sides of the examiner's model. If this occurs, point to the top faces of the blocks and say, "Only the tops of the blocks need to be the same." Do not stop timing when providing this feedback.
- There is also a prompt for children that attempts to construct the design on top of the Stimulus Book. If this occurs, point to the area next to the Stimulus Book and say, "Make yours over here."
- WISC-V Block Design yields a No Time Bonus score similar to WISC-IV. In addition, practitioners have the option to calculate a Partial score, which awards credit for each block that the child places correctly. The score ranges from 0 to 2 on Item 1, 0 to 4 on Items 2–9, and 0 to 12 on Items 10–13 (children who get all nine blocks correct are awarded bonus points). Like the No Time Bonus score, the Block Design Partial score may not be used in the calculation of the VSI or FSIQ.
- There is also a base rate score provided for Rotation Errors, which are recorded on each item and summed in order to get the total raw score.

- Finally, Block Design now provides a Dimension Errors base rate score. A dimension error is made when the child breaks the standard organization of blocks for an item (e.g., 2 × 2, 3 × 3, etc.). An error is judged as made if the child exhibits this behavior *at any time* during the construction of the design.

Matrix Reasoning

- Matrix Reasoning consists of two item types: matrix (2 × 2 or 3 × 3) and serial order (1 × 6). There are two samples items on the WISC-V rather than the three in the WISC-IV, one to introduce children to matrix items, and the other to introduce them to serial order items.
- The prompt given in response to self-corrections or multiple responses has changed from WISC-IV. If this occurs, say, "You (said, pointed to) [*insert child's response*], and you (said, pointed to) [*insert child's response*]. Which one did you mean?"

Picture Concepts

- Much of the item content has changed in Picture Concepts. Practitioners will notice that images are now never repeated across items; this was done to ensure that novel images did not cue the test-taker to the correct answers.
- The prompt given in response to self-corrections or multiple responses is now used on Picture Concepts. If this occurs, say, "You (said, pointed to) [*insert child's response*], and you (said, pointed to) [*insert child's response*]. Which one did you mean?"

Digit Span

- Similar to the WAIS-IV, a Sequencing task has been added to the Forward and Backward conditions. Always administer Digit Span Sequencing, regardless of the child's performance on Digit Span Forward and Backward, as it is required to obtain an overall scaled score for Digit Span.
- Digit Span Sequencing contains a qualifying item for children ages 6–7. If the child does not pass the qualifying item, the Sequencing condition should not be administered and the raw score is equal to 0.
- Several new prompts have been added to Digit Span. If the child responds before you have finished reading a trial, finish reading the trial and allow the child to respond. Score the response and say, "Wait until I stop before you start."
- The prompt in response to a child that asks for an item to be repeated has changed slightly from WISC-IV. If this occurs, say, "I can only say them one time. Just take your best guess."
- Similar to Matrix Reasoning, there is now a prompt for self-corrections or multiple responses. If this occurs, say, "You (said, pointed to) [*insert child's*

response], and you (said, pointed to) [*insert child's response*]. Which one did you mean?"
- Finally, for Digit Span Sequencing *only*, the same number may be included in a single trial more than once. If the child asks if his or her response should include repeated numbers, say, "You may have to say the same number more than one time."

Letter-Number Sequencing

- The structure of the subtest has been altered based on changes that were made in WAIS-IV. Items 1 and 2 have one letter and one number per trial (e.g., 3–C), and there is a demonstration item and sample item preceding them to teach the task. For Items 1 and 2, you do *not* give credit for responses in which the letter is provided before the number, and there is corrective feedback if the child does not get a trial correct. The purpose of this change is to avoid giving credit on floor items where no sequencing has occurred.
- Following Items 1 and 2 is another demonstration and sample item, followed by the remaining test items. For Items 3–10, there is no corrective feedback, and responses with the letters first receive credit.
- Item content has been changed so that rhyming letters and numbers (e.g., "3" and "C") do not appear on the same item. This reduces the likelihood that children with hearing difficulties accidently mishear items.
- Similar to Digit Span, there is a new prompt if the child responds before you have finished reading a trial. If this occurs, finish reading the trial and allow the child to respond. Score the response and say, "Wait until I stop before you start."
- The prompt in response to a child that asks for an item to be repeated has also changed on WISC-V. If this occurs, say, "I can only say them one time. Just take your best guess."
- There is now a longest span score for Letter-Number Sequencing. To calculate this score, count up the number of digits and letters from the longest sequence that the child gets correct (e.g., A–C–1–2 = raw score of 4).

Arithmetic

- The biggest change in Arithmetic is that a single repetition is *not* allowed on Items 1–19.
- Items 20–34 still allow a repetition, but there are two changes from WISC-IV. First, you are required to pause the timer while the item is repeated. Begin timing immediately after saying the last word of the repeated item. Second, you tell the child explicitly that repetitions are allowed before beginning to administer the items.
- You are now required to prompt children when time is running out on an item. If 20 seconds have elapsed and the child has not responded, ask, "Do you have an answer?" Do not stop timing to provide this prompt.

- Watch for the specific query on Item 31 marked with an asterisk. This is a change from WISC-IV Arithmetic, which did not contain any items with unique queries.

Coding

- The symbols have been changed and are designed so that the child can create the symbol without lifting a pencil.
- The item difficulty no longer increases per row. In WISC-IV, the first few rows contain only some of the symbol–number associations. In WISC-V, all symbol–number associations are represented on every row.
- There is a new prompt for cases in which the child begins working on the test items before the instructions are provided. In these cases, say, "Wait until I say 'Go' to start."
- There are no time bonus scores necessary for Coding A or B in WISC-V; whereas the WISC-IV provided a potential time bonus for Coding Form A.
- Examiners now have the option to record the number of times that the child rotates a symbol more than 90°. These rotations are summed and converted into a base rate score describing the total number of rotations on the subtest.

Symbol Search

- The response demands on Symbol Search have changed to permit observation of different error types. Rather than selecting *Yes* if a symbol matches and *No* if none of the symbols match, children are asked to select the matching symbol if it is present and select *No* if none of the symbols match.
- There are several new prompts for Symbol Search. If the child marks a target symbol as a response, say, "Make your marks over here (point to the search group and NO box)."
- If the child makes a mark with anything other than a single slash, point to the error and say, "Draw *one* line to make each mark."
- Similar to Coding, there is a new prompt for cases in which the child begins working on the test items before the instructions are provided. In these cases, say, "Wait until I say 'Go' to start."
- Do not stop the timer while providing any prompts.
- There is a time bonus score for Symbol Search Form A. There is no time bonus score required on Form B.
- The distractor images on Symbol Search were intentionally designed to pull for certain types of errors. For each item, one response option either looks similar to the correct design or matches the correct design but is rotated (children are instructed not to select options that are rotated). Errors in which rotated symbols are selected are recorded and converted into a Rotation Errors base rate score, and errors in which similar symbols are selected get recorded and converted into a Set Errors base rate score.

Cancellation

- There is a new prompt in Cancellation if the child marks an answer using anything other than a single slash. If this occurs, say, "Draw *one* line to make each mark." Do not stop timing while administering this prompt.
- No time bonus score is necessary for the WISC-V.

REFERENCES

Alfonso, V. C., Johnson, A., Patinella, L., & Rader, D. E. (1998). Common WISC-III examiner errors: Evidence from graduate students in training. *Psychology in the Schools, 35*, 119–125.

Belk, M. S., LoBello, S. G., Ray, G. E., & Zachar, P. (2002). WISC-III administration, clerical, and scoring errors made by student examiners. *Journal of Psychoeducational Assessment, 20*, 290–300.

Bowers, P. G., & Wolf, M. (1993). Theoretical links among naming speed, precise timing mechanisms and orthographic skill in dyslexia. *Reading and Writing, 5*(1), 69–85.

Hopwood, C. J., & Richard, D. C. S. (2005). Graduate student WAIS-III scoring accuracy is a function of Full Scale IQ and complexity of examiner tasks. *Assessment, 12*(4), 445–454.

Kail, R., & Hall, L. K. (1994). Processing speed, naming speed, and reading. *Developmental Psychology, 30*(6), 949–954.

Kaufman, A. S. (2009). *IQ testing 101*. New York: Springer Publishing Company.

Klassen, R. M., & Kishor, N. (1996). A comparative analysis of practitioners' errors on WISC-R and WISC-III. *Canadian Journal of School Psychology, 12*, 35–43.

Kuentzel, J. G., Hetterscheidt, L. A., & Barnett, D. (2011). Testing intelligently includes double-checking Wechsler IQ scores. *Journal of Psychoeducational Assessment, 29*(1), 39–46.

Loe, S. A., Kadlubek, R. M., & Marks, W. J. (2007). Administration and scoring errors on the WISC-IV among graduate student examiners. *Journal of Psychoeducational Assessment, 25*, 237–247.

Patterson, M., Slate, J. R., Jones, S. H., & Steger, H. S. (1995). The effects of practice administrations in learning to administer and score the WAIS-R: a partial replication. *Educational & Psychological Measurement, 55*, 32–37.

Platt, T. L., Zachar, P., Ray, G. E., Underhill, A. T., & LoBello, S. G. (2007). Does Wechsler intelligence scale administration and scoring proficiency improve during assessment training? *Psychological Reports, 100*, 547–555.

Ryan, J. J., & Schnakenberg-Ott, S. D. (2003). Scoring reliability on the Wechsler adult intelligence scale—Third edition (WAIS-III). *Assessment, 10*(2), 151–159.

Sattler, J. M. (2008). *Assessment of children—Cognitive foundations* (5th ed.). La Mesa, CA: Author.

Schatschneider, C., Carlson, C. D., Francis, D. J., Foorman, B. R., & Fletcher, J. M. (2002). Relationship of rapid automatized naming and phonological awareness in early reading development: Implications for the double-deficit hypothesis. *Journal of Learning Disabilities, 35*(3), 245–256.

Slate, J. R., & Chick, D. (1989). WISC-R examiner errors: Cause for concern. *Psychology in the Schools, 26*, 78–84.

Slate, J. R., & Jones, C. (1990a). Identifying student errors in administering the WAIS-R. *Psychology in the Schools, 27*, 83–87.

Slate, J. R., & Jones, C. (1990b). Student error in administering the WISC-R: identifying problem areas. *Measurement and Evaluation in Counseling and Development*, *23*, 137–140.

Slate, J. R., Jones, C. H., & Murray, K. A. (1991). Teaching administration and scoring of the Wechsler Adult Intelligence Scale–Revised: An empirical evaluation of practice administrations. *Professional Psychology: Research and Practice*, *22*, 375–379.

Slate, J. R., Jones, C. H., Murray, R. A., & Coulter, C. (1993). Evidence that practitioners err in administering and scoring the WAIS-R. *Measurement and Evaluation in Counseling and Development*, *25*, 156–166.

Wechsler, D. (2014). *WISC-V technical and interpretive manual*. Bloomington, MN: Pearson.

Chapter 3

Practical Considerations in WISC-V Interpretation and Intervention

A. Lynne Beal[1], James A. Holdnack[2], Donald H. Saklofske[3], and Lawrence G. Weiss[4]

[1]Private Practice, Toronto, Ontario, Canada, [2]Pearson Clinical Assessment, Bear, DE, USA, [3]Department of Psychology, University of Western Ontario, London, Ontario, Canada, [4]Pearson Clinical Assessment, San Antonio, TX, USA

INTRODUCTION

Interpretation of the WISC-V scores is typically done in the context of making recommendations for educational interventions for children and adolescents. This chapter provides a guide for interpretation of the WISC-V as a measure of *g* or overall ability, as well as a set of measures of specific abilities. To aid practitioners with developing intervention strategies, the chapter continues by linking interventions to the specific cognitive abilities that WISC-V measures.

In this chapter, we first discuss common challenges to interpreting WISC-V scores for students where there is broad variance among the scores. Next, we present an analogy designed to promote a more intuitive understanding of the abilities measured by each index. Finally, we consider some fundamental suggestions for teachers and parents who have children with weaknesses in one of the primary cognitive abilities. These suggestions, guidelines, and heuristics are drawn from both research and clinical practice to provide further insights into the applications of the WISC-V as an important part of the clinical assessment process. Suggestions are not presented as a clinical "cookbook" of either diagnostic hypotheses or clinical interpretations of the abilities.

LEVELS OF INTERPRETATION: WHEN THE OVERALL ABILITY SCORE DOES NOT TELL THE WHOLE STORY

Tracey's WISC-V scores show that her abilities are not evenly developed. There were significant differences between 3 of the index scores that call into question

L. G. Weiss, D. H. Saklofske, J. A. Holdnack and A. Prifitera (Eds): WISC-V Assessment and Interpretation.
DOI: http://dx.doi.org/10.1016/B978-0-12-404697-9.00003-0

63

the meaningfulness of the FSIQ. But our Director says that this score is needed in order to secure additional funding for special education support for this student.

Wally's teachers have commented on his variable performance across school subjects since entering school 3 years ago. While some earlier test results reporting a summary IQ score indicated that he may have the overall cognitive ability to cope with a regular program, the results of the current assessment suggest that the more relevant focus of his school learning and achievement difficulties may be found in the significant and rarely occurring score differences between his high average VCI, low average WMI and PSI, with borderline scores on the VSI and FRI.

Analysis of the discrepancies among the index score is routinely accepted as good clinical practice, especially when such interpretation occurs in the context of general ability (Flanagan & Kaufman, 2004; Kaufman, 2013; Sattler, 2008). Significant discrepancies among a student's index scores should be interpreted as indications of relative strengths or weaknesses in the cognitive constructs they measure. As most practitioners have observed, an identified strength or weakness in one of these major cognitive abilities will often manifest in classroom behavior. For example, teachers will likely find that a student who has a significant weakness on the Working Memory Index (WMI) tends to forget assignments; or one has who has a weakness on the Processing Speed Index (PSI) takes longer to process instructions than classmates. Such information is beneficial to educational planning.

However, profile analysis of WISC-V index scores is not by itself diagnostic of any particular psychoeducational or clinical disorder. The index scores represent major cognitive abilities. Therefore, a cognitive deficit in one of these areas may be associated with any of several disorders related to that ability. A significant weakness on WMI, for example, may be a common finding in groups with attention-deficit/hyperactivity disorder (ADHD) but also occurs with some frequency in groups with learning disabilities (LD) and traumatic brain injury (TBI). It is for this reason that index score patterns should be considered consistent with but not confirmatory of a diagnosis, and must be combined with other information to rule out alternative diagnostic hypotheses. The cognitive deficits related to such disorders will be discussed further in the final two chapters.

Two examples of a student with a deficit as measured by the WMI demonstrate this concept. For a student referred for possible ADHD, a low WMI, combined with high scores on a parent rating scale for ADHD behaviors, low scores on a continuous performance task of sustained attention, and a developmental and educational history of deficits in attention, impulsivity, or hyperactivity, the practitioner may feel confident in making a diagnosis of ADHD. The preponderance of supporting information along with the low WMI leads to this conclusion. However, for a student athlete who had an on-field concussion referred for reading comprehension problems, a low WMI score would instead warrant further evaluation to investigate a possible traumatic brain injury.

Investigation of Wechsler scores, at all levels, should be conducted within an ecological context (Prifitera, Saklofske, & Weiss, 2005, 2008; Weiss,

Saklofske, Prifitera, & Holdnack, 2006). Interpretation of score patterns may vary depending on the sociocultural background (Georgas, Weiss, van de Vijver, & Saklofske, 2003; Harris & Llorente, 2005), family values, pattern of academic strengths and weaknesses, motivation, and psychiatric and medical history. Interpretation also needs to consider behaviors observed during the test session (Oakland, Glutting, & Watkins, 2005; Sattler & Dumont, 2004). A common mistake is to offer stock interpretations of index score patterns while ignoring the effects of these mediating influences (see Kamphaus, 1998). Consider, for example, two children each having a Full Scale Intelligence Quotient (FSIQ) score of 112, which, by itself, suggests high average ability. The child with a superior Verbal Comprehension Index (VCI) and low average WMI, will certainly present differently in the classroom than a typically developing child with statistically consistent subtest and index scores yielding an FSIQ of 112. The first child may appear much brighter and much less attentive than the second children even though they have the same FSIQ score. Remember that children may perform contrary to expectations on testing. For all of these reasons, the interpretations of WISCV test scores will differ in relation to the examinee's personal context and history. In addition, the examiner's expectations of the likelihood of finding certain patterns will be influenced by the referral questions and hypotheses.

How Important is g, the Measure of Overall Ability?

Curiously, one camp of psychometric researchers argues that the modest portions of variance attributed to the first order factors (the index scores) may be too small to be of clinical importance, should not be used diagnostically, and that therefore FSIQ is the only score worth interpreting (Canivez & Kush, 2013; Canivez & Watkins, 2010). However, data analysis of these studies indicates that the researchers statistically removed g from the index scores and examined only their residual validity. This approach is problematic because an individual's investment of g resources in particular directions results in greater development of those abilities over time (Reynolds & Keith, 2013). Thus, removing the influence of g from the index scores effectively cripples their power, and creates a rather artificial situation. As Schneider (2013) observed:

> ...the independent portion is not the "real Gc". We care about a sprinter's ability to run quickly, not residual sprinting speed after accounting for general athleticism. So it is with Gc: g is a part of the mix. (p. 6)

Another camp of neuropsychological researchers and clinicians argues that FSIQ is a meaningless composite of various disparate abilities and should not be interpreted at all (Hale, Fiorello, Kavanagh, Holdnack, & Aloe, 2007; Kaplan, 1988; Lezak, 1988; Lezak, Howieson, & Loring, 2004). This point demonstrates the incredible diversity of opinion that exists in the field. One camp argues that interpretation of index scores is invalid and recommends interpreting only FSIQ while the other camp argues that interpretation of FSIQ is invalid and recommends interpreting only the index scores.

We do not agree with either camp. Both views have merit, but both views are too one-sided to be workable. We believe that *g* and the broad abilities are both important and that each construct has a place in the practice of assessment.

What is a practitioner to do? We suggest that it depends on the referral question. When the purpose of the evaluation is to efficiently predict a broad range of cognitively driven behaviors, then *g*—as defined by FSIQ—is always the best score to use. Further, we think that heterogeneous tasks, which require integration of multiple abilities for successful performance, will enhance the ecological validity of predicting a broader range of cognitively driven, real-world behaviors. On the other hand, examining particular broad and narrow abilities is necessary when evaluating clients for specific cognitive impairments, neurological conditions, and learning and attentional disorders. Thus, it is not one approach or the other. Strength and weakness interpretations vary in the context of the child's overall level of *g* as evidenced by differing frequencies of discrepant indexes by ability level (Wechsler, 2014).

There is evidence that having one or more low cognitive ability scores is commonly observed among healthy individuals; therefore, practitioners should be cautious when interpreting low scores as conclusive evidence of brain injury or disease in forensic evaluations (Brooks, Holdnack, & Iverson, 2011). The common finding of one or more low index scores in normal subjects, however, suggests that for individuals, *g* does not manifest itself equally across the broad cognitive abilities. Whether for reasons of environmental opportunity or personal and vocational interest, individuals appear to invest *g* resources selectively. They thereby develop some broad abilities at the expense of others over time (cf. Cattell, 1987; Kvist & Gustafsson, 2008; Reynolds & Keith, 2013). This is one reason why clinicians find it difficult to conceptualize the broad abilities independent of *g*—although it is possible to accomplish statistically. As Claeys (2013) observes: "No one is more aware that test factors don't always 'hang together' than those assessing children and adults on a daily basis." How true!

One issue remains. That is, should FSIQ be reported when there is significant variability among the index scores? In other words, is there a statistical or clinical point where FSIQ "fractures" into more meaningful parts, and is no longer a valid measure of general mental ability nor clinically useful for assisting with differential diagnosis or program planning?

The child's overall level of cognitive ability provides a critical backdrop to interpretation of individual differences among the various domains of ability as assessed by the index scores. The calculation of an FSIQ continues to be important for this and several other reasons. From a purely psychometric perspective, a general factor clearly emerges in all studies of intelligence (Carroll, 1993). This fact, combined with the integrity of the five factor structure and the magnitude of the correlations between the index scores make a psychometrically compelling case for the interpretation of the FSIQ.

Further, recent WISC-IV studies suggest that FSIQ may be an equally valid measure of general ability for individuals or groups having highly variable index scores as for those having consistent index scores (Daniel, 2007). WISC-III and WISC-IV studies further suggest that there may be no difference in the predictive validity of FSIQ for low-scatter and high-scatter groups (Watkins, Glutting, & Lei, 2007).

FSIQ is an especially strong predictor of school achievement, occupational success, and memory functioning. FSIQ and achievement correlate more strongly than any two variables known to the behavioral sciences, typically around 0.70. For example, Deary, Strand, Smith, and Fernandes (2007) reported that general mental ability measured at age 11 years is highly correlated ($r = 0.81$) with general educational achievement and further with different subject areas at age 16 years. This means that FSIQ explains about 65% of the variance in achievement. Additional relevant factors likely include the student's perseverance, drive to task mastery, self-regulation toward a goal, and other constructs related to emotional intelligence. Beyond the relationship with achievement, there is considerable ecological and criterion validity for the use of an overall estimate of general intelligence in a variety of areas related to success in life including college readiness, predicting job performance, creativity, and innovation (Gottfredson, 1997, 1998; Kuncel, Hezlett, & Ones, 2004; Squalli & Wilson, 2014).

The Importance of Interpreting the Component Abilities

Although FSIQ has strong psychometric integrity and predictive power, large discrepancies among the component abilities of FSIQ are often observed in clinical practice. We believe that it is these large discrepancies that may provide the most clinically interesting and useful information of relevance to the assessment protocol. In cases of intellectual giftedness or moderate to severe mental retardation, we can expect a relatively flat profile and a summary or FSIQ score can certainly be used to describe the cognitive component of this finding. As well, similar subtest and index scores of a child with FSIQ of 107 certainly allows the psychologist to describe this child as having average ability and further manifesting average Verbal Comprehension (VC), Visual–Spatial (VS), Fluid Reasoning (FR), Working Memory (WM), and Processing Speed (PS) abilities. This would then shift the hypotheses related to poor school performance to other cognitive factors, such as auditory phonemic awareness or long-term memory retrieval; or to noncognitive factors such as work and study skills, personality, motivation, learning style, and the teaching-learning-social environment of the classroom. However, in other cases such as recent lateralized brain trauma, the presence of a large discrepancy between, for example, VC and VS may be very meaningful and should be the focus for interpreting cognitive abilities.

Thus, it is prudent to take the position that the presence of large discrepancies among index scores, reflecting unevenly developed cognitive abilities, makes interpretation of the child's overall intellectual functioning more difficult and complex. Such variability then points to the need to shift test interpretation to the index scores where the most clinically relevant information is more likely to be found. Having five cognitive factors to interpret a child's abilities is a strength of the WISC-V theoretical structure.

Similarly though, any factor-based score such as the PSI becomes more difficult to interpret when the subtest scores within the index are too variable. Significant score differences between the subtests on the same index are clear indicators that the composite does not provide a reliable indication of the child's ability in that domain. Rather than focusing on a less meaningful summary score, determine the clinical relevance of the subtest findings. Assumptions to cover are that the test was properly administered and scored, the testing conditions were adequate, and the examinee was both motivated and seemed to understand the task demands. An example for Processing Speed would show scaled scores of 13 for Symbol Search versus 4 for Coding. These scores might result from differences in the task and the greater requirement for fine motor coordination on Coding. Consider also noncognitive factors, such as interest and motivation or even scoring errors! While careful administration and scoring are essential to providing "valid" data, one should always have enough clinical commonsense to be able to say: "that score can't be right, because the child answered almost all of the items on the Similarities subtest."

Once the analysis of test scores is accomplished in this detailed, bottom-up manner, the interpretation may be made in the traditional top-down manner, whether it begins with the FSIQ or index scores. Top-down and bottom-up approaches can be used in an integrative way to explore various clinical interpretations. Thus, although the FSIQ can be a clinically meaningful summary of a child's overall cognitive functioning, an examination of the subtest scores and index scores can also provide meaning and insight to the assessment process. Targeting the examination to specific abilities can also be informed by information from referral sources. Kamphaus (2001) states that a hypothesized pattern of strengths and weaknesses based on such factors that are subsequently observed in the test data leads to a more meaningful interpretation than the same pattern identified by comparing all possible test scores. Looking for significant differences between all subtest scores is bound to lead to a statistically significant finding simply because of the number of comparisons being made. This possibility is further confounded comparing score differences based on the statistical analyses of a large standardization sample to the single case (nomethetic or generalized versus idiographic or more personalized comparisons).

There has clearly been a change in emphasis in the evolution of the Wechsler tests from primarily measuring IQ only to focusing on the five major cognitive abilities assessed by the VC, VS, FR, WM, and PS indexes. This change brings the WISC-V more in line with the psychologist's current need for a test that has implications for description, diagnosis, and prescription.

Although the standard procedure for investigating and reporting a child's WISC-V profile may begin at the Full Scale level and then proceed with an analysis of the index and subtest scores, invariably there are times when this is not the best practice to follow. In fact extreme discrepancies between scores are the more common finding.

In summary, a general intelligence factor is one of the most robust findings in the history of psychology. A century of evidence shows that it is substantially related to school achievement as well as a wide variety of real-world outcomes. Some psychometric researchers have suggested that *g* is so robust that it fully accounts for all of the broad cognitive abilities and argue that interpretation should be restricted to FSIQ alone. Nonetheless, *g* needs to be interpreted within the context of its component abilities. Since each of the WISC-V subtests is predicated on a broader interpretation of the ability being assessed, it is impossible to separate the overall ability from its components. One cannot remove working memory from fluid reasoning or verbal comprehension. A second order *g* factor also emerges in all other major intelligence tests including but not limited to the Stanford-Binet, Woodcock-Johnson-IV, Differential Abilities Scales-II, Kaufman Assessment Battery for Children-II, and the Das-Luria test battery.

Arguing the opposite, other researchers state that FSIQ should never be interpreted because it is simply a normative averaging of diverse cognitive functions with different neuropsychological underpinnings. Our view is that test results showing significant variance among the index scores or subtest scores are not psychometric or clinical problems at all. Rather, the variance in scores within the ability test provides clinical opportunities to gain insight into a child's unique pattern of strengths and weaknesses. When large discrepancies among index scores are present, we recommend reporting the FSIQ, but focusing interpretation solidly on the index scores. For example:

> *The pattern of Aalyah's scores suggests uneven development across various areas of cognitive ability, even though the combination of her abilities gives an Average FSIQ score of 97. In particular, her verbal conceptualization abilities (VCI 109) are much better developed than her visual spatial abilities (VSI 89). Given her strengths, Aalyah will likely perform much better than her classmates on tasks involving verbal skills, but find it hard to keep up with them on visual spatial tasks. Many children have relatively stronger and weaker areas of ability.*

PERSONIFYING THE PRIMARY ABILITIES: A SIMPLE ANALOGY

In most workplaces, people are hired for specific skills or abilities, and they work together on teams in important ways. Each team member often has a unique ability that is essential to the work the team is performing. Thus, a school team may include a teacher, school psychologist, speech pathologist, nurse, and assistant principal. The team might be asked to determine the best intervention plan for a struggling learner and they each contribute their unique knowledge, skills, and abilities to the collective plan.

At the risk of oversimplifying, the work of the brain is to learn facts and relationships among them, remember them when needed, and use them to quickly and efficiently solve problems in life. In our analogy the brain has at least five primary team members that correspond, more or less, to the five broad abilities measured by the WISC-V. These team members are the librarian, architect, general manager, clerk, and detective.

VCI: The Librarian

The library shelves contain all of the verbal knowledge that has been crystallized in the brain. When someone comes into the library looking for information, an expert librarian can help to solve their problem by recommending certain books, so the person can retrieve them and access knowledge relevant to the problem at hand. The knowledge base of the librarian can be broad and deep, reflecting all of the information that has been acquired through reading, studying, and listening during her or his life. The librarian knows what information may aid in solving a problem.

If the librarian is not effective, the customer will receive information that does not help solve the problem at hand, is only marginally relevant, or maybe misleading. An effective librarian, will not only provide the best information relevant to the question but will do so with the minimum amount of information required to complete the job, thus not wasting the customer's valuable time and limited resources.

The VCI mainly measures crystalized knowledge and some verbal reasoning. But the librarian must also know where the information is stored and how to retrieve it. Thus, verbal comprehension assumes adequate long-term retrieval functions as well.

VSI: The Architect

The architect prepares blueprints to build things by constructing geometric designs based on spatial relationships. They have the ability to see how things fit together to form a whole, and how those things can be rearranged to form something different. In some cases they do this by simply matching pieces and parts together, but for other jobs they may need to see these relationships in their mind's eye and imagine how they might fit together differently. This is why it is necessary to hire a trained architect for these jobs rather than employee a construction site manager who simply matches the job to a blueprint.

An ineffective architect creates blueprints that do not meet building codes and creates structures that are not structurally sound (does not balance structural load), have limited structural lifespan (e.g., selects wrong materials), are not functional for the stated purpose of the space, or may be aesthetically displeasing (uses wrong combination of visual details). An effective architect efficiently designs structures using the most appropriate materials that are structurally sound, efficient for the required usage, and are visually appealing. VSI measures visual–spatial reasoning and requires mental rotation and visual working memory.

WMI: The General Manager

The brain is a very busy workplace. It is barraged minute by minute with requests for previous information, new information that needs to be processed, and decisions that must be made. All of these demands can be loosely thought of as "orders from customers" received at a factory. The general manager controls which customer orders the factory workers pay attention to, based on importance, what work is assigned to which departments within the brain, and in what priority the orders get processed. Once the work is completed, the general manager makes sure the remaining clutter is cleared from the shop floor so the next job can be processed efficiently.

An ineffective manager can slow order processing by not allocating sufficient resources or misallocating resources, not assigning work to the proper groups, not reserving sufficient space for new orders, or not maintaining an organized workflow and work environment. An effective manager devises strategies to handle low and high work volumes, is organized, allows systems for multitasking, and provides the correct amount of resources to get the job completed.

The WMI measures ability to sustain focus on incoming stimuli it assigns to the phonological loop or the visual–spatial sketchpad until completely processed, and to clear out facts that are no longer relevant to the next issue processed in order to avoid proactive interference.

PSI: The Clerk

The clerk is often an entry-level employee who is expected only to complete the assigned work as quickly and accurately as possible. The clerk does not decide what to work on. He or she is not expected to make any really important decisions. The job of the clerk is to do what they are told to do, get it done fast, and not make any mistakes. They then move to the next task assigned by the general manager.

An ineffective clerk can incorrectly fill out forms, fail to notice important missing information, or complete work too slowly for organizational efficiency. An efficient clerk completes tasks quickly and efficiently, identifies incomplete, erroneous, or missing information, and quickly learns and adapts to novel procedures. The PSI measures speed of information processing with visual stimuli.

FRI: The Detective

The detective figures things out by considering all the facts, deducing underlying relationships among them, making inductive inferences, and putting relevant facts together to solve the crime (i.e., the problem). Some facts come from the immediate environment (i.e., the crime scene) whereas other facts are stored in the library (e.g., knowledge of forensics). The detective relies on the librarian for relevant facts stored in the library. He or she relies on the architect to imagine how the items in the room were arranged before the crime. The detective tells the general manager which leads to pursue first, and relies on the general manager to maintain focus on them and selectively ignore facts the detective deems not relevant. The detective relies on the clerk to process all these facts quickly to solve the problem before the criminal gets away.

A good detective knows where to look for clues, quickly integrates complex and sometimes disparate information into a cohesive understanding of the events of the crime. With this information he or she is able to narrow down a list of possible suspects to the one that committed the crime. A hapless detective fails to draw upon relevant knowledge, does not visualize relevant scenarios, cannot prioritize or maintain focus on the most relevant facts, does not process the information in the correct priority while it is still current and relevant, and ultimately draws incorrect conclusions from the various facts at hand—perhaps even arresting an innocent person.

The FRI measures the ability to solve novel problems. It is most closely related to general intelligence, or "g," in that it requires successful integration of multiple cognitive abilities working in concert. For the detective to be successful, the librarian, architect, general manager, and clerk must work together as one team with a common goal of solving the problem.

We hope the reader has appreciated our lighthearted attempt at explaining the primary abilities using personifications that are, of course, somewhat unrealistic. To be sure we are taken seriously, however, we refer the reader to Chapter 4 on theoretical foundations, where we discuss in greater depth the abilities measured by each WISC-V primary index in terms of neuropsychological functions, clinical research, models of cognitive information processing, and theories of intelligence.

ISSUES RELATED TO INTERVENTION

Understanding what ability is measured by an index score is the first step toward planning accommodations for a student who is weak in that ability. Knowing how this weakness would be manifested in daily activities in the classroom is the next step to validating the hypothesized weak ability indicated by the test score.

A first line of intervention is to draw upon the student's strong abilities, be they personal strengths or normative strengths, to compensate for weaker abilities. Now, we suggest classroom modifications and teacher-oriented accommodations for children with weaknesses in each of the five major cognitive abilities measured by WISC-V (verbal comprehension, visual–spatial reasoning, fluid reasoning, working memory, and processing speed). In this regard, weaknesses can either be defined normatively or ipsatively; but it is not necessary that the student be achieving below his or her potential in the context of a discrepancy approach to be considered for one or more of these modifications or accommodations.

Modifications are changes made in the age-appropriate grade-level expectations for a subject or course in order to meet a student's learning needs. These changes might involve developing expectations that reflect knowledge and skills required in the curriculum for a different grade level, or increasing or decreasing the number or complexity of the regular grade-level curriculum expectations, or both. Thus, we may hear a teacher say that, "Given Bill's limited cognitive ability and that he is functioning three grades below his placement in math, he will require a modified arithmetic program over the next year so he can achieve some proficiency with fundamental math operations."

The term *accommodations* is used to refer to the special teaching and classroom assessment strategies, human supports or individualized equipment, or both, required to enable a student to learn and to demonstrate learning. Accommodations do not alter the state curriculum expectations for the grade. The accommodations that the student requires in connection with instruction, assessment, and functioning in the physical environment may be conceptualized as instructional, environmental, or assessment.

Instructional accommodations are adjustments in teaching strategies required to enable the student to learn and to progress through the curriculum (e.g., "Mary will require the use of voice-to-text software to enable her to dictate her assignments to a computer due to her learning disability in written language").

Environmental accommodations are changes or supports in the physical environment of the classroom or the school, or both (e.g., Greg requires modified seating arrangements in the classroom. Provide him with an alternative quiet area or study carrel where distractions from windows, noise, vents, and disruptive students are minimized.)

Assessment accommodations are adjustments in assessment activities and methods required to enable the student to demonstrate learning (e.g., Crystal will require extra time up to 150% of the time to write tests and exams).

This approach to program modifications and accommodations is rooted in a belief that deficits in specific cognitive processes restrict the student's access to the curriculum, and that the cognitive deficit likely cannot be remediated directly. Therefore, the teacher must find ways to teach around the deficit. Empirical support for some of the intervention ideas made in this section is emerging (see Gathercole & Alloway, 2008; Gathercole, Lamont, & Alloway, 2006). Yet, many of these intervention ideas are simply suggested teaching tips intended to be tried and used only if they can be demonstrated to work for an individual student. Thus, single case studies are recommended as one method of providing empirical support for the strategies suggested below on a student by student basis. Methodologies for single case designs exist and are well accepted. In this case, the methodology would include tracking the student's progress on a series of brief academic probes before and after implementation of one or more of the accommodations or modifications suggested below. This can be an effective and powerful methodology for demonstrating empirical support at the student level, and collections of these studies begin to build a body of evidence. If implemented on a school-wide scale, a data management system that charts progress on frequent academic probes as a function of a series of attempted interventions can be a very powerful administrative and scientific tool. One such software system is aimsweb (Pearson, 2012).

Selection from among the tips offered below can be made based on the pattern of classroom behaviors observed (see below) for learners who have not responded to standard group-level educational interventions (i.e., Tier II of a three tier RTI model), or based on patterns of WISC-V test scores for students in special education or being considered for special education (i.e., Tier III of a three tier RTI model).

The hardest part of the job of assessment for the purposes of intervention is to translate test results into appropriate modifications and accommodations to the student's work in the classroom. Yet, this is the function that teachers rely on the most when they refer their student for a psychological assessment. If there is one major criticism that teachers and other educational personnel make about psychological assessment and the reports that follow, it is that they lack sufficient information to guide the teacher on "what to do next or what to do differently" that will have a positive impact on the child (Mastoras, Climie, McCrimmon, & Schwean, 2011; Schwean et al., 2006).

The interventions tips provided here follow directly from the cognitive abilities that are measured by the WISC-V index scores. For many children, these strategies will not be sufficient if applied in isolation. Targeted academic interventions are also necessary for specific learning disabilities. Examples are interventions to address weaknesses found in the academic skills of reading, written language, and mathematics. Excellent sources for such interventions are Mather and Jaffe (2002), Naglieri and Pickering (2003), Wendling and Mather (2008), and Mather and Wendling (2012). Further examples are interventions to address executive skills, such as organization, time management, self-regulation, and others. Excellent resources for interventions on executive functions are Hale and Fiorello (2004) and Dawson and Guare (2004).

Evidence on the effectiveness of specific educational and academic interventions is assessed and rated by the U.S. Department of Education through panels of experts organized by the Institute of Educational Services. These reviews and ratings can be found on a website called the What Works Clearinghouse: ies.ed.gov/ncee/wwc/.

The intervention suggestions in this chapter are not intended to replace more targeted educational interventions for specific academic conditions such as dyslexia or written language disorders. Rather, these general strategies are intended to supplement specific academic instructional interventions by providing simple, practical suggestions for teachers whose students may have a weakness in one of the broader cognitive domains measured by the WISC-V.

Although the intervention suggestions in this chapter focus on academics, we remind the reader to always consider the whole child. Modifications and accommodations may also be needed in the area of social-emotional and interpersonal functioning. Although the cognitive factors do not speak as directly to this, it is important to note that children with cognitive weaknesses may also need accommodation in this emotional area to make them successful in school as well. So a child with low verbal skills may have more difficulty communicating effectively with teachers, parents, and peers. Low FRI scores may mean a child needs more time in understanding and getting comfortable with new social situations, etc. Other factors like inhibitory control, persistence, self-efficacy, grit, and executive functions may play a role in emotions.

The bulleted lists of classroom indicators, modifications, accommodations, and assessment strategies are reprinted with permission from the *Special Education Handbook: A Practical Guide for All Teachers* (Elementary Teachers' Federation of Ontario, 2007). An updated version of this publication is in preparation for 2015.

INTERVENTION SUGGESTIONS RELATED TO VERBAL COMPREHENSION

The VCI measures crystallized knowledge and verbal fluid reasoning. Crystallized intelligence, as measured by the VCI, shows a strong and consistent relationship with the development of reading and math achievement. Contributions of crystallized intelligence to writing achievement are important primarily after age 7. Its contributions to reading, math, and writing achievement become increasingly important for reading and math achievement with age (Berninger & Abbott, 2003; Berninger & Wagner, 2008; Flanagan, Alfonso, Mascolo, & Sotelo-Dynega, 2012; Flanagan & Mascolo, 2005).

A student with needs in these areas has difficulty in understanding oral language, or in expressing himself or herself through oral language, or in both. Classroom indicators of this need in the student's daily performance related to verbal comprehension include:

- Having a limited receptive vocabulary needed to understand words and their meaning, or having a limited expressive vocabulary to express thoughts and ideas using language in terms of correct word meanings, or both
- Having difficulty in listening and comprehending oral language, including gleaning the meanings of phrases, sentences, idiom and colloquialisms, despite adequate attention and auditory processing skills
- Having difficulty in speaking in "real-life" situations in an age-appropriate manner

- Having difficulty with language comprehension and usage, evident in their native language and impacting their learning of a second language in similar ways
- Having a limited range of general knowledge and subject-specific knowledge, despite indicators of adequate memory functioning. This limitation is evidenced by limited expression of the ideas and knowledge through oral language

Possible instructional accommodations for children with low verbal comprehension abilities include:

- Keep the language of instruction as simple as possible.
- Provide definitions for all new terms and concepts before teaching the lesson. Be alert for subject-specific terms that the student does not know. Teach the student to keep a separate page at the back of each subject's notebook to write the new terms and their definitions. Advise the student to study the list regularly.
- Teach new vocabulary in the context of information that the student already knows about the topic. Make explicit links to known vocabulary, information, and concepts.
- Provide models for more elaborate language usage when conversing with the student. Respond to their statements by repeating their utterances with revised vocabulary and sentence structure that is more age-appropriate.
- Teach the student how to use the dictionary to look up words to find their meanings. Use grade-appropriate resources, both in book form and electronic format.
- Teach the student how to use a thesaurus to look up words to find synonyms and related words. Use grade-appropriate resources, both in book form and electronic format.
- Ask the student whether he or she understood instructions that were given orally. If he or she did not understand, then
  - Paraphrase the instruction using more simple language
  - Explain the terms used in the instruction
  - Reduce the complexity of the instruction by breaking it down into parts.
- Teach the student to recognize when he or she has not understood an oral instruction or lesson, and to ask for clarification to build understanding.
- Use instructional strategies that are not reliant on language, or that include other formats, such as:
  - demonstrations and modeling to teach concepts and procedures
  - hand over hand guidance for young students, coupled with verbal explanations
  - pictures, graphs, charts
  - maps, diagrams, flow charts, logic models
  - semantic webbing maps.
- Teach the student to create a visual image of what he or she hears to supplement the language with visual and procedural representations.

- Communicate with parents in writing through notes, the student's agenda book, postings on the class website, or by e-mail.
- Check for knowledge gaps when teaching new information and concepts that rely on prior knowledge. Where gaps occur, teach the material as though it were new.
- Permit the student to make an audio recording of explanations given to clarify assignments and projects so he or she can replay it while working and getting assistance from a parent or tutor.

Environmental accommodations for children with low verbal comprehension abilities include the following considerations:

- Seat the student near the teacher and away from noise sources.
- Reduce the background noise against which oral language is heard in order to reduce the possibility of distortions of the speech stream.

Classroom assessment strategies for children with low verbal comprehension abilities include:

- Confirm that the student understands the instructions and directions before beginning a test or project.
- Use assessment methods with reduced demands on verbal output, such as true/false, multiple choice, or short answer.
- Reduce the demands for language comprehension when assessing competencies in mathematics and sciences. Use language and structures that scores low in reading level.
- Minimize the requirement for oral presentations.
- Assign projects whose products are visual representations, models, charts, and other constructions.

Further intervention strategies related to oral language are available in Dehn (2013).

INTERVENTION SUGGESTIONS RELATED TO VISUAL–SPATIAL PROCESSING

The VSI measures visual processing, which may be important for doing higher-level or advanced mathematics, such as geometry and calculus (Flanagan & Mascolo, 2005). A student with educational needs related to visual processing has difficulty in organizing visual information into meaningful patterns and understanding how they might change as they rotate and move through space.

Indicators of a need in the student's daily performance related to visual processing may include the following behaviors:

- Having difficulty making visual images to "see something in the mind's eye"
- Having difficulty remembering and differentiating left and right

- Having difficulty manipulating simple visual patterns or maintaining their orientation to see things in space
- Having difficulty mentally manipulating objects or visual patterns to see how they would appear if altered or rotated in space
- Having difficulty in combining disconnected, vague, or partially hidden visual information patterns into meaningful wholes
- Having difficulty finding a path through a spatial field or pattern
- Having difficulty in estimating or comparing visual lengths and distances without measuring them
- Having difficulty understanding math concepts in geometry, calculus, and other higher math
- Having difficulty in remembering letter formations and letter patterns
- Having difficulty in reading charts, maps, and blueprints and extracting the needed information
- Having difficulty arranging materials in space, such as in their desks or lockers or rooms at home
- Missing visual details
- Having difficulty copying information from far point, like the blackboard, or from near point, like texts

Possible instructional accommodations for a weakness in visual processing abilities include:

- Reduce the number of visual displays involving manipulative materials, drawings, diagrams and charts that could overwhelm the student, and replace them with clear verbal instructions.
- Explain in words all new skills and concepts, and all graphics and visually-based concepts and tasks.
- Provide the support of clear verbal instructions for tasks requiring spatial organization.
- Encourage the student to use verbal mediation to talk themselves through visual or spatial work.
- Teach the student to write from left to right. Use a green for "go" margin on the left side of the paper where the student begins to write. Use a red for "stop" line at the right edge of the paper.
- Do not require the student to use any visual strategies that he or she finds confusing, such as webs, diagrams, charts, and schemas for math operations.
- Provide activities with manipulative materials, particularly in the primary grades.
- Replace copying from the blackboard with providing copies of the notes or assignments.
- When copying is required, do not require speed. Allow extra time for the student to proofread for accuracy.

- Provide math exercises on worksheets with only a few questions and plenty of white space. Do not require the student to copy problems from the blackboard or textbook.
- Teach the student to use verbal mediation, by saying each word or number or detail when copying from far point to paper.
- Provide extra visual structure on worksheets and assignments. Use organizers like numbered boxes, or colour codes where instructions and similar questions have the same colour.
- Provide graph paper and lined paper to use for completing math exercises while the student learns how to line up numbers by place value.
- Teach the student how to interpret the organization of a page of text having an unusual format by using numbers to identify the sequence, or colours to link related information.
- Provide Direct Instruction in reading and interpreting maps, graphs, charts, and diagrams.

Environmental strategies that may be considered when working with children who have visual processing deficits are:

- Keep work space free from extraneous distractions, by removing all visual clutter that is not necessary to the task.
- Ensure that the student clears his or her desk completely before beginning a task. Remove all visual clutter from the work space before assembling the materials needed for the current task.
- Ensure that presentations using colours have enough contrast to be distinguishable in all light conditions.
- Modify colour usage in visual presentations to avoid reliance on colour coding for students with deficits in colour vision.

Classroom assessment strategies for children with weaknesses in visual processing abilities include the following suggestions:

- Put few math questions on each page, with a lot of white space for calculations on math tests.
- Provide manipulative materials when testing concepts involving spatial relationships.
- Emphasize verbal and written answers, rather than charts, diagrams and maps, where possible.
- Permit students to explain spatial information from their perspective without the requirement to rotate it to the examiner's point of regard.
- Reduce the emphasis on charts and mapping, unless that is the skill being taught and evaluated.
- Relax standards of production for art assignments and accept approximations of accepted criteria.
- Do not penalize the student for placing information incorrectly on a page.

Further intervention strategies related to visual–spatial thinking are available in Dehn (2013).

INTERVENTION SUGGESTIONS RELATED TO FLUID REASONING

The FRI measures fluid reasoning. Fluid reasoning shows a strong relationship with the development of math achievement, and contributes moderately to the development of reading skills. In the elementary grades it contributes moderately to basic writing skills, and at all ages it relates to written expression (Flanagan & Mascolo, 2005). A student with needs related to fluid reasoning has difficulty when faced with relatively novel tasks that require reasoning, recognizing and forming concepts, and drawing inferences (Elementary Teachers' Federation of Ontario, 2007).

Indicators of this need in the student's daily performance related to fluid reasoning may include:

- Having difficulty recognizing, forming, and understanding concepts
- Having difficulty perceiving relationships among patterns
- Having difficulty drawing inferences from information that is presented
- Having difficulty understanding the implications of an issue or an action
- Having difficulty with complex problem solving and concept formation
- Having difficulty understanding and using "and logic"
- Having difficulty understanding and using "or logic"
- Having difficulty with extrapolating, or following a logical pattern through to another conclusion
- Having difficulty with quantitative reasoning needed for understanding and computing mathematics
- Relying heavily on the use of language to aid in their comprehension of concepts and to solve problems that are new to them and cannot be solved automatically
- Having difficulty understanding the Piagetian concepts of conservation and classification
- Having difficulty transferring and generalizing information to new situations

Consider the following instructional strategies when working with children who demonstrate a weakness in fluid reasoning in the perceptual domain:

- Provide verbal instructions to all tasks (assuming verbal skills are adequate).
- Use teaching approaches that promote the development of self-talk to mediate all tasks.
- Rely on the student's verbal memory skills to teach problem-solving through repetition and rote recall.
- Present concepts and procedures verbally, in a straightforward fashion to ensure comprehension.

- Teach strategies for solving problems, paying close attention to the proper sequence of events that can be memorized as verbal instructions.
- Provide repetition and review of concepts to ensure over-learning. Check that a student's memory for material includes comprehension.
- Teach mechanical arithmetic in a systematic, verbal, step-by-step fashion.
- Use real objects and manipulative materials, along with verbal descriptions to teach concepts.
- Teach strategies to increase understanding and retention of concepts, including:
  - self-talk, so the student guides himself or herself through the problem verbally
  - lists of procedures or steps to follow.
- Teach problem-solving techniques in the contexts in which they are most likely to be applied.
- Teach and emphasize reading comprehension skills as early as possible so the student may rely on reading and rereading to ensure comprehension of concepts.
- Teach verbal strategies that will help them to organize their written work into sequential steps.
- Structure and adjust the difficulty level of the task, where possible.
- Explain homework and assignments in a sequential, step by step, fashion.
- When teaching concepts or providing instructions, avoid:
  - complicated and lengthy instructions and directions
  - figurative language, since the student is likely to interpret language literally
  - complex instructions.
- Watch for associated problems with organizational skills and follow instructional strategies for organization, if needed.
- Watch for associated problems with social skills, and provide interventions, if needed.

For children with deficits in fluid reasoning there are no obvious environmental strategies. However, the following classroom assessment strategies may be considered:

- Initially, rely more on verbal instructions and less on charts, maps, and diagrams.
- Pair verbal explanations with visual material to make use of the child's relative strength in verbal reasoning to help them learn how to interpret and organize visual information.
- Ask clear, specific questions, rather than asking open-ended questions or asking students to make inferences.
- Rely more on verbal responses and less on the production of charts, maps, and diagrams.

- Test for knowledge of the material, where possible.
- Ask the student to show all of their work (e.g., complete math calculations, or the outline for a long answer). Give partial marks for the process they followed.
- Provide a scoring rubric to the student so he or she knows how many marks they got for their knowledge, and how many they got for applications and problem solving using the knowledge.
- Use test formats that the student knows to ensure the use of the right problem-solving strategies to answer the questions.

Further intervention strategies related to fluid reasoning are available in Dehn (2013).

INTERVENTION SUGGESTIONS RELATED TO WORKING MEMORY

How do marked working memory deficits affect classroom activities? Two observational studies are informative. The first study involved a group of children with low working memory but typical scores in general ability measures (Gathercole, Alloway, Willis, & Adams, 2006). Compared with classmates with typical working memory skills, the low working memory children frequently forgot instructions, struggled to cope with tasks involving simultaneous processing and storage, and lost track of their place in complex tasks. The most common consequence of these failures was that the children abandoned the activity without completing it. A detailed description of common characteristics of low working memory children in the classroom is in Gathercole and Alloway (2008) and Gathercole et al. (2006). The second observational study by these authors drew a selection of children from the screening study described above. They were observed in mainstream primary classrooms in demographically diverse areas that included children with either low or average working memory skills. Examples of frequently observed behaviors that corresponded to working memory deficits included: "The child raised his hand but when called upon, he had forgotten his response"; "She lost her place in a task with multiple steps"; and "The child had difficulty remaining on task." Children with poor working memory struggled in many classroom activities, simply because they were unable to hold in mind sufficient information to allow them to complete the task. Losing crucial information from working memory caused them to forget many things: instructions they are attempting to follow, the details of what they are doing, where they have got to in a complicated task.

In the observational study described above (Gathercole et al., 2006), children with poor working memory function often gravitated towards lower-level strategies with lower processing requirements resulting in reduced general efficiency. For example, instead of using number aids such as blocks and number lines that are designed to reduce processing demands, these children relied on more error-prone strategies like simple counting instead.

Frequent failures of children with low memory to meet the working memory demands of classroom activities may be at least one cause of the poor academic progress that is typical for them. In order to reach expected attainment targets, the child must succeed in many different structured learning activities designed to build up gradually across time the body of knowledge and skills that they need in areas of the curriculum such as literacy and mathematics. If the children frequently fail in individual learning situations simply because they cannot store and manipulate information in working memory, their progress in acquiring complex knowledge and skills in areas such as literacy and mathematics will be slow and difficult.

For a review of working memory, from theories to assessment approaches and measures, to its impact on various academic skills to intervention strategies for working memory, see Dehn (2008) and Dehn (2015). A further resource is Alloway (2011). Further intervention strategies related to working memory are available in Dehn (2013).

Indicators of a need in the student's daily performance related to difficulties with working memory may include the following behaviors:

- Having difficulty following directions beyond the first steps
- Forgetting what they have to do next
- Difficulty with sentence writing
- Losing his or her place in complex activities
- Having difficulty with writing sentences or paragraphs
- Having difficulty with mathematics computations that involve more than one step, such as long division
- Having difficulty attending to and immediately recalling information they have just seen or heard

Possible interventions and instructional accommodations for children with working memory difficulties are discussed below.

The ideal solution to ameliorate the learning difficulties resulting from impairments in working memory would be to remediate the memory impairment directly. There is increasing evidence that directly training working memory with digital working memory training programs such as CogMed can lead to improvement on nontrained working memory tasks (Holmes, Gathercole, & Dunning, 2009; Klingberg, Fernell, Olesen, Johnson, & Gustafsson, 2005; Klingberg, Forsberg, & Westerberg, 2002), and perhaps in academic attainment as well (Holmes et al., 2009), although some researchers remain unconvinced (Melby-Lervåg & Hulme, 2012), and the debate continues (Shinaver, Entwistle, & Söderqvist, 2014). These programs capitalize on the well-accepted principle of neuroplasticity, which postulates that the brain can grow new connections based on experience. Working memory training programs are indirectly supported by basic neuroimaging research that relates increases in cognitive ability to the development of cortical thickness in healthy children and adolescents (Burgaleta, Johnson, Waber, Colom, & Karama, 2014).

The active ingredients of working memory training programs are carefully constructed tasks that directly stress the working memory structures, algorithms that constantly adjust item difficulty to the upper limit of the student's ability, and effective coaching to keep students motivated during the training. When implemented with fidelity, the CogMed program can be an effective adjunct to a comprehensive psychoeducational intervention program. However, it is unreasonable to expect achievement to improve immediately when working memory abilities remediate. Rather, once the student's working memory capacities increase, the student may be better able to access the curriculum through effective instruction over the following semester.

Thus, in addition to direct training, we recommend a number of classroom management techniques to minimize memory-related failures in classroom-based learning activities frequently experienced by children with working memory impairments.

- First, ensure that the child can remember what he or she is doing, to avoid failure to complete all steps of a learning activity. Strategies include:
  - Use instructions that are as brief and simple as possible. Break instructions down into individual steps where possible.
  - Repeat the instructions frequently.
  - For tasks that take place over an extended period of time, remind the child of crucial information for that phase of the task instead of repeating the original instruction.
  - Ask the child to repeat critical instructions back to you.
  - Since children often have good insight into their working memory failures, check with the child to make sure he or she remembers what to do.
- To help students to follow instructions:
  - Give brief and simple instructions with limited extraneous verbalization.
  - Break down instructions into simple steps when possible. Use numbered points for any sequence.
  - Reduce the number of steps given at one time.
  - Repeat instructions frequently.
  - Ask the child to repeat the instructions to ensure that they are remembered.
  - Give specific reminders targeted to the current step in a multi-step task.
- To prevent a child from losing his or her place in a complex task:
  - Decompose tasks into discreet steps.
  - Encourage older students to practice and actively use memory aids.
  - Provide support for use of external memory aids.
  - Encourage the student to ask for forgotten information.
- To improve the learning successes of individuals with poor working memory skills teach them self-help strategies to promote their development as independent learners who can identify and support their own learning needs. Teach them to develop effective strategies to cope with working memory failures, including:
  - Encourage the child to ask for forgotten information where necessary.

- Train the child in the use of memory aids.
- Encourage the child to continue with a complex task rather than abandoning it, even if some of the steps are not completed due to memory failure.
- Provide supports for spelling frequently occurring words. This will prevent children from losing their place in the complex task of writing activities.
  - Reducing the processing load and opportunity for error in spelling individual words will increase the child's success in completing the sentence as a whole. However, reading off information from spellings on key words on the teachers' board was itself observed to be a source of error in low memory children in our study, with children commonly losing their place within the word.
  - Making available spellings of key words on the child's own desk rather than on a distant board may reduce these errors by making the task of locating key information easier and reducing opportunities for distraction.
  - Develop ways of marking the child's place in word spellings as a means of reducing place-keeping errors during copying.
- For writing tasks:
  - Reduce the linguistic complexity of sentences to be written.
  - Simplify the vocabulary of sentences to be written.
  - Reduce the length of sentences to be written.
  - For older students, introduce use of outlines and techniques to keep place in the outline when writing.
- Teach memory aids, such as verbal mediation or rehearsal, and mnemonic strategies, such as:
  - Dracula's Mother Sucks Blood, to cue the order of operations in long division (Divide, Multiply, Subtract, and Bring down)
  - Every Good Boy Deserves Fudge, for the names of the lines in the treble clef music staff
  - the method of loci to match items with landmarks on the route to school.
- Teach the student to use lists, advance organizers, personal planners as aids to memory.
- Communicate frequently with parents about school activities, equipment needed, homework, and assignments through a communication book or regular e-mail.
- Provide notes to the student from presentations and lectures.

Environmental accommodations for children with working memory problems:

- Reduce opportunities for distraction and reduce the number of distractions in the vicinity.
- Provide visual reminders and other memory supports for multi-step tasks.
- Attach the student's daily schedule or timetable to the notebook cover that the child takes home every day.

- Post the student's daily schedule or timetable on the student's desk or classroom wall. Send a copy of the schedule or timetable home for posting in the student's room or on the fridge.

   Assessment accommodations:

- Allow the student to use appropriate memory supports during testing. Supports would typically provide information about procedures to use, rather than providing content that the student should know.
- Use open-ended questions with more than one correct answer to allow for marks for anything the student remembers.
- Reduce the demands on working memory on tests by providing a structure and outline for responding.

INTERVENTION SUGGESTIONS RELATED TO PROCESSING SPEED

Processing speed shows a strong relationship with the development of reading and math achievement, especially during the elementary school years when children are learning the skills in reading and math, and developing speed and automaticity in their use (Flanagan & Mascolo, 2005). Older school children use these basic academic skills with automaticity, and integrate them with more complex tasks such as problem-solving, subject-focused writing, and complex reading. When mental efficiency in focusing concentration is required, students with slower processing speed have difficulty performing simple cognitive tasks fluently and automatically. Indicators of this need in the student's daily performance related to the speed with which he or she processes information and completes tasks include:

- Being slow to perform basic arithmetic operations, not learning the times tables, and not attaining automaticity in calculations and so uses fingers or counters
- Taking longer to complete assignments in class
- Not finishing tests and exams within the time allotted
- Not finishing a copying exercise within the time allotted
- Reading slowly
- Taking even more time to complete tasks under pressure
- Coming to the right answer, but taking longer to do it

   Consider the following possible instructional accommodations when processing speed is a weakness:

- Allow the student longer response times:
   - to respond orally to questions asked in class
   - to make decisions when offered a choice of activities
   - to complete assignments in class.

- Do not require the student to work under time pressure.
- Reduce the quantity of work assigned in favour of quality productions.
- When copying is required, do not require speed. Allow extra time for the student to proofread for accuracy.
- Provide the student with ample time to complete his or her work, or shorten the assignment so it can be accomplished within the time allotted.
- Provide extra time for the student to complete in-class assignments in a way that does not bring negative attention to him or her.
- Shorten drill and practice assignments that have a written component by requiring fewer repetitions of each concept.
- Provide copies of notes rather than requiring the student to copy from the board in a limited time.
- Provide instruction to increase the student's reading speed by training reading fluency, ability to recognize common letter sequences automatically that are used in print, and sight vocabulary.
- Teach the student how to monitor time spent on each task. The student could use a stopwatch or timer. He or she could record the start and end times on paper. Set a goal for the student to gradually reduce the time needed to do each task.
- Provide timed activities to build speed and automaticity with basic skills, such as:
  - reading a list of high-frequency words as fast as possible
  - calculating simple math facts as fast as possible
  - learning simple math calculations through flash cards and educational software exercises
  - charting daily performance for speed and accuracy.

In the classroom and other settings where the student does tasks such as homework, provide environmental accommodations:

- Reduce environmental distractions to improve performance.

When taking tests in the classroom consider the following strategies for assessment accommodations to obtain maximum performance:

- Emphasize accuracy rather than speed in evaluating the student in all subject areas.
- Do not use timed tests for evaluation. Instead, use assessment procedures that do not rely on speed.
- Allow a specified amount of extra time for tests and exams (usually time and a half).
- Provide supervised breaks during tests and exams.
- Break long tests into more sittings of shorter duration across a few days.
- Provide a reader or text-to-voice app to read test and exam questions to a student to accommodate for slow reading fluency.
- Provide a voice-to-text app to record the student's answers on tests to accommodate for slow writing fluency.

- Use test and exam formats with reduced written output formats to accommodate for slow writing fluency.
  - Examples include: multiple choice formats; true/false formats; and short answer formats where a student fills in the blank.

Further intervention strategies related to processing speed are available in Dehn (2013).

Comment on Intervention Suggestions

Younger children have a lot of support available in the classroom in the form of various aids, such as visual displays of number lines, letters, and rhymes. Once children get older, learning becomes more autonomous and there are fewer opportunities to rely on external supports. For instance, while memory aids such as dictionaries and spelling charts are still available, there is less repetition of instructions, fewer visual cues such as number lines or multiplication tables, and more individual rather than group or supervised activity. At the same time, instructions become lengthier, classroom lessons become more complex, and specific cognitive demands become greater. The combination of these factors can serve to widen the gap in performance between children with average abilities and those with specific impairments as they grow into adolescence and enter middle and high school settings.

The strategies described above for modifying the environment and classroom assessment demands, and differentiating the style of instruction are appropriate for children of all ages. For some children with cognitive processing deficits these modifications and accommodations are necessary to ensure that they have equal access to the curriculum. As these children age, however, they need to be directly taught compensatory strategies that they can employ on their own across environments. Thus, general recommendations for improving the learning successes of children with a weakness in one of the domains of cognitive ability are to encourage them to develop their own learning strategies, and to take advantage of available classroom resources. Strategies may include encouraging the child to ask for forgotten information where necessary, training the child in the use of memory aids, and encouraging the child to continue with complex tasks rather than abandoning them, even if some of the steps are not completed due to memory failure. Providing children with such self-help strategies will promote their development as independent learners able to identify and support their own learning needs. The following case example provides a clear demonstration.

CASE EXAMPLE

Mariana is a 10-year-old girl with an impairment of working memory. Her teacher requested a psychoeducational assessment when she observed that Mariana's achievement and progress in class was somewhat variable. She showed difficulty when required to use both new and previously acquired information to address new questions and especially to continue to build on these themes by revisiting and modifying previous solutions. These difficulties were observed in subjects ranging from social studies to mathematics and seemed to occur mainly when the task involved more "mental" than "paper and pencil" work.

The psychologist reported that Mariana's earned average scores on the WISC-V were VCI (104), VSI (110), FRI (98), and PSI (99). However, her WMI (82) was significantly lower compared to her average scores on the other index scores. The base rate tables showed that very few children in the average ability range demonstrated such a large discrepancy between the WMI, VCI, and VSI. Of particular interest was that Digit Span Backwards (DSB) and Digit Span Sequencing (DSS) were both relatively weak scores for Mariana in contrast to average Digit Span Forward (DSF). Thus, her classroom achievement, under particular learning conditions, was being compromised by her verbal working memory difficulties. Mariana's classroom learning would require support with visual prompts and cues, as well as the pacing of material. She will also require support to develop strategies for managing tasks that required greater demands on verbal working memory.

Mariana was observed in a numeracy lesson in which there were 10 pupils of relatively similar ability who were split into two groups. The lesson began with the children sitting at their tables for the "mental math" session in which the class played "What number am I?" The teacher reminded the children how to play the game as she encouraged them to ask focused questions about the number she was thinking of. She modeled examples of questions that could be asked to help the children work out her number, e.g., "Is the number less than 20?" and emphasized the use of specific mathematical vocabulary before giving volunteers the opportunity to lead the game.

Mariana participated well when asking questions about other pupils' numbers, though she did ask the same type of question each time. Her questions were all based on an example that had been modeled by the teacher, e.g., "If I partition it, will it be 30 and 3? Does it partition into 20 and 4? Does it partition into 70 and 2?" She was also keen to take the leading role part-way through the game. However, as soon as the other pupils began to ask questions about her number, she quickly lost her enthusiasm to participate. When asked, "Does the number have eight 10s?" Mariana did not respond. The teacher repeated the question and reminded her to think of the place value of her number, giving the prompts "Does your number have 10s? Do you know how many 10s there are?" Mariana was evidently struggling to hold the number in mind while attempting to answer questions about it. She eventually told the teacher that she had forgotten it. At this point, the teacher spent a few minutes revising the concept of place value. She referred the children to the 100 square and the place value chart as she asked key questions such as "How many 10s does a number in the 80s have?" and "If a number has six 10s, which row do we point to on the

100 square?" Mariana successfully answered this question, making good use of the visual aids available.

As this took place, the teacher constantly repeated crucial information such as the key vocabulary (more than/less than) and asked target questions to help the children gain greater understanding of the concepts being taught, e.g., "If we are working out 10 more/less than a number, which part of the number changes?" She often directed such questions toward Mariana to support her thinking processes. For instance, "When thinking about 10 less than 307, Mariana, which part of the number will stay the same?"

Mariana correctly stated "7."

"Which part of the number will change?"

Mariana replied: "The 30. It gives 29."

As this main part of the lesson developed, Mariana became increasingly more distracted and appeared to lose total concentration. She began to swing on her chair, talk to her neighbor and shout out random comments unrelated to the task. The teacher reminded Mariana on several occasions to follow the usual classroom routines and actually stopped the class at one point to reinforce her expectations of behavior: "Stop talking. Put your pens down. Listen to me when I'm talking and put your hand up if you have something to say."

These instructions were clearly delineated by the teacher as she simultaneously pointed to the classroom rules displayed on the wall, thus allowing the children time to store and process the information.

During the lesson, students were challenged to perform simple calculations using some of the mental strategies taught in previous lessons. They were encouraged to use the tables' charts, number lines, and 100 square and to note key information on their whiteboards to help them in their calculations. Mariana responded well and made excellent use of these visual strategies to support her working memory. For example, she regularly referred to the poster to help her remember multiplication facts, used her fingers to count on from a given number when performing additions, and used diagrams to calculate divisions.

Here, we see that the teacher regularly repeated key questions to Mariana so that she would not fall behind in understanding the mathematical concepts. This is also a good example of how to encourage children to develop and use strategies to support their learning as Mariana was able to complete the activity on her own.

REFERENCES

Alloway, T. P. (2011). *Supporting improving working memory: Supporting students; learning.* London: Sage Publications Ltd.

Berninger, V., & Abbott, S. (2003). *PAL research supported reading and writing lessons.* San Antonio: Pearson.

Berninger, V., & Wagner, R. (2008). Best practices for school psychology assessment and intervention in reading and writing. In: *Best practices in school psychology V* (Vol. 4, Chapter 74, pp. 1205–1219). Bethesda, WA: National Association of School Psychologists.

Brooks, B. L., Holdnack, J. A., & Iverson, G. L. (2011). Advanced clinical interpretation of the WAIS-IV and WMS-IV: Prevalence of low scores varies by intelligence and years of education. *Assessment, 18*(2), 156–167.

Burgaleta, M., Johnson, W., Waber, D., Colom, R., & Karama, S. (2014). Cognitive ability changes and dynamics of cortical thickness development in healthy children and adolescents. *Neuroimage, 84*, 810–819.

Canivez, G. L., & Kush, J. C. (2013). WISC-IV and WAIS-IV structural validity: Alternate methods, alternate results. Commentary on Weiss et al. (2013a) and Weiss et al. (2013b). *Journal of Psychoeducational Assessment, 31*(2), 157–169.

Canivez, G. L., & Watkins, M. W. (2010). Investigation of the factor structure of the Wechsler Adult Intelligence Scale—Fourth Edition (WISC-IV): Adolescent subsample. *School Psychology Quarterly, 25*, 223–235.

Carroll, J. B. (1993). *Human cognitive abilities: A survey of factor-analytic studies.* New York: Cambridge University Press.

Cattell, R. B. (1987). *Intelligence: Its structure, growth, and action.* New York: North-Holland.

Claeys, J. (2013). Theory and research: The nexus of clinical inference. *Journal of Psychoeducational Assessment, 31*(2), 170–174.

Daniel, M. H. (2007). "Scatter" and the construct validity of FSIQ: Comment on Fiorello et al. (2007). *Applied Neuopsychology, 14*(4), 291–295.

Dawson, P., & Guare, R. (2004). *Executive skills in children and adolescents: A practical guide to assessment and intervention.* New York: The Guilford Press.

Deary, I. J., Strand, S., Smith, P., & Fernandes, C. (2007). Intelligence and educational achievement. *Intelligence, 35*, 13–21.

Dehn, M. J. (2008). *Working memory and academic learning: Assessment and intervention strategies.* New York: John Wiley and Sons, Inc.

Dehn, M. J. (2013). *Essentials of processing assessment* (2nd ed.). New York: John Wiley and Sons, Inc.

Dehn, M. J. (2015). *Essentials of working memory assessment and intervention.* New York: John Wiley and Sons, Inc.

Elementary Teachers' Federation of Ontario, (2007). *Special education handbook: A practical guide for all teachers.* Toronto: Elementary Teachers' Federation of Ontario (ETFO).

Flanagan, D. P., & Kaufman, A. S. (2004). *Essentials of WISC-IV assessment.* New York: Wiley.

Flanagan, D. P., & Mascolo, J. T. (2005). Psychoeducational assessment and learning disability diagnosis. In D. P. Flanagan, & P. Harrison (Eds.), *Contemporary intellectual assessment: Theories, tests, and issues* (pp. 521–544, 2nd ed.). New York: The Guilford Press.

Flanagan, D. P., Alfonso, V. C., Mascolo, J. T., & Sotelo-Dynega, M. (2012). Use of ability tests in the identification of specific learning disability within the context of an operational definition. In D. P. Flanagan, & P. L. Harrison (Eds.), *Contemporary intellectual assessment* (3rd ed.). New York: The Guilford Press.

Gathercole, S. E., & Alloway, T. P. (2008). *Working memory & learning: A practical guide.* London: Sage Press.

Gathercole, S. E., Alloway, T. P., Willis, C., & Adams, A. M. (2006). Working memory in children with reading disabilities. *Journal of Experimental Child Psychology, 93*, 265–281.

Gathercole, S. E., Lamont, E., & Alloway, T. P. (2006). Working memory in the classroom. In S. Pickering (Ed.), *Working memory and education* (pp. 219–240). Elsevier Press.

Georgas, J., Weiss, L. G., van de Vijver, F. J. R., & Saklofske, D. H. (2003). *Culture and children's intelligence: Cross-cultural analyses of the WISC-III.* San Diego: Academic Press.

Gottfredson, L. S. (1997). Why *g* matters: The complexity of everyday life. *Intelligence, 24*, 79–132.

Gottfredson, L. S. (1998). The general intelligence factor. *Scientific American Presents, 9*, 24–29.

Hale, J. B., & Fiorello, C. A. (2004). *School neuropsychology: A practitioners' handbook*. New York: The Guilford Press.

Hale, J. B., Fiorello, C. A., Kavanagh, J. A., Holdnack, J. A., & Aloe, A. M. (2007). Is the demise of IQ interpretation justified? A response to special issue authors. *Applied Neuropsychology, 14*(1), 37–51.

Harris, J. G., & Llorente, A. M. (2005). Cultural considerations in the use of the WISC-IV. In A. Prifitera, D. H. Saklofske, & L. G. Weiss (Eds.), *WISC-IV clinical use and interpretation: Scientist-practitioner perspectives* (pp. 381–413). San Diego: Academic Press.

Holmes, J., Gathercole, S., Place, M., Dunning, D., Hilton, K., & Elliott, J. (2009). Working memory deficits can be overcome: Impacts of training and medication on working memory in children with ADHD. *Applied Cognitive Psychology, 26*(6), 827–836.

Holmes, J., Gathercole, S. E., & Dunning, D. L. (2009). Adaptive training leads to sustained enhancement of poor working memory in children. *Developmental Science, 12*(4), F9–F15.

Kamphaus, R. W. (1998). Intelligence test interpretation: Acting in the absence of evidence. In A. Prifitera, & D. H. Saklofske (Eds.), *WISC-III clinical use and interpretation: Scientist-practitioner perspectives* (pp. 39–57). San Diego: Academic Press.

Kamphaus, R. W. (2001). *Clinical assessment of child and adolescent intelligence* (2nd ed.). Needham Heights, MA: Allyn & Bacon.

Kaplan, E. (1988). A process approach to neuropsychological assessment. In T. Boll, & B. K. Bryant (Eds.), *Clinical neuropsychology and brain function: Research, measurement, and practice* (pp. 129–231). Washington, DC: American Psychological Association.

Kaufman, A. S. (2013). Intelligent testing with Wechsler's fourth editions: Perspectives on the Weiss et al. studies and the eight commentaries. *Journal of Psychoeducational Assessment, 31*(2), 224–234.

Klingberg, T., Fernell, E., Olesen, P. J., Johnson, M., Gustafsson, P., Dahlstrom, K., et al. (2005). Computerized training of working memory in children with ADHD—A randomized, controlled trial. *Journal of the American Academy of Child Adolescent Psychiatry, 44*, 177–186.

Klingberg, T., Forsberg, H., & Westerberg, H. (2002). Training working memory in children with ADHD. *Journal of Clinical and Experimental Neuropsychology, 24*, 781–791.

Kuncel, N. R., Hezlett, S. A., & Ones, D. S. (2004). Academic performance, career potential, creativity, and job performance: Can one construct predict them all? *Journal of Personality and Social Psychology, 86*, 148–161.

Kvist, A. V., & Gustafsson, J. E. (2008). The relation between fluid intelligence and the general factor as a function of cultural background: A test of Cattell's investment theory. *Intelligence, 36*, 422–436.

Lezak, M. D. (1988). IQ: RIP. *Journal of Clinical and Experimental Neuropsychology, 10*, 351–361.

Lezak, M.D., Howieson, D.B., & Loring, D.W. (with Hannay, H. J., & Fischer, J. S.) (2004). *Neuropsychological assessment* (4th ed.). New York: Oxford University Press.

Mastoras, S. M., Climie, E. A., McCrimmon, A. W., & Schwean, V. L. (2011). A C.L.E.A.R. approach to report writing: A framework for improving the efficacy of psychoeducational reports. *Canadian Journal of School Psychology, 26*, 127–147.

Mather, N., & Jaffe, L. E. (2002). *Woodcock-Johnson III reports, recommendations and strategies*. New York: John Wiley & Sons.

Mather, N., & Wendling, B. J. (2012). Linking cognitive abilities to academic interventions: *Contemporary intellectual assessment* (3d ed.). New York: The Guilford Press.

Melby-Lervåg, M., & Hulme, C. (2012). Is working memory training effective? A meta-analytic review. *Developmental Psychology, 49*(2), 270–291.

Naglieri, J. A., & Pickering, E. B. (2003). *Helping children learn: Intervention handouts for use in school and at home*. Baltimore: Paul H. Brookes Publishing Co.

Oakland, T., Glutting, J., & Watkins, M. W. (2005). Assessment of test behaviors with the WISC-IV. In A. Prifitera, D. H. Saklofske, & L. G. Weiss (Eds.), *WISC-IV clinical use and interpretation: Scientist-practitioner perspectives* (pp. 435–463). San Diego: Academic Press.

Pearson (2012). Aimsweb technical manual. Available at: http://www.aimsweb.com/resources/research-articles-and-information.

Prifitera, A., Saklofske, D. H., & Weiss, L. G. (2005). *WISC-IV clinical use and interpretation: Scientist-practitioner perspectives*. San Diego: Academic Press.

Prifitera, A., Saklofske, D. H., & Weiss, L. G. (2008). *WISC-IV clinical assessment and intervention* (2nd ed.). San Diego: Academic Press.

Reynolds, M. R., & Keith, T. Z. (2013). Measurement and statistical issues in child assessment research. In C. R. Reynolds (Ed.), *Oxford handbook of child and adolescent assessment*. New York: Oxford University Press.

Sattler, J. M. (2008). *Assessment of children: Cognitive foundations* (5th ed). San Diego: Author.

Sattler, J. M., & Dumont, R. (2004). *Assessment of children: WISC-IV and WPPSI-III supplement*. San Diego: Author.

Schneider, W. J. (2013). What if we took our models seriously? Estimating latent scores in individuals. *Journal of Psychoeducational Assessment, 31*(2), 186–201.

Schwean, V. L., Oakland, T., Weiss, L. G., Saklofske, D. H., Holdnack, J., & Prifitera, A. (2006). Report writing: A child-centered approach. In L. G. Weiss, D. H. Saklofske, A. Prifitera, & J. Holdnack (Eds.), *WISC-IV advanced clinical interpretation*. San Diego: Elsevier.

Shinaver, C. S., Entwistle, P. C., & Söderqvist, S. (2014). Cogmed WM training: Reviewing the reviewers. *Applied Neuropsychology: Child, 3*(3), 163–172.

Squalli, J., & Wilson, K. (2014). Intelligence, creativity, and innovation. *Intelligence, 46*, 250–257.

Watkins, M. W., Glutting, J. J., & Lei, P. W. (2007). Validity of the full-scale IQ when there is significant variability among WISC-III and WISC-IV factor scores. *Applied Neuropsychology, 14*, 13–20.

Wechsler, D. (2014). *Manual for the Wechsler intelligence scale for children* (5th ed.). San Antonio: Pearson.

Weiss, L. G., Saklofske, D. H., Prifitera, A., & Holdnack, J. A. (2006). *WISC-IV: Advanced clinical interpretation*. San Diego: Academic Press.

Wendling, B. J., & Mather, N. (2008). *Essentials of evidence based interventions*. New York: Wiley.

Part II

Theoretical Considerations

Chapter 4

Theoretical and Clinical Foundations of the WISC-V Index Scores

Lawrence G. Weiss[1], James A. Holdnack[2], Donald H. Saklofske[3], and Aurelio Prifitera[4]

[1]Pearson Clinical Assessment, San Antonio, TX, USA, [2]Pearson Clinical Assessment, Bear, DE, USA, [3]Department of Psychology, University of Western Ontario, London, Ontario, Canada, [4]Pearson Clinical Assessment, Upper Saddle River, NJ, USA

INTRODUCTION

In this chapter we cover advanced topics related to interpretation of the five primary index scores. We conduct a detailed analysis of the cognitive constructs assessed by each of the indexes, how each is related to intelligence through models of cognitive information processing and neuroscience, and how the various cognitive abilities interact with one another and the executive functions in the service of solving problems in real life.

We remind psychologists that although an understanding of the abilities being tapped by the index and subtest scores are fundamental to using this test, these scores must also be placed in the larger context of each child and their "world." There are a huge number of endogenous factors such as genetics and a host of external factors such as culture and education that impact not only the growth and expression of intelligence, but also performance on intelligence tests. This topic is elaborated on in Chapter 5 on societal context.

THE WISC-V INDEX SCORES

Confirmatory Factor Analysis

The original Wechsler model contained only two factors labeled Verbal IQ (VIQ) and Performance IQ (PIQ), together with a composite Full Scale IQ (FSIQ). The modern Wechsler model is based on a five factor theoretical model

L. G. Weiss, D. H. Saklofske, J. A. Holdnack and A. Prifitera (Eds): WISC-V Assessment and Interpretation.
DOI: http://dx.doi.org/10.1016/B978-0-12-404697-9.00004-2

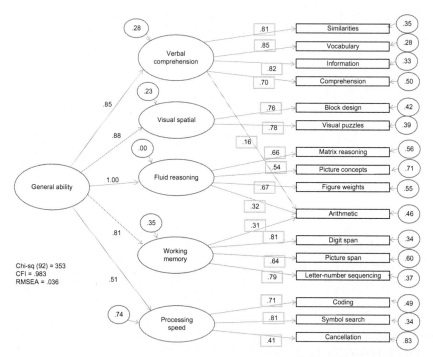

FIGURE 4.1   Arithmetic has moderate loadings on FRI and WMI, and a small loading on VCI due to the use of word problems. *(Data and table copyright Pearson, 2014.)*

of intelligence consisting of the Verbal Comprehension Index (VCI), Visual–Spatial Index (VSI), Fluid Reasoning Index (FRI), Working Memory Index (WMI), and Processing Speed Index (PSI), and retains the composite FSIQ. The contemporary five factor Wechsler model has been shown to fit the data well for all current and recent editions of the Wechsler tests including the WPPSI-IV (Wechsler, 2012), WAIS-IV (Weiss, Keith, Zhu, & Chen, 2013a), WISC-IV (Weiss, Keith, Zhu, & Chen, 2013b), and WISC-V (Wechsler, 2014). Figure 4.1 shows the fit of this five factor model to the WISC-V standardization data (n = 2200). For more information about the evolution of the contemporary Wechsler model, the reader is referred to Chapter 1.

Verbal Comprehension

Tim appears to have a sizeable vocabulary and can recite learned facts but does not appear to reason effectively using words and language. This is also quite obvious in more authentic and everyday tasks that require, for example, comprehending the meaning of stories read in class and in analogical thinking. This is further corroborated by his WISC-V subtest scores for Vocabulary (12) and Information (11) in contrast to Similarities (6) and Comprehension (9).

The VCI reflects an individual's ability to comprehend verbal stimuli, reason with semantic material, and communicate thoughts and ideas with words. Such abilities are imperative for intelligent functioning in modern society.

Although the VCI includes tasks that require prior knowledge of certain words and information, it would be a mistake to consider this index only as a measure of words and facts taught in school. Clearly, some base knowledge of words must be assumed in order to measure verbal reasoning—after all, one could not measure verbal reasoning without using words. Barring a particularly limiting linguistic environment, however, performance on these tasks reflects a person's ability to grasp verbally presented facts typically available in the world around them, reason with semantic constructs, and to express their reasoning with words. Crystallized knowledge is the background within which these abilities are assessed. It is defined as the breadth and depth of a person's acquired knowledge of a culture and the effective application of this knowledge. This store of primarily verbal or language-based knowledge may represent those abilities that have been developed largely through the investment of other abilities during educational and general life experience (McGrew & Flanagan, 1998, p. 20).

The Vocabulary (VC) and Information (IN) subtests require that a fact or the meaning of a word was learned, and can be recalled and expressed coherently. There is no apparent demand to reason in the VC subtest; it is essentially the case that one "knows" the word or in the case of IN, the person has been exposed to, knows, and can recall the "fact." However, VC is one of the highest *g* loaded subtests, and one of the best predictors of overall intelligence. We believe this is due to two reasons. First, higher-order thinking requires analysis of increasingly differentiated verbal constructs and, second, that larger pieces of related information can be chunked into a coherent whole for quicker processing. Individuals with larger vocabularies have words to describe increasingly differentiated views of the world. They can chunk larger concepts into a single word for more efficient reasoning. Although they may have enjoyed a more enriched learning environment, they must also be able to apply their knowledge appropriately. Knowledge of advanced vocabulary words requires the individual to accurately comprehend nuances of situations—which requires a higher level of intelligence. For example, do we say that the AIDS vaccine was "discovered" or "invented"—what is the difference? As another example, consider that to use the word "obviate" appropriately in conversation, one must first perceive that some action will make another action unnecessary. Consider how intelligent one must be to tell the difference between "placating" and "appeasing" another person. Thus, crystallized knowledge is not a simple matter of reciting learned facts or definitions of words, but the ability to acquire higher levels of crystallized knowledge reflects the intelligence necessary to comprehend that knowledge and, furthermore, appropriate application of the stored information requires advanced comprehension of the situation. Finally, adequate vocabulary is necessary for reading comprehension, and reading educational materials can improve crystallized knowledge and facilitate higher order learning. This is how vocabulary development is related to intelligence and higher order reasoning.

The Similarities (SI) and Comprehension (CO) subtests also require a base knowledge of information; however, they are considered to require some reasoning because they involve thinking with crystallized words and facts in ways that may not have been considered previously. For example, CO items typically assume certain facts are known (e.g., cars must have license plates), but the reasons for these facts are typically not taught directly in school. The child must engage in both recall of stored information relevant to the presenting problem and also reasoning to answer the question, "Why must cars have license plates?"

The SI subtest asks how two words representing objects or concepts are alike. The two words are expected to be known, but that their relationship is not usually taught directly in most educational settings and must be reasoned. Consider, for example, the child's response process when the examiner asks how "war" and "peace" are alike. A correct response requires that both concepts have been acquired and stored in long-term memory and the child be able to access that knowledge from semantic memory upon demand. Once these words are recalled, the child can begin the reasoning process to determine how they are similar. This reasoning process appears to take place within a temporary working memory space. The ability to reason in this way may be related to a certain type of working memory capacity and the efficiency with which ideas are worked in this transient memory space before the trace fades or becomes unavailable due to interference—as will be elaborated further in the Working Memory section of this chapter. Similar issues are in play with CO. Thus, the SI and CO subtests require a higher level of reasoning for successful performance than the VC and IN subtests. Students with deficits in crystallized knowledge or retrieval from long-term memory of previously acquired information may score higher on SI and CO than on VC and IN if they have adequate verbal reasoning ability. Conversely, students with an age-appropriate knowledge base that is readily accessible but who have deficits in higher order categorization of abstract verbal concepts may show the reverse score pattern. In these cases, it may then also be instructive to compare performance on SI with Picture Concepts (PCn). Both subtests require categorization of abstract verbal concepts, but PCn does not require that the child verbally explain his or her thinking. Thus, children with good abstract reasoning skills but poor verbal expression may perform better on PCn than SM.

Recall that a low score on an intelligence test such as the WISC-V may reflect low ability, a lack of opportunity to develop particular abilities, or some kind of "interference" that compromises the acquisition or expression of particular abilities (e.g., learning disabilities, auditory processing deficits, traumatic brain injury due to repeated sports-related concussions, etc.), which can also include performance or task demands ranging from speech impediments and motor coordination deficits to test anxiety. Prior to making an interpretation of low verbal ability, the psychologist should also ask: was the knowledge encoded but cannot now be recalled (for several possible reasons), or was it never acquired in the first place? One useful methodology for addressing this issue is the "recognition paradigm." All of the WISC-V VC subtests involve free recall, which is a much more difficult cognitive task than cued recall or recognition. Some students who answered incorrectly because they could not retrieve the information from long-term storage may more readily recall the information if given a clue or recognize the correct information from a set of possible answers. We can see this in our everyday lives when someone tries to recall the name of a colleague by using clues such as what university she is from or the letter-sound her name begins with, but once a possible name is suggested it is instantly recognized as correct or incorrect. In these situations, it may be instructive to consider the child's responses.

Visual–Spatial Organization

Tracey has a history of a somewhat variable pattern of school achievement and fine motor difficulties. A recently administered WISC-V shows that VC, FR, WM, and PS index scores were all in the average range, but that she obtained a much lower score of 82 on VSI.

The WISC-V VSI is a measure of visual–spatial organization. The index is comprised of the Block Design (BD) and Visual Puzzles (VP) subtests. One of the most venerable of the Wechsler subtests, BD is designed to measure the ability to analyze and synthesize abstract visual stimuli. It also involves nonverbal concept formation, visual perception and organization, simultaneous processing, visual–motor coordination, learning, and the ability to separate figure and ground in visual stimuli. For young children, it may also involve visual observation and matching abilities, as well as the ability to integrate visual and motor processes.

Children are given bonus points for completing BD items quickly. A score can also be calculated without time bonuses; however, the Block Design No Time Bonus (BDN) score may not be used to calculate the VSI or FSIQ. This supplemental score may be useful for students whose motor coordination interferes with their ability to manipulate the blocks. In this way, the examiner can evaluate the student's visual–spatial organization abilities somewhat independently from speed of performance. Those who score low only on BD but not BDN may have adequate visual–spatial abilities that require additional time to process. For more severe coordination problems, the WISC-V Integrated includes optional procedures to further analyze these issues.

Visual Puzzles was also designed to measure the ability to analyze and synthesize abstract visual material. Successful performance requires the ability to maintain a visual image in mind temporarily while mentally rotating, inverting, and otherwise manipulating that image and matching the resulting percept to a visual target. Like many tasks on the Wechsler series of tests, VP requires the integration of multiple related cognitive processes including visual perception, simultaneous processing, working memory, spatial visualization, and spatial manipulation.

Visual–spatial stimuli are employed in many fluid reasoning subtests, but the fluid tasks typically place higher demands on reasoning than the pure visual–spatial tasks. As a result, some students with weak visual–spatial abilities may struggle with certain fluid reasoning tasks that employ visual–spatial stimuli. Although it would seem ideal to assess reasoning alone without tapping other domains of cognition, this is patently impossible. Reasoning must take place on some subject. Just like verbal reasoning cannot be assessed without invoking verbal stimuli and therefore some base of crystallized knowledge, fluid reasoning cannot occur in a vacuum. Once any type of stimulus is presented, other factors come into play. Some may view matrix analogies tasks as pure measures of fluid reasoning; however, even the presentation of an abstract visual image that has no known meaning and cannot be verbally encoded will invoke multiple cognitive domains as described above in this section. Although factor analytic studies show that each task loads primarily on one factor, there are often minor loadings on other factors. Indeed, it may be the successful integration of multiple cognitive processes to solve a novel problem that is at the essence of fluid reasoning.

Fluid Reasoning

Maria's mother and teacher report that she appears bright and comes up with good solutions to problems conversationally, but struggles to complete simpler assignments from school. WISC-V testing shows superior scores on FRI and VCI, but relative weaknesses in VSI and PSI.

Fluid reasoning is generally considered to be the ability to solve novel problems for which there is little prior experience, cultural expectation, or crystalized knowledge to guide the solution. This is why visual–spatial stimuli are often employed because they are relatively free of cultural or linguistic expectation and crystallized knowledge. But, fluid reasoning should not be thought of as limited to visual–spatial problems and can take verbal or numerical forms as well.

Importantly, the fluid reasoning factor is virtually synonymous with psychometric g, loading 1.0 in five factor solutions of WISC-IV (Weiss et al., 2013b), WISC-V (Wechsler, 2014), and WAIS-IV (Weiss et al., 2013a).

The FRI is comprised of the Matrix Reasoning and Figure Weights subtests. Arithmetic is a supplemental subtest on the FRI. A standard task on most intelligence batteries, Matrix Reasoning consists of visual analogy problems set in a matrix. It was designed to provide a reliable measure of visual information processing and abstract reasoning skills. MR includes items that tap continuous and discrete pattern completion, classification, analogical reasoning, and serial reasoning.

Figure Weights was designed to measure quantitative and analogical reasoning. Quantitative reasoning tasks involve fluid reasoning processes that can be expressed mathematically, emphasizing either inductive or deductive logic. As such, quantitative reasoning is considered a subtype of fluid reasoning. In a clinical study of adults with focal strokes or cortical excisions, Figure Weights appeared to critically involve the right temporoparietal junction involved in numerical magnitude estimation (McCrea & Robinson, 2011). Although the solution to each Figure Weights item can be expressed with algebraic equations there is no task requirement to do so—thus eliminating demand for acquired knowledge of advanced mathematical equations. Although Figure Weights involves working memory, it reduces this involvement relative to typical quantitative tasks (e.g., mental arithmetic) through the visual presentation of items in a stimulus book that allows the child to continually refresh stimuli held in working memory while solving the problem.

Arithmetic is among the highest g loaded subtest in the Wechsler battery, often first or second depending on the analysis, with Vocabulary in the other position. As a word problem that must be solved mentally, Arithmetic has always been known as a complex task that invokes multiple abilities including verbal conceptualization, working memory, and numerical skill. The task involves performing simple but multiple, sequential mental arithmetic calculations while keeping the word problem in mind and referring back to it for the next step in the problem sequence.

As such, the Arithmetic subtest likely requires examinees to integrate a complex mix of abilities, and this integrative requirement may be responsible for its high g loading. This is consistent with previous research with WISC-IV (Chen, Keith, Chen, & Chang, 2009; Keith, Fine, Taub, Reynolds, & Kranzler, 2006). These findings are also consistent with current research into the theoretical structure of intelligence that documents considerable shared variance between working memory and fluid reasoning (Conway, Cowan, Bunting, Therriault, & Minkoff, 2002; de Jong & Das-Smaal, 1995; Engle, Tuholski, Laughlin, & Conway, 1999; Fry & Hale, 1996, 2000; Kane, Hambrick, & Conway, 2005). Specifically, the cognitive control mechanisms involved in working memory have been identified as the source of the link between working memory and fluid intelligence (Engel de Abreu, Conway, & Gathercole, 2010). This potentially explains the cross-loading of the Arithmetic subtest on the WMI and PRI in four factor solutions, and the movement of Arithmetic from the WMI to the FRI factor in five factor solutions of WISC-IV (Weiss et al., 2013b) and WAIS-IV (Weiss et al., 2013a).

As shown in Figure 4.1, Arithmetic has moderate loadings on FRI and WMI, and a small loading on VCI due to the use of word problems. This is the so-called "problem" of the Arithmetic subtest as a measure of working memory, perceptual reasoning, fluid reasoning, and verbal comprehension (Flanagan, Alfonso, & Reynolds, 2013). From our perspective, the "messy" multidimensionality of Arithmetic is not a problem at all. In fact, the very high loading of Arithmetic on g is an opportunity. Kaufman (2013) also makes an impassioned case for retaining Arithmetic in the Wechsler tests, reminding us that Binet believed multidimensional tasks were the key to intelligence, and that Wechsler knew full well that Arithmetic tapped more than one ability. David Wechsler knew the value of including subtests that had a somewhat broader bandwidth, not only because there was a kind of ecological validity or at least utility to such subtests when assessing intelligence, but they were also more likely to be "correlated" with the very clinical questions of interest to psychologists. Thus, Wechsler, following from Binet, moved away from the much narrower "brass instruments" measures characteristic of the Galton era. We agree completely, and recommend the routine administration of the Arithmetic test. Intriguingly, Schneider (2013) suggests that Arithmetic should contribute to FSIQ directly rather than through any one of the first order factors. Rather than continuing to argue about what factor Arithmetic belongs to, we should seek to understand why the integrative demands of complex multifactorial tasks like Arithmetic are so highly g saturated and which brain pathways are activated when performing such tasks.

At the same time, however, the numerical content of the Arithmetic subtest and its high correlation with mathematics achievement (Wechsler, 2014) are difficult to ignore. The numerical stimuli of the Arithmetic task logically invoke interpretations based partly on numerical skill. Yet, the requisite numerical calculations of Arithmetic are relatively simple and the reasoning requirements are equally compelling. Arithmetic is best interpreted as a measure of Quantitative Reasoning (RQ), which is considered a narrow ability under fluid reasoning in the CHC (Cattell-Horn-Carroll) model of intelligence (Carroll, 1993; see Keith & Reynolds, 2012, pp. 793–795 for a test of the RQ-Gf hypothesis). As reasoning must necessarily occur in the context of some stimuli, QR is essentially fluid reasoning with numerical stimuli and as such requires a base numerical skill. Similarly, MR and VP are essentially fluid reasoning with abstract visual stimuli, and require a base ability of visual–spatial organization.

Working Memory

Mary has such difficulty remembering things that we have been working on in class. I know she is paying attention and her records show that she has earned average scores on group intelligence tests. However, she just can't seem to keep the information in her mind long enough to use it.

Barry's teacher reports that he seems confused when engaging in more complex mental tasks. For example, he can solve printed problems, especially when using paper and pencil or computer presented questions. But, if the same question is orally present to him, he appears to forget parts, asks questions about what he should be doing and generally just "gets lost." Of interest is that his score on the WMI was significantly lower than the average of the five WISC-V index scores. Further, the psychologist noted that Barry required additional repetition and asked for clarification especially on the VCI subtests that placed increasing cognitive demands on his short- and long-term memory and required some reasoning (SI and CO).

The WMI measures attention, concentration, and working memory. Working memory is the ability to hold information in mind temporarily while performing some operation or manipulation with that information, or engaging in an interfering task, and then accurately reproducing the information or updated result. Working memory can be thought of as mental control or focused attention (an executive process) involving reasonably higher-order tasks (rather than rote tasks), and it presumes attention and concentration. As described by Jonides, Lacey, and Nee (2005):

> Working memory is a system that can store a small amount of information briefly, keeping that information quickly accessible and available for transformation by rules and strategies, while updating it frequently. (p. 2)

So, what is the key difference between WM and FR? There is no decision-making involved in WM—only keeping in mind and manipulating whatever stimuli are presented. FR goes further by requiring students to sort out relevant from irrelevant information, determine what order to manipulate the variables first, second, etc., and to do this in the service of solving a novel problem with a correct answer. Fluid reasoning always requires working memory, but working memory does not always result in fluid reasoning. The cognitive control mechanisms of the working memory system appear to constitute the active link between working memory and fluid reasoning.

Baddeley's (2003) seminal model of the working memory system proposes a phonological loop and a visual–spatial sketchpad in which verbal and visual stimuli respectively are stored and refreshed, and a central executive that controls attention directed toward these sources. A fourth component known as the *episodic buffer* was subsequently included in this model. This buffer is assumed to be attentionally controlled by the central executive and to be accessible to conscious awareness. Baddeley regards the episodic buffer as a crucial feature of the capacity of working memory to act as a global workspace that is accessed by conscious awareness. When working memory requires information from long-term storage, it may be "downloaded" into the episodic buffer rather than simply activated within long-term memory (Baddeley, 2003).

The term working memory capacity (WMC) concerns the amount that can be held in immediate memory. Updating or refreshing the information is necessary to keep it active in immediate memory, even for short periods of time. The working memory system involves mechanisms for maintaining information in short-term memory. These mechanisms can be as simple as rehearsing, or chunking information, thereby continuously refreshing the contents of the short-term storage buffer. The working memory system involves processes responsible for cognitive control that regulate and coordinate these maintenance operations. The boundary between short-term and working memory is not always clear. For example, although attending to, storing, and repeating a license plate number may appear only to involve short-term memory, the role of working memory may enter the picture when there is interference from other sources—for example, if the observer is asked to describe the driver and then asked to recall the license plate number. Thus, the distinction between short-term and working memory appears to involve the use of active cognitive control mechanisms.

The WMI subtests of the WISC-V are Digit Span (DS), Picture Span (PSp), and Letter-Number Sequencing (LN). The DS subtest has changed substantially from WISC-IV in order to reflect advances in the understanding of working memory. In WISC-V, Digit Span Sequencing (DSS) was added to the traditional Digit Span Forward (DSF) and Digit Span Backward (DSB) tasks. This was done because of concern that DSF was a measure of short-term and not working memory based on research that indicated different cognitive demands for DSF and DFB (Reynolds, 1997). DSF requires initial registration of the verbal stimuli—a prerequisite for mental manipulation of the stimuli. DSF was retained as part of the subtest to reflect the role of registration in short-term memory as a precursor skill to working memory, and to maintain a set of easier items for evaluation of low functioning students. In some cases, DSF also requires auditory rehearsal to maintain the memory trace until the item presentation is concluded. To the extent that longer spans of digits require the application of a method for maintaining the trace, such as rehearsal or chunking, then some degree of mental manipulation of the stimuli is also involved. The point in the DSF item set at which this is required will vary as a function of age and ability level, and the response processes utilized by the examinee. In DSS, the child must hold the string of presented numbers in short-term memory while reorganizing and reproducing them in the correct sequence from lowest to highest. In DSB, the child must also hold a string of numbers in short-term memory store but this time reverse the given sequence, and then correctly reproduce the numbers in the new order. Both of these subtests area clear examples of mental manipulation.

The developmental level and other cognitive factors such as general mental ability and processing speed (see section below) also may vary the role played by working memory in the DSB item set. For example, short spans of digits backward may tax working memory resources only marginally in older or brighter students. Again, the point at which these students substantially invoke executive control in DSB will vary by age and ability. In DSS, the child hears a string of numbers presented out of order and must repeat them in numerical order. The task is more difficult than it sounds because the numbers presented are not continuous, creating gaps in the rearranged number line, and some numbers are repeated. Thus, the working memory demands of DSB and DSS are similar to each other.

The LN task involves listening to a string of random letters and numbers, and repeating the letters in alphabetical order and the numbers in order of increasing magnitude. Again, this is not as easy as it sounds because some numbers must be retained in the short-term storage buffer while ordering the letters, and then the contents of the buffer updated into conscious awareness before ordering the numbers. Interference is built into the task through occasional repetitions of numbers or letters in the same string, and also by proactive interference of letters and numbers heard in previous strings. Overall, the task demands of LN are very similar to those of DSB and DSS.

Picture Span adds a new dimension to the assessment working memory not previously available in any Wechsler intelligence test. All previous WM subtests relied on verbally presented stimuli pulling for auditory working memory, whereas PSp assesses visual working memory. Thus, while the stimuli may be temporarily stored in the visual–spatial sketchpad rather than the phonological loop, the same executive control mechanisms are invoked to maintain focused attention on the task and overcome distractions. Proactive interference is built into the task by repeating target pictures from previous items as distractors in subsequent items.

A serious deficit in working memory may create difficulties at school and in daily life functioning and also may have major implications for the academic lives of young adults in school or vocational training programs. The role of WM has been implicated in learning and attention disorders. Students diagnosed with learning disabilities (LD) or attention-deficit/hyperactivity disorder (ADHD) may be more likely to experience problems with working memory as suggested by significantly lower scores on this index. Schwean and Saklofske (2005) summarized the results of several studies of children and adolescents with ADHD suggesting that they tended to earn their lowest scores on the WM composite. As always, caution must always be applied when using group data to make diagnostic inferences about individuals. The WISC-V was never intended to be diagnostic of ADHD or LD nor can it be, given the complexity of these disorders. Such nomethetic descriptions should rather be used as another "indicator" supporting or not the eventual diagnosis of any condition in which cognition is implicated. Thus, we are clearly advocating that diagnosis is of an individual, and the test score findings from the WISC-V or any other assessment battery are demonstrated to be relevant to each individual rather than being assumed to apply to all students with a particular diagnosis or being used as a diagnostic "marker" (see Kaufman, 1994).

In What Ways are WM and FR Alike; How are They the Same?

The capacity of one's working memory has been found to account for 50 to 75% of the variance in general fluid intelligence (Kane et al., 2005; Oberauer, Sub, Wilhelm, & Sanders, 2007). As a result, the link between WM and FR is being actively studied by several research teams. These research programs are exploring working memory capacity with the goal of understanding what causes rapid forgetting of information in short-term storage. Several groups of cognitive experimental psychologists employing well-designed studies are finding that rapid forgetting of stimuli is not caused by simple decay of the memory trace over short periods of time (Oberauer & Lewandowsky, 2013), but rather is due to distractions that interfere with the cognitive control mechanisms (Unsworth & Engle, 2005). Purely temporal views of working memory may no longer be adequate to explain forgetting during fluid reasoning tasks.

Engel de Abreu et al. (2010) showed that cognitive control mechanisms are the source of the link with fluid intelligence through their influence on working memory capacity in children as young as 5 to 9 years of age. Thus, the strength of the child's cognitive control mechanisms, such as focused attention, allows him or her to overcome interference from distracting stimuli and successfully complete the steps of the reasoning process, monitor performance, backtrack from wrong paths, and adapt the resolution strategy as performance proceeds. Early evidence suggests that systematic working memory training programs might improve performance on fluid reasoning tasks in typically developing 4-year-olds (Nutley et al., 2011), although not in children with limited intellectual capacity (Soderqvist, Nutley, Ottersen, Grill, & Klingberg, 2012), and much research remains to be accomplished in this area.

With young children, interference can be as simple as seeing the same stimulus as before but this time it is a distractor and not the target stimulus. Interference can also be irrelevant detail, or distractors that are similar to the memory target. In real life, interference can also come from interruptions such as are likely when a student is attempting to focus on homework in a distracting environment, or multitasking between digital social media apps and homework. Consider also the difficulties an ADHD child may have with interference-induced forgetting when continually shifting attention between compelling but irrelevant stimuli in the environment. Further, distractors are not always external environmental events. Some children can be distracted by their own extraneous thoughts, especially if they are anxious or under stress.

The strength of the association between fluid intelligence and working memory has prompted some, including us, to suggest that they might be the same thing (Kyllonen & Christal, 1990; Weiss, Saklofske, & Prifitera, 2005). However, Chuderski (2013) finds that the strength of the association depends on the time demands of the task. He found that working memory and fluid intelligence were indistinguishable under conditions of highly speeded FR tasks, but only moderately correlated when unspeeded tasks were used. Thus, individuals with low working memory capacity may be able to compensate for their capacity limitations through sustained effort over time. This is because low WMC individuals must refresh and retrace their steps in the reasoning logic more frequently as interference-induced forgetting occurs, and this simply takes longer. As Chuderski points out, assessing fluid intelligence with highly speeded tests "…will measure the ability to cope with complexity in a dynamic environment, thus having high real-world validity especially as the technological and informational pressures of the world continue to increases rapidly, but it also may underestimate people who regardless of their limited (working memory) capacity could work out good solutions in less dynamic environments" (p. 260). We would offer that adding time alone may not be sufficient and the individual would also need to have a strong drive to task-mastery motivating them to sustain effort as long as necessary to solve the problem. As recognized by David Wechsler, clinicians should also take note of the noncognitive, or conative, factors that may interact with the cognitive factors being assessed by intelligence tests.

Other groups of experimental neurocognitive researchers are using brain imaging technology to study the neural architecture of cognitive flexibility and fluid intelligence. A recently exploding trend in brain imaging research is to explore the strength of neural connectivity between brain regions as they relate to fluid intelligence. Evidence has emerged that one of the largest networks in the brain—the fronto-parietal control network—is central to cognitive control and fluid reasoning (Cole & Schneider, 2007; Jung & Haier, 2007). Although some researchers in this area are finding that fluid intelligence does not require attentional control and can be reduced to simple short-term storage processes of encoding, maintenance, and retrieval (Martinez et al., 2011), this finding may be related to the particular experimental tasks employed (Engel de Abreu et al., 2010).

More centrally, much of this research highlights the importance of white matter associative tracts, which speed the processing of information along the pathway. Parieto-Frontal Integration Theory (P-FIT) suggests that widespread networks of distal brain areas are involved in g, which requires well-functioning white matter pathways to allow for fast and orchestrated information transfer between brain areas.

Roberto Colom and his colleagues found that cognitive flexibility shares neural substrates with both working memory and processing speed (Barbey, Colom, & Grafman, 2013). They posit that individual differences in fluid intelligence may be related to the integrity (speed and sequencing) of the interactions between brain regions. In our view, this finding allows for both the central executive component of the working memory system and processing speed abilities to play a role in fluid intelligence. Executive or cognitive control mechanisms are central dealing with interference while attending to and sequencing information. Processing speed abilities are central to moving the relevant information quickly between brain regions—before forgetting occurs either due to temporal decay, interference, or both.

Much of this research has been conducted on adults, and until recently it has been unclear when in the course of child neurodevelopment this functional connectivity between brain regions begins to mature. However, this connectivity has now been demonstrated for children between 6 and 8 years of age (Langeslag et al., 2012).

These lines of research and thought are important because cognitive flexibility and fluid abilities are believed to draw upon the combination of conceptual knowledge and executive processes, and so the sequence and speed of communication between areas associated with these capacities is of critical importance. These mechanisms allow the integration and synthesis of crystallized knowledge with supporting cognitive insights, enabling people to see connections that previously eluded them. Recent research suggests that memory places constraints on hypothesis generation and decision-making (Thomas, Dougherty, & Buttaccio, 2014). In our view, both working memory and processing speed may function as rate limiting factors on fluid reasoning. That is, when weak or dysfunctional, they conspire to limit the rate of fluid reasoning in individuals by placing constraints on the number of hypotheses that can be generated and evaluated during the decision-making process. But, when working memory and processing speed abilities are well developed and work in synchrony, they may help to expand the effectiveness of one's fluid reasoning by allowing multiple hypotheses to be generated, retained, and efficiently evaluated. This is why we have referred to the aggregate of the Working Memory and Processing Speed Indexes as the Cognitive Proficiency Index (CPI; see below) (Saklofske, Zhu, Coalson, Raiford, & Weiss, 2010; Weiss, Saklofske, Coalson, & Raiford, 2010; Weiss, Saklofske, Prifitera, & Holdnack, 2006).

In our view, working memory is largely about cognitive control, whereas fluid reasoning is largely about cognitive flexibility. Thus, fluid reasoning always requires working memory. But, working memory does not always result in fluid reasoning. This is because there is no (or little) decision-making involved in working memory tasks—only keeping in mind and manipulating whatever stimuli are presented. The demands of fluid reasoning tasks go further by requiring one to sort out relevant from irrelevant information, determine what order to manipulate the variables first, second, etc., and to do this in the service of solving a novel problem with a correct answer. Further, we think that individual differences in fluid reasoning may be partly a function of individual differences in the speed and sequencing of information transfer between brain regions.

Processing Speed

Rapid transmission of critical information along neural pathways connecting relevant areas of the brain is important to effective fluid reasoning processes, as elaborated in the previous section of this chapter. The Processing Speed Index (PSI) measures the speed of mental processing, using visual stimuli and graphomotor skills, and is importantly related to the efficient use of other cognitive abilities. A weakness in simple visual scanning and tracking may leave a child less time and mental energy for the complex task of understanding new material. Referring to the WISC-V and WAIS-IV, it was for these reasons that PSI along with the WMI were referred to collectively as the Cognitive Proficiency Index (Saklofske et al., 2010; Weiss et al., 2006; Weiss et al., 2010).

The PSI is composed of the Coding (CD), Symbol Search (SS), and Cancellation (CA) subtests. These tasks utilize an apparently simple visual scanning and tracking format. A direct test of speed and accuracy, the CD subtest assesses the child's ability to quickly and correctly scan and sequence simple visual information. Performance on this subtest also may be influenced by short-term visual memory, attention, or visual–motor coordination. Thus, although a low score does raise the question of processing speed, it may also be influenced by graphomotor problems; thus practitioners should be alert to alternative reasons for low scores. Students may complete fewer items on this task if they present with fine motor difficulties, but this does not necessarily imply a problem with processing speed. An obsessive-compulsive child may also earn lower scores on CD, again not due to a processing speed deficit but rather because of a personality disposition.

The SS subtest requires the child to inspect several sets of symbols and indicate if special target symbols appeared in each set. It is also a direct test of speed and accuracy and assesses scanning speed and sequential tracking of simple visual information. Performance on this subtest may be influenced by visual discrimination and visual–motor coordination. Here again we alert the psychologist to use their observation skills and also ensure that the findings from the WISC-V corroborate or are supported by other "clinically relevant" findings. For example, an ADHD child who rushes through this task will likely make sufficient errors that will lower the SS score. Again this is not necessarily due to an underlying processing speed deficit but rather a behavioral correlate (i.e., impulsivity), which impedes performance on the task.

Cancellation is a supplemental processing speed subtest and should in general be used when either of the other two PS subtests cannot be used or are considered invalid. Working within a specified time limit, the examinee scans a structured arrangement of shapes and marks target shapes. It is similar to previously developed cancellation tasks designed to measure processing speed, visual selective attention, vigilance, perceptual speed, and visual–motor ability (Bate, Mathias, & Crawford, 2001; Geldmacher, Fritsch, & Riedel, 2000; Wojciulik, Husain, Clarke, & Driver, 2001). Cancellation tasks have been used extensively in neuropsychological settings as measures of visual neglect, response inhibition, and motor perseveration (Adair, Na, Schwartz, & Heilman, 1998; Geldmacher et al., 2000; Lezak, Howieson, Bigler, & Tranel, 2012; Na et al., 1999).

From a neurodevelopmental perspective, there are large and obvious age-related trends in processing speed that are accompanied by age-related changes in the number of transient connections to the central nervous system and increases in myelination. Processing speed has been shown to mediate the development of general intelligence in adolescents (Coyle, Pillow, Snyder, & Kochunov, 2011), and several previous investigators have found that measures of infant processing speed predict later IQ scores (e.g., Dougherty & Haith, 1997).

Thus, speed of mental processing is more than simply doing a task at a faster or slower rate but in itself is a key cognitive and individual differences variable. There is consistent evidence that both simple and choice reaction time correlate approximately 0.20 or slightly higher with scores from intelligence tests whereas inspection time (hypothesized by some to be a measure of the rate that information is processed) correlates approximately 0.40 with intelligence test scores (see Deary, 2001; Deary & Stough, 1996).

The PSI subtests included in tests such as the WISC-V are relatively simple visual scanning tasks for most students. However, it would be a mistake to think of the PSI as a measure of simple clerical functions that are not relevant or related to intellectual functioning. In matched controlled clinical group studies with the WISC-V, the PSI was observed to have an effect size greater than 1.0 in a group of children with autism spectrum disorder and language impairment (Wechsler, 2014). Yet, we once again caution practitioners from considering these profiles as diagnostic markers; they may guide the clinician to forming hypotheses about a child's cognitive abilities in relation to, say, school difficulties but this should in turn encourage a complete clinical evaluation based on test results combined with observations, history, and background factors.

As operationally defined in WISC-V, the PSI indicates the rapidity with which a child processes simple or routine information without making errors of either omission or commission. Many novel learning tasks involve information processing that is both routine for most students (such as reading at grade level) and complex (such as drawing inferences and predictions based on what was read). When speed of processing information is at least in the average range or a relative strength for a child, this may facilitate both reasoning and the acquisition of new information. Slowness in the speed of processing routine information may make the task of reasoning and integrating novel information more time-consuming and consequently more difficult. It may be hypothesized that students with processing speed deficits learn less material in the same amount of time, or take longer to learn the same amount of material compared to students without processing speed deficits. These children mentally tire more easily at school because of the additional cognitive effort required to perform routine tasks at their desks, perhaps leading to more frequent paper work errors and academic stress. As the months and years pass, these students are likely to spend less time on mentally demanding tasks involving new learning thus leading to smaller stores of crystallized knowledge over time relative to classmates, and possibly less interest in the rigors of further education. Slow PS taxes the entire cognitive network and has wide ranging effects on other cognitive processes that are observable outside the testing room and important consequences in the lives of children.

In some cases, children with serious PS deficits may be slower to comprehend conversation and formulate responses, especially in fast paced conversations that change direction quickly as are characteristic of group interactions in adolescence. Thus, PS strengths and weaknesses can have important implications in the lives of children beyond cognitive functioning, and potentially extend to their social and emotional lives as well. In summary, processing speed interacts in a critical way with other higher-order cognitive functions and may impact reasoning, new learning, general academic performance, and everyday performance.

THE ROLE OF EXECUTIVE FUNCTIONS IN INTELLIGENCE

This is an opportune spot to comment on the influence of other cognitive functions on WISC-V scores. Organization, planning, and other executive functions can impact performance on various WISC-V subtests. But, if we move away from the focus on test performance and consider intelligence in the broader ecology of society, we can at least say that executive functions are inexorably linked with the expression of intelligent behavior at work and in life. Clearly, we all know bright well-educated colleagues whose disorganization and poor planning interferes with their ability to achieve otherwise obtainable career goals. Similarly, many of us can think of friends and relatives whose intently focused attention on work activities has begot considerable success even though they seem no smarter than the rest of us. But, are executive functions really something apart from intelligence—simply mediators of how well one utilizes his or her intelligence in the larger world outside the testing room? To what extent might executive functions be an integral part of an integrated, ecological view of intelligence? To what extent might executive functions even influence the growth of other intellectual abilities during the developmental years? More to the point, what are the theoretical, clinical, and empirical relationships of intelligence and executive function?

Although the term executive function (EF) was not coined at the time, Dr. Wechsler knew that such abilities were importantly related to intelligence because his original tests included tasks that we would call executive functioning today. The WISC-R and WISC-III included a Mazes subtest that was widely believed to measure planning and organization. It was an optional subtest, however, and rarely used by practitioners because of the long administration time. For this and other reasons, Mazes was dropped from the WISC-III. But, the assessment of organization and planning abilities was never replaced by another subtest in the Wechsler model.

EFs as currently conceptualized involve more than planning and organization. Although there is no formally agreed upon definition, executive functioning may be tentatively defined as the effective integration of multiple cognitive processes relevant to goal-directed behavior (Salthouse, 2009). A list of specific cognitive processes included under this umbrella term was offered by Cheung, Mitsis, and Halperin (2004) as planning, decision-making, judgment, working memory, set shifting, and cognitive flexibility, which enables one to orient toward the future and self-regulate toward a goal. Chan, Shum, Toulopoulou, and Chen (2008) similarly offered a wide range of cognitive processes and behavioral competencies including verbal reasoning, problem-solving, planning, sequencing, the ability to sustain attention, resistance to interference, utilization of feedback, multitasking, cognitive flexibility, and the ability to deal with novelty.

In reviewing the extent of the literature on EF, Diamond (2013) groups the core EFs into four categories: inhibition, interference control, working memory, and cognitive flexibility. In this schema, inhibition is more behavioral or emotional and includes response inhibition, self-control, resisting temptations, and resisting acting impulsively. Interference control is more cognitive and includes selective attention and cognitive inhibition. Cognitive flexibility includes the ability to see things from different perspectives, and quickly and flexibly adapting to changed circumstances.

Salthouse (2009) directly addressed the theoretically important question of the relationship of EF and IQ by studying the pattern of convergent and divergent validity between fluid reasoning tasks and three key measures of executive functions, which were inhibition control, switching, and updating in nonclinical samples. Inhibition control involves the ability to focus attention on relevant information and processes while inhibiting irrelevant ones. Switching is described as scheduling processes in complex tasks that require switching of focused attention between tasks. Updating involves checking the contents of working memory to determine the next step in a sequential task and then updating the contents. Salthouse reported that convergent validity among these measures was not significantly higher than the typical correlations among all cognitive abilities—reflecting a lack of homogeneity of the EF construct. More importantly, he showed evidence of divergent validity for inhibition control and fluid reasoning measures, but not for measures of switching or updating with fluid reasoning. Salthouse concluded that the EF construct needs better specification before it finally can be determined if it is a useful construct distinct from fluid reasoning.

It is unknown if evidence of divergent validity between EF and fluid reasoning would emerge in specific clinically disordered samples, or if there is divergent validity between EF and measures of crystallized intelligence. Also, the Salthouse study did not address the emotion regulation aspects of EF. However, his controversial study is important because it raises a key theoretical question about the construct overlap between fluid intelligence and EFs: Are EFs really something different and apart from fluid intelligence?

Diamond (2013) goes further, stating that EFs make possible mentally playing with ideas; taking the time to think before acting; meeting novel, unanticipated challenges; resisting temptations; and staying focused. Rather than asking how EFs influence intelligence, Diamond flips our perspective and argues that what is commonly called fluid intelligence is the reasoning and problem-solving component of EF.

Much work remains to be done in this area. What would a structural model of general cognitive ability look like that included both EF and the five major domains in the contemporary Wechsler model of intelligence as expressed in WISC-V? Perhaps more precisely, which facets of EF have substantial construct overlap with which domains of intelligence, and which EFs serve as moderators or mediators of these domains of intelligence or the dynamic interactions among them? We discuss specific aspects of EF in more detail in the next section, with a focus on their role in facilitating working memory and fluid reasoning.

AN INTEGRATIVE THEORY OF COGNITIVE ABILITIES

In this section we discuss how the five primary cognitive abilities are necessarily interdependent upon each other for successful problem-solving. Any discussion of this topic must begin by considering the role of psychometric *g*;

which is the extent to which all of the subtests in the battery measure a single underlying dimension of general ability. But, psychometric *g* is a mathematically determined definition of general intelligence that is statistically extracted from whatever subtests are included in the battery. *A more theoretically appealing definition of general intelligence involves fluid reasoning as the ability to integrate multiple cognitive abilities from different brain regions in the service of solving novel problems and thereby accumulating crystallized knowledge which, in turn, further advances higher level reasoning.*

As Gregoire (2013) reminds us, fluid and crystallized intelligence have a special status in the original Cattell-Horn model, and should not be considered just one among a set of five or seven equally important broad abilities. *From our perspective, fluid and crystallized intelligence are the epicenter of an integrative model of intelligence, and the remaining broad abilities plus the executive functions operate in their service.* As neuropsychologists have been implying for decades, simply summing scores from a multitude of narrow band abilities certainly is not the same thing as performance on a task that requires real-time integration of those abilities. Perhaps fluid reasoning, when conceptualized as an integrative ability, is the "ecological *g*" that has eluded researchers for more than a century.

Fluid reasoning and working memory are integrally related conceptually and neurologically. The role of the central executive is critical to the relationship between working memory and fluid reasoning. The central executive controls attention to the target task in the face of interfering or distracting stimuli (Engle et al., 1999; Kane, Bleckley, Conway, & Engle, 2001). The more efficiently attention is focused the more effectively working memory is utilized, regardless of working memory capacity. Similarly, the ability to inhibit irrelevant information, or degree to which working memory is "clutter free," also may influence efficient cognitive performance regardless of the size of the working memory space (Lustig, May, & Hasher, 2001). Thus, individual differences in performance on working memory tasks may reflect primarily differences in various EFs such as the ability to sustain focused attention and inhibit competing responses, rather than the size of one's working memory space—particularly in real-life situations outside of the laboratory where interference and distraction are commonplace. The most current research suggests that it may be the cognitive control mechanisms of the central executive that account for the strong relationship between working memory and fluid reasoning tasks, through the mechanism of controlled attention (Chuderski, 2013; Engel de Abreu et al., 2010; Oberauer & Lewandowsky, 2013).

Resolution of novel problems typically requires relational learning. More effective relational learning strategies require the induction of some problem-solving schema to pursue, setting and managing processing goals based on the schema, and strategic control over processing activities to allow backtracking from wrong paths, elimination of irrelevant information, and blocking of competing or distracting stimuli. Failure of the controlled attention mechanisms results in loss of the schema and relevant facts from short-term memory. The individual must then refresh these traces and begin again, which may eventually result in successful resolution of the problem—unless the environmental distractions continue unabated, or if there is a real-life demand to solve the problem quickly.

Together with the central executive, the episodic buffer plays a role in the efficient processing of information in working memory. As the source of controlled attention, the central executive activates long-term memory traces through controlled retrieval and maintains them in buffer storage systems for use by the visual–spatial sketchpad and phonological loop. For any given individual, there are obvious differences in the long-term traces that can be activated in the buffer based on prior knowledge and familiarity with the task at hand. The more crystallized knowledge the person brings to a problem, the less fluid reasoning is required to respond correctly.

Vocabulary and the other VCI subtests are not simply based on facts taught in school, but rather reflect one's ability to comprehend information that is readily available in most environments. Crystallized information in long-term storage can then be accessed and used as inputs into higher-order reasoning processes. This reciprocal relationship between fluid reasoning and crystallized knowledge is one reason these two factors held a special place in the Cattell-Horn model (Cattell, 1963, p. 16). During childhood, fluid ability supports the development of school and cultural abilities. Following a cumulative process, these abilities allow for the acquisition of new abilities, which are gradually integrated into a larger and more organized cluster. Through this process, crystallized intelligence becomes progressively more independent of fluid intelligence; however, Gf and Gc continue to be correlated, even in adulthood (Horn & Cattell, 1966).

Contemporary Wechsler research supports placement of the fluid and crystalized intelligence factors at the epicenter of our integrative model. Recent studies show that the fluid factor is isomorphic with psychometric g loading 1.0 and .99 on g in children and adults, respectively (Wechsler, 2014; Weiss et al., 2013a, 2013b). The field has yet to come to grips with the finding that Gf and g are synonymous. Further, the Vocabulary subtest, as the marker variable for crystallized knowledge, has the highest g loading of any subtest in the WISC-V.

Arithmetic, a quantitatively based fluid reasoning task, is often among the highest g loaded subtest for both children and adults (Wechsler, 2014; Weiss et al., 2013a, 2013b). We interpret this as consistent with our hypothesis that intelligence involves the successful integration of various cognitive abilities toward correct resolution of a problem. Arithmetic requires verbal comprehension of the word problem, controlled attention in completing the steps, and some crystallized knowledge of math facts. Further, the quicker the resolution of the problem, the less of a burden placed on the cognitive control mechanisms in blocking interference. As such, Arithmetic requires the integration of several broad and executive abilities working in tandem—hence the high g loading.

Processing speed is another important cognitive ability that influences the efficiency of working memory functions. Perhaps before their time, Fry and Hale (1996) stated that as students age and mature, the changes that occur in processing speed lead to changes in working memory and "in turn, lead to changes in performance on tests of fluid intelligence" (p. 237). Only moderately correlated with each other, working memory and perceptual processing speed are differentially related to fluid reasoning. Modern neuro-imaging research suggests that processing speed is related to white matter associative tracts involved in transmission of "information" along neural pathways (Barbey et al., 2013; Colom, Martinez-Molina, Shih, & Santacreu, 2011; Martinez et al., 2011; Tang et al., 2010). Thus, processing speed exerts its effect on fluid reasoning indirectly by increasing the quickness of neural transmissions between areas of the brain required to solve the problem at hand. Controlled attention appears to be the active ingredient required for working memory operations to result in fluid intelligence. Quick neural processing speed mediates the relationship between working memory and fluid reasoning by decreasing the demand on the central executive to control attention and block distractors (i.e., focus) during problem resolution. In this way, working memory capacity is more efficiently utilized for higher-order reasoning tasks. Thus, processing speed, working memory, and the EFs combine to support fluid reasoning. If the problem involves perceptual stimuli then the visual–spatial abilities may be invoked to support problem resolution as well.

In short, fluid reasoning may occur in working memory space, but requires the central executive to control the flow of information, and dense white matter to increase the pace of information transmission between relevant areas of the brain. The cognitive control mechanisms sort and sequence relevant information while neural processing speed transfers that information rapidly before the cognitive control mechanisms fail and interference sets in causing forgetting and consequent disruption in the reasoning process.

Crystallized knowledge also may effectively increase fluid reasoning ability. As new facts and ideas are integrated with previously learned knowledge structures, increasingly larger chunks of information can be held in working memory and manipulated or combined with other chunks in novel ways. If an advanced vocabulary word can be retrieved from long-term storage through the episodic buffer and held in the phonological loop to represent a broader set of facts, then there is still time and capacity for other material to be integrated into the thinking process before the memory trace is disrupted and no longer accessible. Such interrelationships among the cognitive abilities are speculative at present, and require further research. But, the effective integration of these and other specific cognitive functions through the central executive may lie at the heart of any neurologically and ecologically valid theory of intelligence.

There is almost no meaningful activity in life that can be successfully performed by one narrow-band cognitive ability in isolation, as was clearly demonstrated by the minimal or zero correlations of the Galton-type tests with such complex factors as school achievement. Research in this area is still unfolding. However, practitioners should keep in mind that scores on factor-based indexes are not necessarily orthogonal; multiple reciprocal interactions are expected among the underlying neurological pathways. Understanding the clinical and behavioral correlates of these reciprocally interacting broad cognitive abilities—including the EFs—is critical to any ecologically meaningful theory of intelligence, including its development during childhood and adolescence, and its application to real-world problems in the classroom and in preparing for college.

An integrative, neurologically, and ecologically valid model of cognitive information processing suggests that impairments—whether developmental or acquired—which interfere with the rapid processing of information, may burden the cognitive control mechanisms of working memory and reduce the student's capacity for reasoning, comprehension, and new learning. For example, traumatic brain injury, perhaps due to repeated sports-related concussions in high school athletes, may reduce processing speed, which reduces effective working memory and thereby makes problem-solving and the acquisition of new learning more effortful and difficult. Even LD and ADHD students with working memory and processing speed deficits seem to mentally tire more easily than others because of the extra cognitive effort required. Some may begin to spend less time studying, and eventually avoid academic environments. This is where personality factors—such as drive to task mastery, resiliency, and motivation—interact with cognitive abilities and cause other students to work even longer and harder despite these cognitive challenges. But, that is a topic for another book!

SUMMARY

In this chapter we address the interpretation of each of the five primary factors measured by the WISC-V, with particular attention to their theoretical, empirical, and clinical foundations. We consider not only how these cognitive abilities differ, but, more importantly, how they relate and interact with each other in the real-life expression of intelligent behavior outside the testing situation. We further consider the relationship of these cognitive abilities to executive functions.

REFERENCES

Adair, J. C., Na, D. L., Schwartz, R. L., & Heilman, K. M. (1998). Analysis of primary and secondary influences on spatial neglect. *Brain and Cognition, 37*, 351–367.

Baddeley, A. (2003). Working memory: Looking back and looking forward. *Nature Reviews/ Neuroscience, 4*, 829–839.

Barbey, A. K., Colom, R., & Grafman, J. (2013). Architecture of cognitive flexibility revealed by lesion mapping. *Neuroimage, 82*, 547–554.

Bate, A. J., Mathias, J. L., & Crawford, J. R. (2001). Performance on the test of everyday attention and standard tests of attention following severe traumatic brain injury. *The Clinical Neuropsychologist, 15,* 405–422.

Carroll, J. B. (1993). *Human cognitive abilities: A survey of factor-analytic studies.* New York: Cambridge University Press.

Cattell, R. B. (1963). Theory of fluid and crystalized intelligence: A critical experiment. *Journal of Educational Psychology, 54,* 1–22.

Chan, R. C. K., Shum, D., Toulopoulou, T., & Chen, E. Y. H. (2008). Assessment of executive functions: Review of instruments and identification of critical issues. *Archives of Clinical Neuropsychology, 23,* 201–216.

Chen, H., Keith, T., Chen, Y., & Chang, B. (2009). What does the WISC-IV measure? Validation of the scoring and CHC-based interpretative approaches. *Journal of Research in Education Sciences, 54*(3), 85–108.

Cheung, A. M., Mitsis, E. M., & Halperin, J. M. (2004). The relationship of behavioral inhibition to executive functions in young adults. *Journal of Clinical and Experimental Neuropsychology, 26,* 393–403.

Chuderski, A. (2013). When are fluid intelligence and working memory isomorphic and when are they not? *Intelligence, 41,* 244–262.

Cole, M. W., & Schneider, W. (2007). The cognitive control network: Integrating cortical regions with dissociable functions. *Neuroimage, 37*(1), 343–360.

Colom, R., Martinez-Molina, A., Shih, P. C., & Santacreu, J. (2011). Intelligence, working memory, and multitasking performance. *Intelligence, 38*(6), 543–551.

Conway, A. R. A., Cowan, N., Bunting, M. F., Therriault, D. J., & Minkoff, S. R. B. (2002). A latent variable analysis of working memory capacity, short-term memory capacity, processing speed, and general fluid intelligence. *Intelligence, 30,* 163–183.

Coyle, T. R., Pillow, D. R., Snyder, A. C., & Kochunov, P. (2011). Processing speed mediates the development of general intelligence in adolescents. *Psychological Science, 22*(10), 1265–1269.

de Jong, P. F., & Das-Smaal, E. A. (1995). Attention and intelligence: The validity of the star counting test. *Journal of Educational Psychology, 81*(1), 80–92.

Deary, I. J. (2001). *Intelligence: A very short introduction.* Oxford: Oxford University Press.

Deary, I. J., & Stough, C. (1996). Intelligence and inspection time: Achievements, prospects, and problems. *American Psychologist, 51,* 599–608.

Diamond, A. (2013). Executive functions. *Annual Review of Psychology, 64,* 134–168.

Dougherty, T. M., & Haith, M. M. (1997). Infant expectations and reaction times as predictors of childhood speed of processing and IQ. *Developmental Psychology, 33*(1), 146–155.

Engel de Abreu, P. M. J., Conway, A. R. A., & Gathercole, S. E. (2010). Working memory and fluid intelligence in young children. *Intelligence, 38,* 552–561.

Engle, R. W., Tuholski, S. W., Laughlin, J. E., & Conway, A. R. A. (1999). Working memory, short term memory, and general fluid intelligence: A latent variable approach. *Journal of Experimental Psychology: General, 128*(3), 309–331.

Flanagan, D. P., Alfonso, V. C., & Reynolds, M. R. (2013). Broad and narrow CHC abilities measured and not measured by the Wechsler Scales: Moving beyond within-battery factor analysis. *Journal of Psychoeducational Assessment, 31*(2), 202–223.

Fry, A. F., & Hale, S. (1996). Processing speed, working memory, and fluid intelligence: Evidence for a developmental cascade. *Psychological Science, 7*(4), 237–241.

Fry, A. F., & Hale, S. (2000). Relationships among processing speed, working memory, and fluid intelligence in children. *Biological Psychology, 54,* 1–34.

Geldmacher, D. S., Fritsch, T., & Riedel, T. M. (2000). Effects of stimulus properties and age on random-array letter cancellation tasks. *Aging, Neuropsychology, and Cognition, 7*(3), 194–204.

Gregoire, J. (2013). Measuring components of intelligence: Mission impossible? *Journal of Psychoeducational Assessment, 31*(2), 138–147.

Horn, J. L., & Cattell, R. B. (1966). Refinement and test of the theory of fluid and crystallized intelligences. *Journal of Educational Psychology, 57*, 253–270.

Jonides, J., Lacey, S. C., & Nee, D. E. (2005). Process of working memory in mind and brain. *Current Directions in Psychological Science, 14*, 2–5.

Jung, R. E., & Haier, R. J. (2007). The Parieto-Frontal Integration Theory (P-FIT) of intelligence: Converging neuroimaging evidence. *Behavioral & Brain Sciences, 30*(2), 135–154.

Kane, M. J., Bleckley, M. K., Conway, A. R. A., & Engle, R. W. (2001). A controlled attention view of working memory capacity. *Journal of Experimental Psychology: General, 130*, 169–183.

Kane, M. J., Hambrick, D. Z., & Conway, A. R. A. (2005). Working memory capacity and fluid intelligence are strongly related constructs: Comment on AcKerman, Beier, and Boyle (2005). *Psychological Bulletin, 131*(1), 66–71.

Kaufman, A. S. (1994). *Intelligent testing with the WISC–III*. New York: Wiley.

Kaufman, A. S. (2013). Intelligent testing with Wechsler's fourth editions: Perspectives on the Weiss et al. studies and the eight commentaries. *Journal of Psychoeducational Assessment, 31*(2), 224–234.

Keith, T. Z., Fine, J. G., Taub, G., Reynolds, M. R., & Kranzler, J. H. (2006). Higher order, multisample, confirmatory factor analysis of the Wechsler intelligence scale for children—Fourth edition: What does it measure? *School Psychology Review, 35*(1), 108–127.

Keith, T. Z., & Reynolds, M. R. (2012). Using confirmatory factor analysis to aid in understanding the constructs measured by intelligence tests. In D. P. Flanagan & P. L. Harrison (Eds.), *Contemporary intellectual assessment: Theories, tests, and issues* (3rd ed.). pp. 758–799. New York: Guilford.

Kyllonen, P. C., & Christal, R. E. (1990). Reasoning ability is (little more than) working memory capacity. *Intelligence, 14*, 389–433.

Langeslag, S. J. E., Schmidt, M., Ghassabian, A., Jaddoe, V. W., Hofman, A., Van der Lugt, A., et al., 2012. Functional connectivity between parietal and frontal brain regions and intelligence in young children: The generation R study. Symposium presented at the Thirteenth Annual Conference of the International Society for Intelligence Research: San Antonio, TX.

Lezak, M. D., Howieson, D. B., Bigler, E. D., & Tranel, D. (2012). *Neuropsychological assessment* (5th ed.). New York: Oxford University Press.

Lustig, C., May, C. P., & Hasher, L. (2001). Working memory span and the role of proactive interference. *Journal of Experimental Psychology: General, 130*, 199–207.

Martinez, K., Burgaleta, M., Roman, F. J., Escorial, S., Shih, P. C., Quiroga, M. A., et al. (2011). Can fluid intelligence be reduced to "simple" short term memory? *Intelligence, 39*(6), 473–480.

McCrea, S., & Robinson, T. P. (2011). Visual puzzles, figure weights, and cancellation: Some preliminary hypotheses on the functional and neural substrates of these three new WAIS-IV subtests. *Neurology*, 1–19.

McGrew, K., & Flanagan, D. P. (1998). *The Intelligence Test Desk Reference (ITDR) Gf–Gc cross-battery assessment*. Boston: Allyn and Bacon.

Na, D. L., Adair, J. C., Kang, Y., Chung, C. S., Lee, K. H., & Heilmand, K. M. (1999). Motor perseverative behavior on a line cancellation task. *Neurology, 52*(8), 1569–1576.

Nutley, S. B., Soderqvist, S., Bryde, S., Thorell, L. B., Humphreys, K., & Klingberg, T. (2011). Gains in fluid intelligence after training non-verbal reasoning in 4-year-old children: A controlled, randomized study. *Developmental Science, 14*(3), 591–601.

Oberauer, K., & Lewandowsky, S. (2013). Evidence against decay in verbal working memory. *Journal of Experimental Psychology: General, 142*(2), 380–411.

Oberauer, K., Sub, H. M., Wilhelm, O., & Sanders, N. (2007). Individual differences in working memory capacity and reasoning ability. In A. R. A. Conway, C. Jarrold, M. J. Kane, A. Miyake, & J. N. Towse (Eds.), *Variation in working memory* (pp. 49–75). Oxford: Oxford University Press.

Reynolds, C. R. (1997). Forward and backward memory span should not be combined for clinical analysis. *Archives of Clinical Neuropsychology, 12*, 29–40.

Saklofske, D. H., Zhu, J. J., Coalson, D. L., Raiford, S. E., & Weiss, L. G. (2010). Cognitive proficiency index for the Canadian edition of the Wechsler intelligence scale for children—Fourth edition. *Canadian Journal of School Psychology, 25*(3), 277–286.

Salthouse, T. A. (2009). Operationalization and validity of the construct of executive functioning. Continuing education workshop presented at the annual meeting of the International Neuropsychological Society: Athens, GA.

Schneider, W. J. (2013). What if we took our models seriously? Estimating latent scores in individuals. *Journal of Psychoeducational Assessment, 31*(2), 186–201.

Schwean, V. L., & Saklofske, D. H. (2005). Assessment of attention deficit hyperactivity disorder with the WISC-IV. In A. Prifitera, D. H. Saklofske, & L. G. Weiss (Eds.), *WISC-IV clinical use and interpretation: Scientist-practitioner perspectives* (pp. 235–280). San Diego: Elsevier.

Soderqvist, S., Nutley, S. B., Ottersen, J., Grill, K. M., & Klingberg, T. (2012). Computerized training of non-verbal reasoning and working memory in children with intellectual disability. *Frontiers in Human Neuroscience, 6*(271), 1–8.

Tang, C. Y., Eaves, E. L., Ng, J. C., Carpenter, D. M., Mai, X., Schroeder, D. H., et al. (2010). Brain networks for working memory and factors of intelligence assessed in males and females with fMRI and DTI. *Intelligence, 38*(3), 293–303.

Thomas, R., Dougherty, M. R., & Buttaccio, D. R. (2014). Memory constraints on hypothesis generation and decision making. *Current Directions in Psychological Science*, 264–270.

Unsworth, N., & Engle, R. W. (2005). Working memory capacity and fluid abilities: Examining the correlation between operation span and Raven. *Intelligence, 33*, 67–81.

Wechsler, D. (2012). *Technical manual for the Wechsler preschool and primary scales of intelligence—Fourth edition (WPPSI-IV)*. San Antonio: Pearson.

Wechsler, D. (2014). *Technical manual for the Wechsler intelligence scales for children—Fifth edition (WISC-V)*. San Antonio: Pearson.

Weiss, L. G., Keith, T. Z., Zhu, J., & Chen, H. (2013a). WAIS-IV clinical validation of the four- and five-factor interpretive approaches. *Journal of Psychoeducational Assessment, 31*(2), 114–131.

Weiss, L. G., Keith, T. Z., Zhu, J., & Chen, H. (2013b). WISC-IV clinical validation of the four- and five-factor interpretive approaches. *Journal of Psychoeducational Assessment, 31*(2), 94–113.

Weiss, L. G., Saklofske, D. H., Coalson, D., & Raiford, S. E. (2010). *WAIS-IV clinical use and interpretation*. San Diego: Academic Press.

Weiss, L. G., Saklofske, D. H., & Prifitera, A. (2005). Interpreting the WISC-IV index scores. In A. Prifitera, D. H. Saklofske, & L. G. Weiss (Eds.), *WISC-IV clinical use and interpretation: Scientist-practitioner perspectives* (pp. 71–100). San Diego: Academic Press.

Weiss, L. G., Saklofske, D. H., Prifitera, A., & Holdnack, J. A. (2006). *WISC-IV: Advanced clinical interpretation*. San Diego: Academic Press.

Wojciulik, E., Husain, M., Clarke, K., & Driver, J. (2001). Spatial working memory deficit in unilateral neglect. *Neuropsycholgia, 39*, 390–396.

Chapter 5

WISC-V Use in Societal Context

Lawrence G. Weiss[1], Victoria Locke[1], Tianshu Pan[1], Jossette G. Harris[2], Donald H. Saklofske[3], and Aurelio Prifitera[4]

[1]*Pearson Clinical Assessment, San Antonio, TX, USA,* [2]*Department of Psychiatry, University of Colorado School of Medicine, Denver, CO, USA,* [3]*Department of Psychology, University of Western Ontario, London, Ontario, Canada,* [4]*Pearson Clinical Assessment, Upper Saddle River, NJ, USA*

Intelligence has been repeatedly shown to be predictive of a wide variety of important life outcomes and is thus of considerable practical importance in our lives; leading to higher educational attainment, job advancement, and career success (Deary, Whiteman, Starr, Whalley, & Fox, 2004; Gottfredson, 2008; Gottfredson & Saklofske, 2009; Lubinski, 2004; Squalli & Wilson, 2014; Sternberg & Grigorenko, 2002). At the societal level, regions with higher IQ citizens have been shown to contribute differentially to innovative ideas in business (Squalli & Wilson, 2014), and the technological and economic progress of nations (Burhan, Mohamad, Kurniawan, & Sidek, 2014). Thus, the measurement of intelligence is of considerable importance at both the individual and societal levels.

An individual's intelligence is traditionally measured relative to a sample of people the same age that is representative of a national population. This helps psychologists answer the question of how a particular person compares to other people across the nation in which that individual lives and competes. However, even though we may live in the United States or Canada or France, no person lives in the country "as a whole." Rather, people live in neighborhoods or communities that can vary along simple dimensions such as size (San Antonio, the Bronx, Ontario), and along more complex dimensions such that communities may reflect unique characteristics that can impact the development and maintenance of cognitive abilities in novel ways. Those who measure intelligence also want to know how the person being tested compares to other people in the local community or culture. This is the essence of *contextual interpretation*. It is contextually informed interpretation of population-based cognitive ability scores in concert with salient demographic and environmental variables.

Most chapters written on intelligence test interpretation conclude with a statement such as, "The examiner should also take into account other factors such as the client's educational, medical, cultural, and family history—as well

L. G. Weiss, D. H. Saklofske, J. A. Holdnack and A. Prifitera (Eds): WISC-V Assessment and Interpretation.
DOI: http://dx.doi.org/10.1016/B978-0-12-404697-9.00005-4

123

as other test scores." This advice has been repeated so frequently that it is often taken for granted, and while most psychologists acknowledge its veracity, not all implement it in practice. With experience, however, many psychologists come to understand that each profile of test scores has a range of meanings depending on the person's history and the context of the evaluation. In fact, one defining characteristic of an expert assessment psychologist may well be the ability to refine standard, cookbook interpretations of test profiles based on environmental, medical, and other relevant contextual issues.

In the *WISC-IV Advanced Clinical Interpretation* book (Weiss, Saklofske, Prifitera, & Holdnack, 2006), we devoted the first chapter to an exploration of the enriching and inhibiting influences of environment on cognitive development of children and adolescents, and some of that ground is revisited in the present chapter. In the *WAIS-IV Clinical Use and Interpretation* book (Weiss, Saklofske, Coalson, & Raiford, 2010) we explored changing environmental issues with respect to various generations of adults. We revisit some of that material because many of these adults are parents who play a major role in shaping the cognitive, physical, social, and emotional development of their children. Just as important, the environmental contexts surrounding adults also may impact cognitive development of their children. For example, changes in parental employment status can affect children's academic performance (Schmitt, Sacco, Ramey, Ramey, & Chan, 1999). Further, the range of physical and psychological stressors on individuals living in war-torn countries, suffering from malnutrition due to famine, or affected by environmental pollutants (e.g., mercury, lead) impacts all humans of all ages, albeit in potentially different ways. On the positive side, and much closer to home, Kaufman and colleagues have recently shown that significant reductions in environmental lead that have occurred in the U.S. due to increasingly tighter government standards over the past several decades can be associated with as much as a 4 to 5 point rise in average IQ scores, even after controlling for urban status and education (Kaufman et al., 2014).

In this chapter, we provide information that may inform the integration of salient cultural and home environmental considerations into clinical assessment practice with children. In doing so, we continue to challenge the belief that the intellectual growth and development of individuals represents the unfolding of a predominantly fixed trait only marginally influenced by the nature and quality of environmental opportunities and experiences. And more so, it is the opportunity to develop and express one's intelligence that is the key issue here. No matter how intellectually gifted a person might potentially be, it is well known from psychological studies over many years (e.g., McVicker Hunt, 1961) that without early environmental stimulation and nurturing that so often comes from parents and caregivers, access to quality education, encouragement for engaging in intellectual and creative activities, etc., children will be restricted in their cognitive growth. Added to this, the effects of poverty, poor nutrition, limited health care and living in unstable environments will further impact the development and expression of one's "genetic" intelligence!

BIAS ISSUES IN INTELLECTUAL ASSESSMENT

Before beginning our discussion of contextually informed interpretation of cognitive test scores, we must devote several pages to the widely held conception that cultural demographic differences in IQ test scores are due to biases built into the test. Our intent in this section of the chapter is to put aside these concerns so that we can focus on contextual mediators of cognitive performance, skill acquisition, and maintenance. Considerable advances have been made since the earlier efforts to produce culture-fair tests (Cattell, 1949; Mercer & Lewis, 1978). We discuss advances in item and method bias research, and show that disproportionate representation of individuals in specific categories or groups is not limited to cognitive and achievement test scores but is present in many areas of life. We acknowledge a legacy of controversy in these areas, and must address it so that we can move forward.

Item bias has been studied extensively, and all reputable test developers take special precaution to avoid it. Best practice in test development first entails systematic reviews of all items for potential bias by panels of cultural experts and such methodology is well documented and practiced (see Georgas, Weiss, Van de Vijver, & Saklofske, 2003). Test developers typically determine representation of ethnic minority examinees in acquiring test cases based upon census percentages, but purposely exceed the percentages so that advanced statistical techniques may be undertaken to detect and replace items that perform differently across ethnic groups. Conceptually, these techniques seek to identify items on which subjects from different demographic groups score differently despite possessing the same overall ability on the particular construct being assessed.

When items are identified as operating differently by examinee group, the reason for any identified differences cannot be determined by these analyses alone. Expert panels commonly predict that certain items will be biased because some groups have less direct experience with the subject of those items than other groups, but then find that various statistical procedures designed to detect bias do not identify the same items as the panel. Perhaps this is because the cultural expert panel is not typically required to provide an evidenced-based theory to explain how culture, as they conceive it, interacts with item content. At the same time, statistical techniques sometimes point to a particular item as problematic when the expert panel can find no contextual reason. This may be due to the very large number of statistical comparisons undertaken (e.g., every test item is evaluated across multiple racial and ethnic group comparisons, and also by gender, region of the country, and educational level) and so even with a $p < 0.01$ criterion there may be some items that randomly test positive for differential functioning when more than a thousand comparisons are made.

For these and other reasons this line of research is no longer referred to as item bias research, but as an analysis of differential item functioning (DIF) because the underlying reasons that items perform differently across groups are not always known. In light of the care taken in the development of items for most modern intelligence tests it seems unlikely that item bias accounts for the bulk of the variance in demographic differences in IQ test scores. However, differential item performance statistics are not very suitable to detect factors that influence entire tests as opposed to single items (van de Vijver & Bleichrodt, 2001). This is because most DIF studies match respondents from different racial/ethnic groups by using total test scores as the indication of ability or intelligence. If one presumes that some aspect of the dominant culture is inherent in the construct being evaluated by the test, and not just in isolated items, then by matching on test scores researchers may be matching on adherence to some unknown aspect of the majority culture. This larger issue can be framed as one of possible construct or method bias in which the construct being tested, or the method used to measure the construct, functions differently across groups.

This type of bias is more general than item bias, and more difficult to study empirically. According to this view, the formats and frameworks of most major intelligence tests are literacy dependent and middle-class oriented. Further, the testing paradigm itself is a stimulus response set that could be considered a social-communication style specific to Western European cultures (Kayser, 1989). The testing paradigm assumes that the test takers will perform to the best of their ability, try to provide relevant answers, respond even when the task does not make sense to them, and feel comfortable answering questions from people who are strangers to them. In some cultures, individuals are expected to greet unfamiliar events with silence or to be silent in the presence of a stranger. Guessing is not encouraged in other cultures and learning takes place through practice rather than explanation. Unfortunately, there are methodological difficulties in determining the amount of variance that may be explained by each of these factors. No studies have attempted to deconstruct the extent to which these influences may be ameliorated by the examinees' experiences within the U.S. educational system where western paradigms are pervasive. At the same time, evidence suggests that amount of U.S. educational experience may explain significant variance in IQ test scores of Hispanic children and adolescents (Wechsler, 2005), as well as immigrant adults (Harris, Tulsky, & Schultheis, 2003).

Therefore, an important question is whether a test measures the same constructs across groups. One common way to examine this question is through factor analysis, and more sophisticated approaches include measurement invariance techniques. Basically, if it can be shown that the various facets (i.e., subtests) of a test correlate with each other in similar ways across groups then such findings are typically taken as evidence in support of the hypothesis that the test is measuring the same constructs across those cultures. A series of studies has shown invariance of the four factor WAIS-III measurement model between large and representative samples of subjects in the U.S., Australia, and Canada, as well as across education levels and age bands (Bowden, Lange, Weiss, Saklofske, 2008; Bowden, Lissner, McCarthy, Weiss, & Holdnack, 2003; Bowden, Lloyd, Weiss, & Holdnack, 2006). Although these studies are important, it must be noted that they are limited to comparisons between English-speaking nations that are westernized, industrialized, and share common historical roots.

In a large international study of 16 North American, European, and Asian nations, Georgas et al. (2003) found reasonable consistency of the factor structure of WISC-III with each nation studied, reporting either three or four factors. In all cases the difference between the three and four factor solutions were due to a single subtest (Arithmetic) cross-loading on two factors (i.e., verbal and working memory). Importantly, these analyses included not only nations from three continents and 16 countries that speak 11 different languages, but also included both westernized and non-westernized societies (i.e., South Korea, Japan, and Taiwan), albeit all were developed countries. Another important finding from this study is that the mean Full Scale Intelligence Quotient (FSIQ) scores for the countries were found to vary systematically with the level of affluence and education of the countries as indicated by key economic indicators such as gross national product (GNP), percent of the GNP spent on education, and percent of the countries' workforce in agriculture. As encompassing as this study is, we again note that there were no pre-industrialized nations included.

Still, examining differences in mean scores across groups is a relatively simple but flawed procedure for assessing cultural bias in tests (see Gottfredson & Saklofske, 2009). A more sophisticated approach is to examine how the relationship of intelligence test scores to important criterion variables differs across groups. This begs the question, however, of what is an appropriate criterion variable for validating an intelligence test. In many, though not all, cultures educational success is considered an important behavioral outcome of intelligence, and thus the prediction of academic achievement from IQ has been studied extensively. Studies have shown a general absence of differential prediction of standardized achievement test scores from IQ scores across racial/ethnic groups for WISC-R (Poteat, Wuensch, & Gregg, 1988; Reschly & Reschly, 1979; Reschly & Saber, 1979; Reynolds & Gutkin, 1980; Reynolds & Hartlage,1979) and this finding has been replicated with WISC-III for nationally standardized achievement tests scores in reading, writing, and math (Weiss & Prifitera, 1995; Weiss, Prifitera, & Roid, 1993). Typically, these regression-based studies show differences in the intercept but not the slope, and this lack of difference in the slopes is taken as evidence in support of a lack of differential prediction. In other words, IQ scores predict scores on standardized achievement tests equally well for all demographic groups studied. Yet, the possibility exists that this finding is attributable to bias being equally present in both the predictor (i.e., the standardized intelligence test) and the criterion (i.e., the standardized achievement test). This question was partially addressed by Weiss et al. (1993) who used teacher assigned classroom grades as the criterion rather than standardized achievement test scores, and again, no differential prediction was observed. A general lack of differential prediction to achievement also was demonstrated more recently with WISC-IV (Konold & Canivez, 2010).

It is unknown if the construct of intelligence as we currently conceptualize it, albeit reliably measured with replicable factor structure across many cultures, predicts behaviors and outcomes that would be uniquely defined as intelligent by each culture and particularly by nonindustrialized cultures. Many researchers weigh as important studies that show a relationship between intelligence and academic achievement because the societies in which they live tend to value education as an important outcome of intelligence. In cultures of pre-industrialized nations, or perhaps some subcultures of industrialized nations where success in school is not necessarily central to success in life, such studies may not be as relevant. Other valued outcomes of intelligence may vary considerably across cultures and might include such behaviors as the ability to resolve conflict among peers, influence one's elders, build useful machines without instructions, survive in a dangerous neighborhood, grow nutritious crops in poor soil, etc. The point is that while tests of intelligence have stable factor structures across groups and predict academic achievement very well, this does not necessarily mean that they predict things that every culture would value as intelligent behavior in real life. Demonstrating the stability of the factor structure across cultures is an important yet insufficient step in demonstrating cross-cultural validity. Further, if we were to design a new test to predict culturally specific outcomes of intelligence we would begin by seeking to understand what constitutes intelligent behaviors as defined by that population and then create tasks designed to predict those behavioral outcomes. If the important outcomes (i.e., the criterion) of intelligence differ across cultures, then we might not end up with the same constructs that comprise most modern tests of intelligence—but, we don't know that.

CONSEQUENCES OF TESTING AND THE FAIRNESS OF TEST USE IN SPECIAL EDUCATION

Some writers have argued that any discussion of test bias is incomplete without commenting on test use, which explicitly involves decisions made about special educational programming based on the test results (Valencia & Suzuki, 2001, p. 145). This view is endorsed in the Standards for Educational and Psychological Testing (American Education Research Association, American Psychological Association, & National Council on Measurement in Education, 2014). This apparently innocuous statement has some inherent dangers. Clearly, studying the consequences of test use is an important area of research. However, we believe that considering the consequences of test use under the heading of test bias runs the risk of confounding the concept of test bias with possible differential need for services across groups. This is because studies have generally found that low SES, culturally and linguistically diverse (CLD) youth are at greater risk for learning delays (Hall & Barnett, 1991; Reid & Patterson, 1991; Schaefer, 2004; Walker, Greenwood, Hart, & Carta, 1994). *If two groups are truly at differential risk for a particular set of problems, then a test that results in a higher percentage of subjects from the at-risk group receiving services should be considered valid rather than biased.* This is an extremely important but frequently ignored issue. Some state education authorities establish proportionate representation criteria by setting acceptable limits around state census targets without regard to risk status. Fair usage is intended to distinguish individuals in need of differential services from those who have been wrongly referred and would not be aided by remedial services. Thus, fair usage should be viewed as a person-level rather than a group-level concept. Much of this chapter concerns taking into account contextual variables in the interpretation of psychological test scores to improve the fairness of individual evaluations. Nonetheless, we continue with a discussion of disproportionate representation of minorities in special educational programs because decisions about entry into these programs lead to claims of unfairness in testing, and because the IDEA legislation contains important provisions designed to reduce overrepresentation of minorities in special education programs (Individuals with Disabilities Education Improvement Act of 2004 [IDEA], 2004).

Despite the general lack of evidence for both item bias and differential prediction of achievement, differences in average IQ test scores between demographic groups persist, even when differences in socioeconomic status (SES) are taken into account. These differences contribute to disproportionate representation in some special educational programs. First, let us examine programs for learning disabilities (LD). At the national level, the percentage of students in each racial/ethnic group enrolled in LD programs is close to the percentage of each racial/ethnic group enrolled in public school.

According to the National Center for Education Statistics (2012a), in the 2011–2012 school year, African-Americans (AAs) comprise 20.2% of students in LD programs, as compared to 15.4% of overall school enrollment. When interpreting data related to the AA population, be aware that researchers commonly identify all Black individuals living in the U.S. as AA, including those who migrated from non-African countries such as Haiti. We use the term AA in the present chapter because it is common practice at the time in which we write, and because Black individuals from different countries of origin were not recorded separately in the majority of the available data. The reader should keep in mind, however, that the AA samples described herein are likely to be more heterogeneous then the label implies.

Twenty-five percent (25.7%) of Hispanics are in LD programs, compared to 23.9% enrolled in school. The percentage of Whites in LD programs is 48.6%, as compared to 51.4% of all students in school. Thus, the national data for the 2011–2012 school year do not support the hypothesis that minorities are grossly overrepresented in LD programs. Hispanics and AAs are overrepresented in LD programs by 1.8% and 4.8%, respectively.

The national picture for both intellectual disability (ID) and gifted/talented (GT) programs, however, is not proportionate to the population percentages by racial/ethnic group. At the national level, AAs are substantially overrepresented in ID programs (27.7% as compared to 15.4% enrolled in school), whereas

Hispanics (19.6%) and Whites (46.8%) are each slightly underrepresented. There is some variation among the states. For example, AAs comprise about one-quarter of the school population in Florida (NCES, 2012b), but approximately 40% of the state's ID enrollment. In Illinois, Hispanics represent 22% of the student population, but 18.4% of the ID enrollment (NCES, 2012c). However, in New York, Hispanics are 22.1% of the school population, but 27.6% of the ID enrollment (NCES, 2012d). Historically, the sparse availability of cognitive ability and adaptive behavior measures in the Spanish language has constrained potential identification of ID in this population. Since these measures are now available, identification of Hispanics in these special education categories may have increased over past numbers.

LD and ID enrollment percentages should be considered in relation to each other because mild ID can sometimes be difficult to differentiate from severe or comorbid learning disorders. Historically, there has been an inverse relationship between the proportion of students identified as LD versus mild (or educable) ID—perhaps as funding sources shifted emphasis or as social acceptance of LD classifications changed over time. Controversies also have been raised regarding the lack of use of adaptive behavior measures when diagnosing ID, and it has been observed that about one-third of mild ID students may be diagnosed with no record of an adaptive behavior measure (Reschly & Ward, 1991). The lack of adaptive behavior measures may call into question the validity of many of the mild ID diagnoses. The relationship of LD and mild ID rates, how they co-fluctuate over time and vary across states, deserves the attention of scholars.

In seeking to understand the relationship between rates of LD and ID, it may be instructive to consider mean scores by demographic groups in combination with established rules for determining eligibility for special education services. In some local education agencies, the ability-achievement discrepancy (AAD) criteria were still a component of eligibility determinations for LD services over the past decade. In other education agencies, however, the Individual Education Plan (IEP) committee is permitted considerable discretion in determining eligibility, which can lead to a lack of standard criteria for deciding which students receive special education services. Typically, students must have a large (usually 15 points or greater) discrepancy between intelligence and achievement, with achievement being lower, in order to qualify for placement in an LD program. Strict application of the AAD criteria may have made LD service less accessible for some low SES AA students whose ability test scores are not above the threshold, or whose ability and achievement test scores were both low and thus not discrepant from each other. Although there are no data on the subject, we speculate that IEP committees may have come to view placement in programs for students with mild ID as the best available option to obtain much needed assistance for some struggling students. The rules for determining eligibility for LD services have been changing over the past decade as school districts have implemented the current IDEA legislation, which no longer requires that the AAD method be used in determining eligibility for LD services.

The IDEA encourages local education agencies to consider other methods of eligibility determination such as response to intervention (RtI), or the student's failure to respond to empirically supported instruction. Even when more contemporary response to intervention or processing strength and weakness methods are used, the student often must have an IQ score above some minimum level, such as 80, in addition to other criteria. Despite promises to the contrary, however, the application of RtI appears to have had no impact on reducing disproportionate representation. Bouman (2010) found that RtI districts in California did not have significantly lower placement rates for CLD students than non-RtI districts. Orosco and Klinger (2010) showed that RtI gives false confidence about removing bias from special education determinations. Hernandez-Finch (2012) concluded that despite recent high-quality studies, insufficient research currently exists to support full implementation of an RtI model with CLD students. Culturally responsive models of RtI have been proposed (Rhodes, 2010; Rhodes, Ochoa, & Ortiz, 2005).

When seeking to understand differential rates of LD it is important to examine the larger process of special education eligibility determination, a process in which test scores play only one role—albeit an important one. Although the process varies across schools, it is almost always the teacher who first identifies a student as needing assistance to keep up with work in the classroom. In most schools, the teacher is then required to demonstrate that one or more instructional modifications have been attempted and were not effective. At that point, other options are considered including after-school tutoring, mentoring programs with community volunteers, retention in the same grade, referral for testing, etc. Researchers and policy advocates are now beginning to examine disproportionate impact in each of the various steps along the way towards placement in LD and ID programs. For example, possible differential rates of teacher referrals for tutoring versus testing by racial/ethnic group.

It is also important to mention that placement in a special education program can be perceived favorably or unfavorably depending on the perspective of the observer. When a student is placed in a special education program, one can either claim that he or she is receiving the help needed, or that the student has been unfairly labeled and segregated. Of students found not eligible for the same special education program, one can argue that they have successfully avoided a stigmatizing label, or that they were unfairly denied access to needed services.

The problem of disproportionate representation is large and complex. The present extent of overrepresentation in some areas is so large that it may not be fully accounted for by the differential rates of risk for cognitive and learning problems between racial/ethnic groups. The extent of overrepresentation that is accounted for by differential risk needs to be better understood. Given that ethnic minority students who are CLD and living in low SES environments are at risk for cognitive and learning problems, we are concerned that enforcing strictly proportionate representation could eventually lead to legal challenges of unfair denial of services. This could occur if CLD children are denied access to special education because the program has exceeded its quota of minorities. We hope that state guidelines will allow local education agencies to take into account differential rates of risk by racial/ethnic group when setting acceptable percentages of minorities in special education. Careful attention to these issues will be important in order to balance both perspectives and ensure that no child is either placed inappropriately or unfairly denied service.

For GT programs, disproportionate representation by racial/ethnic group is evident at the national level. According to the National Center for Education Statistics (2012), in 2006, the last year for which data are available, AAs comprise 9.2% of students in GT programs, as compared to 17.1% of overall school enrollment in Fall 2006. The percent of Hispanics in GT programs is 12.9, compared to 20.5% enrolled in school in Fall 2006. The percentage of Whites in GT programs is 68.4%, while they comprise only 56.5% of all students enrolled in school. In addition to Whites, Asian/Pacific Islanders are also overrepresented in GT programs. Approximately 9.4% of students enrolled in GT programs are Asian/Pacific Islanders, whereas they comprise 4% of all students (Sable & Noel, 2008). Again, there is great variation across states. Enrollment of Hispanics in New York was 20.6% (Sable & Noel, 2008), but only 13.8% of GT students in NY were Hispanic (NCES, 2012). Similarly, enrollment of AAs in North Carolina (NC) was 29.2% (Sable & Noel, 2008), but only 12.1% of GT students in NC were AA (NCES, 2012), and Hispanics were 9.6% of the student population (Sable & Noel, 2008), but 2.7% of GT students in NC (NCES, 2012).

Whenever any group has a lower mean test score than the national average, that group will be overrepresented in programs that require low test scores for eligibility, and underrepresented in programs that require high test scores for admission. However, neither ID nor GT determinations should be made based on the IQ test score alone. As noted above, an ID diagnosis requires that both intelligence and adaptive functioning test scores are significantly below average (by more than two standard deviations); yet there is evidence to suggest that many ID placements are made without any adaptive behavior measure. Similarly, IQ should not be the sole requirement for entrance into GT programs. Starting with Terman (1925), the tendency to equate giftedness solely with high IQ has persisted for several decades, and continues to influence daily practice. Scholars suggest three general characteristics of giftedness (Renzulli, 1986; Winner, 1996). First, there should be evidence of precocious ability in general or in some specific area such as mathematics, guitar, ballet, etc. Second, a strong task commitment to that activity should be obvious, or a "rage to master" the skill. Third, creativity and originality should be evident, or a tendency to "march to one's own drummer" with respect to the gifted skill. It is in the intersection of these three characteristics that true giftedness resides. Although IQ testing has an important role to play in GT determinations, it is not an exclusive role and GT assessments should broaden as our understanding of the concept of giftedness expands.

It is somewhat widely believed that there are different types of intelligences that can be associated with analytical, synthetic, or practical giftedness

(Sternberg, 1997; Sternberg & Davidson, 1986), and it is possible to consider that giftedness is not a stable trait of the person but an interaction between culturally defined opportunities for action and personal talents that are recognized by the gifted person and acted upon (Csikszentmihalyi & Robinson, 1986). These expansions of the construct of giftedness are more inclusionary, and may provide answers to persistent criticisms of the elitist nature of gifted programs (Margolin, 1994).

As with LD and ID programs, understanding disproportionate representation in GT programs requires examination of the larger process. In most cases, teachers nominate students for GT evaluations, although these nominations can be heavily influenced by parent pressure and community expectations. Teachers rely primarily on academic performance, but may include other idiosyncratic criteria. Structured teacher nomination rating scales of observable classroom behavior based on the newer theories of multiple domains of giftedness have been shown to reduce the unreliability inherent in the nomination process and increase valid identification of gifted and talented students (The Gifted Rating Scales, Pfeiffer & Jawarsowik, 2003).

Although the literature on test bias acknowledges the role of SES on intelligence test scores, the literature on disproportionate representation in special education programs has paid insufficient attention to the known effects of poverty on learning and cognitive development. This is a serious oversight because poverty, and the associated effects from physical health to psychological well-being, is known to have an impact on learning and cognitive development, it is disproportionately represented across racial/ethnic groups, and it may explain much of the disproportional representation in special education. This will be discussed in greater detail later in this chapter.

DEMOGRAPHIC DISPARITIES IN VARIOUS AREAS OF LIFE

Disparities exist when differences in outcomes are observed across different groups within a population (Centers for Disease Control and Prevention, 2013). Disparities by racial/ethnic groups within the United States are not limited to disproportionate representation in special education and differences in test scores. Rather they are well documented for a variety of factors including physical and mental health status, infant mortality, longevity, access to health care, educational attainment and opportunities, income, occupational status and job stability, wealth, equality of schools, and more (Hummer, 1996).

These disparities are becoming more important for children's well-being as there has been a wide shift in the demographic composition of the United States population in the last decade, especially in the child population. The U.S. Census Bureau estimates that non-Hispanic Whites (Whites) will be a plurality rather than a majority in the U.S. population between 2040 and 2045 (U.S. Census Bureau, 2013), and this change has already occurred in the young child population (Johnson & Lichter, 2010). These changes are important because the children being assessed with the WISC-V belong to one of the most diverse cohorts of youngsters since David Wechsler published the first edition of this assessment. In 2012, less than 50% of children were born to White non-Hispanic families, and the largest increases are occurring in the Hispanic population (U.S. Census Bureau, 2012). Whereas some of this increase is due to immigration, most of it can be attributed to a higher birthrate among U.S. born Hispanics, as Hispanics on average have more children than the Asian, AA, or White non-Hispanic populations, who have the lowest birth rates. The percentage of children who are White will continue to drop every year in the near future as family size declines and there are fewer White non-Hispanic women in the childbearing years. Although the shifts are widespread, they are not uniform across the country, and they are more pronounced in the west and south than they are in other areas. The southeast in particular has become remarkably more diverse with growing numbers of Hispanics in addition to the historical AA and White non-Hispanic populations (Johnson & Lichter, 2010). For these reasons, this book includes a special chapter on testing Hispanics with WISC-V and WISC-IV Spanish.

Although disparities are present across a wide variety of outcomes, we confine this discussion to areas that are theoretically and conceptually related to children's cognitive development and skill acquisition. Because race/ethnicity and SES are highly correlated (Massey, 2007), it is very difficult to disentangle the two. What may first appear as a racial or ethnic difference may actually be more attributable to poverty and inequality. The premise of this section is that race and ethnicity are socially constructed; yet, they function in society to stratify people across a broad series of outcomes. To illustrate how they are malleable constructs, the U.S. Census has updated the racial/ethnic categories in nearly every decennial census (LaVeist, 2005). In the first census in 1790, it asked for number of White persons, other free persons (typically American Indians), and the number of slaves. In 1850, Mulatto (mixed race) was added, and in 1890, several categories of mixed race were available. However, by 1930, mixed race categories were no longer an option. Until 2000, people could only indicate one category, making it difficult to calculate how many mixed race people there were in the country. Currently, people are asked their race and whether or not they are of Hispanic origin, and they are allowed to check more than one race (U.S. Census Bureau, 2014). This categorization is likely to change again in the next census, and the Census Bureau is currently undertaking research to determine how race and ethnicity will be collected in 2020.

It is also important to recognize that although the racial ethnic groups are grouped into the five categories of White, AA, Hispanic, Asian, and other race/ethnicities, these groups are not homogeneous. AAs include those whose ancestors came to North America nearly 400 years ago, as well as those who have recently arrived from the Caribbean and Africa. Hispanics are an especially heterogeneous group, and there are socioeconomic and linguistic differences depending on the place of origin such as Mexico, Puerto Rico, Dominican Republic, Cuba, and Central and South America. Asians include those whose origins are from areas as diverse as China, Japan, Indonesia, Vietnam, Korea, and India. Other race/ethnicities typically include American Indian and Alaska Natives, and people of mixed ancestry. The exception is people who are mixed race and of Hispanic origin; they are included in the Hispanic category. We realize that some of the terminology for the racial/ethnic groups is controversial, and there is a wide variety of opinion regarding which term is best. We have used the terms AA, Hispanic, Asian, Other, and White (i.e., non-Hispanic), as they appear to be the most current in the literature. Although Latino/a is gaining in prominence, it is not as preferred as Hispanic according to research conducted by the Pew Research Center (Lopez, 2013). This section will explore disparities in four key areas: Education, Income and Occupation, Physical Health Status, and Mental Health Status.

Racial/Ethnic Group Disparities in Education

Group differences in education are important because the education children receive in childhood can have lifelong consequences. Education determines whether or not a person goes to college, and, often, qualifies for a well-paying job with health benefits. That in turn can determine where he or she lives and sends his or her own children to school and the type of education the children receive, and thus the cycle perpetuates.

Racial/ethnic differences in achievement show up at the kindergarten door in reading (Foster & Miller, 2007), social studies and science (Chapin, 2006), and mathematics (Chatterji, 2005). Most of these disparities can be explained by poverty and mother's education (Padilla, Boardman, & Hummer, 2002); however, the impact of poverty can be mediated by parenting style and cognitive stimulation (Guo & Harris, 2000). We will discuss this in more depth later in this chapter.

After a child enters kindergarten, the type of school he or she attends can make a difference in their cognitive development. In many areas of the country, racial/ethnic or socioeconomic residential segregation is persistent, and concentrating AAs or Hispanics into neighborhoods also concentrates poverty (Massey & Fischer, 2000). This in turn impacts the school children attend and the type of education they receive. Most schools are neighborhood schools, especially in the elementary years (Ong & Rickles, 2004), and schools that are predominantly AA and Hispanic also typically serve students who are poor. The National Center for Education Statistics (NCES) considers schools with greater than 75% participation in the free or reduced price lunch program to be high poverty schools, and schools with less than 25% participation are considered to be low poverty schools. Using those criteria, we analyzed data from the NCES Common Core Data File for the school year 2010–2011, and we found that high poverty schools are 80.9% AA or Hispanic, whereas low poverty schools are 75% White (National Center for Education Statistics, 2011). Forty-three percent (43.2%) of AA and 34.9% of Hispanic children attend a high poverty school. Although there are instances of high-achieving, high-poverty schools, it still remains that low-poverty schools typically have higher achievement levels (Harris, 2007). Low poverty schools are in areas with a higher tax base, they have more resources, there are more opportunities for cognitive development than in high poverty schools, and they have higher test scores. Higher poverty schools are often characterized by high faculty turnover, lower achievement, and offer fewer higher-level courses, such as Advanced Placement (AP) classes, in high school.

Poor and minority students also have higher dropout rates, and fewer of these students pursue or finish post-secondary education. Accurate dropout rates are difficult to obtain, because often schools do not know if a student has dropped out or transferred, or has opted for home schooling. What we do know is that some students disappear from the enrollment records. Therefore, we looked at the status dropout rate, which is defined by the NCES as people aged 16–24 who are not enrolled in school, and have not completed a high school diploma or General Education Development (GED). We analyzed data from the U.S. Census Bureau's *American Community Survey (ACS), 2012 1-year period estimates*, available from IPUMS (Ruggles et al., 2010). Hispanics (12.8%) have the highest status dropout rate, followed by AAs (9.0%), Other race/ethnicities (7.1%), Whites (4.7%), and Asians (2.8%). These results are not surprising, as the dropout rate for Hispanics is higher than other groups, and this estimate includes immigrants. When we look at only U.S. born Hispanics, the rate drops to 8.9%, which is very similar to AAs. The difference between the foreign born and U.S. born Hispanics is likely due to either language mastery, socioeconomics, or migration patterns. Often if a student is not proficient in English by high school, he or she will drop out, and some are compelled to leave school early to help support the family. What is notable, however, is how the Hispanic dropout rate has declined in the last decade. In the early 2000s, the percentage of Hispanic children aged 6–16 that had parents with less than a high school diploma was 47%: by 2012 it had dropped to 33.5%. This is a large decrease in the dropout rate, and represents a change for the better in the Hispanic population.

Next, we turn to disparities in undergraduate education. A college degree is becoming increasingly more important as a ticket to the middle class and a well-paying job. In the adult population aged 25–68, Asians have the highest college completion rate at 52.3%, followed by Whites at 34.7%, Others at 26.4%, AAs at 19.5%, and Hispanics at 14.4%. Also worth noting are the differences in the type of degree pursued. Asians (40.4%) are the most likely to complete degrees in the more lucrative STEM fields (Science, Technology, Engineering, and Mathematics), and they are ahead of all other racial/ethnic groups in these fields, including Other race/ethnicities (23.15%), Hispanics (19.9%), and Whites (19.5%). AAs have a lower completion rate in the STEM fields at 16.3%. We will examine these differences again when we discuss variances in occupation and family income.

Table 5.1 shows the percentages of each racial/ethnic group that obtained various levels of education for parents of children in the WISC-V age range, based on data from the *ACS*. These differences are large. For example, 43% of

TABLE 5.1 Educational Attainment by Racial/Ethnic Group

	High School Dropout Rate	College Entrance Rate
White	4%	78%
AA	12%	62%
Hispanic	31%	43%
Asian	8%	78%
Other	7%	72%

Note: Individuals obtaining a GED are considered to have completed high school.
Data and table copyright Pearson 2014. All rights reserved.

Hispanics enter college, whereas 62% of AAs, and 78% of Asians and Whites do so. Among parents of children aged 6–16, 31% of Hispanics drop out of high school while 12% of AAs, 8% of Asians, and 4% of Whites do so.[1]

These differences in educational attainment are important for children's IQ, because there is an increase in FSIQ in every educational category for the WISC-V. Table 5.2 shows the mean FSIQ for children in the WISC-V standardization sample by level of parent education. In this table, we have also added a sixth category for graduate school education, although it was not a stratification variable when the data were collected. Although the children's mean WISC-V FSIQ scores are based on the average parent education, the FSIQ for the graduate level is based on one parent having a graduate degree. The mean FSIQ is similar for both levels of less than high school, but with each increase, there is a jump in the mean FSIQ score. These differences are meaningful, as there is a 22.9-point difference in FSIQ between the lowest and highest education levels, and the difference between the child of a college graduate versus the child of someone with a high school diploma or GED is 14.2 points.

We started with education because it has a profound impact on disparities, starting with income and employability. The U.S. Department of Labor estimates that a college education pays dividends in much higher earnings and lower unemployment (U.S. Department of Labor, 2014). Parent income and occupation often determine whether or not the family has health benefits, and what kind, thus impacting children's access to treatment for physical and mental health issues.

---

1. The *ACS* includes questions on which language a person speaks, and how well a person speaks English if he or she also speaks another language. As it is not good clinical practice to administer the WISC-V to children who do not speak English well, when composing the census targets Pearson (2014) included those children who speak English well or very well in addition to another language, or speak English only. Therefore, the high school dropout rate for Hispanics reported in Table 5.1 (31%) is slightly lower than the one quoted above (33.5%).

TABLE 5.2 Mean FSIQ of Children by Parent Education Level

Parent Education Level	Children's Mean FSIQ
8 years or less	87.8 (10.18) n = 67
9–12 years, no diploma	88.6 (16.24) n = 168
High school diploma or GED	93.8 (13.43) n = 460
Some college or technical school, associate's degree	99.7 (12.45) n = 777
Undergraduate degree or more	108.04 (13.98) n = 726
Graduate degree (at least one parent with a graduate degree)	110.7 (13.03) n = 350

Racial/Ethnic Group Disparities in Income, Occupation, and Poverty Status

Parents' occupations and family income directly impact the SES of families, which relates to IQ test scores of children through various social and psychological mechanisms, which are discussed throughout this chapter. Group differences in occupation and income are difficult topics to discuss as there is evidence that despite a transformation in personal attitudes since the Civil Rights era, AA and Hispanic individuals experience more discrimination in hiring, which has an impact on income and opportunities for promotion. In addition, higher paying jobs typically require more education, and as noted in the previous section, there are strong group differences in educational attainment for parents of young children. For this section, we analyzed data from the 2012 *ACS*.

First, there are disparities in occupational status, and this discussion flows from the differences we discussed in education. Managerial and STEM-related occupations are higher paying, and Whites and Asians predominate in these fields. For people aged 25–68, the overall population is 65.2% White, 5.5% Asian, 12.0% AA, and 15.1% Hispanic, but the highest represented managerial ranks are 70.2% White and 6.8% Asian. Engineers are also White (68.6%) and Asian (14.6%), as are scientists and social scientists at 64.2% White and 17.0% Asian. Health-care workers, who are paid less, are 28.5% AA and 19.6% Hispanic. Food service jobs are also held by Hispanics at 31.0%. One exception for AAs is jobs in legal services, which are better paying. In that profession, AAs are slightly overrepresented at 17.6%. These disparities in occupation stem from educational attainment as the more lucrative managerial and STEM professions require a college education, which may be less accessible to lower income families. In addition, AAs and Hispanics have experienced discrimination in some industries and areas of the country, and may have difficulty gaining promotions into management. With these caveats, we now turn to differences in family income.

From the *ACS*, we selected households that have children aged 6–16, to better understand the differences for children in the WISC-V age ranges. After accounting for households that had a negative income, Asians have the highest median family income at $80,151, with Whites at $72,702. Families of Other race/ethnicities have an income of $45,998, and AAs have the lowest median family income levels at $34,993. The median for all Hispanics is $38,196, but this differs by country of origin. Based on the origin of the head of the household, Dominicans have the lowest median family income at $29,984, Mexican or Mexican-Americans have a median family income of $36,942, which is similar to those whose origin is from Central America, at $36,936, and Puerto Rico at $36,435. South Americans at $45,726 and Cubans at $47,944 have considerably higher incomes. These differences represent different migration patterns over the years. Mexicans, Dominicans, Puerto Ricans, and Central Americans came to the continental United States looking for work and opportunity; and in recent years, people from Mexico and Central America have migrated to escape violence associated with the drug cartels. Political and social issues have historically motivated Cubans and South Americans to come to the United States, and they are better educated with higher college completion rates.

Next, we will demonstrate how disparities in income work across the spectrum, from poverty to prosperity. Poverty is important because the stress of living in a poor household can have a negative impact on cognition, specifically working memory and language. Poor children are more food insecure, move more often, and experience more stress than non-poor children, which can impact their cognitive development (Guo & Harris, 2000). Stress-related hormones such as cortisol have been found to impact learning and memory (van Ast et al., 2013). The differences in the percentage of children living in poverty by race/ethnicity are striking. Whereas 37% of AA children, 23% of other race/ethnicities, and 33% of Hispanic children live at or below the poverty line, only 13% of White and 15% of Asian children are in similar circumstances. Poverty status is based on a combination of income and number of people in the household.

Extreme poverty, where the income is at 50% or more below the poverty line, is an especially harsh environment, and here the numbers bring these disparities even more into focus as 13.3% of AA households with children aged 6–16 have incomes that are at or below 50% of poverty. Next, 11.25% of other race/ethnicity households are in extreme poverty, followed by Hispanics at 9.7%, Whites at 4.6%, and Asians at 5.0%. Equally striking are the differences in wealthier households, as 33.1% of Asians and 27.2% of White children live in households that are 500% or more above the poverty line. In contrast, 16.4% of Other race/ethnicities, 10.7% AAs, and 8.3% of Hispanics live in these prosperous households.

We point out these differences in occupation, income, and poverty because they have an impact on children's home lives, and therefore the opportunities families and children have for cognitive development. They also provide a graphic picture of how disparities are pervasive throughout our economic system, and thus it is not surprising when these disparities show up in special education services.

Racial/Ethnic Group Disparities in Physical Health Status

We now turn to group disparities in the physical health status of both children and adults with the presumption that indirect relationships exist between the physical health of families and the neurocognitive status of children in those families that operate through multiple mechanisms, including prenatal care, visits to the pediatrician, and so on. Physical health may also impact employment and occupational stability, thus limiting parents' ability to provide access to resources if their children are having health or school-related difficulties. Also, we wish to simply point out that group disparities are not restricted to special education programs.

AAs have more health problems than other racial/ethnic groups, and these disparities have a long legacy in the United States. Many AAs have a distrust of the health system due to mistreatment, exploitation, and discrimination (LaVeist, 2005). The disparities for AAs and physical health begin at birth. Low birth weight and infant mortality often serve as benchmarks for comparing living conditions across groups (LaVeist, 2005). AAs have more babies who are born with low birth weight and they also have higher infant mortality, even after accounting for the mother's education. Put plainly, young AA infants die at twice the rate of Whites, Asians, or Hispanics. Infants are fragile, and while they can die from a variety of causes in the early years of life, their environment heavily influences their overall health and survival. Higher neonatal and infant mortality rates may indicate poor maternal health or lack of access to health care, environmental stress, poverty, or other suboptimal living conditions (Centers for Disease Control and Prevention, 2013).

These disparities continue into adulthood. The following information is from the Centers for Disease Control and Prevention Health Disparities and Inequalities Report—United States, 2013. In comparison to Whites, AAs have higher rates of heart disease (47.1%), hypertension, 49.1%, (although they are more likely to be on medication than Whites), colorectal cancer (23.1%), and diabetes (66.2%). For HIV-AIDS, the rate is an astounding 823.1% higher. AAs also have the highest rates of obesity, a recent public health concern, at 37% for men and 53% for women. At the end of life, AAs have the shortest lifespan. Current lifetables available from the CDC indicate that an AA child born today can expect to live 3.5 years less than Whites if female, and 5.0 years less if male.

In contrast, Hispanics often have better health than Whites or AAs despite their SES, and this is known in the health and mortality literature as the *Hispanic Paradox*. Explanations for this paradox include the presumption that generally only healthy people are capable of migrating, thus giving U.S. Hispanics a health advantage. Other explanations include strong family and social ties, psychological and physical resilience, and individual behavior (Ruiz, Steffen, & Smith, 2013), and Hispanics live longer. Current life tables show that a Hispanic baby born today is likely to live 2.3 years longer than a White child, and this is the same for both males and females. Despite their overall better health, they have a higher risk of adult-onset diabetes (69.2%). Their obesity rates are just behind AAs at 44% for women and 35% for men. (Note that these figures are for Mexican-Americans only, data for Hispanics were not available.) Of particular importance is that Hispanics have a high uninsured rate at 41%. It is unknown at this time how their rates of health insurance will change after the implementation of the Affordable Care Act of 2010.

In the CDC report, Whites often served as a referent group, and it is worth noting where some of their health issues reside, as they are more on the behavioral side of health care. Whites are more likely than other groups to report binge drinking than any other group at a 21.1% prevalence rate; they binge more frequently at 4.1 times a month, with an intensity (number of drinks on a binge) at 6.8. This is higher than all other groups, except for American Indians/Alaska Natives. Although American Indians/Alaska Natives report a lower prevalence rate, with less frequency, they report drinking greater quantities during a binge, at 8.4 drinks. White (10.2%) and American Indian/Alaska Native (13.6%) teenagers are also more likely to report they smoke cigarettes, but these percentages even out more in the adult population across groups. Asians have fewer health problems than other groups with the exception of tuberculosis, which is 2388% higher than in Whites.

Health disparities show up in children's home environments. A parent who is not well, either physically or mentally, often will have more difficulty caring and providing for children. We wanted to know if minority children have a higher risk of living with someone with a disability, and the *ACS* asks people if they have any physical or cognitive disabilities, or difficulty caring for themselves. For this analysis, we selected households that have children aged

6–16 years, and we ran a series of logistic regression analyses to calculate racial/ethnic disparities. The sample was restricted to working aged adults 18–68 years, and the outcomes were hearing, physical limitations, mobility, cognitive impairments including memory, difficulty caring for oneself, and sight. After controlling for education and gender, across all types of disabilities except for hearing, AAs and American Indians/Alaska Natives have a higher risk for disabilities than Whites. AAs have a 29% higher risk of physical disabilities, a 24% higher risk of mobility problems, a 13% greater risk of cognitive disabilities, a 38% higher risk of having limitations in caring for themselves, and a 64% higher risk of having sight problems. American Indians/Alaska Natives have a 45% higher risk of physical disabilities, 34% higher risk for mobility, 40% risk of cognitive problems, 54% higher risk of self-care limitations, 88% higher risk for hearing impairments, and 104% higher risk for sight problems. In contrast, and in alignment with the Hispanic paradox, Hispanics have 15–60% lower risk than Whites across all of these categories.

We discuss physical health status not only to demonstrate that disparities exist in other realms beside special education, but also to point out that parents with health difficulties may often have trouble providing care, attention, and financial support for their children as they grow and develop. Physical health also has an impact on employment opportunities and thus family income and available resources to address children's needs.

Racial/Ethnic Group Disparities in Mental Health Status

Disparities in mental health status and services for children are included to further demonstrate that disparities are not restricted to special education services, and to point out that parents with significant mental health concerns may have fewer personal resources available to appropriately attend to the cognitive and academic development of their children.

AAs and Hispanics are less likely to initiate mental health services, and when they do, they receive fewer days of treatment (Cook et al., 2014). The rates of psychological disorders among AA, Whites, and Hispanics appear to be similar after controlling for SES. We analyzed data from the 2011–2012 National Survey of Children's Health (NSCH). This survey was conducted by the CDC, and they interviewed parents about their child's well-being and physical and mental health status. They asked parents if the child currently had autism, ADHD, anxiety, depression, developmental delay, or behavioral problems. These data were self-reported by parents, therefore there are some limitations and the rates should not be considered true prevalence rates. Whites (2.1%) and Asians (1.6%) had the highest rates for autism, and Whites also had the highest rates of ADHD (9.4%). Although AAs had higher reports of developmental delay (3.7%) and behavior problems (4.4%), their risk was not significantly different from Whites after controlling for SES. Compared to children living at 400% above the poverty line, children living in poverty are at greater risk for ADHD

(91%), anxiety (81%), depression (342%), developmental delay (114%), and behavioral problems (453%), indicating that living in poverty has a significant impact on these disorders. These results are consistent with previous research on SES and mental health (Hudson, 2012).

The proportion of individuals with mental illness is much higher among those who are homeless, incarcerated, or in foster care, and AAs are disproportionately represented in these settings. Accurate data on homelessness are difficult to come by given the transient nature of the population. However, the proportion of homeless population who are AAs is estimated at 37%, and 9.7% are Hispanic (SAMHSA, 2011). Families in homeless shelters are 39% AA and 22% Hispanic (Child Trends, 2013). These numbers do not include the unsheltered homeless families, which are difficult to count. Homeless children are more likely to have been abused or neglected.

Abuse and neglect can also lead to a child being placed in foster care, and this may exacerbate their disadvantage. Older children especially may end up in a series of foster homes before they age out of the system (The Annie E. Casey Foundation, 2008). According to the U.S. Department of Health and Human Services (2013), children in foster care are also predominantly AA, although the rates have fallen from 17.4 in 2002 to 10.2 in 2012. AA children are 13.9% of the total child population, yet they represent 25.5% of all children in foster care. American Indians/Alaska Natives are also overrepresented, as they are less than 1% of the population, yet represent 2% of all children in foster care.

Another mental health risk is suicide. According to the CDC, suicide is much more common among Whites, especially males, followed by American Indians/Alaska Natives. All other groups have suicide rates that are substantially lower than Whites. For people aged 10–24, the rate of suicide is much higher for American Indians/Alaska Natives for both males and females, with the male rate being 31.27 for every 100,000 people (Centers for Disease Control and Prevention, 2012).

The Surgeon General distributed a report detailing the disparities in mental health status, and the details in this next section are from that report, except where noted (U.S. Department of Health and Human Services, 2001). The availability of mental health services depends on where one lives and the presence or absence of health insurance. A large percentage of AAs live in areas with diminished access to both physical and mental health-care services, and nearly 25% of AAs have no health insurance as compared to 10% of Whites. Medicaid, which subsidizes the poor and uninsured, covers nearly 21% of AAs.

With respect to Hispanics, most studies support the lack of differences in rates of mental illness as compared to Whites; however, sample size issues have restricted the generalizability of this finding beyond the Mexican-American population. In general, Hispanics underutilize the mental health-care system, and they are the most uninsured of all of the racial/ethnic groups, perhaps because many of them are immigrants (García, 2012). The lifetime prevalence for mental disorders is 25% for Mexican immigrants, but 48% for the U.S. born

Mexican-Americans. Mexican immigrants with less than 13 years of U.S. residence have better mental health than their U.S.-born counterparts and the overall U.S. sample. In general, Hispanics underutilize and in many cases receive insufficient mental health-care services relative to Whites. Approximately 11% of Mexican-Americans access mental health services as compared to 22% of Whites. The trend appears to be that new Mexican immigrants have relatively good mental health, which is consistent with the healthy migrant theory. However, their problems become more prevalent the longer they stay in the United States. Their immigrant status makes access more difficult, particularly in areas that are not used to receiving new immigrants and may have a shortage of clinicians who speak Spanish or understand the culture. Areas that historically have more Mexican immigrants may be more friendly and provide better care (García, 2012). One strength of Mexican immigrants may be their social cohesion and family ties. Research conducted in Arizona found that Hispanics who lived in a neighborhood where they have friends that they trust has a positive impact on both their mental and physical health. People in poorer, more diverse areas had poorer mental health; however, if the poor area was predominantly Hispanic, then the residents had better mental and physical health (Rios, Aiken, & Zautra, 2012), indicating the strength of their social ties.

Another area of strength for Hispanics involves attitudes towards mental health disorders. There appears to be a cultural norm not to hold the person blameworthy and this may predispose people to take care of one another. At least among Mexicans, there appears to be a cultural norm to care for those ill within the family, regardless of physical or mental health status, and this may be reflected in the underutilization of some mental health services.

Implications of Demographic Differences in Various Areas of Life

Some reviewers will undoubtedly critique our overview of racial/ethnic group disparities in various areas of life as too limited to do the topic justice while other readers may wonder why we spent so much time on the topic and how these issues are relevant to intellectual assessment and specifically assessment using the WISC-V. In many cases, the magnitude of the gaps described above is shocking, and have serious political, legal, and economic implications for the United States. Our intention in including this discussion in the current chapter is more modest. First, we wish to make the basic point that disparities between racial/ethnic groups have been observed in many important areas of life, and are not limited to IQ test scores, or special education proportions. We do not imply cause and effect in either direction, but simply note that racial/ethnic group discrepancies are not unique to IQ test scores, or rates of special education.

Second, and much more importantly for our purposes in this chapter, the differences described above suggest, for the most part, that people of different racial ethnic backgrounds have differing levels of opportunity for cognitive growth and development. The effects of these differences on the development of cognitive abilities are critical during childhood but also continue well into middle adulthood depending on level of education, income, mental and physical health, and the resources available in the communities in which they live.

Americans are fond of saying that all children are born with equal opportunity, and that any child can grow up to be President of the United States. The election of Barack Obama as the first African-American U.S. President demonstrates that this is true—although not for immigrant children. Still, although opportunity under the law may be equal, implementation of the law can sometimes vary by jurisdiction for racial/ethnic groups as suggested by differential rates of incarceration. However, this is not the kind of opportunity we are talking about in this chapter. We are talking about opportunity in terms of the development of one's cognitive abilities; the opportunity for a child's mind to grow and expand to its fullest potential through adolescence and into early adulthood.

Even though genetics is a very large factor in determining intelligence (see Neisser et al., 1996), our central tenant is that IQ is not an immutable trait. Rather, it is a basic ability that can be influenced—to some reasonable extent— positively or negatively during the long course of cognitive development beginning in early childhood (if not prenatally) and continuing through adolescence and into early or middle adulthood. Cognitive development can be influenced by the environment in multiple, interactive, and reciprocal ways. When it comes to intellectual development of children, schools and cultures count as integral parts of the environmental mix (Nisbett, 2009). We know that the level of education obtained by the parents is highly correlated with the parent's occupational status and household income. This in turn is related to the quality of schools and libraries available in the neighborhoods that are affordable to the parents, the models for success and advancement present in those neighborhoods, the culturally defined expectations for educational attainment, the expectations for the child's occupational future that surround him or her in the family and community, and the extent to which an adolescent can pursue academic or other cognitively enriching activities free from concerns about economic survival or fears of personal safety that may impede educational progress and career development.

In many ways, education is only a proxy for a host of variables related to the quantity and quality of cognitively enriching activities available to a person, and that parents or care providers can provide for children. Therefore, education is only a gross indicator replete with numerous exceptions. Certainly, there are many individuals with little formal education who are quite successful in business and society, and their success affords critical opportunities to their offspring that belie expectations based on their own education. Similarly, many readers of this chapter will likely know that even advanced academic credentials do not always equate with success in life. What is amazing is that with all of its imperfections, one variable—education—relates so much to cognitive ability.

COGNITIVE DEVELOPMENT, HOME ENVIRONMENT, AND CULTURE

Theoretical Considerations

The family system is the most influential and proximal influence in children's early learning (Bronfenbrenner, 1992). Home environment research findings from developmental psychology have a long history, with roots as far back as Piaget's work in the 1920s. Credited as one of the founders of the Chicago school of family environment research, Bloom (1964) concluded that the preschool years were the most important period for children's intellectual stimulation and that family subenvironments should be identified and researched for unique effects on different aspects of cognitive development. These views were elaborated by several of his students including Wolf (1964) who reported a multiple correlation of .69 between children's measured intelligence and home environment ratings in three subenvironments characterized by the parents' "press" for achievement motivation, language development, and general learning. During the 1970s, a set of international studies based on the Chicago school's approach suggested that ethnicity is a significant variable that should be accounted for in examining the relation between home environment variables and children's intelligence and achievement, and that causal relationships established for one group may not hold for other times, social classes, ethnic groups, or countries (Marjoribanks, 1979; Walberg & Marjoribanks, 1976). In the 1980s, Caldwell and co-investigators developed the Home Observation for Measurement of the Environment (HOME) (Caldwell & Bradley, 1984), which is still the most widely used home environment measure in current research. As summarized by Bradley and Caldwell (1978), HOME scores obtained during the first year of life correlated at low but significant magnitudes with the Mental Development Index of the Bayley Scales of Infant Development at both 6 and 12 months and at moderate to strong levels with Stanford-Binet IQ scores at 36 and 54 months, and moderate to high correlations were found between 24 months HOME scores and 36 month Stanford-Binet IQ scores.

Children with psychological or psychoeducational disorders ranging from ADHD, autism spectrum disorders, intellectual disability, and specific learning disorder provide additional stressors for parents. Although it is common to say that these children need more structure than others, researchers are now systematically studying what this means in terms of home environment. The ability of a family to sustain a daily routine has been shown to be an important factor in the outcome of developmentally delayed children (Weisner, Matheson, Coots, & Bernheimer, 2005). Sustaining meaningful daily routines involves juggling ongoing demands while meeting long-term goals, rather than coping with crises and stress. Difficulty sustaining daily routines was more likely to be encountered in single parent families, expanded families, poor families, and multiply troubled families. When family troubles are high and unpredictable, routines are more difficult to sustain. Although increasing family resources was associated with higher sustainability, families with low income are often able to create and sustain reasonable daily routines even while struggling with limited resources. These low-income families with sustainable daily routines were found to be troubled by no more than one additional issue beyond caring for a delayed child. However, these researchers also point out that the ability of a family to sustain a daily routine is unrelated to the level of stimulation provided the child, or family warmth and connectedness. Quality of interaction is as important as the structure.

If home environment is such a powerful predictor of cognitive development, then one must ask how two children from the same family sometimes can be so different from each another in terms of expressed cognitive ability. Writing from another line of research involving behavior genetics, Plomin and Petrill (1997) offered the concept of shared versus nonshared environment to help explain differences between family members. They argued that during childhood cognitive development is largely influenced by aspects of the home environment that are shared by siblings, whereas by the end of adolescence IQ is largely influenced by nonshared aspects of the environment. However, methodological and other issues have been raised regarding this research (Stoolmiller, 1999), and further studies are needed to fully answer this question.

Certainly, adolescents are more influenced by peers than children. Thus, even children of the same parents may experience different environments as they enter adolescence a few years apart and come under the influence of different circles of friends. Before this period, however, children of the same family may experience different environments as they enter the preschool or preadolescent stages a few years after their older siblings for reasons as varied and normal as changes in job stress, employment status, or marital satisfaction during the intervening years.

Even absent environmentally induced changes in the family, parents often interact differently with each child simply because each is different in personality. Speaking purely as parents we are quite sure that each of our respective children experienced different aspects of ourselves as parents, and thus did not fully share the same developmental environment. We prefer to believe that our changing parental behavior was in response to their unique temperaments (rather than some pathological variability in our own personalities). Although much of the discussion in this literature is one directional concerning how parental behavior influences children's development, practitioners evaluating children in troubled families should keep in mind that children's approaches to the world around them vary greatly and influence parental responses. Simply put, some children are easier to rear than others, which is something that most everyone figures out by the time they become grandparents!

Expert clinicians spend time considering the ways in which each child's unique characteristics interact with the family systems in the home environment, and how these dynamics facilitate or impede the child's unique developmental needs. Many examples exist of children with psychoeducational disorders and/or troubled home environments who turn out to be well adapted.

We relate these positive outcomes, in part, to the characteristic of resiliency. Resiliency involves the extent to which a child is sensitive to perceived environmental threats and the speed with which they recover when upset. These characteristics are important to the child's sense of optimism, self-efficacy, and adaptability. Although the ability to regulate one's own emotions, attention, and behavior may be related to basic temperament, there are also effective strategies for teaching resilience to children at home and in school (Goldstein & Brooks, 2005). Further, resilience is improved with increases in the child's sense of relatedness to others—which is rooted in basic trust, access to support, social comfort, and tolerance of differences—and these drivers are firmly in the family's domain. A measure of resiliency in children and adolescents is available for clinical use (Prince-Embury, 2006; Prince-Embury & Saklofske, 2014).

We have already discussed income inequities by racial ethnic group. Clearly, poverty can have significant consequences on family functioning, thus affecting the home environment. Shah, Mullainathan, and Shafir (2012) suggest that poor individuals often engage in behaviors, such as excessive borrowing, that reinforce the conditions of poverty. Past explanations for these behaviors have focused on personality traits of the poor, or emphasized environmental factors such as housing or financial access. Providing a completely different perspective, Shah and colleagues show in a series of experiments that scarcity necessarily changes how poor people allocate their attention, and suggest that this leads to the poor engaging more deeply in proximal problems while neglecting distal goals. Mani, Mullainathan, Shafir, and Zhao (2013) take this argument one large step further and show that poverty directly impedes cognitive functioning in a set of experiments. These authors suggest that poverty-related concerns consume mental resources, leaving less cognitive capacity for other tasks.

As an added point from a nonresearch point of view, the current authors in their clinical work have observed parents who themselves have limited education, often live in economically impoverished settings and have not realize the impact of "what they do as parents" on their children in the short and longer term. One parent, when asked if she spoke to her young infant or read to her preschool children, simply said "I didn't know I should do that." Such clinical observations are consistent with research showing that vocabulary development of young children varies as a function of maternal speech frequency (Hoff, 2003), and that language development can be enhanced through active exposure to quality auditory stimuli in infancy (Benasich, Choudhury, Realpe-Bonilla, & Roesler, 2014). Parents living in poverty spend less time talking and reading to young children, which negatively impacts the prelinguistic process of acoustic mapping in infancy, and exposes them to fewer new words during later, critical periods of language development.

These findings are consistent with Ruby Payne's popular book (Payne, 2013) in which she proposes a culture of poverty, and describes how this leads people to think differently, sometimes making choices based on immediate needs that may not be in their best long-term interest. Because many teachers are not from a culture of poverty, they sometimes have difficulty understanding the behaviors of their students' parents, and Payne's book provides a framework for that understanding, which is not based on supposed personality flaws of the poor. As such the book has become very popular in workshops for teachers. Valencia (2010) seems to argue that the notion of a culture of poverty, however, leads to deficit thinking, which is just another form of blaming the victim when the real culprit is the flawed educational system.

In our chapter, we seek to blame no one. Our purpose is only to promote an understanding that children's cognitive abilities do not develop by themselves; rather cognitive abilities develop partly in response to physical and social milieus, which support development to varying degrees. The societal and familial issues are far too encompassing for any one experimenter to study in their entirety. Further, the interactions between this myriad of influences are both complex and reciprocal, and so assigning causality is arbitrary and mostly a function of which segment of the problem one is examining at what point in time. In any reciprocally interacting system, the origin of causality is unknowable by definition. Put more simply, we will not debate here which came first, "the chicken or the egg."

Home Environment and African-American Children

Researchers have examined the role of home environment in specific populations. In this way it is possible to explore the hypothesis that the same proximal processes are differentially employed by individuals in different cultures. Several studies correlated home environment and SES ratings with children's measured intelligence and/or academic achievement (Bradley & Caldwell, 1981, 1982; Bradley, Caldwell, & Elardo, 1977; Bradley et al., 1989; Brooks-Gunn, Klebanov, & Duncan, 1996; Johnson et al., 1993; Ramey, Farran, & Campbell, 1979; Trotman, 1977).

Although SES was defined differently across studies, this set of papers generally showed that for AA children the relationship between SES and IQ test scores was not as strong as the relation between home environment and IQ tests scores, nor as strong as the relationship between SES and IQ test scores among White children. This may be because the range of SES within the AA groups was likely both skewed and truncated, regardless of how it was measured (e.g., parent education, income, occupation). This has led some writers to speculate that historical limitations in educational and employment opportunities lead to more variability in parental behavior within the lower SES AA group than within the lower SES White group. In the studies cited above, home environment ratings typically added significant information to the prediction of IQ scores from SES for AA children, and this increment in variance explained was often larger than that for White children.

What this means is that SES, however it is measured, may not be as powerful a predictor of IQ test scores for AA children as it is for White children.

It also means that home environment factors may play a more powerful role in the prediction of IQ test scores for AA than White children.

Home Environment and Mexican-American Children

Several studies examined the relation of home environment and cognitive ability in Mexican-American children (Bradley et al., 1989; Henderson, 1972; Henderson, Bergan, & Hurt, 1972; Henderson & Merritt, 1968; Johnson, Breckenridge, & McGowan, 1984; Valencia, Henderson, & Rankin, 1985).

In general the results of these studies also support the view that parents' in-home behavior is important to cognitive development and academic performance. It has been shown that Mexican-American children with purportedly low educational potential are exposed to a more restricted range of developmental experiences than their high potential Mexican-American counterparts (Henderson & Merritt, 1968). Mexican-American parents who demonstrate higher degrees of valuing language (e.g., reading to the child), valuing school-related behavior (e.g., reinforcing good work), and providing a supportive environment for school learning (e.g., helping the child recognize words or letters during the preschool stage) have children who tend to score higher on tests of basic concepts and early achievement (Henderson et al., 1972), and neither SES nor family size made a significant unique contribution to predicting cognitive ability scores beyond that accounted for by home environment (Valencia et al., 1985).

We must offer a modest word of caution about generalizing these findings. First, these studies do not address the likely impact of parental language on children's test scores. Perhaps English-speaking parents develop more acculturated children who perform better in American schools and on US-based IQ tests. Further, only Mexican-American families were studied and so generalization to Puerto Rican, Cuban, or other Spanish-speaking populations may or may not be valid. As discussed earlier, SES varies systematically with country of origin because of the historical patterns influencing immigration from the various Spanish-speaking nations. The interaction between parent education, home environment and cognitive development has not been fully studied by language status of the parents or country of origin. Yet, there is growing evidence that home environment is an important predictor of cognitive development across cultures.

Home Environment and Academic Achievement

The association of home environment with academic achievement has also been studied. Higher levels of parent involvement in their children's educational experiences at home have been associated with children's higher achievement scores in reading and writing, as well as higher report card grades (Epstein, 1991; Griffith, 1996; Keith et al., 1998; Sui-Chu & Williams, 1996). Research has also shown that parental beliefs and expectations about their children's learning are strongly related to children's beliefs about their own competencies, as well as their achievement (Galper, Wigfield, & Seefeldt, 1997). Improving the home learning environment has been shown to increase children's motivation and self-efficacy (Dickinson & DeTemple, 1998; Mantzicopoulos, 1997; Parker, Boak, Griffin, Ripple, & Peay, 1999).

Fantuzzo, McWayne, Perry, and Childs (2004) extended the above finding in a longitudinal study of very low SES AA children in an urban Head Start program, showing that specific in-home behaviors significantly predicted children's receptive vocabulary skills at the end of the school year, as well as motivation, attention/persistence, and lower levels of classroom behavior problems. Homes with high levels of parent involvement in their children's education were characterized by specific behaviors reflecting active promotion of a learning environment at home. For example, creating space for learning activities at home, providing learning opportunities for the child in the community, supervision and monitoring of class assignments and projects, daily conversations about school, and reading to young children at home.

Home environment influences the learning behaviors demonstrated by children in the classroom, and learning behaviors such as competency, motivation, attention, and persistence are important predictors of academic success. The likelihood of specific learning behaviors has been shown to vary with gender, age, ethnicity, urban residence, parent educational level, and special education classification status (Schaefer, 2004). Researchers have provided data suggesting that differential rates of inattention across racial/ethnic groups may explain as much as 50% of the gap in achievement test scores between AA and White students (Rabiner, Murray, Schmid, & Malone, 2004). Screening attentional behaviors related to learning, such response inhibition in the early grades may be useful additions to school psychology practice.

THE ROLE OF COGNITIVE STIMULATION IN INTELLECTUAL DEVELOPMENT

At this point in the discussion, we elaborate upon our central thesis: *Enriching, cognitively stimulating environments enhance intellectual development, whereas impoverishing environments inhibit that growth.* Further, the factors that inhibit cognitive enrichment interact with each other such that the presence of one factor makes the occurrence of other inhibitory factors more probable. The net result is even worse than the sum of its parts—akin to geometric rather arithmetic increases. Finally, the negative effects of cognitively impoverished environments can accumulate over the course of a child's developmental period and the impact may further worsen with age. The terms enrichment and impoverishment, as used here, are not considered synonymous with the financial status of rich and poor. These terms refer to cognitively enriching versus impoverishing environments, specifically environments that encourage growth, exploration, learning, creativity, self-esteem, etc.

Potter, Mashburn, and Grissmer (2013) state that current explanations of social class gaps in children's early academic skills tend to focus on noncognitive skills that more advantaged children acquire in the family. According to those explanations, social class matters because the cultural resources more abundant in advantaged families cultivate children's repertories and tool kits, which allow them to more easily navigate social institutions, such as schools. Within these accounts, parenting practices matter for children's academic success, but for seemingly arbitrary reasons. Alternatively, Potter and colleagues show that *findings from current neuroscience research indicate that family context matters for children because it cultivates neural networks that assist in learning and the development of academic skills. That is, children's exposure to particular parenting practices and stimulating home environments contribute to the growth in neurocognitive skills that affect later academic performance.* We agree!

Stephen Ceci and Urie Bronfenbrenner have proposed a bioecological model of intellectual development (Bronfenbrenner, 2004; Bronfenbrenner & Ceci, 1994; Ceci, 1996; Ceci & Bronfenbrenner, 2004; Ceci & Williams, 1999). These authors tackle the nature–nurture issue directly, arguing that there is nothing inconsistent about saying a trait is both highly changeable and highly heritable. This is particularly obvious when comparing studies that focus on group averages or means with studies that focus on variances or differences among individuals. They make the point that even when the heritability of a trait is extremely high, such as it is with height, the environment can still exert a powerful influence.

The bioecological model involves (1) the existence of multiple cognitive abilities that develop at different rates from each other, (2) the interactive and synergistic effect of gene–environment developments, (3) the role of specific types of environmental resources (e.g., proximal behavioral processes and distal family resources) that influence how much of a genotype gets actualized in what type of environment, and (4) the role of motivation in determining how much one's environmental resources aid in the actualization of his or her potential. According to this model, certain epochs in development can be thought of as sensitive periods during which a unique disposition exists for a specific cognitive ability to crystallize in response to its interaction with the environment. Not all cognitive abilities are under maturational control, however, as new synaptic structures may be formed in response to learning that may vary widely among people at different developmental periods. Yet, the sensitive period for many abilities appears to be neurologically determined such that the proper type of environmental stimulation must be present during the critical developmental period, and providing that same stimulation at another time may have less impact. In this model, the relative contributions of environment and genetic endowment to intellectual outcome change with developmental stage. For example, general intelligence at age 7 relates to key aspects of home environment at ages 1 and 2, but not at ages 3 or 4 (Rice, Fulker, Defries, & Plomin, 1988). This suggests that it may be difficult to completely compensate for an impoverished early environment by enhancing the child's later environment, although some positive effects from positive environments still may be expected when out of developmental sequence. Where we need more research is in the elucidation of the key paths and the critical developmental timing.

Interestingly, this model does not separate intelligence from achievement because schooling is assumed to elicit certain cognitive potentials that underlie both (see Ceci, 1991). Further, problem-solving as operationalized in most intelligence tests relies on some combination of past knowledge and novel insights. Studies conducted more than 50 years ago have shown structural and biochemical changes in animals after exposure to enriched environments (Diamond et al., 1966; Mollgaard, Diamond, Bennett, Rosenzweig, & Lindner, 1971; Rosenzweig, 1996). We would add that the act of academic learning enhances formation of new synaptic connections and neural networks, and therefore increases intellectual ability directly, in addition to the indirect effect of accumulated knowledge on problem-solving. Thus, schooling and the quality of education play a powerful role in intellectual development. This is part of the reason why achievement and crystallized knowledge exhibit substantial overlap with reasoning ability in psychometric studies of intelligence tests. Although theoretically distinct, these constructs are reciprocally interactive in real life.

Distal resources are background factors such as SES that effect cognitive development indirectly through the opportunities afforded or denied. Proximal processes are behaviors that directly impact cognitive development. Proximal processes occur within the context of distal resources and interact to influence the extent to which cognitive potentials will be actualized. For maximum benefit, the process must be enduring and lead to progressively more complex forms of behavior. Parental monitoring is an example of an important proximal process. This refers to parents who keep track of their children, know if they are doing their homework, who they associate with after school, where they are when they are out with friends, and so forth. Parents who engage in this form of monitoring tend to have children who obtain higher grades in school (Bronfenbrenner & Ceci, 1994). In the bioecological model, proximal processes are referred to as the engines that drive intellectual development, with higher levels of proximal processes associated with increasing levels of intellectual competence.

The distal environment includes the larger context in which the proximal, parent–child behaviors occur. Perhaps the most important distal resource is SES, because it relates to many other distal resources such as neighborhood safety, school quality, library access, as well as the education, knowledge, and experience that the parent brings with him or her into the proximal processes. For example, helping the developing child with homework, an effective proximal process, requires that someone in the home possess enough background knowledge about the content of the child's lessons, a distal environmental resource, to help the child when he or she studies.

Distal resources can place limits on the efficiency of proximal processes because the distal environment contains the resources that need to be imported into the proximal processes in order for them to work to full advantage, and because an adequate distal environment provides the stability necessary for the developing child to receive maximum benefit from the proximal processes over time. Although an educated parent may be able to help a child with algebra homework, a valuable distal resource, a parent with little education can still provide a valuable proximal process of quiet space, a regular time for homework, and ensure that the assigned work is completed. This monitoring and support can be very beneficial.

At the same time, it is unlikely that there is a universal environment whose presence facilitates performance for all children of all cultures, or even for children of all ages. The likelihood of person by environment interactions suggests that there are different developmental pathways to achievement. School and home environments may be benevolent, malevolent, or null with respect to a variety of dimensions. Practitioners conducting clinical assessments with children might include an evaluation of distal environmental resources within the family and community and consider how these factors facilitate or inhibit their parent's expectations for their children, and the children's expectations for themselves.

THE ROLE OF THE CHILD IN ACADEMIC AND INTELLECTUAL DEVELOPMENT

Without detracting from the critical roles that parents and educators play in the cognitive achievement of children, we believe that one also must examine the role of noncognitive individual differences in children's approach to the learning environment. Assuming that proper cognitive stimulation is present at the right time, there are noncognitive characteristics of the developing child that mediate the actualization of cognitive potential. Clearly, cognition plays a role in every aspect of human functioning and thus can never be fully partialled out of the human factor. Yet, the list of possible noncognitive factors is long, and encompasses basic temperament. Some children actively engage with the world around them, drawing inspiration and energy from others, and proactively seeking positive reinforcement from their environment. This stance enhances development of cognitive abilities as well as fostering social emotional development. Others turn inward for energy and insight, passively accommodate to the world around them, and seek only to avoid negative stimulation from the environment. This stance seeks to preserve current status, and if extreme, may inhibit social emotional growth and even cognitive development through restricting cognitive stimulation. This *enhancing* versus *preserving* trait is one of the three basic dimensions of Millon's theory of normal personology (Weiss, 1997, 2002). Children who seek out versus shut off stimulation will have different experiences even in the same environment, and their developmental opportunities for cognitive and social-emotional growth will likewise differ. Some children are receptive to new information, continuously revising and refining concepts based on an open exchange of information with the world around them. This curious, open, perceiving stance may facilitate cognitive growth. Other children prefer to systematize new information into known categories as soon as possible, and shut off further information as soon as an acceptable classification can be made. Although a strong organizational framework can be a positive influence on cognitive development, a closed, judging stance can inhibit intellectual growth if extreme.

Also relevant to cognitive development, learning and the expression of intelligent behavior are general conative (i.e., noncognitive) characteristics such as focus, motivation, and volition. Focus involves directionality of goal. Volition involves intensity toward the goal, or will. Motivation can be proximal or distal. A proximal motivation would be a specific near-term goal. A distal motivation might be a desired state (e.g., to be respected by one's peers) or a core trait (e.g., need for achievement). The list of positive characteristics is long, but includes self-efficacy and self-concept. Self-efficacy is driven by positive self-concept in combination with learned skill sets. Self-efficacy is task specific whereas self-concept is general. Children who have high self-efficacy with respect to intellectual tasks may have experienced initial successes with similar tasks. They also are likely to learn more from new intellectual activities than other children of similar intelligence because they are intellectually engaged in the task and have an internal drive to master it. Intellectual engagement and mastery motivation are critical elements of cognitive growth, along with the ability to self-regulate one's actions toward a goal. Presence of these personal characteristics may enhance cognitive development and the likelihood of success at a variety of life endeavors. However, different factors may be related to success versus failure at intellectual endeavors. After controlling for intellectual level, it may not be simply the absence of positive factors but the presence of specific negative personal factors that are associated with failure to thrive intellectually. Negative predictors may include severe procrastination, extreme perfectionism, excessive rumination, distractibility from goals, rigid categorical thinking, cognitive interference due to social-emotional disorders, or diagnosed psychopathology.

Research into these constructs has been criticized as fragmented in the past. In more recent research programs, many of these constructs are coming together under the umbrella heading of achievement motivation, and various groups of researchers in diverse areas of the world are refining the construct of achievement motivation and validating questionnaires to assess it in different cultures. Some of the current work is based on cultural adaptations of Martin's Motivation and Engagement Scale (Martin, 2008), or Pintrich's original Motivated Strategies for Learning Questionnaire (Pintrich, Smith, Garcia, & McKeachie, 1993). The Martin model clusters these sometimes fragmented skills into four areas: adaptive cognitions (i.e., self-efficacy, mastery motivation, valuing learning); maladaptive cognitions (i.e., anxiety, failure avoidance); adaptive behaviors (i.e., planning, task management, and persistence or effort); and maladaptive behaviors (i.e., disengagement and self-handicapping). The Pintrich model organizes these constructs into the two domains of motivation (i.e., intrinsic and extrinsic value) and learning styles (i.e., self-regulation and strategy use).

Martin and Hau (2010) found that differences in achievement motivation between students in Australia and Hong Kong are primarily ones of degree rather than kind. This suggests that the achievement motivation construct, as it is currently being organized, has some cross-cultural validity and may be more universal than originally thought. In addition, these authors found that enjoyment of school, class participation, positive academic intentions, and academic buoyancy also were importantly related to the motivation to achieve in school. Interestingly, academic buoyancy is much like the concept of resiliency discussed above. Although a significant predictor of achievement test scores, the percent of variance accounted for by motivation is small (Sachs, Law, Chan, & Rao, 2001). We think this is possibly due to complex interactions of student motivation with ability, teaching styles, and home environment.

Lee, Yin, and Zhang (2010) reported that peer learning was importantly related to achievement motivation through the construct of learning strategies in a sample of 12- to 17-year-old students in Hong Kong, and have proposed adding this construct to the Pintrich model. Peer learning involves working on assignments collaboratively with other classmates, explaining material to them, and asking questions of them. Such collaboration skills are increasingly considered important in U.S. education because the ability to work in teams is one of the pillars of twenty-first century skills.

The work of Angela Duckworth and her colleagues on "grit" has received considerable attention with regard to student motivation. Alternately known as self-control or self-regulation, grit is perseverance and passion for a goal that is consistently acted upon over a long period of time; months or years. It is related to the concept of resilience, which involves bouncing back from failure. Resilience and grit overlap when resilience is applied to the pursuit of a goal in the face of failure or obstacles. Grit also bears a relationship to the conscientiousness factor of general personality. But, grit requires neurologically mature executive functioning systems for voluntary self-regulation of emotions, behaviors, and attentional impulses in the face of immediate distractions.

In a longitudinal study of 8th grade students, Duckworth and Seligman (2005) showed that self-control measured in the Fall semester predicted final grades, even after controlling for IQ and achievement test scores. The authors concluded that a major reason for students falling short of their intellectual potential is the failure to exercise self-control. In another longitudinal analysis, Duckworth and colleagues found that measures of self-control predicted report card grades better than IQ, but IQ predicted standardized achievement test scores better than self-control (Duckworth, Quinn, & Tsukayama, 2012). The authors reasoned that self-control helps students study, complete homework, and behave positively in the classroom; whereas IQ helps children learn and solve problems independent of formal instruction.

The seminal work of Carol Dweck shows the importance of having a "growth mindset" with regard to intelligence, rather than a "fixed ability mindset." Individuals with fixed ability mindsets believe that one's intelligence is immutable.

Individuals with growth mindsets believe that one's intelligence can increase with effort. She demonstrates that this mindset differs by culture, with Asian cultures generally having growth mindsets and western cultures having fixed ability mindsets. Fixed ability mindsets respond to intellectual and academic failures with helplessness, whereas growth mindsets respond with a mastery orientation, which fuels persistence or grit. Importantly for applied psychologists, her research shows that having a growth mindset can be taught to children, and leads to increasing IQ test scores over time. This corpus of work earned her an award for distinguished scientific contributions from the American Psychological Association (Dweck, 2012). Dweck's work on growth mindsets speaks of the malleability of cognitive growth as a function of environment and is germane to the central tenant of our chapter; cognitively enriching environments enhance intellectual development.

PATTERNS OF WISC-V IQ SCORES ACROSS CULTURALLY AND LINGUISTICALLY DIVERSE GROUPS

With the above discussion on test bias, fairness, and demographic differences in various areas of life as background, we now present mean WISC-V FSIQ and index scores by racial/ethnic group in Table 5.3. Although we have taken care to elaborate the home environmental and other issues that must be considered when interpreting these data, we are nonetheless concerned that some will take this information out of context and interpret it either as evidence of genetically determined differences in intelligence among the races, or as proof of test bias. We are convinced that such interpretations are scientifically unsound based on the content of this chapter, but also divisive to society and harmful to children.

TABLE 5.3 WISC-V Mean Composite Scores by Racial/Ethnic Group

N	White		African-American		Hispanic		Asian		Other	
	(1,228)		(312)		(458)		(89)		(113)	
	Mean	S.D.	Mean	S.D.	Mean	S.D.	Mean	S.D.	Mean	S.D.
VCI	103.7	14.4	92.1	13.7	94.2	13.5	105.9	15.0	100.3	14.6
VSI	103.0	14.8	90.3	13.2	96.8	13.3	109.8	14.9	99.7	13.2
FRI	102.8	14.8	93.7	14.4	95.6	13.4	107.0	13.3	99.8	16.2
WMI	102.7	14.8	96.1	13.9	94.9	14.5	103.9	13.1	99.5	15.7
PSI	100.9	15.1	96.4	15.5	98.3	14.0	106.5	15.5	101.9	14.3
FSIQ	103.5	14.6	91.9	13.3	94.4	12.9	108.6	14.4	100.4	14.7

As we have shown in Tables 5.1 and 5.2, parent education levels vary systematically by racial/ethnic group and are associated with substantial differences in mean FSIQ scores for children. This fact has critical implications for the collection of standardization samples when developing intelligence, achievement, and other cognitive tests. The first step in defining an appropriate standardization sample is to identify the variables that account for substantial variance in the construct of interest and stratify the sample to represent the population on those variables. For intelligence tests, these variables have traditionally been SES, race/ethnicity, age, gender, and region of the country. These variables may act singly, or in complex interactions such that race/ethnicity may be masking other underlying variables. Most test authors select parent education level as the single indicator of SES when developing tests for children because of its high correlation with direct indicators of SES such as household income and parental occupation, and because it is more reliably reported than income. Given the skewed range of education in the non-White and Hispanic groups resulting from the differential dropout rates and other factors reported above, however, parent education may work as a better indicator of indirect SES effects on test scores for Whites than for children of other groups. This hypothesis will be addressed by analyses presented later in this chapter.

Current practice in test development is to fully cross all stratification variables with each other, and most major intelligence test authors follow this practice. Thus, for example, the percentage of Hispanic or AA children of college educated parents in the standardization sample will be much less than White children of college educated parents. Although this sampling methodology accurately reflects each population as it exists in society, it exaggerates the difference between the mean IQ scores of these groups because the SES levels of the various racial/ethnic samples are not equal. If test authors were to use the same national SES percentage for all racial/ethnic groups, the IQ score gap between groups would be smaller—although not eliminated for all groups as we will demonstrate later in this chapter. At the same time, however, this alternate sampling procedure would obscure the magnitude of societal differences in the developmental milieu of children across racial/ethnic groups.

As shown in Table 5.3, the highest mean FSIQ score was obtained by the Asian sample (108.6), followed by the White (103.5), Hispanic (94.4), and AA (91.9) samples. The largest difference is observed between the Asian and AA groups—more than a full standard deviation (16.7 points). The White/AA difference is 11.6 FSIQ points, and the Hispanic/White difference is 9.1 points. Recall that these data are based on samples matched to the U.S. Census for parent education and region of the country within racial/ethnic group. Thus, these racial/ethnic samples reflect all the educational and social inequities that exist between these groups in the population, as elaborated above. Also noteworthy is that the Other group—consisting of Native American Indians, Alaskan Natives, and Pacific Islanders—obtained mean WISC-V scores very near the population mean at 100.4.

Several additional points are notable concerning differences in the profile of mean index scores across groups. Hispanics—traditionally considered among the most linguistically diverse groups—exhibit VCI scores 2.6 points lower than their mean VSI scores, whereas the AA and White groups exhibit VCI scores slightly higher than their VSI scores. This is important in terms of interpreting index scores in a culturally sensitive manner. For a more complete discussion of this topic, see Chapter 7 on testing Hispanics with WISC-V and WISC-IV Spanish.

It is particularly interesting that the AA sample shows slightly higher VCI than VSI scores because clinical folklore assumes that the verbal subtests are the most biased for AA children due to this group's distance from the dominant culture and use of AA dialect. However, the available data do not support this view. AA children obtained their lowest mean index score on VSI, and highest on PSI. However, no studies to date have examined the linguistic diversity within the group classified as AA, which includes Black immigrants from multiple countries and cultures. While the AA group is traditionally considered monolingual, this assumption may not be valid in all cases. Researchers tend to limit discussion of AA linguistic diversity to dialects. Within the group classified as AA, however, there is the indigenous African-American language (Gullah), as well as French, Spanish, Portuguese, many continental African languages (e.g., Amharic), and Caribbean languages (e.g., Haitian Creole). Because researchers traditionally have assumed that the AA group is monolingual, the influence of language on acculturation and cognitive or achievement test performance has not been adequately investigated.

Although the White group presents reasonably consistent mean scores across the four index scores, the Asian group shows lower scores on WMI and VCI, and highest on VSI. This may be due to the linguistic demands of the VCI subtests, as well as secondary verbal demands in the Digit Span and Picture Span subtests that comprise the WMI. If some linguistically diverse children translate letters and numbers from the English presentation of these stimuli to their first language, then these tasks will tax working memory functions more than for those children who do not translate because their first language is English or because they have become sufficiently proficient in English.

For the Hispanic sample, the highest mean score is observed for the PSI. For the AA group, there is a clear pattern of both WMI and PSI scores higher than VCI and VSI. These findings are interesting for a number of reasons. First, clinical folklore assumes that some minority cultures place less value on speed of performance and may be penalized by tasks with time limits or time bonuses—yet, the PSI score is the highest of the four index scores for both the Hispanic and AA groups. These data suggest that common assumptions about the cultural effects of speed and timed performance among AA and Hispanic children may not be supported by the available data. We previously observed the same trend with WISC-IV data (Weiss, Harris, et al., 2006).

It is also worth pointing out that the AA/White gap in FSIQ scores is about the same in WISC-V as WISC-IV, but much smaller than it was in WISC-III.

The mean FSIQ score for the AA group was 88.6 in WISC-III, but rounds up to 92 in both WISC-IV and WISC-V. At the same time, the White mean remained relatively constant at approximately 103. Thus, the AA/White gap reduced from an almost a full standard deviation (14.9 points) in WISC-III to 11.5 points in WISC-IV, and remained virtually constant in WISC-V at 11.6 points. The mean FSIQ score for Hispanics declined by 1 point from 94.1 to 93.1 between WISC-III and WISC-IV, but increased to 94.4 in WISC-V. The Hispanic/White gap increased slightly, between WISC-III and WISC-IV, by 0.7 points to approximately 10.1 points. In WISC-V the Hispanic/White gap decreased to 9.1 points.

In the early part of the last century, Spearman (1927, cited in Vroon, 1980) hypothesized that group differences in IQ test scores could be explained by innate differences in g between the races, and this position continues to rear its ugly head 70 years later (Jensen, 1998; Murray, 2005). Some will likely follow this antiquated line of reasoning and argue that the AA FSIQ was increased in WISC-IV and WISC-V by increasing the contribution of cognitively less complex subtests with lower g loadings (e.g., Coding and Symbol Search) in the FSIQ, and they could be correct insofar as psychometric studies of g are concerned. However, we would point out that many of the subtests that are purported to be stronger measures of g are also those that are more readily influenced by environmental opportunity, such as Vocabulary. Further, the more abstract tasks found in the fluid reasoning index have also been shown to be susceptible to the effects of changes in environment over time (Flynn, 1984, 1987; Neisser, 1998). In fact, the largest change for AAs was observed between the WISC-III POI (87.5) and WISC-IV PRI (91.4), a difference of approximately 4 points. Conceptual changes in this index between versions of the tests included a reduction in visual organization and an increase in fluid reasoning subtests. As fluid reasoning was separated into its own factor in WISC-V, the AA sample exhibited its lowest mean index score of 90.3 on VSI (composed of Block Design and Visual Puzzles subtests); and a higher mean score of 93.7 points on FRI (composed of the Matrix Reasoning and Figure Weights subtests), which is the index score most closely associated with g.

At this point in our discussion it may be worth stating the obvious: *studies showing between group differences in IQ test scores say nothing about the source of those differences.* As Sternberg, Grigorenko, and Kidd (2005) concluded, the statement that racial differences in IQ or academic achievement are of genetic origin is a "leap of imagination." We have repeatedly noted that race/ethnicity are likely to be proxy variables for a set of active mechanisms that have only been partially identified. In fact, the reason why between-group differences appear to exist may be because the variables that they are substituting for have not been fully identified. Thus, we are not in agreement with Spearman's hypothesis that differences in IQ scores across racial/ethnic groups reflect differences in genotypic ability. We seek to reframe the question in terms of differential opportunity for development of cognitive abilities. Alternatively, cognitively enriched environments may be a synonym for acculturative experiences. Thus, Spearman's hypothesis for IQ score differences across racial/ethnic groups could be reframed either in terms of differential opportunity for cognitive development, or differential acculturation experiences.

In the next section, we report the results of a series of analyses designed to evaluate the extent to which differences in parent education and income are the source of WISC-V FSIQ score differences between racial and ethnic groups. First, however, we review findings from similar studies with WISC-IV and WAIS-IV.

SES MEDIATORS OF FSIQ DIFFERENCES BETWEEN CULTURALLY AND LINGUISTICALLY DIVERSE GROUPS

In this section we explore how SES mediates the gap between racial and ethnic groups in intelligence test scores. This discussion is not about nature–nurture, nor is it about race and IQ. It is about helping people understand why test scores may vary based on contextual factors and using that information to help children.

Previous Findings with WISC-IV and WAIS-IV

We applied a regression-based methodology recommended by Helms, Jernigan, and Mascher (2005), outspoken critics of bias in testing, to examine how much of the variance in test scores can be attributed to racial/ethnic group, and how much that variance is reduced when relevant mediator variables are introduced. We first reported these analyses with WISC-IV data (Weiss et al., 2006). For the AA/White comparison, we reported that race accounted for 4.7% of the variance in WISC-IV FSIQ scores, and that after controlling for parent education and income, race explained only 1.6% of the variance, leaving 6 points of the group difference remaining unexplained after mediation. For the Hispanic/White comparison, we reported that ethnicity accounted for 1.4% of the variance in WISC-IV FSIQ scores, and controlling for parent education and income fully explained the difference. We attributed the fact that controlling for SES did not fully explain the remaining difference in the AA/White comparison to historical inequalities in access to quality education and discrimination in job promotions among the parents of these children.

We then combined the groups and examined the role of parents' expectations for their children's academic success. We were surprised to find that parental expectations explained 30.7% of the variance in children's WISC-IV FSIQ scores, far more than parent education and income combined at 21.3%. After controlling for parent education and income, parental expectations still explained 15.9% of the variance in children's WISC-IV FSIQ scores, far more than explained by race (4.7%) or ethnicity (1.4%) alone. We interpreted these findings as consistent with the view that home environment matters, concluding that demographics is not destiny.

We subsequently reported the same analyses with adults based on WAIS-IV (Weiss, Chen, Harris, Holdnack, & Saklofske, 2010). For the Hispanic/White comparison, we reported that ethnicity accounted for 11.2% of the variance in WAIS-IV FSIQ scores for adults aged 20–90. After controlling for the adult's level of education, occupation, income, gender, and region where they live, ethnicity explained 3.8% of the variance, leaving a 6.5 point difference between the groups unexplained after mediation. For the AA/White comparison, we reported that race accounted for 14.9% of the variance in WAIS-IV FSIQ scores for adults aged 20–90, far more than for children and adolescents. After controlling for other demographics, race still accounted for 9.2% of the variance, leaving an 11 points difference unexplained. This is still quite large, and again we attributed the finding to historical discrimination impacting opportunities for quality education and career advancement.

Across these two studies, we observed that SES variables exhibited much more explanatory power for children and adolescent than adults, possibly suggesting a historical trend across generations. So we examined WAIS-IV FSIQ scores by racial/ethnic group for five birth cohorts from 1917 to 1991. There was a striking trend of increasing FSIQ scores with younger generations. WAIS-IV FSIQ scores increased by more than one-half of a standard deviation for adults born between 1988 and 1991 as compared to those born between 1917 and 1942. During the same period, the gap between AA and White means decreased by 9.3 points, and the gap between Hispanic/White means decreased by 8.6 points. Many historical, legal, and cultural factors have likely contributed to the significant reduction observed in the IQ gap across generations. But, the fact that score gaps remain for younger generations, though significantly reduced in magnitude, suggests that historical discrimination in educational access, employment, and career advancement opportunities continues to impede racial/ethnic equity to some degree even today.

WISC-V Findings

Now, we return our attention to WISC-V. Table 5.4 shows the analyses for the AA/White comparison. In model 1, we regress FSIQ on race. As shown in the table, race accounts for 8.9% of the variance in FSIQ score, or 12.8 points.[2] In model 2, we introduce parent education as a mediator and examine the reduction in variance accounted for by racial group after controlling for parent education.[3] As shown in Table 4, parent education alone accounts for 17.6% of the variance

---

2. The results in these analyses may differ slightly from the mean FSIQ difference reported above based on use of the standardization oversample, which is slightly larger than the standardization sample. The oversample was used because it includes more Hispanic and AA subjects than the standardization sample.

3. Parent education was blocked into four levels as follows: less than 12th grade, high school graduate, some college, and college graduate or higher. When both parents were living in the home, the average of the two levels of education was used.

TABLE 5.4 Regression Analyses of Parent Education (PED) and Income as Mediators of White/African-American Differences in Children's Full Scale IQ ($n = 1804$)

	R-sq	R-sq	Percentage of White/African-American Effect Mediated	Mean Difference Between White/African-American After Mediation
Model 1				
Race	0.089			12.838
Model 2				
PED	0.176			
PED, race	0.210	0.034	61.8%	8.349
Model 3				
PED	0.176			
PED, income	0.208			
PED, income, race	0.227	0.019	78.7%	6.651

in FSIQ between the AA and W samples—which is substantially larger than the variance accounted for by race alone (8.9%). Controlling for parent education level reduces the amount of variance in FSIQ attributed to race alone by 61.8%, from 8.9 to 3.4%. The remaining mean difference between the AA and White samples is 8.3 FSIQ points. As described earlier, parent education is only a rough indicator of SES. Therefore, in model 3 we introduce household income as an additional mediator together with parent education. Parent income explains an additional 3.2% of the variance in FSIQ between groups after controlling for parent education. Together, these two indicators of SES explain 20.8% of the variance in FSIQ scores. Controlling for both parent education and income reduces the variance attributed to race alone by 78.8%. The remaining variance accounted for by racial status is 1.9%. This translates to a mean difference of 6.6 FISQ points between the AA and White samples after taking into account parent education and income. Future researchers should use more sophisticated measures of SES (e.g., zip code or block or residence), and study the incremental effects of controlling for additional variables such as school quality, neighborhood safety, sickle cell disease, etc.

Table 5.5 applies the same methodology to the Hispanic and White, non-Hispanic samples. Model 1 shows that ethnic status accounts for 3% of the variance in FSIQ scores between groups, which amounts to 6.7 FSIQ points.

TABLE 5.5 Regression Analyses of Parent Education and Income as Mediators of White/Hispanic Differences in Children's Full Scale IQ ($n = 1882$)

	R-sq	R-sq	Percentage of White/ Hispanic Effect Mediated	Mean Difference Between White/ Hispanic After Mediation
Model 1				
Ethnicity	0.030			6.702
Model 2				
PED	0.171			
PED, ethnicity	0.172	0.001	96.7%	1.285
Model 3				
PED	0.171			
PED, income	0.188			
PED, income, ethnicity	0.188	0.000	98.6%	0.883

Model 2 shows that parent education alone accounts for 17.1% of the variance, and controlling for parent education reduces the variance in FSIQ accounted for by ethnic group by 96.7%, leaving a mean difference of slightly more than 1 FSIQ point between the Hispanic and White, non-Hispanic samples. In model 3, parent income contributed an additional 1.7% of variance in FSIQ scores, reducing the variance explained by ethnicity by 98.6%. The remaining mean difference between the White and Hispanic FSIQ mean scores was slightly less than 1 point after controlling for parent education and household income.

We next explored the impact of the number of parents living in the home on children's cognitive ability test scores. Table 5.6 shows mean WISC-V FSIQ scores for children in single versus dual parent families by racial/ethnic group. As anticipated, children of dual parent families obtain higher mean FSIQ scores than single parent families of the same race by 4 to 6 points on average. It may be that single parents simply have less time available to engage in linguistically and cognitively stimulating activities with their children. As noted above, single parent families also have more difficulty sustaining daily routines and this has been related to outcome in developmentally delayed children. Alternatively, recent parental separation or divorce may temporarily depress cognitive functioning for some children who are experiencing emotional distress at the time of testing. Further, reduced household income may reduce access to quality

TABLE 5.6 WISC-V FSIQ Scores of Children in Single Versus Dual Parent Families by Racial/Ethnic Group

	Single Parent Families	Dual Parent Families	Difference	t	p	Effect Size
AA	87.2	92.1	4.9	2.97	<.01	0.32
Hispanic	92.8	96.7	3.8	2.74	<.01	0.26
White	96.9	103.5	6.6	6.20	<.01	0.44

schools and other positive environmental influences. Thus, single versus dual parent family status may be another variable contributing to test score differences between racial/ethnic groups.

In our previous research with WISC-IV, we found no effect in the Hispanic group for single versus dual parent families (Weiss et al., 2006). In the present research, an effect was present for Hispanics, but it was smaller than the effect for either AA or Whites. Having one or two parents in the home makes a smaller difference in the cognitive test scores of Hispanic versus AA or White children. This finding requires further research to explain. The possible differential role of extended families across groups may be an appropriate focus of investigation to explain this finding.

In our previous work with WISC-IV, we found that the number of parents living in the home accounts for 2% of the variance in FSIQ between AA and Whites, reducing the AA/White FSIQ difference by 30% (Weiss et al., 2006). However, when parent education and income were entered into the model first, the incremental effect of parental status was zero.

Theoretically, if differential exposure to cognitively enriching environments fully explains IQ test score differences between groups then fully controlling for cognitive enrichment should eliminate the observed score differences. Thus, it is interesting that the effect of parent education and household income almost completely explains the FSIQ gap between the Hispanic and White samples, but only partially explains the gap between AA and White FSIQ scores. This suggests that parent education and income may relate to cognitive ability scores in a somewhat different manner for AAs than Hispanics, or that additional indirect variables remain unaccounted for.

Why do some studies still show differences in IQ test scores between the AA and White groups even after matching for critical variables such as parent education, income, and the number of parents living in the home? Part of the answer is that these variables exert their effects indirectly, and are therefore called distal rather them proximal. Alternatively, unmeasured inequities in societal forces may dampen the positive effects of education and income for AAs.

The indirect nature of the effect, as we discussed above, means that the relationship is not perfect. These are "proxy" variables. That is, they serve as convenient indicators of other variables that are difficult to measure directly. The level of education attained by the child's parent or parents is a powerful demographic variable influencing cognitive ability scores. Although not perfectly correlated with the financial situation of the family, this variable serves as a reasonable proxy for overall socioeconomic status. Parent education is, in turn, related to a host of important variables including the parents' employment opportunities, income level, housing, neighborhood, access to prenatal care, adequacy of nutrition during infancy and early development, and the quality of educational experience available to the child. Much of this may have to do with enriched early stimulation and opportunity to learn and grow in a safe and secure environment. Researchers assume that parents with more education have better access to pediatric care, quality schools, and safe neighborhoods—but this is not always the case. To date, no matched studies have been accomplished that directly control for all medical, societal, legal, environmental, financial, and educational factors known to account for variance in cognitive development. In addition to being limited by the use of proxy variables, the available studies are typically cross-sectional rather than longitudinal.

More generally, results from scholarly studies (such as those reviewed in this chapter) provide invaluable information that informs psychologists, sociologists, political scientists, and others about group characteristics. However, psychology is unique in its commitment to understand an individual's differences. Although research studies may provide helpful insights as to qualities that enhance or attenuate cognitive development for groups, psychologists must not assume that the group data characterize every individual being assessed. When we uncritically apply group-level research findings in our clinical practices we may inadvertently stereotype the very children who were referred to us for help.

It is for all of these reasons that we wish to leave behind the study of racial/ethnic differences in cognitive ability test scores and turn the reader's attention to proximal mediators of children's cognitive development, such as what occurs between parent and child in the home. Our direction is influenced by calls from Helms et al. (2005) to cease the use of race as an independent variable in psychological research. This direction is also consistent with recent advances in the study of the human genome that have led writers from diverse academic disciplines to argue that race is a socially constructed and biologically meaningless concept (Cavalli-Sforza, 2001; Marks, 2002; Schwartz, 2001), whereas others suggest that the division lines between racial/ethnic groups are highly fluid and that far more variation exists within genetic groups than between them (Foster & Sharp, 2002, p. 848). Further, despite the lightening pace of recent advances in genetics, attempts to establish genes for intelligence have so far found only weak effects, been inconclusive, or failed to replicate (Chorney et al., 1998; Hill, Chorney, & Plomin, 2002; Hill et al., 1999; Plomin et al., 1995).

At some point in the future, we expect that researchers will cease using racial/ethnic status groupings because of the fluidity of racial boundaries and the wide variability of culture and language within racial and ethnic groups. Future researchers may wish to study how socially constructed concepts of culture mediate development of the particular cognitive abilities assessed by most major intelligence tests in industrialized countries.

At this point, we leave behind the study of racial/ethnic differences in intelligence, and hope that others will do the same. We now turn the proverbial corner and begin a preliminary discussion of home environment variables that enhance children's cognitive development within and across cultural groups. In the remainder of this chapter, we present initial data regarding home environment and language variables, and impact on cognitive development and cognitive ability test scores.

FURTHER CONSIDERATIONS OF HOME ENVIRONMENT ON INTELLECTUAL AND ACADEMIC DEVELOPMENT OF CHILDREN

Many of the SES-related variables typically studied in intelligence research are assumed to operate on children's development in two ways. First, there are the distal effects of the environment in terms of school quality, neighborhood safety, medical care, etc. Many of these are assumed to be captured indirectly by parent education and income level. Second, there are the proximal effects of how parents interact with children in terms of providing linguistically, intellectually, and academically stimulating and encouraging environments. Parent–child interactions may or may not be related to parent education and income. We treat these variables separately because, unlike SES, parents' behaviors and attitudes are more within their immediate control.

Implicit assumptions are often made about the manner in which more educated mothers interact with their children in different ways from mothers with less formal education. More educated mothers are assumed to provide increased language stimulation to infants and toddlers, read more often to preschool-age children, assist elementary school children more with homework, and generally provide more intellectually stimulating activities throughout childhood and adolescence. This is a broadly sweeping assumption that deserves to be examined in more detail. It is quite possible that there is considerable variability in parenting practices within SES groups, and that this variability influences the cognitive development of children.

Research with the WPPSI-III suggests that three home environment variables play an important role in the development of verbal abilities among young children. These variables are the number of hours per week that the parents spend reading to the child, that the child spends on the computer, and that the child spends viewing television. Mean WPPSI-III Verbal IQ (VIQ) scores increased with number of hours spent reading and on the computer, and decreased with number of hours watching television. There is also a clear relationship between these variables and parent education. Number of hours spent reading and on the computer systematically increased with parent education, whereas number of hours spent watching television decreased. Thus, relative to parents with little formal education, more educated parents read to their children more often, discourage television watching, and encourage computer use. Further, children aged 2½ to 7 who were read to more often, used computers more often, watched less television, and had higher VIQ scores on average (Sichi, 2003). Perhaps SES plays a role in the availability of computers in the home, and the opportunity to interact with children in cognitively stimulating ways (i.e., reading to them versus allowing excessive television watching) in busy single parent versus dual employment families. At the same time, however, there was substantial variability in the frequency of these behaviors within levels of parent education. *Thus, even among young children whose parents have similar levels of education, spending more time reading and using the computer, and less time watching television, is associated with higher verbal ability test scores.*

Next, we explore the proximal effects of parental attitudes on school-age children. We selected four items from a larger questionnaire completed by parents of children in the WISC-V standardization sample ($n = 2419$). Parents were asked four simple questions: How likely is it that your child will achieve good grades in school, graduate from high school, graduate from college, and find better employment than yourself? Each question was rated on a 4-point scale ranging from not likely to very likely. These four questions clearly relate to parental expectations regarding the child's academic and occupational success. We assume that parents communicate these expectations to a child in a multitude of ways, both direct and indirect, during the course of their developmental years.

To analyze the effects of parental expectation on cognitive ability test scores, we return to the mediator analysis methodology described above—but with a different focus. The dependent variable is no longer the *gap* in FSIQ scores between groups, but the FSIQ score itself—for the total group of children combined across all racial and ethnic groups. Thus, we are no longer seeking to explain the gap in FSIQ scores between racial/ethnic groups, but seeking to understand the effect of parental expectations across groups.

Table 5.7 shows these analyses. For all children, the combination of parent education and income explains approximately 22% of the variance in FSIQ scores. Parent expectations alone explain approximately 26.5% of the variance in FSIQ scores across all children. *Thus, parental expectations alone explain more variance in children's FSIQ scores than parent education and income combined.* This is interesting because previous researchers have assumed that parent level of education has the most powerful effect on cognitive test scores. When all three variables are considered in combination (i.e., parent education, income, and expectations) the model explains approximately 37% of the variance in children's FSIQ scores.

But, are parent expectations simply a function of parent education and income? Do more educated and wealthier parents simply have higher expectations for their children? We examine this hypothesis in models 2 and 3 of Table 5.7. In model 2,

TABLE 5.7 Regression Analyses of Parent Expectations as Mediator Among Parent Education and Income on Children's Full Scale IQ

	R-sq	R-sq	Percentage of Effect Mediated
Overall (n = 2419)			
Model 1			
PED, income	0.219		
Model 2			
PEX	0.265		
PEX, PED, income	0.373	0.108	50.7%
Model 3			
PED, income	0.219		
PED, income, PEX	0.373	0.154	41.9%
6–11 Years Old (n = 1328)			
Model 1			
PED, income	0.234		
Model 2			
PEX	0.285		
PEX, PED, income	0.391	0.106	54.7%
Model 3			
PED, income	0.234		
PED, income, PEX	0.391	0.157	44.9%
12–16 Years Old (n = 1091)			
Model 1			
PED, income	0.212		
Model 2			
PEX	0.271		
PEX, PED, income	0.384	0.113	46.7%
Model 3			
PED, income	0.212		
PED, income, PEX	0.384	0.172	36.5%

we find that parent education and income explains only 10.8% of the variance in children's FSIQ scores after parental expectations are controlled. This is a 51% reduction in explanatory power of parent education and income from 21.9 to 10.8% due to the effect of parental expectations.

Next, we examined the reverse question in model 3; how much do parental expectations matter after accounting for parent education and income? As shown in model 3, parental expectations still account for approximately 15.4% of the variance in children's FSIQ scores after controlling for parent education and income. Although the explanatory power of parental expectations declines by 42% after controlling for parent education and income, the size of the remaining effect for parental expectations is substantial.

We were concerned, however, that these data simply reflect the accumulated feedback parents receive about their children's abilities and future potential from various environmental sources such as teachers, community leaders, and even employers for older teenagers. We hypothesized that parents of older children would have received more environmental feedback and would thus have more accurate expectations based on their children's true intellectual abilities. So, we repeated the analyses separately for younger (aged 6–11) and older (aged 12–16) children. Although the explanatory power of parental expectations rose slightly for older children, the increase was relatively small (from 15.7 to 17.2%). More to the point, the effect of parental expectations was substantial for children of all ages.

In our previous work with WISC-IV (Weiss et al., 2006), we regressed FSIQ on parent expectations within levels of parent education. We found that parental expectations were significantly related to FSIQ scores at all levels of parent education, but more so among parents with high school educations ($R^2 = .28$) and least among parents who did not graduate high school ($R^2 = .19$). We interpret these findings in relation to the impact of distal environmental resources on proximal attitudes and behaviors. It may be that real societal and economic factors constrain the power of parent expectations among the lowest SES families. *Still, parent expectations remain a powerful force among all SES groups, just not as powerful among parents who did not graduate high school. Parent expectations appear most influential among middle SES families where parents have graduated high school but not attended college.* Although no data exist to explain this finding, we wonder if children in these families may be mostly on the brink of moving either up or down the SES continuum in adulthood depending on their personal effort, and thus parental expectations are particularly influential.

We also examined the hypothesis that parent expectations operate differently across cultures by examining the effect of parental expectations on the WISC-IV FSIQ gap between racial/ethnic groups after controlling for parent education and income. The remaining variance attributable to parent expectations was approximately 15% for the AA/White FSIQ gap analysis, and 18% for the Hispanic/White FSIQ gap analysis—suggesting that the effect of parent expectations is substantial across cultural and linguistically diverse groups (Weiss et al., 2006).

To recap, parent education and income combined explain approximately 22% of the variance in children's FSIQ, whereas parental expectations alone explain approximately 26.5%. In combination, these three variables explain about 37% of the variability in the measurement of cognitive ability across all children. The effect of parent expectations is only partially accounted for by parent education and income, and the remaining variance attributable to parent expectation is meaningful. Further, parent expectations appear to account for similar amounts of variance in children's FSIQ scores in the AA/White and Hispanic/White comparisons. Although there may be systematic differences in parental expectations across levels of parent education, parental expectations still predict substantial variance in the measurement of children's cognitive abilities within each level of parent education.

The explanatory power of this simple parent expectation variable is both surprising and encouraging. The possibility that parental expectations, attitudes, and behaviors can positively influence the development of cognitive abilities in children of all demographic backgrounds is very exciting, though perhaps a bit naive as well. Do parents express these expectations differently across SES groups? Are there cultural differences in parent expectations that simply mirror differences in standardized test scores? These are all important questions that do not yet have irrefutable data-based answers. However, the analyses above suggest that this may not be the case. Parent's expectations accounted for substantial variance in FSIQ after controlling for two indicators of SES (parent education and income), and a possible indicator of culture (racial/ethnic group). On the other hand, racial/ethnic group is not synonymous with culture, and perhaps more sophisticated measures of cultural or familial beliefs and values will identify systematic differences in parent expectations. For now, however, the data presented above suggest that whatever cultural differences may be captured by simple racial/ethnic group status do not account for substantial differences in the power of parental expectations in children's academic performance.

The psychosocial mechanisms by which parental expectations are translated into specific behaviors in the home, what those behaviors are, whether they vary by culture, and how they increase cognitive ability test scores is an important frontier for potentially fruitful research into contextual interpretation. As Ceci (1996) suggests, these behaviors may differ at different critical stages of cognitive development. Clearly, reading to a preschool child will be more effective than reading to a preadolescent child. Also, playing rhyming games with early elementary children may facilitate the acquisition of phonological awareness, which is critical to the development of early reading skills, but rhyming games with older children who have reading comprehension difficulties may be less effective. When more is known about the timing, and active ingredients of home environment behaviors, and how these may vary across cultures, practitioners will be in a better position to intervene with families of children at risk for cognitive delays or learning disorders.

Jirout and Newcombe (in press) found that when parents engage in interactive play at home with their preschool age-children using blocks, puzzles, board games, and drawing materials the children have significantly better developed visual–spatial abilities. This is particularly useful in light of the finding reported above that AA children tend to score lower on the VSI than the other WISC-V indexes. These authors also found that playing word games had a significant effect, and suggested that parents who engage in playful cognitive interactions with preschool children are facilitating their general intellectual growth. Perhaps these parents have what Carole Dweck called a "growth mindset" with regard to cognitive abilities (see above).

As Gregoire observes (see Chapter 6 on the Flynn effect), the relationship of educational achievement and intelligence is difficult to untangle because it is reciprocal. Intelligence is widely accepted to be the best single predictor of success in school. At the same time, there are positive effects of schooling on the intellectual development of children. Based on several previous studies, Ceci (1996) showed that education stimulates the development of several skills that play an important role in intelligence tests, especially perceptual skills, concept formation, and memory. In fact, this view forms the basis for early intervention and Head Start programs for young children who are developmentally delayed or socioeconomically disadvantaged. Further, improvements to educational systems and access to education are often considered to be one of the primary causes of increases in IQ test scores across the generations, known as the Flynn effect. In a longitudinal study of 2000 identical twins, Ritchie (in press) found that better than average reading skills from age 7 may positively affect children's intellectual abilities in late adolescence. We believe that the rigorous cognitive demands of academic learning in school stimulate development of key cognitive abilities related to intelligence.

These lines of thinking led us to examine the academic monitoring behaviors of parents in relationship to academic achievement test scores on the WIAT-III using data from the WISC-V home environment questionnaire, an unpublished research instrument collected with the standardization sample. We examined a set of 11 questions related to homework routines and parents' academic monitoring behaviors, and identified those with moderate correlations between .20 and .30. How often parents talked to their children about school had a consistently positive effect on achievement test scores for children of all ages. For younger children (aged 6–11), ensuring that they do their homework at the same time each day and asking to see the completed assignments was important. Surprisingly, having a quiet spot to do homework, and turning off electronics while doing homework, was unrelated to achievement at any age.

However, asking older children to see their completed assignments, checking and helping with their assignments, and checking their backpacks for notes and assignments were all inversely related to achievement. Perhaps parents only employ these more intrusive tactics with older children when they are underachieving in school. For older children, asking if they have homework and talking with them about school were positively correlated with achievement. It seems that the simple act of talking with children of any age about school sends an important message that school is important and their parents care about how they do in school. In addition, we found that the amount of time older children spend doing homework was positively correlated with achievement—suggesting that personal factors such as the student's motivation and conscientiousness come into play at these ages, as discussed above.

Still, it is possible that parents know their children's abilities better than anyone, and adjust their expectations and monitoring behaviors accordingly based on feedback from teachers and other sources. We acknowledge that the effect of parent expectations on children's cognitive abilities is probably not unidirectional, but reciprocally interactive. That is, naturally bright children stimulate their parents toward higher quality interactions with them, which, in turn, motivates the child toward intellectually and academically enriching pursuits that further stimulate cognitive development. At the same time, children with limited intellectual endowment may stimulate their parents to have lower expectations for them, monitor them more closely, and steer the child away from intellectual and academic growth activities. There are many factors that may account for the co-variation of parental expectations and FSIQ beyond the parents' education, income, and knowledge of their children's abilities. For example, the parent's motivation for upward mobility or fear of downward mobility is an area for future researchers to investigate. Thus, although parental expectations are worthy of research studies, at the individual level the reasons for those expectations may be far worthier of clinical exploration.

CONCLUSIONS REGARDING HOME ENVIRONMENT AND COGNITIVE DEVELOPMENT

How parental expectations are translated into parental behaviors and the mechanisms by which these behaviors act on children's cognitive development needs further research including more complex modeling and longitudinal studies. But, it seems reasonable to hypothesize that there are both general factors (such as parental monitoring) and specific factors (such as the form of monitoring), which vary by age, developmental level, and familial or cultural context.

In a comprehensive review of intelligence testing and minority students, Valencia and Suzuki (2001) drew several major conclusions and cautions from the literature on home environment (pp. 108–110). First, and most importantly, intellectually stimulating and supportive home environments tend to produce bright children. Although it is easy to assume that the direction of the effect is from parent to child, Valencia and Suzuki remind us that it is equally possible that bright children capture the attention of parents who respond to them in stimulating ways that further the child's cognitive growth. Second, measures of home environment are more accurate predictors of children's measured intelligence than SES. Although SES is a good global predictor, we are reminded that families within each SES stratum differ considerably in the ways in which intellectual climate is structured in the home and in the amounts of stimulation provided. Third, most of the research on minority families has demonstrated significantly positive correlations between home environment and children's intellectual performance. Although there probably are some commonalities in what constitutes a cognitively enriching environment, the specific expression of these characteristics may vary across cultures. Fourth, these studies can be taken together to debunk the view that low SES families cannot raise intelligent children. Clearly, specific in-home behaviors are as important, if not more important, than the parents' income, occupation, or education. Stated succinctly, *what parents do is more important than what they are*. This is critical, because SES can be difficult for families to change. But, as shown in a series of field studies more than a quarter of a century ago, low SES minority parents can be trained effectively to teach specific intellectual skills to their children and to influence their motivation toward academic activities (Henderson & Garcia, 1973; Henderson & Swanson, 1974; Swanson & Henderson, 1976). Such intervention programs, however, must be sensitive to cultural differences in the specific expression of cognitively stimulating behaviors, and the ways in which these are taught and reinforced. The same home environment factors may interact in differing ways in school systems outside the U.S. or when measured by other methods. We also must be cognizant of Ceci's (1996) caution that distal environmental resources can limit the effectiveness of these proximal processes in the home environment. In other words, severely impoverished environments may constrain the influence of parent expectations, but do not eliminate it.

The WISC-V findings reported in this chapter are important and have significant implications for practice. Although SES (as estimated by parent education and income) explains considerable variance in IQ test scores at the group level, these findings suggest that children born into low SES families are not predetermined to have lower cognitive ability and that parents can play an important role in enhancing their children's cognitive development, thus improving their educational and occupational opportunities as young adults. Understanding the types of parental behaviors that enrich or stimulate cognitive development as compared to those that inhibit or stifle intellectual growth is a critical activity for scholars and practitioners alike. But, identifying these behaviors is only the first step. The timing of these behaviors within critical developmental periods must also be understood. Further, developing culturally sensitive models for communicating these findings to parents of different backgrounds and cultures, and for training parents to effectively implement these ideas in their homes, is essential.

These are not new ideas. Most elementary school teachers can easily distinguish students whose parents work with them at home from those who do not. And, teachers will readily empathize with the difficulty of changing parental behavior relating to academic monitoring of children. But, these findings suggest that the benefits for children can be large enough to warrant sustained effort. We strongly encourage psychologists and teachers to speak directly with parents about these in-home behaviors, the benefits of them for their children, doing so at the earliest possible ages, and regular follow-up. Available research suggests that it can be influential to engage parents in conversations about what they do at home to monitor their children's homework and class projects, encouraging quiet time for reading together or independently, limiting time spent watching TV, encouraging computer use (at the local library if necessary), and positively communicating expectations for academic success.

Overall, this is a very positive message for the fields of psychology and education. Initially, we had been concerned that reporting IQ differences between groups of children based on static demographic characteristics such as parent education or income could inhibit the potential of individual children in these groups by reducing expectations for them. But, the variability within these groups combined with the finding that parent's interactions with children in the home can ameliorate the impact of low SES and other relatively fixed demographic characteristics encourages us to give voice to hope. If readers remember only one sentence from this chapter, we would want them to remember this: *Demographics is not destiny.* This is the main contribution of our chapter that began with our previous chapters presented in our books on the WISC-IV and WAIS-IV.

Although we have attempted to make a strong case in favor of interpreting cognitive ability scores in concert with home environment variables, we also believe it is possible to take such interpretations too far. Mercer and Lewis (1978) developed adjusted IQ scores for the WISC-R based on myriad variables including income, urban versus rural status, family size, parent education, etc. Thus, children from families with different incomes and numbers of children would be given "IQ" scores that were different despite answering the same number of questions correctly. Although noble in its intent, this effort served to confuse interpretation of IQ test scores, and researchers did not offer these types of adjustments for subsequent editions of WISC. Our approach with WISC-V is to retain a population-based reference group for the IQ and index scores, while simultaneously providing supplemental information that encourages culturally sensitive interpretation of IQ scores within the context of the child's unique home environment. We refer the reader to Chapter 7 on testing Hispanics.

SUMMARY

In this chapter we lay the foundation for a model of contextual interpretation. Along with others (Saklofske, van de Vijver, Oakland, Mpofu, & Suzuki, in press), we argue that an evaluation of sociocultural-economic context should be part of the nuts and bolts of a general practice model of clinical assessment. Practitioners should pay attention to context in order to test cognitive hypotheses for referral problems in relation to the child's family and community, and to differentiate effective intervention strategies.

We have made a case that while racial/ethnic differences in cognitive ability tests exist, they are not due to item or test bias, nor are they unique with respect to many other areas of life. Further, racial/ethnic differences are likely a proxy for a multitude of other variables that we are just beginning to identify and study. Still, these differences have important implications for individual students in need of educational assistance as well as contribute— along with variability in pre-referral methods and funding mechanisms across local and state education authorities—to disproportionate representation of culturally and linguistically diverse students in special education programs. We make the point that disproportionate representation in special education may partially reflect the disproportionate risk experienced by ethnically diverse children living in low SES environments. We present the case that intelligence tests do not measure pure intelligence, but some combination of innate ability and learning based on interactions with the environment; and that environments vary on critical dimensions that differentially enhance or impede cognitive development. Perhaps most importantly, we argue that cognitive growth is malleable, within limits, based on environmental opportunities for cognitive development. We have shown that SES, as estimated by parent education and income, accounts for a large portion of the variance in children's intelligence test scores between racial/ethnic groups. More importantly, we have shown that substantial variability in cognitive test scores can be explained by home environment behaviors such as parental expectations of children's academic success, even after controlling for parent education and income. Although low SES environments place children at risk for cognitive delay, and many other health factors, the negative cognitive effects of low SES can be mitigated by the expectations that parents have for their children's success, how they interact with children in the home with regard to providing language and cognitive stimulation, reading to children, monitoring schoolwork and learning, and more. It is for these reasons that we offer a voice of hope and encourage practitioners to involve families in the treatment of children at risk for cognitive delays and learning disorders. Similarly, we suggest that researchers systematically study the critical development periods in which specific types of cognitive stimulation are most effectively applied by parents and teachers, and how such interventions may need to be modified for diverse group styles reflected in culture and ethnicity. Therein lies a meaningful life's work!

REFERENCES

American Education Research Association, American Psychological Association, & National Council on Measurement in Education. (2014). *The standards for educational and psychological testing.* Washington, DC: American Psychological Association.

Benasich, A. A., Choudhury, N. A., Realpe-Bonilla, T., & Roesler, C. P. (2014). Plasticity in developing brains: Active exposure impacts prelinguistic acoustic mapping. *The Journal of Neuroscience, 34*(40), 13349–13363.

Bloom, B. S. (1964). *Stability and change in human characteristics.* New York: John Wiley.

Bouman, S.H. (2010). Response to intervention in California public schools: Has it helped address disproportional placement rates for students with learning disabilities? (Unpublished doctoral dissertation). Claremont College, Claremont, California.

Bowden, S. C., Lange, R. T., Weiss, L. G., & Saklofske, D. (2008). Equivalence of the measurement model underlying the Wechsler Adult Intelligence Scale-III in the United States and Canada. *Educational and Psychological Measurement, 68*(6), 1024–1040.

Bowden, S. C., Lissner, D., McCarthy, K. A., Weiss, L. G., & Holdnack, J. A. (2003). Equivalence of WAIS-III standardization data collected in Australia when compared to data collected in the US. CNN Satellite Symposium of the Australian Psychological Society Conference. Perth.

Bowden, S. C., Lloyd, D., Weiss, L. G., & Holdnack, J. A. (2006). Age related invariance of abilities measured with the Wechsler Adult Intelligence Scale–III. *Psychological Assessment, 18*(3), 334–339.

Bradley, R. H., & Caldwell, B. M. (1978). Screening the environment. *American Journal of Orthopsychiatry, 48*, 114–130.

Bradley, R. H., & Caldwell, B. M. (1981). The HOME inventory: A validation of the preschool for Black children. *Child Development, 53*, 708–710.

Bradley, R. H., & Caldwell, B. M. (1982). The consistency of the home environment and its relation to child development. *International Journal of Behavioral Development, 5*, 445–465.

Bradley, R. H., Caldwell, B. M., & Elardo, R. (1977). Home environment, social status, and mental test performance. *Journal of Educational Psychology, 69*, 697–701.

Bradley, R. H., Caldwell, B. M., Rock, S., Barnard, K., Gray, C., Hammond, M., et al. (1989). Home environment and cognitive development in the first three years of life: A collaborative study involving six sites and three ethnic groups in North America. *Developmental Psychology, 28*, 217–235.

Bronfenbrenner, U. (1992). Ecological systems theory. In R. Vasta (Ed.), *Six theories of child development: Revised formulations and current issues* (pp. 187–249). Ithaca, NY: Cornell University Department of Human Development and Family Studies.

Bronfenbrenner, U. (2004). *Making human beings human: Bioecological perspectives on human development*. Thousand Oaks, CA: Sage Publications.

Bronfenbrenner, U., & Ceci, S. J. (1994). Nature–nurture reconceptualized in developmental perspective: A bio-ecological model. *Psychological Review, 101*, 568–586.

Brooks-Gunn, J., Klebanov, P. K., & Duncan, G. J. (1996). Ethnic differences in children's intelligence test scores: Role of economic deprivation, home environment, and maternal characteristics. *Child Development, 67*, 396–408.

Burhan, N. A. S., Mohamad, M. R., Kurniawan, Y., & Sidek, A. H. (2014). The impact of low, average, and high IQ on economic growth and technological progress: Do all individuals contribute equally? *Intelligence, 46*, 1–8.

Caldwell, B. M., & Bradley, R. (1984). *Home observation for the measurement of the environment*. Little Rock, AR: Authors.

Cattell, R. (1949). *Culture free intelligence test, scale 1, handbook*. Champaign, IL: Institute of Personality and Ability.

Cavalli-Sforza, L. L. (2001). *Genes, peoples, and languages*. Berkeley, CA: University of California Press.

Ceci, S. J. (1991). How much does schooling influence general intelligence and its cognitive components? A reassessment of the evidence. *Developmental Psychology, 27*(5), 703–722.

Ceci, S. J. (1996). *On intelligence: A bioecological treatise on intellectual development* (expanded edition). Cambridge, MA: Harvard University Press.

Ceci, S. J., & Bronfenbrenner, U. (2004). Heredity, environment, and the question of "how?". In U. Bronfenbrenner (Ed.), *Making human beings human: Bioecological perspectives on human development* (pp. 150–180). Thousand Oaks, CA: Sage Publications.

Ceci, S. J., & Williams, W. M. (1999). *The nature-nurture debate: The essential readings.* Oxford: Blackwell Publishers Ltd.

Centers for Disease Control and Prevention. (2012). *Suicide rates among persons ages 10–24 years, by race/ethnicity and sex, United States, 2005–2009.* Retrieved from: <http://www.cdc.gov/violenceprevention/suicide/statistics/rates03.html>. Accessed 26.06.14.

Centers for Disease Control and Prevention. (2013). CDC health disparities and inequalities report—United States. *2013 MMWR 2013, 62*(Suppl. 3).

Chapin, J. R. (2006). The achievement gap in social studies and science starts early: Evidence from the early childhood longitudinal study. *Social Studies, 97*(6), 231–238.

Chatterji, M. (2005). Achievement gaps and correlates of early mathematics achievement: Evidence from the ECLS K-first grade sample. *Education Policy Analysis Archives, 13*(46), 1–35.

Child Trends. (2013). *Homeless children and youth.* Retrieved from: <http://www.childtrends.org/?indicators=homeless-children-and-youth>. Accessed 25.06.14.

Chorney, M. J., Chorney, K., Seese, N., Owen, M. J., Daniels, J., McGuffin, P., et al. (1998). A quantitative trait locus associated with cognitive ability in children. *Psychological Science, 9,* 159–166.

Cook, B. L., Zuvekas, S. H., Carson, N., Wayne, G. F., Vesper, A., & McGuire, T. G. (2014). Assessing racial/ethnic disparities in treatment across episodes of mental health care. *Health Services Research, 49*(1), 206–229.

Csikszentmihalyi, M., & Robinson, R. E. (1986). Culture, time, and the development of talent. In R. J. Sternberg & J. E. Davidson (Eds.), *Conceptions of giftedness* (pp. 264–284). New York: Cambridge University Press.

Deary, I. J., Whiteman, M. C., Starr, J. M., Whalley, L. J., & Fox, H. C. (2004). The impact of childhood intelligence on later life: Following up the Scottish mental surveys of 1932 and 1947. *Journal of Personality and Social Psychology, 86*(1), 130–147.

Diamond, M. C., Lay, F., Rhodes, H., Lindner, R., Rosenzweig, M. R., Krech, D., et al. (1966). Increases in cortical depth and glia numbers in rats subjected to enriched environment. *Journal of Comparative Neurology, 128*(1), 117–125.

Dickinson, D. K., & DeTemple, J. (1998). Putting parents in the picture: Maternal reports of preschoolers' literacy as a predictor of early reading. *Early Childhood Research Quarterly, 13,* 241–261.

Duckworth, A. L., & Seligman, M. E. P. (2005). Self-discipline outdoes IQ in predicting academic performance of adolescents. *Psychological Science, 16*(12), 939–944.

Duckworth, A. L., Quinn, P. D., & Tsukayama, E. (2012). What no child left behind leaves behind: The roles of IQ and self-control in predicting standardized achievement test scores and report card grades. *Journal of Educational Psychology, 104*(2), 439–457.

Dweck, C. S. (2012). Mindsets & human nature: Promoting change. *American Psychologist, 67*(8), 614–622.

Epstein, J. L. (1991). Effects on student achievement of teachers' practices of parent involvement. In S. B. Silvern (Ed.), *Advances in reading/language research: Vol. 5. Literacy through family, community, and school interaction* (pp. 61–276). Greenwich, CT: JAI Press.

Fantuzzo, J., McWayne, C., Perry, M. A., & Childs, S. (2004). Multiple dimensions of family involvement and their relations to behavioral and learning competencies for urban, low-income children. *School Psychology Review, 33,* 467–480.

Flynn, J. R. (1984). The mean IQ of Americans: Massive gains 1932 to 1978. *Psychological Bulletin, 95,* 29–51.

Flynn, J. R. (1987). Massive IQ gains in 14 nations. *Psychological Bulletin, 101*, 171–191.

Foster, M. W., & Sharp, R. R. (2002). Race, ethnicity, and genomics: Social classifications as proxies of biological heterogeneity. *Genome Research, 12*, 844–850.

Foster, W. A., & Miller, M. (2007). Development of the literacy achievement gap: A longitudinal study of kindergarten through third grade. *Language, Speech & Hearing Services in Schools, 38*(3), 173–181.

Galper, A., Wigfield, A., & Seefeldt, C. (1997). Head start parents' beliefs about their children's abilities, task values, and performances on different activities. *Child Development, 68*, 897–907.

García, J. I. R. (2012). Mental health care for Latino immigrants in the U.S.A. and the quest for global health equities. Servicios de Salud Mental para los Inmigrantes Latinos en los Estados Unidos y la Lucha por una Igualdad en Salud Global. *Psychosocial Intervention, 21*(3), 305–318.

Georgas, J., Weiss, L. G., Van de Vijver, F. J. R., & Saklofske, D. H. (Eds.), (2003). *Culture and children's intelligence: Cross cultural analysis of the WISC–III*. San Diego, CA: Academic Press.

Goldstein, S., & Brooks, R. B. (2005). *Handbook of resilience in children*. New York: Kluwer Academic/Plenum Publishers.

Gottfredson, L. S. (2008). Of what value is intelligence? In A. Prifitera, D. H. Saklofske, & L. G. Weiss, (Eds.), *WISC-V Clinical Assessment and Intervention*. San Diego, CA: Academic Press.

Gottfredson, L. S., & Saklofske, D. H. (2009). Intelligence: Foundations and issues in assessment. *Canadian Psychology/Psychologie canadienne, 50*(3), 183–195.

Griffith, J. (1996). Relation of parental involvement, empowerment, and school traits to student academic performance. *Journal of Educational Research, 90*, 33–41.

Guo, G., & Harris, K. (2000). The mechanisms mediating the effects of poverty on children's intellectual development. *Demography, 37*(4), 431–447.

Hall, J. D., & Barnett, D. W. (1991). Classification of risk status in preschool screening: A comparison of alternative measures. *Journal of Psychoeducational Assessment, 9*, 152–159.

Harris, D. N. (2007). High-flying schools, student disadvantage, and the logic of NCLB. *American Journal of Education, 113*(3), 367–394.

Harris, J. G., Tulsky, D. S., & Schultheis, M. T. (2003). Assessment of the non-native English speaker: Assimilating history and research findings to guide practice. In S. S. Tulsky, D. H. Saklofske, G. J. Chelune, R. K. Keaton, R. J. Ivnik, & R. Ornstein (Eds.), *Clinical interpretation of the WAIS-III and WMS-III*. San Diego, CA: Elsevier, Inc.

Helms, J. E., Jernigan, M., & Mascher, J. (2005). The meaning of race in psychology and how to change it: A methodological perspective. *American Psychologist, 60*, 27–36.

Henderson, R. W. (1972). Environmental predictors of academic performance of disadvantaged Mexican–American children. *Journal of Consulting and Clinical Psychology, 38*, 297.

Henderson, R. W., & Garcia, A. B. (1973). The effects of a parent training program on the question-asking behavior of Mexican–American children. *American Educational Research Journal, 10*, 193–201.

Henderson, R. W., Bergan, J. R., & Hurt, M., Jr. (1972). Development and validation of the Henderson environmental learning process scale. *Journal of Social Psychology, 88*, 185–196.

Henderson, R. W., & Merritt, C. B. (1968). Environmental background of Mexican–American children with different potentials for school success. *Journal of Social Psychology, 75*, 101–106.

Henderson, R. W., & Swanson, R. A. (1974). Application of social learning principles in a field study. *Exceptional Children, 40*, 53–55.

Hernandez-Finch, M. E. (2012). Special considerations with response to intervention and instruction for students with diverse backgrounds. *Psychology in the Schools, 49*(3), 285–296.

Hill, L., Chorney, M. C., & Plomin, R. (2002). A quantitative trait locus (not) associated with cognitive ability. *Psychological Science, 13*, 561–562.

Hill, L., Craig, I. W., Asherson, P., Ball, D., Eley, T., Ninomiya, T., et al. (1999). DNA pooling and dense marker maps: A systematic search for genes for cognitive ability. *NeuroReport, 10*, 843–848.

Hoff, E. (2003). The specificity of environmental influence: Socioeconomic status affects early vocabulary development Via maternal speech. *Child Development, 74*, 1368–1378.

Hudson, C. G. (2012). Disparities in the geography of mental health: Implications for social work. *Social Work, 57*(2), 107–119.

Hummer, R. A. (1996). Black-white differences in health and mortality: A review and conceptual model. *Sociological Quarterly, 37*(1), 105–125.

Individuals with Disabilities Education Improvement Act of 2004, Pub. L. No. 108-446, 118 Stat. 2647 (2004).

Jensen, A. R. (1998). *The g factor: The science of mental ability.* Westport, CT: Praeger.

Jirout, J., & Newcombe, N. (in press). Building blocks for the development of spatial skills: Evidence from a large representative US sample. *Psychological Science.*

Johnson, D. L., Breckenridge, J., & McGowan, R. (1984). Home environment and early cognitive development in Mexican–American children. In A. W. Gottfried (Ed.), *Home environment and early cognitive development: Longitudinal research* (pp. 151–195). Orlando, FL: Academic Press.

Johnson, D. L., Swank, P., Howie, V. M., Baldwin, C. D., Owen, M., & Luttman, D. (1993). Does HOME add to the prediction of child intelligence over and above SES? *Journal of Genetic Psychology, 154*, 33–40.

Johnson, K. M., & Lichter, D. T. (2010). Growing diversity among America's children and youth: Spatial and temporal dimensions. *Population and Development Review, 36*(1), 151–176.

Kaufman, A. S., Zhou, X., Reynolds, M. R., Kaufman, N. L., Green, G. P., & Weiss, L. G. (2014). The possible societal impact of the decrease in U.S. blood levels on adult IQ. *Environmental Research, 132*, 413–420.

Kayser, H. (1989). Speech and language assessment of Spanish–English speaking children. *Language, Speech, & Hearing Services in Schools, 20*, 226–244.

Keith, T. Z., Keith, P. B., Quirk, K. J., Sperduto, J., Santillo, S., & Killings, S. (1998). Longitudinal effects of parent involvement on high school grades: Similarities and differences across gender and ethnic groups. *Journal of School Psychology, 36*, 335–363.

Konold, T. R., & Canivez, G. L. (2010). Differential relationships among WISC-IV and WIAT-II scales: An evaluation of potentially moderating child demographics. *Educational and Psychological Measurement, 70*(4), 613–627.

LaVeist, T. A. (2005). *Minority populations and health: An introduction to health disparities in the United States.* San Francisco, CA: Jossey-Bass.

Lee, J. C., Yin, H., & Zhang, Z. (2010). Adaptations and analyses of motivated strategies for learning questionnaire in the Chinese setting. *International Journal of Testing, 10*(3), 149–165.

Lopez, M.H. (2013). *Hispanic or Latino? Many don't care, except in Texas.* Retrieved from: <http://www.pewresearch.org/fact-tank/2013/10/28/in-texas-its-hispanic-por-favor/>. Accessed 01.05.14.

Lubinski, D. (Ed.), (2004). Cognitive abilities: 100 years after Spearman's (1904) "General intelligence. Objectively determined and measured" (special section). *Journal of Personality and Social Psychology* (86, pp. 96–199)

Mani, A., Mullainathan, S., Shafir, E., & Zhao, J. (2013). Poverty impedes cognitive function. *Science, 341*(6149), 967–980.

Mantzicopoulos, P. Y. (1997). The relationship of family variables to head start's children's preacademic competence. *Early Education & Development, 8*, 357–375.

Margolin, L. (1994). *Goodness personified: The emergence of gifted children.* New York: Aldine de Gruyter.

Marjoribanks, K. (1979). *Families and their learning environments: An empirical analysis.* London: Routledge & Kegan Paul.

Marks, J. (2002). Folk heredity. In J. M. Fish (Ed.), *Race and intelligence: Separating science from myth* (pp. 95–112). Mahwah, New Jersey: Erlbaum.

Martin, A. J. (2008). *The motivation and engagement scale.* Sydney: Lifelong Achievement Group. Retrieved from: <www.lifelongachievement.com>.

Martin, A. J., & Hau, K. T. (2010). Achievement motivation among Chinese and Australian school students: Assessing differences of kind and differences of degree. *International Journal of Testing, 10*(3), 274–294.

Massey, D. S. (2007). *Categorically unequal: The American stratification system.* New York: Russell Sage Foundation.

Massey, D. S., & Fischer, M. J. (2000). How segregation concentrates poverty. [Article]. *Ethnic & Racial Studies, 23*(4), 670–691.

McVicker Hunt, J. (1961). *Intelligence and experience.* Oxford, England: Ronald.

Mercer, J. R., & Lewis, J. F. (1978). *System of multicultural pluralistic assessment: Technical Manual.* San Antonio, TX: The Psychological Corporation.

Mollgaard, K., Diamond, M. C., Bennett, E. L., Rosenzweig, M. R., & Lindner, B. (1971). Quantitative synaptic changes with differential experience in rat brain. *International Journal of Neuroscience, 2*(3), 113–127.

Murray, C. (2005). The inequality taboo. Commentary, September, 13–22.

National Center for Education Statistics. (2011). *Common core data file.* Retrieved from: <http://nces.ed.gov/ccd/pubagency.asp>. Accessed 26.06.14.

National Center for Education Statistics. (2012). *Digest of education statistics.* Retrieved from: <http://nces.ed.gov/programs/digest/d12/tables_2.asp>. Accessed 30.06.14.

National Center for Education Statistics. (2012a). *Identification of children with disabilities.* Retrieved from: <http://ww2.ed.gov/fund/data/report/idea/partbspap/2013/>. Accessed 30.06.14.

National Center for Education Statistics. (2012b). Retrieved from: <http://www2.ed.gov/fund/data/report/idea/partbspap/2013/fl-acc-stateprofile-11-12.pdf>.

National Center for Education Statistics. (2012c). Retrieved from: <http://www2.ed.gov/fund/data/report/idea/partbspap/2013/il-acc-stateprofile-11-12.pdf>.

National Center for Education Statistics. (2012d). Retrieved from: <http://www2.ed.gov/fund/data/report/idea/partbspap/2013/ny-acc-stateprofile-11-12.pdf>.

Neisser, U. (1998). Introduction: Rising test scores and what they mean. In U. Neisser (Ed.), *The rising curve: Long term gains in IQ and related measures* (pp. 3–22). Washington, DC: American Psychological Association.

Neisser, U., Boodoo, G., Bouchard, T. J., Boykin, A. W., Brody, N., & Ceci, S. J. (1996). Intelligence: Knowns and unknowns. *American Psychologist, 51*(2), 77–101.

Nisbett, R. E. (2009). *Intelligence and how to get it: Why schools and cultures count.* New York: W.W. Norton & Co.

Ong, P. M., & Rickles, J. (2004). The continued nexus between school and residential segregation. *Berkeley La Raza Law Journal, 15*(1), 260–275.

Orosco, M. J., & Klinger, J. (2010). One school's implementation of RtI with English language learners: "Referring into RTI". *Journal of Learning Disabilities, 43*(3), 269–288.

Padilla, Y. C., Boardman, J. D., & Hummer, R. A. (2002). Is the Mexican American "epidemiologic paradox" advantage at birth maintained through early childhood? *Social Forces (University of North Carolina Press)*, *80*(3), 1101–1123.

Parker, F. L., Boak, A. Y., Griffin, K. W., Ripple, C., & Peay, L. (1999). Parent–child relationship, home learning environment, and school readiness. *School Psychology Review*, *28*, 413–425.

Payne, R. K. (2013). *A framework for understanding poverty: A cognitive approach* (5th ed.). Highlands, TX: Aha! Processes, Inc.

Pfeiffer, S., & Jawarsowik, T. (2003). *Gifted rating scale.* San Antonio, TX: Harcourt Assessment, Inc.

Pintrich, P. R., Smith, D. A. F., Garcia, T., & McKeachie, W. J. (1993). Reliability and predictive validity of the Motivated Strategies for Learning Questionnaire (MSLQ). *Educational and Psychological Measurement*, *53*, 801–813.

Plomin, R., Mclearn, G. E., Smith, D. L., Skuder, P., Vignetti, S., Chorney, M. J., et al. (1995). Allelic associations between 100 DNA markers and high versus low IQ. *Intelligence*, *21*, 31–48.

Plomin, R., & Petrill, S. A. (1997). Genetics and intelligence: What's new? *Intelligence*, *24*, 53–77.

Poteat, G. M., Wuensch, K. L., & Gregg, N. B. (1988). An investigation of differential prediction with the WISC–R. *Journal of School Psychology*, *26*, 59–68.

Potter, D., Mashburn, A., & Grissmer, D. (2013). The family, neuroscience, and academic skills: An interdisciplinary account of social class gaps in children's test scores. *Social Science Research*, *42*(2), 446–464.

Prince-Embury, S. (2006). *Resiliency scales for children & adolescents.* San Antonio, TX: Pearson.

Prince-Embury, S., & Saklofske, D. H. (Eds.), (2014). *Resilience interventions for youth in diverse populations.* New York: Springer.

Rabiner, D. L., Murray, D., Schmid, L., & Malone, P. (2004). An exploration of the relationship between ethnicity, attention problems and academic achievement. *School Psychology Review*, *33*, 498–600.

Ramey, C., Farran, D. C., & Campbell, F. A. (1979). Predicting IQ from mother–child interactions. *Child Development*, *50*, 804–814.

Reid, J. B., & Patterson, G. R. (1991). Early prevention and intervention with conduct problems: A social interactional model for the integration of research and practice. In G. Stoner, M. R. Shinn, & H. M. Walker (Eds.), *Interventions for achievement and behavior problems* (pp. 715–739). Bethesda, MD: National Association of School Psychologists.

Renzulli, J. S. (1986). The three-ring conception of giftedness: A developmental model for creative productivity. In R. J. Sternberg & J. E. Davidson (Eds.), *Conceptions of giftedness* (pp. 53–92). New York: Cambridge University Press.

Reschly, D. J., & Reschly, J. E. (1979). Validity of WISC–R factor scores in predicting achievement and attention for four sociocultural groups. *Journal of School Psychology*, *17*, 355–361.

Reschly, D. J., & Saber, D. L. (1979). Analysis of test bias in four groups with the regression definition. *Journal of Educational Measurement*, *16*, 1–9.

Reschly, D. J., & Ward, S. M. (1991). Uses of adaptive behavior measures and overrepresentation of black students in programs for students with mild mental retardation. *American Journal on Mental Retardation*, *96*, 257–268.

Reynolds, C. R., & Gutkin, T. B. (1980). Stability of the WISC–R factor structure across sex at two age levels. *Journal of Clinical Psychology*, *36*, 775–777.

Reynolds, C. R., & Hartlage, L. C. (1979). Comparison of WISC and WISC–R regression lines for academic prediction with black and white referred children. *Journal of Consulting and Clinical Psychology*, *47*, 589–591.

Rhodes, R. L. (2010). Multicultural school neuropsychology. In D. Miller (Ed.), *Best practices in school neuropsychology: Guidelines for effective practice, assessment, and evidence-based intervention* (pp. 61–77). Hoboken, NJ: John Wiley & Sons.

Rhodes, R. L., Ochoa, S. H., & Ortiz, S. O. (2005). *Assessing culturally and linguistically diverse students: A practical guide.* New York: Guilford Press.

Rice, T., Fulker, D. W., Defries, J. C., & Plomin, R. (1988). Path analysis of IQ during infancy and early childhood and the index of the home environment in the Colorado Adoption Project. *Behavior Genetics, 16*, 107–125.

Rios, R., Aiken, L., & Zautra, A. (2012). Neighborhood contexts and the mediating role of neighborhood social cohesion on health and psychological distress among Hispanic and non-Hispanic residents. [Article]. *Annals of Behavioral Medicine, 43*(1), 50–61.

Ritchie, S. (in press). Does learning to read improve intelligence? A longitudinal multivariate analysis in identical twins from age 7 to 16. *Child Development.*

Rosenzweig, M. R. (1996). Aspects of the search for neural mechanisms of memory. *Annual Review of Psychology, 47*, 1–32.

Ruggles, S. J., Alexander, T., Genadek, K., Goeken, R., Schroeder, M. B., & Sobek, M. (2010). *Integrated public use microdata series: Version 5.0 [Machine-readable database].* Minneapolis, MN: University of Minnesota.

Ruiz, J. M., Steffen, P., & Smith, T. B. (2013). Hispanic mortality paradox: A systematic review and meta-analysis of the longitudinal literature. [Article]. *American Journal of Public Health, 103*(3), e52–e60.

Sable, J., & Noel, A. (2008). *Public elementary and secondary school student enrollment and staff from the common core of data: School year 2006–07 (NCES 2009-305).* Washington, DC: National Center for Education Statistics, Institute of Education Sciences, U.S. Department of Education. Retrieved from: <http://nces.ed.gov/pubsearch/pubsinfo.asp?pubid=2009305>. Accessed 29.06.14.

Sachs, J., Law, Y. K., Chan, C. K. K., & Rao, N. (2001). A non-parametric item analysis of the motivated strategies for learning questionnaire and the learning process questionnaire. *Psychologia, 45*, 193–203.

Saklofske, D. H., van de Vijver, F. J. R., Oakland, T., Mpofu, E., & Suszuki, L. A. (2015, in press). Intelligence and culture: History and assessment. In S. Goldstein, J. A. Naglieri, & D. Princiotta (Eds.), *Handbook of intelligence: Evolutionary theory, historical perspective, and current concepts.* New York: Springer.

SAMHSA. (2011). *Current statistics on the prevalence and characteristics of people experiencing homelessness in the United States.* Available at: <http://homeless.samhsa.gov/ResourceFiles/hrc_factsheet.pdf>.

Schaefer, B. (2004). A demographic survey of learning behaviors among American students. *School Psychology Review, 33*, 481–497.

Schmitt, N., Sacco, J. M., Ramey, S., Ramey, C., & Chan, D. (1999). Parental employment, school climate, and children's academic and social development. *Journal of Applied Psychology, 84*(5), 737–753.

Schwartz, R. S. (2001). Racial profiling in medical research. *New England Journal of Medicine, 344*, 1392–1393.

Shah, A. K., Mullainathan, S., & Shafir, E. (2012). Some consequences of having too little. *Science, 338*(6107), 682–685.

Sichi, M. (2003). *Influence of free-time activities on children's verbal IQ: A look at how the hours a child spends reading, using the computer, and watching TV may affect verbal skills.* Poster session presented at the Texas Psychological Association Conference, San Antonio, Texas.

Spearman, C. (1927). *The abilities of man*. New York: Macmillan.

Squalli, J., & Wilson, K. (2014). Intelligence, creativity, and innovation. *Intelligence, 46*, 250–257.

Sternberg, R. J. (1997). A triarchic view of giftedness: Theory and practice. In N. Colangelo & G. A. Davis (Eds.), *Handbook of gifted education* (2nd ed.). pp. 43–53. Boston: Allyn & Bacon.

Sternberg, R. J., & Davidson, J. E. (Eds.), (1986). *Conceptions of giftedness*. New York: Cambridge University Press.

Sternberg, R. J., & Grigorenko, E. L. (Eds.), (2002). *The general intelligence factor: How general is it?* Mahwah, NJ: Erlbaum.

Sternberg, R. J., Grigorenko, E. L., & Kidd, K. (2005). Intelligence, race, and genetics. *American Psychologist, 60*, 46–57.

Stoolmiller, M. (1999). Implications of the restricted range of family environments for estimates of heritability and nonshared environment in behavioral genetic adoption studies. *Psychological Bulletin, 125*, 392–409.

Sui-Chu, E., & Williams, J. D. (1996). Effects of parental involvement on eighth-grade achievement. *Sociology of Education, 69*, 126–141.

Swanson, R. A., & Henderson, R. W. (1976). Achieving home–school continuities in the socialization of an academic motive. *Journal of Experimental Education, 44*, 38–44.

Terman, L. M. (1925). *Genetic studies of genius: Vol. 1. Mental and physical traits of a thousand gifted children*. Stanford, CA: Stanford University Press.

The Annie E. Casey Foundation. (2008). *Data on children in foster care from the census bureau*. Baltimore, MD: William P. O'Hare.

Trotman, F. K. (1977). Race, IQ, and the middle class. *Journal of Educational Psychology, 69*, 266–273.

U.S. Census Bureau. (2012). *2012 National population projections*. NP2012_D2: Projected births by sex, race, and hispanic origin for the United States: 2012 to 2060. US Census Bureau.

U.S. Census Bureau. (2013). Population division, Table 18. Projections of the population by net international migration series, race, and hispanic origin for the United States: 2015 to 2060 (NP2012-T18). Release Date: May 2013.

U.S. Census Bureau. (2014). *History: Index of questions*. Retrieved from: <https://http://www.census.gov/history/www/through_the_decades/index_of_questions/>. Accessed 01.06.14.

U.S. Department of Health and Human Services. (2001). *Head Start FACES: Longitudinal findings on program performance. Third progress report*. Washington, DC: Author.

U.S. Department of Health and Human Services. (2013). *Recent demographic trends on foster care*. Retrieved from: <http://www.acf.hhs.gov/sites/default/files/cb/data_brief_foster_care_trends1.pdf>. Accessed 28.06.14.

U.S. Department of Labor. (March 24, 2014). *Employment projects: Earnings and unemployment by educational attainment*. Retrieved from: <http://www.bls.gov/emp/ep_chart_001.htm>. Accessed 25.06.14.

Valencia, R. R., Henderson, R. W., & Rankin, R. J. (1985). Family status, family constellation, and home environmental variables as predictors of cognitive performance of Mexican–American children. *Journal of Educational Psychology, 77*, 323–331.

Valencia, R. R., & Suzuki, L. A. (2001). *Intelligence testing and minority students: Foundations, performance factors, and assessment issues*. Thousand Oaks: Sage Publications, Inc.

Valencia, R. R. (2010). *Dismantling contemporary thinking: Educational thought and practice*. New York: Routledge.

van Ast, V. A., Cornelisse, S., Marin, M. F., Ackermann, S., Garfinkel, S. N., & Abercrombie, H. C. (2013). Modulatory mechanisms of cortisol effects on emotional learning and memory: Novel perspectives. *Psychoneuroendocrinology, 38*(9), 1874–1882.

van de Vijver, F. J. R., & Bleichrodt, N. (2001). Conclusies [Conclusions]. In N. Bleichrodt & F. J. R. van de Vijver (Eds.), *Diagnosteik bij allochtonen: Mogelijkheden en heperkingen van psychologische tests [Diagnosing immigrants: Possibilities and limitations of psychological tests]* (pp. 237–243). Lisse, The Netherlands: Swets.

Vroon, P. A. (1980). Intelligence on myths and measurement. In G. E. Stelmach (Ed.), *Advances in psychology 3* (pp. 27–44). New York: North-Holland.

Walberg, H. J., & Marjoribanks, K. (1976). Family environment and cognitive models. *Review of Educational Research, 76*, 527–551.

Walker, D., Greenwood, C., Hart, B., & Carta, J. (1994). Prediction of school outcomes based on early language production and socioeconomic factors. *Child Development, 65*, 606–621.

Wechsler, D. (2005). *Wechsler intelligence scale for children—Fourth edition—Spanish.* San Antonio, TX: Harcourt Assessment, Inc.

Weisner, T. S., Matheson, C., Coots, J., & Bernheimer, L. P. (2005). Sustainability of daily routines as a family outcome. In A. E. Maynard & M. I. Martini (Eds.), *Learning in cultural context: Family, peers, and school.* New York: Kluwer Academic/Plenum Publishers.

Weiss, L. G. (1997). The MIPS: Gauging the dimensions of normality. In T. Millon (Ed.), *The Millon inventories: Clinical and personality assessment.* New York: The Guilford Press.

Weiss, L. G. (2002). Essentials of MIPS assessment. In S. Strack (Ed.), *Essentials of Millon inventories assessment* (2nd ed.). New York: John Wiley & Sons, Inc.

Weiss, L. G., Chen, H., Harris, J. G., Holdnack, J. A., & Saklofske, D. H. (2010). WAIS-IV use in societal context. In L. G. Weiss, D. H. Saklofske, D. Coalson, & S. E. Raiford (Eds.), *WAIS-IV clinical use and interpretation.* San Diego, CA: Academic Press.

Weiss, L. G., Harris, J. G., Prifitera, A., Courville, T., Rolfhus, E., Saklofske, D. H., et al. (2006). WISC-IV interpretation in societal context. In L. G. Weiss, D. H. Saklofske, A. Prifitera, & J. A. Holdnack (Eds.), *WISC-IV advanced clinical interpretation.* San Diego, CA: Elsevier Science.

Weiss, L. G., & Prifitera, A. (1995). An evaluation of differential prediction of WIAT achievement scores from WISC-III FSIQ across ethnic and gender groups. *Journal of School Psychology, 33*(4), 297–304.

Weiss, L. G., Prifitera, A., & Roid, G. (1993). The WISC–III and the fairness of predicting achievement across ethnic and gender groups. *Journal of Psychoeducational Assessment*, 35–42.

Weiss, L. G., Saklofske, D. H., Coalson, D. L., & Raiford, S. E. (2010). *WAIS-IV clinical use and interpretation.* San Diego, CA: Academic Press.

Weiss, L. G., Saklofske, D. H., Prifitera, A., & Holdnack, J. A. (2006). *WISC-IV advanced clinical assessment.* San Diego, CA: Elsevier, Inc.

Winner, E. (1996). *Gifted children: Myths and realities.* New York: Basic Books.

Wolf, R. M. (1964). *The identification and measurement of environmental variables related to intelligence.* Unpublished doctoral dissertation. University of Chicago.

Chapter 6

The Flynn Effect and Its Clinical Implications

Jacques Grégoire[1], Mark Daniel[2], Antolin M. Llorente[3], and Lawrence G. Weiss[4]

[1]*Université Catholique de Louvain, Psychological Sciences Research Institute, Louvain-la-Neuve, Belgium,* [2]*Pearson Clinical Assessment, Bloomington, MN, USA,* [3]*Penn State Hershey College of Medicine, Hershey, PA, USA,* [4]*Pearson Clinical Assessment, San Antonio, TX, USA*

WHAT DO WE KNOW ABOUT THE FLYNN EFFECT?

Definition

The *Flynn effect* is undoubtedly one of the most puzzling observations made during the last 30 years in the domain of human intelligence. In 1984, Flynn published an article in which he analyzed 73 U.S. studies (*N* total = 7431) comparing the scores on several intelligence tests across time (Stanford-Binet Intelligence scales and Wechsler scales). All these studies compared the IQs obtained by a sample of individuals on each test and on the previous version of the same test, i.e., using norms collected among the U.S. population at two different points of time. These studies used 10 different norms, collected from 1932 to 1978. Analyzing the data of the comparative studies, Flynn observed a steady evolution of the intellectual level of the U.S. population over 46 years. With one exception, he noted that the individuals get a higher IQ on the tests having the older norms, and vice versa. The performances of the individuals who participated in each study being the same from one test to another, the IQ differences came from a difference of the mean IQ score of the population to which the performances were compared. Flynn's observation corresponded therefore to an increase of the average intellectual level of the population across the time. During a period of 46 years, the average intellectual level of the U.S. population increased by 13.8 IQ points, which represented a difference of nearly one standard deviation between the mean intellectual level of the U.S. population in 1932 and in 1978. Flynn concluded that the average annual gain in the U.S. population was .33 IQ points.

L. G. Weiss, D. H. Saklofske, J. A. Holdnack and A. Prifitera (Eds): WISC-V Assessment and Interpretation.
DOI: http://dx.doi.org/10.1016/B978-0-12-404697-9.00006-6

TABLE 6.1 Evolution of the Average IQ Scores on Raven's Progressive Matrices and of the Scores on a Test of Vocabulary and a Test of Arithmetic in Four European Countries (from Flynn, 1987)

Country	Period	Total and Annual Gains		
		Raven's	Vocabulary	Arithmetic
Holland	1952–1972	12.43 (.62)	–	–
Belgium	1958–1967	7.82 (.87)	4.50 (.50)	4.36 (.48)
France	1949–1974	25.12 (1.01)	9.06 (.36)	9.64 (.39)
Norway	1954–1968	8.80 (.63)	8.40 (.60)	7.90 (.56)
Norway	1968–1980	2.60 (.22)	1.50 (.13)	−3.10 (−.26)

Note: the average annual gain is in brackets.

Flynn's first observation was made only on the U.S. population, based on data coming from tests whose content was often modified from one standardization to another. To better appraise the phenomenon he had revealed, Flynn (1987) extended his first analysis to data sets coming from 14 countries where exactly the same test was used across the time. The most interesting data came from military conscripts, since virtually all 18-year-old men took the same test, often the Raven's Progressive Matrices test, which remained unchanged during a very long period of time. The cohorts being almost identical to the male population of the age group, the problem of potential sampling bias was eliminated. Table 6.1 shows the IQ gain of military examinees on the Raven's Progressive Matrices test in four European countries: the Netherlands, Belgium (Dutch-speaking region), France, and Norway. In three of these countries, the examinees also completed a vocabulary test and an arithmetic test, unchanged over time. To facilitate the comparisons, all the results are expressed on a scale with a mean of 100 and a standard deviation of 15.

In all four countries, the increase of the average IQ measured by the Raven's Progressive Matrices was significant and exceeded, by far, the .33 points observed by Flynn in the U.S. with the Stanford-Binet and the Wechsler scales. This is particularly interesting because the Raven's Progressive Matrices are considered a good measure of fluid intelligence (Gf) and a culturally reduced test. But, during the 1950s and 1960s, the average scores on the Raven's Progressive Matrices grew more rapidly than on tests measuring crystallized intelligence (Gc), influenced more by education and culture. During a rather short period, such an increase of scores on a fluid intelligence measure cannot be a consequence of genetic modifications in the population. Only environmental factors could explain the fast growth of scores on the Ravens Progressive Matrices.

Another interesting observation, mentioned in Table 6.1, is the smaller gain on achievement tests observed in France and Belgium. In these countries, school-related knowledge shows less improvement than performances on a measure of fluid intelligence. However, in Norway, the evolution of the scores on the achievement tests was more correlated to the evolution of the scores on the Raven's Progressive Matrices. Norwegians showed a second feature. The evolution curve of their performances on the Raven's Progressive Matrices changed between the period 1954–1968 and 1968–1980. During the first period, a strong growth of the scores was observed (.63 on average each year), but the growth slowed down during the second period (.22 on average each year). Such an observation was important because it indicated that the evolution of the average IQ is perhaps not a steady or an endless process.

Herrnstein and Murray (1994) suggested that the observation made by Flynn be called "Flynn effect" (FE), even if he was not the very first one to report an increase of the IQ scores across time in developed countries (Lynn, 2013). But, Flynn was the first researcher to systematically analyze this phenomenon. In his publications, Flynn discussed several paradoxes related to IQ gains. Among them, he emphasized the intellectual disability paradox (Flynn, 2007, p. 9): "How can our recent ancestors have been so unintelligent compared to ourselves?" He also questioned the persistence of the IQ gains into the twenty-first century, at least for developed nations. Several of Flynn's questions are discussed in this chapter, bringing into focus the consequences of the FE on the clinical use of intelligence tests, especially the WISC-V.

Variability According to the Intellectual Tasks

As mentioned in the previous section, the FE is not uniform across domains of cognitive ability. Much of the research on the FE among children and adolescents has focused on the overall composite scores from multi-ability batteries (such as the Wechsler scales' Full Scale Intelligence Quotient (FSIQ)), and when lower-level measures have been examined, they often have been the dimensions of fluid reasoning and crystallized ability. The research base is smaller regarding domains such as working memory, spatial ability, and processing speed. Thus, evidence from revisions of the more recent editions of the Wechsler scales, which differentiate these domains in addition to fluid and crystallized intelligence, makes an important contribution to the research base.

To put the findings from the most recent revision (WISC-IV to WISC-V) into context, it helps to review what is known about the patterns of FE by cognitive domain. In a recent meta-analysis of 241 studies from 1909 to 2010, Pietschnig and Voracek (2013) estimated average annual standard-score gains by domain to be 0.29 for overall composites such as FSIQ, 0.42 for fluid reasoning, 0.30 for spatial ability, and 0.26 for crystallized intelligence. Table 6.2 provides more specific information by showing the average annual change for the composite and subtest scores of the WISC and WPPSI in their two most recent revisions (from the second to the third editions, and from the third to the fourth editions). Modifications occurred from one edition to the other, some subtests and subscales being introduced or withdrawn. Therefore several comparisons cannot be done.

TABLE 6.2 Average Annual Standard-Score Change on Composites and Subtests in Recent Revisions of the WISC and WPPSI

Subtests/Composites	WISC		WPPSI	
Editions:	R to III	III to IV	R to III	III to IV
Publication Year:	1991	2003	2002	2012
Full Scale IQ	0.31	0.21	0.09	0.33
Verbal	0.14	0.26	0.03	0.25
Performance/Perceptual	0.44	0.25	0.24	0.28
Working Memory	–	0.13	–	–
Processing Speed	–	0.46	–	0.59
Similarities	0.38	0.29	−0.08	0.55
Comprehension	0.18	0.17	−0.04	0.25
Vocabulary	0.12	0.04	0.08	0.30
Information	−0.09	0.13	−0.04	0.20
Arithmetic	0.09	−0.08	–	–
Matrix Reasoning				0.40
Block Design	0.26	0.42	−0.23	0.15
Picture Concepts				0.20
Picture Completion	0.26	0.29	0.58	–
Picture Arrangement	0.56	–	–	–
Object Assembly	0.35	–	0.42	0.15
Digit Span	0.03	0.04	–	–
Symbol Search/Bug Search	–	0.50	–	0.75
Coding/Animal Coding	0.21	0.29	–	0.20
N	206	244	176	246

Notes: For the WISC-R to WISC-III comparisons, WISC-R VIQ and PIQ were compared to WISC-III VIQ and PIQ, respectively.
For the WISC-III to WISC-IV comparisons, WISC-III VCI was compared to WISC-IV VCI, and WISC-III POI was compared to WISC-IV PRI. For the Working Memory comparison, WISC-III Freedom from Distractibility Index (FDI) was compared to WISC-IV WMI. For the Processing Speed comparison, WISC-III PSI and WISC-IV PSI were used.
For the WPPSI-R to WPPSI-III comparisons, WPPSI-R VIQ and PIQ were compared to WPPSI-III VIQ and PIQ, respectively.
For the WPPSI-III to WPPSI-IV comparisons, WPPSI-III VIQ was compared to WPPSI-IV VCI. For the Performance/Perceptual comparison, the average of the WPPSI-III PIQ/WPPSI-IV VSI and the WPPSI-III PIQ/WPPSI-IV FRI was used. For the Processing Speed comparison, the WPPSI-III Processing Speed Quotient (PSQ) and WPPSI-IV PSI was used. The WPPSI-III PSQ is based on the Symbol Search and Coding subtests. The WPPSI-IV Processing Speed Index (PSI) is based on the Bug Search and Animal Coding subtests.
Source: Test manuals of the WISC-IV (Wechsler, 2003) and WPPSI-IV (Wechsler, 2012).

The higher level of FE for fluid/perceptual rather than crystallized intelligence has been a pervasive and stable finding (Kaufman & Lichtenberger, 2006). In particular, Raven's Progressive Matrices, a highly g-loaded perceptual measure of fluid reasoning, has shown large increases over time, averaging better than 0.50 standard-score points per year, in studies conducted in numerous countries (Flynn, 1987). Consistent with this phenomenon, fairly large FEs have been found for matrices subtests included in cognitive batteries for children, such as the WPPSI (0.40, WPPSI-III to WPPSI-IV) and the Differential Ability Scales (0.31, DAS to DAS-II; Elliott, 2007). However, not all perceptual ability tasks have demonstrated the same high level of FE, as seen in Table 6.2. For example, the Block Design subtest of the Wechsler scales and the similar block-construction subtests of the DAS and the Kaufman Ability Battery for Children (Kaufman & Kaufman, 2004), which are thought to measure a combination of fluid reasoning and spatial ability, show lower FEs: an average of 0.34 on the WISC (second to third, and third to fourth editions), an average of −0.04 on the WPPSI (second to third, and third to fourth editions), and 0.19 and 0.14 on the DAS and K-ABC (first to second editions). Nonverbal-reasoning task types other than Matrices and Block Design (e.g., Picture Concepts or Picture Arrangement) are not sufficiently prevalent on cognitive batteries to support generalizations about their levels of FE.

As noted above, measures of crystallized ability typically have somewhat lower levels of FE than measures of fluid reasoning. As shown in Table 6.2, the FE for the WISC verbal composite (VIQ or VCI) averaged 0.20 in the two most recent revisions, compared with an average of 0.34 for the performance/perceptual composite (PIQ or PRI) of that instrument. A similar pattern was observed on the WPPSI, with average FEs of 0.14 and 0.26 for the verbal and performance/perceptual composites, respectively. Measures of working memory or short-term retrieval have shown varying levels of FE among children and adolescents, with the average level being low to moderate. From WISC-III to WISC-IV the Working Memory Index (WMI) showed an FE of only 0.13, and the K-ABC revision yielded FE values for the Sequential Processing scale of 0.09 (preschool) and 0.31 (child). The Digit Span subtest of the WISC had FEs of 0.03 and 0.04 in the two most recent revisions. On the other hand, high levels of FE have been found for measures of processing speed. In the most recent WISC and WPPSI revisions, the Processing Speed Index (PSI) had FE values of 0.46 and 0.59, respectively. For WISC, these were due mainly to the Symbol Search subtest (0.50) rather than Coding (0.29, as well as 0.21 in the previous WISC revision). Note that the WPPSI-IV PSI is based on two new subtests named Bug Search and Animal Coding that measure the same constructs as Symbol Search and Coding in WPPSI-III, but contain important content differences. In the most recent WPPSI revision, the FE for PSI (0.59) is driven more by Symbol Search/Bug Search (0.75) than Coding/Animal Coding (0.20), and this may be partly due to content differences in addition to generational shifting.

In summary, among children and adolescents, the FE on Wechsler scales mirrors the pattern generally found across ages and instruments, with higher levels for the performance/perceptual scales that measure fluid reasoning and spatial ability, and lower levels for the verbal scales that measure primarily crystallized ability. Short-term or working memory shows a modest FE, whereas there has been rapid change in processing speed.

Variability According to Gender and IQ Level

Is the FE varying as a function of gender or ability level? A differential FE by gender would imply that the female population has changed over time to a different degree than the male population, which is another way of saying that the size of the gender difference in ability would have changed over that time period. Although this would be of theoretical and scientific interest, it would not have practical implications for score interpretation because intelligence tests use combined-gender rather than gender-specific norms. Although the overall FE might be due more to the change in one half of the population than the other, that would have no impact on how one would interpret a particular individual's performance or even how one would adjust an individual's score for the FE, if one chose to do so. Whether the examinee is male or female, their performance is still compared with that of the overall population.

Perhaps counterintuitively, the demographic characteristics (other than age and ability level) of the sample used to study the FE are not helpful in investigating whether there are differential FEs for different population subgroups, nor do they have any influence on the estimate of the size of the FE. This is because the sole function of the individuals in the sample is to provide common-person equating of the two tests being compared. The logic of the analysis rests on the assumptions that each person's true ability is the same during both administrations (setting aside practice effects), and that the two instruments measure the same construct equally accurately. If these assumptions hold, then we can see how a constant level of ability translates to scores based on norms constructed at different time points. If different sizes of FE were observed for the male and female participants in the typical one-point-in-time study—that is, if males and females who obtained equal scores on the more recent test scored differently on the older test—this would be evidence of an interaction between gender and the difference in content between the two tests. It would not have implications regarding the relative amounts of change over time in the latent ability distributions of the male and female populations.

Because the FE has to do with population changes, not individuals, addressing questions about differential FEs for subgroups requires studying subgroup population data from different points in time. However, intelligence instruments typically do not provide subgroup norms, making this line of research challenging. Instead, researchers must identify or collect subpopulation-representative samples from different time periods and compare their rates of change. With respect to gender differences in the FE, the limited amount of research that does exist tends to indicate no sex-related differences in the rate of population change in cognitive abilities. A study conducted by Flynn (1998a) on young Israelis addressed this issue. In Israel, both men and women must perform military service. Between 1976 and 1984, all conscripts completed the Raven's Progressive Matrices test and a verbal intelligence test. Flynn observed that during this period, the average Raven's IQ of men increased by 0.61 points per year and women by 0.64 points per year. During the same period, the average score on the verbal intelligence test increased respectively by 0.37 and 0.35 points. Wai and Putallaz (2011) reported equivalent male and female FEs over three decades among high-ability students taking the Scholastic Assessment Test (SAT), American College Test (ACT), and EXPLORE test. Ang, Rodgers, and Wanstrom (2010) measured the FE as the increase in children's normative scores on a test of mathematical problem-solving as the norms got increasingly out of date, and found no sex difference. All these studies showed that the FE seems independent of gender.

Ability level is not subject to the methodological limitation that applies to studying differential FEs by gender or other subgroups. The question being addressed is whether, as the ability distribution shifts over time, its shape changes. Analyzing differential FEs by level of ability is straightforward, as long as regression artifacts are avoided by using something other than the score being analyzed to form the ability groups. For example, this topic may be addressed by using naturally occurring groups that vary in ability level, or by forming ability subgroups according to an independent test score.

Considerable attention has been given to the question of whether the increase in ability over time has been consistent at different levels of ability. One reason for this interest is that a differential FE by ability level would have practical consequences for test interpretation, because it would mean that the best estimate of the impact of the FE on an individual's score would be a function of that person's level of ability. Another reason is that a nonuniform shift in the ability distribution over time (that is, greater change at some ability levels than others) would be informative regarding causal hypotheses for the FE. For example, a finding that the lower end of the ability distribution had risen quite a bit more than the upper end would lend support to explanations focusing on increasing amelioration of factors that cause low intelligence.

Results of these investigations have been mixed. Some have found greater FEs at lower ability levels. For example, using combined data from four recent Wechsler revisions (involving WPPSI, WISC, and WAIS), Zhou, Zhu, and Weiss (2010) found a significantly larger FE on the Performance IQ/Perceptual Reasoning Index for examinees in the average to low range of verbal ability than for those with above-average verbal ability. Other studies finding greater increase in the low range of the ability distribution include those by Colom, Lluis-Font, and Andrés-Pueyo (2005) and Teasdale and Owen (1989). However, a number of other investigations have found different patterns of effect (e.g., Sanborn,

Truscott, Phelps, & McDougal, 2003; Spitz, 1989). Summarizing the existing data through their meta-analysis, Trahan, Stuebing, Fletcher, and Hiscock (2014) found no relationship between ability level and the FE when all studies were considered. When only studies involving modern tests (those normed since 1972) were included, a statistically significant relationship emerged, with a greater average FE at low ability levels. However, because this result was driven by a few atypical results from studies with nonstandard procedures such as lack of counterbalancing or different floors (lowest possible scores) on the two instruments, the authors consider the finding unreliable.

The hypothesis that the FE is driven to a substantial degree by improvement at the lower end of the ability distribution would predict that the variability of ability scores would decrease over time as scores for the low functioning group move closer to the middle of the distribution (Rowe & Rodgers, 2002). Although this analytical approach has also yielded inconsistent results, the majority of studies have reported decreasing variability (Pietschnig & Voracek, 2013).

Overall, there does not seem to be strong evidence from the presently available studies that the FE varies by ability level; thus there is currently not a good basis for rejecting the assumption that the FE is a uniform upward shift in the ability distribution.

Variation of the Flynn Effect Over Time

The FE does not occur abruptly when new norms are published. It appears gradually, beginning upon publication of new norms. As the characteristics of the population change inexorably, while norms remain fixed, the gap between the two continues to widen between each standardization and the next one. Norms become more and more lenient across time, until the day new norms are set up. Such an evolution of norm validity is a problem for clinical practice, since the value of the cut scores lessens over time and the number of misidentified individuals increases. To solve this problem, Flynn (1998b) suggested correcting the old norms on the basis of an annual change of the average IQ level of the population of .25 points. This adjustment value is a rough estimate based on past observations of the FE, postulating a linear evolution of the population average IQ across time and into the future.

But several recent findings seem to indicate that the shape of the FE could no longer be linear. The FE could have reached a ceiling with the consequence that the future evolution of the population average IQ would be flat. In Table 6.1, reporting Flynn's data collected in Norway, we have already seen that the rate of the FE was slower from 1968 to 1980, compared to the trend from 1954 to 1968. Sundet, Barlaug, and Torjussen (2004) reported more recent data from Norwegian conscripts. They observed that the mean scores of the conscripts on a Raven's-like test stopped increasing in the mid-1990s, and even slightly decreased. Similar observations were made in Denmark (Teasdale & Owen, 2007), Sweden (Rönnlund, Carlstedt, Blomstedt, Nilsson, & Weinehall, 2013) and Finland (Dutton & Lynn,

2013). Two explanations were proposed for the slowdown of the FE in the Nordic countries of Europe. It could be partly attributable to the non-European immigrants with lower education who settled in the north of Europe from the end of the 1960s (te Nijenhuis, de Jong, Evers, & van der Flier, 2004). It could also be the consequence of dysgenic fertility (Nyborg, 2012), i.e., the negative association between fertility and IQ, the families with low IQ having more children than the families with high IQ. The first explanation does not apply to Finland (Dutton & Lynn, 2013) and, consequently, cannot be generalized. The second one is more speculative and needs more empirical data to be supported. Another approach to explaining the FE curve is to consider it as a consequence of several interlinked factors (see "Causes of the Flynn effect," below). These factors are stimulating the development of individual intellectual potential, but their positive influence is likely not infinite and is, therefore, gradually coming to an end. According to a traditional proverb in the stock market: "Trees don't grow to the sky." As a consequence, the shape of the FE is likely to be curvilinear.

Causes of the Flynn Effect

The causes of the Flynn effect have been much debated in the scientific literature. There is no single cause to the FE. This phenomenon should be considered as the consequence of a combination of several factors. The main potential causes are briefly reviewed below, and then concluded with the presentation of a general model proposed by Dickens and Flynn (2001), which explains the FE as the interaction between environmental and genetic factors.

Familiarity with intelligence tests has been suggested as a possible cause of the FE (Jensen, 1998). The FE would be an artifact due to the practice tests. It is true that familiarity with test contents can be a source of bias in testing. Such a risk justifies the confidentiality of test contents and the need to avoid their public release (American Educational Research Association, 1999). The mere completion of a test as a source of learning and short-term memory effects is well documented. For example, the test/retest of the WISC-IV ($N = 247$), with a mean interval of 32 days (Wechsler, 2003), led to an increase of 2.1 points for the VCI, 5.9 points for the PRI, 2.6 points for the WMI, 7.1 points for the PSI, and 5.6 points for the FSIQ. This phenomenon is particularly important in tasks where individuals have to learn associations (e.g., Coding) or strategies (e.g., Block Design). However, the learning effect fades over time and tends to disappear after a year (Canivez & Watkins, 1998). We cannot therefore consider that the familiarity with intelligence tests has significant impact on the FE, especially as in many countries where the testing of intelligence is not systematic and where a large number of individuals never completed an intelligence test.

Education is a serious candidate to explain the FE. Ceci and Williams (1997) collected a large set of data showing the effect of schooling on intelligence. The statistics published by UNESCO highlighted important changes in education around the world during the twentieth century. Illiteracy has decreased and the rate of attendance at preschool, primary, secondary, and higher education has sharply increased, especially in industrial countries where the FE was observed. A Spanish study conducted in 1978–1979 (cited by Fernandez-Ballesteros & Juan-Espinosa, 2001) showed, after controlling for socioeconomic status, a significant advantage ($p < .001$) in intellectual performances for children who attended kindergarten. Based on several previous studies, Ceci (1990) showed that education stimulates the development of several skills that play an important role in intelligence tests, especially perceptual skills, concept formation, and memory. Rönnlund and Nilsson (2008) analyzed a Swedish data set collected from 1989 to 2004. They noted that years of education, height (used as an index of health and nutrition), and number of siblings[1] accounted for more than 94% of FE observed between 1989 and 2004, education being the strongest predictor among the three. They concluded (p. 204) that "education may exert influence on time-related patterns on (broad) fluid (visuospatial ability, episodic memory) as well as crystallized/semantic aspect of cognition."

Changes in family characteristics also play a role in the FE. During the twentieth century, the increase of the average household income, the average level of education, and the professional qualifications of individuals strongly changed the conditions of education within families. Parents have more time and resources to educate their children. They are also better informed about normal child development and the conditions that can foster it. Because of the decrease in family size, more resources can be devoted to the education of fewer children. The quality of the home environment has clearly had an impact on child cognitive development. Espy, Molfese, and DiLalla (2001) conducted a longitudinal study following 105 children between the ages of 3 and 6 years. Each year, these children were tested with the Stanford-Binet-IV Intelligence Scale. The researchers also evaluated the quality of the environment using two measures. The first one was a questionnaire completed by the parents, which assessed the characteristics of the home environment: learning materials, communication skills, physical environment, academic stimulation, behavioral models, variety of experiences, and warmth, tolerance, and acceptance of the child. The second measure assessed the socioeconomic status (educational level, occupation of parents, and family income) as an indirect index of the quality of the home environment. The researchers observed that the two measures of the family environment had a moderate but significant relationship with children's intellectual performances. Characteristics measured by the first questionnaire had an equal relationship with all aspects of intellectual activity measured by the Stanford-Binet. The socioeconomic status measure had a significant effect only on nonverbal intelligence tasks. For a detailed analysis of socioeconomic and home environment variables impacting children's WISC-V test performance, we refer the reader to Chapter 5 on WISC-V use in societal context.

Changes in the family are also related to the increase of technology in everyday life. During the twentieth century, we moved from direct interactions

---

1. The FE is related to a smaller number of siblings.

with reality to interactions mediated by symbolic representations (Fernandez-Ballesteros & Juan-Espinosa, 2001). For example, in the past, washing involved direct interaction with clothes using psychomotor skills. Today, the same task is done through symbolic representations: the instructions to the washing machine. The symbolic mediation reduces the role of psychomotor skills and increases the role cognitive skills. The growing interactions with symbolic representations of the world are very likely a factor explaining the importance of the FE in fluid reasoning tasks as in the Raven's Progressive Matrices. Technology stimulates learning and cognitive development. The unending introduction of new devices, more and more sophisticated, requires continuous learning during all our lives.

Changes in bioenvironmental conditions seem to play a significant role on the FE. The importance of their impact is, however, controversial. Bioenvironmental conditions represent the interactions between the environment and the biophysical characteristics of individuals. Several authors noted, in parallel with the FE, an increase in life expectancy, a reduction in infant mortality, and an increase in average height in the industrialized countries during the twentieth century. Schmidt, Jorgensen, and Michaelsen (1995) analyzed the evolution of the conscript heights between 1960 and 1990 in 11 European countries. In all these countries, a steady increase of the average height of conscripts was observed. For example, in 1960, the average height of the Dutch conscripts was 1.76 meters. In 1990, the average height of the conscripts was 1.81 meters. However, in Holland and the Scandinavian countries, this growth of height has now peaked for several years. The average height of Norwegian and Swedish conscripts has not increased since 1975, but continued its previous rate of growth in the countries of southern Europe, such as Spain and Italy. Schmidt et al. (1995) showed a close relationship between the increase of height and the decrease of postneonatal mortality (death between 28 days and 1 year). This reduction in postneonatal mortality is linked to an improved nutrition and a reduction of the incidence of infectious diseases. Postneonatal mortality reached a floor in the Netherlands and the Nordic countries around the 1970s, whereas in Spain and Italy, this floor was reached only in the 1980s. The authors concluded that the factors that determine the fall of postneonatal mortality are the same as those responsible for the increase in height, namely the improvement of nutrition and the reduction of infectious diseases during early childhood. Many clues suggest that the factors responsible for the increase in height also have an impact on intellectual development. A study of 32,887 Swedish conscripts at age 18 (Tuvemo, Jonsson, & Persson, 1999) showed a significant relationship between the height of the conscripts and their intellectual performances. The intellectual level of the conscripts actually increased in parallel with their height. A longitudinal study of 3733 Americans of Japanese origin (Abbott et al., 1998) lead to the same conclusion. Furthermore, many studies on child malnutrition have clearly demonstrated a negative impact of malnutrition on physical and cognitive development (Pollitt, 2000). It is therefore very likely that during the twentieth century, the improvement of child nutrition and the prevention of infectious diseases contributed to the increases in both height and intellectual performances in industrialized countries.

How can the environmental factors discussed above explain an important IQ gain in a rather short period of time, while many studies show the important role of genes in determining individual differences in intellectual performances? Dickens and Flynn (2001) proposed a solution to this apparent paradox. This solution is close to the bioecological model of Bronfenbrenner and Ceci (1994). Dickens and Flynn postulated that genes and environment do not act independently of each other, but instead are correlated. This correlation is a consequence of reciprocal causal relationships between the intellectual abilities of an individual and its environment. Innate intellectual abilities allow taking advantage of the environment, which stimulates their own growth. Individuals may then look for new environmental conditions suitable for the development of their abilities, and so on. Through this process, small environmental influences can have large effects on the IQ. Dickens and Flynn (2001, p. 347) called this process "the social multiplier." If the genetic potential of the individual finds adequate environmental conditions, it can get into a cycle of positive relationships with this environment. In the industrialized countries, more favorable environmental conditions emerged during the twentieth century, stimulating the development of the intellectual potential of the population. The multiplier effect, which followed, was significant and can easily explain the FE, without denying the role of genetic differences in human intellectual abilities.

It is likely that the stimulating effect of the quality of the environment has some limitations. Even if the conditions for growth are optimal, human intelligence probably has intrinsic limitations that, one day or another, will be achieved. At that moment, the FE will reach a ceiling. Such a phenomenon has already been observed for height (Schmidt et al., 1995). We have seen above that the height of the conscripts peaked around 1975 in Norway and Sweden, but continued to grow in other European countries. It is likely that in the first two countries, the improvement of the bioenvironmental conditions allowed the genetic potential for physical growth to fully express itself. Therefore, the current environmental improvements no longer produce an increase of height comparable to the increase observed in the previous generations. In the case of intelligence, even if an increase of intelligence test scores is no longer observed in some developing countries (see "Variation of the Flynn over time," above), we do not have enough data to say that a ceiling is reached and no future increase could be expected. As Bronfenbrenner and Ceci (1994) emphasized, the amount of the genetic potential that is still to be revealed is unknown and, perhaps, unknowable.

IMPLICATIONS OF THE FLYNN EFFECT FOR PRACTITIONERS

The FE has significant and important repercussions in high-stake, applied academic and legal settings (Hiscock, 2007). Especially as intellectual measures are closely related to the determination of intellectual and learning disabilities (e.g., developmental dyslexia, dyscalculia) the FE could potentially impact access to important constitutional and/or educational rights and resources only available to individuals with these disorders. In the next several sections, this impact is analyzed and possible ways to deal with it are discussed.

Implications for the Identification of Learning and Intellectual Disabilities

In 2004, with the Individuals with Disabilities Education Improvement Act (IDEA), federal regulations adopted a new definition of specific learning disorder (LD). Currently, the most prevalent diagnosis of LD in special education programs is under the Code of Federal Regulations (CFR; 34 CFR §300.8(c)(10)) and is based on clinical findings and specified clinical criteria. Therefore, some schools no longer use the discrepancy between academic achievement and intellectual level as a criterion for LD. However, such a discrepancy is still recommended by many a school district and jurisdictions (Bradley, Danielson, & Hallahan, 2002; Fletcher & Vaughn, 2009) for placement in special educational services. In this case, one standard deviation (i.e., 15 points in the WISC-V) is often considered as a large discrepancy and the criterion of LD. For example, using the discrepancy definition for a reading disorder, if a child's intellectual score on the WISC-V is 100, he will be considered as having a learning disorder if he obtains an overall reading ability score of 84 or lower on a comprehensive test assessing several aspects of reading (decoding, fluency, and comprehension). This example shows the critical role of the global intellectual score as a criterion for specific learning disorders, ultimately leading to the provision of special educational services. In this approach, the intellectual score is considered as an "absolute criterion" (Kaufman & Kaufman, 2001). However, the FE may impact this criterion. The older the norms used as reference, the higher the global intellectual score could be, and the larger the gap between the intellectual level and the current academic achievement. Rejecting the discrepancy criterion is not the solution to avoid the impact of the FE on the LD diagnosis. The FE also affects school districts and jurisdictions that have adopted more contemporary qualifying standards for placement in special education programs and learning disability determinations, such as the processing strengths and weaknesses approach, since intellectual tasks are differentially impacted by FE (see "Variability according to the intellectual tasks," above). For example, visual–spatial tasks often show larger FE than verbal tasks. So, using an older test to compare strength in visual–spatial abilities to weakness in verbal abilities could yield a larger difference due to FE. This difference will be smaller if using a recently restandardized test.

Kanaya and Ceci (2012) recently investigated the potential effects of the FE on the diagnosis of specific learning disorders. This research, similar to previous studies (Gaskill & Brantley, 1996; Truscott & Frank, 2001), used logistic regression analyses for examining the changes in diagnoses of learning disability across time after a new assessment. This study showed a significant decrease in the number of children eligible for special education programs, partially due to the FE. Children who had originally been determined as LD using the discrepancy between IQ and academic achievement were tested using an older version of Wechsler Intelligence Scale for Children (WISC-R; Wechsler, 1974). When they were retested with a more recent version of the same scale (WISC-III; Wechsler, 1991), they showed a decline of their intellectual level, and therefore no longer met the criteria for LD. In other words, the use of the new test led to a decrease of the number of children determined eligible for special education services as LD. Kanaya and Ceci (2012) also observed that, as a consequence of a lower score on the more recent version of the test, some children were no longer determined as LD, but were labeled as "mentally disabled." As a consequence, they failed to qualify for special educational services under a specific learning disability category, but some may have qualified for services as intellectually disabled. Based on this study, it should be pointed out that it would be easier to qualify for services using older IQ tests. When adopting a newly renormed test, districts may therefore find a slightly lower proportion of the student population eligible for services as LD compared to when using the previous edition of the test during its last few years. But, the magnitude of the impact depends on the size of the FE observed when the test is renormed. The FE between WISC-IV and WISC-V is somewhat smaller than between some previous editions, so the impact on the percentage of students eligible, while still present, will be correspondingly smaller with this revision. It is also important to mention that the criteria used by school districts to determine eligibility for special education services as LD are administrative criteria only, and not the same as clinical criteria to diagnose developmental dyslexia. For further discussion on that point we refer the reader to Chapter 9 on LD assessment.

Similar observations were made with regard to the diagnosis of intellectual disabilities according to the criteria of intellectual disability specified by the American Association on Intellectual and Developmental Disabilities (AAIDD) (Schalock et al., 2010) or the *Diagnostic and Statistical Manual of Mental Disorders, Fifth Edition* (DSM-5) (American Psychiatric Association, 2013). Under AAIDD and DSM-5 criteria, a deficit or impairment in intellectual functioning is formally defined as a score on an individually administered test of intelligence that is two standard deviations or less below the test mean, i.e., a score of 70 or below for tests with a mean of 100 and a standard deviation of 15 points. As a consequence of the FE, we could expect that the number of people diagnosed as mentally retarded on the basis of an IQ equal or below 70 should gradually decrease as a function of the aging test norms. On the other hand, this number should increase with the publication of new norms. Based on data from the United States Department of Education, Ceci (2000) showed that this scenario was going only partly as expected. He recorded the number of children diagnosed as intellectually disabled between 1977 and 1995.

Until 1990, these children were usually diagnosed with the WISC-R. As anticipated, the number of children diagnosed as intellectually disabled declined gradually between 1977 and 1990, from 960,000 to 570,000. In 1991, the introduction of the WISC-III should have stimulated a sharp increase of the number of children diagnosed as mentally disabled, but Ceci did not observe this trend. However, the number of children diagnosed as intellectually disabled continued to decline until 1993, and only then rose gradually. Several explanations could be proposed to explain this phenomenon. The most plausible is that practitioners take a while to adopt the new version of a test. A second explanation, not incompatible with the first one, is that practitioners tend to adjust the new norms upward, considering they are harder than the ones previously used. This may be, in part, because this diagnosis also requires that both adaptive and intellectual functioning be two or more standard deviations below the mean. Practitioners seem to be more flexible with the procedures and the scoring criteria of the new test when making such diagnoses.

The available evidence strongly suggests that the shape of the FE curve varies by construct measured, test battery, and country, and may not be as stable across generations as Flynn argued (Kaufman & Weiss, 2010). Thus, FE adjustments for routine evaluations such as LD and ID are not recommended (Weiss, 2010). The best course is to use the most current norms available, and take the standard error of the test into account when making special education eligibility determinations. As the Wechsler intelligence scales are revised about every 10 years, a maximum FE of 3–4 points could be expected before the publication of the next revision. This FE is smaller than the 90% confidence interval that every clinician should report around the observed scores. Consequently, always using the most recent version of the Wechsler scales and mentioning the confidence interval around the observed scores seem to be the best recommendation to avoid adverse consequences of the FE on routine special education evaluations.

Implications for High Stakes Legal Evaluations

Another impact of the FE on the diagnosis of intellectual disability is related the death penalty. Although the majority of jurisdictions in the United States preclude the imposition of capital punishment on children (juveniles or minors prior to the age of 18; c.f., Roper v. Simmons, 543 U.S. 551 (2005)), as it is viewed as "disproportional punishment," adolescents have faced capital punishment and have been executed in the past, and they have been or are currently on Death Row in a select number of states in the U.S. Similarly, with regard to adults, it is common in criminal cases to introduce into evidence archival test scores from the childhood or developmental period of an adult offender who faces capital punishment before a court of law. Therefore, the WISC-V and its predecessors may be relevant in both child and adult criminal cases to prove the presence of intellectual disability or borderline intellectual impairments. This information can be crucial because an impaired intellect is allowable as a mitigating or exculpatory factor, especially in cases associated with capital punishment in the U.S. during the course of an Atkins claim (Atkins v. Virginia, 536 U.S. 304, 321 (2002)). An Atkins claim is raised when a defendant or petitioner, through his or her attorney or legal representative, petitions a court to avoid the imposition of capital punishment on constitutional grounds as a result of intellectual disability. Such claims emerged from the Atkins v. Virginia Supreme Court decision, which deemed unconstitutionally to execute individuals with intellectual disability (Atkins v. Virginia, 2002). The U.S. Supreme Court in the landmark case Atkins v. Virginia (2002) opined that it was inconsistent with "modern standards of decency" and with the Eighth Amendment of the U.S. Constitution, addressing "cruel and unusual punishment," to execute persons with intellectual disability. An Atkins claim requires a valid and reliable assessment of the individual's intelligence, as it is crucial information used by the defense attorney to require the suspension of capital punishment. However, in actual practice, many defendants who appear before a court of law with a petition on the grounds of intellectual disability already may have had their intellect measured many years or even decades before, often with some prior version of WISC. In addition, the individual may have been administered a test of intellect that was published a long time after its original publication For example, the WISC-III (Wechsler, 1991) may have been administered in 2001 a decade after its publication, but before the WISC-IV was available. In such an event, the defendant's IQ score may not meet the criteria for intellectual disability simply because the older norms inflated the obtained score due to the FE.

Interestingly, older norms produce higher scores that favor the state prosecutors whose role in the judicial system is to argue that the convicted felon is not intellectually disabled and therefore may be legally executed (in those states that allow capital punishment). Current norms produce relatively lower scores that favor defense attorneys whose role it is to argue that the convicted felon is intellectually disabled and therefore cannot be legally executed under the Atkins ruling. Further, taking into account the standard error of the test favors the defense attorney's position because scores in the low 70s may still be considered within the mentally retarded range based on the confidence interval. In 2014, however, the U.S. Supreme Court ruled that states must take into account the standard error of measurement of the test when making these determinations (see Hall v. State of Florida). Thus, the IQ scores that school psychologists place into record for children may have far-reaching future consequences for a few children who later commit murder as adults in those states where capital punishment is legal.

Therefore, the question arises whether to adjust the scores obtained using old norms. Some authors remained neutral on this issue (Frumkin, 2006), but several others advocated a systematic correction of the observed test scores because of its life and death implications (e.g., Reynolds, Niland, Wright, & Rosenn, 2010). According to Young (2012), not correcting for the FE across jurisdictions in the U.S. has led to the inconsistent application of the Atkins v. Virginia Supreme Court opinion in American courtrooms in capital punishment cases.

Based on Flynn's observations, Fletcher, Stuebing, and Hughes (2010) supported an adjustment of 3 points per decade. However, such a correction is only a rough estimate from a trend observed in the past on the basis of a selection of intelligence tests. The shape of the FE curve seems not to be linear, but instead curvilinear (see "Variation of the Flynn over time," above). Moreover, the impact of the FE varies from test to test. It is much more important with tests measuring mainly fluid intelligence (e.g., Raven's Progressive Matrices), than with tests measuring several facets of intelligence (e.g., Wechsler intelligence scales). Therefore, using a correction of .30 points per year could be misleading. Sometimes the correction will be too large, but sometimes not enough. In high stakes cases such as the death penalty, using such a generalized estimate has been debated extensively (Kaufman & Weiss, 2010). In our opinion, when using an older test before the new version is available, a generalized estimate of FE based on .30 points per year is reasonable practice in high stakes legal cases. Once the updated norms are available, however, archival scores previously obtained with the older version of the test should be adjusted based on the known FE empirically obtained from studies comparing the two relevant editions of the test. This will more accurately take into account the changing nature of the FE curve over time with different constructs, and in different cultures.

THE FLYNN EFFECT IN THE WISC-V

Flynn and Weiss (2007) studied the FE on the WISC from its first edition to the WISC-IV. The date of reference for the standardization of the first WISC was 1947.5 and it was 2001.75 for the WISC-IV. Therefore, the authors had the opportunity to track the gains of intelligence scores across the different editions of the WISC during a period of 54.25 years. During this period, the FSIQ gain grew from 100.00 to 116.83, i.e., an increase of more than one standard deviation (SD = 15). This global gain corresponds to a gain of roughly .30 points per year. Small variations of the pace of FSQI gain were observed across time: .311 from WISC to WISC-R, .322 from WISC-R to WISC-III, and .300 from WISC-III to WISC-IV. This last gain was calculated using an estimated gain for Object Assembly and Picture Arrangement,[2] which were no longer core subtests of the WISC-IV. Among the subtests remaining in the mainstream from the WISC to the WISC-IV, small gains (less than 1/3 SD) were observed in 50 years for Information (.43), Arithmetic (.46), and Vocabulary (.88). Moderate gains (more than 2/3 SD) were observed for Comprehension (2.20), Picture Completion (2.20), and Block Design (2.34). Large gains (more than 1 SD) were observed for Coding (3.60) and Similarities (4.77). At the subtest level, gains were more erratic across the time than at the Full Scale level.

The standardization of the WISC-V was an opportunity to check if the trend observed between the previous versions of the WISC was continuing at the same

---

2. The estimates were the mean gains observed on the other subtests.

pace. However, the comparisons are now more complex to interpret than in the past because several modifications were introduced in the WISC-V at the subtest and the subscale levels. Some subtests were withdrawn (Word Reasoning and Picture Completion), while new subtests were introduced (Figure Weight, Visual Puzzles, and Picture Span). The Perceptual Reasoning Index was split into a Visual–Spatial Index and a Fluid Reasoning Index. The core subtests for each composite were modified, with the exception of the Processing Speed Index, which was the only index to remain unchanged. Therefore, comparing individual performances between the WISC-IV and the WISC-V should be cautiously done, keeping in mind that the composite scores are calculated from different sets of subtests in the two tests. We should never forget that "A major assumption in comparing manifest scores is that they are measuring the same construct, the same way, across groups" (Beaujean & Sheng, 2014, p. 64). We can reasonably support this assumption for the subtests of the WISC-IV, which remained in the WISC-V, and for the Verbal Comprehension Index, the Working Memory Index, the Processing Speed Index, the Full Scale IQ, the General Ability Index (GAI), and the Cognitive Proficiency Index (CPI). However, such an assumption does not hold for the Perceptual Reasoning Index, which cannot be compared to the new Visual–Spatial and Fluid Reasoning Indexes.

The WISC-V and the WISC-IV were administered to 242 children aged from 6 to 16 in counterbalanced order. The testing for the standardization of the WISC-V started in May 2013 and ended in February 2014, the mid-point being September 2013. Therefore, the reference date for the WISC-V standardization is 2013.75. As the reference date for the WISC-IV standardization was 2001.75, the period between the two standardizations is equal to 12 years. As a consequence, the differences observed between the two tests have to be divided by 12 to have the gain per year. Table 6.3 shows the means of composite and subtests scores of the same children on the WISC-V and the WISC-IV. For the subtests, the scale has a mean of 10 and a standard deviation of 3, while, for the composites, the scale has a mean of 100 and standard deviation of 15. The differences between means and the gains per year are expressed in the same metrics. At the subtest level, the gain per year is always small. The larger gain is observed for Similarities, being equal to 0.7 scaled score per decade (less than ¼ SD). The gain is close to zero for Comprehension, Digit Span, and Symbol Search. A loss is observed for Coding and Cancellation (−0.06 each). At the Composite level, the gain per year for the FSIQ (0.14) is smaller than the gains reported between the previous versions (Flynn & Weiss, 2007). Compared to the gain reported the last 50 years, the current gain is approximately half. This observation seems to indicate that the FE is slowing down. The gain observed for the VCI (0.13) is rather small (less than 1/10 SD), which is consistent with the results of previous studies showing a smaller FE on the verbal comprehension subtests. The trend of the FE on the WMI and PSI is less documented in the literature, since these two indexes are rather new in the Wechsler scales. A small gain is observed for the WMI (0.11) and a small loss for the PSI (−0.11). Interestingly, the larger

TABLE 6.3 Comparisons of Composite Scores and Subtest Scores of the Same Individuals on the WISC-V and WISC-IV

Subtest/ Composite	N	WISC-V		WISC-IV		Difference	Gain/ Year
		Mean	SD	Mean	SD		
Similarities	239	10.57	2.60	11.37	2.46	0.80	0.07
Vocabulary	241	10.46	2.70	10.77	2.55	0.31	0.03
Information	242	10.33	2.41	10.64	2.55	0.31	0.03
Comprehension	242	10.43	2.75	10.39	2.71	−0.04	0.00
Word Reasoning	242	–	–	10.79	2.60	–	–
Block Design	241	10.62	2.71	11.08	2.94	0.46	0.04
Visual Puzzle	242	10.40	2.73	–	–	–	–
Picture Completion	242	–	–	9.64	2.74	–	–
Matrix Reasoning	240	10.96	2.88	11.51	2.92	0.55	0.05
Figure Weight	241	10.50	2.70	–	–	–	–
Picture Concept	241	10.64	2.91	10.95	2.92	0.31	0.03
Arithmetic	241	10.36	2.48	10.69	2.75	0.33	0.03
Digit Span	241	10.50	2.48	10.64	2.72	0.14	0.01
Picture Span	240	10.10	2.78	–	–	–	–
Letter-Number Seq.	241	10.41	2.77	10.71	2.42	0.30	0.03
Coding	241	10.67	2.98	9.99	2.91	−0.68	−0.06
Symbol Search	241	10.61	2.90	10.77	2.82	0.16	0.01
Cancellation	242	11.08	2.94	10.42	3.07	−0.66	−0.06
VCI	238	102.69	12.95	104.30	12.65	1.61	0.13
PRI	242	–	–	107.35	13.89	–	–
VSI	241	102.82	13.24	–	–	–	–
FRI	239	104.28	13.52	–	–	–	–
WMI	239	101.69	12.42	103.05	12.23	1.36	0.11
PSI	240	103.69	14.95	102.39	14.79	−1.30	−0.11
FSIQ	233	104.41	11.74	106.14	11.90	1.73	0.14
GAI	235	104.00	13.33	107.06	12.62	3.06	0.26
CPI	238	103.19	13.03	103.33	12.82	0.14	0.01

Note: The values of the mean columns are the average of the means of the two administration orders. See text for key to abbreviations.

TABLE 6.4 Subtests Gains Per Year from WISC-III to WISCV

Subtest/ Composite	Gain/Year	
	WISC-III to WISC-IV	WISC-IV to WISC-V
Similarities	0.06	0.07
Vocabulary	0.01	0.03
Information	0.03	0.03
Comprehension	0.03	0.00
Block Design	0.08	0.04
Arithmetic	−0.01	0.03
Digit Span	0.01	0.01
Coding	0.05	−0.06
Symbol Search	0.09	0.01

gain is observed for the GAI (0.26), while there is no gain for the CPI (0.01). This last observation is not surprising since the CPI is calculated from the subtest scores of the Working Memory and the Processing Speed Indexes, which showed very small or even negative FE. On the other hand, the GAI is calculated from the scores of the Verbal Comprehension and Fluid Reasoning Indexes, plus Block Design, which showed the larger FE among the WISC-V subtests. It worth noting that the gain per year observed for the GAI is rather close the IQ gain reported by Flynn, which is around 0.30.

To enlighten the trend of the FE from the WISC-III to the WISC-V, the gains per year between WISC-III and WISC-IV and between WISC-IV and WISC-V are presented in Table 6.4. This table shows that the pace of the FE was stable across the time period for Similarities, Information, and Digit Span. It accelerated a little for Vocabulary and Arithmetic. But it slowed down for Comprehension, Block Design, and Symbol Search, and reversed for Coding.

At first glance, the change in the trend for the processing speed subtests seems surprising because the two subtests were apparently unchanged in the WISC-IV and the WISC-V. However, several subtle modifications were introduced in the WISC-V versions of Coding and Symbol Search (e.g., increased complexity of symbols to be drawn, number of search symbols, number of shapes per row, and of rows per page). These modifications made the WISC-V version of both subtests more difficult, weakening their mean raw scores, and perhaps more importantly, increasing extraneous sources of variance such as fine motor skill involved in writing, visual acuity, and visual tracking between rows. Thus, although the WISC-IV and the WISC-V versions of Coding and Symbol Search both primarily measure processing speed, there are subtle but cognitively meaningful differences between them. Clinicians should be aware of the impact of these modifications when interpreting the differences between the performances of the same individuals on the WISC-IV and the WISC-V. According to Nettelbeck and Wilson (2004), the FE has no impact on speed of processing measured by tasks of inspection time. Individuals are becoming smarter, but not faster. Therefore, if the content of Coding and Symbol Search were left unchanged, a similar stagnation of the performances could have been observed across time on both subtests. However, Coding and Symbol Search are more complex than the classical inspection time tasks, involving oculomotor coordination and working memory. Further studies are needed for checking this assumption.

RECOMMENDATIONS

To conclude this chapter, some methodological recommendations are presented for researchers studying generational shifts in intelligence, and for practitioners to take into account the FE in clinical practice.

Recommendations for Researchers

Comparing different versions of tests in FE research creates potential confounds due to changes in test content that are difficult to untangle from changes due to generational shifts in ability. As noted above, Beaujean and Sheng (2014) clarify that a major assumption of FE research is that the test is measuring the same construct in the same way across groups, and we would add, across versions of the test. Zhu and Tulsky (1999) enumerated the myriad of ways that changes in test content between versions can confuse the results of FE studies. Kaufman (2010) gave a specific example of how Flynn's interpretation of large increases on the Similarities subtest scores over fifty years was flawed and more likely due to changes in subtest instructions, administration and scoring rules. For all of these reasons, we strongly recommend that future researchers studying generational increases in ability consider using the same version of a test at two points in time, or empirically demonstrate construct equivalence if different versions of the test are compared.

Recommendations for Clinical Practice

The most important recommendation for clinical practitioners is to use the most recent version of intelligence tests. Each new version provides new norms offsetting the FE. The new norms are an updated photograph of the intellectual abilities of the population, to which an individual's test performance is compared.

However, as photos, norms only provide a static representation of reality at a specific point in time. As soon as they are published, they start aging. During the period between their publication and the next standardization of the same test, the gap between the norms and the true intellectual level of the population is widening. For the Wechsler scales this period is usually around 10 years. During this period, based on previous observations, a difference around 3 points between the norms and the population true scores could be expected for the FSIQ. Earlier, in "The Flynn Effect in the WISC-V" we have seen that the impact of the FE on the FSIQ was smaller (1.40 IQ points per decade). This difference varies according to subscales and subtests, being sometimes smaller or larger.

During the aging period of the norms, correcting for the FE is not recommended because the exact shape of the FE is unknown. Several studies showed that the FE does not follow a straight line. Therefore using a standard correction of .25 or .30 points per year could be misleading. Sometimes it could be an undercorrection, sometimes an overcorrection. To avoid missing the identification of children with LD or intellectual disability because of the FE, with important adverse consequences for the children and their families, the best practice is to always use the most recent version of each test and to report the confidence interval around the observed scores. When a 90% confidence interval is used, it is usually larger than the potential impact of the FE.

However, for high-stake decisions, especially for the death penalty, a correction could be applied. Such a correction should be based on the data of studies comparing the WISC-V scores to those measured with older versions of the test, particularly with the WISC-IV. In this specific case, such a correction is often a better solution than doing a new testing with an updated version of the test. For example, a teenager was tested in 2008 with the WISC-IV when he was 16. At that time, his FSIQ was 71. In 2011, aged 19, he was sentenced to death because of a murder. The defense attorney used the previous test results to advocate the suspension of the death penalty because his client was intellectually deficient. As the WISC-IV was published in 2003 and the testing was done in 2008, a period of 5 years could be taken into account to correct the initial FSIQ for the FE. After the correction, the FSIQ was 69.5 (=71 − (5 × .30)), which is below the cut score for intellectual disability, thus potentially avoiding the death penalty. Another option could have been doing a new testing with a more recent intelligence test, e.g., the WAIS-IV, which was published in 2008. However, even with the WAIS-IV, a correction should apply for the 3-year period between the standardization and the test administration. Moreover, testing intelligence in such a context is not neutral and the risk of faking is high and difficult to control.

A final situation where the FE should be taken into account is when psychologists make comparisons between a client's score reported in a previous evaluation and his or her score obtained on the current evaluation. For example, a child was tested in 2013 with the WISC-IV. In 2015, his intelligence is tested again, but with the WISC-V. As there was a 10-year period between the publication of the

WISC-IV and the testing, an inflation of 1.4 points of the FSIQ should be expected based on data reported in this chapter. Therefore, the FSIQ measured with the new norms of the WISC-V is expected to be lower, as far as the child's true IQ score did not change within the 2 years between the two assessments. If the clinician does not take the FE into account when comparing the two measures of the FSIQ, he could conclude that the child's intellectual abilities deteriorated in the last 2 years. To avoid such a wrong interpretation, any comparisons between intelligence test scores collected with different norms should be done cautiously, taking into account the FE. Again, the best practice should be using confidence intervals when reporting scaled scores. As these intervals are usually larger than the FE, hasty interpretations of differences between scores across the time are prevented.

REFERENCES

Abbott, R. D., White, L. R., Ross, G. W., Masaki, K. H., Snowdon, D. A., & Curb, J. D. (1998). Height as a marker of childhood development and late-life cognitive function: The Honolulu-Asia aging study. *Pediatrics*, *102*, 602–609.

American Psychiatric Association, (2013). *Diagnostic and statistical manual of mental disorders* (5th ed.). Arlington, VA: APA.

Ang, S., Rodgers, J. L., & Wanstrom, L. (2010). The Flynn effect within subgroups in the U.S.: Gender, race, income, education, and urbanization differences in the NLSY-Children data. *Intelligence*, *38*, 367–384.

Beaujean, A., & Sheng, Y. (2014). Assessing the Flynn effect in the Wechsler scales. *Journal of Individual Differences*, *35*, 63–78.

Bradley, R., Danielson, L., & Hallahan, D. P. (Eds.), (2002). *Identification of learning disabilities: Research to practice*. Hillsdale, NJ: Lawrence Erlbaum.

Bronfenbrenner, U., & Ceci, S. J. (1994). Nature-nurture reconceptualized in developmental perspective: A bioecological model. *Psychological Review*, *101*, 568–586.

Canivez, G. L., & Watkins, M. W. (1998). Long-term stability of the Wechsler Intelligence Scale for Children—Third Edition. *Psychological Assessment*, *10*, 285–291.

Ceci, S. J. (1990). *On intelligence … more or less*. Englewood Cliffs, NJ: Prentice Hall.

Ceci, S. J. (2000). So near and yet so far: lingering questions about the use of measures of general intelligence for college admission and employment screening. *Psychology, Public Policy and Law*, *6*, 233–252.

Ceci, S. J., & Williams, W. M. (1997). Schooling, intelligence, and income. *American Psychologist*, *52*, 1051–1058.

Colom, R., Lluis-Font, J. M., & Andrés-Pueyo, A. (2005). The generational intelligence gains are caused by decreasing variance in the lower half of the distribution: Supporting evidence for the nutrition hypothesis. *Intelligence*, *33*, 83–91.

Dickens, W. T., & Flynn, J. R. (2001). Heritability estimates versus large environmental effects: The IQ paradox resolved. *Psychological Review*, *108*, 346–369.

Dutton, E., & Lynn, R. (2013). A negative Flynn effect in Findland, 1997–2009. *Intelligence*, *41*, 817–820.

Elliott, C. (2007). *Differential ability scales* (2nd ed.). Bloomington, MN: Pearson.

Espy, K. A., Molfese, V. J., & DiLalla, L. F. (2001). Effects of environmental measures on intelligence of young children: Growth curve modeling of longitudinal data. *Merrill-Palmer Quarterly*, *47*, 42–73.

Fernandez-Ballesteros, R., & Juan-Espinosa, M. (2001). Sociohistorical changes and intelligence gains. In R. J. Sternberg & E. L. Grigorenko (Eds.), *Environmental effects on cognitive abilities*. Mahwah, NJ: Lawrence Erlbaum.

Fletcher, J. M., Stuebing, K. K., & Hughes, L. C. (2010). IQ scores should be corrected for the Flynn effect in high-stakes decisions. *Journal of Psychoeducational Assessment, 28*, 469–473.

Fletcher, J. M., & Vaughn, S. (2009). Response to intervention: Preventing and remediating academic difficulties. *Child Development Perspectives, 3*, 30–37.

Flynn, J. R. (1984). The mean IQ of Americans: Massive gains 1932 to 1978. *Psychological Bulletin, 95*, 29–51.

Flynn, J. R. (1987). Massive IQ gains in 14 nations: What IQ tests really measure. *Psychological Bulletin, 101*, 171–191.

Flynn, J. R. (1998a). Israeli military IQ tests: Gender differences small; IQ gains large. *Journal of Biosocial Science, 30*, 541–553.

Flynn, J. R. (1998b). WAIS-III and WISC-III gains in the United States from 1972 to 1995: How to compensate for obsolete norms? *Perceptual and Motor Skills, 86*, 1231–1239.

Flynn, J. R. (2007). *What is intelligence?* New York: Cambridge University Press.

Flynn, J. R., & Weiss, L. G. (2007). American IQ gains from 1932 to 2002: The WISC subtests and educational progress. *International Journal of Testing, 7*, 209–224.

Frumkin, I. B. (2006). Challenging expert testimony on intelligence and mental retardation. *The Journal of Psychiatry and Law, 34*, 51–71.

Gaskill, F. W., III, & Brantley, J. C. (1996). Changes in ability and achievement scores over time: Implications for children classified as learning disabled. *Journal of Psychoeducational Assessment, 14*, 220–228.

Herrnstein, R. J., & Murray, C. (1994). *The bell curve. Intelligence and class structure in American life*. New York: Free Press.

Hiscock, M. (2007). The Flynn effect and its relevance to neuropsychology. *Journal of Clinical and Experimental Neuropsychology, 29*, 514–529.

Jensen, A. R. (1998). *The g factor*. New York: Praeger.

Kanaya, T., & Ceci, S. (2012). The impact of the Flynn effect on LD diagnoses in special education. *Journal of Learning Disabilities, 45*, 319–326.

Kaufman, A. S. (2010). "In what way are apples and oranges alike?" A critique of Flynn's interpretation of the Flynn effect. *Journal of Psychoeducational Assessment, 28*(5), 383–398.

Kaufman, A. S., & Kaufman, N. L. (2001). Assessment of specific learning disabilities in the new millennium: Issues, conflicts, and controversies. In A. S. Kaufman & N. L. Kaufman (Eds.), *Specific learning disabilities and difficulties in children and adolescents: Psychological assessment and evaluation* (pp. 433–455). New York: Cambridge University Press.

Kaufman, A. S., & Kaufman, N. L. (2004). *Kaufman assessment battery for children* (2nd ed.). Bloomington, MN: Pearson.

Kaufman, A. S., & Lichtenberger, E. O. (2006). *Assessing adolescent and adult intelligence* (3rd ed.). Hoboken, NJ: Wiley.

Kaufman, A. S., & Weiss, L. G. (2010). Special issue on the Flynn effect. *Journal of Psychoeducational Assessment, 28*(5), 379–510.

Lynn, R. (2013). Who discovered the Flynn effect? A review of early studies of the secular increase of intelligence. *Intelligence, 41*, 765–769.

Nettelbeck, T., & Wilson, C. (2004). The Flynn effect: Smarter not faster. *Intelligence, 32*, 85–93.

Nyborg, H. (2012). The decay of Western civilization: Double relaxed Darwinian selection. *Personality and Individual Differences, 53*, 118–125.

Pietschnig, J., & Voracek, M. (2013). One century of global IQ gains: A formal meta-analysis of the Flynn effect (1909–2010). Available at SSRN 2404239.

Pollitt, E. (2000). Developmental sequel from early nutritional deficiencies: Conclusion and probability judgments. *Journal of Nutrition, 130*, 350–353.

Reynolds, C. R., Niland, J., Wright, J. E., & Rosenn, M. (2010). Failure to apply the Flynn correction in death penalty litigation: Standard practice of today maybe, but certainly malpractice of tomorrow. *Journal of Psychoeducational Assessment, 28*, 477–481.

Rönnlund, M., & Nilsson, L. -G. (2008). The magnitude, generality, and determinants of Flynn effects on forms of declarative memory and visuospatial ability: Time-sequential analyses of data from Swedish cohort study. *Intelligence, 36*, 192–209.

Rönnlund, M., Carlstedt, B., Blomstedt, Y., Nilsson, L. -G., & Weinehall, L. (2013). Secular trends in cognitive test performance: Swedish conscript data 1970–1993. *Intelligence, 41*, 19–24.

Rowe, D. C., & Rodgers, J. L. (2002). Expanding variance and the case of historical changes in IQ means: A critique of Dickens and Flynn (2001). *Psychological Review, 109*, 759–763.

Sanborn, K. J., Truscott, S. D., Phelps, L., & McDougal, J. L. (2003). Does the Flynn effect differ by IQ level in samples of students classified as learning disabled? *Journal of Psychoeducational Assessment, 21*, 145–159.

Schalock, R. L., Borthwich-Duffy, S. A., Bradley, V. J., Buntinx, W. H. E., Coulter, D. L., Craig, E. M., et al. (2010). *Intellectual disability: Definition, classification, and systems of support* (11th ed.). Annapolis, MD: American Association on Intellectual and Developmental Disabilities.

Schmidt, I. M., Jorgensen, H. M., & Michaelsen, K. F. (1995). Height of conscripts in Europe: Is post-neonatal mortality a predictor? *Annals of Human Biology, 22*, 57–67.

Spitz, H. H. (1989). Variations in Wechsler interscale IQ disparities at different levels of IG. Intelligence, 13, 157–167.

Sundet, J. M., Barlaug, D. G., & Torjussen, T. M. (2004). The end of the Flynn effect? A study of secular trends in mean intelligence test scores of Norwegian conscripts during half a century. *Intelligence, 32*, 349–362.

Teasdale, T. W., & Owen, D. R. (1989). Continuing secular increases in intelligence and a stable prevalence of high intelligence levels. *Intelligence, 13*, 255–262.

Teasdale, T. W., & Owen, D. R. (2007). Secular declines in cognitive test scores: A reversal of the Flynn effect. *Intelligence, 36*, 121–126.

te Nijenhuis, J., de Jong, M. -J., Evers, A., & van der Flier, H. (2004). Are cognitive differences between immigrants and majority groups diminishing? *European Journal of Personality, 18*, 405–434.

Trahan, L. H., Stuebing, K. K., Fletcher, J. M., & Hiscock, M. (2014). The Flynn effect: A meta-analysis. *Psychological Bulletin*, 140, 1332–1360.

Truscott, S. D., & Frank, A. J. (2001). Does the Flynn effect affect IQ scores of students classified as LD? *Journal of School Psychology, 39*, 319–334.

Tuvemo, T., Jonsson, B., & Persson, I. (1999). Intellectual and physical performance and morbidity in relation to height in a cohort of 18-year-old Swedish conscripts. *Hormone Research, 52*, 186–191.

Wai, J., & Putallaz, M. (2011). The Flynn effect puzzle: A 30-year examination from the right tail of the ability distribution provides some missing pieces. *Intelligence, 39*, 443–455.

Wechsler, D. (1974). *Wechsler intelligence scale for children*. San Antonio, TX: The Psychological Corporation. Revised.

Wechsler, D. (1991). *Wechsler intelligence scale for children* (3rd ed.). San Antonio, TX: The Psychological Corporation.

Wechsler, D. (2003). *WISC-IV technical and interpretive manual*. Bloomington, MN: Pearson.

Wechsler, D. (2012). *WPPSI-IV technical and interpretive manual*. Bloomington, MN: Pearson.

Weiss, L. G. (2010). Considerations on the Flynn effect. In A. S. Kaufman & L. G. Weiss (Eds.), Special issue of JPA on the Flynn effect. *Journal of Psychoeducational Assessment, 28*(5), 482–493.

Young, G. W. (2012). A more intelligent and just Atkins: Adjusting for the Flynn effect in capital determination of mental retardation or intellectual disability. *Vanderbilt Law Review, 65*, 616–675.

Zhou, X., Zhu, J., & Weiss, L. G. (2010). Peeking inside the "black box" of the Flynn effect: Evidence from three Wechsler instruments. *Journal of Psychoeducational Assessment, 28*, 399–411.

Zhu, J., & Tulsky, D. (1999). Can IQ gain be accurately quantified by a simple difference formula? *Perceptual and Motor Skill, 88*, 1255–1260.

Part III

Clinical Considerations

Chapter 7

Testing Hispanics with WISC-V and WISC-IV Spanish

Lawrence G. Weiss[1], Maria R. Munoz[1], and Aurelio Prifitera[2]

[1]*Pearson Clinical Assessment, San Antonio, TX, USA,* [2]*Pearson Clinical Assessment, Upper Saddle River, NJ, USA*

INTRODUCTION

The U.S. ranks second in the world in number of Hispanics (50.5 million) after Mexico (112 million), as of 2010. By 2060 the Hispanic population will have doubled and one of every three U.S. residents will be of Hispanic origin. Due to the steadily growing Hispanic population in the U.S., culturally sensitive assessment of general intelligence and specific cognitive abilities with Spanish-speaking clients is increasingly important to clinical practice. Yet, it is a complex and multifaceted area of study, and there is no single solution capable of covering all situations. Spanish-speaking clients may share a primary language but represent diverse linguistic and cultural backgrounds. Individuals from different Hispanic cultures vary greatly with regard to country of origin; sociopolitical, economic, and educational experiences; religion; and language(s) spoken. Length of residency in the U.S., from recently immigrated to multiple generations in the U.S., parent ethnicity (Hispanic or other), and family use of Spanish vary widely among Spanish-speaking clients (Elliott, 2012). Many of these variables impact test taking and ultimately test scores. Moreover, these environmental variables in combination with sociological factors may selectively influence the developmental trajectory of specific cognitive abilities in children, as well as the form of expression of intelligent behavior in adolescents. Although there are numerous important issues related to competent psychological assessment of culturally and linguistically diverse clients, in this chapter we restrict our focus to those that are either unique or critical to intellectual assessment with Hispanics. Thus, this chapter should be considered in context with more comprehensive texts on the subject of multicultural assessment (Geisinger, 2014; Rhodes, 2010; Rhodes, Ochoa, & Ortiz, 2005; Suzuki & Ponterotto, 2007).

L. G. Weiss, D. H. Saklofske, J. A. Holdnack and A. Prifitera (Eds): WISC-V Assessment and Interpretation.
DOI: http://dx.doi.org/10.1016/B978-0-12-404697-9.00007-8
215

We realize that some of the terminology for ethnic groups is controversial, and there is a wide variety of opinion regarding which term is best. We have used the term Hispanic as it appears to be the most current in the literature. Although Latino/a is gaining in prominence, it is not yet as preferred as Hispanic according to research conducted by the Pew Research Center (Lopez, 2013).

When assessing intelligence with Hispanic clients, it is important to acknowledge the incremental improvement in U.S. school performance observed as acculturation increases (Lopez, Ehly, & Garcia-Vasquez, 2002). Experience in U.S. schools may be associated with variables known to impact cognitive performance, such as exposure to new learning opportunities and novel intellectual stimulation, and positive changes in socioeconomic environment. Formal education conveys cultural information and conventions for thinking and categorization skills, all of which may affect both verbal and nonverbal test performance. Customs concerning verbal communication may evolve through exposure to U.S. culture and educational settings. For some immigrants, prior experiences with formal education and acculturation may have been limited due to geographic constraints, economic barriers, or sociopolitical constraints affecting access to educational resources. Experience with the testing situation and acquisition of test-taking skills will likely have a positive influence on the individual's performance on cognitive assessments. Experience with U.S. educational culture is likely to facilitate the development of bilingual skills in native Spanish speakers, which may influence performance on cognitive tests. For example, bilingual children exhibit greater inhibitory control and executive functioning skills than observed in monolingual children (Bialystok, Craik, & Luk, 2008; Carlson & Meltzoff, 2008). Younger children acquiring English may take 5 to 7 years, on average, to approach grade level in academic areas (Ramirez, 1991).

Establishing rapport within formal assessment situations involving clients from different cultures cannot be emphasized enough. As elaborated by Elliott (2012), individuals from diverse backgrounds, especially children who face unfamiliar adults in unfamiliar test situations, may be more reluctant to interact and perform at their best. Under some circumstances, parents may be confused or suspicious about the purpose and use of the testing, and directly or indirectly communicate their discomfort to them. This could potentially compromise the child's performance and the validity of the evaluation. Testing may be especially stressful for Hispanic clients residing in the U.S. without documented residency, who may be fearful of any scrutiny by persons in positions of perceived authority. Examiners must be sensitive to these issues. It may be necessary to meet with children and parents over extended periods of time in order to build rapport and to clarify the nature and purpose of an evaluation, the confidential nature of the evaluations, and the manner in which results will be utilized. Such extended effort is well worthwhile as most parents, regardless of immigration status, are very interested in how well their children are adjusting and learning in school.

As Elliott (2012) observes, the issue of what language to test a child in is a critical question; however, the concept of dominant language may be losing favor as proficiency in two languages occurs on a continuum, with bilingual individuals being able to understand or express some concepts better in one language and other concepts in the other language. Proficiency can shift based on context, with some individuals being able to speak fluently about one topic in one language and other topics in the second language. This is especially true for children learning Spanish first as a home language, then English in school. Best practice is to reduce the influence of school experience and secondary language acquisition on test performance, but there is no single best way of accomplishing this goal because of the myriad of potential influences.

We focus first on issues related to appropriate use of the WISC-V with Hispanic clients who speak English, or both English and Spanish. Subsequently in this chapter, we review issues related to testing Spanish-speaking clients in Spanish with the WISC-IV U.S. Spanish edition (Wechsler, 2005).

TESTING HISPANICS WITH WISC-V

The WISC-V (Wechsler, 2014) normative samples included culturally and linguistically diverse individuals who were judged by the examiner to speak English well enough to take the test. All Wechsler norms include Hispanic subjects who speak some Spanish if their English language skills were considered by the examiner to be better than Spanish and adequate for assessment purposes. Clearly, the decision to assess a Spanish-speaking client in English must be made based on numerous factors including but not limited to language spoken as a child or adolescent, years of school in English language classrooms, languages spoken at home, and, for older adolescents, languages spoken at work. Such decisions should be carefully considered in each case and not be made based on the preference of the examiner, nor only due to lack of an available Spanish-speaking examiner. Optimally, this decision would be made by an examiner from the same cultural background or at least very experienced with the client's cultural and linguistic background. Further, results of assessments administered in English should be interpreted with caution, especially when there is concern about the child's English language skills. In this section, we provide some data to encourage more culturally sensitive interpretation of Wechsler intelligence tests administered in English to Hispanic clients who speak English.

The WISC-V normative sample was carefully stratified to represent the U.S. population by race/ethnicity for most groups of Hispanics. Thus, the same percentage of Hispanics is included in the sample as in the population. Because the percentage of U.S. Hispanics has increased over the generations, and differs by region of the country, the research team carefully matched the census data for Hispanics at each age band and within each region. In this way, the regional distribution of Hispanics from different countries of origin was represented. Most importantly, the parent's educational attainment for Hispanic children included in the normative sample was carefully matched to the distribution of educational attainment of Hispanics in the population.

TABLE 7.1 WISC-V Index Score Means for Hispanic Sample

Index	Mean
Primary Indices	
VCI	94.2
VSI	96.8
FRI	95.6
WMI	94.9
PSI	98.3
FSIQ	94.4
Ancillary Indices	
GAI	94.5
CPI	95.8
NVI	95.5
QRI	94.9
AWMI	94.5
Complementary Indices	
NSI	96.9
STI	95.3
SRI	95.2

Note: N = 458.
Data and table copyright Pearson 2014. All rights reserved.

Mean WISC-V Full Scale Index Quotient (FSIQ) and index scores for Hispanics are shown in Table 7.1. The mean scores ranged from 94.2 to 98.3. The lowest and highest mean scores were for Verbal Comprehension Index (VCI) and Processing Speed Index (PSI), respectively, which is the same pattern observed in WISC-IV (Weiss, Prifitera, & Munoz, in press). Some might argue that these means should be 100. They may say that it is possible that these means are depressed to the extent that some individuals tested did not, in fact, speak English well enough to take the test. Although there is no direct way to test this hypothesis with these data, bilingual research assistants carefully reviewed every verbal item response from each individual child in order to identify and eliminate those who exhibited a preponderance of responses in Spanish—although occasional responses in Spanish were accepted, and thus may be accepted in practice. One might also think that biased items were a

TABLE 7.2 Mean WISC-V FSIQ Scores by Parent Education Level

Education Level	FSIQ
8th grade or less	88.2
9th–11th grade	89.4
High school graduate	91.7
Some college	97.3
College graduate	105.0

Note: N = 2200. Individuals with a GED are included as high school graduates. College graduates are considered as 16 or more years of education.

TABLE 7.3 Percentage of Adults Who Did Not Complete High School Versus Those Who Obtained at Least One Year of College

	High School not Completed	Obtained at Least One Year of College
Hispanic	31%	43%
African American	12%	62%
White	4%	78%
Asian	8%	78%

Note: Individuals obtaining a GED are considered to have completed high school. Based on data from the U.S. Census Bureau's 2012 American Community Survey 1-year period estimates.

contributing factor. However, due to the use of expert item bias review panels combined with the sophisticated statistical techniques for detecting differential item functioning by group that is in routine use by most major test developers these days, item bias is unlikely to contribute substantially to the lower scores observed for Hispanics (see Chapter 6 for further discussion).

It is more likely that these differences are due to the overall parent educational level of the Hispanic sample. For example, we know that the correlation of education with the FSIQ is 0.53 for adults. Table 7.2 shows mean FSIQ scores of all children by level of parent education. As expected, children of more educated parents have higher test scores. The differences are dramatic, ranging from 88 to 105 points between children of the most and least educated parents. We also know that the average level of education of Hispanics is substantially less than all other racial/ethnic groups. Table 7.3 shows percentages of educational attainment by group. Hispanic adults who are the parents of WISC-V age children, have a much larger high school dropout rate (approximately 31%) and smaller rate of college entrance (43%) than any other major ethnic group—by far! It should also be mentioned that Hispanics differ significantly with regard to mean educational attainment between subgroups (e.g., Cuban, Mexican, Puerto Rican).

What is most notable, however, is how the Hispanic dropout rate has declined in the last decade. In the early 2000s, the percentage of Hispanic children aged 6–16 that had parents with less than a high school diploma was 47%. By 2012 it had dropped to 33.5%. This large decrease in the dropout rate represents positive change in educational attainment for the Hispanic population. Yet, the Hispanic dropout rate remains much higher than other groups.

Given the large educational disparities between racial/ethnic groups, and the robust correlation between education and intelligence test scores, somewhat lower mean FSIQ scores might be expected in the Hispanic samples. The mean WISC-V FSIQ scores for Hispanic children is 94.4, as shown in Table 7.1. This finding is most likely because samples of Hispanics with generally low educational attainment are being compared to a larger U.S. normative sample with significantly more education on average. If the test performance of Hispanic children was normed relative to a sample of children with the same level of parent educational—regardless of ethnicity—the mean Hispanic FSIQ would be almost identical to 100, as described below and in Chapter 6 of this book. Although some might consider that a fairer approach, we must keep in mind that such an education-adjusted score would tell us nothing about how an individual might be able to succeed in a world made up of largely more educated people. For better or worse, the accepted definition of intelligence involves performance relative to the full population within the country of interest.

To better understand the societal factors underlying these score patterns, Weiss et al. (2006) undertook a systematic investigation of the factors that influence FSIQ scores for Hispanics based on variables available in the WISC-IV standardization data. We showed that ethnicity explained 1.4% of the variance in Hispanic/White FSIQ score differences; whereas 17.5% of the variance was explained by the parents' educational level. Parent income added an additional 3.5% above parent education. More to the point, after controlling for both parent education and income, ethnicity explained no further variance and the magnitude of the difference between Hispanic and White WISC-IV FSIQ scores was reduced to 0.5 points.

We subsequently repeated the above investigation using WISC-V data (Weiss et al., 2014), and found ethnicity alone explained 3.0% of the variance in Hispanic/White FSIQ score differences, whereas 18.8% of the variance was explained by a combination of the parent educational level and income. After controlling for these socioeconomic variables, ethnicity alone explained no further variance, and the magnitude of the difference between Hispanic and White WISC-V FSIQ scores was reduced 0.9 points (see Chapter 6).

Given the above findings, one might expect to see a trend toward higher Hispanic FSIQ scores across generations as children of Hispanic immigrants assimilate into the new culture, gain access to and achieve more education or better paying jobs, and advance in socioeconomic status. Weiss, Chen, Harris, Holdnack, and Saklofske (2010) examined this hypothesis and found it largely supported. We found that average WAIS-IV FSIQ scores (which are age corrected) for Hispanics have increased by 8 points from 85 for those born between 1917 and 1942 to 93 for those born between 1988 and 1991; although the trend was not steadily increasing across all birth cohorts.

All of this means that ethnic status is likely a proxy variable for a host of other structural variables that are more directly related to FSIQ, and when controlling for those variables, ethnicity directly accounts for very little, if any, of the variance in test scores. This view is reinforced by a multinational study which demonstrated a strong relationship between economic factors and education on WISC-III test scores across 12 nations (Georgas, Weiss, van de Vijver, & Saklofske, 2003). We should seek to understand better the underlying societal variables responsible for these differences and cease focus on the surface variable of group membership. Toward this end, we strongly refer the reader to Chapter 5 in which we elaborate how racial/ethnic differences in education, occupation, income, physical, and mental health status impact the cognitive development of children.

Yet, test scores are not completely determined by societal variables. As mentioned above, individual differences in ability likely account for the largest share of the variance, and noncognitive factors such as achievement motivation are important to cognitive development as well. For children and adolescents, home environment and parental behavior toward children are particularly important in terms of enriching or impeding children's cognitive development (see Chapter 6). *This is because even naturally endowed cognitive abilities must grow and develop over time and require proper doses of nurturance and cognitive stimulation at the right time in the developmental sequence.* To begin to test this idea, Weiss et al. (2006) asked parents some very basic questions related to the role of education in the family including how likely they believed it was that their child would get good grades, graduate high school, attend college, etc. Surprisingly, we found that these questions explained 31% of the variance in FSIQ scores—more than parent education and income combined at 21%. We then controlled for parent education and income and found that parent expectations still explained 16% of the variance in FSIQ scores. Thus, although the explanatory power of parent expectations reduces by about half after controlling for parent education and income, the size of the remaining effect is meaningful. Parents with high expectations for the educational attainment of their children typically engage in a wide range of parenting behaviors broadly related to academic and cognitive development such as monitoring and assisting with homework, encouraging exploration, providing meaningful verbal stimulation that improves language development, reading to children and encouraging reading, etc. This finding is supported by the work of Carol Dweck (2012) who has shown that individuals who believe that intelligence can increase based on effort tend to score higher on measures of IQ.

Parent expectations were significantly related to children's FSIQ scores at all levels of parent education, but more so among parents with high school educations, and least among parents who did not graduate from high school. We interpret these findings with regard to the impact of distal environmental constraints on proximal attitudes and behaviors in the home environment. It may be that real societal and economic factors constrain the power of parent expectations among the lowest socioeconomic status families. Still, parent expectations as expressed through parenting behaviors in the home environment remain a powerful force on the cognitive development of children in all families.

HISPANIC BASE RATES FOR WISC-V

With this background firmly in mind, we believe that in clinical practice it is also useful to have a sense of how a client compares to others of the same ethnicity and with similar educational backgrounds. For this reason we provide new Hispanic percentile norms for WISC-V, stratified by the educational distribution of Hispanics living in the U.S. in this chapter. *The Hispanic base rates supplement information derived from the FSIQ, but do not replace the FSIQ. Thus, whenever the Hispanic percentile norms are reported they should be clearly identified as such, and the standard FSIQ should also be reported.*

Hispanic percentile norms for the WISC-V primary, ancillary, and complementary index scores are provided in Tables 7.4 and 7.5, respectively. These tables can be used to determine how a child's score compares to other Hispanic children. For example, a WISC-V VCI score of 85 would be at the 26th percentile compared to other Hispanics, whereas the WISC-V norms tables in the *Administration and Scoring Manual* show that a score of 85 is at the 16th percentile compared to the general population. Both pieces of information are useful. The Hispanic percentile norms provide more culturally specific information to supplement interpretation of test scores.

Tables 7.6 and 7.7 show base rates of WISC-V index score discrepancies for primary, ancillary, and complementary index scores, respectively. Inspection of the mean differences by direction reveals that most Hispanic children and adolescents show a pattern of lower VCI, FRI (Fluid Reasoning Index), and WMI (Working Memory Index) scores, with higher VSI (Visual–Spatial Index) and PSI scores compared to the mean of their own index scores. At the same time, some Hispanic children show the opposite pattern. For example, 21% of the Hispanic sample obtained VCI scores 5 or more points *higher* than their mean index score. The pattern of slightly higher PSI scores is somewhat surprising given common clinical lore that speed of performance is a characteristic of U.S. culture not completely shared by all other cultures. Although this might be true as a cultural value, the present data suggest no differences in the speed of

TABLE 7.4 Percentile Norms from WISC-V Hispanic Sample for the Primary Index Scores

Obtained Score	FSIQ	VCI	VSI	FRI	WMI	PSI
≤70	1.1	1.6	1.2	1.2	1.6	1.3
71	2.5	3.8	2.9	2.7	3.5	2.8
72	3.1	4.7	3.9	3.4	3.9	3.3
73	3.5	5.6	4.7	4.0	4.6	3.7
74	4.0	6.8	5.4	4.5	5.6	4.2
75	5.0	8.2	6.0	5.6	6.9	4.6
76	6.2	9.6	6.7	7.1	8.6	5.7
77	7.3	11.2	7.5	8.6	10.2	7.4
78	9.0	13.1	8.3	10.0	11.9	9.0
79	10.9	14.6	9.1	11.5	13.6	10.3
80	12.3	15.9	9.9	13.0	15.5	11.6
81	13.8	17.3	10.7	14.6	17.8	12.8
82	15.2	19.0	11.9	16.2	20.1	13.9
83	17.3	21.2	13.3	18.3	22.7	15.0
84	20.0	23.4	14.8	20.7	25.7	16.5
85	22.5	26.4	17.2	23.2	28.6	18.6
86	26.0	30.4	20.6	25.8	31.6	20.6
87	29.7	33.6	23.5	28.4	34.5	22.4
88	33.3	36.2	26.1	31.0	37.4	23.9
89	37.1	38.9	28.6	33.9	40.3	25.4
90	39.4	41.9	31.5	37.0	43.1	27.6
91	40.5	45.4	34.6	40.1	46.0	30.2
92	43.3	48.9	37.7	43.2	48.8	32.9
93	47.3	52.0	41.8	46.2	51.5	35.6
94	50.6	54.7	46.8	49.2	54.3	38.2
95	53.8	57.4	50.8	52.5	56.9	40.8
96	57.3	60.1	53.7	56.1	59.4	44.0

(Continued)

TABLE 7.4 (Continued)

Obtained Score	FSIQ	VCI	VSI	FRI	WMI	PSI
97	60.8	62.9	56.6	59.8	61.9	47.7
98	63.5	65.7	59.3	62.7	64.2	51.4
99	65.4	68.8	61.7	65.1	66.3	54.9
100	67.3	72.4	64.1	67.4	68.4	58.0
101	69.9	75.0	66.8	69.7	70.6	60.9
102	72.7	76.6	69.9	71.9	73.0	63.4
103	75.7	78.2	72.5	74.2	75.4	66.0
104	78.2	79.9	74.7	76.1	77.3	69.1
105	80.0	81.6	76.9	77.7	78.7	72.8
106	82.1	83.2	79.0	79.3	80.1	75.8
107	84.2	84.9	81.1	81.2	81.4	78.2
108	86.5	86.7	83.2	83.2	82.8	80.5
109	88.7	87.9	84.9	85.2	84.2	82.5
110	90.0	88.7	86.2	86.8	85.6	84.1
111	91.1	89.4	87.6	87.9	87.0	85.7
112	92.1	90.2	88.9	89.0	88.5	87.1
113	93.1	91.1	90.3	90.2	89.7	88.2
114	94.0	91.9	91.7	91.5	90.5	89.4
115	94.7	92.8	92.8	92.8	91.3	90.8
116	95.1	93.7	93.6	93.9	92.3	92.4
117	95.5	94.6	94.4	94.7	93.5	93.6
118	96.0	95.6	95.1	95.5	95.1	94.3
119	96.2	97.0	95.7	96.9	97.0	95.1
≥120	98.1	98.9	98.0	98.9	98.9	97.7

TABLE 7.5 Percentile Norms from WISC-V Hispanic Sample for the Ancillary Index Scores

Obtained Score	GAI	CPI	NVI	QRI	AWMI	NSI	STI	SRI
≤70	0.9	1.5	1.0	1.4	2.5	3.5	2.7	3.6
71	2.0	3.3	2.3	3.4	5.3	7.0	5.9	7.3
72	2.6	3.7	2.8	4.5	5.8	7.2	6.6	7.8
73	3.8	4.0	3.2	5.5	6.3	7.4	7.4	8.6
74	5.4	4.5	3.4	6.3	7.0	7.9	8.7	9.7
75	6.9	4.9	3.8	7.2	7.9	8.3	9.6	11.5
76	8.1	6.4	4.4	8.4	8.7	9.2	10.2	13.1
77	9.3	8.2	5.1	9.8	9.5	10.2	11.6	13.7
78	10.6	8.8	6.1	11.1	10.3	11.0	13.2	14.4
79	12.1	10.4	7.4	12.5	11.7	12.7	14.4	16.2
80	13.7	12.2	9.6	13.8	13.8	14.5	15.5	17.8
81	14.7	13.5	11.6	15.5	15.8	15.5	16.6	18.8
82	16.8	15.8	12.5	17.5	18.0	17.1	18.3	20.2
83	19.4	18.5	13.5	20.0	20.3	19.3	20.3	22.5
84	21.8	20.6	15.0	22.8	22.6	20.9	22.4	24.1
85	24.5	23.5	18.2	25.7	25.3	23.0	24.8	26.3
86	27.0	26.3	22.7	28.7	28.4	25.4	27.1	28.5
87	30.1	28.3	26.0	31.9	31.4	27.3	29.6	30.7
88	33.3	30.5	28.7	35.1	35.4	28.8	32.0	33.4
89	35.7	33.0	31.4	37.7	40.2	31.8	35.9	36.0
90	37.8	35.4	33.9	39.7	43.7	35.6	40.1	38.4
91	39.7	37.7	37.0	41.8	45.9	37.7	42.5	41.4
92	43.5	41.1	41.6	44.4	48.0	39.5	44.5	45.0
93	47.3	44.6	45.4	47.5	51.0	42.3	46.8	47.8
94	49.2	47.3	47.4	50.6	54.9	44.4	49.3	51.3
95	52.5	50.2	49.8	53.4	58.2	47.4	51.8	53.9
96	55.7	53.1	52.7	55.9	60.9	50.2	53.5	55.8

(Continued)

TABLE 7.5 (Continued)

Obtained Score	GAI	CPI	NVI	QRI	AWMI	NSI	STI	SRI
97	57.6	56.1	56.4	58.4	63.7	51.3	54.9	58.4
98	60.5	59.2	61.0	61.1	66.1	53.0	57.6	60.9
99	64.3	62.1	64.6	64.1	68.2	56.1	61.1	63.1
100	67.4	65.0	66.8	67.1	70.3	59.9	63.7	64.6
101	69.9	68.0	70.0	69.9	72.3	63.4	65.5	67.4
102	72.5	71.1	73.5	72.7	74.2	66.5	67.6	70.9
103	75.3	73.8	76.2	75.5	76.1	68.6	69.3	72.5
104	78.4	76.0	78.1	77.8	78.0	70.7	71.3	74.1
105	82.1	77.9	79.2	79.6	79.7	73.1	73.6	76.1
106	84.6	79.5	80.9	81.4	81.4	75.8	75.4	77.4
107	85.5	81.1	82.6	83.2	83.4	78.0	77.2	78.7
108	87.0	82.5	83.7	85.0	85.4	79.0	79.2	80.2
109	88.5	84.5	85.7	86.9	86.9	79.8	80.8	82.1
110	89.3	86.3	87.6	88.5	87.8	80.9	83.1	83.7
111	89.7	87.3	88.9	90.0	88.7	82.2	85.2	85.6
112	90.6	88.2	90.1	91.4	89.7	83.7	85.9	87.3
113	92.0	88.9	90.9	92.9	90.9	85.4	86.9	88.2
114	92.9	89.9	91.7	94.4	91.8	86.7	88.4	89.1
115	93.1	90.8	92.7	95.3	92.4	88.2	89.5	90.0
116	93.7	91.7	93.3	95.6	92.9	89.5	90.5	90.8
117	94.4	92.9	94.1	95.9	93.6	90.9	91.8	91.4
118	95.9	94.1	95.0	96.5	94.4	92.5	92.6	92.0
119	97.7	94.8	95.6	97.2	95.2	93.6	93.2	93.0
≥120	99.2	97.6	97.9	98.8	97.8	96.9	96.8	96.7

TABLE 7.6 Base Rates of WISC-V Hispanic Sample Obtaining Various Index-Mean Index Score (MIS) Discrepancies

Amount of Discrepancy	VCI-MIS		VSI-MIS		FRI-MIS		WMI-MIS		PSI-MIS	
	VCI > MIS	VCI < MIS	VSI > MIS	VSI < MIS	FRI > MIS	FRI < MIS	WMI > MIS	WMI < MIS	PSI > MIS	PSI < MIS
≥20	0.9	2.4	1.5	1.1	1.5	1.3	1.8	1.1	6.6	1.5
19	1.7	2.8	2.0	1.1	1.5	2.0	2.2	1.3	8.1	2.4
18	2.6	4.1	3.3	1.3	2.6	2.4	2.6	2.2	9.6	3.7
17	3.1	5.5	4.1	2.0	3.5	3.1	2.8	3.7	11.1	5.2
16	3.7	7.0	4.1	2.8	4.1	4.1	4.2	4.6	12.9	5.9
15	3.7	8.3	4.6	3.9	4.4	5.9	5.3	6.1	14.6	7.6
14	5.5	9.8	5.9	4.8	5.9	7.2	7.2	8.8	17.5	8.7
13	6.1	11.1	9.0	5.9	6.8	8.5	7.9	11.2	19.7	9.4
12	6.6	12.9	11.1	6.6	7.4	10.9	10.1	12.9	21.2	11.6
11	8.1	15.5	12.7	8.5	9.4	13.1	11.8	15.3	23.1	13.1
10	10.5	17.7	15.1	10.9	12.0	16.4	12.7	19.0	25.5	14.6

(Continued)

TABLE 7.6 (Continued)

Amount of Discrepancy	VCI-MIS		VSI-MIS		FRI-MIS		WMI-MIS		PSI-MIS	
	VCI > MIS	VCI < MIS	VSI > MIS	VSI < MIS	FRI > MIS	FRI < MIS	WMI > MIS	WMI < MIS	PSI > MIS	PSI < MIS
9	11.8	21.0	17.5	15.1	14.2	18.6	13.6	22.5	27.5	17.9
8	14.8	25.1	20.5	16.4	16.8	21.2	16.4	26.0	31.4	20.1
7	16.4	28.8	24.2	18.3	22.3	24.0	19.5	30.4	33.6	22.1
6	20.3	32.8	28.2	22.1	25.1	26.0	22.8	33.9	37.3	25.3
5	21.6	35.6	32.5	25.5	29.9	31.0	25.6	37.0	42.6	29.0
4	25.5	41.0	37.1	29.7	33.0	34.3	30.4	41.4	45.0	31.7
3	28.8	45.4	43.2	34.3	36.5	38.4	33.3	45.1	48.5	34.9
2	33.8	51.5	46.5	37.1	40.6	41.9	37.0	49.5	52.2	38.6
1	37.3	57.0	52.0	43.7	48.5	47.4	42.0	54.3	55.0	41.7
MEAN	7.1	7.7	7.3	6.7	6.7	7.6	7.5	7.9	10.6	8.4
SD	5.5	5.7	5.2	5.1	5.1	5.4	5.9	5.1	7.9	5.8
MEDIAN	6.0	7.0	6.0	6.0	6.0	7.0	6.0	7.0	8.5	7.0

TABLE 7.7 Base Rates of WISC-V Hispanic Sample Obtaining Various Discrepancies Between Ancillary Composites

Amount of Discrepancy	GAI-CPI		WMI-AWMI		NSI-STI	
	GAI > CPI	GAI < CPI	WMI > AWMI	WMI < AWMI	NSI > STI	NSI < STI
≥20	4.6	7.9	1.1	0.7	12.1	8.9
19	5.3	9.0	1.1	0.7	13.6	10.5
18	6.1	9.4	2.0	1.5	15.0	11.4
17	8.3	11.8	2.2	1.8	17.0	13.4
16	9.2	12.9	3.5	2.2	19.4	14.7
15	10.5	14.7	3.7	3.3	20.1	15.2
14	12.3	16.6	3.9	3.7	21.4	17.0
13	14.2	18.8	6.1	4.4	23.4	19.6
12	16.6	21.2	7.7	7.2	26.1	22.1
11	18.4	23.4	8.5	7.9	28.1	23.7
10	21.0	26.7	11.4	9.6	31.5	25.0

(Continued)

TABLE 7.7 (Continued)

Amount of Discrepancy	GAI-CPI		WMI-AWMI		NSI-STI	
	GAI > CPI	GAI < CPI	WMI > AWMI	WMI < AWMI	NSI > STI	NSI < STI
9	23.2	29.8	13.8	13.1	34.2	27.5
8	24.1	31.1	15.8	16.8	35.7	29.7
7	28.9	34.4	20.4	19.9	37.3	31.0
6	30.2	37.4	25.2	23.0	40.0	34.6
5	34.1	41.4	27.4	25.8	43.1	36.6
4	37.2	42.7	34.1	29.8	46.9	37.9
3	40.5	44.9	37.2	35.0	50.0	39.3
2	42.2	47.7	43.3	39.6	52.2	41.5
1	45.5	51.4	50.5	43.3	53.8	42.6
MEAN	10.0	11.3	6.4	6.7	14.0	14.0
SD	7.0	8.2	5.1	4.6	11.6	10.7
MEDIAN	9.0	10.0	5.0	6.0	11.0	12.0

neurocognitive information processing abilities. This finding is the same pattern as that observed for Hispanic adults on WAIS-IV (Weiss et al., 2010).

These data are important because they may help prevent overinterpretation of low VCI scores when such scores are in fact not uncommon among Hispanics. At the same time, however, some psychologists may tend to overlook even very low verbal scores in Hispanic children on the assumption that such patterns are common due to language variations. The tables presented here provide cultur- ally specific data to aid in these interpretations. As shown in the table, a VCI score that is 11 or more points below the child's own mean could be considered unusual because it was obtained by approximately 15% of the Hispanic sample. In clinical practice, such findings should be interpreted in the context of the child's overall ability, years of education in English-speaking schools, language dominance, and parents' level of education.

TESTING SPANISH-SPEAKING CLIENTS

The WISC-IV Spanish (Wechsler, 2005) is a translation and adaptation of WISC-IV for use with Spanish-speaking Hispanic children aged 6–16 living in the U.S. The trans-adaptation of each item and all subtest directions were reviewed by a panel of expert bilingual psychologists representing the majority of Hispanic countries of origin included in the sample. To assess further the qual- ity of the items across Hispanic cultures, each item was submitted to multiple procedures for identifying differential item functioning (i.e., item bias) among Hispanic children from different countries of origin. Children were excluded from the sample if they reported speaking or understanding English better than Spanish, or if they had been in U.S. schools for more than 5 consecutive years. Intellectually disabled children were excluded if they had been in U.S. schools for more than 7 consecutive years.

As part of the standardization research project, 851 U.S. Hispanic children were tested and this sample was used to evaluate differential item function- ing by country of origin and evaluate results of the norms equating process. The reliability sample ($n = 500$) used to generate the normative information was from Mexico (40%), South/Central America (28%), Dominican Republic (16%), Puerto Rico (12%), and Cuba (4%). Some but not all of the Puerto Rican children were tested in Puerto Rico. All children from all other countries were living in the U.S. when tested. Country of origin was stratified relative to the U.S. Hispanic population within age band, parent educational level, region of U.S., and gender. However, the U.S. Mexican population was intentionally undersampled to ensure that sufficient numbers of subjects from other Hispanic countries of origin were represented in the norms.

The WISC-IV Spanish was designed to produce scores equivalent to the WISC-IV. Thus, children can take the test in Spanish and obtain scores that directly compare them to a representative sample of all children in the U.S. population. Because subtest adaptations for the PRI and PSI were restricted to translation of instructions to the child, the norms for these subtests were adopted directly from the WISC-IV. The adaptation of the verbal and working memory subtests required more modifications, including changes to item content and item order, and scoring rules, in part to account for variations in the Spanish language. Aligning the verbal and working memory subtests distributions to the U.S. norms was accomplished through equipercentile calibration. The method was evaluated by comparing the WISC-IV Spanish-obtained scores to a sample of Hispanics tested with the WISC-IV ($n = 538$ each) matched on parent education level. The mean FSIQ was 92.1 and 94.1 for the WISC-IV Spanish and WISC-IV samples, respectively, and the effect size of the difference was small (.13). The method was further evaluated by comparing the WISC-IV Spanish-obtained scores to a sample of White children on the WISC-IV ($n = 582$ each), matched on parent education level. In this study the mean FSIQs were 94.3 and 98.6 for the WISC-IV Spanish and WISC-IV, respectively, and the effect size was small (.26). An important limitation of both studies is that it was not possible to match the U.S. samples to the Spanish samples on years of U.S. education as all of the education of the U.S. sample was in the U.S. We further discuss issues related to U.S. educational experience on intelligence test scores below.

As described above, it is also useful to compare the performance of Hispanic children to the performance of a subset of children who are culturally similar. Thus, demographically adjusted percentile norms were created for use with WISC-IV Spanish based on the number of years of experience the child had in U.S. schools, and the parent's level of education. These variables combined accounted for 22% of the variance in FSIQ scores, with parent education accounting for the majority of the combined variance. Tables necessary to employ this adjustment can be found in Appendix C of the test's technical manual. First, the number of grades completed in the U.S. is calibrated by the total number of grades completed. This is because 2 years in U.S. schools has a different impact for a 2nd versus 10th grade student. A cross-tabulation of this rating with the parent's level of education yields five categories, each resulting in a different set of adjustments for percentile norms.

In this way, a student's obtained scores on WISC-IV Spanish can be compared to all U.S children using the standardized scores, and then to Hispanic children who have similar experiences in the U.S. educational system and are from similar parent educational backgrounds. Following this method, an 8th grade student with a WISC-IV Spanish FSIQ score of 85, which is at the 16th percentile of the U.S. population, is found to be better than 61% of Hispanic children who obtained two of their seven completed grades in U.S. schools and whose parents obtained between 9 and 11 years of education. The difference between the 16th and 61th percentile makes a huge difference in interpretation. On the one hand, the child scored better than only 16% of all children her age. At the same time, her score was better than 61% of Hispanic children her age who have completed only 2 years of school in the U.S. and whose parents did not graduate high school. *To be clear, this is not an issue of which percentile is more correct. They are both correct, but answer different questions. Both pieces of information are important and are necessary to complete the child's story.*

Obvious limitations of this method include the inability to control for variables related to the language of instruction in the child's U.S. classes (e.g., dual language programs, English immersion programs, etc.), or the quality of the parents' education in the country of origin. Practitioners should consider these issues as they interpret the adjusted percentile scores. Still, this is a useful beginning on the path to more culturally sensitive interpretation of intelligence test scores. It is important because patterns of immigration vary by country of origin and across generations, and these patterns have strong effects on mean test scores. Individuals from some countries come to the U.S. in search of basic skilled or entry level jobs, whereas others have the financial and educational resources to escape oppressive situations (e.g., political repression, economic turmoil, armed conflict, etc.). *The average socioeconomic status of the immigrant populations from each country of origin has a profound impact on the mean intelligence test scores for that group. These patterns of immigration are different for different countries and can change over time for the same country.* For example, the first author (LGW) lives in San Antonio, Texas, where the pattern of immigration from nearby Mexico is changing in part due to the presence of violent conditions widely associated with drug cartels in several regions of that country. Whereas adults with few years of education have historically emigrated from Mexico to Texas in search of basic skilled jobs, the immigration pattern today includes an increasing number of successful Mexican professionals and wealthy business persons moving their families to a safer environment. As foreshadowed by the data presented above in Table 7.2 regarding mean FSIQ scores by level of education, this shift in the pattern of immigration is beginning to have an observable impact on the housing market, local retail businesses, and school systems in upper middle class neighborhoods of the city. Thus, the adjusted percentile norms could be very informative in this situation. Following the example above, this same child with an FSIQ of 85 would be performing better than only 10% of Hispanic children who obtained 2 of their 7 completed years of education in the U.S. *and* whose parents had graduated college. This interpretation is likely the more relevant comparison for this child, and failing to identify her as in need of support would be a disservice to her family.

All of these issues must be considered when evaluating Hispanic children recently arrived in the U.S. and the methods described herein can assist the practitioner in thinking through these issues, but should be considered as guideposts only. Clinical judgment by culturally similar or trained psychologists knowledgeable of changing conditions in the local community is also necessary for competent, culturally sensitive interpretation.

USE OF INTERPRETERS

Best practice is for Spanish-speaking clients to be assessed by a Spanish-speaking examiner administering a validated Spanish edition of the test. Ideally, the examiner would not only speak Spanish but be from the same cultural and linguistic background as the client. However, this procedure is not always feasible. For non-Spanish-speaking examiners, an interpreter may be necessary in order to administer a *validated Spanish edition* such as WISC-IV Spanish. When using interpreters, it is important to be familiar with the ethical guidelines for the use of interpreters, and follow general guidelines for selection, training, and use of interpreters. For example, relatives of the child should not be used as interpreters. Training is required for the interpreter prior to test administration in order to ensure valid results. Interpreters should receive specific instruction in the importance of following standard procedures and not offering subtle hints to the person being tested. The psychologists should observe practice administrations to ensure the interpreter achieves proficiency prior to the actual testing. It is recommended that the examiner manage the stimulus book, timer, and manipulatives, and record responses to nonverbal items, while the interpreter reads the verbal instructions to the child and translates the child's verbal responses without embellishment. The interpreter should also record verbatim responses in Spanish in addition to translating them for the examiner during the assessment, so that after the evaluation they can discuss nuances of scoring based on the written record. If an interpreter is used, the psychologist should note this fact in the psychological report, along with the level of training provided. Although a comprehensive discussion of the use of interpreters is beyond the scope of this chapter, the DAS-II Spanish manual (Elliott, 2012) provides further guidance on this complex topic.

Using interpreters to translate English test questions to Spanish during the evaluation is poor practice. But, the methods described here, and in the DAS-II Spanish manual, can yield acceptable—though not optimal—results when carefully applied with validated Spanish editions of cognitive ability tests. Because the use of interpreters is not best practice, however, these methods generally should not be used in high stakes evaluations such as may result in restrictive placement, or influence child custody decisions.

SUMMARY AND CONCLUSIONS

The complexity of questions relating to language, culture, and educational experience, which impact the development of cognitive abilities in children and their performance on intelligence tests, precludes simple, singular answers. Flexible assessment tools that allow professionals supplemental, alternative perspectives based on the client's unique cultural and linguistic background are a part of best practices in the assessment of culturally and linguistically diverse children. Toward this goal, the present chapter provides Hispanic percentile norms for WISC-V composites, and base rates of index score discrepancies between composites not previously available for Hispanics. The Hispanic percentile norms supplement information derived from the FSIQ, but do not replace the FSIQ. Both pieces of information may be valuable in psychological evaluations. The WISC-IV Spanish edition allows children to be tested in Spanish and their performance compared to the general population of U.S. English-speaking children of the same age through equating. For a discussion of using the WPPSI-IV and WAIS-IV with Spanish-speaking clients, refer to Weiss et al. (in press).

ACKNOWLEDGMENTS

The authors wish to thank Antolin Llorente, Alexander Quiros, and Josette Harris for comments on an earlier draft of this manuscript.

REFERENCES

Bialystok, E., Craik, F., & Luk, G. (2008). Cognitive control and lexical access in younger and older bilinguals. *Journal of Experimental Psychology: Learning, Memory, and Cognition, 34,* 859–873.

Carlson, S. M., & Meltzoff, A. N. (2008). Bilingual experience and executive functioning in young children. *Developmental Science, 11,* 282–298.

Dweck, C. S. (2012). Mindsets & human nature: Promoting change. *American Psychologist, 67*(8), 614–622.

Elliott, C. (2012). *Administration and technical manual for the differential abilities scale—Second edition; Early years Spanish supplement.* San Antonio, TX: Pearson.

Geisinger, K. F. (2014). *Psychological testing of Hispanics* (2nd ed.). Washington, DC: APA Press.

Georgas, J., Weiss, L. G., van de Vijver, F. J. R., & Saklofske, D. H. (2003). *Culture and children's intelligence: Cross-cultural analysis of the WISC-III.* San Diego, CA: Academic Press.

Lopez, E. J., Ehly, S., & Garcia-Vasquez, E. (2002). Acculturation, social support and academic achievement of Mexican and Mexican American high school students: An exploratory study. *Psychology in the Schools, 39*(3), 245–257.

Lopez, M. H. (2013). *Hispanic or Latino? Many don't care, except in Texas.* Retrieved from: <http://www.pewresearch.org/fact-tank/2013/10/28/in-texas-its-hispanic-por-favor/>. Accessed 01.05 14.

Ramirez, J. D. (1991). Executive summary of volumes I and II of the final report: Longitudinal study of structured English immersion strategy, early-exit and late-exit transitional bilingual education programs for language-minority children. *Bilingual Research Journal, 16*(1 & 2), 1–62.

Rhodes, R. L. (2010). Multicultural school neuropsychology. In D. Miller (Ed.), *Best practices in school neuropsychology: Guidelines for effective practice, assessment, and evidence-based intervention* (pp. 61–77). Hoboken, NJ: John Wiley & Sons.

Rhodes, R. L., Ochoa, S. H., & Ortiz, S. O. (2005). *Assessing culturally and linguistically diverse students: A practical guide.* New York: Guilford Press.

Suzuki, L. A., & Ponterotto, J. G. (2007). *Handbook of multicultural assessment: Clinical, psychological, and educational applications.* New York: John Wiley & Sons.

Wechsler, D. (2005). *Wechsler intelligence scale for children—Fourth edition Spanish: manual.* San Antonio, TX: Harcourt Assessment.

Wechsler, D. (2014). *Wechsler intelligence scale for children—Fifth edition: Administration and scoring manual.* San Antonio, TX: Pearson.

Weiss, L. G., Chen, H., Harris, J. G., Holdnack, J. A., & Saklofske, D. H. (2010). WAIS-IV use in societal context. In L. G. Weiss, D. H. Saklofske, D. Coalson, & S. E. Raiford (Eds.), *WAIS-IV clinical use and interpretation.* San Diego, CA: Academic Press.

Weiss, L. G., Harris, J. G., Prifitera, A., Courville, T., Rolfhus, E., Saklofske, D. H., et al. (2006). WISC-IV interpretation in societal context. In L. G. Weiss, D. H. Saklofske, A. Prifitera, & J. A. Holdnack (Eds.), *WISC-IV advanced clinical interpretation*. San Diego, CA: Academic Press.

Weiss, L. G., Locke, V., Pan, T., Harris, J. G., Saklofske, D. H., & Prifitera, A. (2014). WISC-V in societal context. In L. G. Weiss, D. H. Saklofske, & A. Prifitera (Eds.), *WISC-V clinical assessment & interpretation*. San Diego, CA: Academic Press.

Weiss, L.G., Prifitera, A., & Munoz, M. (in press). Intelligence testing with Spanish speaking clients. In K.F. Geisinger (Ed.), *Psychological testing with Hispanics* (2nd ed.). Washington, DC: APA Books.

Chapter 8

WISC-V and the Evolving Role of Intelligence Testing in the Assessment of Learning Disabilities

Donald H. Saklofske[1], Lawrence G. Weiss[2], Kristina Breaux[2], and A. Lynne Beal[3]

[1]*Department of Psychology, University of Western Ontario, London, Ontario, Canada,* [2]*Pearson Clinical Assessment, San Antonio, TX, USA,* [3]*Private Practice, Toronto, Ontario, Canada*

INTRODUCTION

One of the most described and studied groups of exceptional children and adults falls within the broad category of learning disability. Over the past 100 years and particularly in more recent times, considerable progress has made in defining and diagnosing learning disabilities with most emphasis on dyslexia or specific reading disability. As well, advances in cognitive psychology, neuropsychology, and brain sciences have contributed to a greater understanding of the etiology of learning disability (LD), which, in turn, has led to the development of educational programs that can enable persons with LD to develop and use strategies so they may fully function without restriction due to their disability. The incidence and significance of LD has also been addressed in national and state or provincial legislation in countries such as the United States and Canada, which ensures opportunity without restriction in the schools of today.

At the same time as many advances are being made in our understanding of learning disabilities, there remain widely different views on how to operationalize definitions of LD for identification or diagnosis, although there is more agreement on definitions of dyslexia. These differing views are further evident across disciplines within psychology (i.e., neuropsychology, school psychology), as well as across school districts and countries.

Although this book focuses on the WISC-V, its relevance in the assessment and intervention of LD is worthy of a separate chapter. The overview of this

L. G. Weiss, D. H. Saklofske, J. A. Holdnack and A. Prifitera (Eds): WISC-V Assessment and Interpretation.
DOI: http://dx.doi.org/10.1016/B978-0-12-404697-9.00008-X

history, up to contemporary perspectives on LD, is followed by current descriptions of LD, as reflected in definitions derived from research and legislation. From roots in dyslexia and LD research we trace the current cognitive characteristics and subtypes of LD. Links between subtypes of LD and measures of cognitive ability that are logically linked to achievement follow. We acknowledge a 20-year legacy of controversy about the role of IQ tests in LD evaluations, and seek to overview these diverse opinions with a focus on an appropriate role for cognitive assessment and the WISC-V.

Within this context, we introduce WISC-V and the contributions it makes to understanding cognitive processes underlying academic achievement and LD. Data from the clinical studies presented in the WISC-V technical manual illustrate the relevance of this test in a description of specific LDs.

LEARNING DISABILITY: CURRENT DEFINITIONS AND SUBTYPES

Definitions of LD have also evolved over time and in different jurisdictions. Legislation that provides a functional definition in the United States is from the Individuals with Disabilities Education Act (IDEA, 2004). This legislation links children's impairments in academic, cognitive, and other functions to entitlement to special education services. IDEA mandates that states evaluate all children suspected of having a disability by conducting multidisciplinary comprehensive assessments when determining eligibility for special education services under IDEA. "Specific learning disability," according to IDEA (2004) is defined as:

> ...a disorder in one or more of the basic psychological processes involved in understanding or in using language, spoken or written, that may manifest itself in the imperfect ability to listen, think, speak, read, write, spell, or to do mathematical calculations, including conditions such as perceptual disabilities, brain injury, minimal brain dysfunction, dyslexia, and developmental aphasia.

Although U.S. federal regulations provide general guidelines in regard to identification and classification, states have considerable flexibility in how they interpret and institute policies and practices in definitions, classification criteria, assessment processes, and other considerations (Bergeron, Floyd, & Shands, 2008; Reschly & Hosp, 2004). Since 1990 the Office of Special Education Programs (OSEP) has held that the U.S. federal law and regulations do not require documentation of a processing disorder to identify a learning disability. Nonetheless, states are allowed to impose their own understanding of these terms based on the Congressional definition and to require adherence to those guidelines as an additional burden on eligibility groups.

In Canada, provincial and territorial Ministries of Education and advocacy groups promote their own consensus-based definitions within each province (Kozey & Siegel, 2008). In Ontario, for example, in 2014 the Ministry of

Education updated its definition of learning disability that entitles students to a special education program. It defines learning disability as a neurodevelopmental disorder that persistently and significantly has an impact on the ability to learn and use academic and other skills resulting in academic underachievement that is inconsistent with at least average intellectual ability. Significantly, the definition typically associates the academic underachievement with difficulties in one or more cognitive processes, such as phonological processing (Ontario Ministry of Education, 2014).

The definition of the Learning Disabilities Association of Canada (LDAC) (2002) refers to "average abilities essential for thinking and/or reasoning," as distinct from "global intellectual deficiency." It goes on to include, "impairments in one or more processes related to perceiving, thinking, remembering or learning. These include, but are not limited to: language processing, phonological processing; visual–spatial processing, processing speed; memory and attention; and executive functions (e.g., planning and decision-making)." Building on this definition, the Ontario Ministry of Education has adopted the opinion of the Expert Panel on Literacy and Numeracy Instruction for Students with special needs, which notes that, "knowledge about a student's strengths and weaknesses in cognitive processing helps teachers provide appropriate instruction and accommodations for children in their classrooms" (Ontario Ministry of Education, 2005).

Identification of a Learning Disability

A clinical approach to diagnosis that conceptualizes dyslexia as neurobiological in origin is well supported by research (see Chapter 9 on dyslexia). In school psychology settings, the purpose of LD evaluations is to determine eligibility for special education services. These determinations in the United States are typically based on administrative criteria set by the school district in compliance with more general legal criteria set by the state boards of education consistent with federal regulations. Although informed by research, the administrative criteria employed by school districts can diverge from clinical diagnostic criteria set forth in the DSM-V (American Psychiatric Association, 2013), which are followed more closely by neuropsychologists and clinical psychologists. Such differences in criteria for identifying LD can be an area of disagreement between school psychologists and psychologists in private practice who assess students for learning disabilities.

The two primary approaches currently used to identify a learning disability in many school settings are problem-solving (instructional) and intra-individual (cognitive).

A problem-solving approach identifies students with low achievement and provides intervention accordingly, relying on tools such as curriculum-based assessment, progress monitoring, and a response to intervention service delivery model (Fletcher, Morris, & Lyon, 2003). This approach to identification is not concerned with classification or subtypes; rather, the goal is to intervene early and to help as many struggling learners as possible. Challenges associated with this approach involve determining the cut point for defining low achievement (Fletcher, 2012), instability in group membership over time (Francis et al., 2005), and determining the predictors and causes of failure to respond to instruction. Further in-depth critique is found in Reynolds and Shaywitz (2009). If a student fails to respond to instruction, then the assumption is that either the student has a disabling condition (such as LD, attention-deficit hyperactivity disorder [ADHD], or intellectual disability) or the instructional program was inadequate in some way (Vaughn & Fuchs, 2003). At that point, a comprehensive evaluation that includes cognitive and neuropsychological assessment is typically recommended in order to determine the nature of the disabling condition (Hale et al., 2010).

An intra-individual approach to identification focuses primarily on cognitive explanations for learning difficulties (e.g., phonological processing, rapid automatic naming, and working memory) and the identification of intra-individual differences as the marker for unexpected underachievement (Fletcher, et al., 2003). Limitations of this approach may arise from failing to consider important neurological and environmental factors (Hagen, Kamberelis, & Segal, 1991) and focusing on processing skills that are not directly related to intervention (Torgesen, 2002).

Central to the intra-individual approach is the notion that unexpected underachievement, the defining hallmark of a learning disability, is evidenced by a contrast (or discrepancy) between intact and deficient abilities (Kaufman, 2008). According to the specificity hypothesis (Broca, 1865, as cited in Fletcher, Lyon, Fuchs, & Barnes, 2007), individuals with a learning disability exhibit specific, as opposed to general, learning difficulties, whereas normally achieving students exhibit more evenly developed cognitive abilities (Compton, Fuchs, Fuchs, Lambert, & Hamlett, 2011; Fuchs et al., 2008). According to S. Shaywitz (2003), the distinctive learning profile associated with dyslexia may resemble an isolated weakness within a "sea of strengths."

This conceptualization of a learning disability differentiates students with an overall low profile of cognitive and achievement abilities (slow learners or students with intellectual disability) from those who struggle to learn despite average or better IQ. For this reason, traditional definitions of a learning disability have excluded individuals with below average intellectual functioning. In addition to intellectual disability, the exclusionary criteria provided in the IDEA regulations include sensory or motor impairments, emotional disturbance, cultural factors, environmental or economic disadvantage, limited English proficiency, and lack of appropriate instruction in reading [34 CFR 300.307]. However, defining learning disabilities on the basis of such exclusionary criteria has been challenged by many researchers (e.g., Elliott & Gibbs, 2008; Fletcher et al., 2002; Lyon & Weiser, 2013) primarily because such criteria do not meaningfully differentiate struggling learners in terms of information processing skills, neurobiological factors, or instructional requirements. For example, attempts to differentiate between reading disabilities that are environmental as opposed to neurobiological in origin has been criticized because the factors contributing to reading problems are interrelated and complex, and the resulting distinctions may not be worthwhile for education planning (Elliott & Grigorenko, 2014). In addition, differentiating between generally poor readers (with below average IQ) and poor readers with average or better IQ has been challenged by showing that the two groups do not differ in the cognitive processes that underlie academic performance (Fletcher, 2005; Fletcher et al., 1994; González & Espinel, 2002; Maehler & Schuchardt, 2011; Siegel, 1988, 1992).

Subtypes of Learning Disability

An enormous body of research has accumulated with various approaches for identifying subtypes of learning disabilities. Subtyping holds widespread appeal because it offers a way to explain the heterogeneity within the category of LD, and it aims to describe the learning profile of students with LD more specifically in order to plan a more individualized approach to intervention. There is considerable debate over the existence of LD subtypes as distinct categories that can be reliably identified, how best to categorize LD subtypes, and whether instructional implications differ by subtype. However, research programs designed to identify effective interventions for learning disabilities are unlikely to progress without improvements in our understanding and ability to identify LD subtypes.

Inquiry into possible subtypes of learning disabilities began when Johnson and Myklebust (1967) and colleagues (e.g., Boshes & Myklebust, 1964; Myklebust & Boshes, 1960) proposed a nonverbal disability characterized by the absence of serious problems in areas of language, reading, and writing, but with deficiencies in social perception, visual–spatial processing, spatial and right–left orientation, temporal perception, handwriting, mathematics, and executive functions such as disinhibition and perseveration. A nonverbal learning disability is characterized as reflecting a right hemisphere deficit in the neuropsychology literature (Pennington, 1991; Rourke, 1989); however, it remains the least well understood.

According to Fletcher et al. (2003), there are three main approaches to subtyping learning disabilities: achievement subtypes; clinical inferential (rational) subtypes; and empirically based subtypes.

The first approach, achievement subtypes, relies on achievement testing profiles. For example, subgroups of reading difficulties are differentiated by performance on measures of word recognition, fluency, and comprehension. Subgroups of reading disability, math disability, and low ability groups (with IQ scores below 80) exhibit different patterns of cognitive attributes, which were not used to define the groups, and also differ in heritability and neurobiological correlates (Fletcher et al., 2003; Grigorenko, 2001). Compton et al. (2011) found distinctive patterns of strengths and weaknesses in abilities for several LD subgroups, in contrast to the flat pattern of cognitive and academic performance manifested by the normally achieving group. For example, students with reading comprehension LD showed a strength in math calculation with weaknesses in language (listening comprehension, oral vocabulary, syntax); students with word reading LD showed strengths in math problem-solving and reading comprehension with weaknesses in working memory and oral language.

The second approach, clinical inferential, involves rationally defining subgroups based on clinical observations, typically by selecting individuals with similar characteristics, such as a phonological core deficit. The double-deficit model of subtypes (Wolf & Bowers, 1999; Wolf, Bowers, & Biddle, 2000) distinguishes three subtypes: two subtypes with a single deficit in either phonological processing or rapid automatic naming, and a third subtype with a double-deficit in both areas. Another subtype model classifies poor decoders as having either phonological dyslexia, orthographic/surface dyslexia, or mixed dyslexia (phonological and orthographic weaknesses) based on performance on nonword reading and exception (irregular) word reading (Castles & Coltheart, 1993; Feifer & De Fina, 2000).

The third approach, empirically based subtypes of learning disabilities, is based on multivariate empirical classification. It uses techniques such as Q-factor analysis and cluster analysis, and subsequent measures of external validity. Empirical subtyping models have been criticized for being atheoretical and unreliable; however, these models have provided additional support for rational subtyping methods, including the double-deficit model and differentiating garden-variety from specific reading disabilities (Fletcher et al., 2003). A recent example is a study by Pieters, Roeyers, Rosseel, Van Waelvelde, and Desoete (2013), which used data-driven model-based clustering to identify two clusters of math disorder: one with number fact retrieval weaknesses, and one with procedural calculation problems. When both motor and mathematical variables were included in the analysis, two clusters were identified: one with weaknesses in number fact retrieval, procedural calculation, as well as motor and visual–motor integration skills; a second with weaknesses in procedural calculation and visual–motor skills.

The identification and classification of a learning disability relies on either a dimensional or categorical framework. Subtyping efforts are based on evidence that the heterogeneity within learning disabilities is best represented as distinct subtypes. For example, the results by Compton et al. (2011) are used to support the differentiation of reading and math LD because students with reading LD tended to have a relative strength in mathematics, whereas students with mathematics LD tended to have a relative strength in reading. However, some researchers contend that the attributes of reading disability and math disability are dimensional, and efforts to categorize these as distinct subtypes are based on cut scores and correlated assessments (Branum-Martin, Fletcher, & Stuebing, 2013). In the interest of providing tailored intervention to a heterogeneous population of individuals with LD, continued research is needed to advance our understanding of LD subtypes and their instructional implications.

INTELLIGENCE: A KEY LINK IN THE ASSESSMENT AND DIAGNOSIS OF LEARNING DISABILITY

The history of learning disabilities shows an increasingly prominent role of intelligence, or cognitive abilities, as the context for understanding achievement deficits. Through that evaluation, cognitive ability tests have been used to estimate academic potential and to predict response to intervention, although the latter is an area of considerable controversy. Currently, all three alternative research-based approaches to LD identification (i.e., third-method approaches) require that general ability or intelligence is average or better in relation to specific academic and cognitive weaknesses (Flanagan, Fiorello, & Ortiz, 2010). Further, Swanson's (2011) review of three meta-analysis studies revealed that IQ accounts for a substantial amount of the explainable variance in reading performance, ranging from .47 to .58, and there is value in considering IQ as an aptitude measure for identifying learning disabilities in children. Assessment of cognitive ability or cognitive processing has also been defended in order to identify gifted students with learning disabilities (Crepeau-Hobson & Bianco, 2011). As part of a learning disability evaluation, research indicates the importance of measuring verbal reasoning, which is average or better among individuals with reading disability (Berninger et al., 2006), and measuring nonverbal reasoning, which is average or better among individuals with oral and written language learning disability (OWL-LD; Berninger, O'Donnell, & Holdnack, 2008).

However, the use of cognitive ability tests for the identification of learning disabilities is not without controversy. Other researchers contend that, although IQ moderately predicts academic achievement, IQ does not assess aptitude for learning that predicts achievement outcomes for students with LD, and so it should not be used as a benchmark for identifying underachievement (Elliott & Grigorenko, 2014; Fletcher, Coulter, Reschly, & Vaughn, 2004; Sternberg & Grigorenko, 2002). Some of these same critics do recommend the use of cognitive ability testing to provide information about the level of intellectual challenge that is appropriate for a student with learning difficulties, so that teachers can adjust the curricular demands and activities in the classroom accordingly (Elliott & Grigorenko, 2014). Much of this research ignores the longitudinal findings of Ferrer et al. (2010), which shows that IQ and reading ability systematically diverge as individuals with dyslexia grow older, but not for average readers (see Chapter 9).

Similar debate surrounds the use of IQ scores for predicting instructional outcomes. Some studies have shown IQ to be a significant predictor of the response to instruction (e.g., Fuchs, Fuchs, Mathes, & Lipsey, 2000; Fuchs & Young, 2006), whereas many studies assert the opposite finding (e.g., Donovan & Cross, 2002; Gresham & Vellutino, 2010; Stuebing, Barth, Molfese, Weiss, & Fletcher, 2009). Swanson's (Swanson, 2011; Swanson & Hoskyn, 1998; Swanson, 1999) analysis of treatment outcomes showed that IQ has a moderating role in treatment outcomes; and, further, that approximately 15% of the variance in outcomes is related to instruction.

Researchers investigating the specificity hypothesis of LD, the distinctive cognitive profiles of individuals identified with a learning disability, and the possibility of LD subtypes continue to rely on cognitive processing measures to advance scientific understanding. These cognitive processes constitute the broad abilities assessed by most contemporary intelligence tests, including the WISC-V. As we discuss next, intelligence testing in LD evaluations has expanded from an exclusive focus on the composite IQ score to include consideration of each of the broad cognitive processes or abilities that comprise general intelligence.

Beyond the Full Scale Intelligence Quotient (FSIQ): Advances in Intelligence and its Relevance in LD Assessment

Throughout the above discussion, continuous reference has been made to the critical role of intelligence in the definition and diagnosis of learning disabilities. In turn, advances in cognitive science, as well as definitions of LD have directly influenced the evolution of cognitive ability tests in this century (for descriptions of the evolution from theory to practice, see Greenberg, Lichtenberger, & Kaufman, 2013). Advances have moved the science beyond an exclusive focus on a global description of intelligence such as an IQ score as reflected in the early Binet tests or the Wechsler scales until the publication of the WISC-III and WAIS-III. The division of the construct of IQ into a set of distinct yet related cognitive abilities, or indexes, has allowed researchers to link achievement in reading, written language, and mathematics to specific cognitive abilities.

Cattell-Horn-Carroll (CHC) theory (McGrew & Flanagan, 1998) provides a taxonomy for classifying cognitive abilities that is useful for identifying the common abilities measured by different intelligence tests, enabling researchers to communicate and extend findings across studies. McGrew and Wendling's (2010) summary of over 20 years of research on CHC classified cognitive–achievement relation has shown that "cognitive abilities contribute to academic achievement in different proportions in different academic domains, and these proportions change over the course of development."

Some argue that the consistent application of this taxonomy to LD research is necessary if LD assessment is to improve and become more reliable and valid (Flanagan, Ortiz, Alfonso, & Mascolo, 2006). An operational definition of LD that reflects these advances includes the analysis of cognitive ability (Flanagan & Mascolo, 2005). By matching the cognitive processes that underlie success in various academic subjects, practitioners can provide a better understanding of the clear links between deficits in specific cognitive processes and specific academic abilities. Along with the test results, developmental and academic history, tests based on models of cognitive ability provide significant information to draw conclusions about a child's cognitive strengths and deficits, and their implications for education, careers, and other daily activities of the people they assess. A synopsis of the development of specific cognitive ability tests that follow models of cognitive ability is provided by Beal, Willis, and Dumont (2013).

TABLE 8.1 Alignment of the Cattell-Horn-Carroll (CHC) Model to Areas of Information Processing

Cattell-Horn-Carroll Broad Abilities	Areas of Information Processing
Gf Fluid Reasoning	Thinking
Gc Crystallized Intelligence	Language Processing
Gv Visual–Spatial Thinking	Visual–Spatial Processing
Glr Long-term Memory Retrieval	Memory
Ga Auditory Processing	Phonological Processing
Gwm Working Memory	Memory
Gs Processing Speed	Processing Speed

Note: Gwm has replaced Gsm (Short-term Memory) used in earlier models.

A TAXONOMY OF COGNITIVE ABILITIES RELATED TO LEARNING DISABILITIES

The LDAC (2002) definition of LD aligns well with the broad abilities identified in the original CHC model (McGrew & Flanagan, 1998), as shown in Table 8.1. As noted by Horn and Blankson (2012), each broad ability involves learning, and is manifested as a consequence of many factors that can affect learning over years of development.

Links between deficits in particular cognitive abilities that are indicative of learning disabilities in specific academic areas have been demonstrated empirically (Flanagan, Alfonso, & Ortiz, 2012). Table 8.2 shows the CHC abilities most related to reading, math, and writing.

Psychoeducational Relevance of the WISC-V

The Wechsler Intelligence Scale for Children, Fifth Edition (WISC-V) (2014) is the fifth generation of this cognitive abilities test. Since its original edition based on Wechsler's view of clinical tasks that are indicative of intelligence, the test has evolved to reflect models of human cognitive functions that measure processes that could enhance or impair learning. The WISC-V has expanded from an IQ test into a test of multiple cognitive abilities that are easily mapped to six of the seven CHC broad abilities, as follows:

- VCI (Gc)
- VSI (Gv)
- FRI (Gf)

- WMI (Gwm)
- PSI (Gs)
- NSI and STI (Glr)

The five WISC-V primary indexes align with Gc, Gv, Gf, Gwm, and Gs. In addition, Glr is measured by two complementary WISC-V indexes: Naming Speed Index (NSI) and Symbol Translation Index (STI), which are discussed in

TABLE 8.2 CHC Abilities Related to Reading, Math, and Writing

CHC Abilities Most Related to Reading

Ability	Relationship to Reading
Gc	Language development, lexical knowledge, and listening abilities become increasingly important with age
Gwm	Memory span especially within the context of working memory
Ga	Phonetic coding or phonological awareness/processing during the elementary school years
Glr	Naming facility or RAN during the elementary school years
Gs	Perceptual speed, particularly the elementary school years

CHC Abilities Most Related to Math

Ability	Relationship to Math
Gf	Induction and general sequential reasoning at all ages
Gc	Language development, lexical knowledge, and listening abilities become increasingly important with age
Gwm	Within the context of working memory
Gv	Primarily for higher-level or advanced math
Gs	Perceptual speed, particularly during the elementary years

CHC Abilities Most Related to Writing

Ability	Relationship to Writing
Gc	Language development, lexical knowledge, and general fund of information primarily after age 7 become increasingly important with age
Gwm	Memory span especially for spelling skills
	Working memory shows relations with advanced writing skills (e.g., written expression)
Gs	Perceptual speed is related to basic writing and written expression at all ages

detail below. The Wechsler Individual Achievement Test, Third edition (WIAT-III) (Pearson, 2009) Oral Expression and Listening Comprehension subtests also measure Glr.

The WIAT-III Pseudoword Decoding and Early Reading Skills subtests measure grapheme-phoneme knowledge, which is integral to the reading and writing processes. When used together, WISC-V and WIAT-III provide coverage of many of the CHC broad abilities. Many practitioners routinely administer WIAT-III together with WISC-V in LD assessment for this reason, and because they are empirically linked.

Table 8.3 shows the CHC taxonomy in more detail, including both the broad and narrow abilities, and maps the WISC-V and WIAT-III subtests and indexes to the broad and narrow CHC factors. Also shown in this table are the new WISC-V complementary indexes and subtests.

TABLE 8.3 CHC Taxonomy, Including Both the Broad and Narrow Abilities

Broad Ability	Narrow Ability	WISC-V Subtests/Indices	WIAT-III Subtests
Gc		Verbal Comprehension Index	Listening Comprehension; Oral Expression
	LS, K0	Information, Comprehension; Picture Concepts	
	LS		Listening Comprehension; Oral Discourse Comprehension
	VL	Vocabulary; Similarities	Listening Comprehension; Receptive Vocabulary; Oral Expression; Expressive Vocabulary
	LD		Reading Vocabulary; Oral Expression; Sentence Repetition
Gc/Gf		Similarities	
Gf		Fluid Reasoning Index; Quantitative Reasoning Index	Math Problem Solving
	I	Matrix Reasoning; Picture Concepts; Similarities	
	RQ	Figure Weights; Arithmetic, Quantitative Reasoning Index	Math Problem Solving
Gf/Gc		Picture Concepts	
Gf/ Gwm		Arithmetic	

(Continued)

TABLE 8.3 (Continued)

Broad Ability	Narrow Ability	WISC-V Subtests/Indices	WIAT-III Subtests
Ga			Pseudoword Decoding; Early Reading Skills
	PC		Pseudoword Decoding; Early Reading Skills
Gv		Visual–Spatial Index	
	Vz	Block Design; Visual Puzzles	
Gs		Processing Speed Index	Math Fluency Subtests
	R9	Coding; Naming Speed Literacy; Naming Speed Quantity	
	P	Symbol Search, Cancellation	
	N		Math Fluency Addition; Math Fluency Subtraction; Math Fluency Multiplication
Gwm		Working Memory Index, Auditory Working Memory Index	Oral Expression
	MS		Oral Expression: Sentence Repetition
	MS, MW	Digit Span	
	MW	Letter-Number Sequencing, Picture Span, Arithmetic	
Gwm/ Gv		Picture Span	
	MV	Picture Span	
Glr		Naming Speed Index; Symbol Translation Index; Storage and Retrieval Index; Immediate Symbol Translation; Delayed Symbol Translation; Recognition Symbol Translation	Oral expression; Listening Comprehension
	Fl		Oral Expression; Oral Word Fluency

(Continued)

TABLE 8.3 (Continued)

Broad Ability	Narrow Ability	WISC-V Subtests/Indices	WIAT-III Subtests
	MM		Listening Comprehension; Oral Discourse Comprehension
	MA	Immediate Symbol Translation; Delayed Symbol Translation; Recognition Symbol Translation	
	NA	Naming Speed Literacy; Naming Speed Quantity	
Grw			Alphabet Writing Fluency; Early Reading Skills; Word Reading; Pseudoword Decoding; Reading Comprehension; Essay Composition; Sentence Composition; Spelling
	RD		Word Reading; Pseudoword Decoding
	RC		Reading Comprehension
	RS		Oral Reading Fluency; Word Reading; Speed Score; Pseudoword Decoding; Speed Score
	WA		Essay Composition; Sentence Composition
	WS		Alphabet Writing Fluency
	EU		Essay Composition; Sentence Composition
	SG		Alphabet Writing Fluency; Spelling
Gq			Math Problem Solving; Numerical Operations
	KM		Math Problem Solving
	A3		Math Problem Solving; Numerical Operations; Math Fluency Addition; Math Fluency Subtraction; Math Fluency Multiplication

Grw/Gs is how some experts conceptualize the broad ability associated with the actual task.
Cross-loading is not uncommon due to the nature of many cognitive tasks.
The Cognitive Proficiency Index (CPI) can be thought of as Gwm/Gs.

The WISC-V complementary indexes and subtests were specifically designed to inform psychoeducational assessment of children being evaluated for specific learning disorders such as in reading and mathematics. Each WISC-V index score, its component subtests, and their tasks are described next.

Naming Speed Index

The Naming Speed Index (NSI) is comprised of two optional subtests: Naming Speed Literacy (NSL) and Naming Speed Quantity (NSQ). In the NSL subtest the child names elements of various stimuli as quickly as possible. The tasks utilize stimuli and elements that are traditional within rapid naming task paradigms (e.g., colors, objects, letters, and numbers) and that have shown sensitivity to reading and written expression skills and to specific learning disorders in reading and written expression. As described in the WISC-V Technical and Interpretive Manual (Wechsler, 2015), similar tasks are closely associated with reading and spelling skill development, with reading achievement, and with a number of variables related to reading and spelling, and have shown sensitivity to specific learning disorder in reading (Crews & D'Amato, 2009; Korkman, Barron-Linnankoski, & Lahti-Nuuttila, 1999; Korkman, Kirk, & Kemp, 2007; Powell, Stainthorp, Stuart, Garwood, & Quinlan, 2007; Willburger, Fussenegger, Moll, Wood, & Landerl, 2008). Some studies suggest they are also related to mathematics skills, specific learning disorder-mathematics, and a number of other clinical conditions (McGrew & Wendling, 2010; Pauly et al., 2011; Willburger et al., 2008; Wise et al., 2008). In order to ensure sensitivity beyond very early grades, the tasks involve naming multiple dimensions simultaneously and alternating stimuli. Such tasks are also sensitive to a wide variety of other neurodevelopmental conditions such as ADHD (Korkman et al., 2007), language disorders in both monolingual and bilingual children (Korkman et al., 2012), and autism spectrum disorder (Korkman et al., 2007). Children at risk for neurodevelopmental issues have been reported to score lower on similar measures (Lind et al., 2011), which are described as measuring storage and retrieval fluency, and naming facility (Flanagan et al., 2012). These subtests specifically measure the automaticity of visual–verbal associations, which should be well developed in school-aged children.

In the NSQ subtest the child names the quantity of squares inside a series of boxes as quickly as possible. The subtest is similar to tasks in the experimental literature that show greater sensitivity to mathematics skills and specific learning disorders in mathematics than do the traditional rapid automatized naming tasks that are more closely associated with reading- and writing-related variables (Pauly et al., 2011; van der Sluis, de Jong, & van der Leij, 2004; Willburger et al., 2008). Tasks that involve rapid naming of stimuli are described as measuring naming facility, and storage and retrieval fluency (Flanagan et al., 2012).

Symbol Translation Index

The Symbol Translation Index (STI) measures learning associations between unfamiliar symbols and their meanings, and applies them in novel ways.

The subtest consists of three conditions: immediate, delayed, and recognition. In the Immediate Symbol Translation (IST) subtests the child learns visual–verbal pairs and then translates symbol strings into phrases or sentences. Tasks similar to IST are described as measuring verbal–visual associative memory or paired associates learning, storage and retrieval fluency and accuracy, and immediate recall (Flanagan et al., 2012). This is a cued memory paradigm; that is, the child recalls information related to a specific visual cue.

As described in the WISC-V Technical and Interpretive Manual (Wechler, 2015), visual–verbal associative memory tasks similar to the Symbol Translation subtests are closely associated with reading decoding skills, word reading accuracy and fluency, text reading, and reading comprehension (Elliott, Hale, Fiorello, Dorvil, & Moldovan, 2010; Evans, Floyd, McGrew, & Leforgee, 2001; Floyd, Keith, Taub, & McGrew, 2007; Hulme, Goetz, Gooch, Adams, & Snowling, 2007; Lervåg, Bråten, & Hulme, 2009; Litt, de Jong, van Bergen, & Nation, 2013). Furthermore, they are sensitive to dyslexia when they require verbal output (Gang & Siegel, 2002; Li, Shu, McBride-Chang, Lui, & Xue, 2009; Litt & Nation, 2014). Visual–verbal associative memory tasks are also related to math calculation skills and math reasoning (Floyd, Evans, & McGrew, 2003; McGrew & Wendling, 2010).

In the Delayed Symbol Translation (DST) condition the child translates symbol strings into sentences using visual–verbal pairs previously learned during the IST condition. Tasks similar to DST are described as measuring verbal–visual associative memory or paired associates learning, storage and retrieval fluency and accuracy, and delayed recall (Flanagan et al., 2012). This task is a cued memory paradigm.

In the Recognition Symbol Translation (RST) subtest the child views a symbol and selects the correct translation from response options the examiner reads aloud, using visual–verbal pairs recalled from the IST condition. Tasks similar to RST are described as measuring verbal–visual associative memory or paired associates learning, storage and retrieval fluency and accuracy, and delayed recognition (Flanagan et al., 2012). This task constrains the child's responses to words that have been presented in the task and therefore eliminates the possibility of an erroneous word being recalled. This task measures the strength of the associate learning and not the learning of content (e.g., correct words). The examiner may compare performance on this task to the delayed condition to determine the impact of constraining recall on memory performance.

Storage and Retrieval Index

The Storage and Retrieval Index (SRI) is formed by combining the scores from the NSI and the STI. This provides an overall measure of the child's ability to store and retrieve learned information quickly and efficiently.

WISC-V Studies of Children with SLD

The WISC-V Technical and Interpretive Manual reports results from three studies of specific learning disabilities (SLD): SLD in reading (SLD-R), SLD in reading and writing (SLD-RW), and SLD in mathematics (SLD-M). The study samples included 30 children with SLD-R between the ages of 7 and 16, 22 children with SLD-RW between the ages of 6 and 14, and 28 children with SLD-M between the ages of 9 and 16. The sample of SLD-RW were predominantly male (15 males, 7 females), which is expected given that males are at greater risk for writing difficulties than females (Reynolds, Scheiber, Hajovsky, Schwartz, & Kaufman, in submission). The SLD-R and SLD-M groups showed a roughly equal gender split. Control groups of children without a clinical diagnosis were randomly selected from the normative sample and then matched to the clinical groups according to age, sex, race/ethnicity, and parent education level.

Children included in these studies were initially identified as SLD using various criteria, including meeting DSM-5 (2013) criteria, documentation of an ability-achievement discrepancy, a pattern of strengths and weaknesses approach, or eligibility for receiving learning disability services. However, all cases included in these clinical studies were reviewed to ensure that the children met DSM-5 criteria for SLD. These criteria include impairment in reading, reading and writing, or math, as appropriate, which are substantially and quantifiably below those expected for the child's chronological age, causing significant interference with school functioning. Comorbid SLD diagnoses were not permitted with the exception of the SLD-RW group.

The performance of children with SLD-R as compared to matched controls is shown in Table 8.4. The SLD-R group scored significantly ($p < .05$) lower on all the indexes with score differences producing moderate to large effect sizes. All of the global indexes (CPI, FSIQ, NVI, and GAI) showed large effects. The lower index scores obtained by the SLD-R group indicate significant difficulties with working memory, long-term storage and retrieval, verbal comprehension, rapid verbal naming, immediate paired associate learning, and quantitative reasoning. At the subtest level, the largest effect sizes were observed for Picture Span, Digit Span, Similarities, and Arithmetic.

The performance of children with an SLD-RW as compared to matched controls is shown in Table 8.5. Children with SLD-RW scored significantly ($p < .05$) lower on all indexes with the exception of the VSI and PSI. Similar to the SLD-R group, the SLD-RW group demonstrated significant difficulties with long-term storage and retrieval, working memory, rapid verbal naming, quantitative reasoning, immediate paired associate learning, and (to a lesser extent) verbal comprehension. At the subtest level, the largest effect sizes were observed for Naming Speed Literacy, Letter-Number Sequencing, Digit Span, Similarities, Arithmetic, and Immediate Symbol Translation.

The performance of children with an SLD in mathematics (SLD-M) compared to matched controls is shown in Table 8.6. Children with SLD-M scored significantly ($p < .05$) lower on all indexes with the exception of the WMI and NSI. Among the global indexes, large effect sizes were observed for the NVI, FSIQ, and GAI and moderate for the CPI. Consistent with the nature of math disorders, the SLD-M group demonstrated significant difficulties with

TABLE 8.4 WISC-V Mean Performance of Children with SLD-R

Subtest	SLD-R		Matched Control			Group Mean Comparison		
	Mean	SD	Mean	SD	n	Difference	p-Value	Standard Difference
SI	8.2	2.2	10.3	2.4	30	2.07	<.01	.90
VC	7.7	2.6	10.0	3.0	30	2.23	<.01	.79
IN	8.5	1.9	10.1	2.4	30	1.60	<.01	.74
CO	8.6	3.2	10.2	2.9	30	1.60	.03	.52
BD	9.1	2.6	10.3	3.0	30	1.13	.11	.40
VP	8.5	3.1	10.3	2.2	30	1.87	<.01	.70
MR	8.6	2.1	10.4	2.6	30	1.83	<.01	.77
FW	8.9	2.3	10.3	3.0	30	1.37	.08	.51
PC	8.8	3.0	9.5	2.4	30	.70	.35	.26
AR	8.4	2.1	10.7	3.2	30	2.30	<.01	.85
DS	8.2	1.6	10.5	2.3	30	2.33	<.01	1.18
PS	7.7	2.6	10.8	2.1	30	3.10	<.01	1.31
LN	8.2	2.3	9.9	2.1	30	1.73	<.01	.79
CD	8.7	3.1	10.1	3.0	30	1.40	.02	.46
SS	8.8	2.7	10.0	2.9	30	1.23	.07	.44
CA	9.5	3.1	9.5	3.3	29	.03	.97	.01
NSL	88.9	16.3	100.4	12.5	29	11.55	<.01	.80
NSQ	89.7	14.6	102.6	14.1	29	12.83	<.01	.89
IST	91.9	12.6	102.5	12.1	30	10.53	<.01	.85
DST	93.6	11.5	101.5	13.7	30	7.93	.02	.63
RST	93.6	9.9	101.5	11.6	30	7.87	.02	.73
Composite								
VCI	89.1	11.2	100.7	12.6	30	11.63	<.01	.98
VSI	93.3	14.1	101.6	12.4	30	8.27	<.01	.62
FRI	92.5	10.8	101.9	13.5	30	9.40	<.01	.77
WMI	87.8	10.1	104.1	11.2	30	16.23	<.01	1.52
PSI	93.0	15.3	100.3	14.4	30	7.37	.02	.50

(Continued)

TABLE 8.4 (Continued)

Subtest	SLD-R		Matched Control			Group Mean Comparison		
	Mean	SD	Mean	SD	n	Difference	p-Value	Standard Difference
FSIQ	88.9	10.5	102.0	13.9	30	13.07	<.01	1.06
NVI	89.6	11.8	102.6	13.2	30	13.03	<.01	1.04
GAI	90.0	11.0	101.6	13.1	30	11.63	<.01	.96
CPI	88.6	12.6	102.7	13.3	30	14.17	<.01	1.09
QRI	92.2	9.5	102.7	16.1	30	10.57	<.01	.80
AWMI	90.1	9.1	101.2	10.3	30	11.07	<.01	1.14
NSI	88.4	14.0	101.6	13.7	29	13.14	<.01	.95
STI	91.8	11.3	101.5	12.8	30	9.63	<.01	.80
SRI	87.4	11.4	101.9	12.2	29	14.55	<.01	1.23

TABLE 8.5 WISC-V Mean Performance of Children with SLD-RW

Subtest	SLD-RW		Matched Control			Group Mean Comparison		
	Mean	SD	Mean	SD	n	Difference	p-Value	Standard Difference
SI	7.2	2.0	9.1	2.1	22	1.91	<.01	.93
VC	7.8	2.4	8.9	2.9	22	1.09	.23	.41
IN	8.0	1.8	9.3	1.9	22	1.23	.05	.66
CO	7.5	2.1	8.5	2.6	22	.91	.17	.39
BD	9.1	2.8	10.1	2.5	22	1.00	.13	.38
VP	9.6	2.6	9.2	2.8	22	−.45	.49	−.17
MR	8.2	2.2	9.4	2.8	22	1.14	.21	.45
FW	7.8	3.2	9.9	2.8	22	2.14	.03	.71
PC	9.5	3.0	10.6	2.4	22	1.14	.22	.42
AR	7.4	2.0	9.6	2.8	22	2.27	<.01	.93

(Continued)

TABLE 8.5 (Continued)

Subtest	SLD-RW		Matched Control		Group Mean Comparison			
	Mean	SD	Mean	SD	n	Difference	p-Value	Standard Difference
DS	7.2	2.6	10.2	3.1	22	3.05	<.01	1.07
PS	8.0	2.0	9.4	3.0	22	1.36	.01	.53
LN	7.4	2.2	9.8	2.0	22	2.45	<.01	1.17
CD	7.8	3.3	9.0	2.8	22	1.14	.20	.37
SS	9.6	2.9	9.7	2.5	22	.09	.91	.03
CA	9.8	3.3	9.7	3.1	22	−.09	.91	−.03
NSL	85.6	16.2	101.9	8.4	21	16.33	<.01	1.27
NSQ	88.8	14.0	99.7	13.4	21	10.95	.02	.80
IST	88.2	15.1	102.0	14.3	22	13.73	<.01	.93
DST	90.1	16.7	101.1	15.7	22	11.00	.03	.68
RST	87.1	13.0	98.8	12.5	21	11.67	.01	.92
Composite								
VCI	86.5	10.1	94.6	11.7	22	8.09	.02	.74
VSI	96.2	13.3	98.0	12.5	22	1.73	.53	.13
FRI	88.4	12.2	97.8	13.3	22	9.45	.02	.74
WMI	85.8	9.7	98.7	13.9	22	12.95	<.01	1.08
PSI	93.0	15.8	96.3	11.3	22	3.36	.42	.24
FSIQ	84.8	11.1	96.2	10.5	22	11.41	<.01	1.06
NVI	88.6	12.7	95.9	11.5	22	7.27	.02	.60
GAI	87.0	10.9	96.4	12.2	22	9.45	.01	.82
CPI	87.2	12.0	96.8	10.0	22	9.64	<.01	.87
QRI	85.9	12.8	98.5	13.0	22	12.64	<.01	.98
AWMI	85.0	11.1	100.2	12.4	22	15.14	<.01	1.29
NSI	86.2	12.6	100.1	9.0	21	13.86	<.01	1.27
STI	87.1	14.2	100.4	14.3	21	13.29	<.01	.93
SRI	83.9	14.1	100.1	10.2	20	16.15	<.01	1.31

TABLE 8.6 WISC-V Mean Performance of Children with SLD-M

Subtest	SLD-M		Matched Control			Group Mean Comparison		
	Mean	SD	Mean	SD	n	Difference	p-Value	Standard Difference
SI	8.1	2.3	10.3	3.3	27	2.11	<.01	.74
VC	8.1	3.1	9.4	3.1	28	1.32	.04	.43
IN	7.5	2.3	10.3	3.7	27	2.78	<.01	.90
CO	8.0	2.7	10.4	3.0	28	2.43	<.01	.85
BD	7.1	2.3	9.8	3.3	28	2.64	<.01	.93
VP	7.6	2.6	10.3	2.6	28	2.64	<.01	1.02
MR	7.2	3.4	9.6	3.3	28	2.36	.01	.70
FW	6.5	3.2	9.4	2.9	28	2.82	<.01	.92
PC	8.7	2.9	11.0	3.9	28	2.32	.02	.68
AR	6.4	2.4	9.3	3.2	28	2.86	<.01	1.01
DS	7.9	2.7	9.9	3.5	28	1.93	.04	.62
PS	8.2	2.7	9.4	4.1	28	1.18	.21	.34
LN	7.9	2.1	9.7	3.7	27	1.81	.04	.60
CD	7.6	2.6	9.8	3.7	28	2.14	.01	.67
SS	8.8	2.9	9.4	2.9	28	.57	.39	.20
CA	10.3	2.9	10.6	3.2	28	.32	.66	.10
NSL	95.6	15.8	96.6	18.6	28	1.00	.84	.06
NSQ	91.1	15.4	96.0	19.0	28	4.93	.19	.29
IST	88.6	17.0	101.3	16.8	28	12.75	<.01	.75
DST	92.5	16.0	101.3	14.3	28	8.86	.04	.58
RST	90.4	17.0	98.2	15.0	28	7.79	.09	.49
Composite								
VCI	90.3	13.7	99.5	16.4	27	9.19	<.01	.61
VSI	85.4	12.6	100.0	15.3	28	14.61	<.01	1.04
FRI	82.2	15.4	96.7	16.2	28	14.46	<.01	.91
WMI	88.7	13.5	97.7	20.4	28	9.00	.07	.52
PSI	90.2	14.2	97.7	15.6	28	7.46	.03	.50

(Continued)

TABLE 8.6 (Continued)

Subtest	SLD-M		Matched Control			Group Mean Comparison		
	Mean	SD	Mean	SD	n	Difference	p-Value	Standard Difference
FSIQ	83.6	11.9	98.4	16.4	27	14.85	<.01	1.04
NVI	81.5	13.7	97.6	15.9	28	16.11	<.01	1.09
GAI	84.2	12.0	98.6	16.5	27	14.44	<.01	1.00
CPI	87.3	13.9	97.0	16.6	28	9.71	.02	.63
QRI	79.9	13.7	96.2	16.2	28	16.29	<.01	1.09
AWMI	88.3	11.2	99.1	19.2	27	10.78	.02	.69
NSI	92.6	14.2	96.4	18.8	28	3.79	.36	.23
STI	90.1	16.1	100.2	16.0	28	10.07	.02	.63
SRI	89.7	15.7	98.0	14.1	28	8.25	.03	.55

quantitative, conceptual, and spatial reasoning abilities. At the subtest level, the largest effect sizes were observed for Visual Puzzles, Arithmetic, Block Design, Figure Weights, and Comprehension. The low effect size for the NSQ subtest is somewhat surprising. NSQ was expected to provide greater sensitivity to mathematics skills and SLD-M than the traditional rapid automatized naming tasks; however, this expectation was not supported by the SLD-M study. One possibility is that NSQ is low primarily among young children with SLD-M. Unlike the SLD-R and SLD-RW studies, the SLD-M study did not include any children aged 6–8 in the sample, which may represent the grades at which NSQ is most related to the development of math skills. This view is supported by additional data available in the online supplement to the WISC-V Technical and Interpretive Manual (Wechsler, 2014) in which correlations of NSQ with various WIAT-III math subtests are shown to be substantially higher in the younger than older age groups. Another possibility is that NSQ is low only among certain types of math disorders. Further research is needed to investigate possible age or subtype effects among children with SLD-M on the NSQ subtest.

In these studies, across all three SLD groups, low scores with relatively large effect sizes were observed for the FSIQ, GAI, and QRI and, among the subtests, Arithmetic, Similarities, and Immediate Symbol Translation. With the exception of NSQ for older SLD-M students, the results from these studies reveal generally expected trends in performance among each SLD sample, which supports the validity of the WISC-V among children with SLD.

These studies show emerging performance patterns at the group level, while individual score patterns vary. As such, children with various reading difficulties may show a varying, or even contrasting pattern of strengths and weaknesses that cancel out in group data. The value of these clinical studies is in identifying trends in abilities of groups of children with learning disabilities that either confirm expectations or raise important questions. As always, diagnostic classifications are a matter of professional judgment by qualified practitioners. They are based not on any single test score, but on a preponderance of evidence including medical and family histories, cognitive, academic, and neuropsychological test scores, and well as the student's academic progress in response to empirically supported educational interventions.

REVISITING SLD IDENTIFICATION WITH THE WISC-V

The federal definition of SLD in the U.S. has remained the same for the past 30 years; however, the 2006 federal regulations introduced changes to the methods of SLD identification that are being implemented differently across school districts. For example, although the ability-achievement discrepancy (AAD) method continues to be permitted under these regulations, it can no longer be mandated as the sole criteria and some schools have eliminated its use while others continue it as one part of the process. Further, response to intervention (RTI) methods are encouraged by the federal guidelines associated with these regulations, and are now used in many states. At the same time, the regulations allow a so-called "third method," which is an alternative research-based approach to SLD identification that has now been adopted by more than 20 of the 50 states (Sotelo-Dynega, Flanagan, & Alfonso, 2011).

According to IDEA 2004 [Sec.602(30)], SLD means a disorder in "one or more of the basic psychological processes…" These processes are not defined by the law nor does the law require evidence of a processing weakness; however, third-method approaches require the assessment of cognitive processing areas in order to determine if the child's pattern of strengths and weaknesses is consistent with an operational definition of SLD. Research-based methods of SLD identification that are consistent with the third-method approach include Berninger's framework of assessment for intervention, Flanagan and colleagues' operational definition of SLD, Naglieri's Discrepancy/Consistency Model, and Hale and Fiorello's Concordance-Discordance Model (see Flanagan & Alfonso, 2011 for an overview of each method). These approaches share similar features. Each model expects a logical consistency between the achievement weakness and a cognitive processing weakness that is associated with that achievement area (such as performance on a word recognition measure and the NSI or STI). In addition, the models expect statistical discrepancy between the achievement weakness and a cognitive processing strength that is *not* associated with that achievement area (such as performance on a word recognition measure and the VSI). Finally, the models expect statistical discrepancy between the cognitive processing strength and weakness.

According to Berninger's (2011) framework, cognitive assessment is essential for differential diagnosis, especially measures of overall cognitive ability, verbal reasoning, and nonverbal reasoning. Using the WISC-V, these measures would include the FSIQ, VCI, and NVI. As a general estimate of intellectual functioning, the FSIQ is important for ruling out a developmental disability. In addition, measures of verbal and nonverbal intelligence are important for differentiating dyslexia and OWL-LD. In cases of dyslexia, basic reading and spelling are weak in relation to average or better scores on the VCI. The VCI may not be a notable strength in a child with dyslexia, but the score should not be a normative weakness. In cases of OWL-LD, the VCI is often a normative weakness because of the child's language impairments; however, nonverbal reasoning, as measured by the NVI, is at least average. In all three of the WISC-V SLD clinical studies, the VCI was significantly lower than matched controls with mean standard scores of about 89 for SLD-R, 87 for SLD-RW, and 90 for SLD-M. With standard deviations of 10–11 points, the SLD-R and SLD-RW groups included some cases with VCI scores below the average range; a more extensive evaluation would be necessary to confirm whether some of these cases qualified as OWL-LD. Hence, consider the FSIQ, VCI, and NVI scores as one component of an evaluation for determining whether a child may have a developmental disability, a language impairment, or dyslexia.

Pattern of Strengths and Weaknesses

A "third-method" approach to SLD identification, referred to as the Pattern of Strengths and Weaknesses (PSW) approach, is provided in both of Pearson's digital assessment and interpretation systems, Q-interactive and Q-global, for use with the WISC-V and the Kaufman Test of Educational Achievement, Third Edition (KTEA-3) (Kaufman & Kaufman, 2014) or the WIAT-III. This PSW approach most closely aligns with Hale and Fiorello's Concordance-Discordance Model (C-DM) (Hale & Fiorello, 2004).

The PSW approach is a statistically sound methodology for identifying the essential operational marker for SLD: unexpected learning failure, defined as consistency between areas of cognitive processing weakness and academic weakness coupled with a significant discrepancy between areas of cognitive processing strength and cognitive processing weakness (Hale & Fiorello, 2004; Hale, Kaufman, Naglieri, & Kavale, 2006). To use this model, the practitioner selects standardized measures that best represent the student's achievement weakness, cognitive processing strength, and cognitive processing weakness. Index scores with high reliability coefficients are generally preferred, provided that subtest scores within the composites are fairly consistent. Guidelines for selecting measures of strength and weakness include the following: first, the area of achievement weakness should be consistent with the referral concern and cross-validate the low performance with reports from teachers or other measures. Second, the cognitive processing weakness must be clinically or empirically associated with the achievement weakness, so that the student's learning difficulties are reasonably explained, at least in part, by the cognitive processing weakness. Third, the cognitive processing strength should not be strongly associated, clinically or empirically, with the achievement weakness.

Consider an example using the WISC-V and WIAT-III within a PSW approach to evaluate a student referred for reading difficulties. The student demonstrates weaknesses primarily in basic reading skills, as evidenced by a WIAT-III Basic Reading composite score in the below average range (with similarly low scores on both Word Reading and Pseudoword Decoding). Based on prior research (e.g., Fiorello, Hale, & Snyder, 2006; Hale, Fiorello, Kavanagh, Hoeppner, & Gaither, 2001) and given the validity support for the theoretical constructs measured by the WISC-V indexes, it would be appropriate to consider the following WISC-V index scores as cognitive processing weaknesses that could be associated with a weakness in basic reading skills: WMI, PSI, AWMI, STI, SRI, and NSI. Note that phonological processing is also a relevant processing weakness to consider; measures of phonological processing are typically included in diagnostic language and achievement tests. The following WISC-V index scores might be considered as cognitive processing strengths that are not strongly associated with basic reading skills: VCI, VSI, and FRI.

Using the standard error of the difference for statistical comparisons of standard scores, the PSW approach establishes discordance (significant difference) between the cognitive processing weakness and the cognitive processing strength, and between the achievement weakness and the cognitive processing strength. Statistically demonstrating a consistency between the cognitive processing weakness and the achievement weakness is not essential to the PSW approach (see Hale & Fiorello, 2004), but some applications of the C-DM model have included this step (e.g., Hale et al., 2013). If the student has not responded to good quality instruction and the criteria of the PSW model are met, the final step for identification is to determine whether IDEA statutory and regulatory requirements are met to qualify the student for special education services.

By incorporating the PSW approach into Tier 3 of an RTI framework, educators benefit from early identification and intervention for at-risk learners as well as a research-supported approach to SLD identification for nonresponders. IDEA 2004 neither suggested nor implied that practitioners must use either RTI or an intra-cognitive approach to determine SLD; however, gathering both RTI and cognitive assessment data is ideal for accurate SLD identification as well as for individualized interventions (Hale et al., 2006). For the purpose of intervention planning, children with learning disabilities require interventions that are tailored to their cognitive and academic strengths and needs, and although controversial, proponents argue that a PSW approach can provide the necessary information for planning differentiated instruction (Fiorello, Hale, & Wycoff, 2012).

The PSW approach may also be appropriate for the identification of students who are gifted wtih LD, or "twice exceptional." These students are capable of high intellectual and academic performance, but they also have specific processing weaknesses that make achievement difficult in one or more areas (Brody & Mills, 1997). According to some researchers (e.g., Lovett & Sparks, 2011), a learning disability requires below average academic achievement. Others contend that, even though academic performance may be in the average range, these students demonstrate intra-individual variability that is the essence of a learning disability (NJCLD, 2011; Reynolds & Shaywitz, 2009). Using a traditional AAD model of identification, these students are typically not eligible for services because their academic performance is not sufficiently low in an absolute sense. An RTI (or any other) approach to identification that focuses solely on below grade-level performance is similarly problematic for gifted students with LD. Instead, intra-individual strengths and weaknesses must be considered (see Silverman, 2003). According to Crepeau-Hobson and Bianco (2011, 2013), Tier 2 must include targeted assessment of academic, cognitive processing, and social-emotional areas and, at Tier 3, include a comprehensive psychoeducational evaluation to assess intellectual and academic strengths and weaknesses. For educational settings that recognize intra-individual underachievement, a PSW approach is well suited to the identification of twice exceptional students.

Some cautions are warranted, however, regarding use of a PSW model. In particular, Miciak, Fletcher, Vaughn, Stuebing, and Tolar (2013) provide data suggesting there is little agreement in LD classification rates across PSW models, and the models do not adequately identify students who fail to respond to treatment. These authors further argue that there is no evidence that students with unique subtypes respond better to different forms of academic interventions.

When interpreting the PSW analysis results, do not assume that a significant result necessarily indicates SLD or that a nonsignificant result rules out SLD. SLD identification is not a statistical decision; rather, consider the results of this analysis as one component of a comprehensive clinical evaluation (see Chapter 9). The PSW approach should be used within a balanced practice model that incorporates the benefits of RTI (i.e., early intervention with empirically supported interventions and progress monitoring) while ensuring a research-supported approach to SLD identification (Hale, 2006). For children who do not quickly respond to early intervention, a comprehensive evaluation that incorporates a PSW approach may provide information that is relevant for understanding why a student is struggling, what type (or subtype) of learning disability best describes the student's learning profile, and how to tailor interventions accordingly. For example, struggling readers with phonological weaknesses might be instructed differently than those with fluency weaknesses. Only through careful attention to subtyping based on patterns of strengths and weaknesses will it become possible to meaningfully research subtype by treatment interactions.

SUMMARY AND CONCLUDING COMMENTS

The descriptions, conceptualizations, and definitions of dyslexia and other learning disabilities continue to evolve to this day. Lobby groups, researchers, and legislators have defined LD through operational definitions, diagnostic criteria, and legislation for eligibility criteria, resulting in different model conceptualizations and criteria for identification and diagnosis. Concurrent with these descriptions is the expanding and significant role of cognitive psychology and neuropsychology in understanding and defining learning disabilities. Advances in cognitive science have demonstrated empirical links between achievement deficits and deficits in underlying cognitive processes, yet numerous questions and controversies remain. These scientific advances have become increasingly influential in the development and updating of cognitive ability tests whose purpose is to identify strengths and deficits in the human cognitive processes underlying academic achievement. WISC-V, the most recent evolution of the Wechsler Intelligence Scale for Children, is designed to measure the cognitive abilities most related to children's academic learning. The WISC-V is well positioned to become an integral component in a battery of tests designed for the assessment of students with academic difficulties.

With these evolutions came considerable diversity in LD assessment practices across settings and disciplines. Researchers and practitioners who identify LD using a single lens, whether it's neurobiological, instructional, or cognitive, are missing the benefits that a more balanced, hybrid approach might offer. While some school psychologists may undervalue the neuro-cognitive basis of LD, similarly clinical and neuropsychologists need to be more attuned to the academic interventions that must necessarily follow identification of the disorder. Part of the controversy over methods of evaluating students for LD may stem from the use of different criteria for LD identification across settings. In particular, a determination of eligibility for dyslexia services in the school setting is not necessarily the same as a diagnosis of developmental dyslexia in a clinical setting. All parties have much to learn from each other. While some school psychologists may undervalue the neuro-cognitive basis of LD, similarly clinical and neuropsychologists need to be more attuned to the academic interventions that must necessarily follow identification of the disorder. Much research remains to be accomplished in terms of clinically understanding the subtypes of LD and associating more targeted interventions to them.

Contemporary LD assessment should include, but expand beyond, the composite FSIQ score to include consideration of the multiple cognitive abilities measured by most modern IQ tests as part of a processing strengths and weaknesses model. The WISC-V is well suited to this approach to LD assessment. Its five factor theoretical model and new complementary subtests (i.e., Naming Speed and Symbol Translation) are clinically relevant to LD identification and differential diagnosis as well as psychoeducational planning when interpreted together with a valid measure of achievement such as the WIAT-III or KTEA-III. Use of the WISC-V in research and practice holds promise for advancing our understanding of learning disabilities and improving outcomes for children.

REFERENCES

American Psychiatric Association, (2013). *Diagnostic and Statistical Manual of Mental Disorders.* Washington, D.C.: American Psychiatric Publishing.

Beal, A. L., Willis, J. O., & Dumont, R. (2013). Psychological testing by models of cognitive ability. In D. P. Saklofske, C. R. Reynolds, & V. L. Schwean (Eds.), *The oxford handbook of psychological assessment.* New York: Oxford University Press.

Bergeron, R., Floyd, R. G., & Shands, E. I. (2008). States' eligibility guidelines for mental retardation: An update and consideration of part scores and unreliability of IQs. *Education & Training in Developmental Disabilities, 43*(1), 123–131.

Berninger, V. (2011). Evidence-based differential diagnosis and treatment of reading disabilities with and without comorbidities in oral language, writing, and math: Prevention, problem-solving consultation, and specialized instruction. In D. P. Flanagan & V. C. Alfonso (Eds.), *Essentials of specific learning disability identification.* Hoboken, NJ: Wiley.

Berninger, V., Abbott, R., Thomson, J., Wagner, R., Swanson, H. L., & Raskind, W. (2006). Modeling developmental phonological core deficits within a working-memory architecture in children and adults with developmental dyslexia. *Scientific Studies in Reading, 10*, 165–198.

Berninger, V. W., O'Donnell, L., & Holdnack, J. (2008). Research-supported differential diagnosis of specific learning disabilities and implications for instruction and response to instruction. In A. Prifitera, D. H. Saklofske, & L. G. Weiss (Eds.), *WISC-IV clinical assessment and intervention.* San Diego, CA: Elsevier.

Boshes, B., & Myklebust, H. (1964). Neurological behavior study of children with learning disorders. *Neurology, 14*, 7–22.

Branum-Martin, L., Fletcher, J. M., & Stuebing, K. K. (2013). Classification and identification of reading and math disabilities the special case of comorbidity. *Journal of Learning Disabilities, 46*(6), 490–499.

Brody, L. E., & Mills, C. J. (1997). Gifted children with learning disabilities: A review of the issues. *Journal of Learning Disabilities, 30*, 282–296.

Castles, A., & Coltheart, M. (1993). Varieties of developmental dyslexia. *Cognition, 47*(2), 149–180.

Compton, D. L., Fuchs, L. S., Fuchs, D., Lambert, W., & Hamlett, C. (2011). The cognitive and academic profiles of reading and mathematics learning disabilities. *Journal of Learning Disabilities, 45*, 79–95.

Crepeau-Hobson, F., & Bianco, M. (2011). Identification of gifted students with learning disabilities in a response-to-intervention era. *Psychology in the Schools, 48*, 102–109.

Crepeau-Hobson, F., & Bianco, M. (2013). Response to intervention promises and pitfalls for gifted students with learning disabilities. *Intervention in School and Clinic, 48*(3), 142–151.

Crews, K. J., & D'Amato, R. C. (2009). Subtyping children's reading disabilities using a comprehensive neuropsychological measure. *International Journal of Neuroscience, 119*, 1615–1639.

Donovan, M. S., & Cross, C. T. (Eds.). (2002). *Minority students in special and gifted education.* Washington, D.C: National Academies Press.

Elliott, C. D., Hale, J. B., Fiorello, C. A., Dorvil, C., & Moldovan, J. (2010). Differential Ability Scales–II prediction of reading performance: Global scores are not enough. *Psychology in the Schools, 47*(7), 698–720.

Elliott, J. G., & Gibbs, S. (2008). Does dyslexia exist? *Journal of Philosophy of Education, 42*(3–4), 475–491.

Elliott, J. G., & Grigorenko, E. L. (2014). *The dyslexia debate.* Cambridge: Cambridge University Press.

Evans, J. J., Floyd, R. G., McGrew, K. S., & Leforgee, M. H. (2001). The relations between measures of Cattell-Horn-Carroll (CHC) cognitive abilities and reading achievement during childhood and adolescence. *School Psychology Review*, *31*(2), 246–262.

Feifer, S., & De Fina, P. (2000). *The neuropsychology of reading disorders: Diagnosis and intervention*. Middleton, MD: School Neuropsych Press, LLC.

Ferrer, E., Shaywitz, B. A., Holahan, J. M., Marchione, K., & Shaywitz, S. E. (2010). Uncoupling of reading and IQ over time: Empirical evidence for a definition of dyslexi. *Psychological Science*, *21*(1), 93–101.

Fiorello, C. A., Hale, J. B., & Snyder, L. E. (2006). Cognitive hypothesis testing and response to intervention for children with reading problems. *Psychology in the Schools*, *43*(8), 835–853.

Fiorello, C. A., Hale, J. B., & Wycoff, K. L. (2012). Cognitive hypothesis testing: Linking test results to the real world. In D. P. Flanagan & P. L. Harrison (Eds.), *Contemporary intellectual assessment* (3rd ed.). New York: Guilford Press.

Flanagan, D. P., & Alfonso, V. C. (2011). *Essentials of specific learning disability identification*. Hoboken, NJ: Wiley.

Flanagan, D. P., Alfonso, V. C., & Ortiz, S. O. (2012). The cross-battery assessment approach: An overview, historical perspective, and current directions. In D. P. Flanagan & P. L. Harrison (Eds.), *Contemporary intellectual assessment: Theories, tests, and issues* (pp. 459–483, 3rd ed.). New York, NY: The Guilford Press.

Flanagan, D. P., Fiorello, C., & Ortiz, S. O. (2010). Enhancing practice through application of Cattell-Horn-Carroll theory and research: A "third method" approach to specific learning disability identification. *Psychology in the Schools*, *47*, 739–760.

Flanagan, D. P., & Mascolo, J. T. (2005). Psychoeducational assessment and learning disability diagnosis. In D. P. Planagan & P. L. Harrison (Eds.), *Contemporary intellectual assessment: Theories, tests and issues* (pp. 521–544, 2nd ed.). New York: Guilford Press.

Flanagan, D. P., Ortiz, S. O., Alfonso, V. C., & Mascolo, J. T. (2006). *The achievement test desk reference (ATDR): A guide to learning disability identification* (2nd ed.). Hoboken, Wiley.

Fletcher, J. M. (2005). Predicting math outcomes: Reading predictors and comorbidity. *Journal of Learning Disabilities*, *38*, 545–552.

Fletcher, J. M. (2012). Classification and identification of learning disabilities. In B. Wong & D. Butler (Eds.), *Learning about learning disabilities* (pp. 1–26, 4th ed.). New York: Elsevier.

Fletcher, J. M., Coulter, W. A., Reschly, D. J., & Vaughn, S. (2004). Alternative approaches to the definition and identification of learning disabilities: Some questions and answers. *Annals of Dyslexia*, *54*(2), 304–331.

Fletcher, J. M., Lyon, G. R., Barnes, M., Stuebing, K. K., Francis, D. J., Olson, R. K., et al. (2002). Classification of learning disabilities: An evidence-based evaluation. *Identification of Learning Disabilities: Research to Practice*, 185–250.

Fletcher, J. M., Lyon, G. R., Fuchs, L. S., & Barnes, M. A. (2007). *Learning disabilities: From identification to intervention*. New York: Guilford.

Fletcher, J. M., Morris, R. D., & Lyon, G. R. (2003). Classification and definition of learning disabilities: An integrative perspective. In H. L. Swanson, K. R. Harris, & S. Graham (Eds.), *Handbook of learning disabilities* (pp. 30–56). New York: Guilford.

Fletcher, J. M., Shaywitz, S. E., Shankweiler, D. P., Katz, L., Liberman, I. Y., Stuebing, K. K., et al. (1994). Cognitive profiles of reading disability: Comparisons of discrepancy and low achievement definitions. *Journal of Educational Psychology*, *86*(1), 6.

Floyd, R. G., Evans, J. J., & McGrew, K. S. (2003). Relations between measures of Cattell-Horn-Carroll (CHC) cognitive abilities and mathematics achievement across the school-age years. *Psychology in the Schools*, *40*(2), 155–171.

Floyd, R. G., Keith, T. Z., Taub, G. E., & McGrew, K. S. (2007). Cattell-Horn-Carroll cognitive abilities and their effects on reading decoding skills: *g* has indirect effects, more specific abilities have direct effects. *School Psychology Quarterly, 22*(2), 200–233.

Francis, D. J., Fletcher, J. M., Stuebing, K. K., Lyon, G. R., Shaywitz, B. A., & Shaywitz, S. E. (2005). Psychometric approaches to the identification of LD IQ and achievement scores are not sufficient. *Journal of Learning Disabilities, 38*(2), 98–108.

Fuchs, D., Fuchs, L. S., Mathes, P. G., & Lipsey, M. W. (2000). Reading differences between low-achieving students with and without learning disabilities: A meta-analysis. *Contemporary special education research: Syntheses of the knowledge base on critical instructional issues*, 81–104.

Fuchs, D., & Young, C. L. (2006). On the irrelevance of intelligence in predicting responsiveness to reading instruction. *Exceptional Children, 73*(1), 8–30.

Fuchs, L. S., Compton, D. L., Fuchs, D., Hollenbeck, K. N., Craddock, C. F., & Hamlett, C. L. (2008). Dynamic assessment of algebraic learning in predicting third graders' development of mathematical problem solving. *Journal of Educational Psychology, 100*(4), 829.

Fuchs, L. S., Fuchs, D., Stuebing, K., Fletcher, J. M., Hamlett, C. L., & Lambert, W. (2008). Problem solving and computational skill: Are they shared or distinct aspects of mathematical cognition? *Journal of Educational Psychology, 100*(1), 30–47.

Gang, M., & Siegel, L. S. (2002). Sound-symbol learning in children with dyslexia. *Journal of Learning Disabilities, 35*(2), 137–157.

González, J. E. J., & Espinel, A. I. G. (2002). Strategy choice in solving arithmetic word problems: Are there differences between students with learning disabilities, GV poor performance and typical achievement students? *Learning Disability Quarterly, 25*(2), 113–122.

Greenberg, D., Lichtenberger, E. O., & Kaufman, A. S. (2013). The role of theory in psychological assessment. In D. H. Saklofske, V. L. Schwean, & C. R. Reynolds (Eds.), *The Oxford handbook of child psychological assessment* (pp. 3–29). New York: Oxford University Press.

Gresham, F. M., & Vellutino, F. R. (2010). What is the role of intelligence in the identification of what is the role of intelligence in the identification of specific learning disabilities?: Issues and clarifications. *Learning Disabilities Research & Practice, 25*(4), 194–206.

Grigorenko, E. L. (2001). Developmental dyslexia: An update on genes, brains, and environments. *Journal of Child Psychology and Psychiatry, 42*(1), 91–125.

Hagen, J. W., Kamberelis, G., & Segal, S. (1991). A dimensional approach to cognition and academic performance in children with medical problems or learning difficulties. In L. V. Feagans, E. J. Short, & L. Meltzer (Eds.), *Subtypes of learning disabilities: Theoretical perspectives and research* (pp. 53–82). Hillsdale, NJ: Erlbaum.

Hale, J., Alfonso, V., Berninger, V., Bracken, B., Christo, C., Clark, E., et al. (2010). Critical issues in response-to-intervention, comprehensive evaluation, and specific learning disabilities identification and intervention: An expert white paper consensus. *Learning Disability Quarterly, 33*(3), 223–236.

Hale, J. B. (2006). Implementing IDEA with a three-tier model that includes response to intervention and cognitive assessment methods. *School Psychology Forum: Research and Practice, 1*, 16–27.

Hale, J. B., & Fiorello, C. A. (2004). *School neuropsychology: A practitioner's handbook.* New York: Guilford Press.

Hale, J. B., Fiorello, C. A., Kavanagh, J. A., Hoeppner, J. B., & Gaither, R. A. (2001). WISC-III predictors of academic achievement for children with learning disabilities: Are global and factor scores comparable? *School Psychology Quarterly, 16*, 31–55.

Hale, J. B., Hain, L. A., Murphy, R., Cancelliere, G., Bindus, D., & Kubas, H. (2013). The enigma of learning disabilities: Examination via a neuropsychological framework. In C. Noggle & R. S. Dean (Eds.), *The neuropsychology of psychopathology.* New York, NY: Springer Publishing.

Hale, J. B., Kaufman, A., Naglieri, J. A., & Kavale, K. A. (2006). Implementation of IDEA: Integrating response to intervention and cognitive assessment methods. *Psychology in Schools*, *43*, 753–770.

Horn, J. L., & Blankson, A. N. (2012). Foundations for better understanding of cognitive abilities. In D. P. Flanagan & P. L. Harrison (Eds.), *Contemporary intellectual assessment. Theories, tests and issues* (3rd ed.). New York: The Guilford Press.

Hulme, C., Goetz, K., Gooch, D., Adams, J., & Snowling, M. J. (2007). Paired-associate learning, phoneme awareness, and learning to read. *Journal of Experimental Child Psychology*, *96*, 150–166.

Individuals with Disabilities Education Improvement Act of 2004 (IDEA 2004), Pub. L. No. 108–446, 118 Stat 2647 (2004).

Johnson, D. J., & Myklebust, H. (1967). *Learning disabilities: Educational principles and remedial approaches*. New York, NY: Grune & Stratton.

Kaufman, A. S. (2008). Neuropsychology and specific learning disabilities: Lessons from the past as a guide to present controversies and future clinical practice. In E. Fletcher-Janzen & C. Reynolds (Eds.), *Neuropsychological perspectives on learning disabilities in an era of RTI: Recommendations for diagnosis and intervention* (pp. 1–13). Hoboken, NJ: Wiley.

Kaufman, A. S., & Kaufman, N. (2014). *Technical manual for the kaufman test of educational achievement* (3rd ed.). Minneapolis, MN: Pearson.

Korkman, M., Barron-Linnankoski, S., & Lahti-Nuuttila, P. (1999). Effects of age and duration of reading instruction on the development of phonological awareness, rapid naming, and verbal memory span. *Developmental Neuropsychology*, *16*(3), 415–431.

Korkman, M., Kirk, U., & Kemp, S. (2007). *NEPSY–II*. Bloomington, MN: Pearson.

Korkman, M., Stenroos, M., Mickos, A., Westman, M., Ekholm, P., & Byring, R. (2012). Does simultaneous bilingualism aggravate children's specific language problems? *Acta Pædiatrica*, *101*, 946–952.

Kozey, M., & Siegel, L. S. (2008). Definitions of learning disabilities in Canadian provinces and territories [Special issue]. *Canadian Psychology/Psychologie Canadienne*, *49*, 162–171.

Learning Disabilities Association of Canada (2002). *LD defined: Official definition of learning disabilities*. Retrieved from: <http://www.ldac-acta.ca/learn-more/ld-defined/official-definition-of-learning-disabilities>.

Lervåg, A., Bråten, I., & Hulme, C. (2009). The cognitive and linguistic foundations of early reading development: A Norwegian latent variable longitudinal study. *Developmental Psychology*, *45*(3), 764–781.

Li, H., Shu, H., McBride-Chang, C., Liu, H. Y., & Xue, J. (2009). Paired associate learning in Chinese children with dyslexia. *Journal of Experimental Child Psychology*, *103*, 135–151.

Lind, A., Korkman, M., Lehtonen, L., Lapinleimu, H., Parkkola, R., Matomäki, J., et al. (2011). Cognitive and neuropsychological outcomes at 5 years of age in preterm children born in the 2000s. *Developmental Medicine & Child Neurology*, *53*(3), 256–262.

Litt, R. A., de Jong, P. F., van Bergen, E., & Nation, K. (2013). Dissociating crossmodal and verbal demands in paired associate learning (PAL): What drives the PAL–reading relationship? *Journal of Experimental Child Psychology*, *115*, 137–149.

Litt, R. A., & Nation, K. (2014). The nature and specificity of paired associate learning deficits in children with dyslexia. *Journal of Memory and Language*, *71*, 71–88.

Lovett, B. J., & Sparks, R. L. (2011). The identification and performance of gifted students with learning disability diagnoses: A quantitative synthesis. *Journal of Learning Disabilities*, 1–13.

Lyon, G. R., & Weiser, B. (2013). The state of the science in learning disabilities: Research impact on the field from 2001 to 2011. In H. L. Swanson, K. R. Harris, & S. Graham (Eds.), *Handbook of learning disabilities* (2nd ed., pp. 118–144). New York: Guilford Press.

Maehler, C., & Schuchardt, K. (2011). Working memory in children with learning disabilities: Rethinking the criterion of discrepancy. *International Journal of Disability, Development and Education*, *58*(1), 5–17.

McGrew, K. S., & Flanagan, D. P. (1998). *The intelligence test desk reference (ITDR): Gf-Gc cross-battery assessment*. Boston, MA: Allyn & Bacon.

McGrew, K. S., & Wendling, B. J. (2010). Cattell–Horn–Carroll cognitive-achievement relations: What we have learned from the past 20 years of research. *Psychology in the Schools*, *47*(7), 651–675.

Miciak, J., Fletcher, J. M., Vaughn, S., Stuebing, K. K., & Tolar, T. D. (2013). Patterns of cognitive strengths and weaknesses: Identification rates, agreement, and validity for learning disabilities identification. *School Psychology Quarterly*, *29*, 21–37.

Myklebust, H., & Boshes, B. (1960). Psycholoneurological learning disorders in children. *Rehabilitation Literature*, *77*, 247–278.

National Joint Committee on Learning Disabilities (NJCLD) (2011). Learning disabilities: Implications for policy regarding research and practice. Retrieved from: <www.ldonline.org/njcld>.

Ontario Ministry of Education (2005). Education for all, the report of the expert panel on literacy and numeracy instruction for students with special education needs, kindergarten to grade 6. Retrieved from: <http://www.edu.gov.on.ca/eng/ppm/ppm8.pdf>.

Ontario Ministry of Education (2014). Program/Policy Memorandum 8. Retrieved from: <http://www.edu.gov.on.ca/eng/ppm/ppm8.pdf>.

Pauly, H., Linkersdörfer, J., Lindberg, S., Woerner, W., Hasselhorn, M., & Lonnemann, J. (2011). Domain-specific rapid automatized naming deficits in children at risk for learning disabilities. *Journal of Neurolinguistics*, *24*, 602–610.

Pearson (2009). *Wechlser individual achievement test–III*. San Antonio, TX: Pearson.

Pennington, B. F. (1991). *Diagnosing learning disorders: A neuropsychological framework*. New York: Guilford Press.

Pieters, S., Roeyers, H., Rosseel, Y., Van Waelvelde, H., & Desoete, A. (2013). Identifying subtypes among children with developmental coordination disorder and mathematical learning disabilities, using model-based clustering. *Journal of Learning Disabilities*, 0022219413491288.

Powell, D., Stainthorp, R., Stuart, M., Garwood, H., & Quinlan, P. (2007). An experimental comparison between rival theories of rapid automatized naming performance and its relationship to reading. *Journal of Experimental Child Psychology*, *98*(1), 46–68.

Reschly, D. J., & Hosp, J. L. (2004). State SLD identification policies and practices. *Learning Disabilities Quarterly*, *27*(4), 197–213.

Reynolds, C. R., & Shaywitz, S. E. (2009). Response to intervention: Ready or not: Or, from wait-to-fail to watch-them-fail. *School Psychology Quarterly*, *24*, 130–145.

Reynolds, M.R., Scheiber, C., Hajovsky, D.B., Schwartz, B., & Kaufman, A.S. (In submission). Gender differences in academic achievement: Is writing an exception to the gender similarities hypothesis?

Rourke, B. P. (1989). *Nonverbal learning disabilities the syndrome and the model*. New York: The Guilford Press.

Shaywitz, S. E. (2003). *Overcoming dyslexia: A new and complete science-based program for reading problems at any level*. New York: Alfred A. Knopf.

Siegel, L. S. (1988). Evidence that IQ scores are irrelevant to the definition and analysis of reading disability. *Canadian Journal of Psychology é Revue Canadienne De Psychologie*, *42*, 201–215.

Siegel, L. S. (1992). An evaluation of the discrepancy definition of dyslexia. *Journal of Learning Disabilties*, *25*, 618–629.

Silverman, L. K. (2003). Gifted children with learning disabilities. In N. Colangelo & G. A. Davis (Eds.), *The handbook of gifted education* (pp. 533–543, 3rd ed.). Boston, MA: Allyn & Bacon.

Sotelo-Dynega, M., Flanagan, D. P., & Alfonso, V. C. (2011). Overview of specific learning disabilities. In D. P. Flanagan & V. C. Alfonso (Eds.), *Essentials of specific learning disability identification*. Hoboken, NJ: Wiley.

Sternberg, R. J., & Grigorenko, E. L. (2002). Difference scores in the identification of children with learning disabilities: It's time to use a different method. *Journal of School Psychology, 40*(1), 65–83.

Stuebing, K. K., Barth, A. E., Molfese, P. J., Weiss, B., & Fletcher, J. M. (2009). IQ is not strongly related to response to reading instruction: A meta-analytic interpretation. *Exceptional Children, 76*(1), 31–51.

Swanson, H. L. (1999). Instructional components that predict treatment outcomes for students with learning disabilities: Support for a combined strategy and direct instruction model. *Learning Disabilities Research and Practice, 14*(3), 129–140.

Swanson, H. L. (2011). Learning disabilities: Assessment, identification, and treatment. In M. A. Bray & T. J. Kehle (Eds.), *The Oxford handbook of school psychology.* New York: Oxford University Press.

Swanson, H. L., & Hoskyn, M. (1998). Experimental intervention research on students with learning disabilities: A meta-analysis of treatment outcomes. *Review of Educational Research, 68*(3), 277–321.

Torgesen, J. K. (2002). Empirical and theoretical support for direct diagnosis of learning disabilities by assessment of intrinsic processing weaknesses. In R. Bradley, L. Danielson, & D. P. Hallahan (Eds.), *Identification of learning disabilities: Research to practice* (pp. 565–613). Mahwah, NJ: Lawrence Erlbaum.

van der Sluis, S., de Jong, P. F., & van der Leij, A. (2004). Inhibition and shifting in children with learning deficits in arithmetic and reading. *Journal of Experimental Child Psychology, 87*(3), 239–266.

Vaughn, S., & Fuchs, L. S. (2003). Redefining learning disabilities as inadequate response to instruction: The promise and potential problems. *Learning Disabilities Research & Practice, 18*(3), 137–146.

Wechsler, D. (2014). *Wechsler intelligence scale for children–V.* San Antonio, TX: Pearson.

Wechsler, D. (2014). WISC-V technical & interpretive manual supplement: Special group validity studies with other measures, and additional tables. Available from: <http://downloads.pearson-clinical.com/images/Assets/WISC-V/WISC-V-Tech-Manual-Supplement.pdf>.

Willburger, E., Fussenegger, B., Moll, K., Wood, G., & Landerl, K. (2008). Naming speed in dyslexia and dyscalculia. *Learning and Individual Differences, 18*, 224–236.

Wise, J. C., Pae, H. K., Wolfe, C. B., Sevcik, R. A., Morris, R. D., Lovett, M., et al. (2008). Phonological awareness and rapid naming skills of children with reading disabilities and children with reading disabilities who are at risk for mathematics difficulties. *Learning Disabilities Research & Practice, 23*(3), 125–136.

Wolf, M., & Bowers, P. G. (1999). The double-deficit hypothesis for the developmental dyslexias. *Journal of Educational Psychology, 91*, 415–439.

Wolf, M., Bowers, P. G., & Biddle, K. (2000). Naming-speed processes, timing, and reading: A conceptual review. *Journal of Learning Disabilities, 33*(4), 387–407.

Chapter 9

Translating Scientific Progress in Dyslexia into Twenty-first Century Diagnosis and Interventions

Bennett A. Shaywitz[1], Lawrence G. Weiss[2], Donald H. Saklofske[3], and Sally E. Shaywitz[1]

[1]Yale Center for Dyslexia & Creativity, Yale University School of Medicine, New Haven, CT, USA, [2]Pearson Clinical Assessment, San Antonio, TX, USA, [3]Department of Psychology, University of Western Ontario, London, Ontario, Canada

INTRODUCTION

Dyslexia (or specific reading disability) is the most common and extensively studied of the learning disabilities, affecting 80% of all individuals identified as learning disabled (Lerner, 1989). Not only is dyslexia the most thoroughly characterized of all learning disabilities but it is historically the oldest. In fact, the first description of dyslexia in children preceded the first mention of "learning disability" by over 60 years; dyslexia was first described in 1896 while the term "learning disability" was not used until 1962!

EVOLUTION OF DYSLEXIA AS AN UNEXPECTED DIFFICULTY IN RELATION TO INTELLIGENCE

The observation that seemingly otherwise healthy men and women could lose the ability to read had been made as early as the seventeenth century (see Shaywitz, 2003) and by the nineteenth century a number of reports described educated adults who suddenly found themselves unable to read, a condition referred to as "acquired alexia." The most prominent of these cases were described in the early 1890s by the French neurologist Jules Dejerine (Dejerine, 1891, 1892), who showed that acquired alexia was the result of a stroke involving posterior brain systems in the parieto-temporal and occipito-temporal regions. It was a

L. G. Weiss, D. H. Saklofske, J. A. Holdnack and A. Prifitera (Eds): WISC-V Assessment and Interpretation.
DOI: http://dx.doi.org/10.1016/B978-0-12-404697-9.00009-1
269

report by Hinshelwood (1895), an ophthalmologist in Glasgow, Scotland, of an adult with acquired alexia that served as the impetus for the first report of developmental dyslexia by Dr. W. Pringle Morgan of 14-year-old Percy F. in the *British Medical Journal* on November 7, 1896 (Morgan, 1896): "… He has always been a bright and intelligent boy, quick at games, and in no way inferior to others his age. His great difficulty has been—and is now—his inability to read." Following Hinshelwood's diagnosis of word blindness in adults, Morgan labeled this condition congenital word blindness, emphasizing that the young boy, Percy, had good vision and was intelligent, commenting that "The schoolmaster who has taught him for some years says that he would be the smartest lad in the school if the instruction were entirely oral."

In the years immediately following these early reports, there were many further documented cases of unexpected reading difficulties in children, many from Britain, Europe, and the United States (Shaywitz, 2003). In fact, Hinshelwood (1917) went on to describe a number of other children with dyslexia, noting, for example, that one boy with the "condition" learned very well if the lessons were oral and reporting that his mother believed he was, in many ways, brighter than her other children, except for his inability to learn to read. Hinshelwood also emphasized the unexpected nature of the reading difficulty; it was not due to a generalized deficit in intelligence, but to a "localized" problem affecting reading so that affected children also manifest strengths as well as the weakness in reading. He also observed that the disorder, like most other physiological entities, occurred in gradations rather than as an all or none phenomenon, a finding that more recent research has validated (Shaywitz, Escobar, Shaywitz, Fletcher, & Makuch, 1992).

By the early part of the twentieth century, clinicians had elaborated descriptions, possible causes, and potential treatments for developmental dyslexia, with perhaps the most cogent described by the physician Samuel Torrey Orton. In his 1937 monograph, *Reading, Writing and Speech Problems in Children*, Orton (1937) noted a number of characteristics of dyslexia that we have come to know 80 years later. These include the observation that though some dyslexic individuals may learn to read, their reading remains slow compared to their peers in age and intelligence, a phenomenon we have come to appreciate as lack of reading fluency. He further knew that although their reading could often appear normal for their age, it was below what was expected for their intelligence. Orton also described characteristic poor spelling as well as how often it was that the smaller function words caused the most trouble in reading. Finally, Orton described how children with difficulty learning to read in the lower grades often had trouble learning a foreign language at adolescence (Orton, 1937, pp. 91–95).

Consistent in the original descriptions by the pioneers who described dyslexia was that they all noted that the reading problem in dyslexic children was *unexpected* in relation to their intelligence. As we review below, the unexpected nature of the reading problem was also the hallmark of what came to be known as learning disabilities (LD).

A decade or two after Orton's prescient descriptions of dyslexia, astute clinicians were beginning to elaborate an entity that came to be known as the brain-injured child (Strauss & Lehtinen, 1947; Strauss & Werner, 1942) and which by 1962 had evolved into what Clements and Peters (1962) described as minimal brain dysfunctions (MBD). The first finding mentioned was specific learning deficits and the first symptoms noted were failure to read and making dyslexic errors along with poor spelling. In the same year, Kirk and Bateman (1962) first used the term "learning disability," and illustrated the evaluation of a learning disability with the steps in diagnosing a reading disability. From this very first paper, which used the words learning disability, the concept of a discrepancy between the child's ability and his achievement was prominent. Thus, Kirk and Bateman (1962) noted the very first step in determining if the child has a learning disability is to determine the child's reading capacity, a measure reflecting IQ. Then, actual reading achievement is determined, and the "discrepancy between the capacity for reading and actual achievement in reading is examined."

Myklebust (1968) emphasized the hallmark of learning disability as a discrepancy between potential and actual success in learning resulting in significant underachievement. Learning disability continued to be defined as a deficiency in learning despite adequate intelligence.

By the 1970s parents of thousands of children in the United States knew about LD "... even if professional educators and psychologists and pediatricians did not" (Cruickshank, 1972). But this was changing, and within a decade LD had become one of the most frequently diagnosed conditions in children referred for problems learning in school. Writing in 1985, Kavale and Forness (1985) emphasized that the IQ-achievement discrepancy is essential to the diagnosis of LD and can be reliably determined. At the same time they reviewed many of the methodological challenges associated with defining LD on the basis of an IQ-achievement discrepancy. More about these problems can be found below.

More than two decades ago Hammill (1990) reviewed the then published proposals for defining LD. He found that the concept of underachievement was the most consistent element in all the definitions: underachievement within the individual child, i.e., underachievement of the child in relation to that child's inherent abilities. But how is underachievement to be determined? Not surprisingly, many of the definitions suggest that underachievement is indicated by the presence of an ability-achievement discrepancy as we have discussed above, that is, a significant difference between intellectual ability (usually represented by an IQ) and performance in, for example, reading achievement.

This historical review emphasizes that for over 100 years in the case of dyslexia and over 50 years in the case of LD, the most consistent and enduring core of the definition is the concept of dyslexia (and LD) as *unexpected* underachievement. The most up-to-date, scientifically supported definition of dyslexia is that introduced by Rep. Bill Cassidy (now Sen. Cassidy) in 2014: "Dyslexia is defined as an unexpected difficulty in reading in an individual who has the intelligence to be a much better reader, dyslexia reflects a difficulty in getting to the individual sounds of spoken language which typically impacts speaking (word retrieval), reading (accuracy and fluency), spelling, and often, learning a second language."

For the first time there is now empirical data confirming the unexpected nature of dyslexia. These data come from the Connecticut Longitudinal Study, a project involving a sample survey of Connecticut schoolchildren representative of those children entering public kindergarten in Connecticut in 1983. All subjects were children whose primary language was English. This cohort, assembled from a two-stage probability-sample survey, has been followed longitudinally beginning in kindergarten, and each was given individualized tests of cognitive abilities and achievement annually up through 12th grade. The racial and ethnic composition of this sample from Connecticut was similar to that of the nation at the time of the study (Statistical abstract of the United States: 1986, 1985).

Using the Connecticut Longitudinal Study, Ferrer, Shaywitz, Holahan, Marchione, and Shaywitz (2010) demonstrated that in typical readers, reading and IQ are dynamically linked over time. Not only do reading and IQ track together over time, they also influence one another. Such mutual interrelationships are not perceptible in dyslexic readers, suggesting that reading and cognition develop more independently in dyslexia (Figure 9.1) (Ferrer et al., 2010).

Furthermore, these data of an uncoupling between IQ and reading in dyslexia provide evidence to support the conceptual basis of dyslexia as unexpected

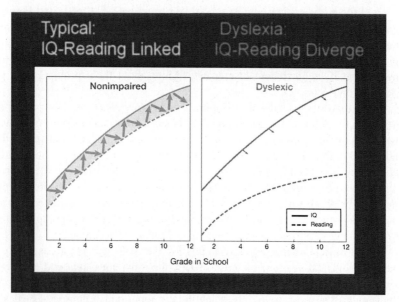

FIGURE 9.1 Mutual interrelationships are not perceptible in dyslexic readers, suggesting that reading and cognition develop more independently in dyslexia. (*Based on Ferrer et al., 2010*).

underachievement. Based on dynamic models, the uncoupling of reading and cognition demonstrate that in dyslexia the reading difficulty is unexpected for an *individual's* level of intelligence, that is, the difficulty is defined as existing *within* the individual. The implication is that for individuals who are dyslexic, the appropriate comparison is between a person's ability and his/her reading. These findings provide the long-sought empirical evidence for the seeming paradox involving cognition and reading in dyslexia. Thus, in dyslexia, a highly intelligent person may read at a level above average but below that expected, based on his/her intelligence, education, or professional status.

Many confuse the impact of dyslexia with an almost total inability to read. While that may occur, most commonly and certainly as defined legally and supported by scientific evidence, there is no reading level below which an individual, student or adult, must score to be diagnosed as dyslexic. Rather, the central point is *how* the individual reads, the effort and work that must go into the reading process for him or her to decipher the word accurately and fluently. Think of a motor disability. The question is not whether the person can cross a street, but rather what he or she must do to get to the other side, i.e., use a cane or a wheelchair.

NEUROBIOLOGICAL EVIDENCE SUPPORTING DYSLEXIA

Making a Hidden Disability Visible

In the early descriptions of dyslexia and LD, there was serious concern over whether there was evidence of "brain dysfunction." Many of the early reports of dyslexia and LD attempted to demonstrate nervous system involvement using the methodology available at the time, methodology that is relatively primitive by current standards. The emergence of functional brain imaging using positron emission tomography (PET) in the 1980s and then functional magnetic resonance imaging (fMRI) in the 1990s has provided the critical evidence the pioneers who described dyslexia and LD were hoping for. Using these technologies, primarily fMRI, converging evidence from many laboratories around the world has demonstrated a "neural signature for dyslexia," that is, an inefficient functioning of posterior reading systems during reading real words and pseudowords (see Figure 9.2).

This evidence from fMRI has for the first time made visible what previously was a hidden disability. For example, in one of the first studies of fMRI in dyslexia, Shaywitz et al. (2002) used fMRI to study 144 children, approximately half of whom had dyslexia and half were typical readers. Results indicated significantly greater activation in posterior reading systems in typical readers than in readers with dyslexia during a task tapping phonologic analysis. These findings align with the classic nineteenth century reports by Dejerine (1891, 1892) of acquired alexia caused by left hemisphere lesions in the parieto-temporal areas as well as areas around the fusiform gyrus.

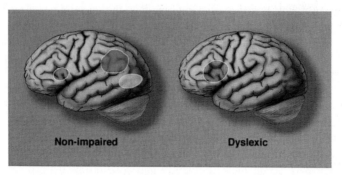

FIGURE 9.2   Neural signature for dyslexia: disruption of posterior reading systems. (© *Shaywitz, 2003*).

These data from fMRI studies in groups of children with dyslexia have been replicated in reports from many investigators and show a failure of left hemisphere posterior brain systems to function properly during reading, particularly the systems in the left hemisphere occipito-temporal region (see Peterson & Pennington, 2012; Price & Mechelli, 2005; Richlan, Kronbichler, & Wimmer, 2009, 2011; Shaywitz & Shaywitz, 2005). Similar findings have been reported in German (Kronbichler et al., 2006) and Italian (Brambati et al., 2006) readers with dyslexia. Some studies in Chinese readers with dyslexia show brain abnormalities in left occipito-temporal and anterior frontal regions (Siok, Niu, Jin, Perfetti, & Tan, 2008; Siok, Perfetti, Jin, & Tan, 2004; Siok, Spinks, Jin, & Tan, 2009) similar to those found in dyslexia in alphabetic orthographies. Other studies of Chinese dyslexia have reported reduced activation in *bilateral* occipito-temporal regions and left middle frontal gyrus (Siok et al., 2004; Siok et al., 2008; Siok et al., 2009), regions not generally found in fMRI studies of dyslexia in alphabetic orthographies. A more recent study demonstrated reduced activation for Chinese dyslexics in right occipital cortex, consonant with a language-specific role of right visual cortex in Chinese reading and suggesting a deficit in holistic visuo-orthographic analysis in Chinese dyslexia (Liu et al., 2012).

Connectivity analyses of fMRI data represent the most recent evolution in characterizing brain networks in dyslexia. Measures of functional connectivity are designed to detect differences in brain regions with similar magnitudes of activation but whose activity is differentially synchronized with other brain systems across subject groups or types of stimuli. Most recently Finn et al. (2013) report that compared to typical readers, dyslexic readers showed reduced connectivity in the visual word-form area, a part of the left fusiform gyrus specialized for printed words.

Thus, these findings from brain imaging provide still further support for viewing dyslexia as a distinct neurobiological entity, diagnosed by unexpected underachievement and now with a neural signature.

NECESSITY AND CHALLENGE OF BRINGING DIAGNOSIS OF DYSLEXIA INTO THE TWENTY-FIRST CENTURY

As stated by one us (Dr. S. Shaywitz in her testimony before the Congressional Committee on Science, Space and Technology hearing on the Science of Dyslexia in September, 2014), "Education must, and can be, aligned with science. We must ensure that scientific knowledge is translated into policy and practice and that ignorance and injustice do not prevail. We know better, we must act better." Dr. Shaywitz further emphasized that "Dyslexia differs markedly from all other learning disabilities. Dyslexia is very specific and scientifically validated: we know its prevalence, cognitive and neurobiological origins, symptoms, and effective, evidence-based interventions. Learning disabilities is a general term referring to a range of difficulties which have not yet been delineated or scientifically validated. Learning disabilities are comparable to what in medicine are referred to as 'infectious' diseases, whereas dyslexia is akin to being diagnosed with a strep throat—a highly specific disorder in which the causative agent and evidence-based treatment are both known and validated."

A range of scientific studies delineate dyslexia as an unexpected difficulty, that is, there is an uncoupling of reading and intelligence so that one may have average or high intelligence but, at the same time, read at an unexpectedly lower level. Today, in 2015, we know even more that can be used to diagnose dyslexia—the major problem relates to a difficulty in phonological processing, that is, accessing the individual sounds of spoken language. This knowledge, in turn, pinpoints the major symptoms to look for that are caused by this difficulty, as described earlier in this chapter.

Dyslexia is a specific, scientifically supported condition affecting as many as 20% of our student (and adult) population. It is unacceptable to have different groups of professionals ignore the scientific definition of dyslexia and use various administrative criteria to define and diagnose the disorder. Its unexpected nature and its phonological basis must be reflected in any definition used. If particular practitioners or groups of practitioners wish to use additional measures, that is their prerogative. However, we must respect the evidence and base any diagnosis of dyslexia on demonstration of the unexpected nature and of a phonological deficit.

Operationalizing "Unexpected"

More challenging has been the question of how to operationalize the unexpected nature of dyslexia. In fact, the difficulty has been not with the concept of unexpected underachievement, but rather with the real-life practical effect of implementation in a school setting; some have attempted to capture the "unexpected" nature of dyslexia by requiring a discrepancy of a certain degree between a child's measured IQ and his or her reading achievement. In some cases, schools adopted simplified rules, for example, criteria based on a discrepancy, most commonly one or one-and-one-half standard deviations between standard scores on IQ and reading tests, or even more commonly a 20 or 22 point discrepancy between IQ and reading test scores.

Critiques of the methodology were voiced just as soon as the ability achievement discrepancy was codified into PL 94-142 in 1975 and into regulations in 1977 (Kavale & Forness, 1985). One of the first problems that became apparent was that children who were clearly struggling as early as kindergarten or first grade had to wait, often until third grade or later, until their failure in reading was of such a magnitude that they met discrepancy requirements. In other words, in the beginning grades, the use of an ability-achievement discrepancy seemed to reduce the chances of early reading intervention because the child had to fall behind his or her expected reading achievement before he or she would be eligible for services. As a result, identification was often delayed and services were denied until the requisite discrepancy had developed, resulting in what has been described as a "wait-to-fail" approach. By the time a child was identified, he or she might be far behind peers in reading skill. In addition, the size of the required discrepancy varied among states, as well as among school districts within states. Thus, a child might be identified as dyslexic or LD in one school district, but not in another.

More importantly, although these criticisms were directed to *how* the discrepancy was operationalized, they did not negate the construct of *unexpected* underachievement nor did they negate the use of an ability-achievement discrepancy as one component of an overall clinical assessment, one that considers and puts to use the knowledge gained from the scientific study of dyslexia delineating its unexpected nature, its basic difficulty, its impact on, for example, the individual's spoken language, reading, spelling, and even learning a second language.

Diagnosing Dyslexia: Operationalizing "Unexpected" in Young Children

Difficulties in identifying younger children based solely on a discrepancy score bring into focus that dyslexia is a clinical diagnosis. Although it may not yet be possible to demonstrate a quantitative disparity between ability and achievement in the early grades, it is still possible to demonstrate the fundamental concept of an unexpected difficulty in reading.

In *Overcoming Dyslexia*, Shaywitz (2003) conceptualizes dyslexia as a weakness in phonology (getting to the sounds of spoken words) surrounded by a sea of strengths in higher-order thinking. In younger children there is an encapsulated weakness in decoding surrounded by strengths in, for example, problem-solving, critical thinking, concept formation, and reasoning. In older children, adolescents, and adults it may be thought of as an encapsulated weakness in fluent reading surrounded by these strengths in higher-order thinking.

Given that dyslexia is defined on the basis of scientific evidence as an unexpected difficulty in reading in a child or an adult in relation to intelligence, it is not surprising that a measure of intelligence, the Wechsler Intelligence Scale for Children—Fifth Edition (WISC-V) (Wechsler, 2014), is a critical component of a comprehensive assessment of the child (aged 6–16 years) with dyslexia. Very often an intelligence test can reveal areas of strength, particularly in areas of abstract thinking and reasoning, which are very reassuring to parents and especially to the child him/herself. They also indicate that the reading difficulty is isolated and not reflective of a general lack of learning ability or intellectual disability.

Currently, most children with dyslexia are not diagnosed until they are in third grade or about 9 years old, although it is possible to recognize children at risk for dyslexia as young as 4–5 years of age. As shown in Box 9.1, from *Overcoming Dyslexia* (Shaywitz, 2003), signs and symptoms of children at risk for dyslexia can be observed even before formal reading begins in school.

These clues, along with a positive family history, represent significant risk factors for dyslexia.

The assessment approach we focus on here and elaborated in more detail in Dr. Sally Shaywitz's new edition of *Overcoming Dyslexia* (forthcoming) is an in-depth evaluation of the skills (especially phonologic) known to be related to reading success. This evaluation is appropriate for preschool, kindergarten, and first grade children who may have signs of a potential reading problem, and is carried out on an individual basis by a professional knowledgeable about reading and dyslexia: a speech and language pathologist, a learning disabilities specialist, an experienced psychologist, or even a teacher trained to recognize and understand dyslexia and to administer the tests.

We and other researchers have begun to recognize that one source of potentially powerful and highly accessible screening information that has thus far been ignored is the teacher's judgment about the child's reading and reading-related skills. Remarkably, we found that teachers' response to a small subset of questions [Dyslexia Screening Measure (© Sally Shaywitz, 2014) comprising 10 items from the kindergarten and 12 items from the first grade Multigrade Inventory for Teachers (© Sally Shaywitz, 1987)] predict children at high risk for dyslexia with a high degree of accuracy, with good sensitivity and specificity.

BOX 9.1 Clues to Children at Risk for Dyslexia

- Delayed language
- Trouble learning common nursery rhymes such as "Jack and Jill" and "Humpty-Dumpty"
- A lack of appreciation of rhymes
- Mispronounced words; persistent baby talk
- Difficulty in learning (remembering) names of letters and numbers
- Failure to know the letters in his own name

From Shaywitz (2003).

Development and Assessment of Phonological Processing

Because difficulties in phonological processing are so central to dyslexia, it is imperative that educators and evaluators become more knowledgeable about the developmental progression of children's phonological abilities; these follow a natural progression and so are relatively straightforward to assess across development, beginning at about age 4 (Shaywitz, 2003). In general, what the examiner is looking for is the development of phonological sensitivity that refers to the ability of the child to focus on the sounds, rather than on the meaning, of spoken words. For example, the child can tell what word rhymes with cat rather than simply if a cat is a kind of animal. Phonological skills develop gradually over time and in a predictable, logical sequence. Awareness of this sequence and its timing makes it possible to recognize when a child is veering off course. We know that, in general, as children develop phonological skills, they gain the ability to focus on smaller and smaller parts of the word, rather than on the word as a whole, indivisible unit. At the same time, they also work their way from attending to the outside or ends of words to the inside or middle parts of words. And so at first children are able to separate out only the beginning sounds of words, then the end sounds, and, finally, the inside parts of words. Penetrating the inside of a word is much more difficult than noticing either end. And it is the ability to notice and to code each of the parts within a word that marks the maturing reader.

In describing a child's phonological skills, two terms are often used: phonological awareness and phonemic awareness. Phonological awareness is a more general and more inclusive term that includes all levels of awareness of the sound structure of words; it is also used to refer to the earliest stages of developing an awareness of the parts of words, for example, sensitivity to rhyme or noticing larger parts of words such as syllables. Phonemic awareness is a much more specific term; it refers to the more advanced ability to notice, to identify, to think about, and to manipulate the smallest particles of language making up a word, phonemes. Phonemic awareness has the strongest relationship to later reading and most tests focus on this level of awareness. The most helpful measures in the young child include: (1) sound comparison; (2) segmentation; and (3) blending.

For sound comparison, we would ask a child: "Tell me which word begins with the same first sound as bat: dog, sat, or boy?" For segmentation, we might ask a child to count or pronounce the individual parts of a word, for example, "Can you count the sounds you hear in pan?" (three) Alternatively, we can ask him to blend together the parts of a word that has already been pulled apart: "What word do the sounds /k/ /a/ /t/ make? (cat)." In addition, as he develops increasing phonemic awareness, we can have him add, move around, or delete part of a word by asking, for example, "What word remains if you take the "r" sound away from frog? (fog)."

In addition to tests of phonemic awareness, there are two other related tests that add valuable information about a young child's readiness for reading.

The first, which measures phonological memory, evaluates a child's ability to temporarily store bits of verbal information; we see how well he can remember a series of numbers or words that were just presented to him orally. (Both spoken numbers and words are stored as phonemes.) In this type of test, a child may be asked, "Can you repeat these numbers to me, five-seven-three-one-six?" This type of memory plays an important role in reading at every level, even for a first grader as he is trying to sound out a word. As a child reads a sentence, he has to hold several bits of information in mind in order to put it all together and make sense of what he has just read. Think of the process: he first decodes the letters into sounds, then holds these sounds in his memory as he tries to decode the remaining letters in the word, and then he takes these stored sounds, blends them together, and forms the word. Words are stored primarily on the basis of their sounds, so the ability to hold words temporarily is really a kind of phonological skill. And the clearer the phonemes, the more efficiently words (or letters or numbers) can be retrieved.

A second kind of test, the rapid automatic naming test, or RAN, examines still another aspect of phonological processing, what is technically referred to as "phonological access." The RAN tries to determine how easily and rapidly a child can retrieve verbal information held in long-term storage. Here, the child is typically shown a card with several rows of pictures of familiar objects and asked to name these, one after another, as quickly as he can. Highly familiar stimuli are used so that this does not turn into a test of the child's vocabulary. Both accuracy and speed are measured. The child's facility in rapid naming is related to just the sorts of processes he must perform as he reads, when he must be able to go into his long-term memory storage and rapidly retrieve the stored phonemes.

Tests Helpful in the Evaluation of Children with Dyslexia

Phonological Processing

Given that phonological processing represents the core weakness in dyslexia, it is fortunate that a robust range of measures are now available for assessment of each of its components. Such tests can be very useful for young children and continuing as the child matures. For example, specific core and primary WISC-V (Wechsler, 2014) subtests and indexes may be useful in dyslexia evaluations. The Digit Span Forward task evaluates phonological memory, the child's ability to temporarily store bits of verbal information—a basic step in the reading process as described above. Further, the Working Memory Index evaluates the child's ability to hold several bits of verbal information in mind and put it all together to make sense of what has just been heard or read.

With its addition of the complementary Naming Speed Index and subtests, the new WISC-V can be used to aid in the assessment of a range of a young child's phonological capabilities. More specifically, the WISC-V was designed to provide insights into phonological processing with its measure of phonological access, rapid automatic naming, specifically, the Naming Speed Literacy (NSL) subtest, a component of the Naming Speed Index (NSI). The test requires the child to name colors, objects, letters, and numbers as quickly as possible. For further details about Naming Speed Literacy, please see Chapter 1.

Clinicians and researchers also use the Comprehensive Test of Phonological Processing, now in its second edition (CTOPP-2) (Wagner, Torgesen, Rashotte, & Pearson, 2013), to test for the full range of phonological skills. Specifically, in children 4–6 years of age, awareness of and access to the phonological structure of oral language may be assessed by three subtests of the CTOPP-2 referred to as phonological awareness composite: Elision, Blending Words, and Sound Matching. In older children and young adults 7 through 24 years of age, phonology is assessed also by the phonological awareness composite but with Sound Matching replaced by Phoneme Isolation. Phoneme Isolation measures the ability to isolate individual sounds within words. For example, "Where does the /t/ sound occur in the word cat, beginning, middle or end of the word?" Other components of the CTOPP-2 assess phonological memory and rapid automatic naming.

Letter Knowledge

Though not as robust as tests of phonological awareness in predicting whether the young child is at risk for dyslexia, a child's knowledge of letter names and sounds may also serve as a helpful guide to how ready he or she is to read. Testing letter knowledge is straightforward; it can be assessed informally by asking the child to name letters presented one at a time on a card. Similarly, knowledge of letters and sounds is tested by asking the child, "Can you tell me the sound(s) this letter makes in words?" More formal testing can be obtained by using a reading test that contains a letter-identification section, for example, the letter-word subtest on the Wechsler Individual Achievement Test—Third Edition (WIAT-III) (Wechsler, 2009); the Kaufman Test of Educational Achievement—Third Edition (KTEA-III) (Kaufman & Kaufman, 2014); or the Woodcock-Johnson IV Tests of Achievement (WJ-IV Achievement) (Schrank, McGrew, Mather, & Woodcock, 2014).

In addition, it is often helpful to assess a child's familiarity with the conventions of print (i.e., that there are spaces between words and that books are read from top to bottom and from left to right), to ensure that a young child is aware of what books are and how they work.

Academic Achievement

Overall, in the school-age child, reading is assessed by measuring accuracy, fluency, and comprehension. Specifically, in the school-age child, one important element of the evaluation is how accurately the child can decode words (i.e., read single words). This is measured with standardized tests of single real word and pseudoword reading. Because pseudowords are unfamiliar and cannot be memorized, each nonsense word must be sounded out. Tests of nonsense word reading are referred to as "word attack." Reading fluency, the ability to read accurately, rapidly, and with good prosody, an often overlooked component of reading, is of critical importance because it allows for the automatic, attention-free recognition of words.

The WIAT-III, KTEA-III, and WJ-IV are each reliable, valid, and comprehensive measures of academic achievement. Each measure includes multiple tasks designed to evaluate early reading skills such as letter identification, word reading, pseudoword decoding, as well as reading fluency, and comprehension tasks. Only the WIAT-III and KTEA-III have been empirically linked to the WISC-V. In addition, fluency also may be assessed by asking the child to read *aloud* using the Gray Oral Reading Test—Fifth Edition (GORT-5) (Wiederholt & Bryant, 2012). This test consists of increasingly difficult passages, each followed by comprehension questions; scores for accuracy, rate, fluency, and comprehension are provided. Such tests of oral reading are particularly helpful in identifying a child who is dyslexic; by its nature oral reading forces a child to pronounce each word. Listening to a struggling reader attempt to pronounce each word leaves no doubt about the child's reading difficulty. In addition to reading passages aloud, single word reading efficiency may be assessed using, for example, the Test of Word Reading Efficiency, 2nd edition (TOWRE-2) (Torgesen, Wagner, & Rashotte, 2013), a test of speeded oral reading of individual real words and pseudowords. Children who struggle with reading often have trouble spelling; spelling may be assessed with the WIAT-III, KTEA-III, or WJ-IV spelling test.

DIAGNOSIS OF DYSLEXIA IN ADOLESCENTS AND YOUNG ADULTS

The developmental course of dyslexia has now been characterized. First, dyslexia is persistent, it does not go away; on a practical level, this means that once a person is diagnosed as dyslexic there is no need for re-evaluation following high school to confirm the diagnosis. Second, over the course of development, skilled readers become more accurate and more automatic in decoding; they do not need to rely on context for word identification. Dyslexic readers, too, become more accurate over time, but they do not become automatic in their reading. Residua of the phonological deficit persist so that reading remains effortful and slow, even for the brightest of individuals with childhood histories of dyslexia. Failure to either recognize or measure the lack of automaticity in reading represents, perhaps, the most common error in the diagnosis of dyslexia in accomplished young adults. It is often not appreciated that tests measuring word accuracy are inadequate for the diagnosis of dyslexia in young adults at the level of college, graduate, or professional school and that, for these individuals, timed measures of reading must be employed in making the diagnosis.

Since they often are able to read words accurately (albeit very slowly) dyslexic adolescents and young adults may mistakenly be assumed to have "outgrown" their dyslexia (Bruck, 1998; Lefly & Pennington, 1991; Shaywitz, 2003). Data from studies of children with dyslexia who have been followed prospectively support the notion that in adolescents, difficulties with reading fluency and, often, poor spelling may be especially useful clinically in diagnosing dyslexia in students in secondary school and college, and even graduate and professional schools. It is important to remember that these older dyslexic students may be similar to their typically reading peers on untimed measures of word recognition yet continue to suffer from the phonological deficit that makes reading less automatic, more effortful, and slow. Thus, the most consistent and telling sign of dyslexia in an accomplished young adult is slow and laborious reading and writing.

Essential Components of Diagnosis in Adolescents and Young Adults

Lack of Automaticity

The failure either to recognize or to measure the lack of automaticity in reading is, along with the failure to assess intelligence, perhaps one of the two most common errors in the diagnosis of dyslexia in older children and in accomplished young adults. Tests relying on the accuracy of word identification alone are inappropriate to use to diagnose dyslexia in accomplished young adults; tests of word identification reveal little to nothing of their *struggles* to read. It is important to recognize that, since they assess reading accuracy but not automaticity, the kinds of reading tests commonly used for school-age children may provide misleading data on bright adolescents and young adults. The most critical tests are those that are timed; they are the most sensitive to a phonological deficit in a bright adult. However, there are very few standardized tests for young adult readers that are administered under timed and untimed conditions; the Nelson-Denny Reading Test (Brown, Fishco, & Hanna, 1993) represents an exception. Any scores obtained on testing should be considered relative to peers with the same degree of education or professional training. Clinicians and researchers have recognized that in bright young adults a history of phonologically based reading difficulties, requirements for extra time on tests, current slow and effortful reading, i.e., signs of a lack of automaticity in reading, and indications of an unexplained difficulty in reading are the sine qua non of a diagnosis of dyslexia.

Measure of Intelligence

The failure to include a test of intelligence such as the WISC-V represents one of the two most common and harmful errors made in the diagnosis of dyslexia. As discussed throughout this chapter, the demonstration of an unexpected difficulty in reading in relation to intelligence is a key hallmark of dyslexia. Dyslexia is an unexpected difficulty in reading that is best and most reliably and clearly demonstrated by performance on a test of intelligence, on the WISC-V, most often observed using the VCI, though the Full Scale IQ may also be useful.

Use of a reliable test of intelligence such as the WISC-V to diagnose dyslexia is of fundamental importance. It is one of the definitive steps necessary to identifying dyslexia. Once individuals knows their diagnosis, the "world changes." Often following years of frustration, disappointment, and self-doubt, of thinking that they are dumb, there is suddenly an explanation and a name to the difficulties. It is not a problem of "not trying hard enough" or "a lack of intelligence," it is because a phonological deficit, in spite of their average or high intelligence and strong effort, prevents them from reading and achieving at a level and rate according to their intellect.

Here is how celebrated and dyslexic writer John Irving describes the experience of an undiagnosed, bright dyslexic student: "I wasn't diagnosed as dyslexic at Exeter; I was seen as just plain stupid ... I wish I'd known, when I was a student at Exeter, that there was a word for what made being a student so hard for me; I wish I could have said to my friends that I was dyslexic. Instead, I kept quiet or—to my close friends—I made bad jokes about how stupid I was" (quoted in Shaywitz, 2003, p. 346).

Self-awareness and self-knowledge, gained by an accurate diagnosis of dyslexia, bring in the light and allow the person to understand himself, to know how he functions and learns, the nature of his difficulties, and how to help himself. One of us (S. Shaywitz) has personally shared the results of a full evaluation for dyslexia, including measures of intelligence, reading, phonological processing, and other components, and witnessed the individual's face light up, sadness slowly transition to at least a half smile, and the outpouring of energy and excitement at being told that she was dyslexic and, indeed, intelligent, often highly intelligent. If, as a result of failure to diagnose dyslexia, everything that is happening in school tells them they are "dumb" or "stupid" because they are not reading well or fluently, we as a society are negligent, if not unethical, in denying such individuals this important information about themselves. Similarly, all educators want their students to learn; it is wrong to deny teachers twenty-first century, truly evidence-based knowledge of why a particular student is not progressing in reading. Such knowledge is a critical key to providing that student with the evidence-based reading instruction that now exists.

SUMMARY

Awareness of the historical background of dyslexia, now joined together with twenty-first century scientific advances, provides powerful evidence to address the needs of the large segment of our children who are dyslexic, and who, in turn, represent the overwhelming majority of students labeled as learning disabled. Dyslexia can be reliably identified using twenty-first century knowledge and assessment tools, including its unexpected difficulty in reading and its phonological basis. It cannot be stressed enough that to ensure accurate diagnosis, the unexpected nature, the phonological deficit, and the lack of reading fluency in dyslexia must be taken into account, both in making a reliable and timely diagnosis and to ensure that those who require identification and effective interventions are not overlooked.

Currently, we are failing large numbers of our children by failing to identify the many who are dyslexic and who can be helped. A dyslexic child who is not identified cannot be counted, will not receive effective interventions, and, perhaps even more importantly, cannot know he or she is not dumb and can have a fulfilling future.

To address the needs of our dyslexic children, accurate diagnosis and effective intervention must both be in place. We have focused on scientifically based approaches to diagnosis; we must do no less when implementing interventions for dyslexia. For education to truly align with twenty-first century science, we must ensure that modern concepts of evidence-based reflecting randomized clinical trials are the standard in choosing programs, whether professional development, reading programs, or in educating educators about dyslexia. When selecting any of these programs, we must not succumb to received wisdom or tightly held belief systems, but continually ask "Show me the evidence!" Putting into practice twenty-first century advances in the science of dyslexia so that this common condition is reliably identified and effectively treated will mark a major positive turning point in meeting the needs of the one in five children who are dyslexic, serving not only the children but their parents, educators, and society as well.

ACKNOWLEDGMENTS

Much of the material in this chapter is based on or have appeared in: *Overcoming Dyslexia* (Shaywitz, 2003), or will appear in the forthcoming second edition of this book; chapters in *Swaiman's Textbook of Child Neurology*; and pediatric texts.

REFERENCES

Brambati, S., Termine, C., Ruffino, M., Danna, M., Lanzi, G., Stella, G., et al. (2006). Neuropsychological deficits and neral dysfunction in familial dyslexia. *Brain Research, 1113*(1), 174–185.

Brown, J., Fishco, V., & Hanna, G. (1993). *Nelson Denny reading test—Manual for scoring and interpretation (forms G and H)*. Itaca, IL: Riverside Publishing.

Bruck, M. (1998). Outcomes of adults with childhood histories of dyslexia. In C. Hulme & R. Joshi (Eds.), *Reading and spelling: Development and disorders* (pp. 179–200). Mahwah, NJ: Lawrence Erlbaum Associates.

Clements, S., & Peters, J. (1962). Minimal brain dysfunctions in the school-age child: Diagnosis and treatment. *Archives of General Psychiatry, 6*(3), 185–197.

Cruickshank, W. (1972). Some issues facing the field of learning disability. *Journal of Learning Disabilities, 5*, 380–388.

Dejerine, J. (1891). Sur un cas de cecite verbale avec agraphhie, suivi d'autopsie. *C. R. Societe du Biologie, 43*, 197–201.

Dejerine, J. (1892). Contribution a l'etude anatomo-pathologique et clinique des differentes varietes de cecite verbale. *Memoires de la Societe de Biologie, 4*, 61–90.

Ferrer, E., Shaywitz, B., Holahan, J., Marchione, K., & Shaywitz, S. (2010). Uncoupling of reading and IQ over time: Empirical evidence for a definition of dyslexia. *Psychological Science, 21*(1), 93–101.

Finn, E., Shen, X., Holahan, J., Scheinost, D., Lacadie, C., Papademetris, X., et al. (2014). Disruption of functional networks in dyslexia: A whole-brain, data-driven approach to fMRI connectivity analysis. *Biological Psychiatry, 76*(5), 397–404.

Hammill, D. (1990). On defining learning disabilities: An emerging consensus. *Journal of Learning Disabilities, 23,* 74–84.

Hinshelwood, J. (1895). Word-blindness and visual memory. *The Lancet, 2,* 1564–1570.

Hinshelwood, J. (1917). *Congenital word blindness.* London: Lewis, HK.

Kaufman, A. S., & Kaufman, N. L. (2014). *Kaufman test of educational achievement* (3rd ed.). Bloomington, MN: NCS Pearson.

Kavale, K., & Forness, S. (1985). Learning disability and the history of science: Paradigm or paradox? *Remedial and Special Education, 6,* 12–24.

Kirk, S., & Bateman, B. (1962). Diagnosis and remediation of learning disabilities. *Exceptional Children, 29*(2), 73–78.

Kronbichler, M., Hutzler, F., Staffen, W., Mair, A., Ladurner, G., & Wimmer, H. (2006). Evidence for a dysfunction of left posterior reading areas in German dyslexic readers. [Comparative Study Research Support, Non-U.S. Gov't]. *Neuropsychologia, 44*(10), 1822–1832.

Lefly, D., & Pennington, B. (1991). Spelling errors and reading fluency in compensated adult dyslexics. *Annals of Dyslexia, 41,* 143–162.

Lerner, J. (1989). Educational interventions in learning disabilities. *Journal of the American Academy Child Adolescent Psychiatry, 28*(3), 326–331.

Liu, L., Wang, W., You, W., Li, Y., Awati, N., Zhao, X., et al. (2012). Similar alterations in brain function for phonological and semantic processing to visual characters in Chinese dyslexia. *Neuropsychologia, 50,* 2224–2232.

Morgan, W. (1896). A case of congenital word blindness. *British Medical Journal,* 1378.

Myklebust, H. R. (1968). Learning disabilities: Definition and overview. In H. R. Myklebust (Ed.), *Progress in learning disabilities* (Vol. 1, pp. 1–15). New York: Grune & Stratton, Inc.

Orton, S. T. (1937). *Reading, writing, and speech problems in children.* New York: Norton.

Peterson, R., & Pennington, B. (2012). Developmental dyslexia. *The Lancet, 379*(9830), 1997–2007.

Price, C., & Mechelli, A. (2005). Reading and reading disturbance. *Current Opinion in Neurobiology, 15,* 231–238.

Richlan, F., Kronbichler, M., & Wimmer, H. (2009). Functional abnormalities in the dyslexic brain: A quantitative meta-analysis of neuroimaging studies. *Human Brain Mapping, 30,* 3299–3308.

Richlan, F., Kronbichler, M., & Wimmer, H. (2011). Meta-analyzing brain dysfunctions in dyslexic children and adults. *NeuroImage, 56,* 1735–1742.

Schrank, F., McGrew, K. S., Mather, N., & Woodcock, R. (2014). *Woodcock-Johnson-IV.* Rolling Meadows, IL: Riverside Publishing.

Shaywitz, B., Shaywitz, S., Pugh, K., Mencl, W., Fulbright, R., Skudlarski, P., et al. (2002). Disruption of posterior brain systems for reading in children with developmental dyslexia. *Biological Psychiatry, 52*(2), 101–110.

Shaywitz, S. (2003). *Overcoming dyslexia: A new and complete science-based program for reading problems at any level.* New York: Alfred A. Knopf.

Shaywitz, S., Escobar, M., Shaywitz, B., Fletcher, J., & Makuch, R. (1992). Evidence that dyslexia may represent the lower tail of a normal distribution of reading ability. *New England Journal of Medicine, 326*(3), 145–150.

Shaywitz, S., & Shaywitz, B. (2005). Dyslexia (specific reading disability). *Biological Psychiatry, 57,* 1301–1309.

Siok, W., Niu, Z., Jin, Z., Perfetti, C., & Tan, L. (2008). A structural-functional basis for dyslexia in the cortex of Chinese readers. *Proceeding of the National Academy of Science—USA, 105,* 5561–5566.

Siok, W., Perfetti, C., Jin, Z., & Tan, L. (2004). Biological abnormality of impaired reading is constrained by culture. *Nature, 431*, 71–76.

Siok, W., Spinks, J., Jin, Z., & Tan, L. (2009). Developmental dyslexia is characterized by the coexistence of visuospatial and phonological disorders in Chinese children. *Current Biology, 19*, R890–R892.

Statistical abstract of the United States: 1986. (1985) (46). Washington, DC: US Government Printing Office.

Strauss, A., & Lehtinen, L. (1947). *Psychopathology and education of the brain-injured child.* New York: Grune and Stratton.

Strauss, A. A., & Werner, H. (1942). Disorders of conceptual thinking in the brain-injured child. *Journal of Nervous and Mental Disease, 96*(2), 153–172.

Torgesen, J., Wagner, R., & Rashotte, C. (2013). *TOWRE-2: Test of word reading efficiency* (2nd ed.). Austin, TX: PRO-ED.

Wagner, R., Torgesen, J., Rashotte, C., & Pearson, N. (2013). *CTOPP-2: Comprehensive test of phonological processing* (2nd ed.). Austin, TX: PRO-ED.

Wechsler, D. (2009). *Wechsler individual achievement test* (3rd ed.). San Antonio, TX: Psych Corp.

Wechsler, D. (2014). *Wechsler intelligence scale for children-V.* San Antonio, TX: Pearson.

Wiederholt, J., & Bryant, B. (2012). *GORT-5 examiner's manual.* Austin, TX: PRO-ED, Inc.

Chapter 10

Issues Related to the WISC-V Assessment of Cognitive Functioning in Clinical and Special Groups

Jessie L. Miller[1], Donald H. Saklofske[2], Lawrence G. Weiss[3], Lisa Drozdick[3], Antolin M. Llorente[4], James A. Holdnack[5], and Aurelio Prifitera[6]

[1]Pearson Clinical Assessment, Toronto, Ontario, Canada, [2]Department of Psychology, University of Western Ontario, London, Ontario, Canada, [3]Pearson Clinical Assessment, San Antonio, TX, USA, [4]Penn State Hershey College of Medicine, Hershey, PA, USA, [5]Pearson Clinical Assessment, Bear, DE, USA, [6]Pearson Clinical Assessment, Upper Saddle River, NJ, USA

INTRODUCTION

David Wechsler's definition of intelligence has sustained the test of time: "the global capacity of a person to act purposefully, to think rationally, and to deal effectively with his environment" (Wechsler, 1944, p. 3). On the heels of the publication of the fifth edition of the *Wechsler Intelligence Scale for Children* (WISC-V) (Wechsler, 2014), Dr. Wechsler's legacy remains as integral and important a factor in the description of individual differences as ever. Intelligence was initially viewed and conceptualized as a continuum of the capacity to think, learn, and act in a way that could then be used to describe individual differences in ability along a range of performance from the most intellectually impaired to the most extreme of genius. With time it was further observed that all individuals fall along this continuum and regardless of the diagnosed condition, cognitive functioning could be more fully understood by examining the patterns of scores that comprised the tests such as the Wechsler and Binet scales. Contemporary views of intelligence (see Neisser et al., 1996), have expanded the breadth of construct coverage of intelligence tests to include key performance factors that together define general mental ability. Although the first intelligence tests were mainly used for classification, selection, and placement, the role of intelligence tests has broadened to include profile analysis that may characterize groups of

L. G. Weiss, D. H. Saklofske, J. A. Holdnack and A. Prifitera (Eds): WISC-V Assessment and Interpretation.
DOI: http://dx.doi.org/10.1016/B978-0-12-404697-9.00010-8

patients with particular diagnoses and alternatively to use such information to recognize individual differences that may translate to targeted intervention planning. Intelligence tests play a dominant role in the "strengths-based" models of today.

The study and measurement of intelligence is significantly impacted by current cultural and societal issues (as discussed in Chapter 5), in addition to advances in scientific research (as discussed in Chapter 4). This fact has never been clearer than now with the WISC-V five factor model. The research and development leading to the WISC-V coincides with a period of tremendous change in cognitive assessment. Less than 18 months after the publication of the widely debated fifth edition of the *Diagnostic and Statistical Manual of Mental Disorders* (DSM; APA, 2013), the WISC-V emerged to a professional landscape marked by uncertainty and opportunity in assessment, measurement, and diagnosis of neurocognitive disorders. The changes to the diagnostic criteria detailed in the most recent DSM-5 have impacted practitioners and research scientists in diverse ways. For some, the question has been the translation of these new diagnostic categories to clinical practice. For instance, how to keep pace with changes to insurance billings and discordance among rules for eligibility of services by region. For others, it has meant a paradigm shift in our understanding of the etiology of mental health disorders and as such, the theoretical basis of the methodologies employed in psychological research. Perhaps most importantly, it has spurred a wave of new research focused on investigating the reliability and validity of these new definitions in the identification, classification, and treatment of mental disorders. Debate over the classification of mental health disorders is far from new: this debate spans more than a century in the literature, before even the first publication of the DSM in 1952. Yet, the momentum with which this latest revision has sparked discussion among professionals working in education and mental health is intriguing. Without question, the push for new research to address the controversial new organization of psychological disorders will serve to advance our understanding in the field.

One of the more significant changes to the DSM-5 was the consolidation of autism, Asperger's, and pervasive developmental disorders. While DSM-IV used distinct categories for these classifications, DSM-5 has combined these disorders into one broad category of autism spectrum disorders (ASD). What were formerly termed "autistic disorder" and "Asperger's disorder" can still be readily distinguished by identifying the level of language impairment in the nosology of the disorder. Still, this change to the grouping of autism and Asperger's disorders reflects a dynamic shift in the theoretical underpinning of the DSM and in the etiology of mental health disorders. Although the field of psychology has been gradually moving towards a continuum theory of mental health disorders since the DSM-III, the integration of autism and Asperger's disorders is the first time a neurodevelopmental disorder has been reflected by a continuum model similar to the prevailing conceptualization of personality disorders among leading personality theorists. This change is influenced by advanced research in genetic and family studies of children with autism, along with the need to approach interventions for both autism and Asperger's from a common core deficit.

A continuum approach to describing neurocognitive disorders is necessary among theorists seeking an explanation for the shared behavioral and cognitive profiles of categorically distinct disorders. It is also necessary for making sense of the substantial comorbidity that occurs among disorders, particularly when comorbid disorders also share common phenotypes. In fact, the lack of specificity among disorders has necessarily relegated Kraepelin's 1913 categorical approach to defining mental health disorders to a small fraction of researchers and practitioners investigating latent class and taxonomic evidence of distinct group membership (Watson & Clark, 2006; Widiger & Samuel, 2005).

With advances in assessment such as the development of WISC-V, researchers and clinicians now have the necessary tools to measure atypical profiles across cognitive domains, allowing researchers to map overlapping phenotypes among disorders. Though atypical neurocognitive profiles have been documented in the literature for decades, the empirical studies emerging in more recent literature are bolstered by advances in cognitive neuroscience, brain imaging, epidemiology, and genetic studies. The profiles of cognitive impairment shared within the attention, language, and motor skills disorders, as well as the cluster symptoms in executive dysfunction observed in attention-deficit hyperactivity disorder (ADHD), oppositional defiant disorder (ODD), and conduct disorder (CD) or the common verbal deficits between ASD and specific language impairment (SLI), are more recent examples (Dyck & Piek, 2014; Kjelgaard & Tager-Flusberg, 2001; Lewis, Murdoch, & Woodyatt, 2007; Rapin, Dunn, Allen, Stevens, & Fein, 2009). For some researchers these co-occurrences in cognitive deficits are an indication of a common underlying etiologic factor. Others suggest the lack of neurocognitive specificity is evidence that cognitive dysfunction is not the common denominator among disorders and that these common weaknesses are superficial correlations (Taylor, Mayberry, Grayndler, & Whitehouse, 2014; Whitehouse, Barry, & Bishop, 2008; Williams, Minshew, & Goldstein, 2008). Evidence that interventions aimed at improving the cognitive weakness in disorders such as ADHD do little to explain or reduce core behavioral symptoms (Coghill, Hayward, Rhodes, Grimmer, & Matthews, 2014; Klingberg et al., 2005; Sonuga-Barke et al., 2013) seems to support this argument. Similarly, findings that the behavioral phenotypes of many mental health problems are also strongly correlated to cognitive deficits in typically developing children suggest an alternate model of causation (Dyck & Piek, 2014). This is a complex question and current evidence is not conclusive. Whether cognitive deficits contribute to impairment and symptomology or are rooted in the causal mechanism of the disorder, future research using tools such as the WISC-V, which can accommodate both comprehensive and targeted assessment of performance along with process analysis, are needed to address this issue. Contributions from brain imaging and functional magnetic resonance imaging studies will also add significantly to an understanding of the phenotypic overlap among neurocognitive disorders.

THE RELEVANCE AND PURPOSE OF COGNITIVE ASSESSMENT

The role of intelligence in understanding individual variations in children's learning and behavior cannot be overstated. Whether from the perspective of diagnostic frameworks such as DSM-5, eligibility criteria from schools determining special education classifications, or the teacher working to identify the unique strengths of a child with ADHD, intelligence tests like the WISC serve an important role in providing information that will guide more effective identification and intervention planning. In the following sections, selected special group studies included in the development of the WISC-V are discussed with respect to the neurocognitive factors associated with each disorder's symptoms and impairment. This is followed by a summary of the results of the special group studies on the WISC-V subtests and composites. The complete data for all special group studies are presented in the *WISC-V Technical and Interpretive Manual* and the *WISC-V Technical and Interpretive Manual Supplement*. The results from the special group studies may serve as guideposts at a group level so that psychologists might use the results of the WISC-V to determine a child's cognitive strengths and weaknesses both in relation to the normative sample and also for particular clinical groups. This is important information because of the variability within and between groups, and while the tables in the manual for the various special group studies are not representative of all clinical populations, they do show average patterns of performance on the various indexes and subtests of the WISC-V that can be used to inform and guide the clinician's investigation of diagnostic hypotheses.

Still, although certain WISC-V profiles of cognitive strengths and weaknesses are repeatedly observed in group research relating to specific diagnostic conditions, similar patterns also occur in other disorders, especially those that are related neurocognitively. Thus, clinicians must bear in mind that although deficits (or strengths) in specific cognitive abilities can be reliably identified in individual patients using the WISC-V, the presence of such patterns is not a conclusive indicator of a specific DSM-5 diagnosis, and other disorders with similar cognitive profiles must be systematically ruled out by the clinician. Conclusive diagnoses cannot be made based on the pattern of scores in WISC-V, or any other single test. As always, clinical diagnosis is a matter of professional judgment informed by scores from all relevant tests administered and combined with information from the clinical interview, parents, teachers, medical history, and educational records.

CLINICAL AND SPECIAL GROUPS: GENERAL DESCRIPTION AND INTELLECTUAL FUNCTIONING

Intellectual Disability

The assessment of intellectual disability within the context of psychological assessment has a long and, in some instances, controversial history (Sattler, 2008). As noted by Spruill, Oakland, and Harrison (2005), a "diagnosis involving mental retardation" (intellectual disability, ID) "can have a profound impact on a person's life," particularly on a child. Such a diagnosis can have a significant impact on the types of services legally afforded to a child or those they fail to receive. A diagnosis of intellectual disability, whether correct or incorrect, can be carried by a child for the rest of their life. Clinicians must weigh this burden and exercise caution when diagnosing a child with this condition. In addition, such a diagnosis should only be reached after a careful evaluation has been conducted involving a comprehensive investigation of the child's intellectual and adaptive skills from various sources and environments in which a child is required to function. An extensive review of records associated with the child's abilities and functioning is also required.

The most recent and frequently used definitions of intellectual disability are from the American Association on Intellectual and Developmental Disabilities (AAIDD, 2010; Schalock et al., 2010) and the American Psychiatric Association under DSM-5 (APA, 2013). They define intellectual disability as the presence of intellectual impairment that occurs concurrent with the presence of adaptive deficits during the developmental period (APA, 2013; Schalock et al., 2010), defined as before 18 years of age historically. Currently only one adaptive domain needs to be impaired in the conceptual, social, or practical areas, unlike earlier more restrictive definitions associated with intellectual disability where greater adaptive deficits, or a deficit in overall adaptation, was required. A deficit or impairment in intellectual functioning under AAIDD and DSM-5 criteria is confirmed following a complete clinical assessment, which includes standardized tests of intelligence and adaptive functioning. For tests with a mean of 100 and a standard deviation of 15 points, identical to the properties of the WISC-V, a score of 70 or below is sufficiently impaired to be considered intellectually disabled when adaptive functioning is also impaired. Scores as high as 75 also may meet criteria as these account for errors in test measurement, as a result of a set margin of approximately +5 points (AAIDD, 2010; APA, 2013).

Intellectual disability is characterized by a failure to achieve developmental milestones in cognitive, language, motor, and other domains including self-care skills, especially when compared to same age peers. Intellectual disability is further defined by academic problems, problems adapting or adjusting to new environments, problems understanding and following social rules, and other more complex problems involving social situations. According to AAIDD (2010), intellectual disability impacts approximately 1–3% of the U.S. population, and this prevalence rate seems to be supported globally (Maulik, Mascarenhas, Mathers, Dua, & Saxena, 2011). It should be noted that ID is based on a set of criteria, which in and of themselves are not a specific disorder or condition. There are many risk factors and causes of ID such as central nervous system (CNS) disorders and other types of infections. ID can result from many genetic and environmental consequences, but most commonly results from a combination of polygenetic expression coupled with environmental risk factors (e.g., malnutrition; Sattler, 2008). In addition, Madduri et al., (2006) have shown that increases in genetic involvement are associated with increases in cognitive disability, at least in one genetic disorder. Increases in the number of and exposure severity to risk factors tend to be associated with increased morbidity. Under DSM-5 (APA, 2013), the level of ID continues to be described as Mild, Moderate, Severe, and Profound using identical criteria as that of DSM-IV (APA, 2000).

Variability in performance across the cognitive abilities tends to decrease the further one moves below the mean ability level of the general population (Nunes et al., 2012). That is, cognitive deficits become more global as you move from mild to moderate to severe and profound functioning levels of ID. For instance, Schuchardt, Gebhardt, and Maehler (2010) found working memory deficits significantly increased with the degree of intellectual disability, among adolescents with borderline and mild ID, compared to matched controls. Adolescents with mild ID exhibited the most impairment. Similar results have been found in tests of motor performance and perceptual organization among children and adolescents with mild and borderline ID (Di Blasi, Elia, Buono, Ramakers, & Di Nuovo, 2007; Vuijk, Hartman, Scherder, & Visscher, 2010; Wuang, Wang, Huang, & Su, 2008). Moreover, the discrepancies between verbal and nonverbal performance decrease with decreasing ability levels (Gordon, Duff, Davidson, & Whitaker, 2010). Put another way, variability in performance across different domains of cognitive ability is more likely to be observed among borderline and mild than moderate or severe ID patients.

Although impairment is less severe among borderline and mild forms of ID, performance on measures of cognitive ability are still reliably able to distinguish from control groups. For instance, Bonifacci and Snowling (2008) compared speed of information processing among typically developing children, children with dyslexia, and children with borderline ID. The children with borderline functioning were slower and more error prone compared to the other two groups and also showed greater variability in performance within tasks, even after outliers had been removed. Alloway (2010) found greater verbal and visuospatial working memory deficits among individuals with borderline ID compared to typically developing children aged 7 to 11 years. Van der Molen, Van Luit, Jongmans, and Van der Molen (2007) found adolescents 13–17 years with mild ID exhibited greater impairment in phonological functioning (storage), but not in automatic rehearsal compared to children matched on chronological age. Schuchardt et al. (2010) found similar results for adolescents with mild and borderline ID compared to children matched on chronological and mental age.

Global deficits in cognitive functioning are the major defining factor among moderate and severe intellectual disabilities. This trend is similar for children with mild ID also but more variability occurs in the cognitive profile of mild ID than in moderate or severe ID, particularly as the child ages. Based on previous findings among mild and moderate ID in children using the WISC–IV and WPPSI–IV, significant discrepancies are typically found across all cognitive domains including verbal, perceptual/visuospatial and fluid reasoning, working memory and processing speed. When compared to typically developing children, the largest effect sizes tend to occur across verbal subtests and composites followed by working memory, perceptual/visuospatial, and fluid reasoning, with the smallest differences appearing in processing speed subtests (Wechlser, 2003, 2004, 2012a, 2012b).

Intellectual Giftedness

Although clearly not a clinical disorder, we include intellectual giftedness (IG) in this discussion as it is the opposite end of the intellectual spectrum from ID, and because it is a common referral question involving WISC-V evaluations.

Sir Francis Galton was one of the first individuals to note the broad and divergent nature of mental abilities. In one of his seminal works, "Classification of men according to their gifts," Galton (1869) set forth to delineate the tremendous variability that exists in individuals' cognitive abilities and their hereditary factors, after having examined the records ("Scale of merit") of over 200 students who obtained "mathematical honors" at Cambridge University in England. In doing so, he started a scholarly and intellectual dialogue and debate that sometimes has verged on argument, controversy, and heated discord that permeates to this day.

This controversy has sometimes overflowed into the gifted and talented (GT) arena, partially as a result of the difficulty in its definition and actual identification (Pfeiffer, 2002; Stephens & Karnes, 2000). For example, the National Society for the Gifted and Talented (NSGT) uses the definition set forth by the U.S. Department of Education in 1993 noting that: "Children and youth with outstanding talent who perform or show the potential for performing at remarkably high levels of accomplishment when compared with others of their age, experience, or environment." In contrast, the National Association for Gifted Children is more precise in its definition of GT, noting that "Gifted individuals are those who demonstrate outstanding levels of aptitude (defined as an exceptional ability to reason and learn) or competence (documented performance or achievement in top 10% or rarer) in one or more domains. Domains include any structured area of activity with its own symbol system (e.g., mathematics, music, language) and/or set of sensorimotor skills (e.g., painting, dance, sports)." Finally, Public Law (P.L. 103–382, Title XIV) defines GT as those children and adolescents who "show evidence of high performance capability in areas such as intellectual, creative, artistic, or leadership capacity, or in specific academic fields, and who require services or activities not ordinarily provided by the school in order to fully develop such capabilities."

Conceptual disagreement in the definition of giftedness extends into operational criteria. For example, educational entities and school districts do not agree on the actual cut-off score to use when employing a specific IQ score to define giftedness. One district may use an IQ score representing the top 2% of the population of children, whereas another may use an IQ score representing the top 5% of a population of children (Stephens & Karnes, 2000). This debate notwithstanding, most operationalized definitions of GT use high intelligence as a primordial characteristic and as a result the Wechsler scales have historically and continually played a major role.

The intellectual profile of children identified as intellectually gifted typically manifests in greater than average performance on measures of intellectual ability compared to the general population (Wechsler, 2002, 2003, 2004, 2012a, 2012b). However, many gifted children do not display uniformly superior cognitive abilities across all domains (Lohman, Gambrell, & Lakin, 2008; Pfeiffer, 2005; Sweetland, Reina, & Tatti, 2006). Although some gifted children obtain higher scores across all cognitive areas compared to same-aged peers, others demonstrate lower relative scores on measures of processing speed and working memory (Rimm, Gilman, & Silverman, 2008; Rowe, Kingsley, & Thompson, 2010). These lower scores are still higher than the population average but are typically weaker relative to their verbal and perceptual reasoning abilities (Raiford, Weiss, Rolfhus, & Coalson, 2005).

Conversely, there is evidence for a group of GT spatial learners with weak verbal skills that are worth noting. Individuals with high spatial ability often have relative weaknesses in verbal ability and as a result of verbally-loaded Full Scale Intelligence Quotient (FSIQ) measures, may obtain FSIQ scores below cut-off score requirements for gifted programs (Andersen, 2014; Mann, 2005, 2006; Silverman, 2002).

Children who are gifted and learning disabled have been described as 'twice exceptional learners'. These children have a disability or dysfunction in at least one cognitive domain despite superior cognitive abilities across all other domains (Nicpon, Allmon, Sieck, & Stinson, 2011). Thus, whereas scores on a measure of cognitive ability are typically above average across all domains for children who are gifted, performance will fluctuate depending on the presence (masked or identified) or absence of comorbid learning disorders in the sample.

Autism Spectrum Disorder

The cardinal characteristics of autism spectrum disorder (ASD) are pervasive and protracted deficits in social communication and social interaction across multiple environments, accompanied by repetitive and extremely restrictive profiles of activities, behavioral repertoire, and personal interests (APA, 2013). Children with ASD either fail to reach or regress in their social and communicative abilities when compared to typically developing children. For example, children with ASD frequently exhibit difficulties responding to their own name, fail to develop the ability to make gestures and use imitative play (e.g., make-believe play), may develop echolalia (exact repetition or echoing), or refer to themselves using the third pronoun ("he" or "she" third pronoun reversal). Also common are pragmatic language difficulties or idiosyncratic usage of words for things that only make sense to them or those close to them (APA, 2013; Naigles, 2013). On the other hand, children with high functioning autism are characterized by mostly adequate linguistic skills with some pragmatic difficulties particularly around reacting to social and more abstract linguistic cues. Perseverations about topics that represent favorite subjects only to them or deficits with prosody are also common.

Children with ASD exhibit deficits interacting with others and reciprocally engaging others in social "give-and-take" exchanges. For example, children with ASD tend to exhibit little or no eye contact and research has indicated that they tend to pay attention to different visual cues relative to healthy children (APA, 2013). Children with ASD frequently exhibit incongruent nonverbal social cues as they interact with others, such as inappropriate facial expressions, grimaces, or gestures and their linguistic prosody does not match the feelings expressed or the content of their speech. As a result it is difficult for other individuals to understand their social cues and body language. Many children with ASD also exhibit problems understanding other individuals' point of view (APA, 2013; Baron-Cohen, 1989).

Children with ASD also exhibit unusual motor behaviors such as hand flapping, unique sounds (e.g., "digy, diggy, diggy"), walking patterns (e.g., tiptoe walking without suffering from hypertonia), or other idiosyncratic behaviors (APA, 2013). Children with ASD often exhibit overly focused interests in specific features of objects or persons while ignoring other important parts or the rest of the object or person. Similarly, they tend to align objects in a row rather than playing or using the objects for their intended play or function. Perseverations, sometimes misconstrued as obsessions, with specific objects or parts of objects such as road signs, toys, or specific aspects of the weather, are often exhibited.

ASD is perhaps one of the most heterogeneous and complex neurocognitive disorders in the DSM. Although a substantial percentage of individuals with ASD fall into the intellectually disabled IQ range (i.e., approximately 2–3 SDs below the mean; Baird et al., 2000; Kielinen, Linna, & Moilanen, 2000), there is substantial support for average, above average, and even superior "peaks" of ability in areas of fluid reasoning, visuospatial performance, working memory, verbal reasoning, and processing speed (Dawson, Soulières, Gernsbacher, & Mottron, 2007; Muth, Hönekopp, & Falter, 2014; Scheuffgen, Happeé, Anderson, & Frith, 2000; Shah & Frith, 1983, 1993). Indeed, the specifiers in the new DSM-5 include "with or without accompanying intellectual impairment" (APA, 2013, p. 51) and an understanding of the uneven intellectual profile of a child or adult with ASD. Cognitive functioning in ASD is inversely related to symptom severity (Matson & Shoemaker, 2009). Thus, as symptom severity increases, IQ decreases (Matson, Mahan, Hess, & Fodstad, 2010; Szatmari, White, & Merikangas, 2007). Mayes and Calhoun (2011) found IQ to be the most highly correlated variable to symptom severity among those with ASD.

Across cognitive domains, ability levels are best described as atypical among individuals with ASD. For example, visuospatial ability has been shown to be a relative strength for children with ASD in some studies (Mayes & Calhoun, 2008; Osmon, Smerz, Braun, & Plambeck, 2006; Wechsler, 2003, 2008, 2012a), but not in others (Bölte, Holtmann, Poustka, Scheurich, & Schmidt, 2007; White & Saldaña, 2011). Typical visuospatial tasks used in research on ASD include Figure Disembedding (Witkin, Oltman, Raskin, & Karp, 1971), Block Design (Wechsler, 1974), Mental Rotation (Shepard & Metzler, 1971), and Navon Figures (Navon, 1977). Several decades ago Shah and Frith (1983) postulated an explanation for the variable performance observed across visuospatial tasks in ASD by deconstructing the two components involved in visuospatial processing: orientation and visualization. Orientation refers to the comprehension of the arrangement of elements within a stimulus pattern and is necessary for tasks such as Block Design, Figure Disembedding, and Object Assembly. Visualization involves the ability to mentally manipulate a pictured stimulus through some form of rotation or inversion. Visualization is also necessary for tasks such as Block Design, Object Assembly, Mental Rotation, and Visual Puzzles. Shah and Frith (1983) suggested that among children with autism, orientation abilities are good but visualization abilities are weak. Evidence cited to support this hypothesis was the speed and accuracy with which children with autism were able to find embedded figures in their 1983 experiment. Other research seemed to support this notion of greater visuospatial weaknesses for the ability to hold or form mental images (Hammes & Langdell, 1981; Hermelin, 1978; O'Connor & Hermelin, 1975). Over the decades since Shah and Frith published their research, other studies have found performance peaks on tasks involving both orientation and visualization, but less evidence of superior performance on tasks involving strict mental rotation. A recent meta-analysis of visuospatial performance among ASD found support for superior performance on both Block Design and Figure Disembedding, but less clear support for Mental Rotation and Navon Figures (Muth et al., 2014).

Like visuospatial performance, working memory abilities show substantial variability among children with ASD. Discrepancies in the literature seem to indicate this variability is the result of the task choice used to measure working memory (Vogan et al., 2014) and the complexity of the material to be remembered (Williams, Goldstein, & Minshew, 2006a). Although basic working memory abilities seem to be intact for materials with low levels of structure, working memory is impaired for materials with more complex levels of organization (Williams et al., 2006a). For verbal working memory, Fein et al. (1996) found young children with autism had the least difficulty recalling digits, some difficulty recalling sentences, and the most difficulty recalling information from stories. Other studies report intact verbal working memory among individuals with ASD, but deficits in visuospatial working memory (Ozonoff & Strayer, 2001; Russell, Jarrold, & Henry, 1996; Steele, Minshew, Luna, & Sweeney, 2007). This is noteworthy insofar as verbal working memory in particular has been described as a core cognitive deficit in ASD (Pennington et al., 1997), and performance on some measures of visuospatial ability are relatively superior in ASD (Muth et al., 2014). Again, the conflicting evidence seems to be modulated by the complexity of the visual stimuli, with basic visual discrimination a relative strength among ASD, whereas sequencing and visual discrimination tasks with greater cognitive loads are a relative weakness in ASD (Williams et al., 2006a). For example, Williams, Goldstein, and Minshew (2006b) compared 38 children with high functioning autism to a matched control sample on the WRAML (Sheslow & Adams, 1990) and found significant differences between measures of visual and verbal memory involving syntactic and discourse elements. However, there were no differences between the high functioning autism and control groups on measures of associative memory or immediate memory span tasks. Of the WRAML subtests compared across these two groups, the Finger Windows test, a measure of spatial working memory, was the most powerful discriminator between the comparison groups. Most of these studies described used DSM-IV criteria to define study groups. Studies of visuospatial ability under the new DSM-5 categorization of ASD are needed in order to address the role of language deficits and intellectual disability in the outcome of visuospatial task performance among children with ASD.

Language impairment is another cognitive domain where performance can vary significantly among ASD. Deficits in social communication are one of the hallmark characteristics of ASD. However, impairment in language is not universal across ASD and in fact can be somewhat normal among high functioning autism. For this reason the DSM-5 requires a specifier of "with or without language impairment" in the diagnosis of ASD. In general, ASD with language impairment is associated with poor performance on most measures of verbal ability and lower global IQ scores. Conversely, ASD without language impairment is associated with higher global IQ (Lindgren, Folstein, Tomblin, & Tager-Flusberg, 2009; Mayes & Calhoun, 2007; Rice, Warren, & Betz, 2005). However, even among non-language impaired ASD groups the development of structural language is frequently atypical and there are subtle yet persistent anomalies among even the highest performers (Boucher, 2012). For instance, individuals classified as language normal ASD, high functioning autism, and former classifications of Asperger's, show poor performance on tests of comprehension, have difficulty applying commonalties among category members, and show deficits in morphology, pragmatics, and semantics in some studies (Boucher, 2012; Howlin, 2003; Mayes & Calhoun, 2007; McGregor et al., 2012; Rice et al., 2005). Conversely, these same groups demonstrate normal understanding of basic word meaning, have intact performance across letter-cued word fluency tasks, and overall good expressive language abilities (articulation and syntax) (Howlin, 2003; Kjelgaard & Tager-Flusberg, 2001; Koning & Magill-Evans, 2001; Minshew, Goldstein, & Siegel, 1997; Rice et al., 2005; Saalasti et al., 2008; Seung, 2007; Williams et al., 2006b).

One area of cognitive weakness that tends to be a more consistent deficit among children diagnosed with ASD is motor processing speed. Children with

ASD tend to perform poorly on graphomotor and processing speed subtests fairly consistently in the literature (Calhoun & Mayes, 2005; Green et al., 2002; Mayes & Calhoun, 2003a, 2003b; 2007; Nydén, Billstedt, Hjelmquist, & Gillberg, 2001). This is not surprising given the comorbidity of motor incoordination disorders and dysgraphia observed among children with ASD (Green et al., 2002; Mayes & Calhoun, 2003a, 2003b, 2007; Szatmari, Archer, Fisman, Streiner, & Wilson, 1995; Wechsler, 2003).

Given the degree of heterogeneity in performance on intelligence tests among children with ASD, a comprehensive examination of all domains measured by the WISC-V may be necessary. The subtests necessary for obtaining the FSIQ will be important for identifying the presence of an intellectual disability; however, administration of all primary and secondary subtests is recommended as they will be important for analysis of strengths and weaknesses. For instance, in cases where language impairment is suspected, administration of Picture Span and Visual Puzzles is recommended as this will allow for interpretation of the nonverbal index, which may provide a better strength-based estimate than the traditional full-scale or general ability index. Even for cases where language impairment is not a primary feature, subtle deficits in pragmatics and comprehension tend to occur. Thus, targeted intervention planning will require administration of secondary verbal subtests (Information and Comprehension) for identifying verbal weaknesses even among high functioning ASD.

Attention-Deficit/Hyperactivity Disorder

ADHD is categorized, using an epidemiological perspective, as a "high prevalence, low morbidity" condition. Its high prevalence emerges out of the fact that ADHD is one of the most commonly occurring childhood disorders, with varying degrees of severity and developmental expression into adolescence and adulthood. ADHD includes difficulty maintaining sustained focus, disinhibition, or the diminished ability to control one's own behavior or impulsivity, coupled in certain cases with heightened levels of activity labeled as hyperactivity (APA, 2013; Barkley, 1997). In addition, in order to reach a diagnostic threshold, the presenting symptoms of ADHD have to have negative repercussions for the child such as impact in the school environment and socialization with other children, adolescents or adults, or at home (APA, 2013). It is also imperative to note that the conceptualization of ADHD as a low morbidity condition may be greater than once thought, with detrimental effects on a child's overall level of functioning and future outcomes (e.g., driving accidents, marriage outcome, vocational achievement; APA, 2013).

Given its high prevalence, ADHD has been one of the most researched conditions worldwide (Barkley, 2007). Relatively recent studies from several lines of research are better informing investigators about the broad functional effects of ADHD and its psychopathophysiological effects on CNS functions. For example, recent neuroimaging studies have indicated that children with ADHD exhibit normal CNS maturation, but with delays in development by approximately

3 years (Shaw, Eckstrand, & Sharp, 2007). These studies suggest that the delay is most pronounced in CNS regions involved in attention and regulatory skills, planning, and higher order functions. Recent studies additionally have noted delays in overall cortical maturation (Shaw et al., 2012) and in particular in a brain area important for functional inter-hemispheric communication (Gilliam, Stockman, & Malek, 2011). From a neurochemical standpoint, studies of the association between neurotransmitter levels and tasks of executive functioning have emerged, similar to the original literature (Ashton-Jones, Rajkowsky, & Alexinsky, 1994; Usher, Cohen, Servan-Schreiber, Rajkowski, & Aston-Jones, 1999). One study found performance on a reaction time task of visual sustained attention-discrimination was positively associated with levels of norepinephrine (NE) but not dopamine (DA) in children with ADHD, with poorer reaction time scores associated with lower levels of NE (Llorente et al., 2006). Similarly, a visual sustained attention-discrimination task that included alternating attention with exploratory behavior (goal-directed search) was also associated with levels of NE as well as DA among children with ADHD (Llorente et al., 2012). Again poorer scores on this procedure were correlated with lower levels of these metabolites. These neurochemical abnormalities may be useful in understanding underlying functional deficits and symptoms observed in ADHD and help to explain how the disorder may come to develop and impact CNS maturation and subsequent functional problems.

From DSM-IV to DSM-5 the specific diagnostic criteria of ADHD did not change. Thus, the same 18 symptoms under DSM-IV exist in DSM-5, and they continue to be organized across two subdomains termed inattention and hyperactivity-impulsivity. Like DSM-IV, a diagnosis of ADHD in DSM-5 requires at least six symptoms to be met in each applicable subdomain. Substantial clinical heterogeneity can emerge within ADHD because of the possible permutations that result from a diagnostic requirement of six from 18 symptoms. This issue remains problematic from a nosological standpoint and needs to be addressed in future DSM revisions.

Although clinical symptoms did not change with the revision to the DSM, several other aspects of the diagnostic criteria did and these changes have an impact on the neurocognitive profile of ADHD under DSM-5 criteria. The cross-situational or cross-environmental requirement has been given greater focus under the new system in order to underscore the importance of several symptoms occurring in each setting. Additionally, age of onset of the disorder changed. DSM-IV required "symptoms that caused impairment before 7 years of age" whereas DSM-5 uses "several inattentive or hyperactive-impulsive symptoms that have to be present prior to 12 years of age." This change is in many respects a positive one as many children are not referred for evaluation until school age, particularly those with primarily inattentive symptoms. Another major change that took place under DSM-5 is that the various clinical "subtypes" (e.g., Predominantly Inattentive Type) were changed and replaced with "presentation specifiers" to delineate the prior subtypes. This was a welcome change as the neuropsychological literature suggests that there may be many more "subtypes" than those previously noted under DSM-IV. In addition, unlike DSM-IV, a comorbid diagnosis with ASD is now permitted under DSM-5. Finally, a major change under DSM-5, partially to address the adoption of the future ICD-11 system, ADHD was placed in the neurodevelopmental disorders chapter to reflect a CNS disorder.

Intellectual ability among children with ADHD is typically lower than children without ADHD (Carte, Nigg, & Hinshaw, 1996; Clark, Prior, & Kinsella, 2000; Kuntsi et al., 2004; Mariani & Barkley, 1997; Melnick & Hinshaw, 1996; Rucklidge & Tannock, 2001; Schachar & Logan, 1990). One large population-based twin study of 5-year-olds found a difference of nine IQ points between children with ADHD and those without. This study used Vocabulary and Block Design subtests of the WPPSI–R as measures of IQ, and although it sampled children below the WISC age range, the results were consistent with previous literature using older children and adolescents (Fergusson, Horwood, & Lynskey, 1993; Goodman, Simonoff, & Stevenson, 1995; Rapport, Scanlan, & Denney, 1999; Rucklidge & Tannock, 2001). Cognitive impairment in ADHD is frequently implicated through its relation to deficits in executive functioning skills-the inability to plan and execute a strategy (Willcutt, Doyle, Nigg, Faraone, & Pennington, 2005). Children with both inattentive and hyperactive specifiers of ADHD consistently perform poorly on measures of attention, executive function, and processing speed (Calhoun & Mayes, 2005; Clark et al., 2000; Clark, Prior, & Kinsella, 2002; Naglieri, Goldstein, Iseman, & Schwebach, 2003; Nydén et al., 2001; Saklofske, Schwean, Yackalic, & Quinn, 1994; Seidman, 2006; Willcutt et al., 2005; Wodka et al., 2008). Many also have dysgraphia or problems with motor coordination (Gillberg & Kadesjo, 2000; Karatekin, Markiewicz, & Siegel, 2003; Pitcher, Piek, & Hay, 2003; Tannock, 2000; Tseng, Henderson, Chow, & Yao, 2004). Relevant WISC-V subtests that tap these domains include Digit Span, a measure of auditory working memory, Coding, a graphomotor processing speed measure, and Symbol Search, a measure of processing speed.

Poor performance on tests of verbal fluency or rapid naming tasks are also frequently reported in studies comparing typically developing children to children with ADHD, with similar deficits occurring across both combined and inattentive specifiers (Chhabildas, Pennington, & Willcutt, 2001; Geurts, Verté, Oosterlaan, Roeyers, & Sergeant, 2005; Hinshaw, Carte, Sami, Treuting, & Zupan, 2002; Lockwood, Marcotte, & Stern, 2001; Nigg, Blaskey, Huang-Pollock, & Rappley, 2002; Pasini, Paloscia, Alessandrelli, Porfirio, & Curatolo, 2007; Riccio, Homack, Jarratt, & Wolfe, 2006). Paired-Associate Learning (PAL), which combines both verbal fluency and working memory, has been similarly shown to be weaker in ADHD samples compared to control groups (Chang et al., 1999; Douglas & Benezra, 1990).

Pragmatic language difficulties are frequently found among children with ADHD, at levels commensurate with those reported for the former Asperger's syndrome (Bishop & Baird, 2001; Geurts, Verté, Oosterlaan, Roeyers, & Sergeant, 2004). Mulligan et al. (2009) found that ADHD was most strongly associated with neurocognitive difficulties, including language disorder, among children with more autism symptoms, highlighting the phenotypic overlap between the two disorders. Similarly, Geurts and Embrechts (2008) found pragmatic deficits among ADHD children 7 to 14 years of age that were indistinguishable from children with ASD. The added complexity of comorbid ASD with ADHD makes it difficult to identify these deficits as belonging to one disorder or the other; however, phenotypic overlap is a common theme among neurocognitive disorders and an accurate reflection of the current state of research in both these disorders.

Disruptive Behavior Disorders (DBD)

Conduct disorder (CD) and oppositional defiant disorder (ODD) form the DBD category of the DSM. ODD is characterized by age-inappropriate and persistent displays of angry, defiant, irritable, and oppositional behaviors whereas CD includes far more aggressive and antisocial behaviors such as inflicting pain, denial of the rights of others, and status offenses (Hinshaw & Lee, 2003). Both CD and ODD are highly comorbid with ADHD, and this comorbidity is an important factor in the neurocognitive profile of DBD. Low intelligence is often considered a precursor to DBD given the correlation between behavior disorders and poor academic achievement (Farrington, 1995; Frick et al., 1991). In addition some research has found persistent low intelligence and deficits in executive functioning among delinquent children compared to the general population (Frick & Viding, 2009; Lynam & Henry, 2001; Moffitt, 2006). However, some experts have argued that studies showing a significant relation between deficits in executive functioning or low IQ and behavior disorders have failed to control for comorbid ADHD (Burke, Loeber, & Birmaher, 2002; Hogan, 1999). Indeed, when studies control for ADHD, the relation between ODD and CD to weak neuropsychological functioning tends to either disappear or become nonsignificant (Clark et al., 2000; Klorman et al., 1999; Kuhne, Schachar, & Tannock, 1997; Mayes & Calhoun, 2007; van Goozen et al., 2004).

Still, a consistent deficit in receptive vocabulary has been observed among children with antisocial behaviors (Kaufman & Kaufman, 1990; Lansing et al., 2014; Lynam, Moffitt, & Stouthamer-Loeber, 1993; Moffitt & Caspi, 2001; Rosso, Falasco, & Koller, 1984). Additionally, there seems to be evidence that weaknesses in spatial and perceptual forms of cognitive processing may be related to early onset of antisocial behaviors (Lansing et al., 2014; Raine, Yaralian, Reynolds, Venables, & Mednick, 2002). However, in all other domains, the evidence supports average cognitive functioning for DBDs. For instance, DBD groups do not differ significantly from community control children on measures of graphomotor or processing speed tasks (Mayes & Calhoun, 2007). In fact, some studies have shown the opposite trend, with higher intelligence associated with increased conduct problems in children with persistent antisocial behavior, and at minimum, commensurate intelligence levels with community control groups (Christian, Frick, Hill, Tyler, & Frazer, 1997; Lahey et al., 1995). Thus, incorporating more recent evidence on neurocognitive functioning and DBDs, significant difficulties with attention, executive function, learning, or memory would not be expected among children with DBD, assuming no comorbid ADHD was present (Mayes & Calhoun, 2007; Oosterlaan, Scheres, & Sergeant, 2005; Pennington & Ozonoff, 1996; Pickering & Gathercole, 2004).

Traumatic Brain Injury

Traumatic brain injury (TBI) is an acquired injury resulting from sudden trauma causing damage to the brain (Hayden, Jandial, Duenas, Mahajan, & Levy, 2007; McCrea, 2007). Although several nosological systems exist (e.g., ICD–10; American Academy of Neurology), the U.S. Department of Defense, and Department of Veterans Affairs (2008) provides one of the most comprehensive and updated criteria for classification purposes associated with such injuries. Using this nosological system TBIs are classified as "mild," "moderate," or severe" depending on the Glasgow Coma Scale (GCS) score, length of loss of consciousness (LOC), and length of post-traumatic amnesia (PTA). Traumatic brain injuries can also be classified as open (penetrating) or closed (non-penetrating, blunt). In general and basic terms, a closed TBI results when the head violently hits an object or when an object violently and suddenly hits the head, without piercing the skull. In contrast, an open TBI results when perforation of the skull takes place and a projectile enters (or the head violently hits an object) impacting brain tissue (brain parenchyma). TBI can range from mild concussion to severe TBI and the resulting symptoms depend on the extent of the damage to the brain and other parameters as noted above (Hayden et al., 2007). A child with a mild TBI may remain conscious or may experience a brief loss of consciousness (LOC) for a few seconds or minutes. Sports-related concussion is a common form of mild TBI that has been widely overlooked historically, but is now receiving focused attention in schools at all levels. The effects of even mild TBI can be exacerbated if the student athlete is allowed to return to play the sport before fully recovering, or if he or she suffers multiple mild concussions. Diagnosis of more severe TBIs requires greater alterations in conscious states as well as the presence of other indicators (lower score on the GCS, greater length of PTA, etc.; McCrea, 2007).

TBI is associated with a broad array of neuropsychological deficits in language skills (verbal reasoning, verbal fluency), visual–perceptual and constructional skills, attention and memory, executive functions, and speeded tasks (Ries, Potter, & Llorente, 2007; Slomine et al., 2002; Yeates, 2000; Yeates et al., 2002). Although there is variability associated with the age of insult, as well as the location and the severity of the insult, longitudinal and prospective studies support the notion that these deficits are persistent for moderate to severe TBIs, with only minor or partial recovery occurring in the first year post-injury for some children (Anderson, Catroppa, Morse, Haritou, & Rosenfeld, 2000; Catroppa, Anderson,

Morse, Haritou, & Rosenfeld, 2007; Chadwick, Rutter, Brown, Shaffer, & Traub, 1981; Chadwick, Rutter, Shaffer, & Shrout, 1981; Jaffe, Polisar, Fay, & Liao, 1995; Knights et al., 1991; Yeates et al., 2002). The level of impairment as well as the long-term outcome of cognitive functioning following childhood TBI is worse for younger children with severe injury compared to both older children with severe injury and all children with mild or moderate injuries (Anderson, Brown, Newitt, & Hoile, 2009, 2011). Age of the child at injury is an important predictor of post-injury ability according to Catroppa et al. (2007) because the interruption on an emerging cognitive ability during critical developmental periods may prevent normal development of this ability following injury.

INTELLECTUAL ASSESSMENT WITH THE WISC-V IN DIAGNOSTIC AND TREATMENT PLANNING

The general structure of the WISC-V expands upon the traditional WISC-IV index and subtest score offering. While it retains the FSIQ and factor-based index scores, it also provides multiple theoretically driven composite scores that are not included in the FSIQ assessment. In addition, the WISC-V introduces complementary subtests and index scores that measure abilities related to academic achievement domains but are not direct measures of intellectual abilities. The evolution of the test structure, domain coverage, and scores provided reflects the changes within psychological assessment and education over time (see Chapters 1–3 of this book).

The WISC-V, along with its predecessors, includes an overall estimate of general intellectual ability, FSIQ. In the early versions of the instrument, FSIQ was used as the main score for diagnostic and interpretive purposes. The main development goal was to produce an instrument whose global score could accurately differentiate among individuals of varying overall intellectual ability. Children with high overall ability were often classified as intellectually gifted and those with low overall ability were classified as intellectually disabled (previously mental retardation). Although a Verbal IQ and Performance IQ were provided, the FSIQ was the main product of intellectual assessment. The FSIQ was used as an estimate of the general mental ability of a child and was used to make educational placement decisions. A global measure of cognitive ability has remained in the WISC and most other measures of intelligence despite criticism and concerns over the clinical utility of combining different cognitive abilities into a single score. Psychometric and clinical research continues to support a general factor of mental ability, and many contemporary theories of intelligence include overall ability. In addition, an overall estimate of ability is required for diagnoses of intellectual disability and evaluations of intellectual giftedness. The FSIQ is frequently used not just as an estimate of overall ability but as a comparison measure (e.g., memory, achievement), allowing other scores to be interpreted within the context of overall ability. In other words, the FSIQ provides an overall estimate to which the index and other scores can be compared to determine whether ability within a specific domain is higher or lower than the individual's overall ability.

As psychological assessment matured and educational systems accommodated greater intellectual variability in mainstream classes, the role of the overall estimate of ability changed and the focus of interpretation shifted to factor- and theory-based index scores describing more specific cognitive abilities. The four-factor index model was introduced in the WISC-III and provided scores for domains covering verbal comprehension, perceptual organization, working memory, and processing speed. This allowed practitioners to expand their evaluation beyond overall ability to specific cognitive domains within the context of overall ability. This was particularly beneficial in cases in which subtest and index scores varied across the domains. The FSIQ is a composite score; the interpretation of the score depends on the similarity of the scores from which it is derived. The more similar the contributing scores, the more the global score reflects consistent functioning across the cognitive domains included. The more dissimilar the contributing scores, the greater the clinical utility of analyzing patterns of strengths and weaknesses. As assessment began to focus on narrower cognitive domains, the primary purpose of using an intelligence assessment also changed. In addition to assigning classifications to children for educational placement purposes, practitioners began to assess children to provide recommendations on appropriate accommodations and interventions. This shift required greater description of a child's specific abilities to allow for more refined diagnoses and interventions. Beginning with the WISC-IV, the focus of interpretation shifted from the FSIQ to the primary index scores. Research on the performance of various clinical groups on the four cognitive domains demonstrated the clinical utility of the index scores. Score differences across the factors varied across clinical groups and provided valuable information on cognitive abilities within and across clinical groups. The benefits of examining subtest scores and process scores to further delineate the cognitive strengths and weaknesses of a child were also recognized. Flanagan and Harrison (2012) describe several contemporary theories on interpretation of intelligence assessment results that utilize index and subtest-level scores to provide detailed descriptions of an individual's cognitive strengths and weaknesses. The neuropsychological tradition (Kaplan, 1988; Lezak, 2004) has long promoted an approach looking at subtest-level performance rather than composite scores and assessments that were more flexible and personalized rather than a strict battery approach. Also the Patterns of Strengths and Weaknesses (PSW) model (Hale & Firoello, 2004) advocates for a more flexible and customized approach to assessment with less focus on overall FSIQ.

All of these theoretical, educational, practical, and clinical elements were examined and considered in the development of the WISC-V. The WISC-V continued the movement toward more cognitively specific indexes, expanding the four-factor model to five, including a separate index score to measure fluid reasoning. It further expanded the number of index scores available by introducing theory-based index scores called Ancillary Index Scores. These scores expand the domains measured by the WISC-V beyond the factor-based primary indexes and include the Quantitative Reasoning Index (QRI), Auditory Working Memory Index (AWMI), Nonverbal Index (NVI), General Ability Index (GAI), and Cognitive Processing Index (CPI). The theoretical foundations of these indexes are described in greater detail in Chapter 4. The AWMI is comprised of the same subtests as the WISC-IV WMI, allowing a direct comparison of working memory ability across the two editions. The NVI, GAI, and CPI provide comprehensive measures of abilities, which can be interpreted independently or compared to the FSIQ for various clinical purposes.

A further enhancement in the WISC-V is the development and inclusion of complementary subtests and indexes. These are not part of the main battery and are not directly related to the primary indexes or FSIQ. Instead, they measure skills and abilities related to the development of reading, writing, and mathematics and are included to enhance the evaluation of children with learning disabilities and other clinical conditions. Because they were not designed to measure intellectual ability, performance on these tasks may differ from performance on traditional intellectual measures. The development of the WISC-V primary, ancillary, and complementary index scores allows greater flexibility and content coverage to practitioners utilizing the WISC-V. It enhances the ability of the practitioner to focus the assessment on the cognitive abilities related to the needs of the child while retaining the global ability and index scores required for a comprehensive intellectual assessment.

WISC-V PERFORMANCE IN SPECIAL GROUPS

The WISC-V subtest and composite data for selected special groups with matched control comparisons are provided in Tables 10.1–10.9. An overview of the pattern of index and subtest scores observed for each of the selected special groups now follows.

Intellectual Giftedness

Children in the intellectually gifted (GT) group were selected for inclusion if they had previously obtained global scores of intelligence at least 2 standard deviations above the mean on any standard measure of cognitive ability. In addition, all children in the GT sample were currently receiving services in school for intellectual giftedness. Data for the GT group is shown in Table 10.1.

On the WISC-V, the GT group obtained a mean FSIQ score of 127.5. Consistent with previous research using the WISC-IV among gifted children, the highest index score was observed on the VCI and the lowest score on the PSI. All primary index scores were greater than 1 standard deviation (SD) above the mean, with the exception of the PSI. A similar pattern is observed among the subtest scores, with the highest subtest scores observed in the verbal

TABLE 10.1 Mean Performance of Intellectually Gifted and Matched Comparison Groups

Subtest/ Process/ Composite Score	Intellectually Gifted		Matched Control			Group Mean Comparison			
	Mean	SD	Mean	SD	n	Difference	t Value	p Value	Standard Difference[a]
SI	15.1	2.4	10.9	2.7	95	−4.16	−10.53	<.01	−1.63
VC	14.9	2.3	11.2	2.8	95	−3.77	−9.62	<.01	−1.47
IN	14.6	2.5	11.0	2.8	95	−3.53	−9.93	<.01	−1.33
CO	14.1	2.5	10.9	2.9	95	−3.19	−7.64	<.01	−1.18
BD	13.9	2.4	10.9	2.6	95	−3.03	−9.50	<.01	−1.21
VP	13.5	2.1	11.0	2.4	95	−2.47	−6.97	<.01	−1.10
MR	13.3	2.8	10.9	2.6	95	−2.38	−6.19	<.01	−.88
FW	13.8	2.5	10.8	2.4	95	−2.95	−8.55	<.01	−1.20
PC	12.3	2.9	10.5	2.9	95	−1.76	−3.81	<.01	−.61
AR	13.9	2.5	10.6	2.4	95	−3.24	−8.67	<.01	−1.32
DS	14.0	2.5	11.0	2.6	95	−3.00	−7.69	<.01	−1.18
PS	12.3	2.9	10.4	2.5	95	−1.93	−4.52	<.01	−.71

LN	14.3	2.5	11.1	2.8	93	-3.20	-7.91	<.01	-1.21
CD	12.1	2.7	9.9	2.6	94	-2.19	-5.78	<.01	-.83
SS	12.5	2.7	10.2	2.9	91	-2.27	-5.23	<.01	-.81
CA	11.8	3.2	9.8	2.9	95	-2.01	-4.68	<.01	-.66
VCI	127.7	12.3	105.8	12.9	95	-21.97	-11.09	<.01	-1.74
VSI	121.2	11.5	105.2	12.2	95	-15.98	-9.55	<.01	-1.35
FRI	120.3	12.0	105.1	12.3	95	-15.26	-8.80	<.01	-1.26
WMI	117.9	11.7	104.0	12.1	95	-13.86	-7.33	<.01	-1.16
PSI	112.9	13.5	100.4	13.5	90	-12.44	-6.05	<.01	-.92
FSIQ	127.5	8.8	105.7	12.2	94	-21.85	-13.19	<.01	-2.05
QRI	122.1	11.8	104.1	11.4	95	-18.04	-10.41	<.01	-1.55
AWMI	123.0	12.9	105.9	13.0	93	-17.13	-8.49	<.01	-1.32
NVI	122.9	10.5	104.6	11.8	94	-18.28	-10.80	<.01	-1.64
GAI	127.1	9.6	106.3	12.4	95	-20.83	-12.54	<.01	-1.88
CPI	118.8	11.0	102.1	12.4	90	-16.73	-8.71	<.01	-1.43

[a]The Standard Difference is the difference of the two test means divided by the square root of the pooled variance; computed using Cohen's (1996) Formula 10.4.

comprehension and working memory domains, and the lowest scores in the processing speed domain. All primary subtest scores, with the exception of Picture Span and the processing speed subtests, were more than 1 SD above the mean.

Among the ancillary index scores, a significant difference is observed between the GAI and CPI with the mean score on the GAI approximately 8 points higher than the mean score on the CPI. As discussed in previous chapters, GAI includes the verbal conceptualization, visual–spatial, and fluid reasoning subtests; whereas CPI includes the working memory and processing speed subtests. For this reason, some practitioners prefer using GAI rather than FSIQ to identify GT in students who perform relatively low on the processing speed tasks (which are excluded in the GAI). This may be appropriate when PSI is low due only to the student's meticulous behavioral approach to the Coding subtest, and there is other evidence that cognitive processing speed is strong. Using GAI rather than FSIQ may qualify more students as GT, but could also result in selecting some students for GT programs who have clinically significant weaknesses in processing speed or working memory. As discussed in Chapter 4, each of the primary cognitive abilities is an important facet of intelligence and no area should be ignored in an overall evaluation of intellectual capacity. Issues related to interpretation of GAI are discussed in more detail in Chapter 1.

The AWMI is higher than the WMI due to higher subtest scores on the auditory working memory tasks than on Picture Span. Scores on the complementary subtests and indexes were above average for the symbol translation subtests and index and in the average range on the naming speed subtests and index, possibly reflecting the more basic than advanced cognitive processes measured by these tasks, or lower performance on speeded tasks.

Intellectual Disability—Mild and Moderate

Children in the intellectual disability groups (ID-Mild, ID-Moderate) were included in the sample if they met the DSM-5 criteria for intellectual disability or obtained full scale scores on a standard measure of cognitive ability that were at least 2 SDs below the mean for the ID-Mild group and 3 SDs below the mean for the ID-Moderate group. Data for the ID-Mild and ID-Moderate groups are shown in Tables 10.2–10.3.

On the WISC-V, the ID-Mild group obtained a mean FSIQ of 60.9 and the ID-Moderate group obtained a mean FSIQ score of 49.7. Among the primary index scores, performance across cognitive domains was low with the highest relative scores occurring on the PSI composite and associated processing speed subtests, including Cancellation and Symbol Search. Additionally, relatively high scores were also observed in the fluid reasoning domain and on Picture Span, compared to the low performance occurring across all other domains. Scores among the ancillary index scores were relatively similar to the primary index scores with scores in the low 60s for the ID-Mild group and in the low to mid-50s for the ID-Moderate group. Performance on the AWMI

TABLE 10.2 Mean Performance of Intellectual Disability-Mild Severity and Matched Control Groups

Subtest/ Process/ Composite Score	Intellectual Disability- Mild Severity		Matched Control			Group Mean Comparison			Standard Difference[a]
	Mean	SD	Mean	SD	n	Difference	t Value	p Value	
SI	3.8	2.1	9.5	3.2	74	5.74	13.92	<.01	2.12
VC	3.9	1.9	9.0	3.2	74	5.07	12.40	<.01	1.93
IN	3.8	1.9	9.6	3.1	74	5.76	15.00	<.01	2.24
CO	4.0	1.9	8.7	2.9	74	4.69	12.37	<.01	1.91
BD	3.9	2.2	10.1	2.9	74	6.22	14.18	<.01	2.42
VP	4.1	1.6	10.3	2.9	74	6.22	16.03	<.01	2.66
MR	4.1	2.6	10.0	3.4	74	5.89	11.62	<.01	1.95
FW	4.3	2.1	9.8	3.3	74	5.46	11.96	<.01	1.97
PC	4.7	2.5	9.7	3.4	74	5.03	10.16	<.01	1.69
AR	3.2	1.8	9.6	3.2	74	6.34	13.39	<.01	2.44
DS	3.4	1.9	9.9	2.8	73	6.51	15.55	<.01	2.72
PS	4.3	2.3	9.7	2.9	74	5.42	11.49	<.01	2.07

(Continued)

TABLE 10.2 (Continued)

Subtest/ Process/ Composite Score	Intellectual Disability- Mild Severity		Matched Control			Group Mean Comparison			
	Mean	SD	Mean	SD	n	Difference	t Value	p Value	Standard Difference[a]
LN	3.5	2.1	9.7	2.7	73	6.18	14.23	<.01	2.56
CD	4.6	2.9	9.6	2.8	70	5.00	11.06	<.01	1.75
SS	5.3	3.3	9.5	2.2	67	4.15	8.51	<.01	1.48
CA	6.1	3.4	10.8	2.5	73	4.67	8.61	<.01	1.56
VCI	66.0	10.9	96.1	16.4	74	30.14	14.21	<.01	2.16
VSI	66.0	9.9	101.1	14.6	74	35.14	16.72	<.01	2.82
FRI	67.0	11.0	99.3	16.1	74	32.34	13.49	<.01	2.35
WMI	65.1	10.5	98.7	14.6	73	33.60	14.93	<.01	2.64
PSI	71.6	16.2	97.3	10.9	67	25.78	11.45	<.01	1.87
FSIQ	60.9	8.9	98.0	15.6	69	37.07	16.22	<.01	2.92
QRI	64.2	9.7	98.1	15.1	74	33.86	15.16	<.01	2.67
AWMI	62.2	11.5	99.2	13.8	72	36.96	15.96	<.01	2.91
NVI	62.1	8.7	99.5	15.2	70	37.40	16.46	<.01	3.02
GAI	63.5	8.8	97.9	15.7	74	34.46	15.95	<.01	2.71
CPI	63.4	12.3	97.6	13.4	67	34.19	14.75	<.01	2.66

[a]The Standard Difference is the difference of the two test means divided by the square root of the pooled variance; computed using Cohen's (1996) Formula 10.4.

TABLE 10.3 Mean Performance of Intellectual Disability-Moderate Severity and Matched Control Groups

Subtest/ Process/ Composite Score	Intellectual Disability-Moderate Severity		Matched Control			Group Mean Comparison			
	Mean	SD	Mean	SD	n	Difference	t Value	p Value	Standard Difference[a]
SI	2.2	1.9	10.1	3.5	37	7.89	11.65	<.01	2.80
VC	2.4	1.7	9.6	3.1	37	7.22	11.75	<.01	2.89
IN	2.3	1.8	9.6	2.7	37	7.30	13.42	<.01	3.18
CO	2.6	2.4	9.5	2.9	37	6.89	11.37	<.01	2.59
BD	2.4	1.5	9.5	2.9	37	7.14	13.18	<.01	3.09
VP	2.8	1.9	9.3	3.0	37	6.51	12.72	<.01	2.59
MR	2.4	2.1	9.7	3.3	37	7.30	11.16	<.01	2.64
FW	3.2	2.1	9.4	3.6	36	6.17	9.24	<.01	2.09
PC	3.1	2.5	9.9	3.0	37	6.81	10.76	<.01	2.47
AR	2.2	1.5	10.0	2.9	37	7.81	14.87	<.01	3.38
DS	2.0	1.4	9.7	3.0	34	7.74	13.32	<.01	3.31
PS	3.5	2.3	10.2	3.4	36	6.69	9.94	<.01	2.30

(Continued)

TABLE 10.3 (Continued)

Subtest/ Process/ Composite Score	Intellectual Disability-Moderate Severity		Matched Control			Group Mean Comparison			
	Mean	SD	Mean	SD	n	Difference	t Value	p Value	Standard Difference[a]
LN	2.6	1.7	9.9	3.0	33	7.27	11.72	<.01	2.98
CD	3.1	2.6	10.4	2.7	37	7.32	10.86	<.01	2.76
SS	3.2	2.7	9.9	2.8	37	6.73	10.05	<.01	2.45
CA	4.6	3.5	10.2	2.8	37	5.68	8.56	<.01	1.79
VCI	55.2	11.3	99.4	15.2	37	44.19	13.37	<.01	3.30
VSI	56.8	9.6	96.6	14.6	37	39.86	14.71	<.01	3.23
FRI	58.6	12.0	97.1	17.3	36	38.44	11.36	<.01	2.58
WMI	58.3	10.6	99.4	17.0	33	41.09	11.48	<.01	2.90
PSI	59.3	15.8	101.1	12.6	37	41.76	11.31	<.01	2.92
FSIQ	49.7	8.9	98.5	16.8	33	48.79	13.72	<.01	3.63
QRI	57.1	10.6	98.2	15.2	36	41.08	13.15	<.01	3.14
AWMI	54.1	9.4	99.0	15.2	32	44.94	14.12	<.01	3.56
NVI	53.4	10.1	98.0	17.2	35	44.54	13.27	<.01	3.16
GAI	54.3	9.4	97.8	16.4	36	43.50	13.40	<.01	3.25
CPI	52.5	12.7	99.9	15.8	33	47.45	12.26	<.01	3.31

[a]The Standard Difference is the difference of the two test means divided by the square root of the pooled variance; computed using Cohen's (1996) Formula 10.4.

was lower than the WMI for both ID groups. Scores on the complementary subtests and indexes, while still low in comparison to matched controls, were relatively higher than those observed for the primary index scores and FSIQ, with mean scores 10 to 15 points higher than the mean FSIQ. Overall the ID groups obtained scores roughly 2–3 SDs below the mean with the exception of the PSI and complementary index scores, which were relatively higher. Both the Mild-ID and Moderate-ID groups were statistically significantly different from the matched control groups on all subtests and composites and all effect sizes were large.

Borderline Intellectual Functioning

Children in the Borderline Intellectual Functioning (BIF) group were included if they had prior FSIQ scores between 71 and 84 on a standardized measure of ability or met DSM-5 criteria for a diagnosis of borderline intellectual functioning. Data for the BIF group are shown in Table 10.4.

On the WISC-V, the borderline group obtained a mean FSIQ of 80.4, which was statistically significantly lower than the matched control group. The pattern of scores on the primary indexes was similar to those observed in the Mild and Moderate ID groups, although with higher means as expected. The highest score was obtained on the PSI, followed by the FRI, with lower scores across the other three domains. The ancillary index scores were similar to the primary index scores with mean scores in the 75–85 range. Unlike the Mild and Moderate ID groups, scores on the AWMI were not lower than scores on the WMI. In general, complementary subtest and index scores were similar to those observed on the primary and ancillary subtest and index scores. In addition, as noted earlier in the chapter and consistent with prior research, variability in group performance across subtests decreased as severity of disability moved from borderline to mild to moderate levels of intellectual functioning. The range of mean scores across subtests for the BIF group was 5.7–10.4, whereas it was 3.2–6.1 for Mild-ID and 2.0–4.6 for Moderate-ID.

Attention-Deficit Hyperactivity Disorder

Children were included in the WISC-V ADHD sample if they met the DSM-5 criteria for a current diagnosis of ADHD (any subtype), had obtained clinically significant parent ratings on the Brown Attention-Deficit Disorder Scales® for Children and Adolescents (Brown, 2001), and had an estimate of general cognitive ability at least in the average range (FSIQ ≥ 80). Any children prescribed psycho-stimulant medication were required to be off medications for at least 24 hours prior to testing. Data for the ADHD group are shown in Table 10.5.

The ADHD group obtained primary index and subtest scores that, while in the average range, were still statistically significantly lower than the matched control group on the WMI, PSI, and FSIQ. The VCI, VSI, and FRI were not

TABLE 10.4 Mean Performance of Borderline Intellectual Functioning and Matched Control Groups

Subtest/ Process/ Composite Score	Borderline Intellectual Functioning		Matched Control			Group Mean Comparison			
	Mean	SD	Mean	SD	n	Difference	t Value	p Value	Standard Difference[a]
SI	7.0	1.4	9.0	2.9	20	2.00	2.59	0.02	.88
VC	6.2	2.0	8.7	2.9	19	2.53	3.33	<.01	1.02
IN	6.8	2.2	9.1	2.7	20	2.30	2.86	0.01	.93
CO	6.6	2.3	9.2	3.1	20	2.60	3.25	<.01	.95
BD	6.8	2.1	9.6	2.5	20	2.85	4.53	<.01	1.23
VP	7.1	1.7	9.4	2.4	20	2.30	3.15	<.01	1.11
MR	8.5	3.3	9.8	2.2	20	1.30	1.44	0.17	.46
FW	7.1	1.9	9.3	1.8	20	2.25	3.39	<.01	1.22
PC	7.3	2.7	10.6	3.1	20	3.30	3.94	<.01	1.14
AR	6.5	2.2	9.7	2.7	20	3.20	4.38	<.01	1.30
DS	5.9	2.6	9.6	2.8	20	3.75	5.10	<.01	1.39
PS	6.5	2.3	9.4	2.9	19	2.84	3.57	<.01	1.09

LN	5.7	2.0	9.7	3.3	20	4.05	5.00	<.01	1.48
CD	9.4	2.2	9.3	2.7	20	-.10	-.13	0.90	-.04
SS	8.9	3.0	9.5	3.0	19	.53	.63	0.54	.18
CA	10.4	2.5	11.1	3.2	20	.70	.70	0.49	.24
VCI	81.7	7.6	93.1	13.8	19	11.42	3.08	<.01	1.03
VSI	83.1	8.3	97.2	11.6	20	14.10	5.06	<.01	1.40
FRI	87.1	11.7	97.3	9.0	20	10.25	2.88	<.01	.98
WMI	78.2	11.9	97.1	14.2	19	18.95	5.10	<.01	1.45
PSI	95.1	11.9	96.4	13.1	19	1.37	.33	0.75	.11
FSIQ	80.4	5.7	94.5	9.2	19	14.16	5.53	<.01	1.85
QRI	81.3	7.8	97.1	10.4	20	15.75	4.97	<.01	1.71
AWMI	76.6	11.1	98.0	14.9	20	21.35	6.07	<.01	1.63
NVI	82.1	7.9	95.0	8.6	19	12.89	4.18	<.01	1.56
GAI	80.8	7.5	94.6	11.8	19	13.79	4.26	<.01	1.39
CPI	84.0	10.4	95.7	11.5	19	11.74	3.33	<.01	1.07

[a]The Standard Difference is the difference of the two test means divided by the square root of the pooled variance; computed using Cohen's (1996) Formula 10.4.

TABLE 10.5 Mean Performance of Attention-Deficit/Hyperactivity Disorder and Matched Control Groups

Subtest/ Process/ Composite Score	Attention-Deficit/ Hyperactivity Disorder		Matched Control			Group Mean Comparison			
	Mean	SD	Mean	SD	n	Difference	t Value	p Value	Standard Difference[a]
SI	9.6	2.2	10.3	3.0	48	.67	1.27	0.21	.25
VC	9.6	2.4	10.7	2.4	48	1.17	2.41	0.02	.49
IN	9.6	2.7	10.3	2.7	48	.71	1.34	0.19	.26
CO	9.5	2.8	10.3	2.7	48	.79	1.61	0.11	.29
BD	9.4	3.1	9.8	2.4	48	.35	.70	0.49	.13
VP	9.6	3.3	10.8	2.7	48	1.13	1.94	0.06	.37
MR	9.4	2.5	10.4	2.4	48	1.02	2.14	0.04	.42
FW	9.8	3.0	10.5	3.0	48	.73	1.18	0.24	.24
PC	8.9	2.8	10.4	2.9	48	1.42	2.38	0.02	.50
AR	8.5	2.6	10.6	2.4	48	2.19	4.31	<.01	.88
DS	9.2	2.6	10.5	2.3	47	1.23	2.99	<.01	.50
PS	8.9	2.8	10.1	2.8	48	1.23	2.08	0.04	.44

LN	9.0	3.0	10.0	2.7	47	1.02	1.64	0.11	.36
CD	8.4	2.7	10.0	2.5	48	1.69	3.48	<.01	.65
SS	9.5	3.0	9.9	2.7	47	.36	.57	0.57	.13
CA	9.5	2.6	10.0	2.8	48	.52	.99	0.33	.19
VCI	97.8	11.4	102.7	13.2	48	4.90	1.98	0.05	.40
VSI	97.3	16.7	101.5	12.4	48	4.17	1.51	0.14	.28
FRI	97.6	13.4	102.6	13.1	48	5.04	1.94	0.06	.38
WMI	94.8	13.3	101.7	12.3	47	6.91	2.98	<.01	.54
PSI	94.2	13.9	99.9	12.5	47	5.70	2.19	0.03	.43
FSIQ	95.6	11.7	102.2	10.2	47	6.66	3.20	<.01	.61
QRI	94.8	14.2	103.1	12.7	48	8.33	3.13	<.01	.62
AWMI	95.2	13.3	101.4	11.5	47	6.23	2.73	<.01	.50
NVI	94.4	13.1	101.7	12.3	48	7.29	3.01	<.01	.57
GAI	97.1	13.3	102.3	11.1	48	5.21	2.23	0.03	.43
CPI	92.8	12.6	100.8	12.2	46	8.00	3.18	<.01	.65

[a]The Standard Difference is the difference of the two test means divided by the square root of the pooled variance; computed using Cohen's (1996) Formula 10.4.

statistically significantly different between groups, although Vocabulary and Matrix Reasoning were statistically significantly lower for the ADHD group compared to controls. The lowest scores were obtained on the Arithmetic and Coding subtests. All ancillary index scores were statistically significantly lower than the matched control group. The CPI was lower than the GAI, as expected, given the PSI and WMI domains contribute to the CPI. The AWMI was similar to the WMI; lower than other index scores but within the average range. The lowest index score across all primary, ancillary, and complementary indexes was on the Naming Speed Index (NSI). Performance on the NSI was 8 points lower than on the Symbol Translation Index. Overall the lowest scores were observed on measures involving processing speed and working memory. This is consistent with the extant literature on ADHD, which demonstrates greatest weaknesses in domains tapping executive functioning.

Disruptive Behavior Disorder

Children included in the DBD group were diagnosed with oppositional defiant disorder or conduct disorder, or identified as having a high degree of parent-rated conduct problems (e.g., T score > 70) on the Behavior Assessment System for Children, Second Edition (BASC-2; Reynolds & Kamphaus, 2004). Children with a comorbid ADHD diagnosis or ADHD symptoms were excluded. Data for the DBD group are shown in Table 10.6. Mean scores across the primary, secondary, and ancillary index and subtest scores are in the average range of intellectual functioning and were relatively similar. Results show no statistically significant differences between DBD and matched control groups on any WISC-V subtest or composite measure. In line with previous research, the neurocognitive profile of DBD is unremarkable once ADHD has been controlled for.

Traumatic Brain Injury

TBI is one of the leading causes of cognitive disability in children. However, unlike other clinical groups, the cognitive sequelae of TBI are expected to vary across individuals due to injury-specific factors, such as location and severity of the injury, type of injury, functioning and age at injury, and length of time since the injury. Children in the TBI group were diagnosed with a moderate to severe TBI in the 6–18 months prior to the WISC-V assessment. A premorbid intelligence estimate above the range for intellectual disability (i.e., FSIQ > 70) was also required. Comorbid diagnoses of ADHD, conduct disorder, and anxiety or mood disorders were allowed as were speech services for language difficulties related to the TBI. Data on the TBI group are shown in Table 10.7.

Mean scores across the primary, secondary, and ancillary index and subtest scores are in the low average range of intellectual functioning and were relatively similar. Consistent with previous research and results on the WISC-IV, the PSI was the lowest index score on the WISC-V. The lowest subtest scores were obtained on Arithmetic, Coding, and Symbol Search. On the

TABLE 10.6 Mean Performance of Disruptive Behavior Disorder and Matched Control Groups

Subtest/ Process/ Composite Score	Disruptive Behavior		Matched Control			Group Mean Comparison			
	Mean	SD	Mean	SD	n	Difference	t value	p value	Standard Difference[a]
SI	9.4	2.6	10.4	3.5	21	1.00	1.10	0.28	.32
VC	8.4	2.3	8.9	2.8	21	.52	.89	0.38	.20
IN	9.0	3.0	9.9	2.5	21	.90	1.17	0.25	.33
CO	9.3	3.3	9.5	3.1	21	.19	.18	0.86	.06
BD	9.5	2.7	8.2	2.9	21	−1.24	−1.34	0.20	−.44
VP	9.5	2.7	9.1	2.6	21	−.43	−.57	0.58	−.16
MR	9.2	3.1	9.4	2.7	21	.19	.26	0.80	.07
FW	8.8	2.8	9.2	2.8	21	.38	.50	0.62	.14
PC	9.4	2.6	9.3	2.1	21	−.14	−.20	0.84	−.06
AR	9.0	3.1	9.3	3.3	21	.29	.31	0.76	.09
DS	9.3	3.4	9.4	3.1	21	.10	.09	0.93	.03
PS	9.0	3.0	8.8	2.6	21	−.24	−.24	0.81	−.09

(Continued)

TABLE 10.6 (Continued)

Subtest/ Process/ Composite Score	Disruptive Behavior		Matched Control			Group Mean Comparison			
	Mean	SD	Mean	SD	n	Difference	t value	p value	Standard Difference[a]
LN	8.7	3.8	9.3	2.2	21	.62	.55	0.59	.20
CD	8.7	3.2	8.2	3.4	21	-.52	-.55	0.59	-.16
SS	8.8	3.2	9.0	3.1	21	.24	.24	0.81	.08
CA	9.6	2.4	9.4	2.4	21	-.19	-.24	0.82	-.08
VCI	94.1	11.8	98.2	13.3	21	4.14	1.27	0.22	.33
VSI	97.1	13.9	92.6	13.3	21	-4.52	-1.10	0.29	-.33
FRI	94.4	15.2	95.9	13.3	21	1.52	.44	0.66	.11
WMI	95.3	13.7	95.0	13.2	21	-.29	-.06	0.95	-.02
PSI	92.8	17.1	92.1	16.5	21	-.62	-.12	0.91	-.04
FSIQ	93.3	12.4	93.5	12.8	21	.19	.06	0.96	.02
QRI	93.8	13.7	95.5	13.7	21	1.71	.47	0.64	.12
AWMI	94.5	18.0	96.6	13.1	21	2.10	.39	0.70	.13
NVI	93.6	12.5	91.3	12.7	21	-2.29	-.73	0.48	-.18
GAI	94.1	12.0	95.1	13.2	21	.95	.31	0.76	.08
CPI	92.8	14.3	92.6	14.7	21	-.24	-.05	0.96	-.02

[a]The Standard Difference is the difference of the two test means divided by the square root of the pooled variance; computed using Cohen's (1996) Formula 10.4.

TABLE 10.7 Mean Performance of Traumatic Brain Injury and Matched Control Groups

Subtest/ Process/ Composite Score	Autism Spectrum Disorder with Language Impairment		Matched Control			Group Mean Comparison			
	Mean	SD	Mean	SD	n	Difference	t Value	p Value	Standard Difference[a]
SI	6.5	3.3	10.9	2.8	29	4.38	5.22	<.01	1.43
VC	6.1	3.6	10.6	2.6	29	4.48	5.64	<.01	1.43
IN	5.8	3.5	11.2	2.9	29	5.34	6.39	<.01	1.66
CO	4.8	3.0	11.1	3.0	30	6.23	8.56	<.01	2.08
BD	7.2	4.1	10.5	2.8	30	3.30	3.67	<.01	.94
VP	6.7	4.3	11.1	2.4	29	4.45	4.86	<.01	1.28
MR	7.1	4.2	10.3	2.2	30	3.13	3.77	<.01	.93
FW	7.4	3.6	10.3	3.5	30	2.93	3.07	<.01	.83
PC	6.3	4.4	11.6	2.2	29	5.21	6.60	<.01	1.50
AR	5.4	3.5	10.6	2.5	30	5.23	6.68	<.01	1.72
DS	5.4	3.9	10.8	2.8	30	5.43	6.37	<.01	1.60
PS	6.9	3.8	10.7	3.0	30	3.77	4.07	<.01	1.10

(Continued)

TABLE 10.7 (Continued)

Subtest/Process/Composite Score	Autism Spectrum Disorder with Language Impairment		Matched Control			Group Mean Comparison			
	Mean	SD	Mean	SD	n	Difference	t Value	p Value	Standard Difference[a]
LN	5.0	3.6	10.3	2.3	29	5.24	7.40	<.01	1.73
CD	5.2	3.5	9.3	3.2	29	4.07	4.94	<.01	1.21
SS	6.2	3.7	9.9	2.7	26	3.69	5.30	<.01	1.14
CA	5.8	3.4	9.7	3.0	29	3.93	4.92	<.01	1.23
VCI	80.4	18.2	104.1	13.6	28	23.68	5.51	<.01	1.47
VSI	82.8	22.3	104.4	13.4	29	21.62	4.49	<.01	1.18
FRI	84.3	20.6	101.6	13.9	30	17.30	3.75	<.01	.98
WMI	77.6	19.4	104.1	13.9	30	26.47	6.05	<.01	1.57
PSI	75.8	19.0	96.9	14.8	26	21.12	5.41	<.01	1.24
FSIQ	76.3	19.1	102.1	14.5	28	25.82	5.75	<.01	1.52
QRI	78.9	19.2	102.5	15.8	30	23.67	5.07	<.01	1.35
AWMI	72.3	21.6	102.4	12.6	29	30.14	7.14	<.01	1.70
NVI	79.9	20.1	102.8	13.8	28	22.86	4.78	<.01	1.33
GAI	81.8	18.6	102.9	14.2	28	21.18	4.82	<.01	1.28
CPI	74.4	18.4	100.0	13.5	26	25.62	6.24	<.01	1.59

[a]The Standard Difference is the difference of the two test means divided by the square root of the pooled variance; computed using Cohen's (1996) Formula 10.4.

complementary scores, naming speed subtests were not significantly different compared to performance by the matched control group whereas performance on the symbol translation subtests were significantly lower. Overall, this group demonstrated relatively weaker processing speed abilities, resulting in a lower CPI than GAI.

Autism Spectrum Disorder

Children in the two ASD groups, those *with* accompanying language impairment and those *without* accompanying language impairment, were included in the WISC-V clinical sample if they met the DSM-5 criteria for ASD. Those *with* accompanying language impairment (ASD-L) were excluded if they had existing general cognitive ability scores more than 2.67 SDs below the mean (e.g., FSIQ < 60) or if they did not have adequate communication skills to complete testing. Those *without* accompanying language impairment (ASD-NL) were excluded if they had existing general cognitive ability scores more than 2 SDs below the mean (e.g., FSIQ < 70).

Data for the ASD-L group is shown in Table 10.8, and the ASD-NL group in Table 10.9. In the ASD-L group all primary and ancillary index scores were below 85 and all were statistically significantly lower than the matched control group. The lowest primary index scores were observed on PSI and WMI, although the largest effect sizes when compared to matched controls were observed on VCI and WMI. Comparatively, FRI and VSI scores were higher, supporting the literature that has indicated visuospatial ability is a relative strength for some children with autism. Deficits in auditory working memory were greater than visual working memory, with a relatively high score on Picture Span in comparison to Digit Span and Letter-Number Sequencing. The highest subtest score was obtained on Figure Weights and the lowest on Comprehension. Scores on the NVI and GAI were higher than the FSIQ, reflecting the language difficulties in this group. All complementary indexes were significantly lower than matched controls and naming facility resulted in lower scores than symbol translation subtests. Effect sizes for the complementary subtests were large.

In the ASD-NL group, scores on the primary indexes were not statistically significantly different from the matched control group except for the WMI. The PSI was lower than the other index scores but not significantly different than the control group. The lowest subtest scores were on Coding, Symbol Search, Letter-Number Sequencing, and Comprehension. Among the ancillary index scores, AWMI and CPI were the lowest scores, in line with the previous research on verbal working memory deficits as a core cognitive deficit in ASD. The CPI was nearly 10 points lower than the GAI. On the complementary subtests, the NSI was 16 points lower than the STI, likely due to the processing speed deficits observed on PSI. Consistent with findings reported by Williams et al. (2006b), impairment in associative memory tasks was not found for the group of high functioning autism (ASD-NL) compared to matched controls.

TABLE 10.8 Mean Performance of Autism Spectrum Disorder with Language Impairment and Matched Control Groups

Subtest/ Process/ Composite Score	Autism Spectrum Disorder With Language Impairment		Matched Control			Group Mean Comparison			
	Mean	SD	Mean	SD	n	Difference	t Value	p Value	Standard Difference[a]
SI	6.5	3.3	10.9	2.8	29	4.38	5.22	<.01	1.43
VC	6.1	3.6	10.6	2.6	29	4.48	5.64	<.01	1.43
IN	5.8	3.5	11.2	2.9	29	5.34	6.39	<.01	1.66
CO	4.8	3.0	11.1	3.0	30	6.23	8.56	<.01	2.08
BD	7.2	4.1	10.5	2.8	30	3.30	3.67	<.01	.94
VP	6.7	4.3	11.1	2.4	29	4.45	4.86	<.01	1.28
MR	7.1	4.2	10.3	2.2	30	3.13	3.77	<.01	.93
FW	7.4	3.6	10.3	3.5	30	2.93	3.07	<.01	.83
PC	6.3	4.4	11.6	2.2	29	5.21	6.60	<.01	1.50
AR	5.4	3.5	10.6	2.5	30	5.23	6.68	<.01	1.72
DS	5.4	3.9	10.8	2.8	30	5.43	6.37	<.01	1.60
PS	6.9	3.8	10.7	3.0	30	3.77	4.07	<.01	1.10

LN	5.0	3.6	10.3	2.3	29	5.24	7.40	<.01	1.73
CD	5.2	3.5	9.3	3.2	29	4.07	4.94	<.01	1.21
SS	6.2	3.7	9.9	2.7	26	3.69	5.30	<.01	1.14
CA	5.8	3.4	9.7	3.0	29	3.93	4.92	<.01	1.23
VCI	80.4	18.2	104.1	13.6	28	23.68	5.51	<.01	1.47
VSI	82.8	22.3	104.4	13.4	29	21.62	4.49	<.01	1.18
FRI	84.3	20.6	101.6	13.9	30	17.30	3.75	<.01	.98
WMI	77.6	19.4	104.1	13.9	30	26.47	6.05	<.01	1.57
PSI	75.8	19.0	96.9	14.8	26	21.12	5.41	<.01	1.24
FSIQ	76.3	19.1	102.1	14.5	28	25.82	5.75	<.01	1.52
QRI	78.9	19.2	102.5	15.8	30	23.67	5.07	<.01	1.35
AWMI	72.3	21.6	102.4	12.6	29	30.14	7.14	<.01	1.70
NVI	79.9	20.1	102.8	13.8	28	22.86	4.78	<.01	1.33
GAI	81.8	18.6	102.9	14.2	28	21.18	4.82	<.01	1.28
CPI	74.4	18.4	100.0	13.5	26	25.62	6.24	<.01	1.59

[a]The Standard Difference is the difference of the two test means divided by the square root of the pooled variance; computed using Cohen's (1996) Formula 10.4.

TABLE 10.9 Mean Performance of Autism Spectrum Disorder without Language Impairment and Matched Control Groups

Subtest/ Process/ Composite Score	Autism Spectrum Disorder without Language Impairment		Matched Control			Group Mean Comparison			
	Mean	SD	Mean	SD	n	Difference	t Value	p Value	Standard Difference[a]
SI	10.8	3.2	10.3	2.4	31	−.55	−.98	0.34	−.19
VC	9.9	3.0	11.5	2.6	32	1.56	2.13	0.04	.56
IN	10.5	3.7	10.8	2.5	32	.31	.47	0.64	.10
CO	8.9	2.9	10.1	3.2	32	1.19	1.48	0.15	.39
BD	9.4	3.6	11.2	2.9	32	1.78	2.34	0.03	.54
VP	10.8	2.9	10.0	3.2	32	−.84	−1.22	0.23	−.28
MR	10.2	3.2	10.6	2.2	32	.47	.63	0.53	.17
FW	10.2	3.5	10.5	2.9	32	.38	.49	0.62	.12
PC	9.9	3.2	10.9	2.6	32	.97	1.28	0.21	.33
AR	10.4	3.8	10.8	2.8	32	.31	.38	0.71	.09
DS	9.2	3.2	10.4	2.3	32	1.22	1.69	0.10	.44
PS	9.3	3.4	11.0	2.7	32	1.75	2.74	0.01	.57

LN	8.7	3.7	10.9	3.0	32	2.22	2.61	0.01	.66
CD	7.8	3.4	10.0	3.0	31	2.23	2.39	0.02	.70
SS	8.4	3.4	9.3	3.0	32	.91	1.02	0.32	.28
CA	9.8	3.4	9.7	2.8	32	-.09	-.11	0.91	-.03
VCI	102.5	14.4	104.8	11.6	31	2.26	.77	0.45	.17
VSI	100.7	17.1	103.4	14.5	32	2.72	.77	0.44	.17
FRI	100.9	17.5	103.5	12.7	32	2.53	.65	0.52	.17
WMI	95.4	16.8	104.3	12.1	32	8.81	2.52	0.02	.60
PSI	89.4	18.4	98.0	14.7	31	8.58	1.79	0.08	.52
FSIQ	98.3	17.4	105.0	11.9	30	6.63	1.75	0.09	.44
QRI	101.7	19.1	103.5	12.4	32	1.78	.47	0.64	.11
AWMI	94.1	17.2	103.8	12.2	32	9.78	2.59	0.01	.66
NVI	97.5	17.7	104.4	13.9	31	6.87	1.72	0.10	.43
GAI	101.1	17.0	105.5	11.9	31	4.45	1.31	0.20	.30
CPI	91.0	17.9	101.4	13.0	31	10.32	2.35	0.03	.66

[a]The Standard Difference is the difference of the two test means divided by the square root of the pooled variance; computed using Cohen's (1996) Formula 10.4.

The WISC-V in Context

Results from standardized intelligence tests like the WISC-V are used to inform clinical evaluations, identify appropriate placement options, target appropriate resource and funding opportunities, and guide intervention planning. However, the manner in which the results of standardized intelligence tests are used is changing. Increased recognition of the neurocognitive heterogeneity of many clinical profiles has spurred a movement to modify the process for identification of cognitive impairment and determination of service eligibility. Procedures for identifying children needing intervention rely less often on global estimates of intellectual functioning exclusively. Rather, greater weight is placed on contrasting strengths and weaknesses within and across domains of ability. Expanded construct coverage in the WISC-V facilitates this form of assessment and is particularly relevant for children presenting with atypical profiles. Although the focus of clinical interpretation now rests on the five factor-based primary cognitive abilities, a global assessment of functioning (i.e., FSIQ score) continues to be useful for evaluation and comparison with other scores. Most practitioners utilize FSIQ alongside other scores and schools frequently use FSIQ for determining eligibility in gifted identification (McClain & Pfeiffer, 2012). Despite varying criteria for determining service need, the WISC-V has evolved to accommodate most definitions of eligibility, whether it is based on multi-method assessment, single score cut-offs, cross-battery profile analysis, ability-achievement discrepancy, or intra-individual patterns of strengths and weaknesses.

Comparing and contrasting performance across a wider array of broad and narrow cognitive abilities is increasingly seen as a diagnostically relevant method for capturing the complexity of atypical clinical profiles during an evaluation (McGrew & Flanagan, 1998). Examining pairwise comparisons across and within all cognitive domains, which are diagnostically relevant to the case at hand, provides both breadth in construct coverage and depth in the interpretation of task-specific weaknesses. For instance, an examination of discrepancies within a domain such as between Similarities and Vocabulary will inform appropriateness of using the VCI for index-level comparisons as well as identify specific verbal weaknesses, such as whether verbal ability is stronger for tasks relying on abstract reasoning or lexical knowledge. Where significant discrepancies exist between Similarities and Vocabulary, use of the VCI in index-level pairwise comparisons may be difficult to interpret, leading the clinician to limit the number of comparisons with VCI in their scoring and reporting. However, additional pairwise comparisons are available for clinicians to evaluate both relative and absolute weaknesses. Index and subtest pairwise comparisons promote more targeted diagnosis and intervention planning. When comparing scores, practitioners should take into account the base rates, confidence intervals, and tests of statistically significant differences found in the test manual to facilitate interpretation of the frequency of these discrepancies in the normal population.

Subtest-level discrepancies at the primary index or FSIQ level may not tell the whole story, however, and clinicians may need to administer secondary or complementary subtests in addition to primary subtests in order to obtain a comprehensive assessment. Each WISC-V index score is comprised of two primary subtests, but additional subtests are available to substantiate a hypothesized weakness that is based either on clinical observation or on the extant literature. For example, when language impairment is observed in children with ASD, the greatest weakness often appears in Comprehension, rather than Similarities or Vocabulary, as Comprehension requires social reasoning and tasks involving theory of mind are relative weaknesses for this group (Mayes & Calhoun, 2008; Zayat, Kalb, & Wodka, 2011). However, since the VCI is comprised of the Similarities and Vocabulary subtests, interpretation of the VCI will denote the child's relative strengths but not their relative weaknesses. Given the importance of understanding both ability and disability for intervention planning, the optional administration of the Comprehension subtest in ASD is one example of the utility of including secondary subtests in the WISC-V battery.

Neurocognitive disorders typically result in mixed cognitive profiles that cannot be easily explained using a measure of full-scale intelligence. Thus, a GAI and a CPI were developed and published post-WISC-IV to assist with describing less homogeneous clinical populations (Weiss, Saklofske, Prifitera, & Holdnack, 2006). The GAI and CPI are now included in the array of index scores available with the WISC-V. The GAI does not incorporate working memory or processing speed subtests, thus it represents a cognitive ability score that may provide increased clarity in evaluations of, for example, gifted children who show superior intellect in conceptual thinking and problem solving but who may perform poorly on processing speed and working memory tasks (Assouline & Whiteman, 2011; Baum & Owen, 2004; Brody & Mills, 1997). The GAI may be particularly appropriate for identification of children who are gifted and learning disabled, i.e., twice exceptional, as weaknesses in working memory and processing speed tasks are characteristic of some learning and attention disorders (Saklofske, Prifitera, Weiss, Rolfhus, & Zhu, 2005). In these scenarios, the resulting GAI would be higher than the FSIQ (Rowe et al., 2010) with the interpretation being that the GAI is capturing maximum potential of the child being assessed. Maximum potential might be observed in environments where the task demands an emphasis on the child's strengths, but practitioners should keep in mind that maximum potential is not typical performance. The GAI can also be used with the FSIQ or the CPI in an index-level pairwise comparison for assessing intelligence among children with TBI who tend to have weaknesses on processing speed and working memory. The CPI estimates cognitive ability without factoring in language-laden subtests or fluid reasoning measures. Therefore it provides a good option for contrasting and explaining the strengths and weaknesses of individuals with ASD or borderline intellectual disability.

The NVI is a composite measure of general ability that eliminates the need for productive language in order to respond to the test item. As described in Chapter 1, the NVI is formed by six subtests: Block Design, Visual Puzzles, Matrix Reasoning, Figure Weights, Picture Span, and Coding. Five of these are primary subtests. Thus, calculating the NVI requires administration of one secondary subtest (Visual Puzzles). The NVI is useful for evaluating cognitive functioning among children with reduced language abilities such as children with ASD or children with intellectual disability. The opportunity to assess cognitive ability by minimizing productive language is important given the reorganization of the neurodevelopmental disorders. The ASD category in the DSM-5 requires clinicians to specify "with or without language impairment" as well as "with or without intellectual impairment." The complex assessment of intelligence in ASD can be informed by interpretation of the NVI in comparison to FSIQ and VCI.

The QRI and AWMI may be useful in assessing gifted or ADHD children with comorbid learning disorders. QRI is formed by Figure Weights and Arithmetic, and thus requires administration of one secondary subtest (i.e., Arithmetic). This index may be useful when evaluating possible comorbid SLD-Math in gifted children, along with the complementary Naming Speed Quantity subtest. The AWMI consists of Digit Span and Letter-Number Sequencing, and thus requires administration of one secondary subtest (i.e., Letter-Number Sequencing). Comparing WMI to AWMI allows clinicians to determine domain-specific working memory impairment in various clinical disorders where the sensitivity to detect discrepancies between complex visual–spatial working memory versus verbal working memory may be clinically meaningful.

When significant discrepancies exist within a factor, for example verbal comprehension, the clinician may choose one of these ancillary index scores that reduce the demand on language abilities from the estimate of overall ability, such as the NVI, or the CPI, in order to estimate the maximum potential of cognitive ability for an individual child. Thus, secondary indexes may be clinically useful because they focus on specific abilities. Although informative, however, estimates of maximum potential based on secondary indexes should generally not be considered as better estimates of general intelligence than the FSIQ because all five primary abilities are essential components of general intelligence (see Chapter 4), and are necessary to represent typical performance across a wider range of environmental demands. The obvious exception is when speech, vision, or motor skills interfere with performance, or if the child was clearly not attentive or engaged for some subtests.

Analysis of patterns of strengths and weaknesses among the index scores is important and widely accepted as part of modern clinical assessment practice. Yet, some cautions are warranted when implementing index-level profile analysis with individual students or patients. Despite the fact that common profiles tend to emerge in diagnostic group research, the presence of a particular WISC-V profile in an individual should not be considered diagnostic of that disorder, and the absence of that profile should not rule out the disorder. This is because there is considerable heterogeneity within diagnostic groups such that not all individuals with the same diagnosis show the same pattern. Furthermore, similar profiles may be observed in other diagnostic groups that are related neurocognitively. For example, profiles with low WMI are often found in groups of patients diagnosed with ADHD, ASD, and some forms of LD (see Chapter 8 on learning disabilities). So, while a significantly low score on WMI clearly indicates that the child has a weakness in working memory, which needs to be described in the report and addressed in the treatment plan, it does not by itself indicate a specific diagnosis. Rather, it suggests a range of possible diagnoses that are related to deficits in that ability. The final diagnosis is a matter of clinical judgment on the part of a trained and experienced practitioner after careful consideration of all DSM-5 criteria based on a comprehensive evaluation including other appropriate tests, clinical interview, behavioral observations, family and medical histories, etc.

The WISC-V is a five factor model of cognitive ability that aligns more closely to existing theory and other measures of neurocognitive assessment including the WPPSI-IV and recent factor analyses of the WAIS-IV (Benson, Hulac, & Kranzler, 2010; Keith, Fine, Taub, Reynolds, & Kranzler, 2006; Weiss, Keith, Zhu, & Chen, 2013a, 2013b). Comparisons of subtests and composites within Wechsler tests will be more clinically useful with this alignment of factor models across preschool, school-aged, and adult measures of intelligence. One particular population where this utility will be most valued is in TBI. Repeat assessments following a TBI are necessary given that many short-term cognitive deficits will abate in the years following the TBI. Mutable cognitive impairment necessitates repeated assessments for children with a TBI to ensure ongoing eligibility of services, which is tied to funding and intervention planning.

From a scientist-practitioner perspective, continuity of measurement with the new five factor model of the WISC-V is an important advancement in the field as it ensures the integrity of data collected across time during research. Again the TBI population serves as a key example of where research will benefit the most from the improved continuity of measurement of the WISC-V. Longitudinal studies are the most robust methodological design for studying the post-injury outcomes of children who sustain TBI (Fletcher, Ewing-Cobbs, Francis, & Levin, 1995; Yeates et al., 2002). The need for continuity of measurement in these multi-year research studies is clear. The overlap in factor structure across the WPPSI-IV and the WISC-V will permit clinicians and researchers to ensure continuity of measurement as developing children require ongoing assessment through adolescence and beyond.

SUMMARY

This chapter has provided an overview of general issues related to identification of specific clinical disorders and special groups according to the DSM-5 with an emphasis on variability in cognitive functioning. WISC-V data for particular groups including intellectually gifted, mild and moderate intellectual disability, borderline intellectual functioning, ADHD, DBD, ASD with and without language impairment, and TBI have been presented to aid clinicians in understanding the profiles of various clinical and special groups.

The WISC-V is a tool for clinicians to use when evaluating a given child's strengths and weaknesses as it relates to the overall clinical profile and presenting concerns. A test such as the WISC-V should be used by experienced professionals who understand the properties of the measure, including its limitations. Any measure a clinician uses to diagnose or interpret must be applied within the boundaries of best practice recommendations, which stipulate that multiple sources of information and clinical judgment are necessary for interpretations of ability or disability. With the WISC-V there is a larger offering of subtests, more comparison options, and more index scores available for assisting with interpretation of ability. The addition of process scores, contrast scores, and error scores to the WISC-V further assists clinicians with understanding the contextual details of task performance. The information that can be obtained by administering the WISC-V constitutes much more than a single IQ score, but as always, must be framed within the full family, medical, behavioral, and academic record of the child.

REFERENCES

Alloway, T. P. (2010). Working memory and executive function profiles of individuals with borderline intellectual functioning. *Journal of Intellectual Disability Research, 54,* 448–456.

American Association on Intellectual and Developmental Disabilities, (2010). *Intellectual disability: Definition, classification, and systems of supports* (11th ed.). Washington, D.C.: American Association on Intellectual and Developmental Disabilities.

American Psychiatric Association, (2000). *Diagnostic and statistical manual of mental disorders* (4th ed., Text Revision). Washington, D.C.: American Psychiatric Association.

American Psychiatric Association, (2013). *Diagnostic and statistical manual of mental disorders* (5th ed.). Arlington, VA: American Psychiatric Association.

Andersen, L. (2014). Visual–spatial ability: Important in STEM, ignored in gifted education. *Roeper Review, 36,* 114–121.

Anderson, V., Brown, S., Newitt, H., & Hoile, H. (2009). Educational, vocational, psychosocial, and quality-of-life outcomes for adult survivors of childhood traumatic brain injury. *The Journal of Head Trauma Rehabilitation, 24,* 303–312.

Anderson, V., Brown, S., Newitt, H., & Hoile, H. (2011). Long-term outcome from childhood traumatic brain injury: Intellectual ability, personality, and quality of life. *Neuropsychology, 25,* 176.

Anderson, V., Catroppa, C., Morse, S., Haritou, F., & Rosenfeld, J. (2000). Recovery of intellectual ability following traumatic brain injury in childhood: Impact of injury severity and age at injury. *Pediatric Neurosurgery, 32,* 282–290.

Assouline, S. G., & Whiteman, C. S. (2011). Twice-exceptionality: Implications for school psychologists in the post-IDEA 2004 era. *Journal of Applied School Psychology, 27,* 380–402.

Aston-Jones, G., Rajkowsky, J., & Alexinsky, J. (1994). Locus coeruleus neurons in monkey are selectively activated by attended cues in a vigilance task. *The Journal of Neuroscience, 14,* 4467–4480.

Baird, G., Charman, T., Baron-Cohen, S., Cox, A., Swettenham, J., Wheelwright, S., et al. (2000). A screening instrument for autism at 18 months of age: A 6-year follow-up study. *Journal of the American Academy of Child & Adolescent Psychiatry, 39*, 694–702.

Barkley, R. A. (1997). Behavioral inhibition, sustained attention, and executive functions: Constructing a unifying theory of ADHD. *Psychological Bulletin, 121*, 65–94.

Barkley, R. A. (2007). *Attention-deficit hyperactivity disorder: A handbook for diagnosis and treatment* (3rd ed.). New York, NY: The Guilford Press.

Baron-Cohen, S. (1989). The autistic child's theory of mind: A case of specific developmental delay. *Journal of Child Psychology and Psychiatry, 30*, 285–297.

Baum, S., & Owen, S. (2004). *To be gifted and learning disabled: Strategies for helping bright students with LD, ADHD, and more*. Mansfield, CT: Creative Learning Press.

Benson, N., Hulac, D. M., & Kranzler, J. H. (2010). Independent examination of the Wechsler Adult Intelligence Scale—Fourth Edition (WAIS-IV): What does the WAIS-IV measure? *Psychological Assessment, 22*, 121.

Bishop, D. V., & Baird, G. (2001). Parent and teacher report of pragmatic aspects of communication: Use of the Children's Communication Checklist in a clinical setting. *Developmental Medicine & Child Neurology, 43*, 809–818.

Bölte, S., Holtmann, M., Poustka, F., Scheurich, A., & Schmidt, L. (2007). Gestalt perception and local-global processing in high-functioning autism. *Journal of Autism and Developmental Disorders, 37*, 1493–1504.

Bonifacci, P., & Snowling, M. J. (2008). Speed of processing and reading disability: A cross-linguistic investigation of dyslexia and borderline intellectual functioning. *Cognition, 107*, 999–1017.

Boucher, J. (2012). Research review: Structural language in autistic spectrum disorder—Characteristics and causes. *Journal of Child Psychology and Psychiatry, 53*, 219–233.

Brody, L. E., & Mills, C. J. (1997). Gifted children with learning disabilities: A review of the issues. *Journal of Learning Disabilities, 30*, 282–296.

Brown, T. E. (2001). *The Brown attention-deficit disorder scales*. San Antonio, TX: Psychological Corporation.

Burke, J. D., Loeber, R., & Birmaher, B. (2002). Oppositional defiant disorder and conduct disorder: A review of the past 10 years, part II. *Journal of the American Academy of Child & Adolescent Psychiatry, 41*, 1275–1293.

Calhoun, S. L., & Mayes, S. D. (2005). Processing speed in children with clinical disorders. *Psychology in the Schools, 42*, 333–343.

Carte, E. T., Nigg, J. T., & Hinshaw, S. P. (1996). Neuropsychological functioning, motor speed, and language processing in boys with and without ADHD. *Journal of Abnormal Child Psychology, 24*, 481–498.

Catroppa, C., Anderson, V. A., Morse, S. A., Haritou, F., & Rosenfeld, J. V. (2007). Children's attentional skills 5 years post-TBI. *Journal of Pediatric Psychology, 32*, 354–369.

Chadwick, O., Rutter, M., Brown, G., Shaffer, D., & Traub, M. (1981). A prospective study of children with head injuries: II. Cognitive sequelae. *Psychological Medicine, 11*, 49–61.

Chadwick, O., Rutter, M., Shaffer, D., & Shrout, P. E. (1981). A prospective study of children with head injuries: IV. Specific cognitive deficits. *Journal of Clinical Neuropsychology, 3*, 101.

Chang, H. T., Klorman, R., Shaywitz, S. E., Fletcher, J. M., Marchione, K. E., Holahan, J. M., et al. (1999). Paired-associate learning in attention-deficit/hyperactivity disorder as a function of hyperactivity-impulsivity and oppositional defiant disorder. *Journal of Abnormal Child Psychology, 27*, 237–245.

Chhabildas, N., Pennington, B. F., & Willcutt, E. G. (2001). A comparison of the neuropsychological profiles of the DSM-IV subtypes of ADHD. *Journal of Abnormal Child Psychology, 29*, 529–540.

Christian, R. E., Frick, P. J., Hill, N. L., Tyler, L., & Frazer, D. R. (1997). Psychopathy and conduct problems in children: II. Implications for subtyping children with conduct problems. *Journal of the American Academy of Child & Adolescent Psychiatry, 36*, 233–241.

Clark, C., Prior, M., & Kinsella, G. (2002). The relationship between executive function abilities, adaptive behaviour, and academic achievement in children with externalising behaviour problems. *Journal of Child Psychology and Psychiatry, 43*, 785–796.

Clark, C., Prior, M., & Kinsella, G. J. (2000). Do executive function deficits differentiate between adolescents with ADHD and oppositional defiant/conduct disorder? A neuropsychological study using the Six Elements Test and Hayling Sentence Completion Test. *Journal of Abnormal Child Psychology, 28*, 403–414.

Coghill, D. R., Hayward, D., Rhodes, S. M., Grimmer, C., & Matthews, K. (2014). A longitudinal examination of neuropsychological and clinical functioning in boys with attention deficit hyperactivity disorder (ADHD): Improvements in executive functioning do not explain clinical improvement. *Psychological Medicine, 44*, 1087–1099.

Cohen, B. H. (1996). *Explaining psychological statistics*. Pacific Grove, CA: Brooks & Cole.

Dawson, M., Soulières, I., Gernsbacher, M. A., & Mottron, L. (2007). The level and nature of autistic intelligence. *Psychological Science, 18*, 657–662.

Department of Defense and Department of Veterans Affairs (2008). *Traumatic brain injury task force*. Available from: <http://www.cdc.gov/nchs/data/icd9/Sep08TBI.pdf>.

Di Blasi, F. D., Elia, F., Buono, S., Ramakers, G. J., & Di Nuovo, S. F. (2007). Relationships between visual-motor and cognitive abilities in intellectual disabilities. *Perceptual and Motor Skills, 104*, 763–772.

Douglas, V. I., & Benezra, E. (1990). Supraspan verbal memory in attention deficit disorder with hyperactivity normal and reading-disabled boys. *Journal of Abnormal Child Psychology, 18*, 617–638.

Dyck, M. J., & Piek, J. P. (2014). Developmental delays in children with ADHD. *Journal of Attention Disorders, 18*, 466–478.

Farrington, D. P. (1995). The development of offending and antisocial behaviour from childhood: Key findings from the Cambridge Study in Delinquent Development. *Journal of Child Psychology and Psychiatry, 36*, 929–964.

Fein, D., Dunn, M. A., Allen, D. M., Aram, R., Hall, N., Morris, R., et al. (1996). Neuropsychological and language findings. In I. Rapin (Ed.), *Preschool children with inadequate communication: Developmental language disorder, autism, low IQ* (pp. 123–154). London: Mac Keith Press.

Fergusson, L., Horwood, L. J., & Lynskey, M. T. (1993). The effects of conduct disorder and attention deficit in middle childhood on offending and scholastic ability at age 13. *Journal of Child Psychology and Psychiatry, 34*, 899–916.

Flanagan, D. P., & Harrison, P. L. (Eds.), (2012). *Contemporary intellectual assessment: Theories, tests, and issues*. New York: The Guilford Press.

Fletcher, J. M., Ewing-Cobbs, L., Francis, D. J., & Levin, H. S. (1995). Variability in outcomes after traumatic brain injury in children: A developmental perspective. In S. H. Broman & M. E. Michel (Eds.), *Traumatic head injury in children* (pp. 3–21). New York: Oxford University Press.

Frick, P. J., Kamphaus, R. W., Lahey, B. B., Loeber, R., Christ, M. A. G., Hart, E. L., et al. (1991). Academic underachievement and the disruptive behavior disorders. *Journal of Consulting and Clinical Psychology, 59*, 289.

Frick, P. J., & Viding, E. (2009). Antisocial behavior from a developmental psychopathology perspective. *Development and Psychopathology, 21*, 1111–1131.

Galton, F. (1869). *Hereditary genius*. London: Macmillan.

Geurts, H. M., & Embrechts, M. (2008). Language profiles in ASD, SLI, and ADHD. *Journal of Autism and Developmental Disorders, 38,* 1931–1943.

Geurts, H. M., Verté, S., Oosterlaan, J., Roeyers, H., & Sergeant, J. A. (2004). How specific are executive functioning deficits in attention deficit hyperactivity disorder and autism? *Journal of child Psychology and Psychiatry, 45,* 836–854.

Geurts, H. M., Verté, S., Oosterlaan, J., Roeyers, H., & Sergeant, J. A. (2005). ADHD subtypes: Do they differ in their executive functioning profile? *Archives of Clinical Neuropsychology, 20,* 457–477.

Gillberg, C., & Kadesjo, B. (2000). Attention deficit hyperactivity disorder and developmental co-ordination disorder. In T. E. Brown (Ed.), *Attention deficit hyperactivity disorder and comorbidities in children, adolescents and adults* (pp. 393–406). Washington, D.C: American Psychiatric Press.

Gilliam, M., Stockman, M., Malek, M., et al. (2011). Developmental trajectories of the corpus callosum in attention-deficit/hyperactivity disorder. *Biological Psychiatry, 69,* 839–846.

Goodman, R., Simonoff, E., & Stevenson, E. (1995). The impact of child IQ, parental IQ and sibling IQ on child behavioural deviance scores. *Journal of Child Psychology and Psychiatry, 36,* 409–425.

Gordon, S., Duff, S., Davidson, T., & Whitaker, S. (2010). Comparison of the WAIS–III and WISC–IV in 16-year-old special education students. *Journal of Applied Research in Intellectual Disabilities, 23,* 197–200.

Green, D., Baird, G., Barnett, A. L., Henderson, L., Huber, J., & Henderson, S. E. (2002). The severity and nature of motor impairment in Asperger's syndrome: A comparison with specific developmental disorder of motor function. *Journal of Child Psychology and Psychiatry, 43,* 655–668.

Hale, J. B., & Fiorello, C. A. (2004). *School neuropsychology: A practitioner's handbook.* New York: Guilford Press.

Hammes, J. G. W., & Langdell, T. (1981). Precursors of symbol formation and childhood autism. *Journal of Autism and Developmental Disorders, 11,* 331–346.

Hayden, M. G., Jandial, R., Duenas, H. A., Mahajan, R., & Levy, M. (2007). Pediatric concussions in sports: A simple and rapid assessment tool for concussive injury in children and adults. *Child's Nervous System, 23,* 431–435.

Hermelin, B. (1978). Images and language. In M. Rutter & E. Schoppler (Eds.), *Autism: A reappraisal of concept and treatment* (pp. 141–154). New York: Plenum.

Hinshaw, S. P., Carte, E. T., Sami, N., Treuting, J. J., & Zupan, B. A. (2002). Preadolescent girls with attention-deficit/hyperactivity disorder: II. Neuropsychological performance in relation to subtypes and individual classification. *Journal of Consulting and Clinical Psychology, 70,* 1099.

Hinshaw, S. P., & Lee, S. S. (2003). Conduct and oppositional defiant disorders. *Child Psychopathology, 2,* 144–198.

Hogan, A. E. (1999). Cognitive functioning in children with oppositional defiant disorder and conduct disorder. In: *Handbook of disruptive behavior disorders* (pp. 317–335). United States: Springer.

Howlin, P. (2003). Outcome in high-functioning adults with autism with and without early language delays: Implications for the differentiation between autism and Asperger syndrome. *Journal of Autism and Developmental Disorders, 33,* 3–13.

Jaffe, K. M., Polissar, N. L., Fay, G. C., & Liao, S. (1995). Recovery trends over three years following pediatric traumatic brain injury. *Archives of Physical Medicine and Rehabilitation, 76,* 17–26.

Kaplan, E. (1988). A process approach to neuropsychological assessment. In T. J. Boll & B. K. Bryant (Eds.), *Clinical neuropsychology and brain function: Research, measurement, and practice* (pp. 129–167). Washington, D.C: American Psychological Association.

Karatekin, C., Markiewicz, S. W., & Siegel, M. A. (2003). A preliminary study of motor problems in children with attention-deficit/hyperactivity disorder. *Perceptual and Motor Skills, 97,* 1267–1280.

Kaufman, A. S., & Kaufman, N. L. (1990). *Kaufman brief intelligence test.* Circle Pines, MN: American Guidance Service.

Keith, T. Z., Fine, J. G., Taub, G. E., Reynolds, M. R., & Kranzler, J. H. (2006). Higher order, multisample, confirmatory factor analysis of the Wechsler Intelligence Scale for Children—Fourth Edition: What does it measure? *School Psychology Review, 35,* 108–127.

Kielinen, M., Linna, S. L., & Moilanen, I. (2000). Autism in northern Finland. *European Child & Adolescent Psychiatry, 9,* 162–167.

Kjelgaard, M. M., & Tager-Flusberg, H. (2001). An investigation of language impairment in autism: Implications for genetic subgroups. *Language and Cognitive Processes, 16,* 287–308.

Klingberg, T., Fernell, E., Olesen, P. J., Johnson, M., Gustafsson, P., Dahlström, K., et al. (2005). Computerized training of working memory in children with ADHD—A randomized, controlled trial. *Journal of the American Academy of Child & Adolescent Psychiatry, 44,* 177–186.

Klorman, R., Hazel-Fernandez, L. A., Shaywitz, S. E., Fletcher, J. M., Marchione, K. E., Holahan, J. M., et al. (1999). Executive functioning deficits in attention-deficit/hyperactivity disorder are independent of oppositional defiant or reading disorder. *Journal of the American Academy of Child & Adolescent Psychiatry, 38,* 1148–1155.

Knights, R. M., Ivan, L. P., Ventureyra, E. C., Bentivoglio, C., Stoddart, C., Winogron, W., et al. (1991). The effects of head injury in children on neuropsychological and behavioural functioning. *Brain Injury, 5,* 339–351.

Koning, C., & Magill-Evans, J. (2001). Social and language skills in adolescent boys with Asperger syndrome. *Autism, 5,* 23–36.

Kraepelin, E. (1913). *Psychiatrie,* 3, Leipzig: Barth.

Kuhne, M., Schachar, R., & Tannock, R. (1997). Impact of comorbid oppositional or conduct problems on attention-deficit hyperactivity disorder. *Journal of the American Academy of Child & Adolescent Psychiatry, 36,* 1715–1725.

Kuntsi, J., Eley, T. C., Taylor, A., Hughes, C., Asherson, P., Caspi, A., et al. (2004). Co-occurrence of ADHD and low IQ has genetic origins. *American Journal of Medical Genetics Part B: Neuropsychiatric Genetics, 124,* 41–47.

Lahey, B. B., Loeber, R., Hart, E. L., Frick, P. J., Applegate, B., Zhang, Q., et al. (1995). Four-year longitudinal study of conduct disorder in boys: Patterns and predictors of persistence. *Journal of Abnormal Psychology, 104,* 83.

Lansing, A. E., Washburn, J. J., Abram, K. M., Thomas, U. C., Welty, L. J., & Teplin, L. A. (2014). Cognitive and academic functioning of juvenile detainees implications for correctional populations and public health. *Journal of Correctional Health Care, 20,* 18–30.

Lewis, F. M., Murdoch, B. E., & Woodyatt, G. C. (2007). Linguistic abilities in children with autism spectrum disorder. *Research in Autism Spectrum Disorders, 1,* 85–100.

Lezak, M. D. (Ed.), (2004). *Neuropsychological assessment.* New York: Oxford University Press.

Lindgren, K. A., Folstein, S. E., Tomblin, J. B., & Tager-Flusberg, H. (2009). Language and reading abilities of children with autism spectrum disorders and specific language impairment and their first-degree relatives. *Autism Research, 2,* 22–38.

Llorente, A. M., Voigt, R. G., Bhatnagar, P., Jensen, C. L., Heird, W. C., Williams, J., et al. (2012). Simultaneous visual sustained attention-discrimination and goal-directed search are associated with excretion of catecholaminergic metabolites in children with attention-deficit/hyperactivity disorder. *Journal of Pediatric Biochemistry, 2*, 115–122.

Llorente, A. M., Voigt, R. G., Jensen, C. L., Berretta, M. C., Fraley, J. K., & Heird, W. C. (2006). Performance on a visual sustained attention and discrimination task is associated with urinary excretion of norepinephrine metabolite in children with attention-deficit/hyperactivity disorder (AD/HD). *Clinical Neuropsychology, 20*, 133–144.

Lockwood, K. A., Marcotte, A. C., & Stern, C. (2001). Differentiation of attention-deficit/hyperactivity disorder subtypes: Application of a neuropsychological model of attention. *Journal of Clinical and Experimental Neuropsychology, 23*, 317–330.

Lohman, D. F., Gambrell, J., & Lakin, J. (2008). The commonality of extreme discrepancies in the ability profiles of academically gifted students. *Psychology Science, 50*, 269.

Lynam, D., Moffitt, T., & Stouthamer-Loeber, M. (1993). Explaining the relation between IQ and delinquency: Class, race, test motivation, school failure, or self-control? *Journal of Abnormal Psychology, 102*, 187.

Lynam, D. R., & Henry, B. (2001). The role of neuropsychological deficits in conduct disorders. In J. Hill & B. Maughan (Eds.), *Conduct disorders in childhood and adolescence* (pp. 235–263). Cambridge, UK: Cambridge University Press.

Madduri, N., Peters, S. U., Voigt, R. G., Llorente, A. M., Lupski, J. R., & Potocki, L. (2006). Cognitive and adaptive behavior profiles in Smith-Magenis syndrome. *Journal of Developmental & Behavioral Pediatrics, 27*, 188–192.

Mann, R. L. (2005). Gifted students with spatial strengths and sequential weaknesses: An overlooked and underidentified population. *Roeper Review, 27*, 91–97.

Mann, R. L. (2006). Effective teaching strategies for gifted/learning-disabled students with spatial strengths. *Prufrock Journal, 17*, 112–121.

Mariani, M. A., & Barkley, R. A. (1997). Neuropsychological and academic functioning in preschool boys with attention deficit hyperactivity disorder. *Developmental Neuropsychology, 13*, 111–129.

Matson, J. L., Mahan, S., Hess, J. A., & Fodstad, J. C. (2010). Effect of developmental quotient on symptoms of inattention and impulsivity among toddlers with autism spectrum disorders. *Research in Developmental Disabilities, 31*, 464–469.

Matson, J. L., & Shoemaker, M. (2009). Intellectual disability and its relationship to autism spectrum disorders. *Research in Developmental Disabilities, 30*, 1107–1114.

Maulik, P. K., Mascarenhas, M. N., Mathers, C. D., Dua, T., & Saxena, S. (2011). Prevalence of intellectual disability: A meta-analysis of population-based studies. *Research in Developmental Disabilities, 32*, 419–436.

Mayes, S. D., & Calhoun, S. L. (2003a). Analysis of WISC-III, Stanford-Binet IV, and academic achievement test scores in children with autism. *Journal of Autism and Developmental Disorders, 33*, 329–341.

Mayes, S. D., & Calhoun, S. L. (2003b). Ability profiles in children with autism: Influence of age and IQ. *Autism, 7*, 65–80.

Mayes, S. D., & Calhoun, S. L. (2007). Learning, attention, writing, and processing speed in typical children and children with ADHD, autism, anxiety, depression, and oppositional-defiant disorder. *Child Neuropsychology, 13*, 469–493.

Mayes, S. D., & Calhoun, S. L. (2008). WISC-IV and WIAT-II profiles in children with high-functioning autism. *Journal of Autism and Developmental Disorders, 38*, 428–439.

Mayes, S. D., & Calhoun, S. L. (2011). Impact of IQ, age, SES, gender, and race on autistic symptoms. *Research in Autism Spectrum Disorders, 5,* 749–757.

McClain, M. C., & Pfeiffer, S. (2012). Identification of gifted students in the United States today: A look at state definitions, policies, and practices. *Journal of Applied School Psychology, 28,* 59–88.

McCrea, M. (2007). *Mild traumatic brain injury and post-concussion syndrome: The new evidence base for diagnosis and treatment (American Academy of Clinical Neuropsychology Workshop Series).* New York: Oxford University Press.

McGregor, K. K., Berns, A. J., Owen, A. J., Michels, S. A., Duff, D., Bahnsen, A. J., et al. (2012). Associations between syntax and the lexicon among children with or without ASD and language impairment. *Journal of Autism and Developmental Disorders, 42,* 35–47.

McGrew, K. S., & Flanagan, D. P. (1998). *The intelligence test desk reference (ITDR): Gf-Gc cross-battery assessment.* Boston, MA: Allyn & Bacon.

Melnick, S. M., & Hinshaw, S. P. (1996). What they want and what they get: The social goals of boys with ADHD and comparison boys. *Journal of Abnormal Child Psychology, 24,* 169–185.

Minshew, N. J., Goldstein, G., & Siegel, D. J. (1997). Neuropsychologic functioning in autism: Profile of a complex information processing disorder. *Journal of the International Neuropsychological Society, 3,* 303–316.

Moffitt, T. E. (2006). Life course persistent versus adolescence-limited antisocial behavior. In D. Cicchetti & D. J. Cohen (Eds.), *Developmental psychopathology* (vol. 3, 2nd ed., pp. 570–598). New York: Wiley.

Moffitt, T. E., & Caspi, A. (2001). Childhood predictors differentiate life-course persistent and adolescence-limited antisocial pathways among males and females. *Development and Psychopathology, 13,* 355–375.

Mulligan, A., Anney, R. J., O'Regan, M., Chen, W., Butler, L., Fitzgerald, M., et al. (2009). Autism symptoms in attention-deficit/hyperactivity disorder: A familial trait which correlates with conduct, oppositional defiant, language and motor disorders. *Journal of Autism and Developmental Disorders, 39,* 197–209.

Muth, A., Hönekopp, J., & Falter, C. M. (2014). Visuo-spatial performance in autism: A meta-analysis. *Journal of Autism and Developmental Disorders, 44,* 3245–3263.

Naglieri, J. A., Goldstein, S., Iseman, J. S., & Schwebach, A. (2003). Performance of children with attention deficit hyperactivity disorder and anxiety/depression on the WISC-III and Cognitive Assessment System (CAS). *Journal of Psychoeducational Assessment, 21,* 32–42.

Naigles, L. R. (2013). Input and language development in children with autism. *Seminars in Speech and Language, 34,* 237–248.

Navon, D. (1977). Forest before trees: The precedence of global features in visual perception. *Cognitive Psychology, 9,* 353–383.

Neisser, U., Boodoo, G., Bouchard, T. J., Jr., Boykin, A. W., Brody, N., Ceci, S. J., et al. (1996). Intelligence: Knowns and unknowns. *American Psychologist, 51,* 77.

Nicpon, M. F., Allmon, A., Sieck, B., & Stinson, R. D. (2011). Empirical investigation of twice-exceptionality: Where have we been and where are we going? *Gifted Child Quarterly, 55,* 3–17.

Nigg, J. T., Blaskey, L. G., Huang-Pollock, C. L., & Rappley, M. D. (2002). Neuropsychological executive functions and DSM-IV ADHD subtypes. *Journal of the American Academy of Child & Adolescent Psychiatry, 41,* 59–66.

Nunes, M. M., Honjo, R. S., Dutra, R. L., Amaral, V. A. S., Oh, H. K., Bertola, D. R., et al. (2012). Assessment of intellectual and visuo-spatial abilities in children and adults with Williams syndrome. *Universitas Psychologica, 12,* 581–589.

Nydén, A., Billstedt, E., Hjelmquist, E., & Gillberg, C. (2001). Neurocognitive stability in Asperger syndrome, ADHD, and reading and writing disorder: A pilot study. *Developmental Medicine & Child Neurology*, *43*, 165–171.

Oosterlaan, J., Scheres, A., & Sergeant, J. A. (2005). Which executive functioning deficits are associated with AD/HD, ODD/CD and comorbid AD/HD+ ODD/CD? *Journal of Abnormal child Psychology*, *33*, 69–85.

Osmon, D. C., Smerz, J. M., Braun, M. M., & Plambeck, E. (2006). Processing abilities associated with math skills in adult learning disability. *Journal of Clinical and Experimental Neuropsychology*, *28*, 84–95.

Ozonoff, S., & Strayer, D. L. (2001). Further evidence of intact working memory in autism. *Journal of Autism and Developmental Disorders*, *31*, 257–263.

O'Connor, N., & Hermelin, B. (1975). Modality-specific spatial coordinates. *Perception and Psychophysics*, *17*, 213–216.

Pasini, A., Paloscia, C., Alessandrelli, R., Porfirio, M. C., & Curatolo, P. (2007). Attention and executive functions profile in drug naive ADHD subtypes. *Brain and Development*, *29*, 400–408.

Pennington, B. F., & Ozonoff, S. (1996). Executive functions and developmental psychopathology. *Journal of Child Psychology and Psychiatry*, *37*, 51–87.

Pennington, B. F., Rogers, S. J., Bennetto, L., Griffith, E. M., Reed, D. T., & Shyu, V. (1997). Validity tests of the executive dysfunction hypothesis of autism. In J. Russell (Ed.), *Autism as an executive disorder* (pp. 143–178). Oxford, England: Oxford University Press.

Pfeiffer, S. I. (2002). Identifying gifted and talented students: Recurring issues and promising solutions. *Journal of Applied School Psychology*, *1*, 31–50.

Pfeiffer, S. I. (2005). Assessment of children who are gifted with the WISC-IV. In A. Prifitera, D. H. Saklofske, & L. G. Weiss (Eds.), *WISC-IV clinical use and interpretation: Scientist-practitioner perspectives* (pp. 281–298). New York: Elsevier Academic Press.

Pickering, S. J., & Gathercole, S. E. (2004). Distinctive working memory profiles in children with special educational needs. *Educational Psychology*, *24*, 393–408.

Pitcher, T. M., Piek, J. P., & Hay, D. A. (2003). Fine and gross motor ability in males with ADHD. *Developmental Medicine & Child Neurology*, *45*, 525–535.

Raiford, S. E., Weiss, L. G., Rolfhus, E., & Coalson, D. (2005). General ability index [WISC–IV Technical Report No. 4]. Retrieved from: <http://www.Pearsonassessments.com/NR/rdonlyres/1439CDFE-6980-435F-93DA-05888C7CC082/0/80720_WISCIV_Hr_r4.pdf>.

Raine, A., Yaralian, P. S., Reynolds, C., Venables, P. H., & Mednick, S. A. (2002). Spatial but not verbal cognitive deficits at age 3 years in persistently antisocial individuals. *Development and Psychopathology*, *14*, 25–44.

Rapin, I., Dunn, M. A., Allen, D. A., Stevens, M. C., & Fein, D. (2009). Subtypes of language disorders in school-age children with autism. *Developmental Neuropsychology*, *34*, 66–84.

Rapport, M. D., Scanlan, S. W., & Denney, C. B. (1999). Attention-deficit/hyperactivity disorder and scholastic achievement: A model of dual developmental pathways. *Journal of Child Psychology and Psychiatry*, *40*, 1169–1183.

Reynolds, C. R., & Kamphaus, R. W. (2004). *BASC-2: Behavior assessment system for children* (2nd ed. manual.). Bloomington, MN: Pearson.

Riccio, C. A., Homack, S., Jarratt, K. P., & Wolfe, M. E. (2006). Differences in academic and executive function domains among children with ADHD predominantly inattentive and combined types. *Archives of Clinical Neuropsychology*, *21*, 657–667.

Rice, M. L., Warren, S. F., & Betz, S. K. (2005). Language symptoms of developmental language disorders: An overview of autism, down syndrome, fragile X, specific language impairment, and Williams syndrome. *Applied Psycholinguistics*, *26*, 7–27.

Ries, J., Potter, B., & Llorente, A. M. (2007). Multicultural aspects of neuropsychological rehabilitation and intervention. In S. J. Hunter & J. Donders (Eds.), *Pediatric neuropsychological
intervention.* New York: Cambridge University Press.

Rimm, S., Gilman, B., & Silverman, L. (2008). Alternative assessments with gifted and talented
students. In J. L. VanTassel-Baska (Ed.), *Nontraditional applications of traditional testing*
(pp. 175–202). Waco, TX: Prufrock Press.

Rosso, M., Falasco, S. L., & Koller, J. R. (1984). Investigations into the relationship of the
PPVT-R and the WISC-R with incarcerated delinquents. *Journal of Clinical Psychology, 40,*
588–591.

Rowe, E. W., Kingsley, J. M., & Thompson, D. F. (2010). Predictive ability of the general ability index
(GAI) versus the full scale IQ among gifted referrals. *School Psychology Quarterly, 25,* 119–128.

Rucklidge, J. J., & Tannock, R. (2001). Psychiatric, psychosocial, and cognitive functioning of
female adolescents with ADHD. *Journal of the American Academy of Child & Adolescent
Psychiatry, 40,* 530–540.

Russell, J., Jarrold, C., & Henry, L. (1996). Working memory in children with autism and with moderate learning difficulties. *Journal of Child Psychology and Psychiatry, 37,* 673–686.

Saalasti, S., Lepistö, T., Toppila, E., Kujala, T., Laakso, M., Nieminen-von Wendt, T., et al. (2008).
Language abilities of children with Asperger syndrome. *Journal of Autism and Developmental
Disorders, 38,* 1574–1580.

Saklofske, D. H., Prifitera, A., Weiss, L. G., Rolfhus, E., & Zhu, J. J. (2005). Clinical interpretation
of the WISC-IV FSIQ and GAI. In A. Prifitera & D. Saklofske (Eds.), *WISC-IV clinical use and
interpretation.* San Diego, CA: Academic Press.

Saklofske, D. H., Schwean, V. L., Yackalic, R. A., & Quinn, D. (1994). WISC-III and SB: FE performance of children with attention deficit disorder. *Canadian Journal of School Psychology,
10,* 167–171.

Sattler, J. M. (2008). *Assessment of children: Cognitive foundations.* San Diego, CA: Jerome M.
Sattler Publications.

Schachar, R., & Logan, G. D. (1990). Impulsivity and inhibitory control in normal development and
childhood psychopathology. *Developmental Psychology, 26,* 710.

Schalock, (2010). *Intellectual disability: Definition, classification, and systems of support*
(11th ed.). Annapolis, MD: AAIDD.

Scheuffgen, K., Happeé, F., Anderson, M., & Frith, U. (2000). High "intelligence," low "IQ"? Speed
of processing and measured IQ in children with autism. *Development and Psychopathology,
12,* 83–90.

Schuchardt, K., Gebhardt, M., & Maehler, C. (2010). Working memory functions in children with
different degrees of intellectual disability. *Journal of Intellectual Disability Research, 54,*
346–353.

Seidman, L. J. (2006). Neuropsychological functioning in people with ADHD across the lifespan.
Clinical Psychology Review, 26, 466–485.

Seung, H. K. (2007). Linguistic characteristics of individuals with high functioning autism and
Asperger syndrome. *Clinical Linguistics & Phonetics, 21,* 247–259.

Shah, A., & Frith, U. (1983). An islet of ability in autistic children: A research note. *Journal of Child
Psychology and Psychiatry, 24,* 613–620.

Shah, A., & Frith, U. (1993). Why do autistic individuals show superior performance on the block
design task? *Journal of Child Psychology and Psychiatry, 34,* 1351–1364.

Shaw, P., Eckstrand, K., Sharp, W., et al. (2007). Attention-deficit/hyperactivity disorder is characterized by a delay in cortical maturation. *Proceedings of the National Academy of Science USA,
104,* 19649–19654.

Shaw, P., Malek, M., Watson, B., Sharp, W., Evans, A., & Greenstein, D. (2012). Development of cortical surface area and gyrification in attention-deficit/hyperactivity disorder. *Biological Psychiatry, 72,* 191–197.

Shepard, R. N., & Metzler, J. (1971). Mental rotation of three-dimensional objects. *Science, 171,* 701–703.

Sheslow, D., & Adams, W. (1990). *WRAML: Wide range assessment of memory and learning.* Wilmington, DE: Jastak Assessment Systems.

Silverman, L. K. (2002). *Upside down brilliance: The visual-spatial learner.* Denver, CO: DeLeon Publishing.

Slomine, B. S., Gerring, J. P., Grados, M. A., Vasa, R., Brady, K. D., Christensen, J. R., et al. (2002). Performance on measures of executive function following pediatric traumatic brain injury. *Brain Injury, 16,* 759–772.

Sonuga-Barke, E. J., Brandeis, D., Cortese, S., Daley, D., Ferrin, M., Holtmann, M., et al. (2013). Nonpharmacological interventions for ADHD: Systematic review and meta-analyses of randomized controlled trials of dietary and psychological treatments. *American Journal of Psychiatry, 170,* 275–289.

Spruill, J., Oakland, T., & Harrison, P. (2005). Assessment of mental retardation. In A. Prifitera, D. H. Saklofske, & L. G. Weiss (Eds.), *WISC-IV clinical use and interpretation: Scientist–practitioner perspectives* (pp. 299–331). San Diego, CA: Elsevier.

Steele, S. D., Minshew, N. J., Luna, B., & Sweeney, J. A. (2007). Spatial working memory deficits in autism. *Journal of Autism and Developmental Disorders, 37,* 605–612.

Stephens, K. R., & Karnes, F. A. (2000). State definitions for the gifted and talented revisited. *Exceptional Children, 66,* 219–238.

Sweetland, J. D., Reina, J. M., & Tatti, A. F. (2006). WISC-III verbal/performance discrepancies among a sample of gifted children. *Gifted Child Quarterly, 50,* 7–10.

Szatmari, P., Archer, L., Fisman, S., Streiner, D. L., & Wilson, F. (1995). Asperger's syndrome and autism: Differences in behavior, cognition, and adaptive functioning. *Journal of the American Academy of Child & Adolescent Psychiatry, 34,* 1662–1671.

Szatmari, P., White, J., & Merikangas, K. R. (2007). The use of genetic epidemiology to guide classification in child and adult psychopathology. *International Review of Psychiatry, 19,* 483–496.

Tannock, R. (2000). Attention deficit disorders with anxiety disorders. In T. E. Brown (Ed.), *Attention-deficit disorders and comorbidities in children, adolescents and adults* (pp. 125–175). New York: American Psychiatric Press.

Taylor, L. J., Mayberry, M. T., Grayndler, L., & Whitehouse, A. J. (2014). Evidence for distinct cognitive profiles in autism spectrum disorders and specific language impairment. *Journal of Autism and Developmental Disorders, 44,* 19–30.

Tseng, M. H., Henderson, A., Chow, S. M., & Yao, G. (2004). Relationship between motor proficiency, attention, impulse, and activity in children with ADHD. *Developmental Medicine & Child Neurology, 46,* 381–388.

Usher, M., Cohen, J. D., Servan-Schreiber, D., Rajkowski, J., & Aston-Jones, G. (1999). The role of the Locus Coeruleus in the regulation of cognitive performance. *Science, 283,* 549–554.

Van der Molen, M. J., Van Luit, J. E. H., Jongmans, M. J., & Van der Molen, M. W. (2007). Verbal working memory in children with mild intellectual disabilities. *Journal of Intellectual Disability Research, 51,* 162–169.

Van Goozen, S. H., Cohen-Kettenis, P. T., Snoek, H., Matthys, W., Swaab-Barneveld, H., & Van Engeland, H. (2004). Executive functioning in children: A comparison of hospitalised ODD and ODD/ADHD children and normal controls. *Journal of Child Psychology and Psychiatry, 45,* 284–292.

Vogan, V. M., Morgan, B. R., Lee, W., Powell, T. L., Smith, M. L., & Taylor, M. J. (2014). The neural correlates of visuo-spatial working memory in children with autism spectrum disorder: Effects of cognitive load. *Journal of Neurodevelopmental Disorders, 6*, 1–15.

Vuijk, P. J., Hartman, E., Scherder, E., & Visscher, C. (2010). Motor performance of children with mild intellectual disability and borderline intellectual functioning. *Journal of Intellectual Disability Research, 54*, 955–965.

Watson, D., & Clark, L. A. (2006). Clinical diagnosis at the crossroads. *Clinical Psychology: Science and Practice, 13*, 210–215.

Wechsler, D. (1944). *The measurement of adult intelligence* (3rd ed.). Baltimore, MD: Williams & Wilkins.

Wechsler, D. (1974). *Manual for the Wechsler intelligence scale for children–revised.* San Antonio, TX: The Psychological Corporation.

Wechsler, D. (2002). *Wechsler preschool and primary scale of intelligence* (3rd ed.). San Antonio, TX: Pearson.

Wechsler, D. (2003). *Wechsler intelligence scale for children* (4th ed.). San Antonio, TX: Pearson.

Wechsler, D. (2004). *Wechsler intelligence scale for children* (4th ed.). Toronto, ON, Canada: Harcourt Assessment.

Wechsler, D. (2008). *Wechsler adult intelligence scale* (4th ed.). Bloomington, MN: Pearson.

Wechsler, D. (2012a). *Wechsler preschool and primary scale of intelligence* (4th ed.). Bloomington, MN: Pearson.

Wechsler, D. (2012b). *Wechsler preschool and primary scale of intelligence* (4th ed.). Toronto, ON, Canada: Pearson.

Wechsler, D. (2014). *Wechsler intelligence scale for children* (5th ed.). Bloomington, MN: Pearson.

Weiss, L. G., Keith, T. Z., Zhu, J., & Chen, H. (2013a). WAIS-IV clinical validation of the four- and five-factor interpretive approaches [Special edition]. *Journal of Psychoeducational Assessment, 31*, 94–113.

Weiss, L. G., Keith, T. Z., Zhu, J., & Chen, H. (2013b). WISC-IV and clinical validation of the four- and five-factor interpretive approaches [Special edition]. *Journal of Psychoeducational Assessment, 31*, 114–131.

Weiss, L. G., Saklofske, D. H., Prifitera, A., & Holdnack, J. A. (2006). *WISC-IV advanced clinical interpretation.* Burlington, MA: Academic Press.

White, S. J., & Saldaña, D. (2011). Performance of children with autism on the Embedded Figures Test: A closer look at a popular task. *Journal of Autism and Developmental Disorders, 41*, 1565–1572.

Whitehouse, A. J. O., Barry, J. G., & Bishop, D. V. M. (2008). Further defining the language impairment of autism spectrum disorders: Is there a specific language impairment subtype? *Journal of Communication Disorders, 41*, 319–336.

Widiger, T. A., & Samuel, D. B. (2005). Diagnostic categories or dimensions? A question for the diagnostic and statistical manual of mental disorders—fifth edition. *Journal of Abnormal Psychology, 114*, 494.

Willcutt, E. G., Doyle, A. E., Nigg, J. T., Faraone, S. V., & Pennington, B. F. (2005). Validity of the executive function theory of attention-deficit/hyperactivity disorder: A meta-analytic review. *Biological Psychiatry, 57*, 1336–1346.

Williams, D. L., Goldstein, G., & Minshew, N. J. (2006a). The profile of memory function in children with autism. *Neuropsychology, 20*, 21–29.

Williams, D. L., Goldstein, G., & Minshew, N. J. (2006b). Neuropsychologic functioning in children with autism: Further evidence for disordered complex information-processing. *Child Neuropsychology, 12*, 279–298.

Williams, D. L., Minshew, N. J., & Goldstein, G. (2008). Memory within a complex information processing model of autism. In J. Boucher & D. Bowler (Eds.), *Memory in autism* (pp. 125–142). New York: Cambridge University Press.

Witkin, H. A., Oltman, P. K., Raskin, E., & Karp, S. A. (1971). *A manual for the embedded figures test*. Palo Alto, CA: Consulting Psychologists Press.

Wodka, E. L., Mostofsky, S. H., Prahme, C., Gidley Larson, J. C., Loftis, C., Denckla, M. B., et al. (2008). Process examination of executive function in ADHD: Sex and subtype effects. *The Clinical Neuropsychologist, 22*, 826–841.

Wuang, Y. P., Wang, C. C., Huang, M. H., & Su, C. Y. (2008). Profiles and cognitive predictors of motor functions among early school-age children with mild intellectual disabilities. *Journal of Intellectual Disability Research, 52*, 1048–1060.

Yeates, K. O. (2000). Closed-head injury. In K. O. Yeates, M. D. Ris, & H. G. Taylor (Eds.), *Pediatric neuropsychology: Research, theory, and practice* (pp. 92–116). New York, NY: Guilford Press.

Yeates, K. O., Taylor, H. G., Wade, S. L., Drotar, D., Stancin, T., & Minich, N. (2002). A prospective study of short- and long-term neuropsychological outcomes after traumatic brain injury in children. *Neuropsychology, 16*, 514.

Zayat, M., Kalb, L., & Wodka, E. L. (2011). Brief report: Performance pattern differences between children with autism spectrum disorders and attention deficit-hyperactivity disorder on measures of verbal intelligence. *Journal of Autism and Developmental Disorders, 41*, 1743–1747.

Part IV

Current and Future Directions

Chapter 11

Digital Assessment with Q-interactive

Dustin Wahlstrom[1], Mark Daniel[2], Lawrence G. Weiss[1], and Aurelio Prifitera[3]
[1]Pearson Clinical Assessment, San Antonio, TX, USA, [2]Pearson Clinical Assessment, Bloomington, MN, USA, [3]Pearson Clinical Assessment, Upper Saddle River, NJ, USA

INTRODUCTION

Q-interactive® is a digital system built to support and enhance a clinician's use of individually administered tests such as the WISC-V. This type of computer-assisted testing is distinct from the more familiar computer-administered testing in which the examinee sees test items on a computer screen and answers using a keyboard, mouse, or touchscreen. That technology, which has been used for many years in psychology, education, and the workplace, is well suited to instruments such as self-report inventories or multiple-choice tests that have consistent, unspeeded, and fairly simple administration and response formats (Butcher, Perry, & Hahn, 2004; Mead & Drasgow, 1993). By contrast, in individually administered testing the examinee interacts with a skilled examiner who presents test items, records and scores responses, and provides feedback or guidance as needed to make sure that the examinee is demonstrating his or her best performance. Individual administration of this type is invaluable when it is considered critical to obtain a valid measure of the examinee's abilities on a performance task; when the examinee must provide motoric or vocal responses; or when assessing an individual who, because of age, disability, or clinical condition, cannot be tested without assistance. Q-interactive is perhaps the first system to enlist digital technology to improve and enhance the practice of individually administered assessment.

Consistent with this focus on assessment as an interaction between two people, the heart of Q-interactive is a test-administration component based on two tablets, one for the examinee and the other for the examiner. The examinee's tablet takes the place of the traditional printed stimulus booklet, and also

L. G. Weiss, D. H. Saklofske, J. A. Holdnack and A. Prifitera (Eds): WISC-V Assessment and Interpretation.
DOI: http://dx.doi.org/10.1016/B978-0-12-404697-9.00011-X

captures touch responses (from a finger or stylus). The examiner's tablet has multiple functions: it shows the item administration and scoring instructions typically provided in an examiner's manual, captures and scores item responses, shows the examinee's touch responses, performs timing, implements administration rules such as start and discontinue points, records examiner notes, calculates a score, and saves a record of the administration. The two devices are connected via Bluetooth, with the examiner controlling what is displayed on the examinee device.

The overarching goal of Q-interactive is to leverage advances in both hardware and software to improve the assessment experience and the quality of assessment results. Elements of that goal that were emphasized in the initial generation of Q-interactive tests are:

1. *Accuracy*. Automating subtest rules (start points, discontinues, etc.), automating aspects of scoring, presenting all item-specific administration and scoring reference information in a single location, and reducing the amount of materials an examiner has to juggle, all serve to remove common sources of examiner error.
2. *Portability and accessibility*. Having an entire test library self-contained within two tablets is significantly more convenient than transporting several paper test kits, and provides easy access to a larger amount of test content.
3. *Efficiency*. By streamlining the workflow and automating tasks such as scoring, Q-interactive can save the clinician time.
4. *Flexibility*. The system makes it easy to add or subtract subtests from a test battery, and has the potential to provide real-time data to help inform those decisions. This enables more personalized assessments and accurate diagnosis (see Chapter 12).
5. *Examinee engagement*. Children find technology more engaging than paper, giving greater confidence that the child's performance is a valid indicator of their ability.
6. *Focus on the examinee*. Examiners can pay more attention to examinee behavior because the system simplifies their task by automating distracting, mundane activities.

Notably, four of these five goals have to do with the examiner, not the examinee. This reflects the initial focus of Q-interactive, which has been to preserve the examinee's test-taking experience so that their performance on a subtest can be expected to be the same in either format—that is, the two versions will be raw-score equivalent. Thus, in its initial form, the test administration component of Q-interactive can be thought of as a new and improved medium for providing the same test-taking experience as the standard version of the test.

However, that is soon to change. WISC-V was the thirteenth instrument to be incorporated into Q-interactive since the system was launched in 2012. Although it is true that in the initially released version of the WISC-V all of the subtests are faithful analogues of their paper-based counterparts, new versions of some of the Processing Speed subtests are being developed that are designed to have fully digital interfaces that will differ, by necessity, from the paper versions but maintain or enhance reliability and validity. Looking ahead, it is inevitable that tests will soon be created that can only be administered digitally—that is, they will not have a paper-based counterpart.

This chapter describes the Q-interactive system, explains how it was conceived and developed, gives an overview of its research base including findings for the WISC-V, and explores some of the implications of the system for the science and practice of clinical assessment.

OVERVIEW OF COMPONENTS AND WORKFLOW

Q-interactive is digital tool and a system that supports and gives access to multiple tests, serving as a central hub for a practitioner's assessment activities. These two major components of Q-interactive are called *Central* and *Assess*. Central is a website that the examiner typically will access through a laptop or desktop computer in order to create clients, manage his or her test library, set up assessment sessions, generate reports, and store data long-term for review. Assess is the tablet application, described above, where testing takes place.

The entire Q-interactive workflow consists of a few basic steps:

1. In Central, the practitioner creates a client and assigns a set of tests in an administration sequence; the combination of the client and the set of tests is called the *Assessment*.
2. The Assessment is sent wirelessly to Assess (i.e., to the examiner tablet).
3. The testing session takes place within Assess, using two tablets.
4. Once all items are scored, the assessment data are sent back wirelessly to Central for long-term storage, and are removed from the examiner tablet.
5. The practitioner generates reports in Central.

The user must be connected to the internet in order to access Central (Steps 1 and 5) and to transfer information between Central and Assess (Steps 2 and 4). However, the test administration itself (Step 3) can take place without an internet connection, with no loss of functionality (i.e., tests are still scored, and clinicians can add new tests to their session, even without internet connectivity).

The following section describes the Assess component of Q-interactive, including its primary features, the principles guiding its development, and what has been learned through research on WISC-V and other tests. This is followed by a discussion of some of the features of Central including security, flexible assessment, and data visualization.

ASSESS

At a high level, subtest administration within Assess follows a consistent workflow. The examiner will already have downloaded the Assessment (the set of

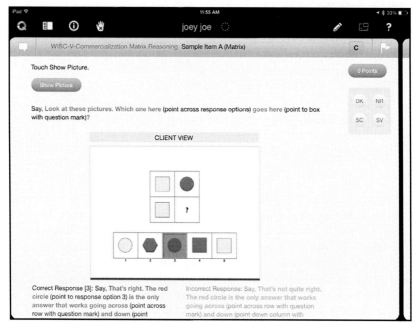

FIGURE 11.1 Examiner screen for a WISC-V Matrix Reasoning item.

tests for the client) to the examiner's tablet. From that point until completion of the administration, all work is carried out using the examiner and examinee tablets, and there is no need for an Internet connection.

The examiner initiates a subtest by opening it on the examiner tablet, and placing the other tablet (if used) in front of the examinee. Administration instructions for the item appear on the examiner's screen, which is positioned so that the examinee cannot see it. The examiner brings up the stimulus image on the examinee tablet by touching a button; this image is also displayed in a portion of the examiner screen so that the examiner knows what the examinee is seeing. Another button is available for starting the timer, if performance is timed.

The examiner may capture responses in a number of ways, depending on the nature of the subtest and on the examiner's preference. On a subtest such as Matrix Reasoning where the examinee chooses one or more images on the screen, the examinee's touch is recorded and also shows up on the examiner's screen (shown in Figure 11.1). The examiner can touch the option(s) to ensure that the examinee's intended response is captured. The sequence of touches can also be captured, if that is a factor in scoring (such as on CELF-5 Linguistic Concepts).

On most subtests, touch response is not used; instead, the examiner tablet is the only device needed to score and record responses. There are three ways of capturing response information on the examiner tablet: touch, handwriting (preferably with a stylus, although the fingertip may be used), and audio recording.

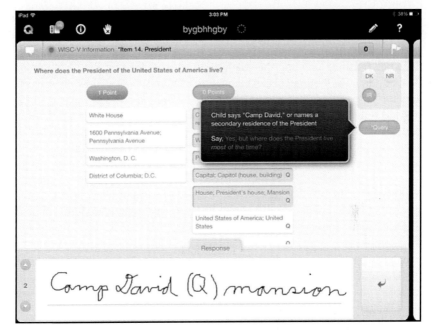

FIGURE 11.2   Examiner screen for a WISC-V Information item.

Many of the Q-interactive capture screens have a number of buttons representing different responses or response characteristics. For example, the screens for the WISC-V Verbal Comprehension subtests display buttons for each item's sample responses, grouped by score. Figure 11.2 illustrates this screen design for the WISC-V Information subtest. Where appropriate, there is a handwriting area on the screen that provides unlimited room for writing verbatim responses. And on subtests with oral responses, the examiner tablet automatically (unless intentionally disabled) makes a digital audio recording of what the examinee says. This recording can be reviewed by the examiner at any time until the entire administration session is completed, checked, and uploaded to Central, at which time the audio files are erased from the tablet. (Audio files are not uploaded.) In addition, there are numerous tools on the examiner tablet such as timers, buttons for recording important events such as querying or self-correction, and a "notes" tool that lets the examiner record comments about an item, a subtest, or the entire assessment session.

In most cases, the examiner assigns item scores. Only for multiple-choice subtests such as Matrix Reasoning does the system assign a score, but even in that case the examiner can override the score. On the Verbal Comprehension subtests that have sample-response buttons grouped by score level, the examiner must decide what score to give for each item, because an examinee's response to an item may be complex. If the examiner is not sure what score to assign he or she can assign a tentative score but also touch the "flag" button, which high-lights the item for review at the end of the assessment session (along with any unscored items).

After finishing an item, the examiner moves to the next item by swiping. At that point, the system checks the pattern of item scores against the standard administration rules (discontinue, reversal, etc.) and notifies the examiner if a rule has been met, giving the examiner the choice of what to do next; this allows the examiner to test the limits, for example. So as long as each item is scored accurately, the system guides the examiner through a correct administration.

Once the examiner decides to end the subtest, the system shows a summary report for that subtest. If any items have flags or were left unscored, they are highlighted in the "To Do" section. The examiner can look at any item's capture screen, including the handwriting, and listen to any audio recordings, in order to check and complete scoring. After all items are scored, the screen shows the subtest raw and scaled scores. This provides instant feedback regarding the examinee's performance, which can be used to adjust the test battery on the fly via Q-interactive's "Edit Battery" functionality. During the testing session, the examiner may decide to confirm an unexpectedly low score on the Vocabulary subtest by adding the optional Comprehension subtest into the test battery.

Finally, when the test session is complete and all subtest scoring is finished, the examiner can choose to remove the assessment from the tablet, which trans-fers all of the data wirelessly to Central and deletes them from the examiner tablet. However, not all activities for an assessment have to be completed in one sitting. An assessment can be administered and scored over the course of days or weeks, during which time the data remain on the tablet.

Phases of Assess Evolution

As noted earlier, the goals of the Assess interface design are evolving. This development may be divided into three phases. Phase 1 aims to achieve raw-score equivalence to the paper version by maintaining a consistent examinee experience. Phase 2 allows the examinee experience to differ (to take advantage of technology) but preserves construct equivalence. Finally, in Phase 3 digitally native tasks are created that may not have paper counterparts.

In Phase 1, the objective is for the Q-interactive administration to produce the same raw scores as the standard paper administration, so that not only the existing norms but also the existing research base on reliability and validity can be used. This entails a cautious and conservative approach to digital adapta-tion that sometimes results in Assess not taking advantage of all the features that the Q-interactive technology offers. For example, in this phase, manipu-latives such as Block Design blocks and Processing Speed response booklets must be retained. Essential to this phase is demonstrating raw-score equivalence between digital and paper formats, on the assumption that if examinees obtain the same raw scores regardless of which version they take (and if the interface appears to provide the same examinee experience as the paper administration), the reliability and validity of the score are the same with either format.

Phase 2, like Phase 1, is aimed at obtaining the same assessment information provided by standard paper-format tests, but it gives up the benefits of raw-score equivalence in order to obtain the benefits offered by the digital medium such as more accurate administration and scoring, the convenience and accessibility of being entirely digital, and greater examinee engagement. Its goal is to develop a digital subtest that measures the same or nearly the same construct as a paper-format subtest, with comparable or superior reliability. An example of Phase 2 development would be a version of the WISC-V Symbol Search subtest where the examinee responds by touching the tablet rather than marking a paper response booklet. As in Phase 1, the examinee experience should appear to be nearly the same as in the paper format in all ways thought to be construct-relevant; differences in examinee experience that are considered construct-irrelevant are permitted, and in fact such a difference may be desirable if it means that the digital version is a purer measure of the target construct. (In the example just given, removing the need for pencil control might be seen as a benefit for assessing visual processing speed in young children.) However, in Phase 2 it is assumed that the digital and paper versions will not be raw-score equivalent. The nature and extent of evidence needed to support the reliability and validity of scores will depend on a number of factors including the magnitude of the correlation between the digital and paper versions. Essentially, judgments must be made about the kind of supporting data required to enable practitioners to interpret scores with confidence. Depending on the closeness of the correspondence between the digital and paper scores, norms may be derived through equating (if the clinical construct being measured is substantially the same in both versions) or through independent sampling. Phase 2 research studies are currently under way for versions of the WISC-V Symbol Search and Coding subtests, which require the examinee to perform the task on the tablet.

Phase 3 is the development of new digitally native tests that do not necessarily have a close relationship with existing paper tests. This phase requires the same development methods, including explorations of reliability and validity, as are needed for any new test in any format.

Because nearly all of the Q-interactive development work to date has been in Phase 1, the following sections focus on the approaches that have been taken to achieving raw-score equivalence and the research evidence that has been collected.

Design Requirements (Phase 1)

Two overarching requirements drove the design and development of Assess. The first was raw-score and construct equivalence, which is a precondition for valid interpretation of scores (International Test Commission, 2005). The second was clinical flexibility, i.e., giving the examiner as much control over the administration as when using the standard paper materials. The role of Assess is to support the examiner by performing mundane aspects of the administration process, without taking over control or imposing limitations on what the examiner can do. Individual administration remains a skilled clinical activity involving judgment and flexibility.

Equivalence

For some tests, the threats to equivalence posed by digitization are fairly obvious. For example, one could imagine a version of Block Design in which the examinee drags images of blocks across the tablet screen in order to create a design. Although such a task may be conceptually appealing and might ultimately be implemented on Q-interactive, from the point of view of equivalence a change this major raises a number of questions: Does the new task measure the same core ability? To what extent are scores influenced by extraneous abilities or skills different from those involved in the standard (paper) version? Are scores similarly reliable? What impact might these potential differences have for interpretation? Some of these same questions apply as well to other types of subtests where there is less apparent difference between the paper and digital versions.

Three ways in which the design of a Q-interactive subtest could threaten equivalence are:

1. Changing how the examinee interacts with the test (e.g., by changing how they view or manipulate test stimuli), such as in the Block Design example above.
2. Changing how the examiner interacts with the test (e.g., by changing how the examiner accesses administration and scoring information, records examinee responses, etc.). These tasks are intentionally quite different on Q-interactive than when using paper materials. Assess presents item-specific administration instructions, provides an entire screen for capturing the response to an item, and offers new methods for response capture such as pick lists and audio recording. While these may improve accuracy, they represent a significant change in the examiner's task.
3. Interaction of the two, whereby a change in how either the examiner or examinee interacts with the test affects the other. An example will illustrate this concept. In early development work, the team prototyped the examiner's use of an external keyboard to record oral responses (such as on WISC Vocabulary). Examiners took longer to type responses than to write them on paper, and this (possibly in combination with the sounds of the keyboard) led examinees to purposefully shorten their responses, as if in an attempt to assist the struggling examiners. For this reason, the development team made the decision not to support capturing verbatim responses by typing in the Q-interactive system.

How did the identification of these equivalence threats affect the design process? First, it drove the decision that what the examinee hears, sees, and touches needs to be similar enough to the paper format not to threaten equivalence. Thus, test manipulatives (such as Block Design blocks or NEPSY-II Animal Sorting cards) and response booklets (such as for the WISC Processing Speed subtests) were retained, despite the fact that digital tasks without the manipulatives could have been designed. This decision also applied to visual stimuli presented on the examinee tablet. It was important to maintain the size and clarity of images wherever possible, although slight concessions were made to accommodate the size of the tablet screen.

An illustrative example of the importance of image consistency occurred during development of WAIS-IV Picture Completion. The original equivalence study suggested slightly poorer performance on the digital version of the task than with the paper version, despite the fact that the images appeared to the development team to be comparable. After weeks of investigation, a staff member taking the paper and digital versions side by side reported a subjective sense of wanting to solve the paper items because the clarity of the images made the problems seem easier. It turned out that subtle fuzziness in areas of the digital image unrelated to solving the problem nevertheless was distracting because examinees thought it might be significant. Improving the clarity of the digital images eliminated the difference in raw scores obtained from digital and paper versions of Picture Completion.

Another example concerns touch feedback on the examinee screen. The screen flashes momentarily when the examinee touches a response selection, which of course is unlike the behavior of the paper stimulus book. Nevertheless, examinees know that their touch is being captured, and they are used to seeing feedback on touchscreen devices. If there were no feedback at all, they might be concerned about whether their touch had registered. So this difference between digital and paper interfaces was accepted as being necessary to remove a possible source of distraction. This design feature has been supported by equivalence data across several subtests.

Clinical Flexibility and Robustness

The second major driver of Q-interactive design was the need to accommodate the dynamic nature of the clinical assessment process. The importance of this consideration was documented through interviews and observations of hundreds of users. Tests such as the WISC-V are governed by standard administration rules that are relatively easy to program. However, as important as the rules themselves is the requirement to deviate from them when appropriate. For example, clinicians should start at earlier start points if they suspect that an individual is lower functioning, give items past the discontinue point if the examinee is answering questions correctly with additional time, and come back to administer previously administered items if the pattern of responses indicates unexplained inconsistency. The innumerable possible paths in the test-administration workflow, driven by clinical judgment, cannot be captured in a linear program. Thus, the Q-interactive system must be flexible.

This flexibility was built into Assess in a number of ways. For example, on most subtests each item is presented on its own screen, which enables flexible navigation through items in either forward or reverse direction and the ability to jump to another item. Also, although start points by age or grade are programmed into the system, examiners can override these for special cases. The same is true for discontinue points, which are flagged by the system but do not prevent the examiner from continuing with additional items if desired.

Scoring is also flexible. For example, the examinee can change his or her touch response on a task like Matrix Reasoning as many times as needed. On all subtests and items, the examiner has ultimate control of scoring and can override the examinee's touch response (for the case in which the examinee touches option 5 but says, "I mean 1"). This does not have to occur while the item is being administered, but can be done after the assessment is complete; item responses and scores can be updated at any time. These design features build in a level of flexibility that is intended to match that available with paper-based administration.

One distinctive aspect of designing an application for clinical assessment is the fact that giving a test is usually a "one-shot" event. The clinician typically has a single try to administer a test: for example, once Block Design has been administered to an individual, it cannot be administered again for quite a while because practice effects can influence the score. Thus, the capture of information about every item administration must be robust. This requirement was reflected in the design of functional characteristics such as the transfer and saving of data. For example, Assess is usable without an internet connection so that Q-interactive can be employed in rural, forensic, government, and other settings where wireless connections may not be available or reliable. When Assess is used in offline mode, data are saved on the examiner tablet after every item to ensure that data are maintained even if the application or tablet were to unexpectedly close. If this occurs, the examiner can simply turn the device back on, enter the assessment session, and pick back up where he or she left off, with all data up to that point saved.

Development Steps

Because Q-interactive is the first system of its kind, its development required confronting many novel system-design questions. What started as a concept slowly took the form of a design, a prototype, and eventually a functional system. In general, the steps taken to create Q-interactive fall into the following activities:

1. Designing and prototyping
2. Evaluating equivalence
3. Beta testing

Designing and Prototyping

One of the first steps in designing Assess for a subtest was to map its administration into a logical, programmable workflow called a "logic map." Figure 11.3

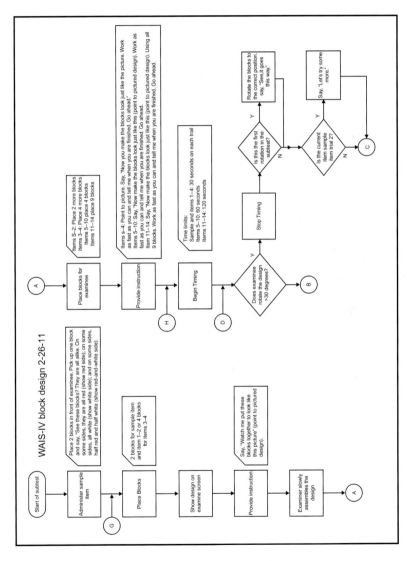

FIGURE 11.3 Partial workflow map of the Block Design subtest.

illustrates a small section of the logic map for the WAIS-IV Block Design administration process. This reveals the numerous steps and decision points that make up an administration, each of which is performed intuitively by seasoned examiners. The logic map showed each possible step and its relationships to other actions and events, in order to enable the software team to design the architecture supporting Assess.

The next step in the design process was to lay out the interfaces of individual subtests—what would the examinee see, how would the examiner read instructions, and how would responses be recorded and scored? This was approached systemically. A wide cross-section of subtests were grouped according to the type of response required on the part of the examinee (e.g., verbal, touch, arranging manipulatives, etc.), and the type of information recorded by the examiner (e.g., verbatim verbal response, a score, etc.).

Once these groupings were complete, common design concepts were created for each group. This had two benefits. First, it simplified the system and improved usability by letting examiners transfer learnings from one subtest to others within that same group, reducing the overall training burden. Second, it allowed the development team to evaluate possible format effects in interface design concepts used in common across multiple subtests, increasing the power of the research designs.

Proposed design concepts were prototyped using basic implementations of those designs and updating as necessary to ensure that they met the needs of clinicians. This was a key element of the development process, which heavily influenced the final designs. Essentially, an experimental approach was taken to selecting designs for many of the specific functions incorporated in the interfaces.

A good illustration of this process was the development of the examiner interface for the California Verbal Learning Test (CVLT-II). On the immediate recall trials, the examiner says a list of 16 words to the examinee at a rate of approximately one word per second. The examinee is then asked to say as many of the words as possible, in any order. This is repeated for a total of five trials, which provides an index of how well the examinee learns over multiple presentations of the stimuli. (There are also an interference-list trial and several delayed-recall trials.) On the recall trials the examiner must record each word that the examinee says (whether correct or incorrect) to allow for the calculation of various process scores. Given the rapid pace with which examinees respond, examiners using paper materials have developed tricks in order to keep up, such as writing down only the first three letters.

These requirements meant that the Assess design had to enable quick recording of verbatim responses, both correct and incorrect. This ruled out a simple interface containing a button for each word on the list. The first design approach (see Figure 11.4) was prototyped to answer the question: If examiners had to write on a tablet like they do on paper, could they keep up with the examinee?

The answer provided by prototyping was clearly "No." Almost every person who tested the interface reported that they could not keep up with the examinee.

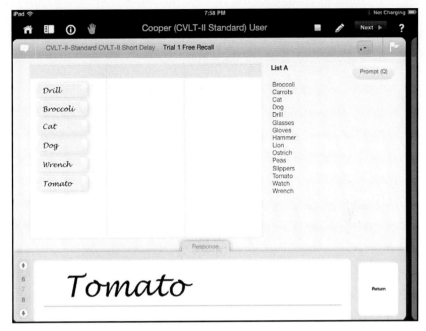

FIGURE 11.4   First CVLT-II prototype.

This was due in part to the novelty of writing on a digital interface, but also to a half-second lag when the examiner hit the "Return" button to begin writing a new word. The next design attempt was a hybrid model with buttons for the list words and the handwriting area for nonlist words. Although this improved response capture, the "Return" lag still presented a problem. Finally, the designers invented a clever solution (shown in Figure 11.5) with two handwriting areas. Once a word was written in one area, the examiner could begin writing in the second, which automatically cleared the first area and committed the word to the list. This switching back and forth eliminated the need for a "Return" button, and in conjunction with buttons for correct words, achieved the needed level of speed of response capture. (Audio recording is also enabled on this subtest as a backup for extreme cases.)

Evaluating Equivalence

Once the prototyping process was completed, the next step was to conduct equivalence studies to determine whether the Q-interactive format yielded the same raw scores as the standard paper version. It is important to distinguish between equivalence studies and norming studies. Norming is a matter of sampling from a defined population. By contrast, an equivalence study is an experiment designed to answer the question whether an individual would be expected to obtain the same raw score regardless of which format was used.

FIGURE 11.5   Final CVLT-II Implementation with "dual capture" design.

The two types of undertaking require different kinds and amounts of data. The Q-interactive equivalence studies (described in technical reports available on www.helloq.com) used several types of experimental designs, as appropriate to the characteristics of the test being studied and the types of threats to equivalence that those characteristics might present.

Several principles guided the design and conduct of the equivalence studies:

- An *a priori* definition of "equivalent": The team set an operational standard for equivalence as an effect size of 0.20 or less. Effect size is the difference in scores obtained using Q-interactive and paper formats, expressed in terms of the population standard deviation (e.g., 3 for Wechsler subtest scaled scores). Effect sizes of 0.20 are traditionally classified as small in the research literature, whereas effect sizes of 0.50 and 0.80 are classified as medium and large, respectively (Cohen, 1988). An effect size of 0.20 is equal to 0.6 scaled-score points, or 3 points on the composite-score metric that has a mean of 100 and standard deviation of 15. This is roughly equivalent to the SEM of the Full Scale Intelligence Quotient on WISC-V (2.90) and smaller than the SEM for the primary index scores (which range from 3.89 to 5.24).
- Focus on plausible threats: The first step in planning an equivalence study was to do a logical analysis of the examinee and examiner tasks to identify aspects that might affect scores. This led to choosing a study design that would be capable of revealing these effects.

- Begin with the general population: The initial question was whether there is anything inherent in the format that affects scores. This needs to be answered first with typical examinees before turning to the question of whether equivalence also obtains in subgroups such as clinical populations.
- One administration per examinee: Usually, each examinee takes the test only once. The experience in a second administration can be different than in the first, because the examinee already understands the task and may remember how to solve particular items or what overall strategy was helpful. Counterbalancing the format sequence may not effectively control for these effects. For example, if the Q-interactive presentation of a test were less clear than the paper presentation, we would not see that in examinees taking the Q-interactive format second.
- Adequate sample size: The studies should have good statistical power to detect an effect size of 0.20 (at an alpha level of .05).
- Video record administrations: We need to be able to determine the cause of any observed format effect. Is there a difference in examinee behavior? Or is there a difference in how the examiner or the Q-interactive system captures or scores that behavior? When a format effect is found, we do not know which format is more accurate. Video recordings provide a reference point to answer this question, and also may reveal differences in how examinees behave, which can provide insights into interface design. Without this record, diagnosing the cause of a format effect would often be speculative.

Three types of experimental designs have been used. In the *equivalent-groups design*, one group takes the test in the standard paper format and a second, comparable group takes it in the digital format, and the scores obtained by the two groups are compared. Comparability of the groups may be obtained through stratified-random assignment to format, or through a combination of demographic matching and statistical control from covariate tests. This design is suitable for any type of test, and it has high ecological validity because each subject's testing experience is similar to what they would have in clinical practice. Relatively large samples (several hundred examinees) are required to provide good statistical power.

In the second design type, *retest*, each examinee takes the test in both formats, in counterbalanced order. Because this design violates the single-administration design principle described above, it has been used only for tests where it is thought that the examinee uses the same cognitive processes the second time as the first. Types of tests that have been studied using the retest design include tests of short-term memory for nonmeaningful stimuli (e.g., digit span or spatial patterns) and tests of processing speed. Offsetting the limitations of this design is its high degree of statistical power with small samples, due to the fact that examinees serve as their own controls. This efficiency is enhanced by starting with demographically matched pairs of examinees whose members are randomly assigned to the two format sequences.

Like the retest design, the third type of design, called *dual capture*, is also highly efficient but limited to tests with certain characteristics. A small number of test administrations are video-recorded from the examiner's viewpoint, showing only the examinee. Each video recording is then scored by many examiners, some using the standard paper materials and the others using Q-interactive. The analysis looks for any differences between scores obtained using the two formats. This design focuses on possible threats to equivalence arising from the response/capture interface on the examiner tablet. It is appropriate for tests in which there is no interaction between examiner and examinee during item administration, and where the examinee does not respond on the examinee tablet.

The initial Q-interactive studies evaluated all of the subtests in a battery because little was known about the effects that the Q-interactive format might have. As studies were completed, knowledge accumulated about the behavior of certain kinds of interface features. As a result, in later studies a subtest might not be evaluated if the only possible threats to equivalence were interface features that had already been shown to be benign. This knowledge base relied on the categorization of interface features described earlier.

As described above, all research designs have their relative strengths and weaknesses, and none provide a perfect test of the given hypotheses. When large numbers of effects are evaluated in an experiment, random positive results may occur based on the law of probabilities. This is why it is commonly stated in all beginning statistical textbooks that significant findings should be reliably replicated across multiple studies before finally being accepted. For all of these reasons, the Q-interactive development team focused on trends in the overall research program across multiple subtests with very similar digital interface demands, rather than findings from individual subtests in single studies.

To date, 75 subtests from 10 instruments (including WISC-V) have been studied, permitting some general conclusions about how various types of Q-interactive interfaces perform with respect to equivalence. Overall, 73 of the 75 effect sizes were within the range of -0.20 to 0.20, which is considered to indicate equivalence, and the mean effect size was 0.01. Table 11.1 reports the average effect sizes separately for each of six different interface types.

Interface types in which the examinee tablet is not used, or is used only to display a visual stimulus with no touch response, have been found to have average effect sizes very close to zero (between -0.03 and 0.04), with no individual effect sizes exceeding 0.20 in absolute value. This indicates that the examiner interfaces are functioning as intended, even when response capture is complex.

For subtests involving a touch response by the examinee, there is a slight tendency toward higher scores when using Q-interactive, and the two subtests that have shown effect sizes greater than 0.20 (WISC-IV Matrix Reasoning and WISC-IV Picture Concepts) are of this type. Although the reason for this tendency is not known, evidence from the video recordings of the administrations rules out administration or scoring errors with either the paper or the digital formats, or any obvious differences in examiner behavior. The effect is subtle,

TABLE 11.1 Average Q-interactive Format Effect Sizes by Type of Interface, for All Studies

Type of Interface (WISC-V Example)	No. Subtests	Effect Size		
		Mean	SD	Range
No examinee interface:				
Oral response, captured by examiner (Vocabulary)	27	−0.03	0.09	−0.20 to 0.12
Time, captured by examiner (Coding)	7	0.04	0.14	−0.07 to 0.13
Errors and time, captured by examiner (Digit Span)	8	0.04	0.09	−0.08 to 0.18
Visual display, no touch response (Block Design)	20	−0.03	0.12	−0.19 to 0.20
Visual display, single touch (Matrix Reasoning)	6	0.15	0.10	−0.02 to 0.27
Visual display, multiple touches (Picture Concepts)	7	0.06	0.10	−0.08 to 0.21
Total	75	0.01	0.11	−0.20 to 0.27

Note: Data from studies of CELF-5, CMS, CVLT-II, D-KEFS, NEPSY-II, WAIS-IV, WIAT-III, WISC-IV, WISC-V, WMS-IV.

and is likely related to the increased level of examinee engagement reported by Q-interactive users.

The consistency of the effect sizes reported in Table 1 lends support to the adequacy of the designs and the sample sizes used in the equivalence studies. Had samples been too small, we would have seen random variability in results due to the increased sampling error, probably resulting in more effect sizes outside the range of −0.20 to 0.20.

WISC-V was the most recent instrument to be evaluated for equivalence of Q-interactive administration. The study, described in Q-interactive Technical Report 8 (Daniel, Wahlstrom, & Zhang, 2014), used a randomly-equivalent-groups design with 350 examinees (175 demographically matched pairs). The findings are shown in Table 11.2. Effect sizes for the 13 primary and ancillary cognitive subtests (not including the Processing Speed subtests) ranged from −0.20 to 0.20 with a mean of 0.03 (SD = 0.13). (The Processing Speed subtests are not included because their Q-interactive versions were under development at the time of the study.) The complementary psychoeducational subtests had the same mean effect size but a smaller standard deviation (0.05). The pattern of results by type of interface resembles the pattern for all 75 subtests shown in Table 11.1.

TABLE 11.2 Q-interactive Format Effect Sizes for WISC-V Subtests

Subtest by Interface Type	Effect Size
No examinee interface: oral response	
Arithmetic	−0.16
Comprehension	−0.20
Information	−0.05
Similarities	0.04
Vocabulary	−0.13
No examinee interface: errors and time	
Digit Span	0.08
Letter-Number Sequencing	0.09
Examinee interface: display only	
Block Design	0.20
Immediate Symbol Translation	0.03
Delayed Symbol Translation	0.01
Recognition Symbol Translation	0.00
Naming Speed Literacy	0.12
Naming Speed Quantity	−0.02
Examinee interface: display and single touch	
Figure Weights	0.16
Matrix Reasoning	0.17
Examinee interface: display and multiple touches	
Picture Concepts	0.02
Picture Span	0.07
Visual Puzzles	0.04

WISC-V Comprehension (an optional subtest) and Block Design each show an effect size of 0.20. Although these findings technically show equivalence in that they are within the *a priori* criteria of 0.20 or less, they are close enough to the cut off to warrant special attention. Note, first, that these two subtests show effects in opposite directions: one (Block Design) shows an effect favoring digital administration and the other (Comprehension) shows an effect favoring paper administration. Furthermore, neither of these tasks requires the examinee to inter-act with the tablet, and no logical explanation for the differences could be identi-fied based on a careful review of the examiner interface by licensed psychologists on the Q-interactive development team who observed numerous video-recorded administrations. More importantly, equivalence studies of WISC-IV showed no format effects for Comprehension or Block Design, and the interface demands of these subtests are virtually identical in WISC-IV and WISC-V. Taken together, these studies suggest that the marginal format effects reported for WISC-V are small in magnitude, limited to two subtests, occur in different directions, have no logical explanation, and are not replicable across studies.

Equivalence for Subgroups

Even if subtests are found to be raw-score equivalent in studies of large samples of typical individuals, it is reasonable to wonder whether this finding holds for all subgroups. For example, might examinees of low ability, or the very young or very old, or those from low socioeconomic environments experience dif-ficulties when tested using digital tablets? It was possible to examine this ques-tion in the equivalence studies that used the randomly equivalent groups design (WISC-IV and WISC-V), because that design uses large samples. We evaluated whether the "format effect" (that is, the difference between actual and expected Q-interactive subtest scores) was related to age, gender, ethnicity, parent edu-cation, or score level on that subtest. Among the total of 165 analyses, only seven (4%) were statistically significant at the .05 level, fewer than the number expected by chance if there were no true effects. In other words, there appear to be no differences in format effect between males and females, between younger and older examinees, between examinees with above-average and below-aver-age levels of parental education, among examinees of different race/ethnicity groups, or for examinees at different levels of ability on the construct being measured. Interestingly, however, preliminary research on the Q-interactive ver-sion of WPPSI-IV found children aged 2 or 3 to sometimes be distracted by the tablet or by the visual feedback to touch responding, and this is being addressed through design changes for tests used with very young children.

Beta Testing

Once equivalency studies were complete, the final development activity prior to the launch of the platform was a beta study. The goals of this study were threefold:

1. Test the platform in a real-world environment to ensure that the design met the needs of the individuals using the test in clinical practice and to identify any desired features that may have been previously overlooked,
2. By having the system used daily at several locations, get further information regarding the integrity and robustness of the design and implementation in order to identify and fix any previously unidentified issues, and
3. Learn about the training and support needs for new users of the system.

The participants were carefully selected to represent a broad cross-section of practice environments, including schools, large hospitals, private practice, and forensic settings. Furthermore, participants varied widely in their technological experience and proficiency. Some were already tablet users who were very familiar with its functionality, while others were self-proclaimed luddites whose experience consisted of little more than checking email.

As expected, the reaction of beta testers varied based on their technological proficiency, and the study confirmed the need for a range of levels of training and support. Feedback from beta test participants identified some new requirements that were added to Assess. For example, many participants expressed a need to be able to swipe back to the previous item to deal with self-correction, examiner error, etc., and so that capability was added.

As Q-interactive has matured, the process for obtaining practitioner feedback has changed. Rather than conducting periodic, formal beta studies, the development team is in regular contact with clinicians who provide feedback regarding what they like and what they want to see changed in new releases of Q-interactive.

CENTRAL

The ultimate vision for Central is to be the practitioner's full-service resource for all assessment activities. However, in the early iterations of Q-interactive it has focused on supporting the three core functions of setting up clients, creating assessments, and receiving and storing data. This section discusses three of the most important functions that Central had to perform in order to meet clinicians' needs: security, flexible test selection, and data visualization.

Security

The ways in which Q-interactive protects client information are based on industry best practices and are in compliance with all applicable security and privacy regulations required by the Health Insurance Portability and Accountability Act (HIPAA) and Health Information Technology for Economic and Clinical Health Act (HITECH). Several types of safeguards (administrative, physical, and technical) are employed to protect data. It is helpful to think of three different aspects of security, each relevant to a different part of the Q-interactive workflow: during administration, during data upload to Central, and when data are stored.

During Administration

While a test is being administered on Assess, all data entered into the app are saved to an encrypted directory within the device. The Bluetooth connection between the two tablets is not encrypted because it does not transmit any identifiable information that needs to be protected (it conveys only basic information such as a numerical value associated with an examinee response). Access to

Assess is safeguarded via two layers: the application is protected with a complex password, and the examiner tablet itself can be protected with a complex password. In the case of a lost or stolen examiner device, there are numerous enterprise applications that allow the user to wipe their device remotely. If Wi-Fi is enabled during test administration, score data are frequently uploaded to Central during testing, so even in the event of needing to perform a remote wipe before finalizing an administration, data can still be preserved.

During Data Upload

When data are being transferred wirelessly between Assess and Central, it is secured using Secure Socket Layer (SSL) technology, the same technology used in banking and e-commerce.

Storage

Data are stored on an encrypted Pearson server, which is hosted in a secure facility where physical and virtual access is restricted to authorized personnel. Data are continually backed up, and auditing procedures are in place to ensure that no unauthorized activity takes place on the server. Only the database administrator has access to the data on the server.

Flexible Test Selection

One of the basic requirements for Q-interactive was for the clinician to be able to customize a test battery at the *subtest* level. This is important because it is rare to administer a complete battery; more often, a clinician will give perhaps 10 or 12 of the 19 WISC-V subtests to a child, depending on the referral question. In a climate where clinicians are pressured to obtain more information in less time, testing is becoming more hypothesis driven and focused rather than open-ended and exploratory (see Chapter 12). This requires a flexible battery approach, such as Edith Kaplan's Boston Process Approach (Millberg, Hebben, & Kaplan, 2009), which is dependent on subtest-level customization.

In Central, clinicians are able to configure customized batteries that include any subtest available in the test library regardless of which test kit it is part (e.g., WISC-V, NEPSY-II, KTEA-3, etc.). These custom batteries can be named, saved for later use, and even shared with colleagues within an organization. The purpose of this last feature is to support settings where standard batteries are given for research or specific referral questions. Rather than recreating a custom battery for every session, practitioners can all use the same pre-existing configuration, reducing set-up time and ensuring standardization across examiners.

Even when a clinician enters an assessment session with a custom battery in mind, their plan may change in light of the examinee's performance or other new information. Thus, Q-interactive must allow the clinician to modify the battery *during* the testing session. Assess contains an "edit battery" function that allows subtests to be subtracted, added, and reordered, even when there is no internet connectivity. This functionality, when combined with real-time scoring and access to a broad library of tests, enables clinicians to personalize an assessment battery during the assessment session. The reader is referred to Chapter 12 for a complete description of personalized approach to the assessment of learning disabilities, which can be implemented most efficiently with a computer-assisted assessment platform such as Q-interactive to guide and support clinical decisions in real time during the assessment session.

Data Visualization

A major and obvious benefit of Q-interactive is the ability to automate much of the scoring process, both to reduce scoring time and also to provide immediate score results so that clinicians can use the flexible testing capability described above. In addition, after data have been uploaded to Central, Q-interactive automatically feeds data into sophisticated reporting engines including ones that are able to combine data from different tests (e.g., WISC-V and WIAT-III).

In Central, the clinician needs to be able to review the record of an examinee's responses in a more efficient and convenient format than the one-screen-per-item format used in Assess. That format is optimal for administration accuracy and efficiency but is bulky and cumbersome for storage and review, and does not permit the clinician to look at patterns across items as well as details within items. For these reasons, Central displays response data on an "Item-Level Data" screen that formats the information in a similar way as a paper record form. For example, the Block Design screen shows all items and includes each item's score, the design that the examinee constructed, the correct design, and the completion time. Likewise, the Similarities screen displays each item's score, any sample response buttons that the examiner selected, and the examiner's handwritten transcriptions (Figure 11.6). This format allows the examiner to ascertain exactly what the examinee did on each item, while seeing patterns in behavior across items.

IMPLICATIONS FOR PROFESSIONAL PRACTICE

A radically new platform for assessment is bound to have numerous consequences for clinical practice, including some that were not anticipated during development. This section highlights three areas of impact that we believe are particularly significant: (1) examinee engagement, (2) training, and (3) the use of examinee data to create novel scores and clinical profiles.

Examinee Engagement

Given the widespread use of digital technology in schools, on the job, in commercial transactions, and at home, it would be reasonable to expect examinees to find a digital interface not only familiar but also appealing. This is likely to

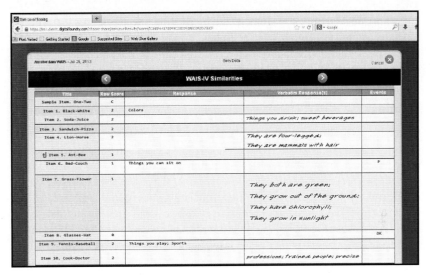

FIGURE 11.6   Sample Item-Level Data screen for WISC-V Similarities.

be particularly true of children, who have grown up in a technology-rich environment; in 2013, 75% of American children aged 8 and younger had access to a mobile device (Rideout & Saphir, 2013). To learn more about how children referred for assessment react to the digital format, in 2013 the Q-interactive team surveyed practitioners who had been administering WISC-IV with Q-interactive, and obtained 95 responses (a 38% response rate; Daniel, 2013). Approximately 70% of the respondents indicated that Q-interactive affected examinee behavior, and over 90% of these described the impact as positive (e.g., "more engaged," "more attentive," "increased interest," "more willing to respond," "more focused"). Five percent of those who saw an effect on behavior described it as negative or neutral (e.g., "more distracted and want to play with the computer," "some become preoccupied trying to get the items to light up," "they like to push the buttons that light up—sometimes this is good, but sometimes distracting"). When respondents were asked about the impact on children with particular clinical conditions (attention-deficit/hyperactivity disorder (ADHD), autism spectrum disorders, and intellectual disability), the results mirrored the overall findings, with the vast majority of clinicians reporting that Q-interactive increased engagement in each of these groups.

The significance of these findings for clinical practice is substantial. A lack of engagement or effort, especially among individuals with clinical conditions such as ADHD, is a major threat to the validity of test results. When interpreting low scores, practitioners have to consider whether they might reflect a reluctance to engage with a task or to persevere when items increase in difficulty. (It is possible that any slightly higher scores that may have been observed in the equivalence studies for subtests in which the examinee interacts with the tablet are due to greater engagement and motivation.) To the degree that a digital modality such as Q-interactive facilitates rapport and effort, practitioners can have greater confidence that results reflect the child's true potential on the constructs measured by these tasks.

Training

Given their role in preparing the next generation of clinicians, it is not surprising that many graduate school trainers have watched the development of Q-interactive with great interest. In addition to seeing the need to incorporate new digital technology into their coursework, they perceive a tension in the implications for the future role of psychologists. Trainers have expressed excitement that they will be able to spend less instructional time on the mechanics of assessment and more on the nuances of observation and clinical judgment. Some have commented that Q-interactive's modeling of correct administration and scoring practices should help ensure that students learn to give tests accurately. On the other hand, some trainers are concerned that students may not fully understand test administration rules and test data if they do not invest the requisite effort to internalize basic concepts and procedures such as applying reversal and discontinue rules and calculating subtest and composite scores. At the same time, however, trainers can use the audio recorded oral responses to evaluate how well students are using the rules for prompting and scoring.

A balance of these considerations is probably the ideal training approach. Practitioners need to understand why start points and discontinue points are used and have a general understanding of how they function so that they can smoothly anticipate test events. Similarly, examiners must understand how item raw scores roll up to subtest and composite scaled scores, so that they can interpret data responsibly. To obtain this knowledge, they may need to administer and score a test several times in paper format.

Training is also an issue for clinicians already in practice, in two different ways. First, of course, those who transition from giving a test with the paper materials to giving the same test (or its revision) with Q-interactive will need to learn how Assess works for that test and practice with it sufficiently so that it becomes comfortable. Even when a subtest is implemented in Q-interactive with no change in administration procedures, the examiner's actions can be quite different than with paper materials, and it takes time to develop the "motor memory" that allows the examiner to move smoothly through the administration. Becoming fluent in giving a test is a similar process with Q-interactive as it is with paper.

A second training consideration arises from the fact that Q-interactive offers easy, immediate, and relatively inexpensive access to a large and growing number of tests, and is designed to encourage and facilitate flexible administration. However, the available tests that might be attractive for a particular situation may include some that the practitioner has not used before. Because Q-interactive is a tool to *support* individual administration and personalized assessment, not a replacement for the clinician, there is still an ethical requirement for the examiner to study and practice a test before giving it to a client.

Novel Data and Analyses

Technology makes it possible to capture new types of test data and share data in ways that are difficult or impossible with paper materials. These capabilities can lead to new scores and interpretive information that may help clinicians better serve their clients.

The ability of digital tablets to capture fine-grained response-time information has the potential to transform the scoring of tests that rely on speed. For example, performance on the Wechsler Coding subtest is currently measured by the number of correct symbols that the examinee draws in the allotted time, but this is a simple measure that ignores other information that may be of interest. Does the examinee speed up, slow down, or maintain a consistent pace over the course of the task? Is the time between symbols consistent or variable? Answering these questions would be tedious when using paper and a stopwatch, but in a digital environment these scores could be readily extracted from the system, standardized, and converted into scores that might be clinically useful. For example, intra-individual variability (i.e., trial-by-trial fluctuations of performance on speeded tasks) has been shown to be an important construct in ADHD, brain injury, and dementia (MacDonald, Nyberg, & Bäckman, 2006).

For practical reasons, scores generated from individual administration of paper-based tests are not easily used to generate new knowledge that would contribute to the quality of test interpretation. In collaboration with clinicians, a digital system such as Q-interactive has the potential to aggregate and analyze de-identified test information about the relationship of test performance to clinical conditions, and disseminate what is learned to the professional community. The benefit of this ongoing, collaborative research is clear, because clinical validation is an ongoing process that is never fully complete. In a digital world, Q-interactive practitioners could submit data from various populations, including those that are rare, and these data could be aggregated and provided back to clinicians in the form of specific clinical profiles or unique process scores in order to enhance practice. Furthermore, clinical decision support tools based on analyses of large data sets can add a wealth of information for improved hypothesis testing and assessment by the clinician (see Chapter 12).

FUTURE DIRECTIONS

The current version of Q-interactive affords several benefits to practitioners: it is efficient, accurate, flexible, portable, and engaging for examinees. However, its greatest potential contribution to assessment probably lies in the development of digitally native tests that take advantage of technology to improve the measurement of familiar constructs and open the door to measuring constructs different from those measurable with print materials. That is, Q-interactive is in a transition stage with one foot in the world of traditional tests and the toe of the other beginning to dip into the pool of novel measures. This is a gradual process that fortunately is supported by the digital technology itself, which enables new tests or subtests to be distributed to practicing clinicians on a continuing basis rather than only when an entire new kit is published. WISC-V is attempting to move this process forward through the research and development work presently being done on Q-interactive versions of the Coding and Symbol Search processing speed subtests that, for the first time, are not replicas of the paper versions.

Test data are critical components of the nomological networks that support inferences about latent constructs such as intelligence (Cronbach & Meehl, 1955). To the extent that technology changes the observable variables we can measure, it may also change our fundamental understanding of these constructs. The possible implications of this for assessment and intervention are profound. It could improve the diagnostic accuracy of assessment, clarify our understanding of brain/behavior relationships, and generate new hypotheses for treatment and remediation. In this respect, Q-interactive will hopefully share a legacy with the original Wechsler intelligence tests, which revolutionized the practice of psychological assessment in the twentieth century.

REFERENCES

Butcher, J. N., Perry, J., & Hahn, J. (2004). Computers in clinical assessment: Historical developments, present status, and future challenges. *Journal of Clinical Psychology, 60,* 331–345.

Cohen, J. (1988). *Statistical power analysis for the behavioral sciences* (2nd ed.). Hillsdale, NJ: Erlbaum.

Cronbach, L. J., & Meehl, P. E. (1955). Construct validity in psychological tests. *Psychological Bulletin, 52,* 281–302.

Daniel, M. H. (2013). *User survey on Q-interactive examinee behavior.* Bloomington, MN: Pearson.

Daniel, M. H., Wahlstrom, D., & Zhang, O. (2014). *Equivalence of Q-interactive® and paper administrations of cognitive tasks: WISC®-V.* (Q-interactive Technical Report 8). Bloomington, MN: Pearson.

International Test Commission. (2005). *International guidelines on computer-based and internet delivered testing* (Version 2005). Author.

MacDonald, S. W. S., Nyberg, L., & Bäckman, L. (2006). Intra-individual variability in behavior: links to brain structure, neurotransmission, and neuronal activity. *TRENDS in Neurosciences, 29*(8), 474–480.

Mead, A. D., & Drasgow, F. (1993). Equivalence of computerized and paper-and-pencil cognitive ability tests: A meta-analysis. *Psychological Bulletin, 114,* 449–458.

Millberg, W. P., Hebben, N., & Kaplan, E. (2009). The Boston Process Approach to neuropsychological assessment. In I. Grant & K. Adams (Eds.), *Neuropsychological assessment of neuropsychiatric and neuromedical disorders* (pp. 42–65). New York: Oxford University Press.

Rideout, V., & Saphir, M. (2013). *Zero to eight: Children's media use in America 2013.* San Francisco, CA: Common Sense Media.

Chapter 12

WISC-V and the Personalized Assessment Approach

James A. Holdnack[1], Aurelio Prifitera[2], Lawrence G. Weiss[3], and Donald H. Saklofske[4]

[1]*Pearson Clinical Assessment, Bear, DE, USA,* [2]*Pearson Clinical Assessment, Upper Saddle River, NJ, USA,* [3]*Pearson Clinical Assessment, San Antonio, TX, USA,* [4]*Department of Psychology, University of Western Ontario, London, Ontario, Canada*

INTRODUCTION

At the center of a psychological evaluation of any type is the individual child or adolescent who is experiencing difficulties in his or her life. Understanding each individual child/adolescent in the assessment process is a challenge because most tests and test batteries are designed around a construct or measurement model rather than understanding the uniqueness of an examinee. Therefore, the assessment process can easily become more about the test and what the test scores mean rather than about the individual.

The future of psychological assessment revolves around the concept of individualized, tailored assessments that are designed to understand the unique interactions of psychosocial environment (as described in Chapters 5 and 8) and personal combinations of problems, risk factors, strengths, weaknesses, and support systems (Matarazzo, 1990). This model proposes a fluid, flexible, and interactive model in which initial evaluation plans are modified on the fly based on child/adolescent test performance and response to the evaluation process. The goal of the evaluation is to best pinpoint the child's cognitive, emotional, social, and behavioral difficulties and strengths to identify more targeted interventions and accommodations.

At the heart of this model are the concepts of probability, risk factors, and multiplicity. The concept of probability, in regards to this model, recognizes the limitations of our tools and techniques for an exact identification of a specific disorder and outcome. Probabilities help us conceptualize the *most likely* disorder, potential short- and long-term outcomes, and the interventions that have the best chance of being effective. The identification of risk factors provides a

L. G. Weiss, D. H. Saklofske, J. A. Holdnack and A. Prifitera (Eds): WISC-V Assessment and Interpretation.
DOI: http://dx.doi.org/10.1016/B978-0-12-404697-9.00012-1

framework for making recommendations for diagnostic conclusions, the potential impact of identified cognitive risk factors, and potential unexpected consequences of the disorder (e.g., children with language disorders are at greater risk for social isolation). Multiplicity recognizes that developmental disorders have high rates of comorbidity, that additional risk and protective factors may be present that can affect the expression of a disorder and its consequences, and that individual strengths and weaknesses in cognition, behavior, temperament, and psychosocial environment influence are important in the expression of symptoms and outcomes of a clinical condition. A failure to identify the multiple influencing factors can result in misdiagnosis and inappropriate prognosis or ineffective intervention.

This chapter discusses the application of the personalized assessment approach with a focus on the WISC-V in conjunction with a variety of other measures. First, the process of developing an initial evaluation plan based on the reason for referral, background information, and parent and teacher rating scales to ensure comprehensive evaluation of the child's potential cognitive and emotional issues. Second, the assessment plan is derived targeting high probability problem areas and using those results to branch into more in-depth coverage of specific areas of weakness or to branch into other possible cognitive/emotional difficulties not previously considered. Third, integrating test information to be child centered rather than test centered. Finally, the utilization of the test data to develop a treatment plan addressing the examinees' unique profile of skills, abilities, and risk factors.

OBTAINING AND REFINING INITIAL IMPRESSIONS OF THE CHILD

Prior to evaluation of any examinee, information, though often not well formulated, about their current psychosocial environment is made available to the clinician. This is the clinician's first glimpse at how the world views the child, usually framed by a set of "problems." It is easy for the "problems" to come to define the child or be synonymous with their personality, abilities, and potential. Additionally, the clinician starts to glean environmental factors that may influence the child's presenting problems. Unfortunately, there is often insufficient time or resources for the clinician to obtain all the critical information about the child prior to the date of the evaluation.

This section discusses the importance of pre-assessment planning and refinement of pre-testing hypotheses. Although some clinicians may feel it is better not to be biased by the impressions of others prior to engaging with the child personally, it is of critical value for establishing an assessment plan that is tailored to the child and flexible during the course of the evaluation. *A priori* hypothesis generation is not a prejudgment of the child but helps the examiner focus in on all critical areas of concerns rather than focusing on only what is perceived to be the most critical problems (e.g., learning problems in the face of other difficulties such as social difficulties and family problems). The pre-assessment phase can be generally divided into four key areas: referral, collecting background information, parent and teacher ratings (classroom observation if possible), and assessment planning.

Reason for Referral

The quality of the reason for referral varies tremendously among referral agents. There are many reasons for the variability among referral agents including experience working with psychologists; level of familiarity with the child, child's family, and current difficulties; time spent formulating referral; knowledge of what information would be helpful to the psychologist; and general knowledge of factors influencing specific child difficulties. Many requests for evaluation, such as: "what is John Smith's level of functioning?", "are there cognitive difficulties?", "learning difficulties" and "evaluate behavior problems," are too vague for the clinician to be able to glean any direction for the evaluation. And in some cases, referral questions, such as: "John Smith is referred for a Rorschach test," "neuropsychological testing," and "Does Johnny have moral reasoning capacity," can be too vague and specific at the same time. Although these referral questions provide a vague notion of why the child needs an evaluation, the psychologist cannot effectively plan for the assessment or understand the social forces driving the request.

The most important elements in the referral question relate to the anticipated outcome from the evaluation and identification of risk factors. Frequently, the referral agent has multiple outcomes they desire from obtaining an evaluation. Without knowing those desired outcomes, it is easy to complete an evaluation that does not directly answer the needs of the referral agent. There are many reasons for referrals, such as diagnostic/classification questions, functional level, placement or intervention. The selection of tests can vary based on the required outcomes for the evaluation.

In addition to tailoring the evaluation to the specific needs of the referral agent, the referral question also helps the psychologist formulate some initial hypotheses about what problems the child may have. If the question is about social functioning, the psychologist can initially focus on factors related to poor social functioning. Also, the psychologist will be certain to include measures that could help identify autism spectrum disorders (ASD). In this way, the referral question starts the process of the evaluation.

The psychologist can help referral agents improve their requests for psychological assessment in many ways. One method is to provide referral agents with a *brief* checklist with sections related to diagnostic or classification concerns, specific problematic behaviors, and placement questions. These should be tailored to the psychologist's practice setting. When possible, it can be very informative to interview the referral agent about their responses to gain a more nuanced understanding of the areas of concern. Additionally, the psychologist can help educate the referral source through direct contact. Asking for clarification about the specific behaviors that are a primary source of concern versus secondary issue can help the referral source focus their questions and concerns for an individual child. Although a good referral question is not a requirement for performing a personalized assessment, it improves the psychologist's ability to plan ahead for which tests may be most appropriate and which tests are required.

Background Information and *a priori* Hypothesis Building

There are two types of background information that are required to develop *a priori* hypotheses in order to develop an effective assessment plan. There is background information specific to the child/adolescent and there is background information related to specific developmental, medical, and psychiatric disorders, behavioral issues, and psychological symptoms. It would seem counterintuitive to apply information collected from research studies that typically use group-level data rather than individual performance when performing a personalized assessment. However, information about specific disorders can provide an excellent starting point for an assessment. That is because there are not an infinite number of possible disorders and the probabilities that a child or adolescent has a specific disorder is knowable. For example, the probability that a child with attention problems has attention-deficit hyperactivity disorder (ADHD) versus childhood onset of schizophrenia would strongly favor ADHD unless some other symptom (e.g., auditory hallucinations) was also present. An assessment plan that focuses initially on more probable outcomes versus a global assessment of all possible outcomes can result in a more detailed evaluation of the factors related to the presenting symptoms and potentially provide better information for intervention and accommodation.

Background Research

It is beyond the scope of this chapter to provide a comprehensive research review of all possible disorders of childhood and adolescence. This chapter focuses on the types of information that are helpful when planning an assessment. These can be roughly categorized as epidemiological, phenomenology, and cognitive profile. These different categories of information should not be considered as independent but each is important in planning for an assessment and provides a different perspective on possible outcomes.

Epidemiological information in this model refers to information about the prevalence of a disorder, heritability, and environmental factors that may contribute to the expression of the disorder and biological and genetic factors that modify the expression of the disorder. Some of this information is organized and presented in the *Diagnostic and Statistical Manual of Mental Disorders*—5th edition (DSM-5). Prevalence rates for common developmental and psychiatric disorders are frequently reported here. The Centers for Disease Control and Prevention website CDC.gov provides prevalence data for some developmental conditions. Understanding the relative base rate of a disorder is important for initial assessment planning. In most cases, children will present with more common rather than rare conditions and these need to be evaluated and ruled in or out.

Epidemiological data regarding heritability and genetics of a disorder may be helpful not only in the initial stages of an evaluation but also when making decisions regarding probable diagnosis and intervention. For instance, in families with a history of reading disorder, the probability that a child in that family will also have a reading disorder is approximately 34%, whereas in families with no history of reading disorder the risk is approximately 6% (Pennington & Lefly, 2001). This is not a precise estimation of the risk factor; however, it is strong evidence that if there is a family history of reading problems it increases the probability that the child may also have some reading issues. Also, from an intervention standpoint, it may be important to know if a parent has a learning difficulty because it may affect their ability to help their child in that domain.

Epidemiological data regarding the base rates of comorbid disorders is of critical importance. For example, we know that a high proportion of children suffering from depression also suffer from significant symptoms of anxiety, therefore if a child is referred for depression we must also evaluate anxiety symptoms. Similarly, in a large sample of children diagnosed with a learning disability, it was found that comorbid disorders were ADHD (33%), anxiety disorder (28%), developmental coordination disorder (17.8%), language disorder (11%), and mood disorder (9%) (Margari et al., 2013). Again, these are estimates of the actual rates of comorbidity; however, it makes clear that children being referred for reading, math, or writing problems also need evaluation of other possible comorbid disorders that can impact the child's functioning and possibly affect the type of intervention required.

The expression of a disorder or the severity of impairments is multifactorial. Knowing the factors that may modify or alter the expression of a disorder is helpful as this can impact the sensitivity and specificity of our diagnostic criteria. In one study, girls that had a high number of autism spectrum traits were less likely to be diagnosed with ASD than boys unless comorbid intellectual impairments and more severe behavioral disturbance were also present (Dworzynski, Ronald, Bolton, & Happé, 2012). This may be a sample-specific finding but it alerts clinicians that there may be some bias or sex-based moderation in the identification of ASD. Other factors affecting the expression of a disorder are related to psychosocial or medical issue such as socioeconomic status, early language environment, abuse, pre-natal exposure to substances of abuse, poor nutrition, premature birth, etc. Factors that create additional behavioral or cognitive deficits or increase the severity of psychological or behavioral symptoms can cloud the overall diagnostic impression by the appearance of symptoms or symptom severity that seems inconsistent with a specific disorder. In addition, protective factors and individual resiliency can reduce symptom severity or expression of a disorder.

The phenomenological aspects of a disorder refer to the characteristic feature and expressions associated with that disorder. For example, the manifestation of

ADHD is typically exemplified by excessive motor activity that is inconsistent with the child's age, difficulty paying attention when the child is not interested in the situation, a failure to follow rules due to poor behavioral control not a lack of understanding of rules or a general disregard for authority, and frequent feelings of frustration. Others frequently experience these children as "lazy," "hyper," "forgetful," "defiant," "messy," etc. Although these are the core features of the disorder, additional behavioral, psychosocial, and emotional issues are frequently present. The difficulty for the clinician is identifying the core symptoms when these symptoms may be present in other relevant clinical conditions (e.g., attention issues in ASD, problems following rules in oppositional defiant disorder (ODD), poor frustration tolerance in depressive disorders). Fortunately, the expression of a symptom and underlying causes of common symptoms can help differentiate core versus comorbidity issues. In ADHD, inattentiveness is not pervasive but situational. Children can attend to highly stimulating environments or when a task is of interest or value to them. In ASD, the inattention is often expressed as a hyperfocus on objects or concepts of interest to them to exclusion of attending to the environment more generally. The expression of a common symptom can vary quite a bit between disorders and can aid in differential diagnosis. The intervention for ADHD inattentiveness might be very different than the intervention in ASD inattentiveness depending on the expression of symptomatology.

Epidemiology and phenomenology help us understand the personal and psychosocial consequences of having a disorder. Children and adolescents diagnosed with ADHD are at greater risk of academic difficulties due to inefficient learning and behavior problems, comorbid psychiatric disorders (e.g., depression and anxiety), substance abuse, injury due to accidents, stressful interpersonal relationships, and long-term employment difficulties (Barkley, 2002). Children diagnosed with language disorder are at risk of social difficulties (Snowling, Bishop, Stothard, Chipchase, & Kaplan, 2006), academic issues (Beitchtman et al., 1996), social phobia (Beitchtman et al., 2001), victimization from peers (Redmond, 2011), behavioral disorder (Lindsay, Dockrell, & Strand, 2007), depression and anxiety (Conti-Ramsden & Botting, 2008), long-term academic struggles, and reduced educational attainment and occupational success (Johnson, Beitchman, & Brownlie, 2010). A failure to recognize the risk for negative social experiences associated with early language problems (which differ from the social problems associated with ASD) can have long-term implications for the child's development. Knowledge of the risk factors posed by each disorder improves the assessment and intervention planning for children with specific disorders. It is clear from epidemiological research that psychiatric and social problems are significant risk factors for children with developmental disorders. The presence of these problems may make it more difficult to identify the primary diagnosis; therefore, the clinician must be very knowledgeable about the differences in expression of these problems across clinical groups.

Planning an assessment requires an understanding of the cognitive deficits associated with specific disorders and how those specific cognitive weaknesses are a risk factor for academic, social, and behavioral difficulties. Cognitive difficulties are, in some cases, a common pathway for observed problems. In ADHD, research suggests that deficits in executive functioning are an important domain of cognitive weakness, specifically difficulties with response inhibition, sustained attention, spatial working memory, and planning (Willcutt, Doyle, Nigg et al., 2005). ADHD is also associated with intra-individual variability in cognitive performance within and across tasks (Castellanos, Sonuga-Barke, Milham, & Tannock, 2006), processing speed deficits (Shanahan et al., 2006), problems with response-selection and working memory (Jacobson et al., 2012), and verbal learning (Cutting, Koth, Mahone, & Denckla, 2003). In addition to specific and general cognitive difficulties, children with ADHD obtain lower scores on standardized measures of reading and math (Frazier, Youngstrom, Glutting, & Watkins, 2007; Loe & Feldman, 2007), and spelling with effect sizes in the moderate range in each domain (Frazier et al., 2007). Deficits in executive functioning are associated with increased grade retention (Biederman et al., 2004) and reduced word reading (Bental & Tirosh, 2007), and working memory and inhibitory control deficits predict math difficulties (Bull & Scerif, 2001).

By comparison, children with reading disorder show deficits in phoneme awareness (Willcutt et al., 2001); naming speed, phonological processing (Wolf & Bowers, 1999); orthographic processing (Berninger, Abbott, Thomson, & Raskin, 2001), morphology (Berninger et al., 2006), word and nonword reading (Castles, Datta, Gayan, & Olson, 1999), processing speed (Shanahan et al., 2006), verbal working memory (Willcutt et al., 2001), and verbal learning (Kramer, Knee, & Delis, 2000). Reading difficulties are a core feature of reading disorder and these occur due to a combination of linguistic, processing speed, memory, and working memory issues. Because there are common cognitive deficits across the groups, the clinician needs to understand how the specific and nonspecific cognitive difficulties relate to differential diagnosis and outcomes. Two children may both present with reading difficulties but the underlying reasons for those problems can be quite different and would warrant very different interventions. Therefore, the clinician must know the cognitive risk factors for mild versus severe reading problems to facilitate diagnosis and treatment planning.

ADHD and reading disorder were used as examples here due to their relatively high rate of comorbidity (Willcutt, Pennington, Olson, Chhabildas, & Hulsander, 2005). There are unique and overlapping cognitive difficulties between the groups; a common finding among developmental disorders. There are also many commonalities among the symptom presentation of children with developmental disorders including academic achievement issues, social difficulties, behavioral problems, and often depression and anxiety. Because there is so much overlap in presentation, clarification of the referral question and obtaining pre-assessment specifics about the nature of academic and behavior issues help the clinician plan for an effective assessment. Parent and teacher rating scales provide some clarification of the nature of the presenting problem. When possible, it is helpful to obtain these measures prior to the evaluation.

Parent and Teacher Ratings

Internet-based assessment platforms such as Pearson's Q-Global™ have simplified the process of obtaining parent and teacher ratings. In the past, to obtain these ratings before the assessment, it was necessary to mail response forms to each person and for him or her to complete and return the forms via standard mail. The process is not efficient and posed problems with lost forms, delayed forms, or even lost forms containing personal information. It was more practical to have the parent complete the rating scales in the office. Teacher ratings could be more directly obtained by psychologists working in the school; however, community and hospital-based clinicians had more difficulty obtaining these important assessments. With Internet-based platforms, it is possible to send both parents and teachers a secure link to complete one or more rating scales. The scales are then ready for immediate scoring and reporting. The improved practicality of obtaining pre-assessment ratings of the child's behavior can help the clinician formulate an assessment plan.

There are numerous rating scales that can be used by clinicians. Most clinicians have a set of scales they use consistently and can easily interpret. In general, there are no recommendations for a specific scale to be used in pre-assessment planning, rather the recommendation is related to the type of information that is useful to obtain at this stage. For pre-assessment planning, a broad range behavior screener such as the *Behavior Assessment Scales for Children*—2nd edition (Reynolds & Kamphaus, 2004) is helpful in capturing a broad dimension of possible problem areas. The behavioral domains that are important in pre-assessment planning include activity level, attention, learning problems, characteristics of social functioning, unusual social or behavior problems, mood disturbance, aggressive behavior, opposition/conduct problems, and problems related to adaptive functioning.

Obtaining information about the specific nature of the child's academic difficulties is also useful assessment planning. Scales such as the Academic Competency Evaluation Scale (ACES: DiPerna & Elliot, 2000) provides more detailed information from the child's teacher regarding the domains (e.g., reading, math, language, and critical thinking) and type of academic problems within the domain, and factors related to school/learning engagement (e.g., study skills, motivation, etc.). This type of scale can identify pervasive from more specific learning difficulties from the teacher's perspective.

Combining information from these types of scales, the examiner is armed with information about the cognitive domains that have the highest probability of contributing to the observed difficulties. This does not indicate that the examiner does not assess other domains of cognitive functioning; rather the examiner uses this information to formulate an assessment plan to insure the appropriate depth of content coverage in specific areas.

An Assessment Plan

The assessment plan helps the examiner organize materials needed for an evaluation or in the case of the Q-interactive™ platform enables the examiner to select a battery of tests for iPad administration. The assessment plan requires the examiner to have knowledge of a variety of tests in a broad domain of cognitive functions; and within each domain the subset of cognitive skills important for differential diagnosis and treatment planning. There are no professionally proscribed sets of domains that should be evaluated, rather the domains assessed should be driven by the research related to specific conditions or in some cases theoretical models can be applied depending on the clinician's experience and training with using those models.

The personal assessment approach recommends a primarily research-based approach for the purposes of preparing for an assessment. The recommended domains of assessment in this approach are language, attention/executive functioning, working memory, academic skills, social cognition/pragmatic language, memory, processing speed, spatial/constructional, reasoning/problem-solving, and sensory-motor. These domains should not be considered as unique, unrelated processes, as there can be considerable overlap in the cognitive processes evaluated across domains, as described more fully in Chapter 5. For example, working memory is a process that crosses almost all domains, as working memory is frequently required to solve most types of problem-solving and information processing. Within a domain such as memory, there can be visual–spatial or verbally mediated tasks and processing speed tests may require fine motor control. The categories are not set up as boundaries but reflect core and secondary domains that impact symptom presentation, outcomes, daily functioning, and differential diagnosis. It is expected that children with diagnosable conditions will likely have low scores in more than one domain and as the severity of the disorder increases so will the number of deficits within and across domains increase.

Assessment of cognitive functions in each category may not be required for any particular child and attempting to assess all areas thoroughly is often not practical from a workflow or child-friendliness perspective. In some cases, it will be important to assess one domain very intensely, with less focus on some domains, and no focus on others. Comprehensive evaluation in this model is a comprehensive evaluation of the presenting problems, discovered prior to and during the assessment, rather than an evaluation of all possible problems. In neuropsychology, this is similar to the concept of a flexible versus standard battery approach. The focus of the evaluation is not strictly cognitive as evaluation of behavioral, emotional, and family functioning is imperative for proper diagnosis and treatment planning. It is beyond the scope of this chapter to present assessment plans for all possible referrals and conditions. Instead, a description of some of the general rules that are based on research and diagnostic criteria are presented here.

Language

Language functioning is a critical ability that impacts multiple aspects of cognitive, academic, social, and behavioral functioning. Language difficulties should be considered in any child referred for academic issues (e.g., slower than expected reading, writing, or math development), social difficulties (e.g., isolation or atypicality), behavior problems (e.g., aggressive or oppositional behavior), or adaptive behavior delays. The nature of the language difficulty may be a moderate to severe general impairment in understanding and using language or in other cases more subtle difficulties with language that are secondary to problems in concrete thinking (e.g., problems understanding figurative language or colloquialisms), social deficits (e.g., pragmatic language deficits), or attention, working memory, or auditory processing difficulties (e.g., does not hear well or has poor memory for communicated information).

The number of measures planned would be influenced by any history of language delay or disorder, any observation of communication difficulties, and reported problems with reading or writing. Additionally, a family history of language or learning disabilities or ASD would warrant at a least an initial plan for intensive language assessment. Due to the importance of this ability domain, a screening for language issues should be a part of all evaluations. For that purpose, at least two measures from the WISC-V Verbal Comprehension index should be included in most evaluations. These measures are aimed at complex aspects of language use and are rarely performed well by children with significant language impairment (Holdnack, Weiss, & Entwistle, 2006), though children with more subtle language deficits may do well or inconsistently across these measures. If the child has a significant history of language delay or diagnosis of a language disorder, a comprehensive assessment of language functioning is indicated, whereas children presenting with only reading or writing problems in the absence of any history of language delays need a more focused evaluation of phonology and morphology. Children referred for attention or working memory problems or oppositional behavior can be evaluated with measures of sentence repetition and ability to follow multistep commands to identify or rule out impact of linguistic contributions to these observed behaviors.

A large number of published tests of language functioning exist and it is beyond the scope of this chapter to present all possible selections. Each clinician will develop a set of tools that meets their needs and should identify tests that cover the important linguistic domains that help with differential diagnosis, targeting interventions, and informing about potential outcomes (e.g., probability or reading, social problems, etc.). Not all language tests are developed for the same purpose; subsequently their content will vary considerably. Many language tests are affected by more than one linguistic or cognitive process. When deciding to use specific language measures, it is essential to determine the intended population of children the test was designed for evaluating (i.e., language disorder, learning disabled, or severe aphasia), as the content and cognitive processes of the tasks will vary depending on proposed use. This section briefly categorizes subtests from the CELF-V (Wiig, Semel & Secord, 2013), NEPSY-II, Wechsler Individual Achievement Test—3rd) (Wechsler, 2012), Delis–Kaplan Executive Functioning Scale (D-KEFS) (Delis, Kaplan, & Kramer, 2001), Process Assessment of the Learner-Reading and Writing—2nd edition (PAL-RW) (Berninger, 2007), Peabody Picture Vocabulary Test—3rd edition (PPVT-III) (Dunn & Dunn, 2007), Kaufmann Test of Educational Achievement-III (KTEA) (Kaufman & Kaufman, 2014), and Boston Naming Test (BNT) (Goodglass, Kaplan, Weintraub, & Siegel, 2001) into specific language functions. Profiling of language scores can help decision-making regarding the severity of language deficits, the nature of the language problems, and diagnostic considerations.

1. Phonological decoding
   WIAT-II: Pseudoword Decoding, Word Reading
   PAL-RW: Pseudoword Decoding
   KTEA-III: Nonsense Word Decoding
   KTEA-III: Letter and Word Recognition
2. Phonemic/phonological awareness/processing
   NEPSY-II: Phonological Processing
   DAS-II: Phonological Processing
   PAL-RW: Rimes, Phonemes, Syllables, Rhyming
   WIAT-III: Early Reading Skills
   KTEA-III: Phonological Processing
3. Morphology
   PAL-RW: Are They Related? Does It Fit? Morphological Decoding Fluency
4. Rapid automatic naming
   NEPSY: Speeded Naming
   PAL-RW: Rapid Automatic Naming, Rapid Automatic Switching
   WISC-V: Naming Speed Literacy
   WISC-V: Naming Speed Quantity
   DAS-II: Rapid Naming
5. Semantic knowledge
   WISC-V: Vocabulary
   DAS-II: Word Definition
   PPVT-III
   KTEA-III: Reading Vocabulary
6. Relational semantic knowledge
   CELF-V: Word Classes
   WISC-V: Similarities
7. Confrontation naming
   BNT
8. Ability to follow multistep commands
   NEPSY-II: Comprehension of Instruction
   CELF-V: Following Directions

9. Syntactic knowledge
   CELF-V: Linguistic Concepts, Word Structure, Sentence Assembly
   PAL-RW: Sentence Structure
10. Comprehending increasingly complex semantics and syntax
    CELF-V: Sentence Comprehension, Understanding Paragraphs, Semantic Relationships
    WIAT-III: Listening Comprehension
    KTEA-III: Listening Comprehension
11. Language production
    CELF-V: Formulated Sentences (controlled production requires good control of semantic and syntactic structure)
    CELF-V: Sentence Assembly (controlled production with syntactic structures)
    WIAT-III: Oral Expression (production of organized, cohesive language)
    NEPSY-II: Word Generation Initial Letter (access to word knowledge using orthographic prompts)
    NEPSY-II: Word Generation Semantic (access to word knowledge using semantic prompts)
    D-KEFS: Letter Fluency (access to word knowledge using orthographic prompts)
    D-KEFS: Semantic Fluency (access to word knowledge using semantic prompts)
    KTEA-III: Associational Fluency
    KTEA-III: Oral Expression
12. Flexibility in language production and comprehension
    CELF-IV: Sentence Assembly (requires flexible use of syntax and semantics)
    D-KEFS: Semantic Switching (requires mental switching between semantic categories)
    WISC-V: Comprehension (requires abstraction and flexibility)
13. Repetition of language
    NEPSY: Sentence Repetition, Word List Interference
    CELF-V: Recalling Sentences

Attention/Executive Functioning

There are a variety of abilities that are subsumed under the concept of attention. For the purposes of this chapter, the focus will be on sustained attention, which is the ability to maintain attention on an intrinsically uninteresting task for an extended period of time. Executive functions refer to a broad range of cognitive abilities that enable individuals to effectively manage his or her behavior and regulate the performance of other cognitive abilities. These skills include but are not limited to: inhibitory control, cognitive flexibility, behavioral productivity, maintenance of cognitive set, self-monitoring, planning, and abstract reasoning. Inhibitory control is the ability to stop a pre-potent, or automatic thought, behavior, or emotion (e.g., overlearned, stimulus bound, emotional reaction, etc.) in order to consider and apply a better (e.g., behaviorally or emotionally appropriate or a correct versus incorrect response to a problem) response to a situation, problem, or cognitive process. Cognitive flexibility is the capacity to think about a problem in more than one way. It is the ability to change a behavior in consideration of changes in the environment (adaptive) or to see different bits of information in a single stimulus (abstraction). Behavioral productivity refers to the process by which an individual is able to initiate and maintain problem-solving behavior. Maintenance of cognitive set refers to the ability to understand and apply the rules of a task or situation and the ability to monitor his or her behavior to avoid violating the rules. Planning is a process by which the individual identifies the necessary steps to reach a goal and maintains their behavior toward the goal. Abstract reasoning is the ability to understand a stimulus beyond its obvious, physical properties, and the ability to see a problem beyond the immediate constraints. These cognitive skills related to the efficiency of problem-solving, the adaptability of the individual, the capacity to regulate and control one's behavior, and the ability to solve complex problems.

Attention and executive function deficits are an important aspect of the expression of many neurodevelopmental disorders. Children diagnosed with ADHD show mild to moderate difficulties with inhibitory control and planning (Corbett, Constantine, Hendren, Rocke, & Ozonoff, 2009; Willcutt et al., 2005) and sustained attention; autistic children show difficulties with planning (Geurts, Verté, Oosterlaan, Roeyers, & Sergeant, 2004), cognitive flexibility (Corbett et al., 2009; Geurts et al., 2003), and sustained attention and inhibitory control (Corbett et al., 2009); and math disability is associated with inhibitory regulation (Geary, 2004). Both autism and Asperger's syndrome show some executive functioning deficits (Verté, Geurts, Roeyers, Oosterlaan, & Sergeant, 2006). ODD and conduct disorder (CD) are not necessarily associated with executive functioning impairments, but given the high rate of comorbidity with ADHD, children with ODD or CD may show executive function deficits similar to children with ADHD (Geurts et al., 2004). Cognitive flexibility and inhibitory control deficits are associated with increased repetitive and restrictive behaviors in autistic children (Lopez, Lincoln, Ozonoff, & Lai, 2005). Inhibitory control problems are associated with poor math functioning (Bull & Scerif, 2001) and to academic performance in general (Bull, Espy, & Wiebe, 2008). Inhibitory control deficits may indirectly influence the potential aggressive behaviors (Hoaken, Shaughnessy, & Pihl, 2003). The behavioral manifestations associated with attention and executive functioning problems are off-task behaviors, distractibility, impulsivity, poor frustration tolerance, disorganization, rigid behavior or thinking, difficulty adapting to new situations or changes in routine, concrete thinking, aggressiveness, and high rates of errors in school work due to working too quickly or making mental mistakes. These behaviors may, incorrectly, be attributed to personality style or "willfulness" rather than due to cognitive limitations.

Pre-assessment information in which behavior control problems or attention problems are present (i.e., not necessarily primary) indicates that one or more measures of executive functioning should be part of the assessment plan. Academic difficulties due to sloppy, disorganized work, or failure to automatize basic skills (e.g., simple calculation skills, as opposed to difficulties learning academic concepts or procedures (e.g., decoding procedures for reading words)), also indicates that one or more executive functioning measures should be employed. For children showing attention problems, measures of sustained attention should be considered. On rating scales, elevations on measures of activity, impulsivity, adaptability, social difficulties, aggressive or explosive behaviors, poor study skills, and oppositional or conduct-related problems warrants a plan to use executive functioning measures. *Next to language functioning, deficits in attention and executive functioning may be the most common causes of problems in academic achievement and psychosocial functioning.*

A large number of published tests of executive functioning exist. However, few of these tests have large stratified normative samples. Executive functioning measures vary in content and method from one another. They often have low correlation with each other. It is important to recognize that measures that purport to measure similar constructs can give very different results. In the case of executive functioning, the rules of the task are very important. The more rules to follow, the greater the amount of self-monitoring and cognitive control required to complete the task. This section briefly categorizes subtests from the D-KEFS, NEPSY-II, California Verbal Learning Test for Children (CVLT-C: Delis, Kramer, Kaplan, & Ober, 1994), and the Wisconsin Card Sorting Test (WCST: Heaton, Chelune, Talley, Kay, & Curtiss, 1993) into general categories.

1. Verbal productivity
   D-KEFS: Verbal Fluency
   NEPSY-II: Word Generation
2. Visual productivity
   D-KEFS: Design Fluency
   NEPSY-II: Design Fluency
3. Conceptual productivity
   D-KEFS: Card Sorting
   NEPSY-II: Animal Sorting
4. Cognitive flexibility
   D-KEFS: Trail-Making Switching
   D-KEFS: Design Fluency Switching
   D-KEFS: Verbal Fluency Category Switching
   D-KEFS: Color–Word Interference Switching
   D-KEFS: Sorting Test
   NEPSY-II: Card Sorting
   Wisconsin Card Sorting Test (particularly when assessing for emotional response and frustration tolerance)
   CELF-IV: Sentence Assembly

5. Inhibitory control
   NEPSY-II: Inhibition
   D-KEFS: Color–Word Interference Test
6. Planning
   D-KEFS: Tower Test
7. Organization
   CVLT-C: Cluster Scores
8. Abstract/conceptual reasoning
   WISC-V: Matrix Reasoning
   WISC-V: Similarities
   D-KEFS: Card Sorting
   D-KEFS: 20 Questions
   D-KEFS: Proverbs
   NEPSY-II: Card Sorting
9. Self-monitoring and cognitive control
   D-KEFS: Trail Making
   D-KEFS: Verbal Fluency
   D-KEFS: Design Fluency
   D-KEFS: Color–Word Interference
   D-KEFS: Sorting Test
   D-KEFS: Tower Test
   CVLT-C (error scores)
   Wisconsin Card Sorting Test
10. Attention: sustained
    NEPSY-II: Auditory Attention and Response Set
11. Attention: registration
    DAS-II: Digits Forward
    WISC-V: Digits Forward
12. Attention: visual scanning
    WISC-V: Cancellation
    D-KEFS: Trail-Making Test Visual Scanning

Working Memory

Working memory is often associated with attention and executive functioning skills. Like attention and executive functions, working memory has a significant influence in cognitive efficiency, learning, and academic performance. In Baddeley's model (2009, 2012) of working memory, there are three main functional components: the phonological loop, visual sketchpad, and the central executive. This system interacts with long-term memory in the episodic buffer to retrieve previously learned information needed for problem-solving and to help process new information for long-term storage. The phonological loop keeps auditory information active in consciousness for the purpose of immediate problem-solving. The visual sketchpad allows people to keep visual images and spatial information active in the mind for problem-solving. The central executive component allocates cognitive resources, focuses attention that is needed to solve problems, and controls cognitive interference (Baddeley, 2012; Baddeley, Eysenck, & Anderson, 2009). This top-down executive attention is the central mechanism common to working memory functions across both the auditory and visual domains, as described more fully in Chapter 5. Working memory has been identified as a key cognitive function in learning, and deficits in working memory problems often contribute to development of learning disabilities and are often found in many neurodevelopmental disorders.

A brief review of the research shows that working memory has an impact on learning, and deficits in working memory are often found in children with learning disabilities. Verbal working memory longitudinally predicts language functioning whereas spatial working memory predicts math and language test performance in school children (Gathercole, Pickering, Knight, & Stegmann, 2004; St Clair-Thompson & Gathercole, 2006) and is moderately related to cognitive functioning in general (Ackerman, Beier, & Boyle, 2005). Children diagnosed with ADHD (Martinussen, Hayden, Hogg-Johnson, & Tannock, 2005) or math (McLean & Hitch, 1999) show greater deficits in spatial and executive components of working memory than in verbal working memory. Children diagnosed with dyslexia show deficits on verbal working memory measures and not spatial working memory (Jeffries & Everatt, 2004). Reading comprehension deficits are also associated with verbal working memory, particularly those having a high attention load (Carretti, Borella, Cornoldi, & De Beni, 2009). The role of working memory in ASD is less clear though some studies have found visual–spatial but not verbal working memory deficits in children with ASD (Steele, Minshew, Luna, & Sweeney, 2007; Williams, Goldstein, & Minshew, 2006). Working memory difficulties are commonly associated with learning difficulties and developmental disorders.

Clinicians will likely use one or more working memory measures in most clinical evaluations. In any case where a child is referred for attention or learning problems, difficulties in working memory will be suspected and need to be assessed. On parent and teacher rating scales, high scores on attention problems or academic issues will indicate that working memory measures should administered.

A number of working memory measures are available as subtests within larger batteries. These tests typically measure components of the phonological loop, visuospatial-sketchpad, and central executive. This section briefly categorizes subtests from the WISC-V and Integrated, NEPSY-II, CELF-V, Children's Memory Scales (CMS: Cohen, 1997) into general working memory categories.

1. Verbal Working Memory
   WISC-V: Digit Span
   WISC-V: Arithmetic
   DAS-II: Recall of Digits Backward
   DAS-II: Recall of Sequential Order

NEPSY-II: Word List Interference Repetition
NEPSY-II: Sentence Repetition
CELF-V: Sentence Repetition
CMS: Sequences
2. Visual Working Memory
WISC-V: Picture Span
WISC-V Integrated: Spatial Span
CMS: Picture Locations
3. Central Executive
NEPSY-II: Word List Interference Test Recall

Academic Skills

Academic performance issues are a common problem in children referred for psychological evaluation. Even in cases where behavioral regulation or emotional problems is the primary concern, academic issues are often a secondary or co-primary area of difficulty. All psychological assessments of children are likely to include at least two basic academic measures such as word reading and math computations. Additional measures of academic functioning are included when academic performance is a primary concern of the referral.

A number of standardized academic achievement batteries are available. These tests typically measure multiple reading, math, and writing skills. This section briefly categorizes academic achievement measures from the WIAT-III and Kaufmann Test of Educational Achievement-III (KTEA).

1. Word Reading
WIAT-III: Word Reading
KTEA-III: Letter & Word Recognition
2. Reading Comprehension
WIAT-III: Reading Comprehension
KTEA-III: Reading Comprehension
3. Reading Fluency
WIAT-III: Oral Reading Fluency
KTEA-III: Silent Reading Fluency
4. Math Computations
WIAT-III: Numerical Operations
KTEA-III: Math Computation
5. Math Reasoning
WIAT-III: Math Problem Solving
KTEA-III: Math Concepts & Applications
6. Math Fluency
WIAT-III: Math Fluency Addition, Subtraction, Multiplication
KTEA-III: Math Fluency

7. Spelling
   WIAT-III: Spelling
   KTEA-III: Spelling
8. Written Expression
   WIAT-III: Essay Composition
   KTEA-III: Written Expression

Social Cognition/Pragmatic Language Skills

Social cognition refers to a broad spectrum of concepts and measures. In this section, it refers to the ability to understand emotional expressions from facial expressions or vocal intonation, discriminate and recognize faces, remember a face/name association, and understand the perspective of another person. Pragmatic language refer to the skills needed for social communication such as appropriate use of gestures and body language, ability to track and stay on topic in a conversation, and metalinguistic aspects of language. Impairments in social cognition and pragmatic language skills are most often associated with ASD; however, children diagnosed with other neurodevelopmental conditions may experience difficulties in one or more areas of social information processing.

Research studies show that children diagnosed with autism show impairments in face recognition from an early age (Dawson et al., 2002) and brain activation is similar to processing objects rather than faces (Schultz et al., 2000). When viewing social scenes, children with ASD tend to focus on the mouth, body, or an object that is negatively associated with social competence (Klin, Jones, Schultz, Volkmar, & Cohen, 2002). ASD is associated with reduced ability to understand facial expressions of emotion (Kuusikko et al., 2009) with general deficits in face perception and memory (Weigelt, Koldewyn, & Kanwisher, 2012). Compared to typically developing children, individuals diagnosed with ASD also fail to activate expected brain regions during prosody recognition (Wang, Lee, Sigman, & Dapretto, 2007), have difficulties with language pragmatics (Wilkinson, 1998), and do not understand the perspective of others (e.g., theory of mind; Baron-Cohen, 2001). Individuals with antisocial tendencies show deficits in processing facial expressions of fear (Marsh & Blair, 2008) and adolescents diagnosed with conduct disorder show decreased ability to recognize specific emotions (Fairchild, van Goozen, Calder, Stollery, & Goodyer, 2009). Despite their importance in the development of social skills, face processing, emotion recognition, and language pragmatics are not as well researched in developmental disorders compared to other domains of cognition. Deficits in these domains are often associated with ASD and to a lesser degree conduct-related problems.

The use of face processing, theory of mind, emotion recognition, or language pragmatics should be considered when the referral question is directly related to questions of autism. Also, in cases where there are clear social difficulties, either aggression or isolation. On parent or teacher ratings, elevations on the atypicality scale, aggression, or poor social skills would warrant investigation of social cognitive abilities. There are fewer options available for assessing this cognitive domain; however, subtests from the NEPSY-II, CMS, CELF-V, and CELF-V metalinguistic batteries can be helpful.

1. Theory of Mind
   NEPSY-II: Theory of Mind
2. Face Recognition
   NEPSY-II: Face Memory
   CMS: Memory for Faces
3. Facial Affect Recognition
   NEPSY-II: Affect Recognition
4. Language Pragmatics
   CELF-V: Pragmatics Profile
5. Metalinguistics
   CELF-V: Metalinguistics

Memory

Memory functioning refers to intentional (explicit) or unintentional (implicit) acquisition of information of long-term storage and access. This differs from working memory functions, which involve maintaining focus and manipulating information in active short-term storage. Most clinical memory measures evaluate the child's or adolescent's ability to explicitly store and retrieve verbal and visual information from long-term memory. Key concepts include multi-trial versus single-trial learning, encoding versus retrieval, visual versus verbal, and memory errors (Cohen, 1997). Pure amnesia is a rare phenomenon in neurodevelopmental disorders. There are subtle memory difficulties, which can contribute to academic difficulties. ADHD is associated with subtle deficits in single- and multi-trial learning (Muir-Broaddus, Rosenstein, Medina, & Soderberg, 2002). Children with reading disorder (Kramer et al., 2000) and those with language disorder (Shear, Tallal, & Delis, 1992) show reduced learning rate compared to controls.

The decision to use additional memory measures is more difficult to determine based on psychosocial history or behavioral reports from teachers and parents. Since severe memory disorders are associated with brain injury and neurological conditions more than specific developmental disorders, and reports of poor memory functioning by parents and teachers often reflect difficulties with working memory and prospective memory, it may be difficult to determine which memory measures to use for academic or behavioral referrals. Forgetfulness is often due to immediate mental operations, but in many of these children they remember information adequately or perhaps very well. Prospective memory is a memory difficulty associated with forgetting to do things at a future time, such as remembering that a report is due in 2 weeks.

This is a memory skill but it is often not assessed in memory batteries. When memory problems exist, they often occur in the context of other impaired cognitive skills, such as language and executive functioning. And, memory problems are often masked by these other cognitive difficulties or are attributed to the other cognitive impairments. While co-occurring with other processing deficits, the presence of memory problems should not be ignored. Rather, observed memory deficits likely contribute to the child's difficulty developing their knowledge base and general academic skills.

When the psychosocial history of the child is not well known, teacher observations may be helpful; specifically, children that appear to lose acquired knowledge after they have gained a new skill appear to remember information only when prompted or provided a cue, or perhaps have inconsistent memory functioning. An observation of "forgetfulness" can implicate a number of cognitive problems, so asking more direct questions about information recall is important. Teacher reports may be insufficient for identifying memory problems, so the clinician will need to consider including additional memory-based observations and test results.

The clinician has a variety of options for measuring memory functioning using standardized batteries. There is considerable overlap between many memory tests although variations in content and administration rules impact the skills that are being measured. For example, there are many list learning tasks, such as the California Verbal Learning Test—Children's Version, NEPSY-II—List Learning Subtests, CMS—List Learning subtest, and Wide Range Assessment of Memory and Learning—List Learning subtest. The subtests vary considerably in the details of administration, such as using full reminding versus selective reminding, organization of content by semantic category, interference trials, and delayed free, cued, and recognition trials. There are more memory batteries available than can be reported here, so a brief list is reviewed by category: Children's Memory Scale (Cohen, 1997), NEPSY Memory subtests (NEPSY-II: Korkman, Kirk, & Kemp, 2007), California Verbal Learning Test—Children's Edition (CVLT: Delis et al., 1994), and the Wide Range Assessment of Memory and Learning—2nd edition (Sheslow & Adams, 2003).

1. Memory for organized verbal information
   CMS: Stories
   NEPSY-II: Story Memory
   WRAML-II: Story Memory
2. Verbal-associative learning (effects of repeated exposure) and memory
   CMS: Word Pairs
3. Rote verbal learning (repeated exposure) and memory
   CMS: List Learning
   CVLT-C
   NEPSY: List Learning
   WRAML-II: List Learning

4. Verbal encoding versus retrieval
   CMS
   CVLT-C
5. Encoding strategy and organization
   CVLT-C
6. Interference effects (proactive and retroactive)
   CVLT-C
7. Verbal recall, self-monitoring control/accuracy of recall, and recognition (intrusions/perseverations/false positives)
   CVLT-C
   CMS
   NEPSY
8. Visual–spatial memory and learning
   DAS-II: Recall of Designs
   CMS: Dots
   WRAML: Design and Picture Memory
   NEPSY-II: Design Memory
9. Memory for faces
   CMS
   NEPSY-II
10. Associative verbal–visual memory
    WISC-V: Symbol Translation
    CMS: Family Pictures
    WRAML: Sound Symbol
    NEPSY-II: Memory for Names

Processing Speed

Processing speed is the ability to identify, discriminate, integrate, make a decision about information, and to respond to visual and verbal information. Response processes for speeded tests are typically motoric (e.g., written response, check a response, etc.) or oral (e.g., saying an object's name, reading numbers or letters aloud). Processing speed measures provide an estimation of how efficiently a child can perform basic, overlearned tasks or tasks that require processing of novel information. These tests usually do not assess higher-level thinking; however, they frequently require some degree of simple decision-making. Some anxious children may perform slowly on such tasks because of a lack of confidence or certainty in decision-making. Generally, performance on these tests reflects how well (speed and accuracy) the examinee can perform a specific procedure (e.g., simple math calculation, naming, visual identification, etc.), which can indicate the automaticity of that process, accessibility to that information, efficiency of early stages of information processing (e.g., visual or auditory discrimination), and speed of decision-making.

Processing speed deficits have been associated with autism (Mayes & Calhoun, 2007), reading disorder (Shanahan et al., 2006), and ADHD (Mayes &

Calhoun, 2007; Shanahan et al., 2006) but not anxiety, depression, or oppositional defiant disorder (Mayes & Calhoun, 2007). Processing speed is often the
lowest or one of the lowest index scores on the Wechsler intelligence scales
for children in neurological and neurodevelopmental disorders with the exception of intellectual disability (Calhoun & Mayes, 2005; Wechsler, 2003, 2014).
Rapid naming tests measure aspect of visual–verbal association and automaticity of semantic retrieval (Denckla & Cutting, 1999) and poor performance
on these tasks is associated with learning impairments (Waber, Wolff, Forbes
et al., 2000). Slow performance on rapid automatic naming tasks is often associated with reading (Wolf & Bowers, 1999) but not math disorder (Willburger,
Fussenegger, Moll, Wood, & Lander, 2008). Examinees diagnosed with ADHD
without a reading disorder may show slower performance on color naming tasks
compared to controls and similar to children with reading disorder (Tannock,
Martinussen, & Frijters, 2000); however, children with reading disorder are
slower and make more errors on letter and number naming than do ADHD
children (Semrud-Clikeman, Guy, Griffin, & Hynd, 2000). Processing speed as
measured by visual–perceptual/motor tasks are sensitive to many clinical conditions while rapid automatic naming tasks are more specifically associated reading and learning difficulties.

Because of their overall sensitivity to clinical conditions, the WISC-V processing speed subtests may be used on a routine basis. These tests work like a
doctor's thermometer or blood pressure monitor. A positive sign suggests there
may be a disorder present but the results require further testing to identify the
nature of the problem. The rapid automatic naming tasks are typically used
when there is a question related to a learning problem, particularly if a reading
disorder is suspected. These will be used in many evaluations due to the commonality of academic problems in referred populations.

Rapid automatic naming tasks can be found on a number of test batteries
including the NEPSY-II, PAL-II, and KTEA-III.

Visual–Spatial and Fluid Reasoning

Visual and spatial reasoning tasks cover a variety of measures and cognitive
processes. There are very few developmental disorders in which a deficit in
visual–spatial reasoning is a primary deficit; however, difficulties in this domain
can be found in many clinical conditions. Tasks identified as fluid reasoning
measure, though not always visual in nature, are typically based on using novel
visual information to solve a complex task. Spatial tasks can involve mental
construction, manipulation, rotation of objects in working memory, and ability
to identify angles. Constructional tasks typically require the examinee to make a
design based on a model (e.g., drawing or block constructions) or from memory.

Clinical research-related visual processes are not as developed as other
cognitive domains. Studies evaluating spatial and visual functioning in children and adolescents with clinical disorders often focus on working memory

component rather than reasoning. Studies indicate that some children diagnosed with ADHD have lower performance than typically developing controls on fluid reasoning tasks due to a fast but inaccurate problem-solving approach (Tamm & Juranek, 2012) or due to inattention (Semrud-Clikeman, 2012). Like fluid reasoning, performance on visual–spatial tasks was negatively affected by inattention in children with ADHD (Semrud-Clikeman, 2012). Spatial processing deficits have been also associated with math disorder (Osmon, Smerz, Braun, & Plambeck, 2006). Low scores on fluid reasoning measures correlate with lower scores on math reasoning tests but were not related to computational skills in children with math disorder (Proctor, Floyd, & Shaver, 2005). In contrast to the math disorder findings, fluid reasoning has been found to be a cognitive strength in some children diagnosed with ASD (Hayashi, Kato, Igarashi, & Kashima, 2008; Soulières et al., 2009). Aspects of visual–perceptual and visual–spatial processing have also been identified as cognitive strengths for some children with ASD (Caron, Mottron Rainville, & Chouinard, 2004; Falter, Plaisted, & Davis, 2008). Research suggests that some children with developmental disorders may have diminished abilities on fluid and spatial reasoning tasks, which may put them at risk for math difficulties. Among children with ASD, these types of tasks may be relatively intact or a cognitive strength.

A referral question would rarely specify a need for visual–spatial, visual–perceptual, or fluid reasoning tasks to be administered. In clinical questions related to potential global impairments in cognitive functioning (e.g., intellectual disability), questions specifically related to understanding and problem-solving (e.g., Reading Comprehension and Math Reasoning), and questions regarding math functioning more generally would indicate the use of one or more visual processing measures. Also, in children where significant language or social difficulties are a primary concern, visual measures can be helpful in identifying relative strengths in reasoning or other aspects of visual processing.

The clinician has a variety of options for measuring visual perceptual and fluid reasoning skills. The WISC-V, DAS-II (Elliot, 2007) and NEPSY-II batteries have various measures of visual perceptual and reasoning tests.

1. Fluid Reasoning
   WISC-V: Matrix Reasoning
   WISC-V: Figure Weights
   DAS-II: Matrices
   DAS-II: Sequential and Quantitative Reasoning
2. Quantitative Reasoning
   WISC-V: Figure Weights
   DAS-II: Sequential and Quantitative Reasoning
3. Visual–Constructional (Spatial and Details)
   WISC-V: Block Design
   WISC-V: Visual Puzzles
   DAS-II: Pattern Construction

NEPSY-II: Design Copying
NEPSY-II: Block Construction
4. Visual–Spatial
NEPSY-II: Arrows
NEPSY-II: Geometric Puzzles
5. Visual–Details
NEPSY-II: Picture Puzzles

Sensory and Motor Tests

Sensory and motor assessment is indicated for children with obvious fine or gross motor processing deficits, and writing difficulties, referrals specifically related to developmental coordination disorder or for determining if occupational therapy services are indicated. Gross and fine motor testing can be accomplished using the Bruininks-Oseretsky Test of Motor Proficiency, Second Edition (BOT-2: Bruininks & Bruininks, 2005). On NEPSY-II, fine motor speed, motor coordination, motor imitation, and visuo-motor speed and integration are assessed with the Finger-Tip Tapping, Manual Motor Series Imitating Hand Positions, and Visuomotor Precision subtests. The PAL-II provides measures of sensory discrimination with the Finger Recognition subtest.

Research studies have identified fine motor problems in children diagnosed with ADHD (Meyer & Sagvolden, 2006; Pitcher, Piek, & Hay, 2003) and gross motor problems in children with ADHD-combined type (Piek, Pitcher, & Hay, 1999). Severity of inattention and impulsivity symptoms is associated with more fine and gross motor deficits (Tseng, Henderson, Chow, & Yao, 2004). Motor control issues in ADHD are more pronounced in left versus right hand (Rommelse et al., 2007). ADHD children with comorbid disorders are more likely to exhibit motor difficulties than those with ADHD only (Kooistra, Crawford, Dewey, Cantell, & Kaplan, 2005). Like ADHD, fine and gross motor difficulties or motor delays co-occur at a higher rate in children with language impairment (Bishop, 2002; Hill, 2001) and in ASD (Jansiewicz et al., 2006; Noterdaeme, Wriedt, & Höhne, 2010) compared to the general population. There is little research linking reading and math disorders to fine or gross motor deficits; though motor issues can occur independently. Motor delays or deficits commonly co-occur in children with developmental disorders.

Referral questions specifically focusing on fine or gross motor delays are not typical in psychological evaluations, as these referral questions are typical completed by occupational therapists. However, given the high rate of comorbidity between developmental disorders and motor problems, psychologists will often include drawing tasks (e.g., design copying) to screen for fine motor problems. In pre-assessment planning, if there is information from the parent or teacher that this is a concern (e.g., sloppy handwriting, clumsiness, accident prone, etc.), then planning to administer one or more motor measures is recommended. If there are no reports of any motor issues, then it is recommended to use a single screening test such as NEPSY-II: Visuomotor Integration or Design Copying subtests.

Example of Pre-Assessment Planning

On the surface, it would appear that developing an assessment plan prior to interviewing and interacting with the child or adolescent is contrary to the notion of a personalized assessment. Historical data, parent and teacher reports of concerns and symptoms, and referral information provide a probabilistic set of potential cognitive strengths and weaknesses. Without any *a priori* information, the clinician has to assume the child/adolescent could have any disorder from transient stress-related emotional difficulties with no cognitive deficits to intellectual deficits with significant comorbid psychiatric symptoms. The assessment plan is not designed to be a sum total of measures to be administered but is simply a starting point from which the clinician may start ruling in or out cognitive difficulties and possible diagnoses. The clinician can organize the materials from multiple batteries or set up an electronic battery via Q-interactive that has the tests that will be required. If additional information is gathered during the parent/child interview, the assessment may be modified prior to initiating the assessment.

Background

Marcus Smith, a 10-year-old, African-American male, is referred for psychoeducational evaluation from his 4th grade teacher Ms. W. The initial referral question is academic difficulties. Further discussion with the teacher revealed that Marcus, a friendly, sociable boy, was struggling with math, particularly math computations. Reading and writing skills were not a primary concern. Ms. W. also reported concerns regarding off-task behavior, inattentiveness, and over-talkativeness. No obvious social difficulties were reported. Ms. W. completed the ACES (a rating scale that assesses specific areas of academic strengths and weaknesses) and BASC-II (a rating scale designed to identify behavioral difficulties) teacher rating scales. On the ACES, Marcus was rated as below grade level for math only. Specifically, items identifying computation, mental math, breaking down complex problems, and problem-solving were identified as weaknesses. Additional difficulties were reported for reading fluency, spelling, investigating problems, and developing solutions to problems, though the index-level scores for reading/language and critical thinking were at grade level. Academic enabler scores indicated low interpersonal skills related to the learning process, low academic motivation, and underdeveloped study skills. Specific concerns related to listening, following classroom rules, working effectively in groups, managing frustration, motivation to learn, quality of classroom work, task persistence, goal-orientation, staying on task, completing homework, correcting own work, completing work on time, preparing for class, and paying attention in class.

The BASC-II teacher rating showed elevations on attention and learning problems and to a lesser extent hyperactivity. Social skills were not identified as being problematic indicating that the social issues noted on the ACES were restricted to those related to academic functioning. Additionally, conduct-related problems were not identified again suggesting that compliance issues are specific to classroom learning situations rather than a general problem with oppositional behavior. Study skills were identified as an area of concern consistent with the ACES scale. Attention, learning problems, and study skills appear to be the core issues.

Prior to the evaluation, Marcus's mother Mrs. Smith completed the BASC-II parent rating form. On the parent rating form there were significant elevations on study skills and learning problems, with slight elevations on attention, anxiety, and depression. No compliance or social skills issues were identified. Marcus completed the BASC-II self-report form. Marcus reported greater than average negative attitudes towards school and teachers. He feels that he is not in control of his life, feels inadequate, and experiences feelings of anxiety and depression. Marcus did not report problems with attention or hyperactivity or social interactions.

Based on the pre-referral information, the differential diagnostic considerations are math disorder, ADHD inattentive type, and mood disorder. The academic skills in question are math computations and reasoning with some additional concerns regarding reading fluency, spelling, and problem-solving. The cognitive abilities associated with the academic and behavioral concerns are sustained attention, working memory, verbal comprehension, processing speed, executive functioning particularly inhibitory control and self-monitoring, automatic quantity naming, spatial processing, and fluid/quantitative reasoning.

The Assessment Plan

Based on the information acquired from Marcus's teacher and mother, the psychologist determined that the assessment plan should evaluate cognitive skills associated with ADHD, math disorder, mood disorder, and to a lesser degree word reading. She decided not to pursue testing in other areas because she considered the probability of other disorders such as intellectual deficiency, autism, conduct disorder, etc. to be quite low given the reported academic, social, and behavioral issues. In consideration of the observed academic difficulties and the diagnostic probabilities, she selected measures of executive functioning, attention, working memory, fluid/quantitative reasoning, spatial processing, specific language measures, processing speed, and math and word reading skills. Additional assessment of depression and anxiety during the interview and through self-reports is also indicated.

For this evaluation, the following tests were included as part of the initial assessment plan: NEPSY-II Inhibition, Auditory Attention and Response Set, Word List Interference, Speeded Naming, Phonological Processing; WISC-V

Vocabulary, Similarities, Digit Span, Figure Weights, Matrix Reasoning, Block Design, Coding; CELF-V Following Directions; WISC-IV Integrated Spatial Span; WIAT-III Numerical Operations, Math Problem Solving, Math Fluency, Word Reading, and Spelling; and Beck Youth Scales. These measures provide an *estimation* of executive functioning, attention, language, academic, visual–perceptual, reasoning, and processing speed abilities. They also provide an estimation of Full Scale Intelligence Quotient, if that is required, even though the probability of intellectual disability is quite low.

These measures provide an overview of cognitive processes that may influence math performance, attention, and emotional issues. However, these are not necessarily the only tests that will be administered. During the clinical interview with the parent and child, additional concerns may be uncovered or observations of the child may point to other cognitive issues (e.g., gaze aversion, motor signs, language use/comprehension) and indicate evaluation of other cognitive skills (e.g., social perception, motor, or general language assessment) should be considered. During the assessment, the examiner uses obtained scores on specific measures to determine if additional measures within that domain or a different cognitive domain may be required. This process is facilitated when the Q-interactive platform is used as it gives immediate normative results as the tests are administered; however, this process can also be completed with examiner on-the-fly scoring and performance observations.

On-the-Fly Adjustments to the Assessment

The heart of the personalized assessment approach is the tailoring of the overall assessment to the specific needs of the individual child. The pre-assessment and clinical interview work provide only a direction based on probabilities related to reported symptoms, referral question, and academic issues; clinical research; and the perception of individuals that know the child. However, the individual strengths and weaknesses for each child are manifest during the actual assessment process. It is only the psychological assessment process in which the child's symptoms and issues can be invoked. Clinical interviews, teacher consultations, and family reports often hint at but do not get at the underlying cognitive issues. In the assessment process, the child is challenged both cognitively and emotionally and often the emotional response to the testing process is as telling as the actual test performance.

Completing on-the-fly adjustments during testing requires the examiner to have many batteries and tools available. They need to complete real-time scoring and have a strong sense of which tests will help them to understand the child's limitations. It is possible to build a comprehensive, fixed, assessment battery that can be used in all situations and covers all the relevant cognitive domains; however, this makes the testing process long and arduous for both examiner and examinee and then requires the examiner to score and interpret large amounts of information. This section briefly describes a general process for on-the-fly assessment; however, a full discourse on the topic is beyond the scope of this chapter.

There are a number of interpretive issues that affect the decision to include additional tests or to change the course of testing. These issues relate to identifying low scores, cognitive variability, multivariate base rates, and expected level of performance. Each of these topics has been the subject of research and disagreement among professionals as to the best approaches and meaning of the information. These topics are briefly recounted here to illustrate the complexity of the process of making on-the-fly changes to the assessment plan.

Identifying Low Scores

Defining a cut-off or model for identifying what level of performance constitutes a *low score* is a challenge for clinicians, schools, administrators, and researchers. There are some clear parameters that most psychologists would agree upon such as IQ scores 70 or below or subtest scaled scores 4 and below, which are indeed low scores. However, there is considerable debate as to whether an index score of 90, 85, or 80 or subtest scores of 8, 7, or 6 should be considered cut-offs for identifying a low score. Establishing a definition of a low score is important in on-the-fly assessments because it directs the examiner to pursue or to stop assessing a specific set of cognitive functions.

The answer to the question of defining a low score is that 'it depends.' It depends on the nature of the problem being assessed and the questions that need to be answered. Consider that in research studies an effect size above .8 is considered large, which translates into scaled scores of approximately 7.5. Moderate effect sizes are .4 to .8 or scaled scores of 7.6 to 8.8. These effect sizes would represent the mean performance of the clinical sample on a specific subtest for which there is a large or moderate effect size. If the clinical question is regarding intellectual disability, then we would expect scores in the large effect range. For mild intellectual disability (ID), the average subtest scaled scores on the WISC-V range from 3.2 for Arithmetic to 6.1 for Cancellation. Children with ID will have scores that fall in the 5, 6, and 7 scaled score range. Setting a strict cut-off of 4 scaled score points would result in many children with ID not being identified. In children with learning disabilities, working memory, an area that is often considered a significant weakness, and large effect sizes are observed compared to match controls, the mean scores across groups are in the scaled score 7–8 range indicating that many children with learning disabilities will have scores in the 8, 9, or 10 range. Similarly, ADHD is associated with slow processing speed. The effects are moderate and mean scores for PSI subtests are in the 8–9 range indicating that many children diagnosed with ADHD will score in the 9, 10, and 11 range on these measures.

On-the-fly assessment requires using scaled scores to make decisions about which tests to administer, to add, or to drop. Clearly, using highly restrictive scaled score cut-offs will result in problems with identifying deficits. By the same token, using very relaxed criteria may result in overtesting. Additional research lines help in the development of some basic logic for conducting on-the-fly changes to the assessment plan.

Multivariate Base Rates

There is a substantial body of research demonstrating that obtaining one or more low scores in a battery of tests is commonly observed in healthy children and adults (Brooks, Holdnack, & Iverson, 2011; Brooks, Iverson, Sherman, Holdnack, & Feldman, 2009). Obtaining scaled scores of 5, 6, 7, and 8 in a battery of tests does not occur at the rate implied by the percentile rank of the test (5%, 9%,16%, and 25%), rather the observed rates are closer to 44%, 60%, 77%, and 89%, respectively (Brooks et al., 2011). Conceptually, obtaining a score of 8 or less on a measure would never in and of itself indicate a clear cognitive deficit because an occasional low subtest score is often observed in individuals without any cognitive dysfunction. However, it is unusual for typically developing children and healthy adults to obtain more than one or two low scores, and the probability or normality diminishes the more low scores that are obtained in a particular cognitive function. This phenomenon can be used to the clinician's advantage. Children with mild ID are not identified by the presence of a single score of 4 or less; rather there is a consistent pattern of low scores across all or most measures such that the probability of obtaining that many low scores is nearly 0 in typically developing children and even among children with less severe cognitive disorders. Identifying a cognitive weakness within a domain may require the administration of three or more measures to clearly identify actual deficits versus a random low score in the overall testing profile.

Cognitive Variability

Like multivariate base rates, there is a substantial body of literature demonstrating that cognitive variability is common in typically developing children and adults (see Holdnack, Drozdick, Weiss, & Iverson, 2013 for review). Cognitive variability in and of itself is not diagnostic of the presence of a clinical condition. In fact, in some cases (e.g., mild ID and intellectual functioning) variability might be evidence against a specific diagnosis. Large discrepancies between scores will occur in most test batteries. On the WISC-IV, the average highest score obtained by children in the standardization sample was 13.5 and the average lowest score was 6.5; subsequently the mean difference between highest and lowest scores on the core WISC-IV subtests is 7 points, more than 2 standard deviations. The size of the discrepancy is exacerbated when very high scores are obtained. This finding holds true for index scores and is also observed on the WISC-V (e.g., average scatter is 7 points).

Variability in itself is not diagnostic of clinical conditions; however, aspects of variability are important in the assessment process. In clinical conditions, variability typically occurs in a specific pattern across domains rather than within a domain. Children with reading disorder may do poorly on reading measures associated with the nature of their reading problem but perform reasonable well on math measures. Children suffering a traumatic brain injury may do well on verbal intellectual tasks but do poorly on memory measures. Knowing the research literature related to specific conditions enables clinicians to explore the domains that are strengths or weaknesses for that condition and to determine if the pattern of scores is expected or maybe due to general cognitive variability observed in most individuals. Also, the concept that an absence of variability is diagnostically important cannot be underestimated. If a child with suspect reading problems performs below average on WIAT-III Word Reading but performs in the high average on the WRAT-III Word Reading test, the clinician might question if there is a true reading disorder or some other issue affecting the child's functioning.

When doing an assessment that contains tests from multiple batteries, there are some important practical issues that need to be considered. Variability across batteries is difficult to assess when they are not co-normed. Difference in norming techniques, the time at which the norms were collected, and the procedures (e.g., sampling strategy) used to obtain the sample may affect score consistency across measures. Variability in scores is also a function of the correlation between two measures. Low correlation between tests will yield high rates of large discrepancies than tests that have a high degree of correlation. Regression to the mean effects will also impact observed profile variability with the presence of very high scores (e.g., scaled scores >15) likely to produce significant differences with other subtest scores. The reliability of the tests and the number of tests administered also have an impact on consistency of performance. The clinician needs to use caution so as not to overinterpret test scores as being diagnostic but to use variability as one piece of evidence for decision-making.

Performance Indexing

Performance indexing is the process by which the clinician determines if a particular score is below what is expected for the individual child. This is a variation on the concept of cognitive variability but encompasses additional inferences. A standard example of performance indexing is the IQ-Achievement discrepancy. In this approach, performance on the achievement test is compared to performance on ability to measure if a specific score is unexpectedly low. Since cognitive ability and academic achievement are moderately to highly correlated, it would be expected that there would be some consistency between the scores. So, unexpectedly low reading compared to general cognitive functioning suggests that reading scores are unexpectedly low and this may indicate a reading problem. Similarly in a processing strengths and weaknesses model, a large discrepancy between Listening Comprehension and Reading Comprehension might indicate a specific reading problem. However, as noted in the previous section, such discrepancies may occur in any cognitive profile and factors other than an actual weakness in reading may be responsible for the large difference (e.g., IQ = 160 and Reading = 130 may be due to regression to the mean or ceiling effects on the reading test). Similarly, an absence of a difference between Listening Comprehension and Reading Comprehension scores may reflect the presence of both reading problems and attentional problems impacting listening, rather than an absence of an actual reading difficulty.

Background information is frequently used as a tool for gauging if an individual's score is unexpectedly low or not. A child whose parents have advanced degrees may be expected to have higher scores than children whose parents have very low levels of academic achievement. A score of 8 might be expected for one child but be considered somewhat low for another based on background information. In fact, multivariate base rates of low scores do vary based on background variables of the individual and using this information can improve the sensitivity and specificity of the test (Brooks et al., 2011). However, that information may not always be available for a specific set of measures. In Chapter 8 we make this information available for WISC-V with Hispanic examinees.

The most important aspect of indexing may not necessarily be in finding one large difference between two measures or an overall ability estimate and specific test scores. One large difference may or may not indicate a problem and a failure to find such a difference does not necessarily indicate that specific cognitive deficits are not present. Like the research being published related to multivariate base rates, similar research will be explored to show that small but very consistent differences between critical skills is a better indicator of a cognitive weakness than a single large difference. This is in part due to the fact that most tests do not measure one specific ability and isolating the nature of the problem requires observation of consistent findings.

General Concepts for On-the-Fly Assessments

There are no exact numerical values or precise model for completing an on-the-fly assessment. Based on the information presented earlier in this section and in this chapter generally, some basic concepts can be established. These concepts can be loosely identified as: setting multivariate criteria; assessing high probability and important functions; drop and pursue logic; and verification. The processes reported here are not necessarily independent but can be described as discrete decision-making points.

Setting Multivariate Criteria

In this model, the goal is to identify a cognitive domain that may be impacting the child's performance. Therefore, the goal is not to identify a single low score or single anomalous result. This is important because it reduces the likelihood of overinterpreting a single finding. Despite not having specific data about the multivariate base rates of the tests being used, there is research that provides some general rules. Brooks, Holdnack, and Iverson (2013) provide an extensive volume of tables for the WAIS-IV/WMS-IV by cognitive domain. Although the tests may be somewhat different, the multivariate base rate effects are generally pretty consistent across batteries of test (Brooks et al., 2013). For example, in the WAIS-IV sample, 13% of examinees had three working memory subtests at or below a score of 8 whereas only approximately 9% had two or more scores of 7 or less. A single score of 8 may not indicate a deficit in working memory but three or more scores or 8 or 2 or more scores of 7 suggest difficulties in this domain. The base rates for immediate memory on the WMS-IV are 11% have three scaled scores of 8 or less and 14% have two scores of 7 or less. A general rule, three or more scaled scores of 8 or 2 or more scaled scores of 7 on subtests measuring the same domain suggest a possible cognitive deficit in that area. Once the threshold is obtained, further assessment within that domain may not be required at that time and other domains can be pursued.

Assessing High Probability and Important Functions

For many disorders, there is a research literature that identifies the cognitive domains that are most likely to result in learning difficulties, behavioral problems, or social relatedness issues. Factors such as language functioning are so critical to overall academic and social development that these tests should be administered first in the sequence of an assessment. These include general language skills and those specific language skills associated with the referral question (e.g., phonological processing for reading, pragmatic for social issues, etc.). Working memory functioning is also an important ability associated with academic functioning and after deficits in language functioning have been identified or ruled out, working memory skills could be evaluated next, depending if the research question is primarily academic or behavioral. In cases where behavioral issues are predominant, executive functioning or social perception tasks may be administered subsequent to the language assessment. Therefore, for each assessment, a hierarchy of measures can be determined and applied. In some cases, certain tests have to be administered in a certain sequence (e.g., long-delay memory 30 minutes after immediate) such that not all subtests in a domain can be given sequentially.

Creating a hierarchy is also helpful in guiding the interpretation and recommendation process. If highly probable and important skills are identified as weaknesses, these can be targeted hierarchical for intervention. Also, if probable cognitive deficits are not observed, then standard intervention models may not be indicated. Further, diagnostically, it enables the clinician to rule out the most probable disorders early and to focus on alternative hypotheses in more detail. Or, in cases where the child is unable to complete a long test session, it increases the probability of identifying core versus secondary problems.

Drop and Pursue Logic

This concept pertains to the idea that once a problem domain is ruled out or ruled in, further assessment in that domain may not be required and other domains can be pursued. The logic for these decisions is associated with the multivariate base rate and cognitive variability models. Performance in a cognitive domain in which multiple low scores have been observed meets the criteria for a cognitive problem and a consistent deficit. These two factors are very important, having a few low scores but a high degree of inconsistency within a domain does not indicate a deficit in that domain. Rather, some specific aspect of one task may have invoked an extraneous cognitive factor not present in the other task, assuming attention and effort remained consistent across tasks. If Vocabulary is in the high average range and Similarities is in the low average range it is not possible to know if verbal skills are problematic or not. Additional tests would be required. If Information is then administered and in the high average range, there is evidence for Similarities to be an anomalous finding and there is strong evidence that a language disorder is unlikely. However, the clinician may wish to explore the finding further by administering Comprehension. If Comprehension is also low, then there is evidence that some aspects of language or some other cognitive skill is affecting language performance. In this case, Similarities and Comprehension require a greater verbal response, more abstract reasoning, and cognitive flexibility compared to Vocabulary and Information. Additional language measures such as CELF-V Formulated Sentences and Sentence Assembly may help identify difficulties using language flexibly.

The decision to stop testing relates to a clear finding of problems in a specific cognitive domain that are defined by multiple low scores that are atypical in the general population and are consistently low across measures. Similarly, multiple consistently high scores is a general rule out for problems in that domain and further testing may be stopped. A decision to pursue an alternate assessment path can occur when scores in a domain show multiple low and high scores and general inconsistency in performance in that domain. Pursuing additional measures that cross domains or are in a different cognitive domain that is known to influence performance on the tests that are low versus those that are high might be indicated. The pursue decision helps the clinician to fine tune the assessment of the child's overall cognitive weaknesses and helps identify which cognitive difficulties may be core versus secondary.

The pursue option may also occur from behavioral observations (e.g., the child appears to forget instructions, or is inattentive, etc.). Also, performance on a test itself strongly suggests a specific cognitive process is affecting test performance (e.g., the child makes impulsive or sloppy errors on a math test but generally has knowledge of how to obtain the correct answer).

Verification

Verification is the process by which additional tests are given in a specific domain to be certain that an actual deficit is present. In some cases, two low scores might be identified and the examiner moves onto the next set of tests. If tests performed later in the assessment seem to contradict the finding or a specific cognitive problem, then the clinician may wish to add one or two additional tests in that domain to verify that there is a deficit in that domain. An example of such a scenario would be if two scores of 7 were obtained on Digit Span and Picture Span. The examiner may have decided that this was a domain of cognitive difficulties and moved to another cognitive domain. However, at some point later in the assessment, if the child does really well on tests that the examiner knows require relative intact working memory (e.g., first learning trial on a word list task), then he or she may decide to re-evaluate that the observed cognitive difficulty was due to some other process (e.g., mental sequencing) or variable attention, or other issue.

Interpreting the Test Scores

The brain is complex with multiple integrated pathways simultaneously and sequentially processing information, as described in Chapter 5. The concept that a specific cognitive weakness will always yield a predictable outcome is not supported in most clinical studies. Rather, cognitive weaknesses should be treated as risk factors for potentially negative or positive outcomes related to academic, behavior, and psychosocial functioning. The relationship between cognition and daily functioning is not deterministic but probabilistic (Pennington, 2006). Let us take an example from cardiology; having a high cholesterol level does not guarantee that a person will have a heart attack but it increases the risk for having a heart attack. Having high blood pressure is a risk for heart attack and stroke but it does not indicate imminent heart attack or stroke; however, the presence of both high cholesterol and high blood pressure increases the risk of heart attack. The presence of additional risk factors such as family history, obesity, smoking, and diabetes can dramatically increase the probability that the person will have a heart attack but it is not deterministic. In psychology, most children diagnosed with a clinical condition have multiple cognitive deficits or weaknesses and there is not just a single cognitive factor that causes reduced efficiency in one or more aspects of psychosocial functioning. The constellation of cognitive weaknesses allows us to identify the diagnosis for which the child is at risk and the risk for short- and long-term psychosocial outcomes. Consistent with the application of the risk factor model for cognitive assessment, Berninger et al. (2006) showed that the number and types of linguistic deficits was related to the type and severity of reading difficulties in children and adults.

If the assessment process reveals cognitive difficulties in just phonological processing, the child would be considered at risk for developing reading problems; however, the overall risk would be relatively low. If the child has deficits in both phonological processing and automaticity of semantic retrieval, the risk factor for reading problems is higher but there is no certainty that they would develop reading issues. As more cognitive difficulties are found, the probability that observable difficulties would be present increases and the probability that a diagnosable disorder is present also increases. This is why it is critical to identify all cognitive difficulties and to verify that the deficits are true and not due to chance or other factors.

Once the clinician has identified primary and secondary cognitive difficulties and any comorbid emotional difficulties, they can identify the most relevant domains for intervention. Also, the clinician can identify potential short- and long-term consequences of the cognitive difficulties. For example, children identified with language, executive functioning, and social perception deficits are at high risk for long-term difficulties establishing close interpersonal relationships. This does not mean that he or she is not capable of doing so but the presence of specific cognitive factors may increase the risk of such problems occurring. Identifying those risks helps the parent to seek interventions or to prepare for possible issues in that area.

Subsequently, the treatment recommendations follow from the identification of the risk factors in an attempt to improve or ameliorate the impact of those risk factors, to provide accommodations where necessary, and to focus on the child's and family's overall quality of life, which is the essence of evidence-based clinical practice. Using a client-centered approach helps the clinician identify the important domains of limitations and helps identify the potential risks and negative consequences of these problem areas.

SUMMARY

This chapter lays the foundation for a research-based approach to personalizing psychological evaluations based on the particular referral question, in context with a child's unique developmental, phenomenological and psychosocial context. The process begins with a careful pre-assessment investigation of relevant informants together with consideration of family history and epidemiological likelihood of various possible conditions to create an initial assessment plan tailored for the individual. The initial assessment plan is then adjusted on-the-fly by dropping subtests planned in some areas and adding subtests in other areas based on the child's performance during the session. Such on-the-fly decisions require the clinician to be informed of research regarding the cognitive correlates of specific problem areas as described in the chapter, and is made more feasible with digitally assisted assessment systems that provide immediate scoring during the session (see Chapter 4). Advanced measurement issues are discussed including interpretation of multivariate data, and statistical and clinical expectations about variability of performance as related to diagnosis.

REFERENCES

Ackerman, P. L., Beier, M. E., & Boyle, M. O. (2005). Working memory and intelligence: The same or different constructs? *Psychological Bulletin, 131*, 30–60.

Baddeley, A. (2012). Working memory: theories, models, and controversies. *Annual Review of Psychology, 63*, 1–29.

Baddeley, A., Eysenck, M. E., & Anderson, M. C. (2009). *Memory*. Florence, KY: Psychology Press.

Barkley, R. A. (2002). Major life activity and health outcomes associated with attention-deficit hyperactivity disorder. *Journal of Clinical Psychiatry, 63*(Suppl. 12), 10–15.

Baron-Cohen, S. (2001). Theory of mind and autism: A review. *International Review of Research in Mental Retardation, 23*, 169–184.

Beichtman, J. H., Wilson, B., Brownlie, E. B., Walters, H., Inglis, A., & Lancee, W. (1996). Long-term consistency in speech/language profiles: II. Behavioral, emotional, and social outcomes. *Journal of the American Academy of Child & Adolescent Psychiatry, 35*, 815–825.

Beichtman, J. H., Wilson, B., Johnson, C. J., Atkinson, L., Young, A., Adalf, E., et al. (2001). Fourteen-year follow-up of speech/language-impaired and control children: Psychiatric outcome. *Journal of the American Academy of Child & Adolescent Psychiatry, 40*, 75–82.

Bental, B., & Tirosh, E. (2007). The relationship between attention, executive functions and reading domain abilities in attention deficit hyperactivity disorder and reading disorder: A comparative study. *Journal of Child Psychology and Psychiatry, 48*, 455–463.

Berninger, V. W. (2007). *Process assessment of the learner—Test battery for reading and writing.* Bloomington, MN: NCS Pearson, Inc.

Berninger, V. W., Abbott, R. D., Thomson, J. B., & Raskin, W. H. (2001). Language phenotype for reading and writing disability: A family approach. *Scientific Studies of Reading, 5*, 59–106.

Berninger, V. W., Abbott, R. D., Thomson, J., Wagner, R., Swanson, H. L., Wijsman, E. M., et al. (2006). Modeling phonological core deficits within a working memory architecture in children and adults with developmental dyslexia. *Scientific Studies of Reading, 10*, 165–198.

Biederman, J., Monuteaux, M. C., Doyle, A. E., Seidman, L. J., Wilens, T. E., Ferrero, F., et al. (2004). Impact of executive function deficits and attention-deficit/hyperactivity disorder (ADHD) on academic outcomes in children. *Journal of Consulting and Clinical Psychology, 72*, 757–766.

Bishop, D. V. M. (2002). Motor immaturity and specific speech and language impairment: Evidence for a common genetic basis. *American Journal of Medical Genetics (Neuropsychiatric Genetics)* (114), 56–63.

Brooks, B., Holdnack, J., & Iverson, G. (2011). Advanced clinical interpretation of the WAIS-IV and WMS-IV: Prevalence of low scores varies by level of intelligence and years of education. *Assessment, 18*, 156–167.

Brooks, B., Iverson, G. L., & Holdnack (2013). Understanding multivariate base rates. In J. A. Holdnack, L. W. Drozdick, L. G. Weiss, & G. L. Iverson (Eds.), *WAIS-IV, WMS-IV, and ACS advanced clinical interpretation.* San Diego, CA: Academic Press.

Brooks, B. L., Iverson, G. L., Sherman, E. S., Holdnack, J. A., & Feldman, H. H. (2009). Healthy children and adolescents obtain some low scores across a battery of memory tests. *Journal of the International Neuropsychological Society, 15*, 613–617.

Bruininks, R. H., & Bruininks, B. D. (2005). *Bruininks-Oseretsky test of motor proficiency* (2nd ed.). Bloomington, MN: Pearson, Inc.

Bull, R., Espy, K. A., & Wiebe, S. A. (2008). Short-term memory, working memory, and executive functioning in preschoolers: Longitudinal predictors of mathematical achievement at age 7 years. *Developmental Neuropsychology, 33*, 205–228.

Bull, R., & Scerif, G. (2001). Executive functioning as a predictor of children's mathematics ability: Inhibition, switching, and working memory. *Developmental Neuropsychology, 19*, 273–293.

Calhoun, S. L., & Mayes, S. D. (2005). Processing speed in children with clinical disorders. *Psychology in the Schools, 42*, 333–343.

Caron, M. J., Mottron, L., Rainville, C., & Chouinard, S. (2004). Do high functioning persons with autism present superior spatial abilities? *Neuropsychologia, 42*, 467–481.

Carretti, B., Borella, E., Cornoldi, C., & De Beni, R. (2009). Role of working memory in explaining the performance of individuals with specific reading comprehension difficulties: A meta-analysis. *Learning and Individual Differences, 19*, 246–251.

Castellanos, F. X., Sonuga-Barke, E. J. S., Milham, M. P., & Tannock, R. (2006). Characterizing cognition in ADHD: Beyond executive dysfunction. *Trends in Cognitive Sciences, 10*, 117–123.

Castles, A., Datta, H., Gayan, J., & Olson, R. K. (1999). Varieties of developmental reading disorder: Genetic and environmental influences. *Journal of Experimental Child Psychology, 72*, 73–94.

Cohen, M. (1997). *Children's memory scale.* Bloomington, MN: Pearson, Inc.

Conti-Ramsden, G., & Botting, N. (2008). Emotional health in adolescents with and without a history of specific language impairment (SLI). *Journal of Child Psychology and Psychiatry, 49*, 516–525.

Corbett, B. A., Constantine, L. J., Hendren, R., Rocke, D., & Ozonoff, S. (2009). Examining executive functioning in children with autism spectrum disorder, attention deficit hyperactivity disorder and typical development. *Psychiatry Research, 166*, 210–222.

Cutting, L. E., Koth, C. W., Mahone, E. M., & Denckla, M. B. (2003). Evidence for unexpected weaknesses in learning in children with attention-deficit/hyperactivity disorder without reading disabilities. *Journal of Learning Disabilities, 36*, 259–269.

Dawson, G., Carver, L., Meltzoff, A. N., Panagiotides, H., McPartland, J., & Webb, S. J. (2002). Neural correlates of face and object recognition in young children with autism spectrum disorder, developmental delay, and typical development. *Child Development, 73*, 700–717.

Delis, D. C., Kaplan, E., & Kramer, J. (2001). *Delis-Kaplan executive function system.* Bloomington, MN: NCS Pearson, Inc.

Delis, D. C., Kramer, J. H., Kaplan, K., & Ober, B. A. (1994). *California verbal learning test—Children's edition.* Bloomington, MN: NCS Pearson, Inc.

Denckla, M. B., & Cutting, L. E. (1999). History and significance of rapid automatized naming. *Annals of Dyslexia, 49*, 29–42.

DiPerna, J. C., & Elliot, S. N. (2000). *Academic competency evaluation scale.* Bloomington, MN: NCS Pearson, Inc.

Dunn, L. M., & Dunn, L. M. (2007). *Peabody picture vocabulary test* (3rd ed.). Bloomington, MN: NCS Pearson, Inc.

Dworzynski, K., Ronald, A., Bolton, P., & Happé, F. (2012). How different are girls and boys above and below the diagnostic threshold for autism spectrum disorders? *Journal of the American Academy of Child and Adolescent Psychiatry, 51*, 788–797.

Elliot, C. (2007). *Differential ability scales* (2nd ed.). Bloomington, MN: Pearson, Inc.

Fairchild, G., Van Goozen, S. H. M., Calder, A. J., Stollery, S. J., & Goodyer, I. M. (2009). Deficits in facial expression recognition in male adolescents with early-onset or adolescence onset conduct disorder. *Journal of Child Psychology and Psychiatry, 50*, 627–636.

Falter, C. M., Plaisted, K. C., & Davis, G. (2008). Visuo-spatial processing in autism—testing the predictions of extreme male brain theory. *Journal of Autism and Developmental Disorders, 38*, 507–515.

Frazier, T. W., Youngstrom, E. A., Glutting, J. J., & Watkins, M. W. (2007). ADHD and achievement meta-analysis of the child, adolescent, and adult literatures and a concomitant study with college students. *Journal of Learning Disabilities, 40*, 49–65.

Gathercole, S. E., Pickering, S. J., Knight, M., & Stegmann, Z. (2004). Working memory skills and educational attainment: Evidence from national curriculum assessments at 7 and 14 years of age. *Applied Cognitive Psychology, 40*, 1–16.

Geary, D. C. (2004). Mathematics and learning disabilities. *Journal of Learning Disabilities, 37*, 4–15.

Geurts, H. M., Verté, S., Oosterlaan, J., Roeyers, H., & Sergeant, J. A. (2004). How specific are executive functioning deficits in attention deficit hyperactivity disorder and autism? *Journal of Child Psychology and Psychiatry, 45*, 836–854.

Goodglass, H., Kaplan, E., Weintraub, S., & Siegel, O. (2001). In T. X. Austin (Ed.), *Boston naming test*. Pro-ed Inc.

Hayashi, M., Kato, M., Igarashi, K., & Kashima, H. (2008). Superior fluid intelligence in children with Asperger's disorder. *Brain and Cognition, 66*, 306–310.

Heaton, R. K., Chelune, G. J., Talley, J. L., Kay, G. G., & Curtiss, G. (1993). *Wisconsin card sorting test manual: Revised and expanded*. Lutz, FL: PAR, Inc.

Hill, E. L. (2001). Non-specific nature of specific language impairment: A review of the literature with regard to concomitant motor impairments. *International Journal of Language and Communication Disorders, 36*, 149–171.

Hoaken, P. N. S., Shaughnessy, V. K., & Pihl, R. O. (2003). Executive cognitive functioning and aggression: Is it an issue of impulsivity? *Aggressive Behavior, 29*, 15–30.

Holdnack, J. A., Drozdick, L. W., Weiss, L. G., & Iverson, G. L. (2013). *WAIS-IV/WMS-IV/ACS: Advanced clinical interpretation*. San Diego, CA: Elsevier Science.

Holdnack, J. A., Weiss, L. W., & Entwistle, P. (2006). Using the WISC-IV Integrated with other measures. In L. W. Weiss, A. Prifitera, D. H. Saklofske, & J. A. Holdnack (Eds.), *WISC-IV: Advanced clinical interpretation*. San Diego, CA: Elsevier Science, Inc.

Jacobson, L. A., Ryan, M., Martin, R. B., Ewen, J., Mostofsky, S. H., Denckla, M. B., et al. (2012). Working memory influences processing speed and reading fluency in ADHD. *Child Neuropsychology, 17*, 209–224.

Jansiewicz, E. M., Goldberg, M. C., Newschafler, C. J., Denckla, M. B., Landa, R., & Mostofsky, S. H. (2006). Motor signs distinguish children with high functioning autism and Asperger's syndrome from controls. *Journal of Autism and Developmental Disorders, 36*, 613–621.

Jeffries, S., & Everatt, J. (2004). Working memory: Its role in dyslexia and other specific learning difficulties. *Dyslexia, 10*, 196–214.

Johnson, C. J., Beitchman, J. H., & Brownlie, E. B. (2010). Twenty-year follow-up of children with and without speech-language impairments: Family, educational, occupational, and quality of life outcomes. *American Journal of Speech-Language Pathology, 19*, 51–65.

Kaufman, A. S., & Kaufman, N. L. (2014). *Kaufman test of educational achievement* (3rd ed.). Bloomington, MN: NCS Pearson Inc.

Klin, A., Jones, W., Schultz, R., Volkmar, F., & Cohen, D. (2002). Visual fixation patterns during viewing of naturalistic social situations as predictors of social competence in individuals with autism. *Archives of General Psychiatry, 59*, 809–816.

Kooistra, L., Crawford, S., Dewey, D., Cantell, M., & Kaplan, B. J. (2005). Motor correlates of ADHD contribution of reading disability and oppositional defiant disorder. *Journal of Learning Disabilities, 38*, 195–206.

Korkman, M., Kirk, U., & Kemp, S. (2007). *NEPSY: A developmental neuropsychological assessment* (2nd ed.). Bloomington, MN: NCS Pearson, Inc.

Kramer, J. H., Knee, K., & Delis, D. C. (2000). Verbal memory impairments in dyslexia. *Archives of Clinical Neuropsychology, 15*, 83–93.

Kuusikko, S., Haapsamo, H., Jansson-Verkasalo, E., Hurtig, T., Mattila, M. L., Ebeling, H., et al. (2009). Emotion recognition in children and adolescents with autism spectrum disorders. *Journal of Autism and Developmental Disorders, 39*, 938–945.

Lindsay, G., Dockrell, J. E., & Strand, S. (2007). Longitudinal patterns of behaviour problems in children with specific speech and language difficulties: Child and contextual factors. *British Journal of Educational Psychology, 77*, 811–828.

Loe, I. M., & Feldman, H. M. (2007). Academic and educational outcomes of children with ADHD. *Journal of Pediatric Psychology, 32*, 643–654.

Lopez, B. R., Lincoln, A. J., Ozonoff, S., & Lai, Z. (2005). Examining the relationship between executive functions and restricted, repetitive symptoms of autistic disorder. *Journal of the American Academy of Child & Adolescent Psychiatry, 44*, 377–384.

Margari, L., Buttiglione, M., Craig, F., Cristella, A., de Giambattista, C., Matera, E., et al. (2013). Neuropsychopathological comorbidities in learning disorders. *BMC Neurology, 13*, 198.

Marsh, A. A., & Blair, R. J. R. (2008). Deficits in facial affect recognition among antisocial populations: A meta-analysis. *Neuroscience and Biobehavioral Review, 32*, 454–465.

Martinussen, R., Hayden, J., Hogg-Johnson, D. C. S., & Tannock, R. (2005). A meta-analysis of working memory impairments in children with attention-deficit/hyperactivity disorder. *Journal of the American Academy of Child & Adolescent Psychiatry, 44*, 377–384.

Matarazzo, J. D. (1990). Psychological assessment versus psychological testing: Validation from Binet to the school, clinic, and courtroom. *American Psychologist, 45*, 999–1017.

Mayes, S. M., & Calhoun, S. L. (2007). Learning, attention, writing, and processing speed in typical children and children with ADHD, autism, anxiety, depression, and oppositional-defiant disorder. *Child Neuropsychology: A Journal on Normal and Abnormal Development in Childhood and Adolescence, 6*, 469–493.

McLean, J. F., & Hitch, G. J. (1999). Working memory impairments in children with specific arithmetic learning difficulties. *Journal of Experimental Child Psychology, 74*, 240–260.

Meyer, A., & Sagvolden, T. (2006). Fine motor skills in South African children with symptoms of ADHD: Influence of subtype, gender, age, and hand dominance. *Behavioral and Brain Functions, 2*(3), 3.

Muir-Broaddus, J. E., Rosenstein, L. D., Medina, D. E., & Soderberg, C. (2002). Neuropsychological test performance of children with ADHD relative to test norms and parent behavioral ratings. *Archives of Clinical Neuropsychology, 17*, 671–689.

Noterdaeme, M., Wriedt, E., & Höhne, C. (2010). Asperger's syndrome and high-functioning autism: Language, motor and cognitive profiles. *European Child and Adolescent Psychiatry, 19*, 475–481.

Osmon, D. C., Smerz, J. M., Braun, M. M., & Plambeck, E. (2006). Processing abilities associated with math skills in adult learning disability. *Journal of Clinical and Experimental Neuropsychology, 28*, 84–95.

Pennington, B. F. (2006). From single to multiple deficit models of developmental disorders. *Cognition, 101*, 385–413.

Pennington, B. F., & Lefly, D. L. (2001). Early reading development in children at family risk for dyslexia. *Child Development, 72*, 816–833.

Piek, J. P., Pitcher, T. M., & Hay, D. A. (1999). Motor coordination and kinaesthesis in boys with attention deficit–hyperactivity disorder. *Developmental Medicine & Child Neurology, 41*, 159–165.

Pitcher, T. M., Piek, J. P., & Hay, D. A. (2003). Fine and gross motor ability in males with ADHD. *Developmental Medicine & Child Neurology, 45*, 525–535.

Proctor, B. E., Floyd, R. G., & Shaver, R. B. (2005). Cattel-Horn-Carroll broad cognitive ability profiles of low math achievers. *Psychology in the Schools, 42*, 1–12.

Redmond, S. M. (2011). Peer victimization among students with specific language impairment, attention-deficit/hyperactivity disorder, and typical development. *Language, Speech, and Hearing Services in Schools, 42*, 520–535.

Reynolds, C. R., & Kamphaus, R. W. (2004). *Behavioral assessment system for children* (2nd ed.). Bloomington, MN: NCS Pearson, Inc.

Rommelse, N. N. J., Altink, M. E., Oosterlaan, J., Buschgens, C. J. M., Buitelaar, J., De Sonneville, L. M. J., et al. (2007). Motor control in children with ADHD and non-affected siblings:

Deficits most pronounced using the left hand. *Journal of Child Psychology and Psychiatry*, *48*, 1071–1079.

Schultz, R. T., Gauthier, I., Klin, A., Fulbright, R. K., Anderson, A. W., Volkmar, F., et al. (2000). Abnormal ventral temporal cortical activity during face discrimination among individuals with autism and Asperger syndrome. *Archives of General Psychiatry*, *57*, 331–340.

Semrud-Clikeman, M. (2012). The role of inattention on academics, fluid reasoning, and visual–spatial functioning in two subtypes of ADHD. *Applied Neuropsychology: Child*, *1*, 18–29.

Semrud-Clikeman, M., Guy, K., Griffin, J. D., & Hynd, G. W. (2000). Rapid naming deficits in children and adolescents with reading disabilities and attention deficit hyperactivity disorder. *Brain and Language*, *74*, 70–83.

Shanahan, M. A., Pennington, B. F., Yerys, B. E., Scott, A., Boada, R., Willcutt, E. G., et al. (2006). Processing speed deficits in attention deficit/hyperactivity disorder and reading disability. *Journal of Abnormal Child Psychology*, *34*, 585–602.

Shear, P. K., Tallal, P., & Delis, D. C. (1992). Verbal learning and memory in language impaired children. *Neuropsychologia*, *30*, 451–458.

Sheslow, D., & Adams, W. (2003). *Wide range assessment of memory and learning* (2nd ed.). Lutz, FL: PAR, Inc.

Snowling, M. J., Bishop, D. V. M., Stothard, S. E., Chipchase, B., & Kaplan, C. (2006). Psychosocial outcomes at 15 years of children with a preschool history of speech-language impairment. *Journal of Child Psychology and Psychiatry*, *47*, 759–765.

Soulières, I., Dawson, M., Samson, F., Barbeau, E. B., Sahyoun, C., Strangman, G. E., et al. (2009). Enhanced visual processing contributes to matrix reasoning in autism. *Human Brain Mapping*, *30*, 4082–4107.

St Clair-Thompson, H. L., & Gathercole, S. E. (2006). Executive functions and achievements in school: Shifting, updating, inhibition, and working memory. *The Quarterly Journal of Experimental Psychology*, *59*, 745–759.

Steele, S. D., Minshew, N. J., Luna, B., & Sweeney, J. A. (2007). Spatial working memory deficits in autism. *Journal of Autism and Developmental Disorders*, *37*, 605–612.

Tamm, L., & Juranek, J. (2012). Fluid reasoning deficits in children with ADHD: Evidence from fMRI. *Brain Research*, *17*(1465), 48–56.

Tannock, R., Martinussen, R., & Frijters, J. (2000). Naming speed performance and stimulant effects indicate effortful, semantic processing deficits in attention-deficit/hyperactivity disorder. *Journal of Abnormal Child Psychology*, *28*, 237–252.

Tseng, M. H., Henderson, A., Chow, S. M. K., & Yao, G. (2004). Relationship between motor proficiency, attention, impulse, and activity in children with ADHD. *Developmental Medicine & Child Neurology*, *45*, 525–535.

Verté, S., Geurts, H. M., Roeyers, H., Oosterlaan, J., & Sergeant, J. A. (2006). The relationship of working memory, inhibition, and response variability in child psychopathology. *Journal of Neuroscience Methods*, *151*, 5–14.

Waber, D. P., Wolff, P. H., Forbes, P. W., & Weiler, M. D. (2000). Rapid automatized naming in children referred for evaluation of heterogeneous learning problems: How specific are naming speed deficits to reading disability? *Child Neuropsychology: A Journal on Normal and Abnormal Development in Childhood and Adolescence*, *6*, 251–261.

Wang, A. T., Lee, S. S., Sigman, M., & Dapretto, M. (2007). Reading affect in the face and voice: Neural correlates of interpreting communicative intent in children and adolescents with autism spectrum disorders. *Archives of General Psychiatry*, *64*, 698–708.

Wechsler, D. (2003). *The Wechsler intelligence scale for children* (4th ed.). Bloomington, MN: NCS Pearson, Inc.

Wechsler, D. (2012). *Wechsler individual achievement test* (3rd ed.). Bloomington, MN: NCS Pearson, Inc.

Wechsler, D. (2014). *The Wechsler intelligence scale for children* (5th ed). Bloomington, MN: NCS Pearson, Inc.

Weigelt, S., Koldewyn, K., & Kanwisher, N. (2012). Face identity recognition in autism spectrum disorders: A review of behavioral studies. *Neuroscience and Biobehavioral Reviews, 36,* 1060–1084.

Wiig, E. H., Semel, E., & Secord, W. A. (2013). *Clinical evaluations of language fundamentals* (5th ed.). Bloomington, MN: NCS Pearson, Inc.

Wilkinson, K. M. (1998). Profiles of language and communication skills in children with autism. *Mental Retardation and Developmental Disabilities, 4,* 73–79.

Willburger, E., Fussenegger, B., Moll, K., Wood, G., & Lander, K. (2008). Naming speed in dyslexia and dyscalculia. *Learning and Individual Differences, 18,* 224–236.

Willcutt, E. G., Doyle, A. E., Nigg, J. T., Faraone, S. V., & Pennington, B. F. (2005). Validity of the executive function theory of attention-deficit/hyperactivity disorder: A meta-analytic review. *Biological Psychiatry, 57,* 1336–1346.

Willcutt, E. G., Pennington, B. F., Boada, R., Ogline, J. S., Tunick, R. A., Chhabildas, N., et al. (2001). A comparison of cognitive deficits in reading disability and attention-deficit/hyperactivity disorder. *Journal of Abnormal Psychology, 130,* 157–172.

Willcutt, E. G., Pennington, B. F., Olson, R. K., Chhabildas, N., & Hulsander, J. (2005). A comparison of cognitive deficits in reading disability and attention-deficit/hyperactivity disorder. *Journal of Abnormal Psychology, 130,* 157–172.

Williams, D. L., Goldstein, G., & Minshew, N. J. (2006). The profile of memory function in children with autism. *Neuropsychology, 20,* 21–29.

Wolf, M., & Bowers, P. G. (1999). The double-deficit hypothesis for the developmental dyslexias. *Journal of Educational Psychology, 91,* 415–438.

Index

Note: Page numbers followed by "*f*" and "*t*" refer to figures and tables, respectively.

C

California Verbal Learning Test, 358, 360*f*, 392–393
California Verbal Learning Test for Children (CVLT-C), 386–387
Cancellation, 14, 47, 61, 111
Cattell–Horn–Carroll (CHC) theory of intelligence, 5, 244, 245*t*, 246*t*, 247*t*–249*t*
CELF-V, 382–384, 388–391
Central, 349, 366–368
  data visualization, 368
  flexible test selection, 367–368
  security, 366–367
    during administration, 366–367
    during data upload, 367
    storage, 367
Central executive component, 387–388
Child, initial impressions of, 374–407
  academic skills, 389–390
  attention/executive functioning, 384–387
  background information and *a priori* hypothesis building, 376–382
    assessment plan, 381
    background research, 376–380
    parent and teacher ratings, 380–381
  language, 382–384
  memory functioning, 391–393
  on-the-fly adjustments to the assessment, 399–407
    cognitive variability, 401–402
    concepts for, 403–407
    identifying low scores, 400–401
    multivariate base rates, 401
    performance indexing, 402–403
  pre-assessment planning example, 397–399
  processing speed, 393–394
  reason for referral, 375–376
  sensory and motor tests, 396–397
  social cognition/pragmatic language skills, 390–391
  visual–spatial and fluid reasoning, 394–396
  working memory, 387–389
Children
  in foster care, 143
  homeless, 143
  intellectual and academic development, home environment on, 167–173
  mental health risk in, living in poverty, 142–143
  parent involvement in their development, 147, 150–151
  with psychological/psychoeducational disorders, 146–147
  role in academic and intellectual development, 154–157
Children with SLD, WISC-V studies of, 251–258
Children's Memory Scales (CMS), 388–393
Classroom assessment strategies
  for children with low verbal comprehension abilities, 77
  for children with weaknesses in visual processing abilities, 79
Classroom management techniques
  to minimizing memory-related failures, 84–85
Clerk, 71
Code of Federal Regulations (CFR), 199
Coding, 6, 13, 45–47, 60
CogMed program, 83–84
Cognitive abilities, 66–68, 88, 171, 173, 244, 329–331, 398
  development of, 123
  integrative theory of, 114–118
Cognitive deficits, 64, 289–290, 292
Cognitive development, 124, 145, 174–176, 221–222
  and home environment, 146–149, 173–175
Cognitive flexibility, 109, 113, 384–385
  and inhibitory control deficits, 385
Cognitive functioning, 287
  in clinical and special groups, 291–303
    attention-deficit/hyperactivity disorder (ADHD), 298–301
    autism spectrum disorder (ASD), 294–298
    disruptive behavior disorders (DBD), 301–302
    intellectual disability, 291–293
    intellectual giftedness, 293–294
    traumatic brain injury (TBI), 302–303
  intellectual assessment with WISC-V in diagnostic and treatment planning, 303–305
  relevance and purpose of cognitive assessment, 290
  WISC-V performance in special groups, 305–331
    attention-deficit hyperactivity disorder, 313–318
    autism spectrum disorder (ASD) groups, 323
    Borderline Intellectual Functioning (BIF) group, 313